SOLUTIONS
and other
PROBLEMS

Also by Allie Brosh

Hyperbole and a Half

SOLUTIONS
and other
PROBLEMS

Allie Brosh

Gallery Books

New York   London   Toronto   Sydney   New Delhi

GALLERY
BOOKS

Gallery Books
An Imprint of Simon & Schuster, Inc.
1230 Avenue of the Americas
New York, NY 10020

First Gallery Books hardcover edition September 2020

GALLERY BOOKS and colophon are registered trademarks
of Simon & Schuster, Inc.

For information about special discounts for bulk purchases,
please contact Simon & Schuster Special Sales at 1-866-506-1949
or business@simonandschuster.com.

The Simon & Schuster Speakers Bureau can bring authors to your
live event. For more information or to book an event, contact
the Simon & Schuster Speakers Bureau at 1-866-248-3049
or visit our website at www.simonspeakers.com.

Interior design by Jaime Putorti

Manufactured in the United States of America

10 9 8 7 6 5 4 3

Library of Congress Control Number: 2020940967

ISBN 978-1-9821-5694-7
ISBN 978-1-9821-5696-1 (ebook)

Copyright strictly enforced by
the Copyright monster.

For Kaiti. There's so much I wish I could have said to you.

Contents

Introduction: Balloon

I saw a balloon going 90 miles per hour.

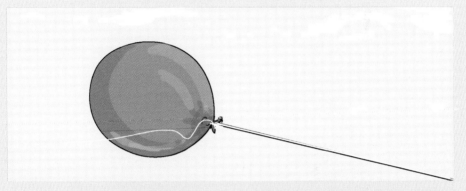

It was tied to a truck, so there was an explanation for it, but I don't know … I guess you still just never expect to see a balloon going that fast. Balloons aren't designed for that. They aren't aerodynamic enough. This one was wobbling all around in spastic little circles, making a sound like *wp-wp-wp-wp-wp-wp-wp-wp-wp-wp-wp-wp-wp-wp-wp-wp-wp*. It seemed genuinely out of control.

I was laughing so hard I had to pull over.

I feel just like that balloon.

1. BUCKET

The first time I can remember feeling truly powerless, I was three, and I was trapped sideways in a bucket in the garage.

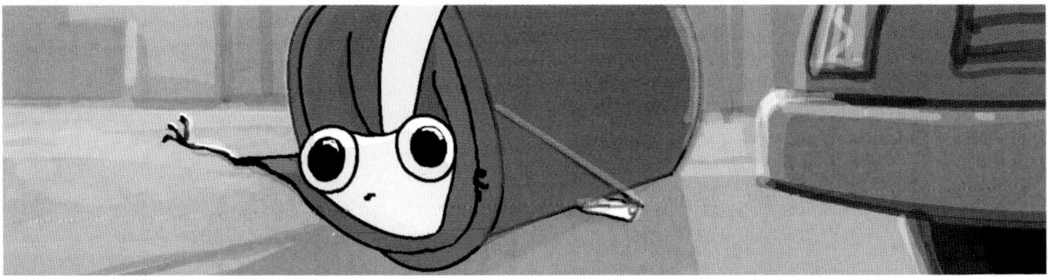

The bucket belonged to my dad. He used it for washing the car.

I don't remember exactly how or why this started, but through some contortion of childhood logic, I decided that I needed to get my entire body into the bucket.

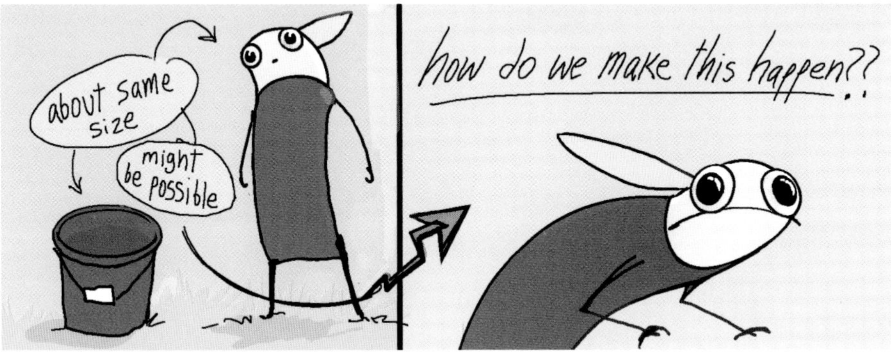
about same size
might be possible
how do we make this happen??

The bucket had other plans.

real close, but whole body is not in, so cannot be considered legitimate victory →

Maybe I had something to prove. Maybe there was a compelling reason to need to be entirely inside the bucket that I don't remember. But I couldn't let it go. The fact that I couldn't fit my whole body into the bucket infuriated me.

Initially, attempts were confined to car-washing days. Slowly, though, I sought out opportunities to make extracurricular assaults. I'd sneak into the garage by myself to try out different configurations.

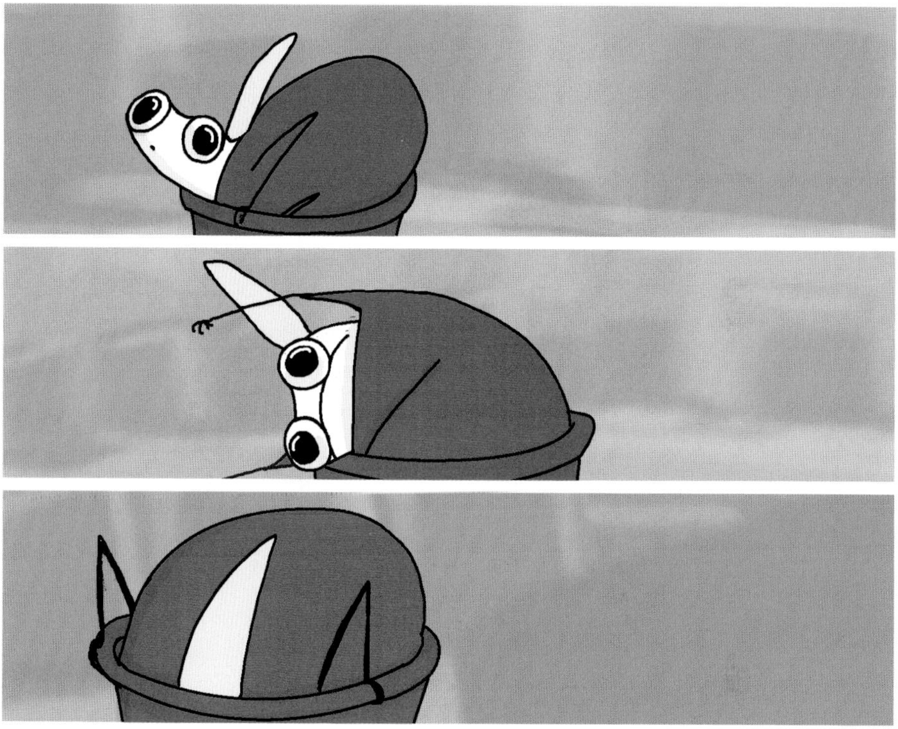

That's how I ended up alone in the garage trapped in the bucket.

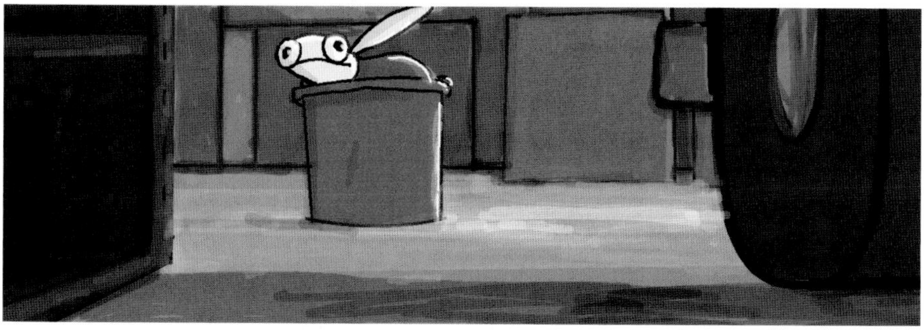

When both my shoulders finally dropped below the bucket's rim, I felt only the briefest flash of triumph before the sensation of being trapped kicked in.

I had done it: my entire body was in the bucket.

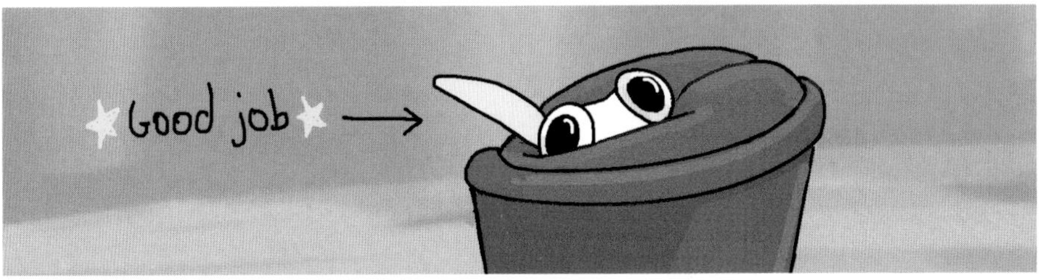
Good job

Except now, the only thing I wanted was to not be in there anymore.

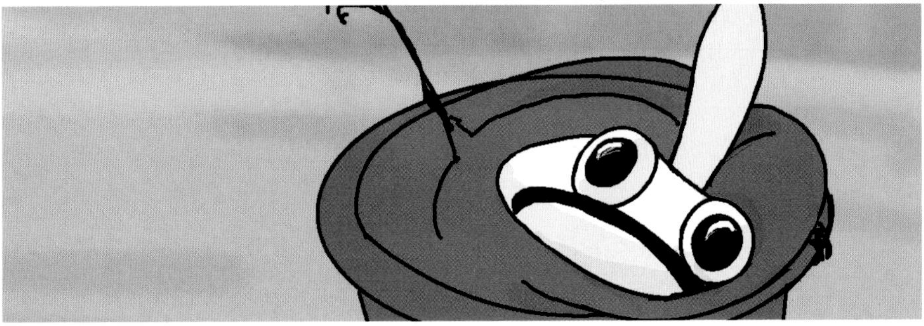

No amount of thrashing could free me, but it did make the bucket tip over.

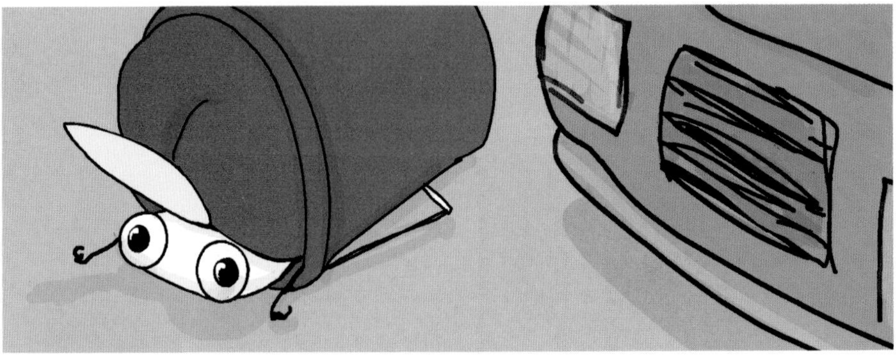

And suddenly, there I was—sideways, four limbs deep in a plastic car-wash bucket—only three years old, and already doomed to spend my life scooting around like the world's saddest upside-down hermit crab.

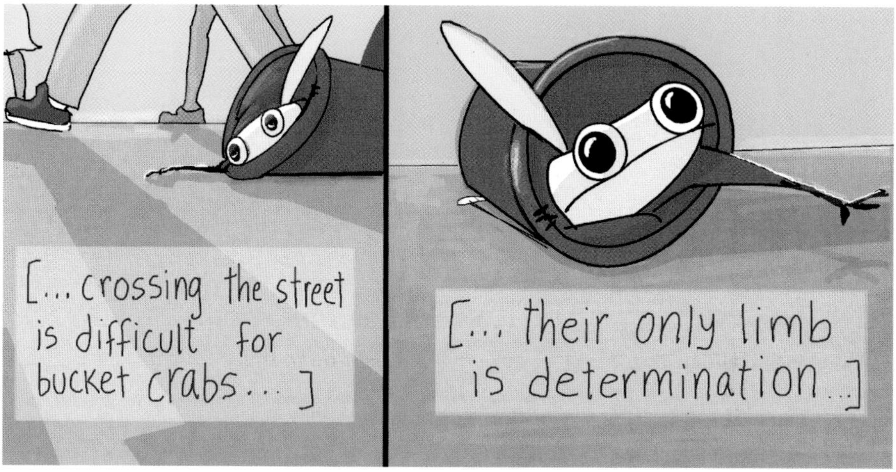
[... crossing the street is difficult for bucket crabs...]
[... their only limb is determination...]

This is not what I'd been trying to accomplish. I didn't even realize it was possible. That's the scary thing about decisions: you don't know what they are when you're making them.

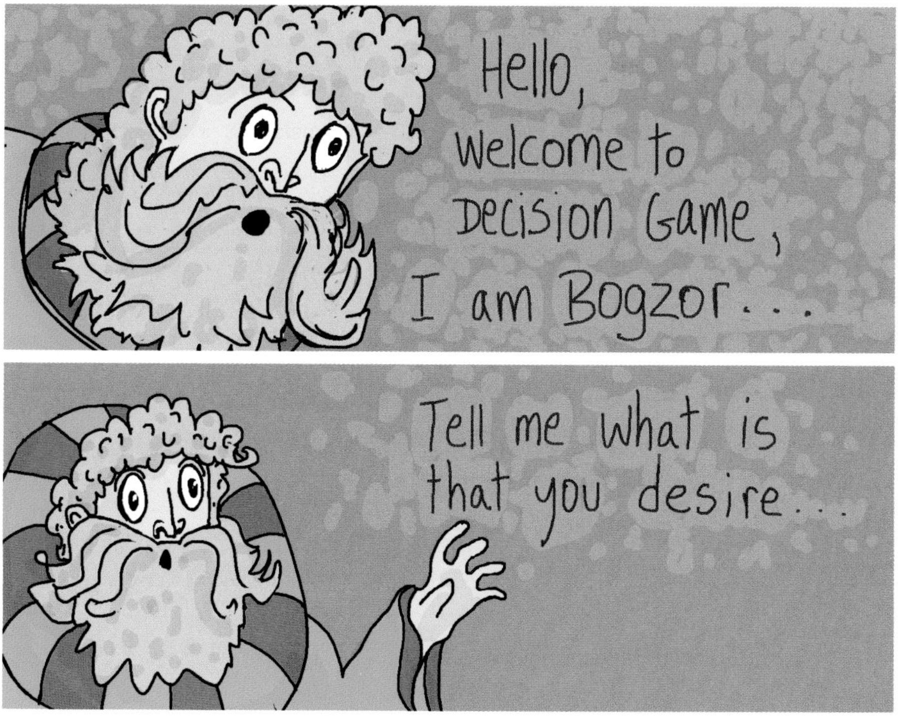
Hello, welcome to Decision Game, I am Bogzor...
Tell me what is that you desire...

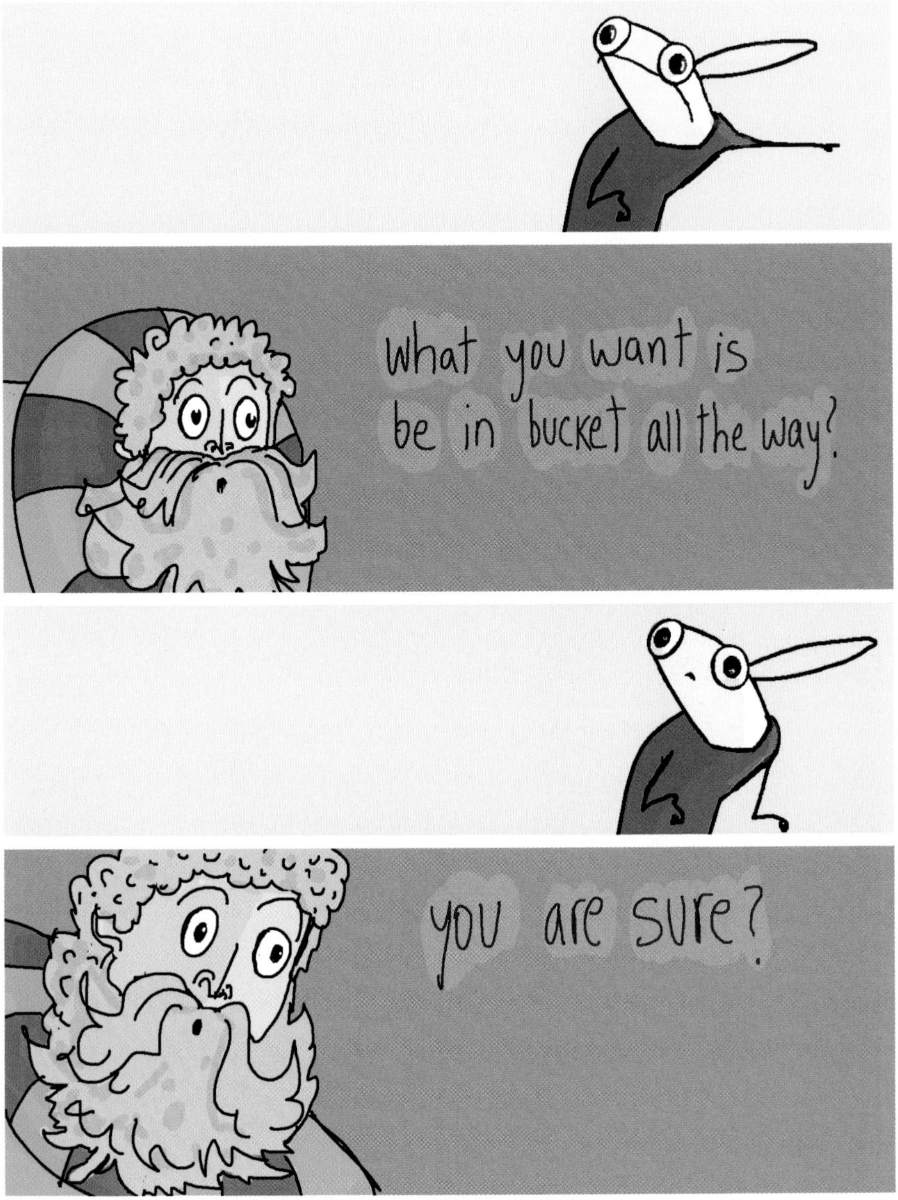
what you want is
be in bucket all the way?
you are sure?

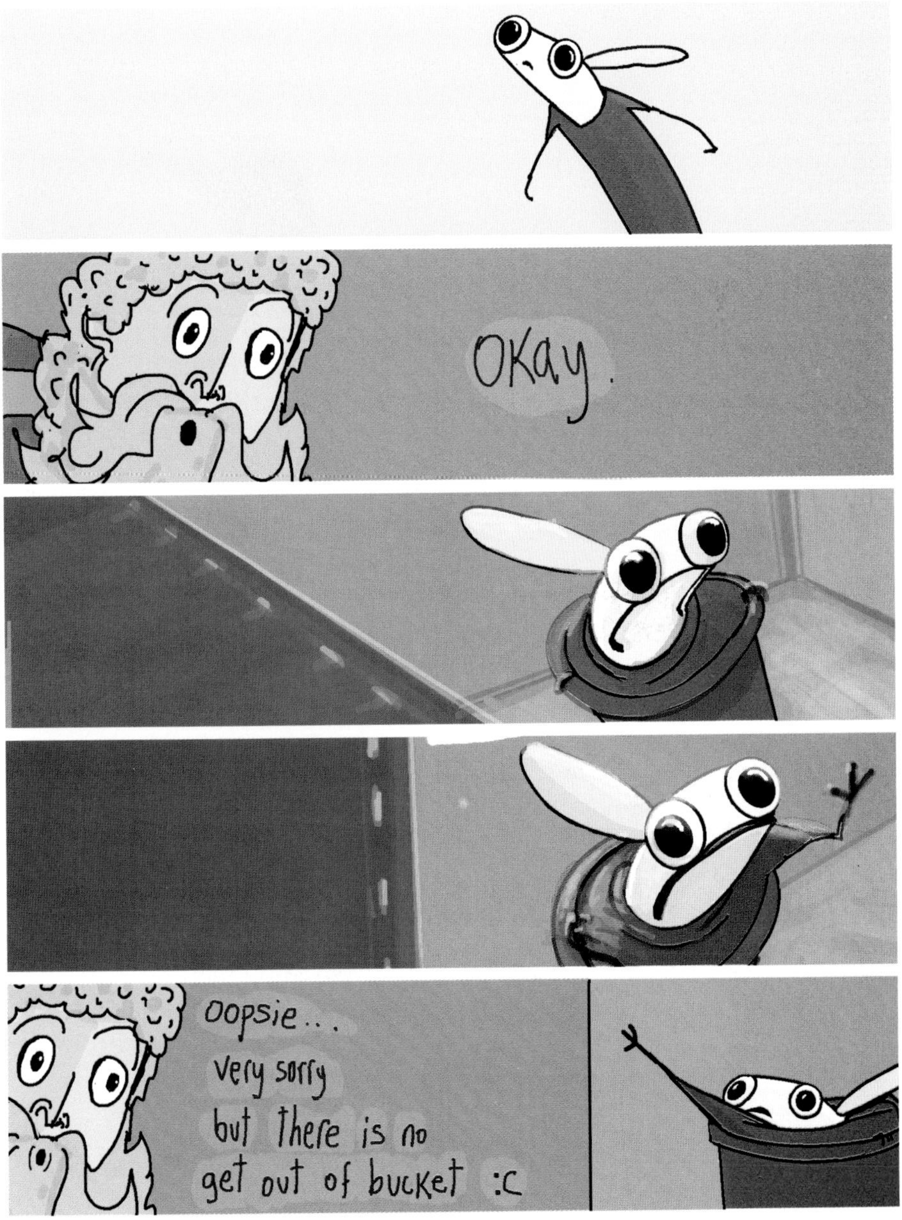
OKay.
oopsie...
very sorry
but there is no
get out of bucket :c

Fortunately, it wasn't permanent. I was rescued when my parents accidentally walked close enough to the garage to detect screaming.

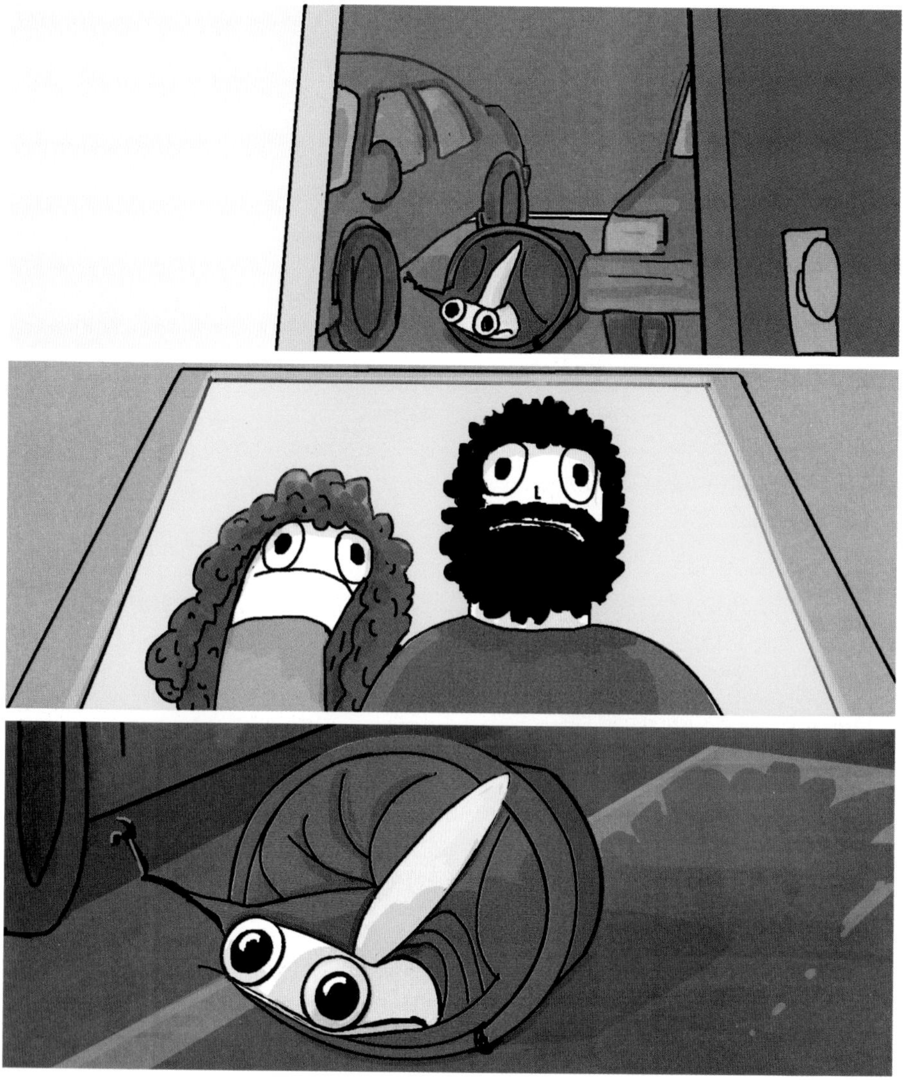

And the bucket was relocated to a high shelf to prevent me from interacting with it.

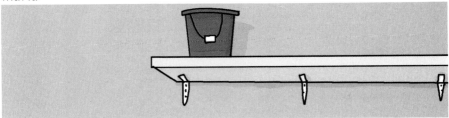

It wasn't enough.

The incident had only strengthened the drive to exert my will upon the bucket. I wouldn't be content with anything less than total domination now. A bucket shouldn't be able to stop a person, and I was willing to do whatever had to happen to prove it.

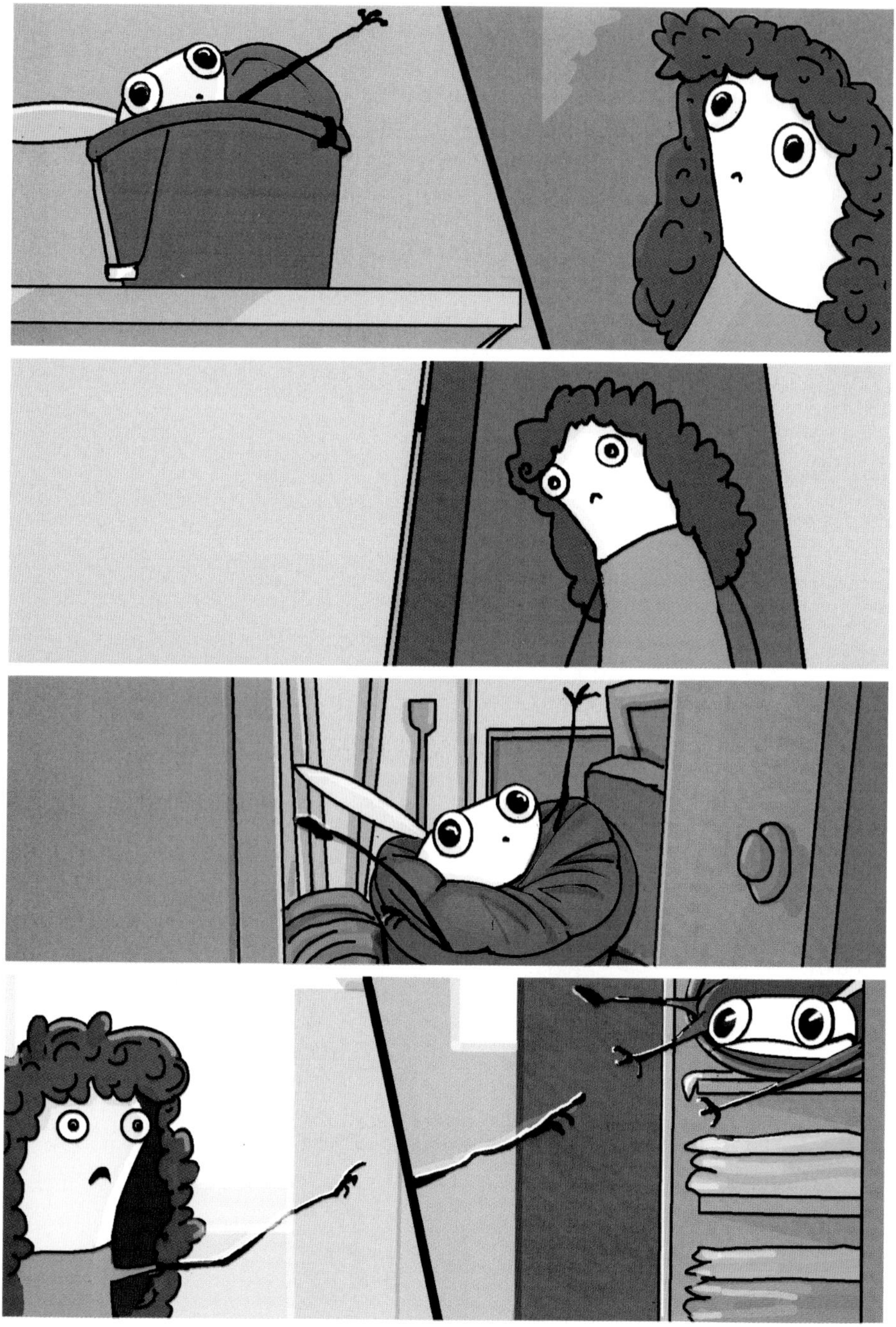

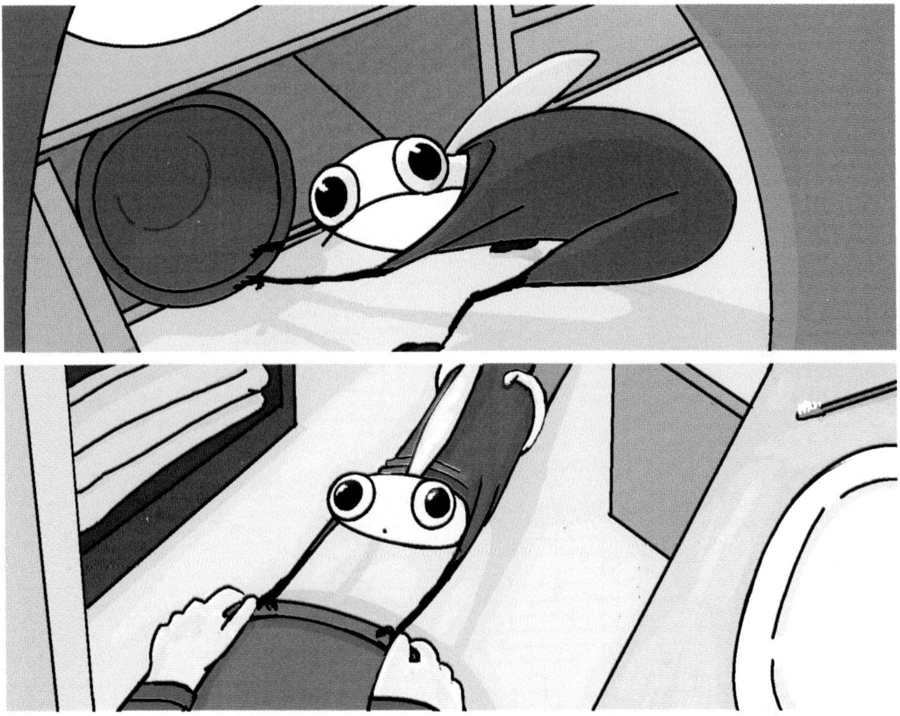

The only thing worse than getting trapped in the same bucket nineteen times is surrender.

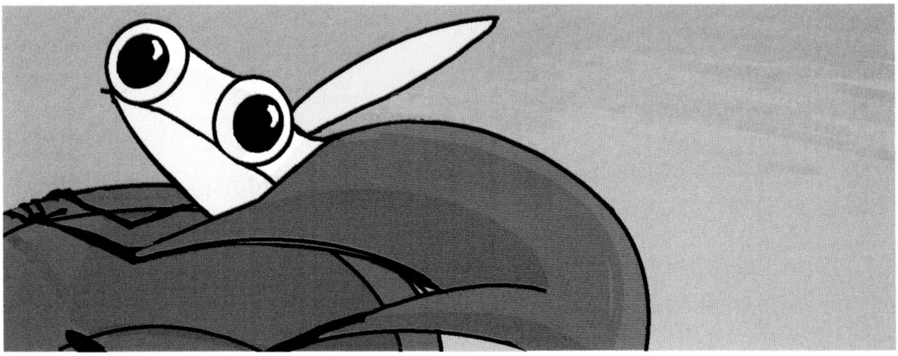

Explanation

That was the first chapter. The second chapter is next. It is loosely related to the first, but this isn't some perfectly sequential masterpiece of order where every segue makes sense.

For the sake of trust building, the third chapter will follow the second. But then we will jump directly to chapter five, do you understand? _No chapter four_. Why? Because sometimes things don't go like they should. This is an inescapable property of reality, which we all must learn to accept. There just isn't enough power in the universe for everybody to have all of it.

Anyway, the numbering structure will continue as normal thereafter. This was a charitable decision on my part, and we should take a moment to appreciate the fact that I did not explore the full extent of my power. And believe me, I could have. I could have made these chapters be any number I wanted. I could have invented a totally unrecognizable number system based on snake pictures. Shit, I could've called them all chapter 2 and refused to acknowledge that I did that.

But we are civilized, friendly people, and sometimes it is best to restrain ourselves.

2. RICHARD

For the first few years of my life, the only people I knew how to find lived in my house.

People: where do they live?
US
our house

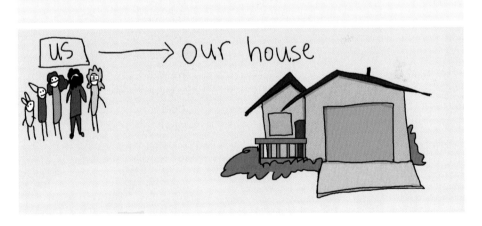

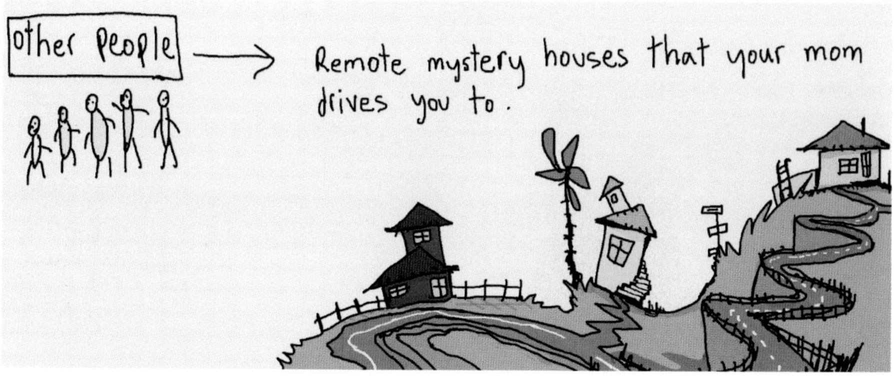
other people
Remote mystery houses that your mom drives you to.

We had a neighbor, Richard. But Richard was quiet and rarely outside for long, so I didn't know about him.

One afternoon, though, Richard went outside.

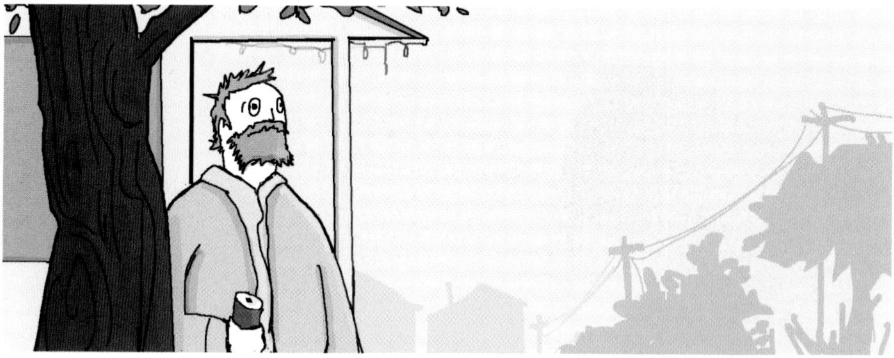

That's how I found out about him.

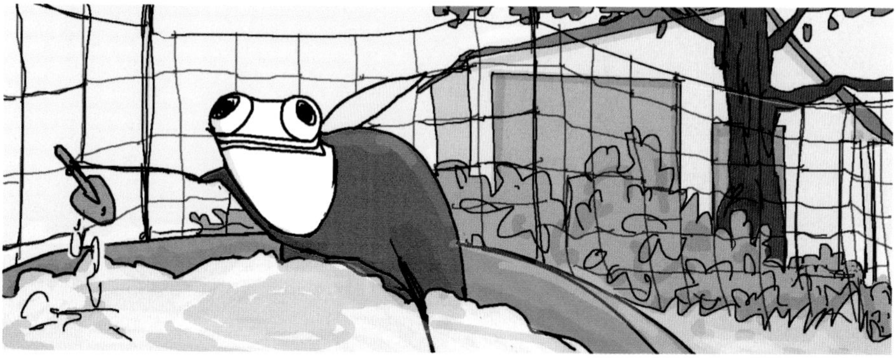

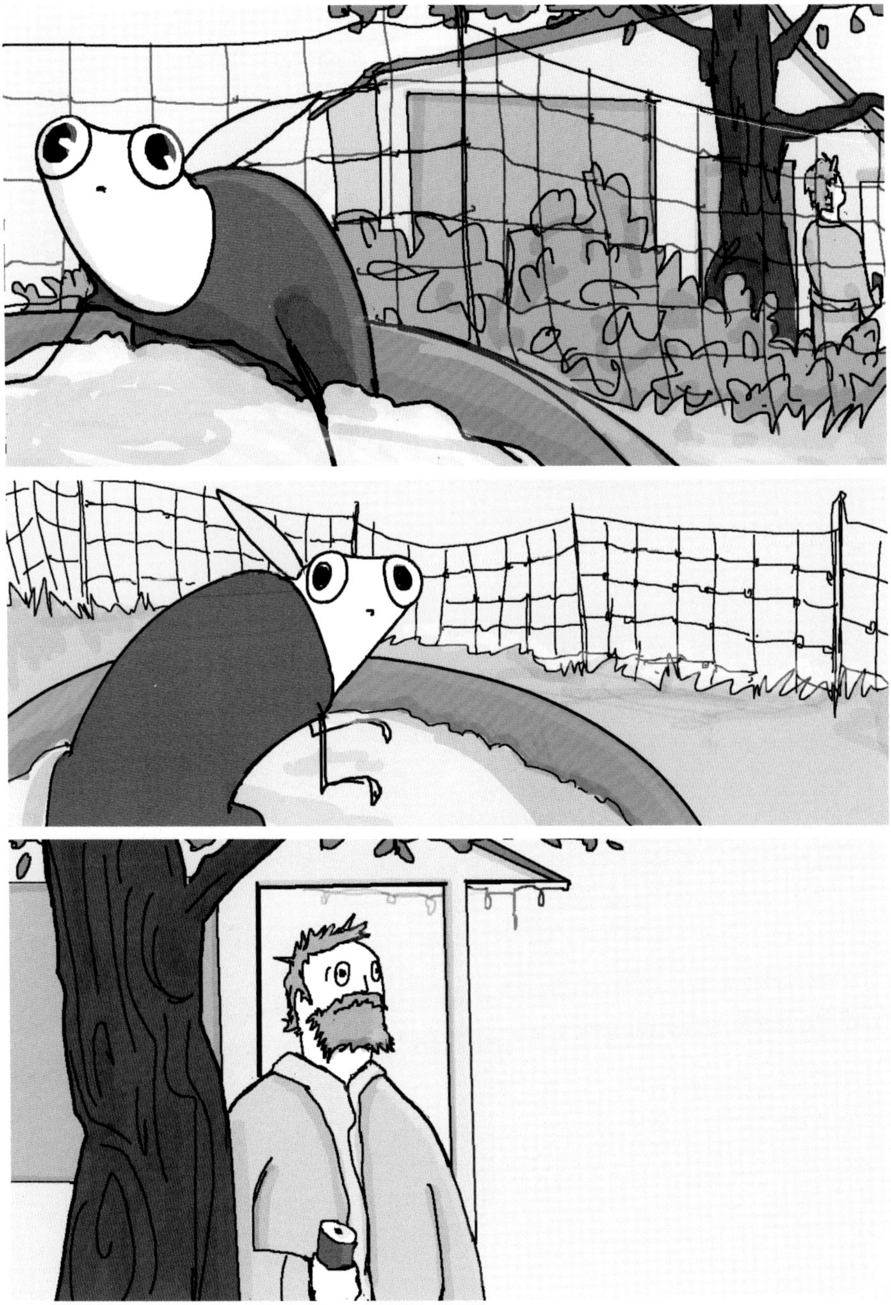

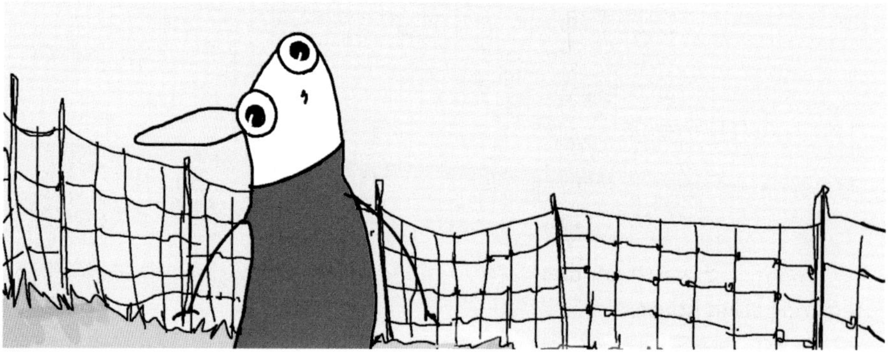

I did not interact with Richard. I just saw him. He probably didn't even know. He stood in his driveway for a minute or two and then went back into his house. But I saw him. I think that was the main thing.

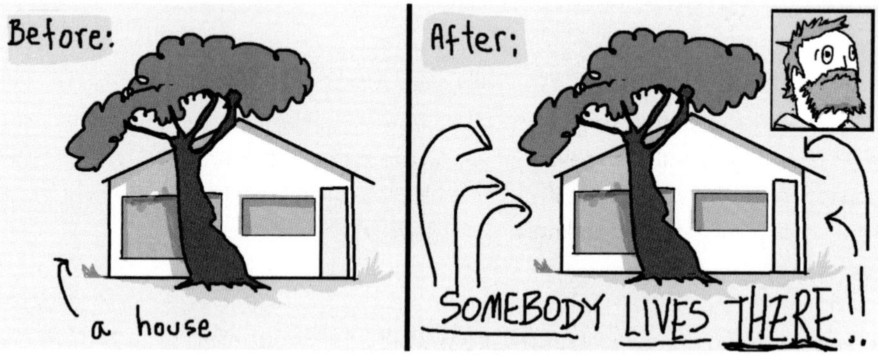

Before:
a house
After:
SOMEBODY LIVES THERE!!

It was very exciting. A person lives next to us! A *person*! He lives right there! And I SAW him! When will he go outside again? What else does he do? Does he know about Dad? Who is his friend? Does he like whales? Is his house the same as ours? Which room does his grandma live in?

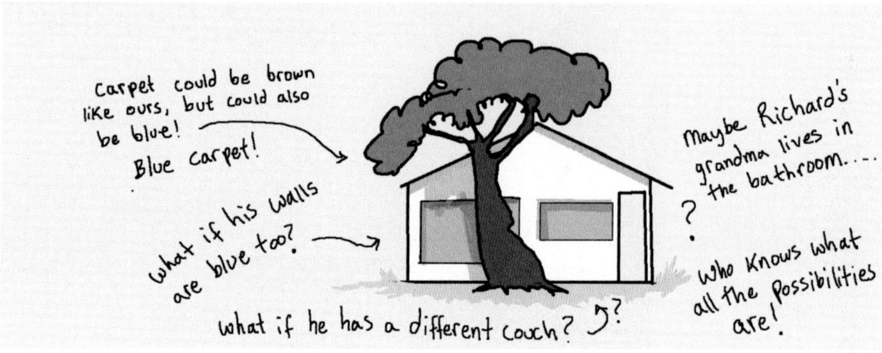

Carpet could be brown like ours, but could also be blue!
Blue carpet!
what if his walls are blue too?
what if he has a different couch?
Maybe Richard's grandma lives in the bathroom....
?
Who Knows what all the Possibilities are!

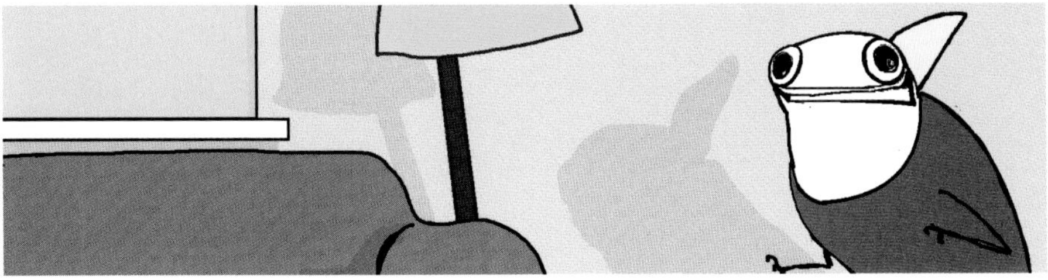

Desperate to catch another glimpse of him, I'd lurk near the windows all day, just staring at his house.

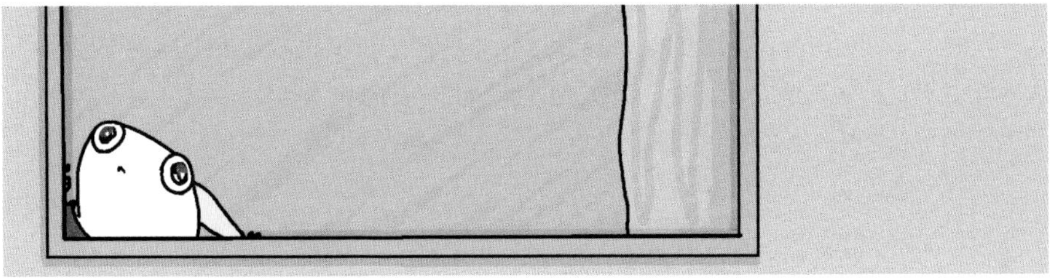

I think I expected it to go somewhere. You can't find out there's a person living right next to you and then never get any answers. Maybe if you're 100 years old and you know everybody, but not if you're 3. Not when it's the first stranger you know how to find. I just wanted to know more. Anything.

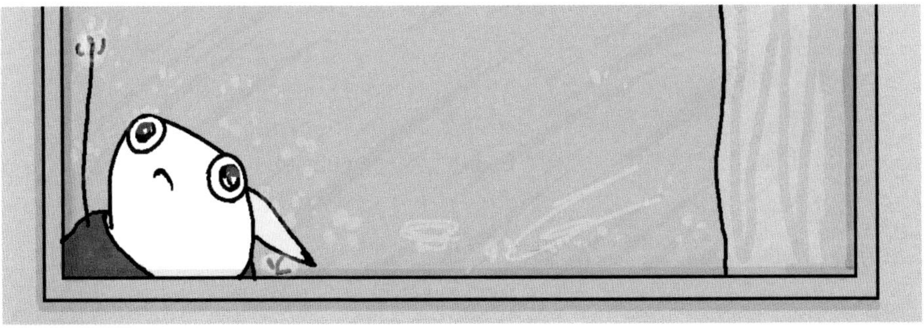

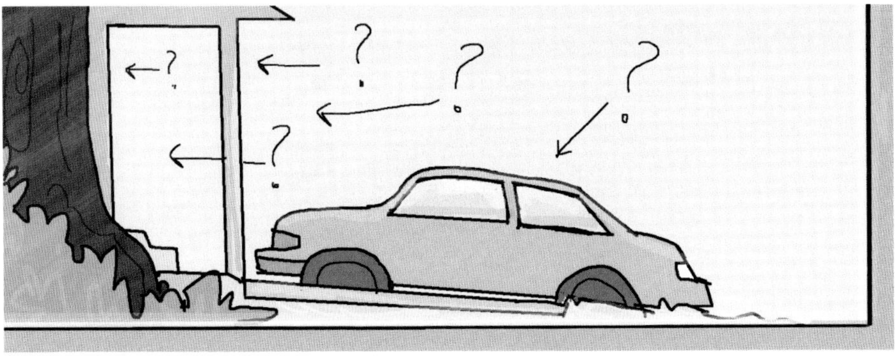

And this is as far as it would have been able to go if it wasn't for the dog door.

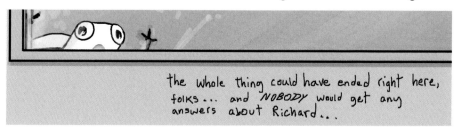

the whole thing could have ended right here, folks... and *NOBODY* would get any answers about Richard...

My grandma usually supervised me while my parents were at work. She'd drink screwdrivers and do the crossword, I'd run around the house and do whatever. If she hadn't seen me in a while, she'd check to make sure I still had all my fingers, but escaping wasn't a big concern. The doors were locked. Just in case, there were jingle bells on the handles.

The dog door was the single weak point in the fortress.

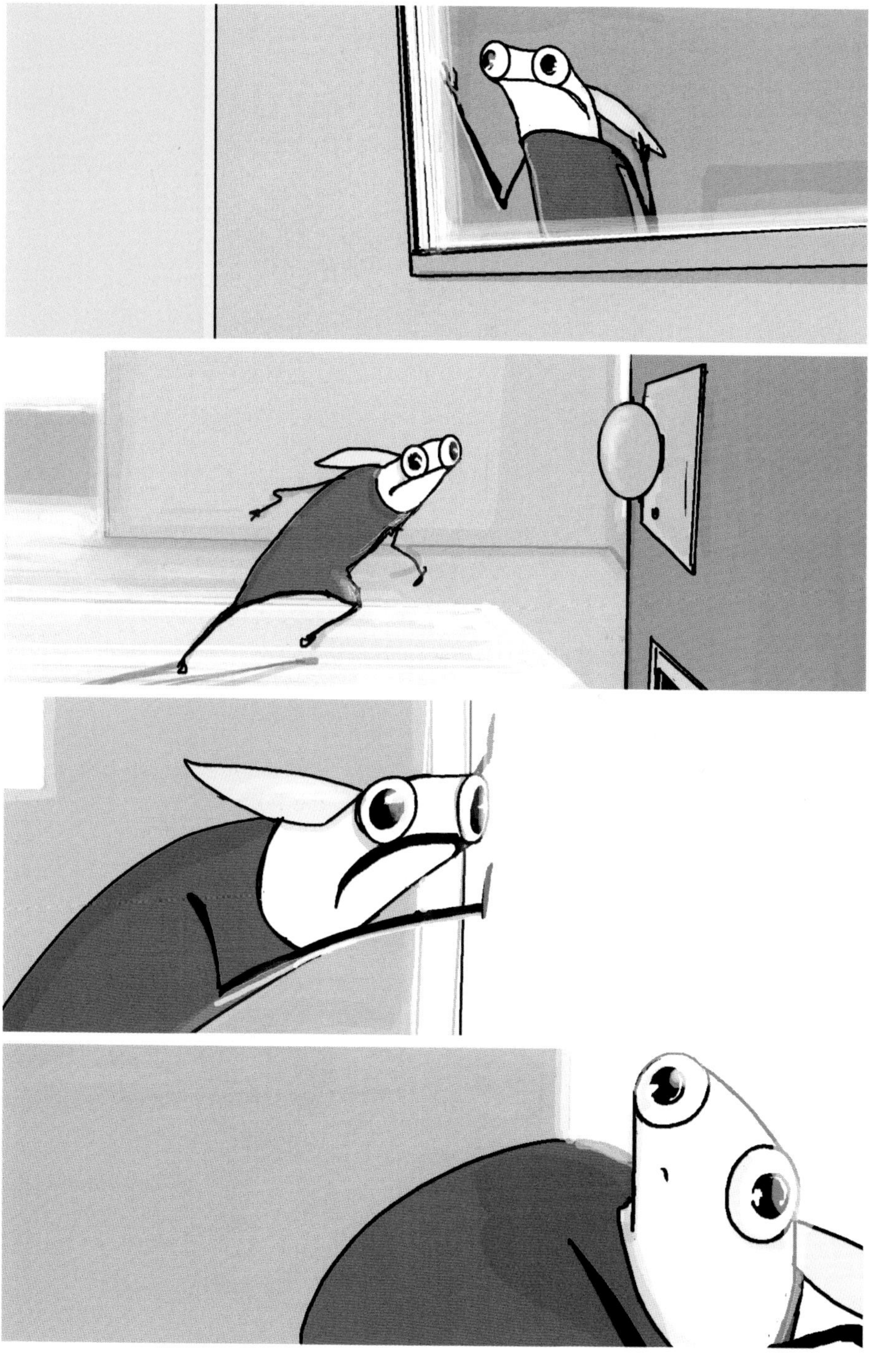

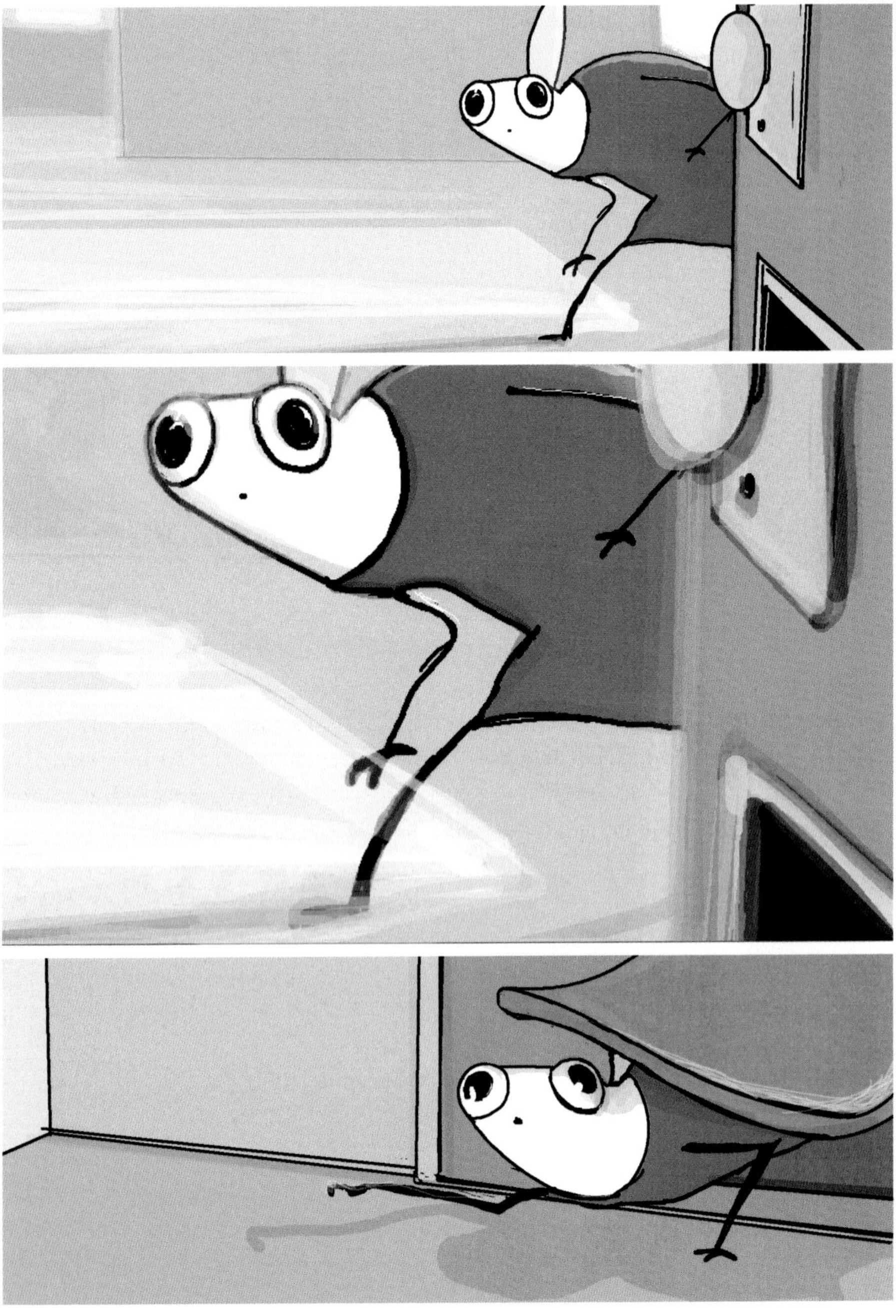

The revolutionary impact the dog door had on my ability to observe Richard was second only to the discovery of Richard himself.

I was cautious at first.

I just wanted to get a little closer. Just a little. I'd sneak out through the dog door and go stare at his house from the edge of our driveway, hoping this would summon him. When it didn't, I'd sneak a little closer. *Maybe it'll work if I stand in Richard's driveway … or, actually, maybe I'll just go over to this little window here and see what I can see …*

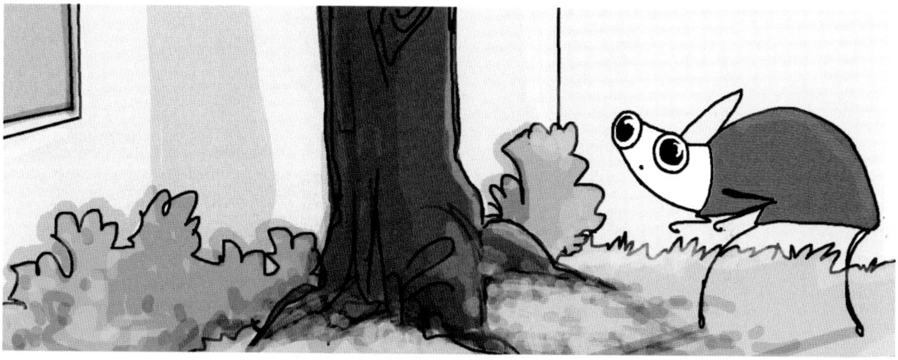

I started sneaking out more frequently. I started sneaking out at night. And the fact that I was *sneaking* seems to suggest I might've been at least partially aware that this type of behavior should be a secret, but I don't think I'd reached that crucial developmental point where you're capable of recognizing how creepy you're being.

However, on the night I found the cat door in Richard's garage, even my undeveloped, fish-level brain could sense that a boundary was about to be crossed. A tiny, instinctual trace of doubt—the wisdom of my ancestors whispering through the ages: *This might be too weird of a thing to do …*

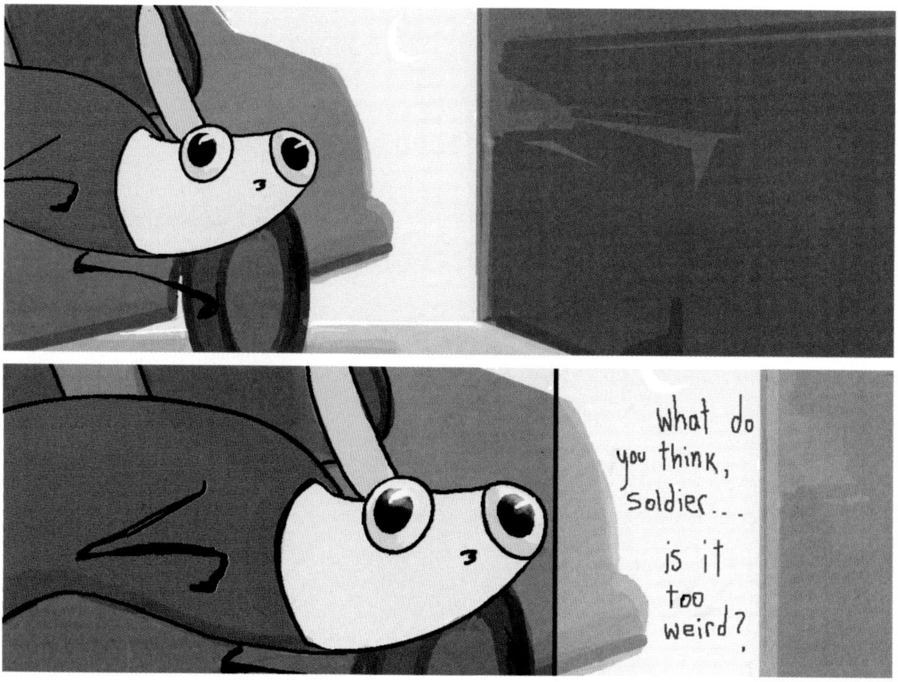
what do you think, soldier…
is it too weird?

Of course, one of the main features of undeveloped, fish-level brains is poor impulse control, and before I could complete the thought, I was in Richard's living room.

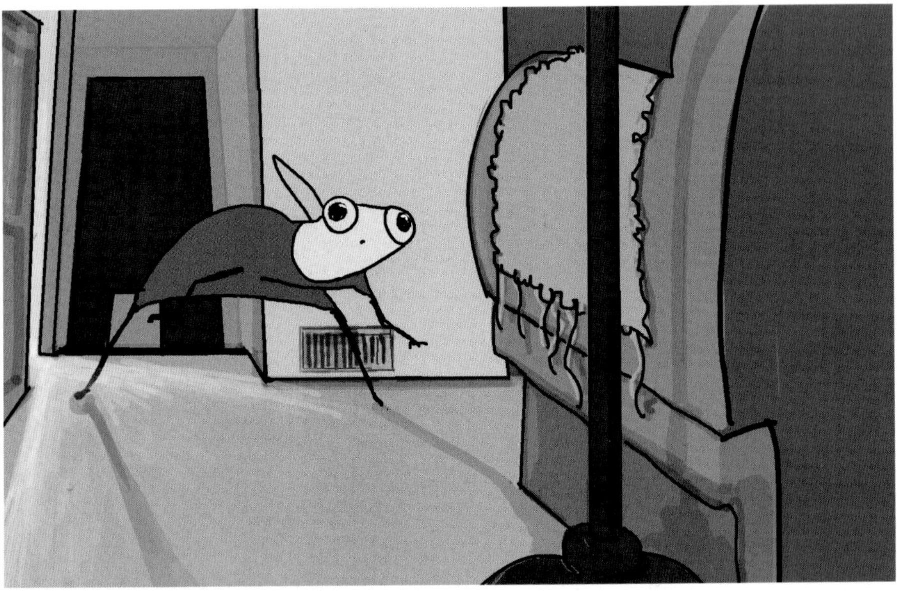

I hadn't prepared for this possibility. I'd dreamed of it, sure. But I wasn't expecting it to *HAPPEN*. So I just stood there for a little while and then retreated to regroup.

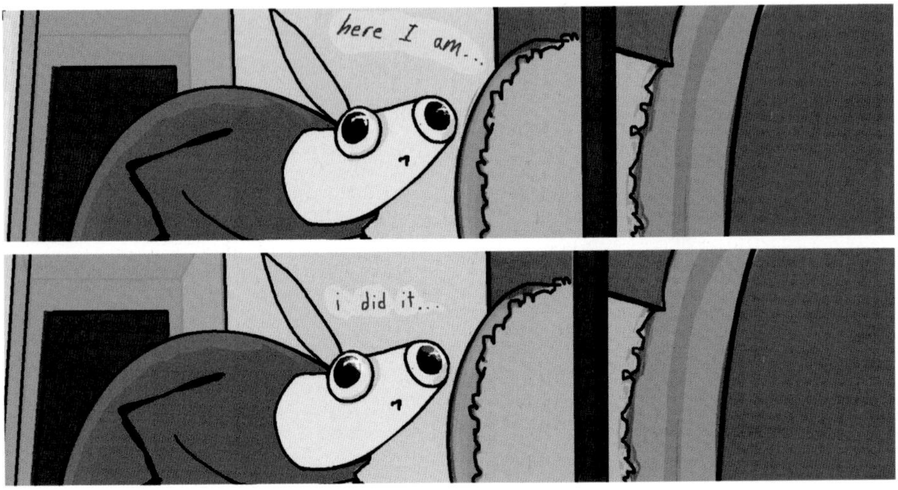
here I am...
i did it...

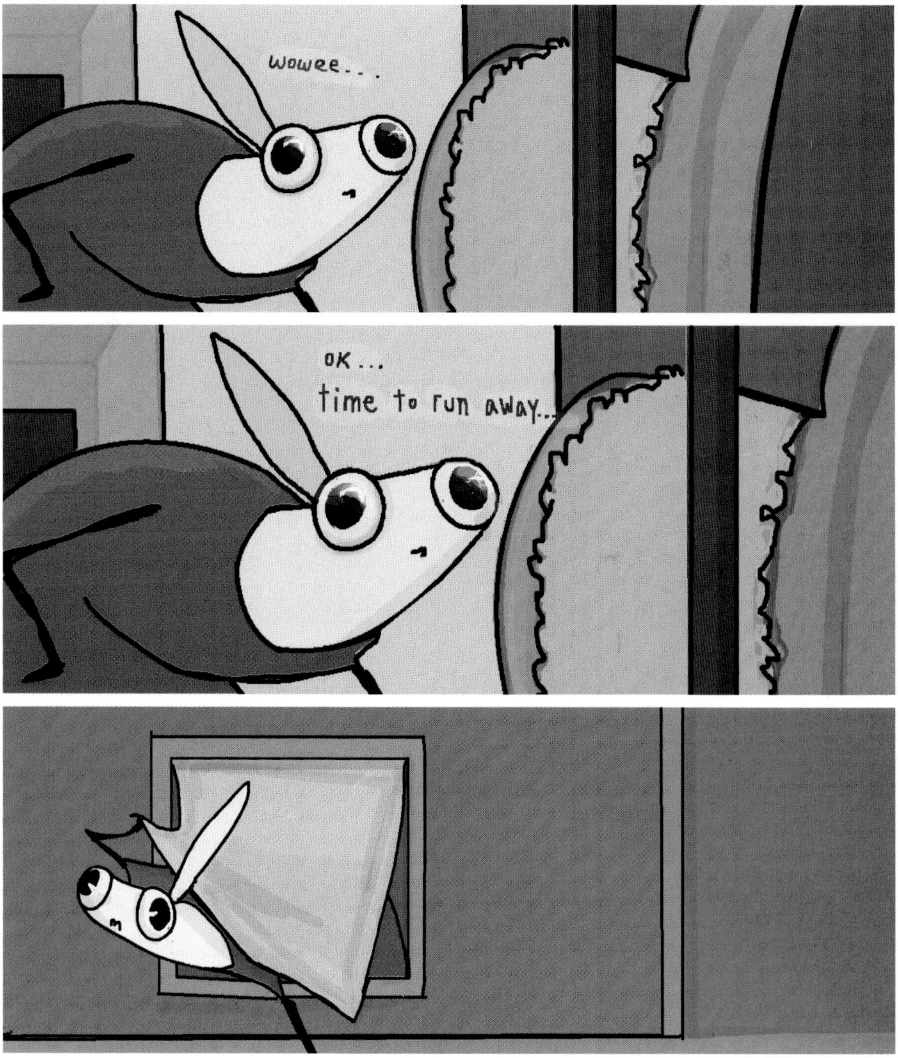
wowee...
ok...
time to run away...

A concrete objective never emerged, but the missions became bolder and more frequent. I started bringing things back with me. Richard's things.

They seemed valuable, somehow. Richard likes these things... Perhaps they contain the secret to Richard...

A nonsensical collection of Richard's possessions slowly accumulated at the back of my toy drawer.

This would prove to be my downfall.

Long before that, though, my mom noticed that I'd mysteriously disappear sometimes. She wasn't worried yet because she didn't think I knew how to get out of the house, but one day she asked me where I'd been.

And I said:

"Hanging out with Richard."

"Hanging out" was a misnomer—Richard had been hanging out by himself, and I had been standing in his hallway just out of view—but this was concerning news to my parents. They didn't even know that I knew Richard, let alone that we'd been "hanging out." They went over and knocked on Richard's door and asked him about it, probably with thinly veiled suspicion regarding Richard being a child predator. And Richard, who was still somehow unaware of all the hanging out we'd been doing, told them he didn't know anything about that.

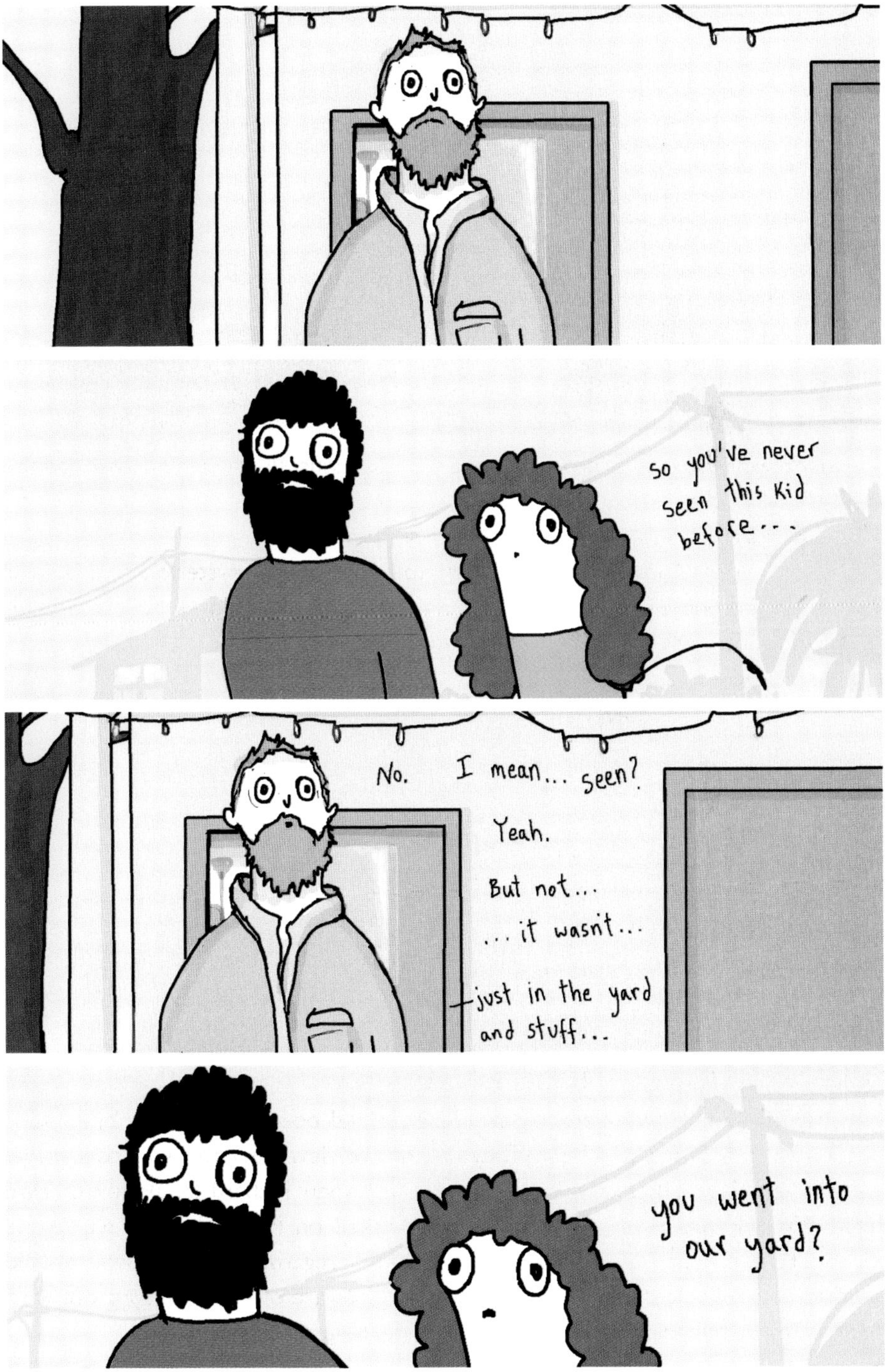
So you've never seen this Kid before...
No. I mean... seen?
Yeah.
But not...
... it wasn't...
just in the yard and stuff...
you went into our yard?

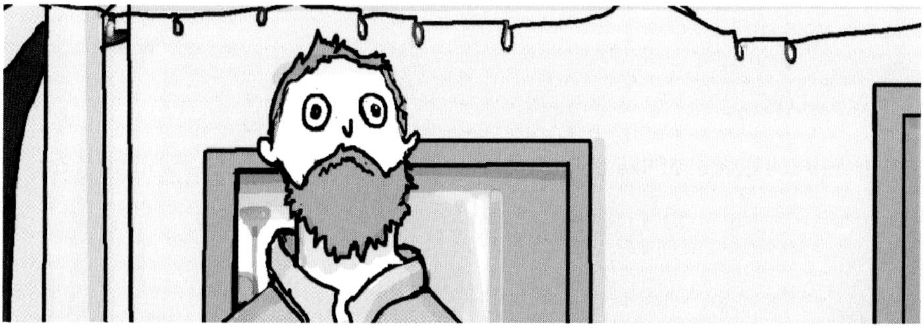

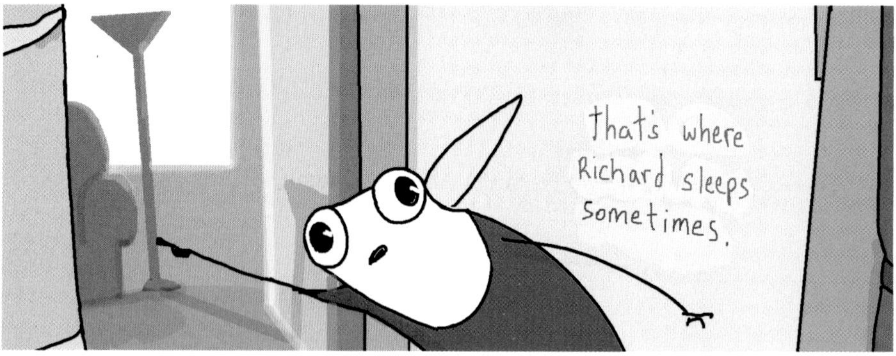
that's where Richard sleeps sometimes.

I imagine things were tense for a bit. The suggestion that I'd been hanging out with Richard was disturbing for both my parents and Richard. But the clues piled up. I couldn't control myself. I took more things, bigger things. I also branched over into hiding things for Richard to find. Pretty rocks, pieces of string, letters I'd tried to write. At that age, I didn't know how to spell very many words, so the messages were fairly cryptic: *the entire alphabet, followed by the word "Mom" and a drawing of the sun. Rampant scribbling, hundreds of tiny circles, and . . . is this a spider??*

The spider was supposed to be Richard. I hadn't figured out how many arms and legs people are supposed to have yet, so I just put a whole bunch on there and hoped it was enough. I didn't want him to feel offended because I shortchanged him on legs.

 ← Look how **beautiful** You are, Richard !!

It must've come off like being haunted by a defective but well-meaning ghost.

The connection should have been obvious. But, when faced with a mystery like, "Where did my remote control go? Why is there a piece of paper with a child's handwriting on it hiding in the VCR? And how do these rocks keep getting in here?" almost no rational adult would jump to the conclusion "because a child has been sneaking in through my cat door and leaving these for me to discover." Not even with clues. I don't know what theory Richard came up with to explain it, but it almost certainly wasn't that one.

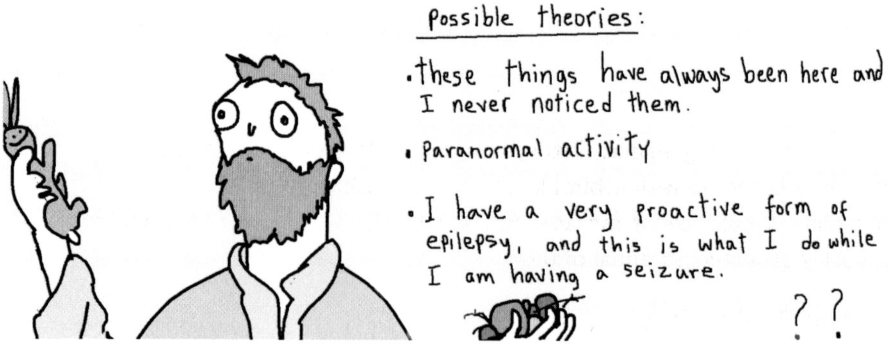
possible theories:
• these things have always been here and I never noticed them.
• paranormal activity
• I have a very proactive form of epilepsy, and this is what I do while I am having a seizure.
??

Similarly, when faced with a mystery like "Why does our child keep disappearing? And why has our child been 'hanging out' with our 40-year-old neighbor?" almost no rational adult would jump to the conclusion "because our child has become obsessed with our 40-year-old neighbor, and 'hanging out' is a loose term to describe the activity of spying."

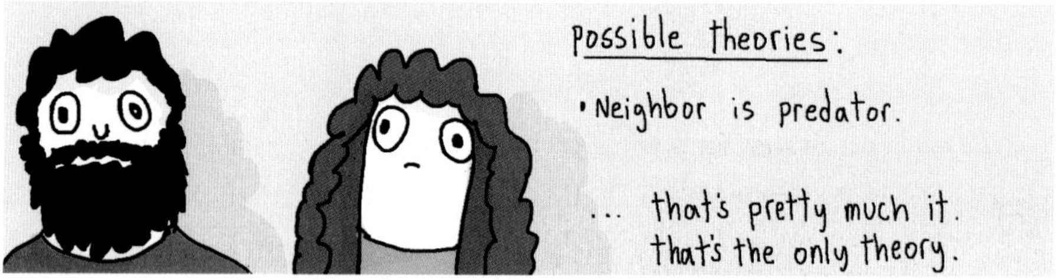
possible theories:
• Neighbor is predator.
... that's pretty much it. that's the only theory.

The thing that finally blew my cover was stealing Richard's cat.

Stealing it wasn't the original plan. The opportunity presented itself, I seized it.

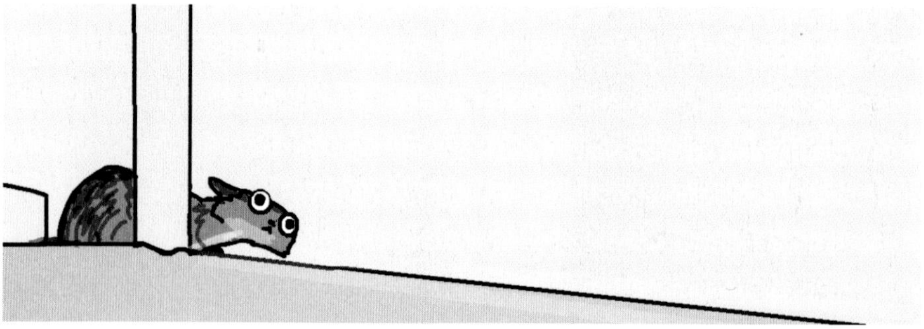

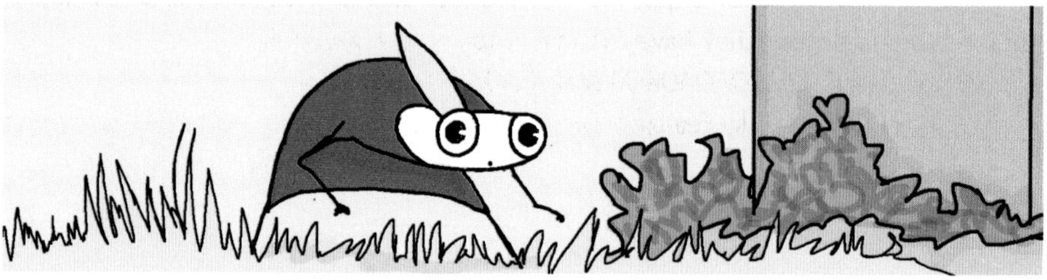

It was a strong animal. Getting it into the drawer was difficult. I didn't have a plan for what to do with it, but I knew I had something valuable. And I think the idea was that I should save it for later. For when I figured out how to capitalize on the probably unlimited potential of this.

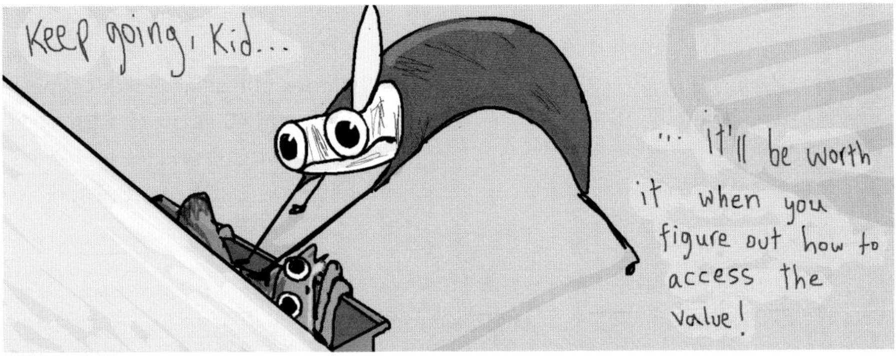
Keep going, Kid...
... it'll be worth it when you figure out how to access the value!

It lived in the drawer for a while. I don't know how long. Hours, probably.

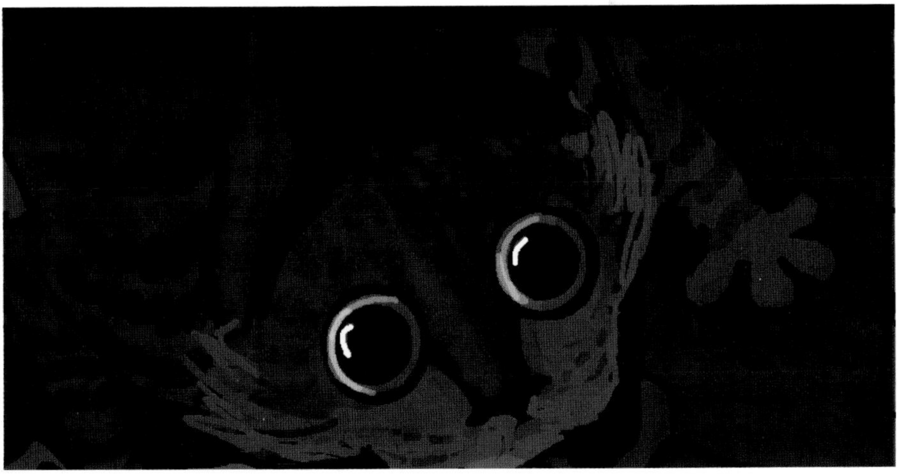

And now it is time for a quick fact about cats: cats aren't good secrets, because, under extreme duress, they have the ability to make a sound like:

YAOAOAOAOAOAOAOAOAOAOAOAOAOAOAOAOAOAOAOAOAO

My parents eventually realized the sound was coming from inside the house and located the source of it.

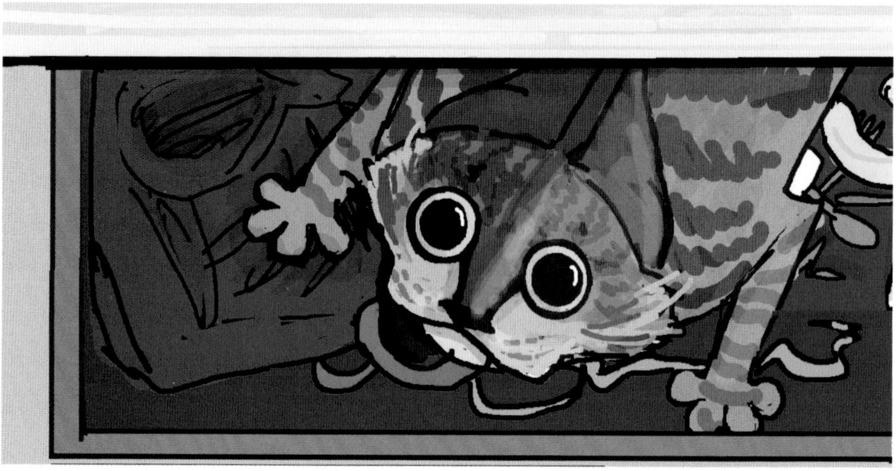

They weren't expecting to find quite so many of Richard's things.

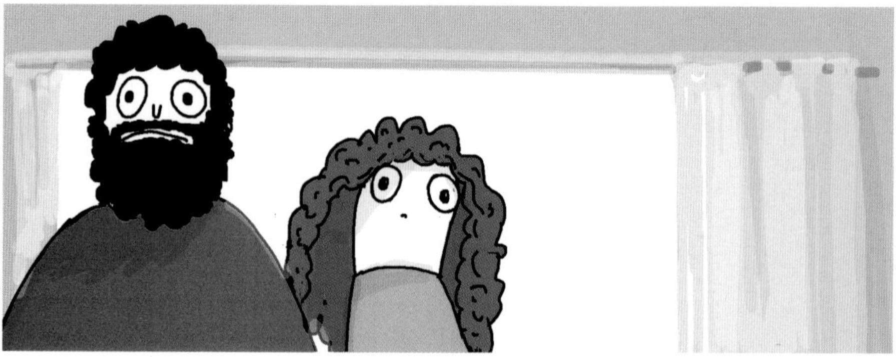

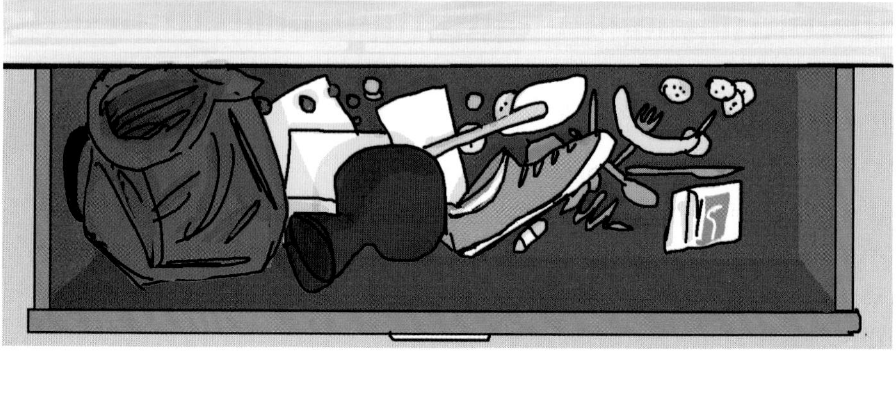

I don't know if they put the pieces together immediately, or processed them individually as they came up—*"First of all, there's a cat in this drawer; how about that. Next up: there appear to be a considerable number of objects under the cat. This one is a shoe. This one is a piece of bread. This one is a credit card bill. Huh ... it's addressed to 'Richard the Neighbor ...'"*—inching closer to the truth with every clue until the ultimate answer to "What does 'hanging out with Richard' mean?" was revealed. There was more than enough evidence to answer the question.

That's got to be a strange moment for a parent. There's this omnipresent fear of predators and monsters, and you just ... you never quite expect to find out the monster is your kid.

They confronted me after a strategy meeting about how the fuck to handle this. That's not something the books prepare you for. There's no chapter on what to do if you suspect your child is a predator. There's no Hallmark card for "Sorry we accused you of being a molester; we didn't realize our kid was sneaking into your house and stealing your spoons and animals and watching you while you sleep. We're really, really sorry."

That primal shame instinct I'd felt in Richard's garage flickered back online a little bit. Looking at the objects, and the freaked-out cat, and my parents' confused faces, I realized that, yeah, maybe this had been a weird thing to do.

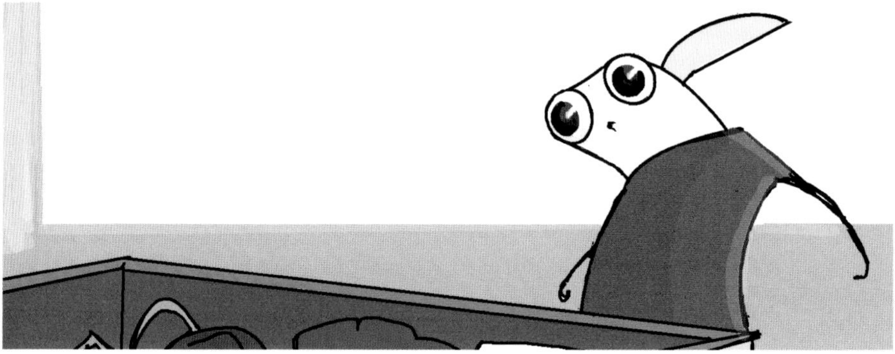

I felt like I should explain why I had done this, but I didn't know either. So we all just stood there, feeling weird about ourselves and each other.

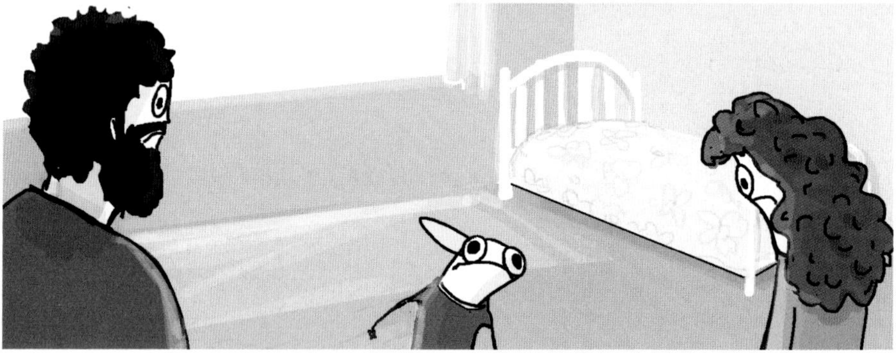

The cat was stoked to be free, though.

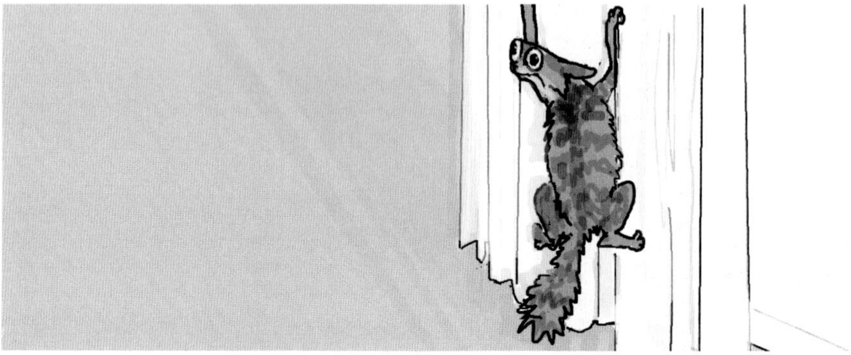

Karma

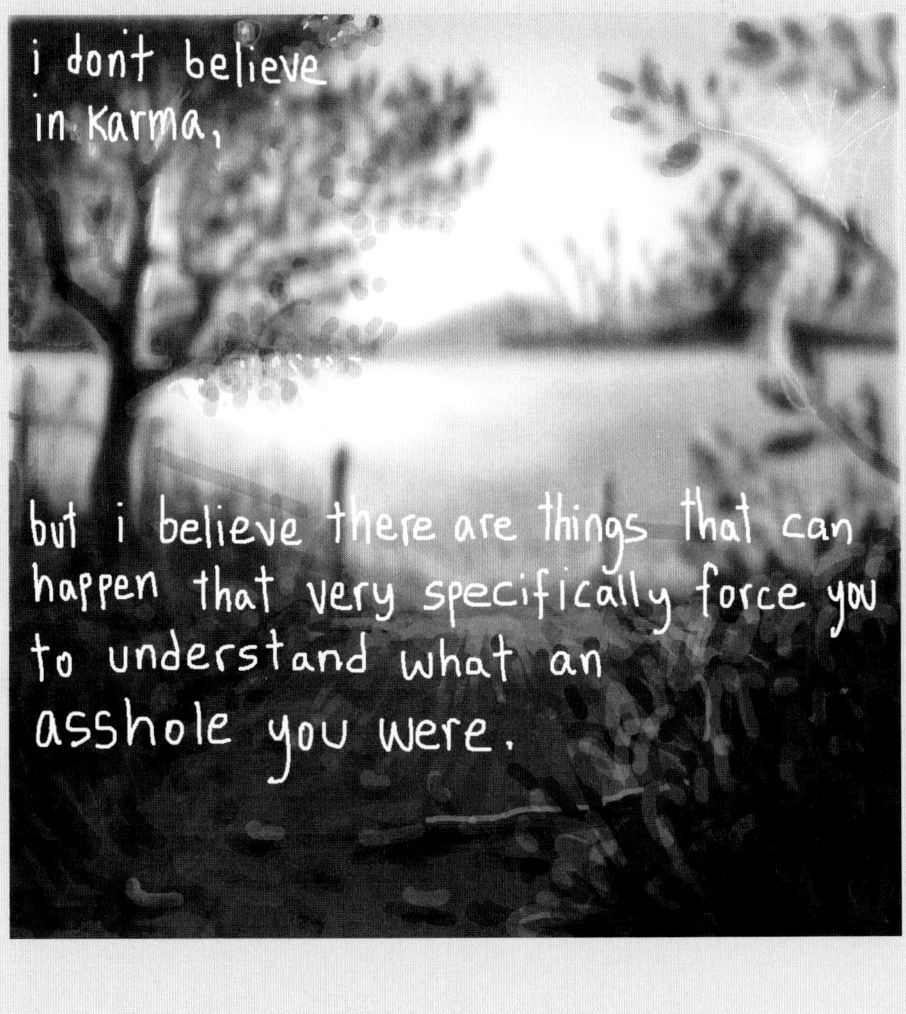
i don't believe
in Karma,
but i believe there are things that can
happen that very specifically force you
to understand what an
asshole you were.

3. NEIGHBOR KID

My neighbor's 5-year-old is a social juggernaut.

I can't leave my apartment unless I figure out how to deal with her. She gets up at 5 in the morning and hangs out directly in front of my door like a bridge troll—all who wish to pass must answer her riddles, and the only riddle she knows is *Do you want to see my room?*

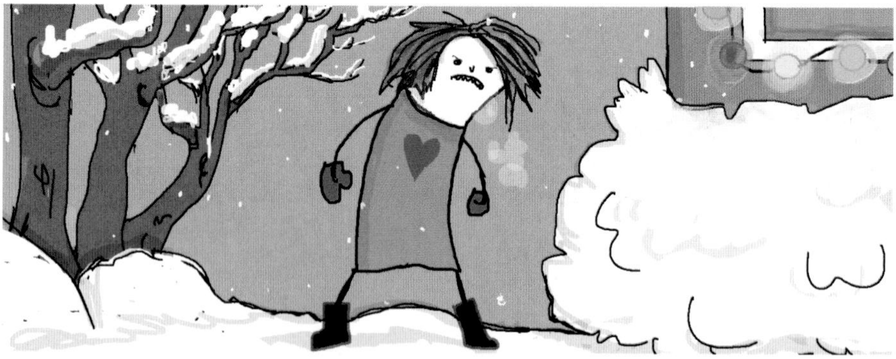

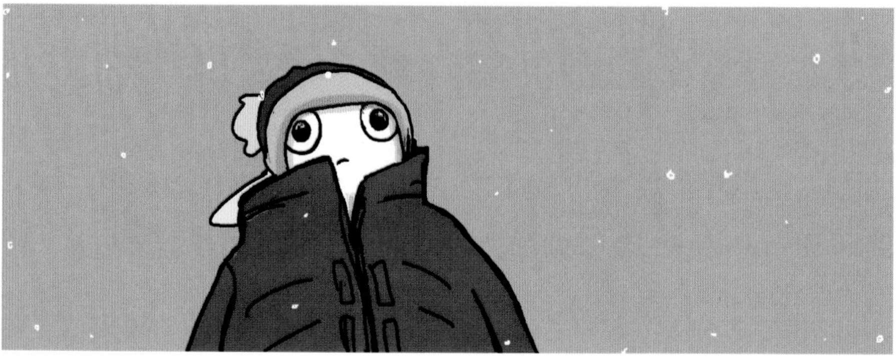

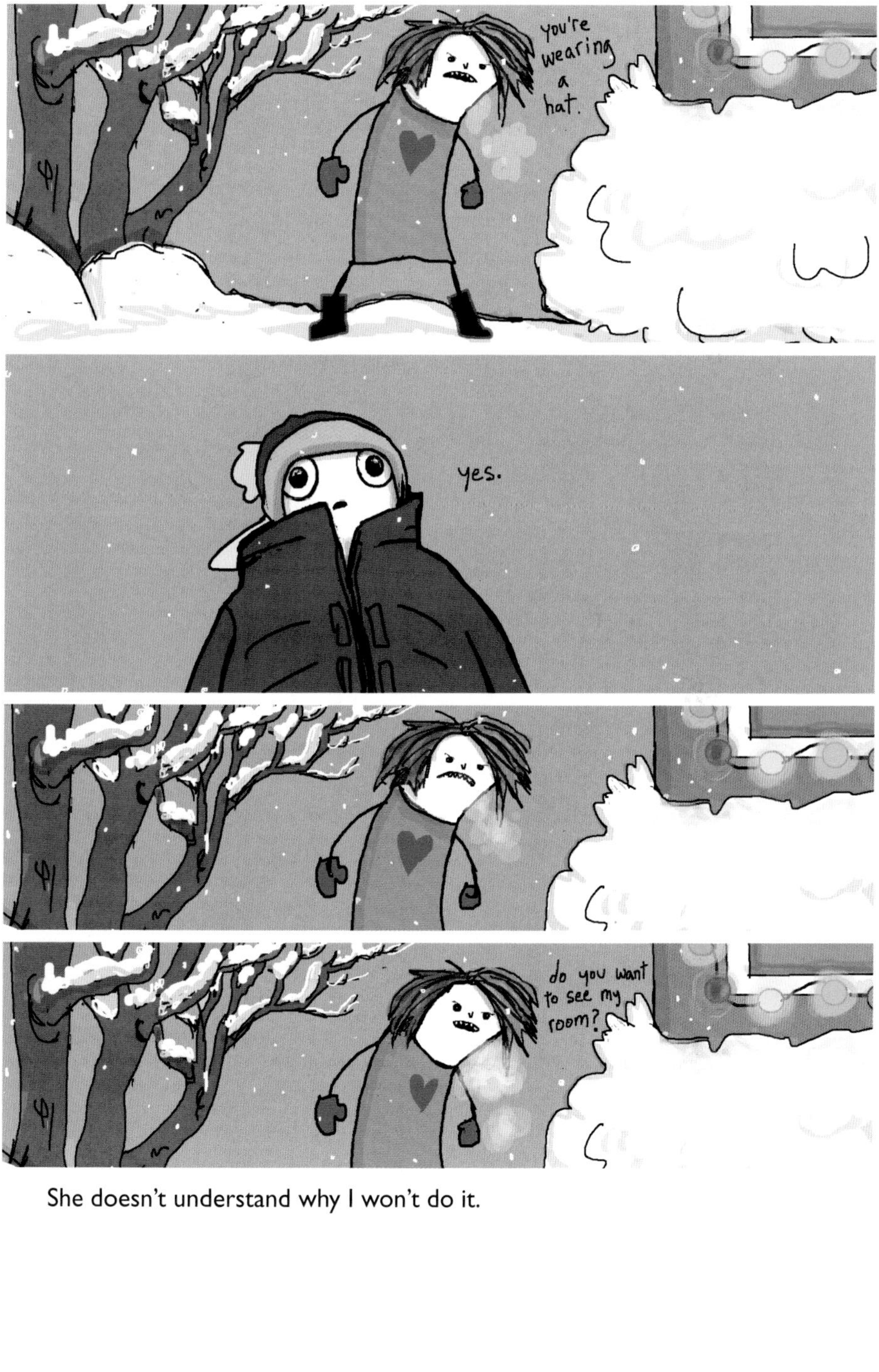
you're wearing a hat.
yes.
do you want to see my room?

She doesn't understand why I won't do it.

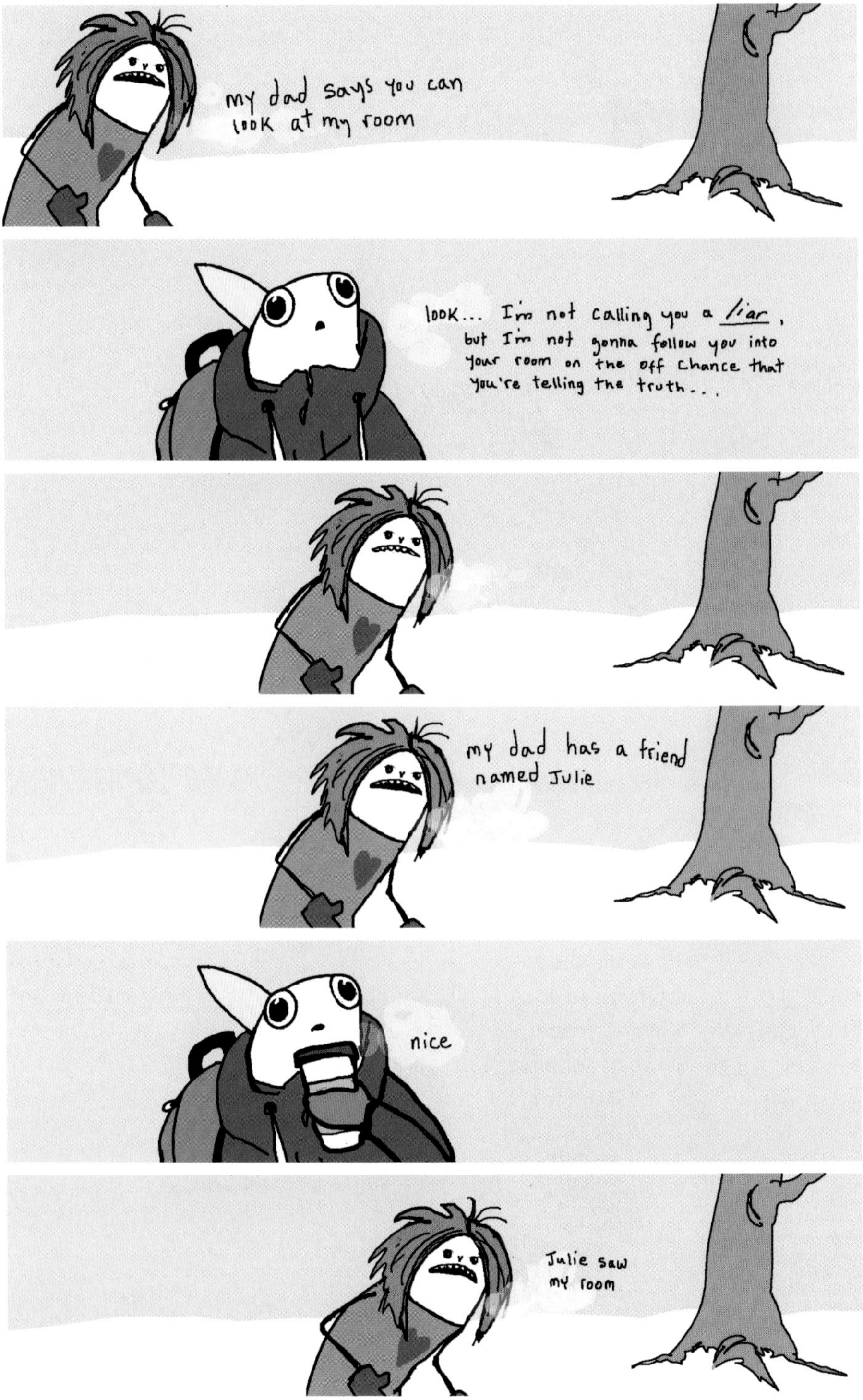
my dad says you can look at my room
look... I'm not calling you a liar, but I'm not gonna follow you into your room on the off chance that you're telling the truth...
my dad has a friend named Julie
nice
Julie saw my room

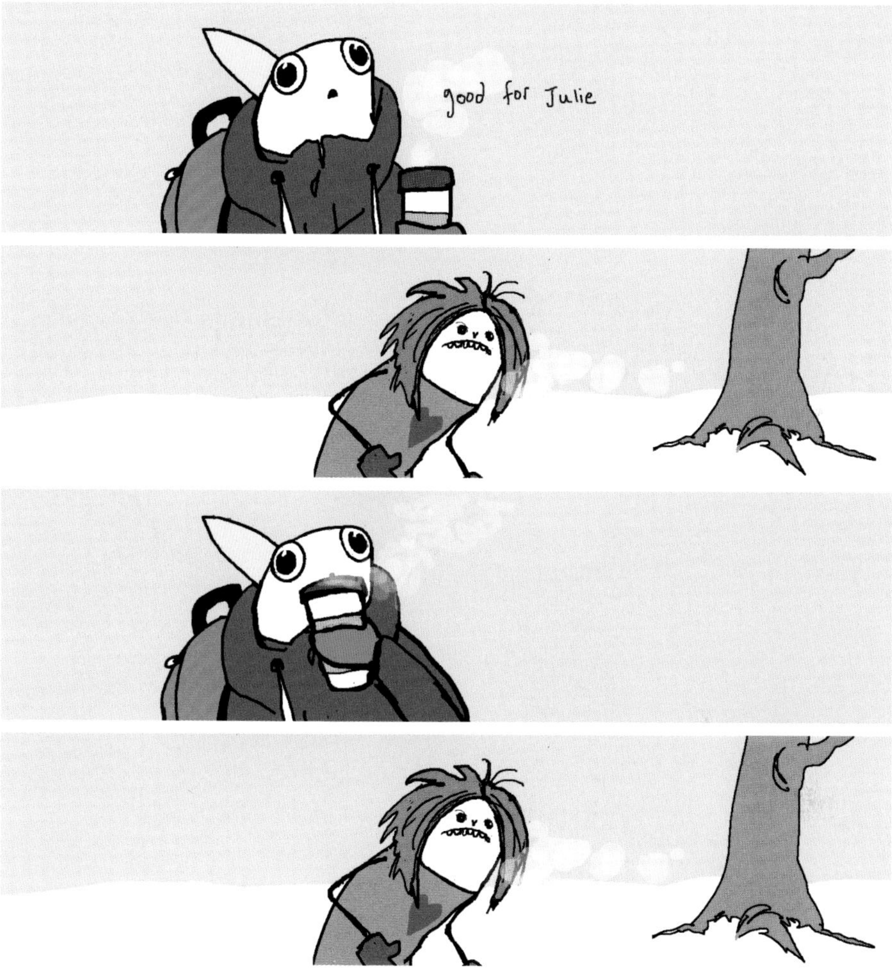
good for Julie

Permission isn't really the main issue. Her dad, Julie, and everybody she knows could give me permission to look at her room while crawling on their bellies and begging me to look at her room, and I still wouldn't do it. This isn't the kind of situation where you want to set a precedent for caving under pressure. I mean, what's gonna happen? I go look at her room and then she leaves me alone forever?

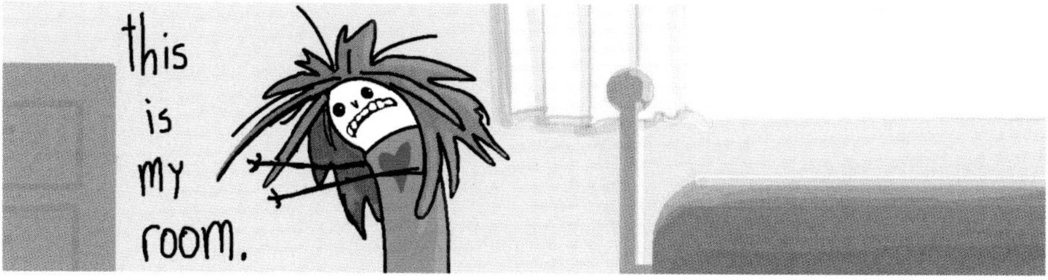
this is my room.

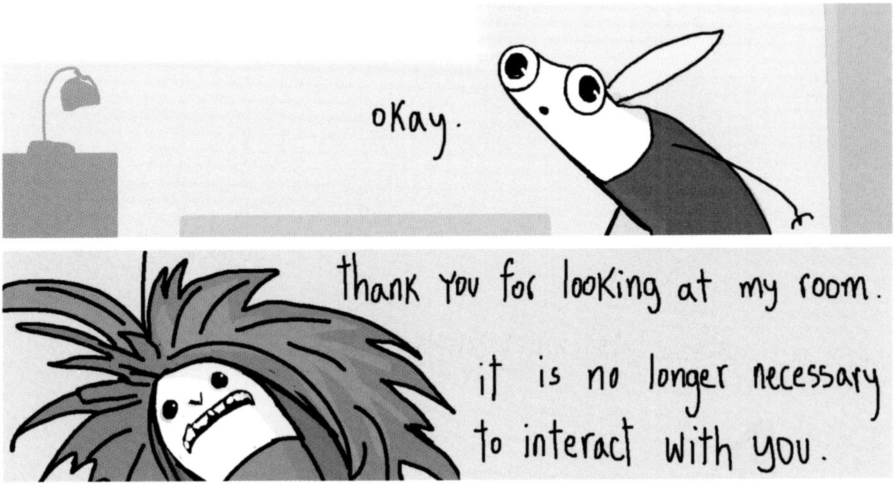
okay.
thank you for looking at my room.
it is no longer necessary to interact with you.

I thought it would die down after a few weeks of nonstop rejection, but she is *relentless*.

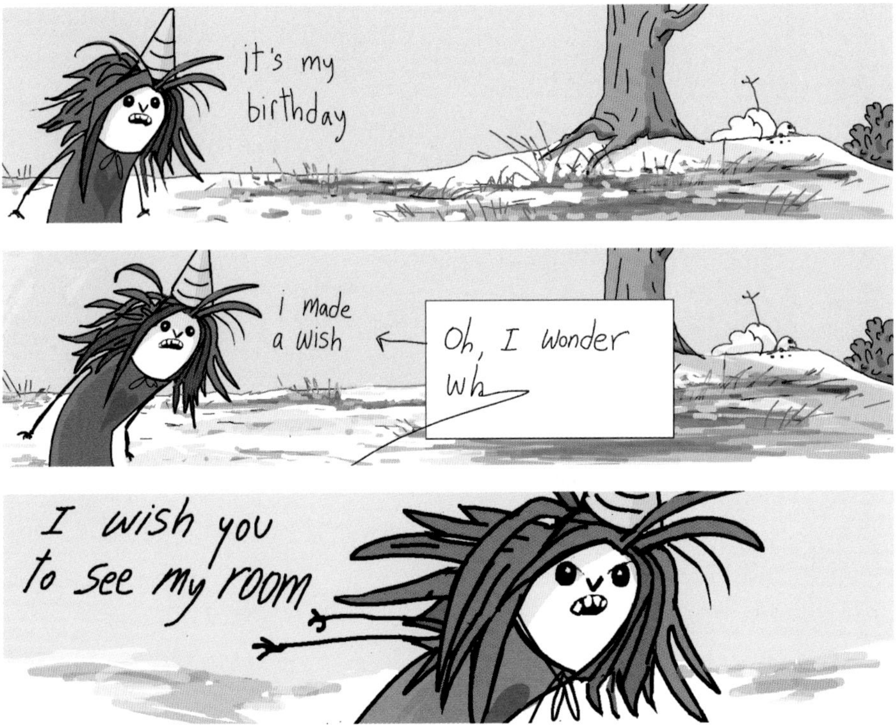
it's my birthday
i made a wish
Oh, I wonder wh
I wish you to see my room

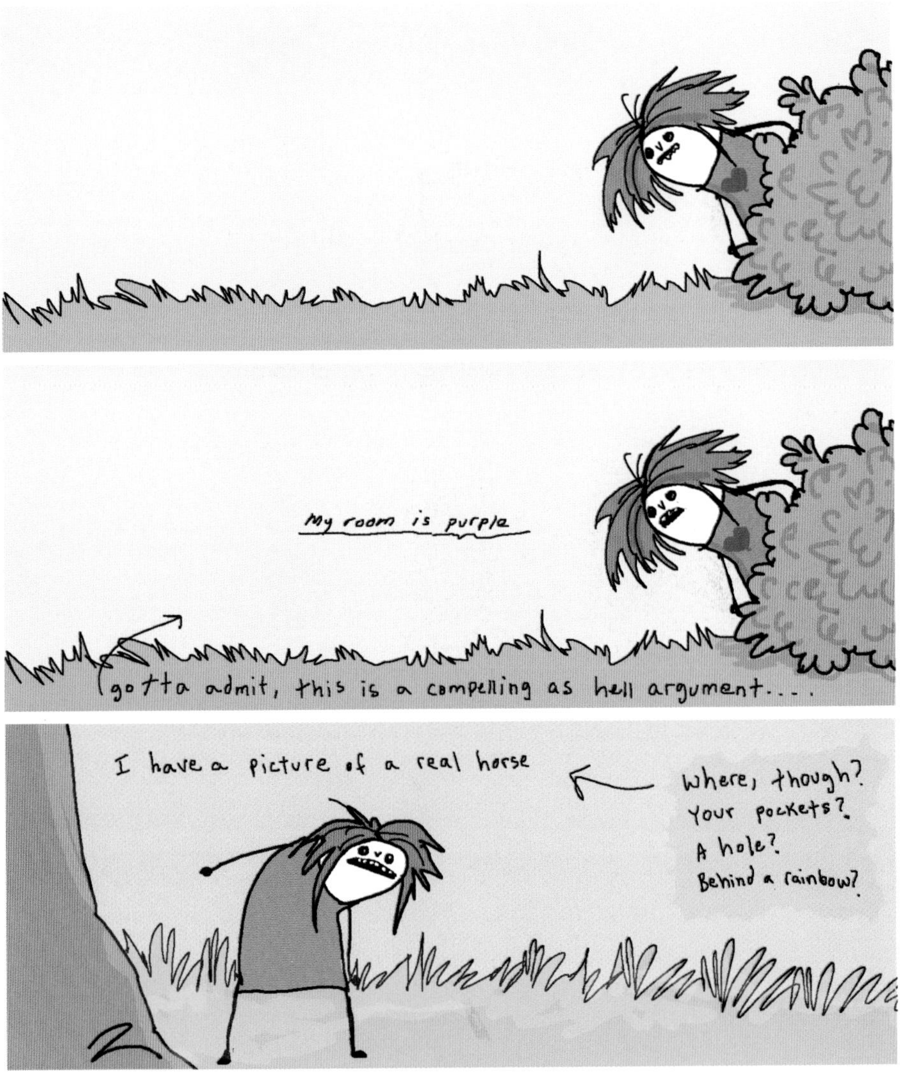
my room is purple
gotta admit, this is a compelling as hell argument....
I have a picture of a real horse
where, though? Your pockets? A hole? Behind a rainbow?

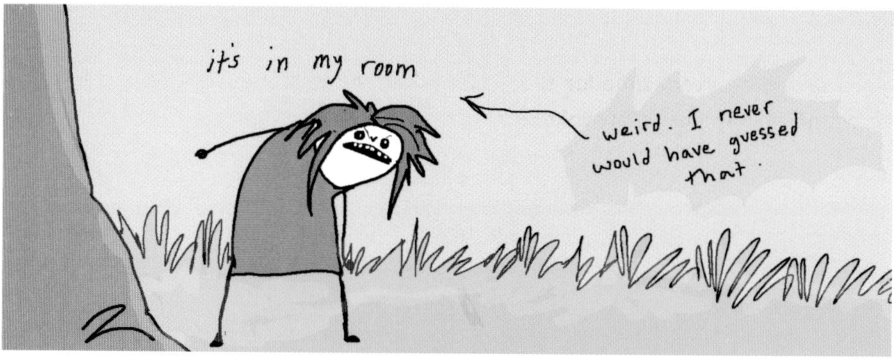
it's in my room
weird. I never would have guessed that.

She's always telling me how great it is, wildly exaggerating the number of lamps she has like it's gonna change my mind after seven consecutive months of saying no.

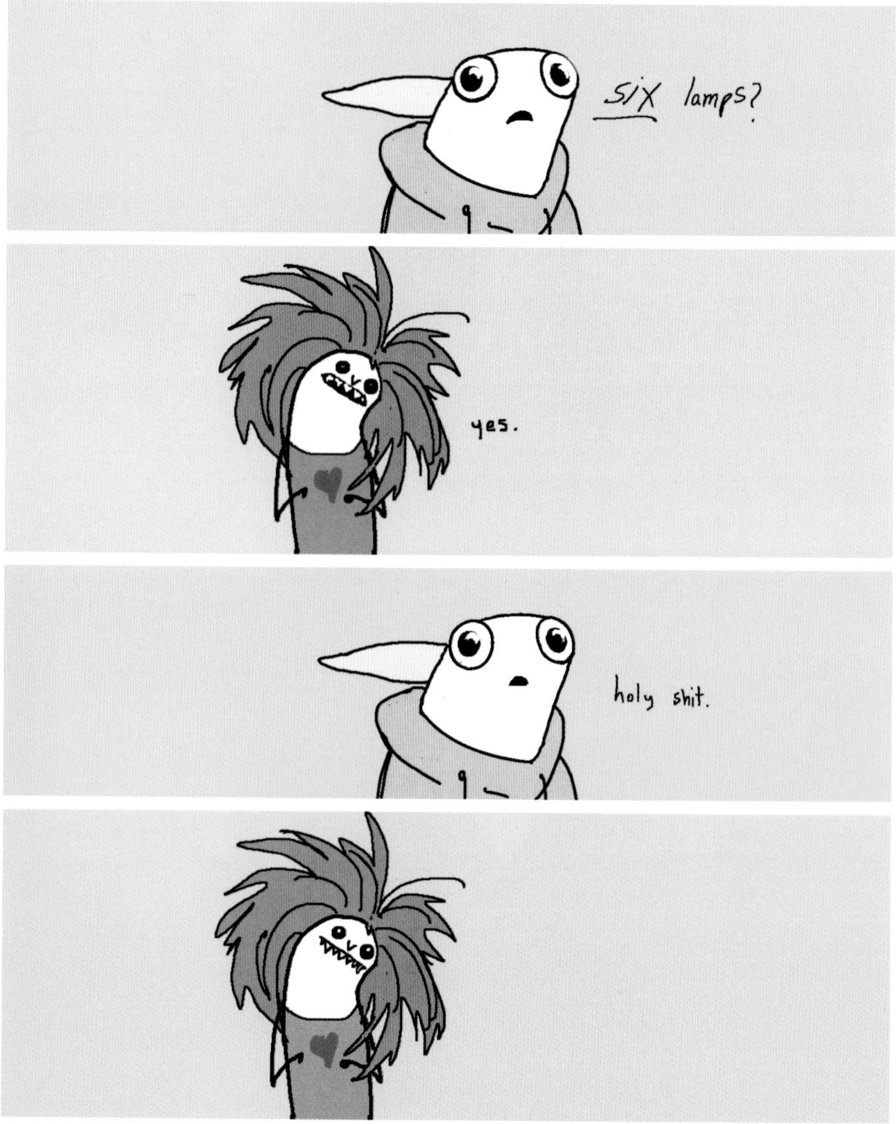
six lamps?
yes.
holy shit.

I've said no every time for the whole seven months. She won't take it. In fact, a direct no only seems to provoke her.

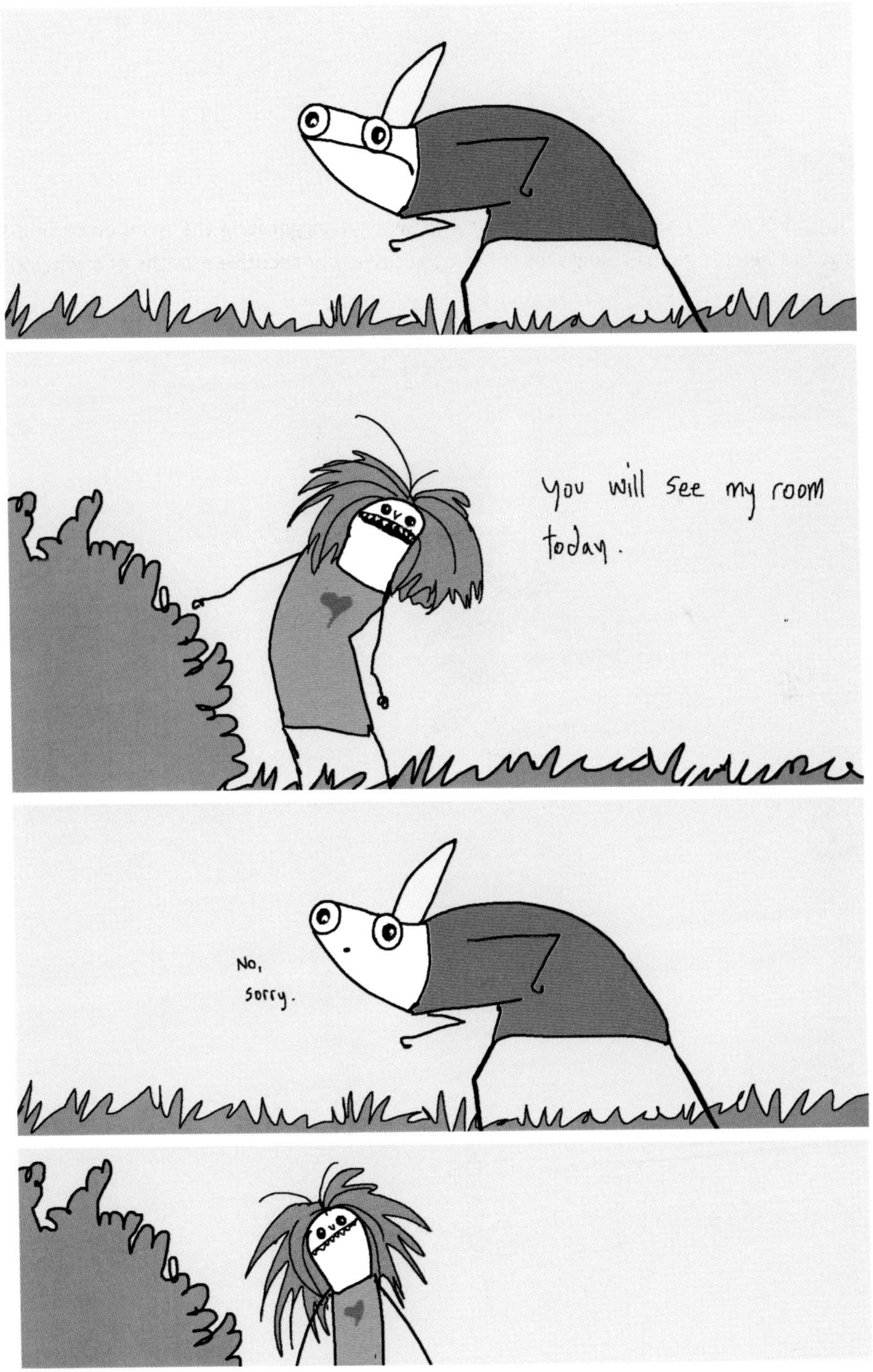
you will see my room today.
No, sorry.

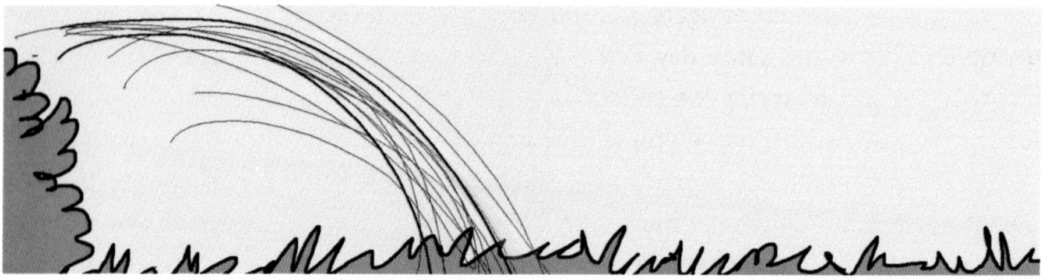

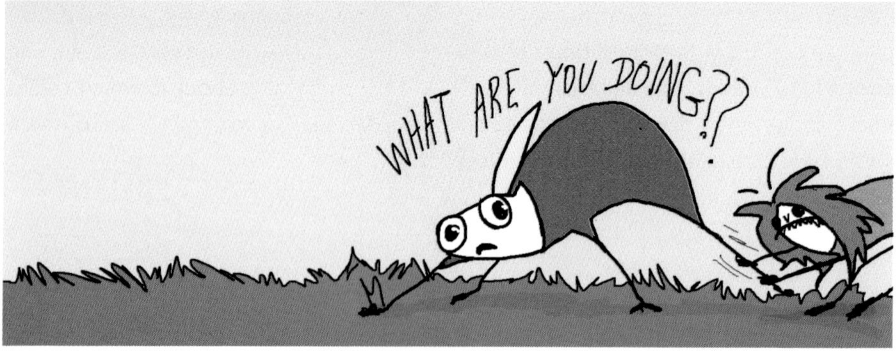
WHAT ARE YOU DOING??

Is this how negging works? I act like this kid's room is no big deal, and she becomes singularly obsessed with proving her room's value?

I have never met anybody who is this determined about anything. I honestly don't understand where she finds the motivation to keep going.

Here's the thing, though: part of me is legitimately starting to wonder what the fuck is so special about this room. Is there a portal in there? Is this a cry for help? Does she really have six lamps? What on earth could anybody need that many lamps for?

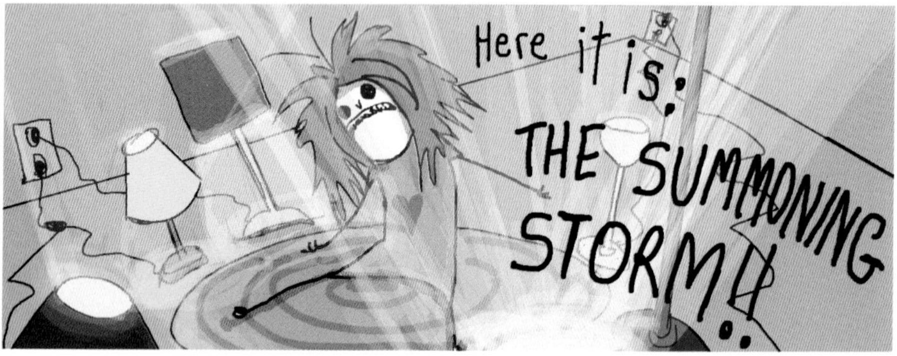
Here it is:
THE SUMMONING STORM!!

She's the weirdest person I know. If anybody's got a magical bedroom, it'd be her.

But this kid's a one-way friendship train with no brakes. I can't risk encouraging her. The second she senses weakness, she'll be crawling in through my windows.

It's getting hard to navigate around. I see her at least twice a week. Sometimes multiple times in the same day. The interactions are tense, only barely avoiding the fact that she's been asking me to look at her room for seven months, and somehow it hasn't happened yet. We're gonna have to deal with it eventually.

In the meantime, it's a precarious balance between not provoking her and not destroying her self-esteem. I mean, the easiest way to end the interaction would be to ignore her and use my superior strength to overpower her attempts to restrain me—I don't have to answer her questions. But she'd keep trying, and you can't brutally reject a kid at least two times every week and expect it to not leave a dent. This poor kid is already weirder than anybody. So I try to be nice about it, which means I have to lie. Every day, this kid comes at me harder and harder, and I have to invent some fable to explain why I still can't look at her room.

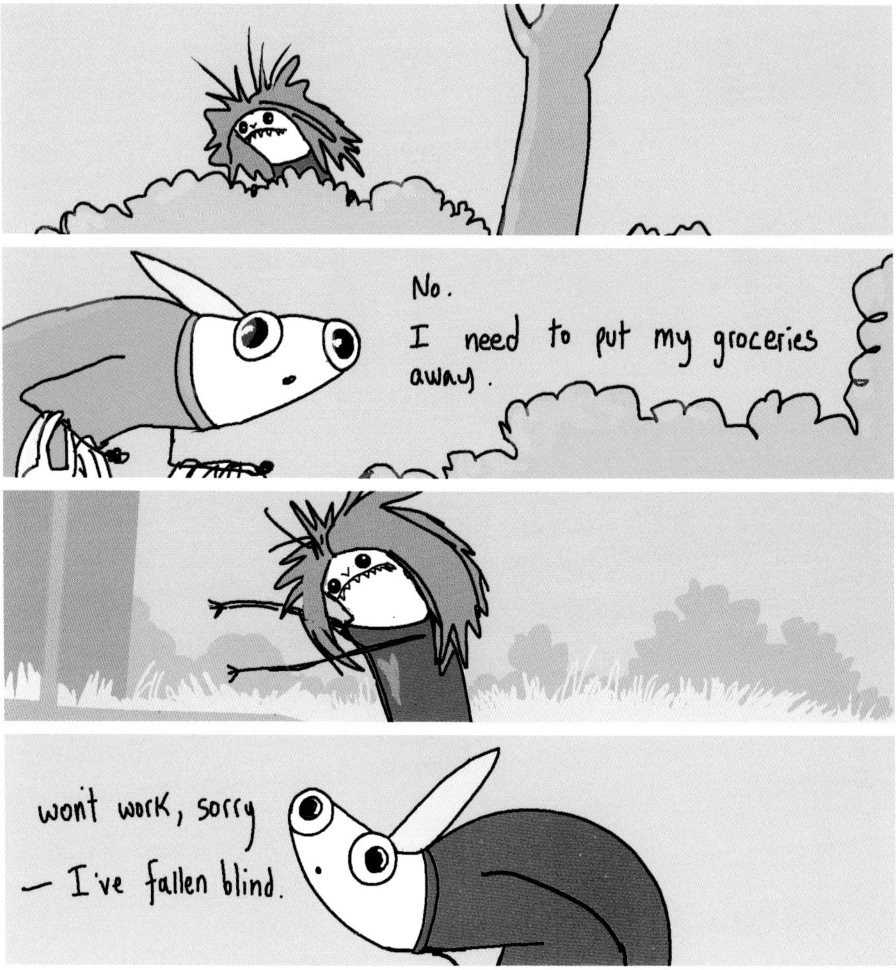
No.
I need to put my groceries away.
wont work, sorry
— I've fallen blind.

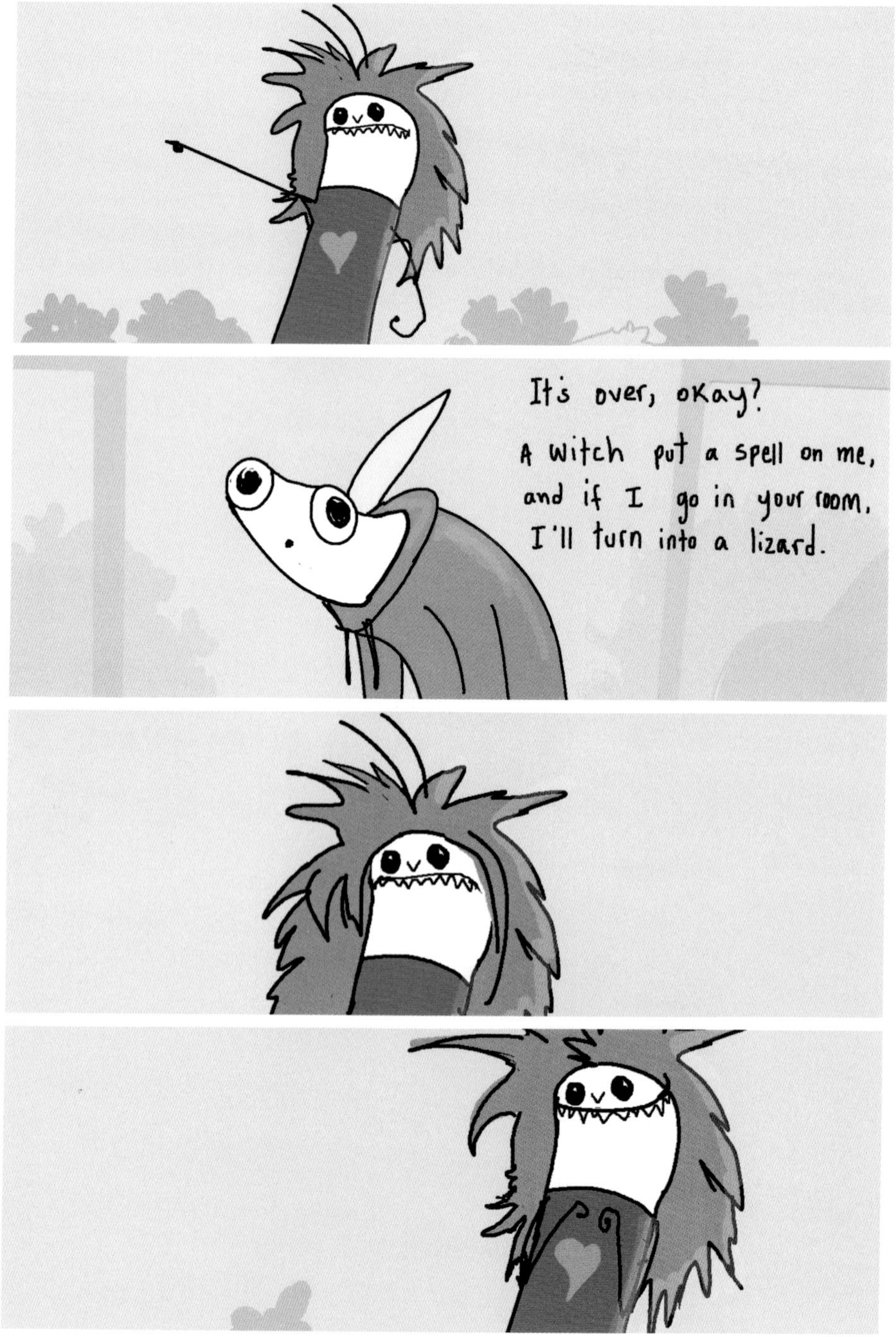
It's over, okay?
A witch put a spell on me, and if I go in your room, I'll turn into a lizard.

I have to leave 20 minutes early to have enough time for the debate.

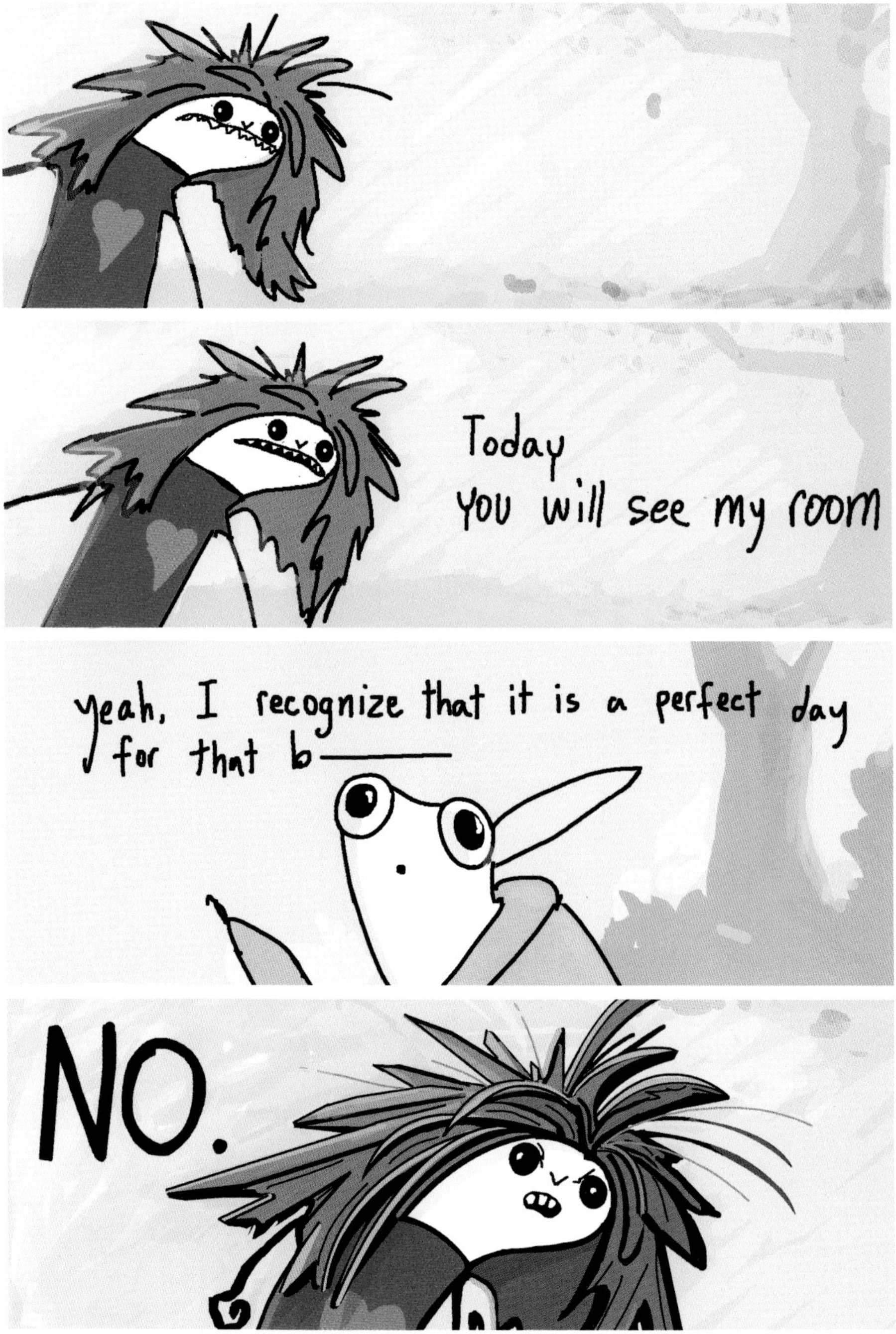
Today
you will see my room
yeah, I recognize that it is a perfect day for that b———
NO.

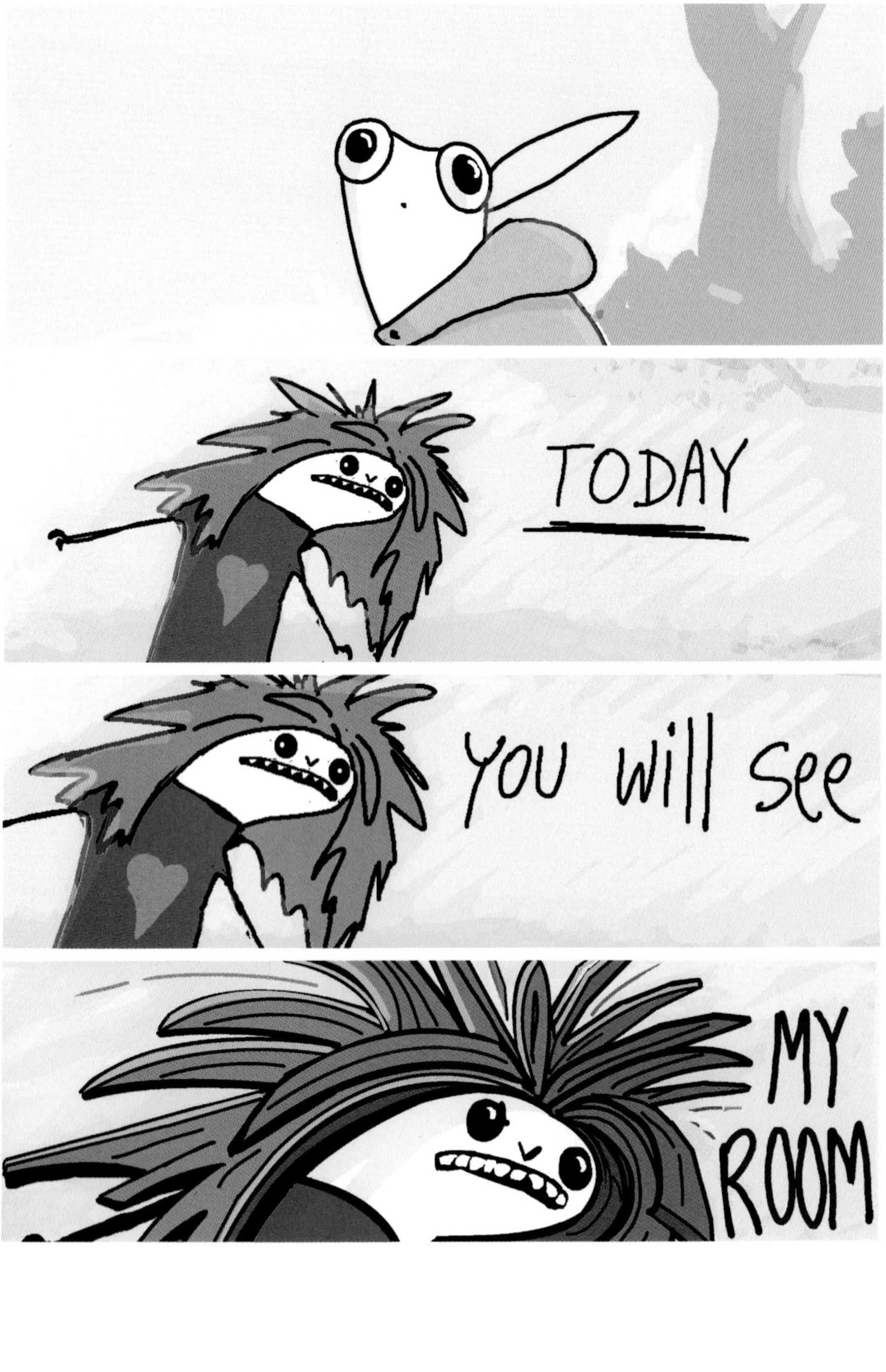
TODAY
YOU WILL SEE
MY ROOM

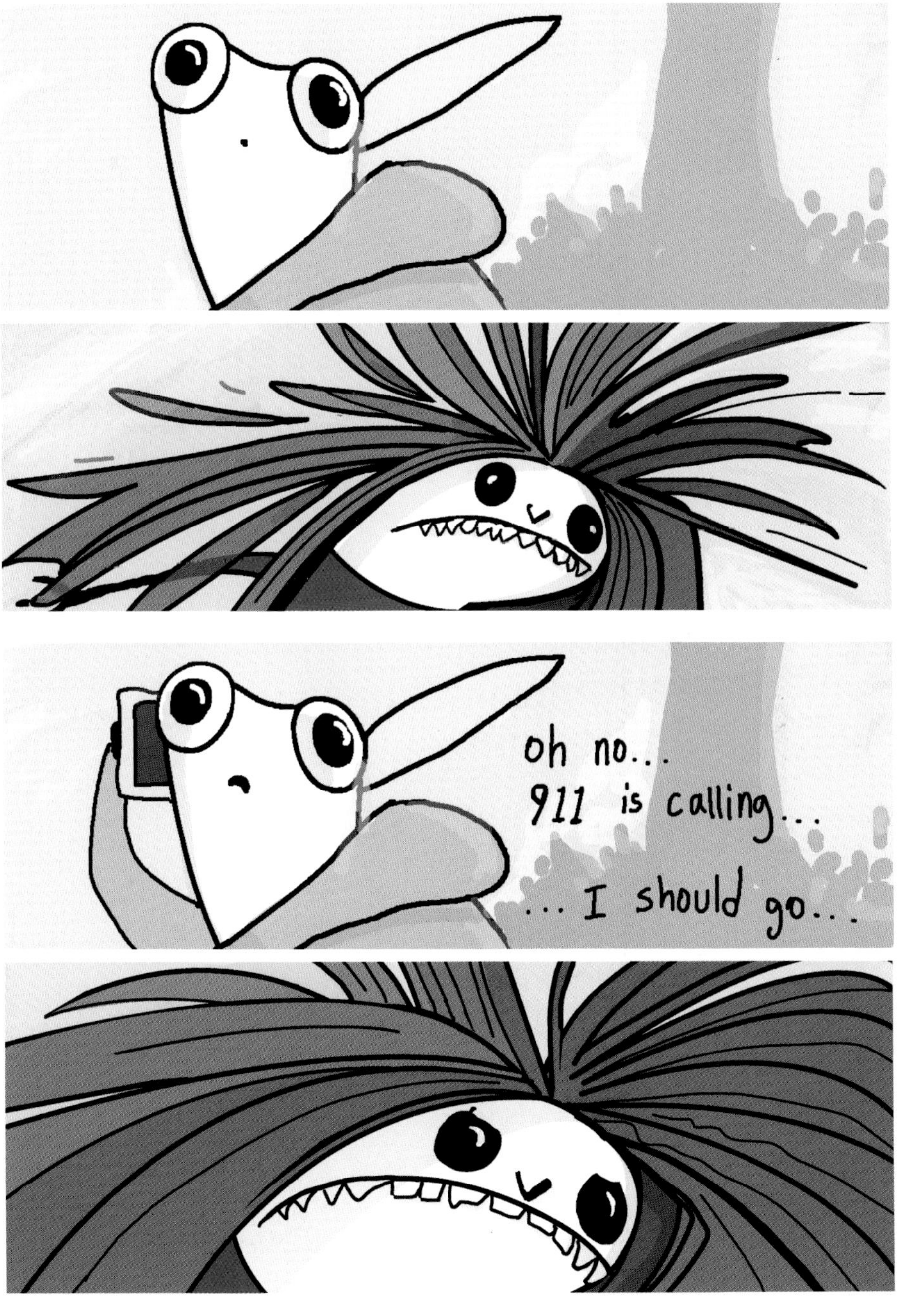
oh no...
911 is calling...
...I should go...

Saying no to a socially considerate adult is hard enough. If saying no to a socially considerate adult is like fighting a serpent, this would be like fighting a serpent, but you can't use your arms or legs, and you can't touch the serpent or hurt the serpent's feelings. Also, the serpent doesn't understand the words "no" or "sorry."

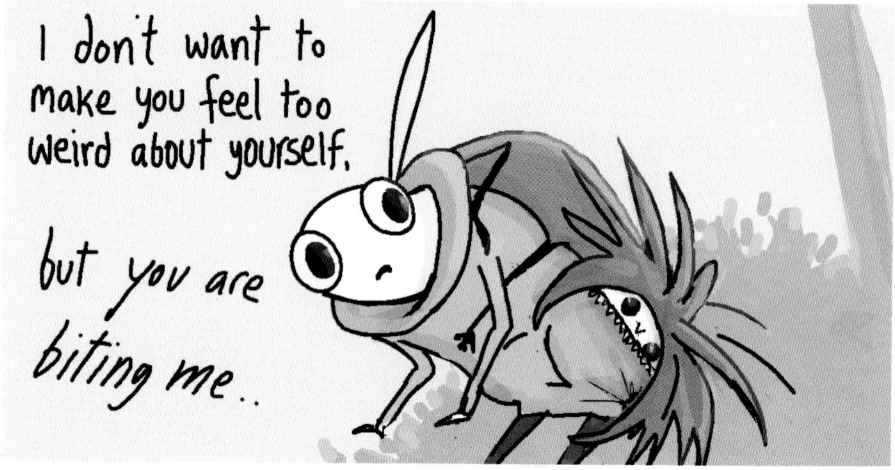
I don't want to make you feel too weird about yourself,

but you are biting me..

And now we are going to pause the story and tell the rest of it later. Don't worry—no matter how unrelated it seems, it'll loop back. I'll give you a signal when it's about to happen. A symbol.

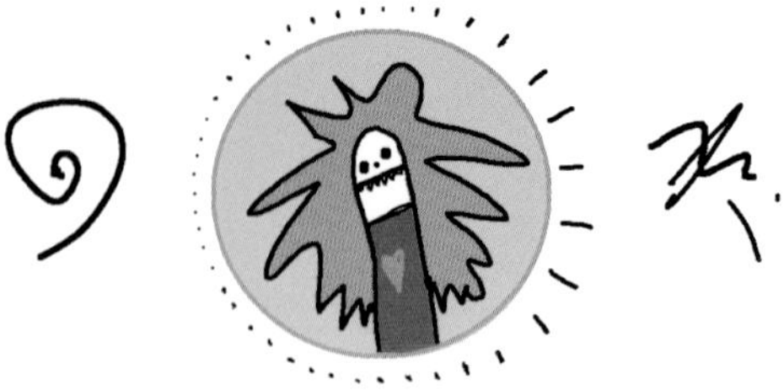

All you have to do is remember that this:

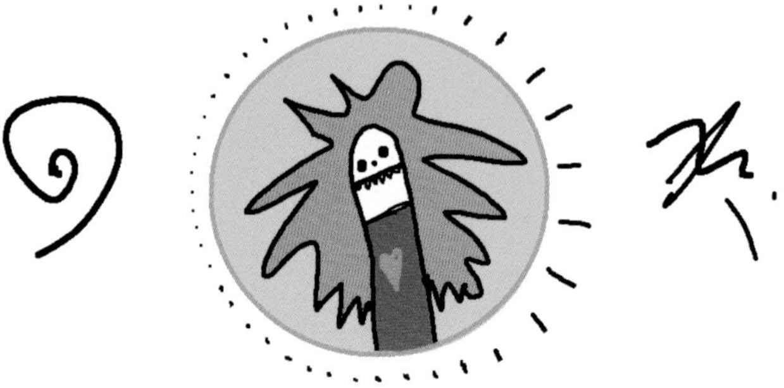

is the symbol for when it is four seconds away from happening.

We're doing it like this because it'll be closer to the actual experience if it comes out of nowhere.

Relax for a little bit, though. It isn't going to happen right away.

Mistake

A kid said hi to me.

I said hello, how are you?

She said good, how about you?

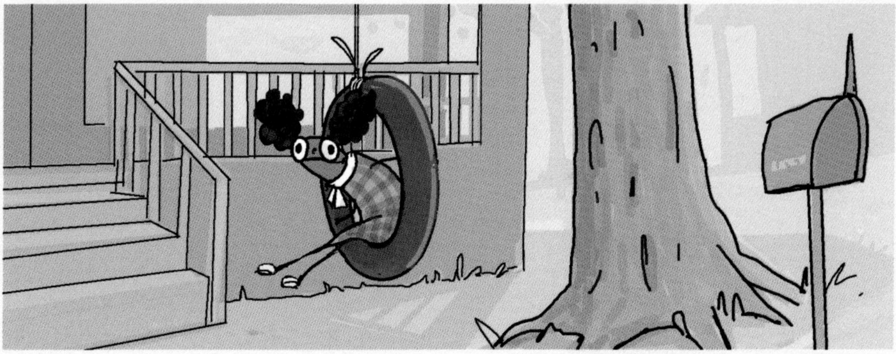

And I said:

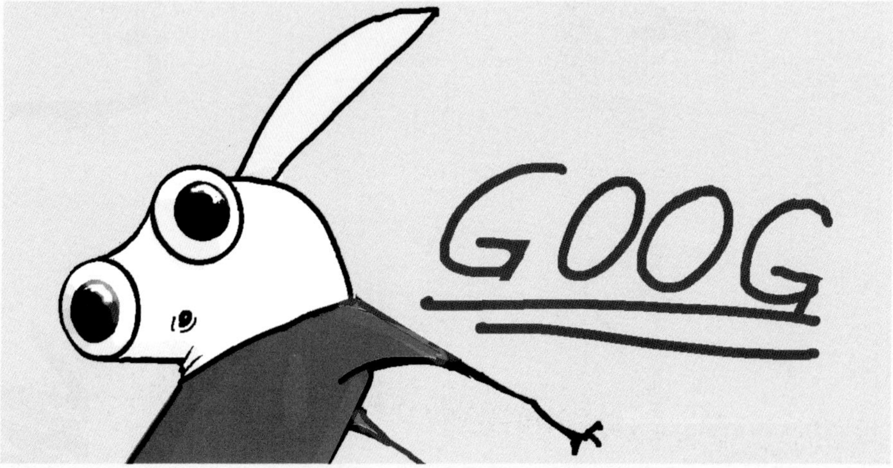
GOOG

And then I walked away, because there's no coming back from that. What am I gonna do? Explain myself?

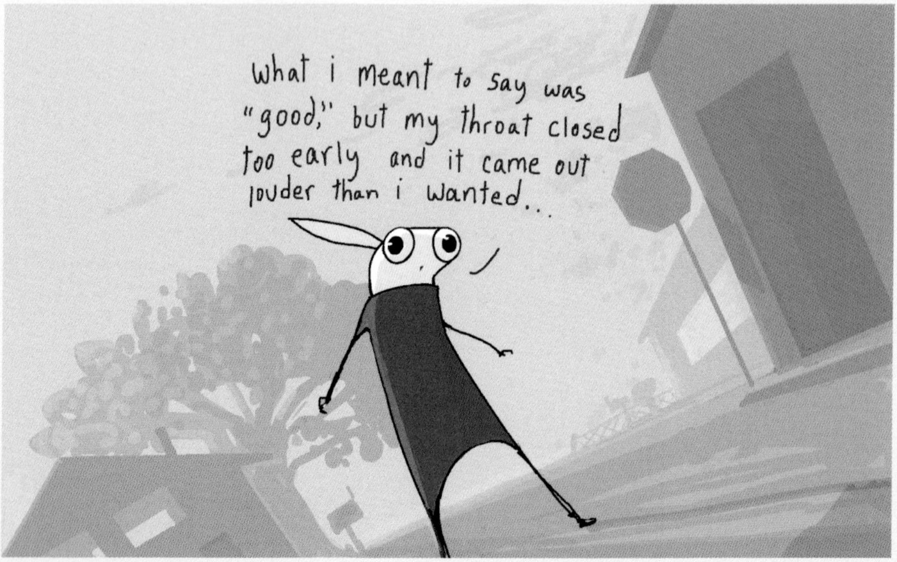
what i meant to say was "good," but my throat closed too early and it came out louder than i wanted...

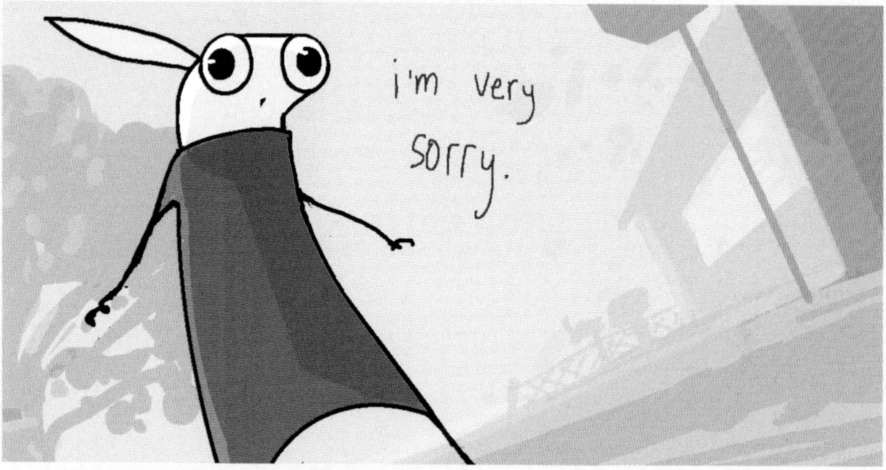
i'm very sorry.

I was thinking about it for an hour. I must have seemed *insane* to that kid …

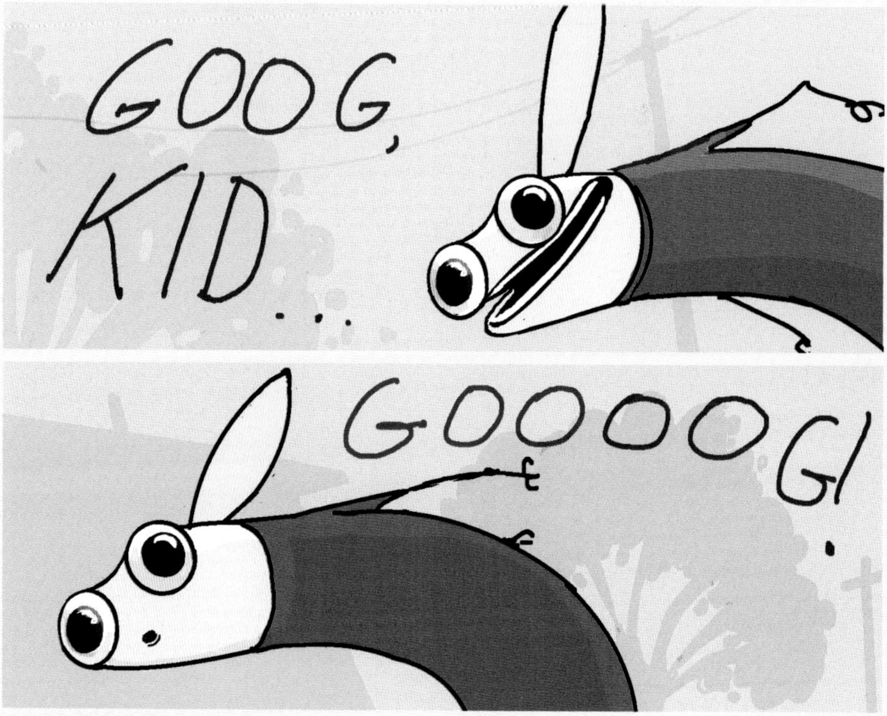
GOOG, KID . . .
GOOOOG!

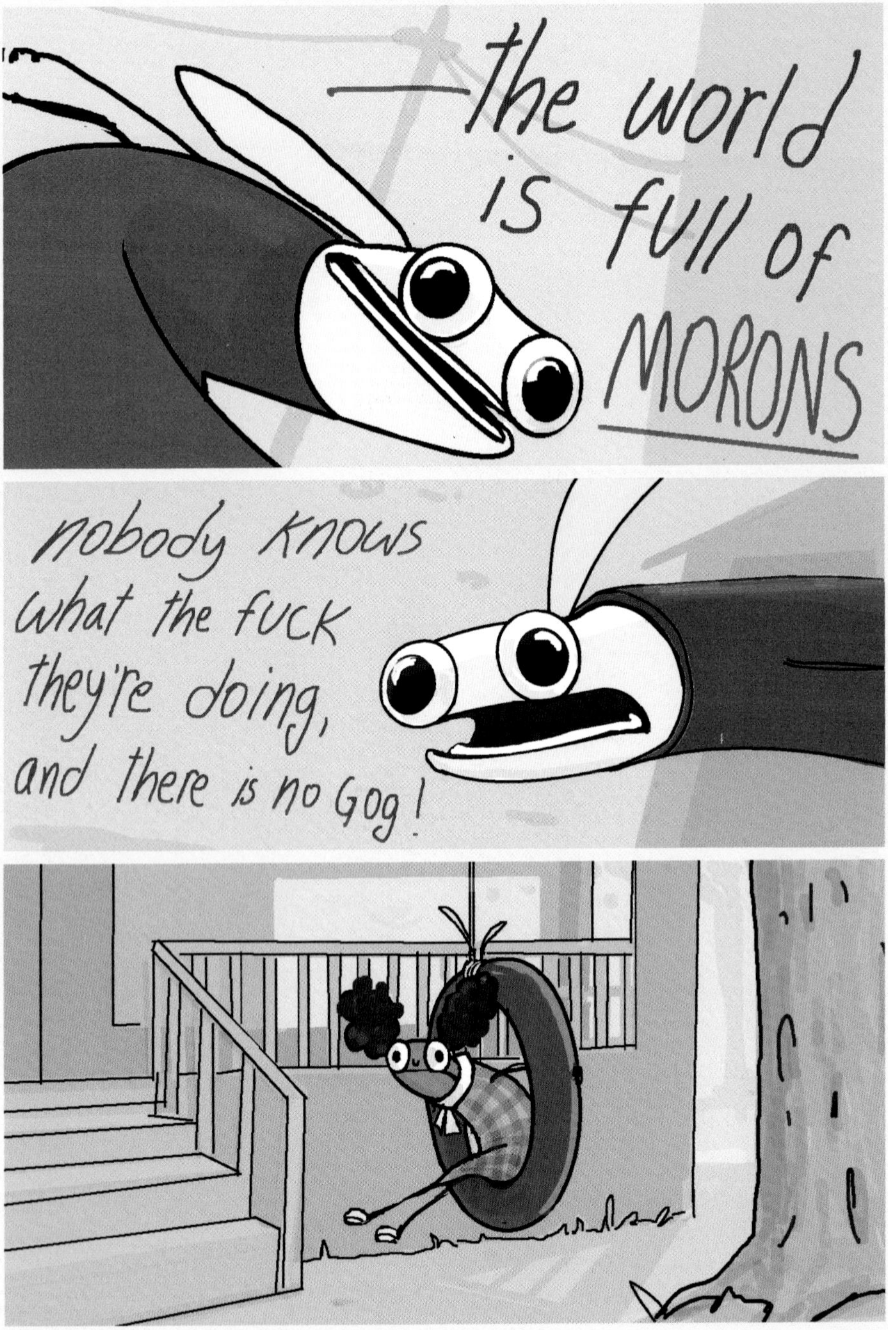

—the world is full of MORONS
nobody knows what the fuck they're doing, and there is no Gog!

5. POOP MYSTERY

OCTOBER 1997.

Winter's first snow blankets the remains of autumn.

And inside the house, for the third morning in a row, there is poop just *everywhere.*

It appears to be horse poop.
No one knows why it's there, but it's a pattern at this point.

Naturally, the first suspects were the horses.

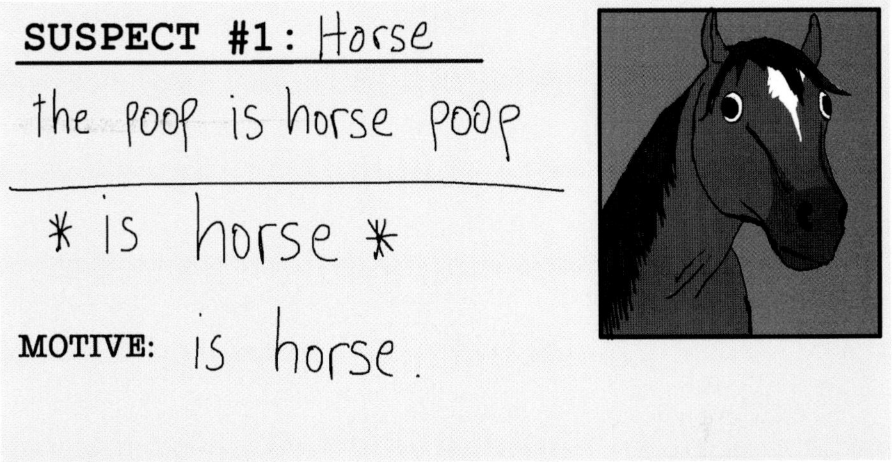
SUSPECT #1: Horse
the poop is horse poop
* is horse *
MOTIVE: is horse.

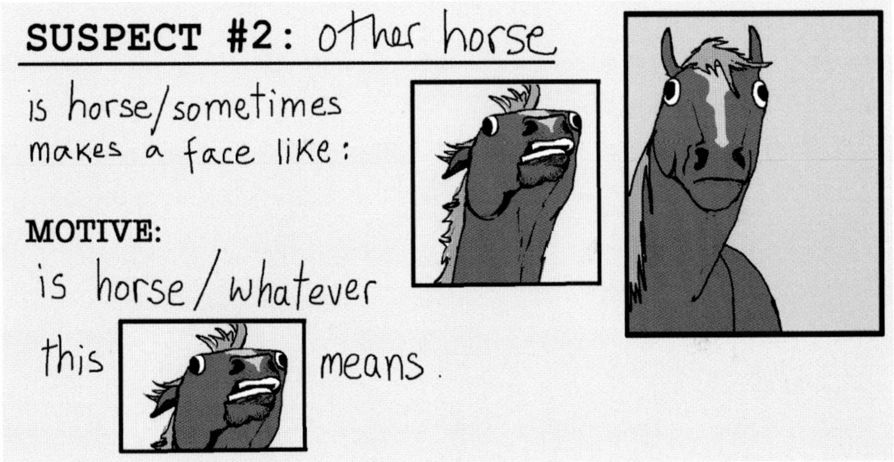
SUSPECT #2: other horse
is horse/sometimes makes a face like:
MOTIVE:
is horse/whatever this
means.

The first theory was that sometime during each of the three nights, the smaller, weirder horse wandered into the house, ran around everywhere trying to figure out how to escape, and was just shitting the entire time.

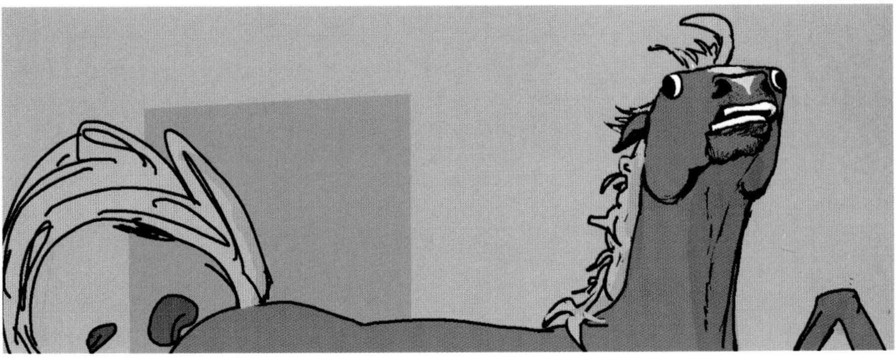

However, horses weigh roughly a thousand pounds and basically have rocks for feet, so pulling this off undetected would have been impossible. The horses were therefore temporarily ruled out as suspects, and we broadened our investigation to include the other pets and family members.

SUSPECT #3 : Charlie

Charlie is 19 years old and incapable of moving quickly enough to scatter horse poop over so many locations in a single night.
But Charlie is still somehow alive, so Charlie is a suspect.

MOTIVE: possibly in contract with demon?

SUSPECT #4 : Murphy

Suspect has an extensive history of crimes within the household, but all of them were food-related, as Murphy is on a diet and doesn't want to be.

MOTIVE: retaliation

SUSPECT #5 : Maddy

- seems guilty at all times
- basically lives under the table

* history of bringing random objects
  into the house:

—— rocks, pine cones, dead mice, grass, grasshoppers, tiny sticks, etc.

MOTIVE: who knows. Nobody understands maddy.

SUSPECT #6 : larger child

has previously been accused of:

- drawing on the floor • drawing on
the wall • collecting scabs in a jar
- regularly eating toothpaste.

MOTIVE: the larger child does not need a motive.
Will do unimaginably weird things for basically no reason.

SUSPECT #7: smaller child

no incidents on record.
the small child is suspiciously
well-behaved.

MOTIVE: spends the most time with
the horses = possibly horse whisperer/
spiritually linked with the horses. may have
committed crime while under mind control of horses.

SUSPECT #8: Mom and Dad

previously convicted of being:
• the easter bunny
• santa
• "skeleton man"
• the tooth fairy
* 64 incidents of stealing teeth and
  keeping them in a box on top of the piano
MOTIVE: display of dominance?

SUSPECT #9: grandma Margo

grandma regularly antagonizes
the family for sport.

MOTIVE: entertainment.

As usual, Maddy seemed guilty.

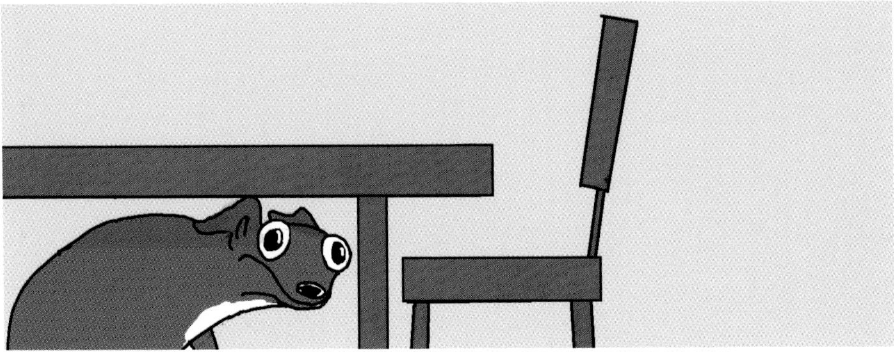

Murphy and Charlie were harder to get a read on.

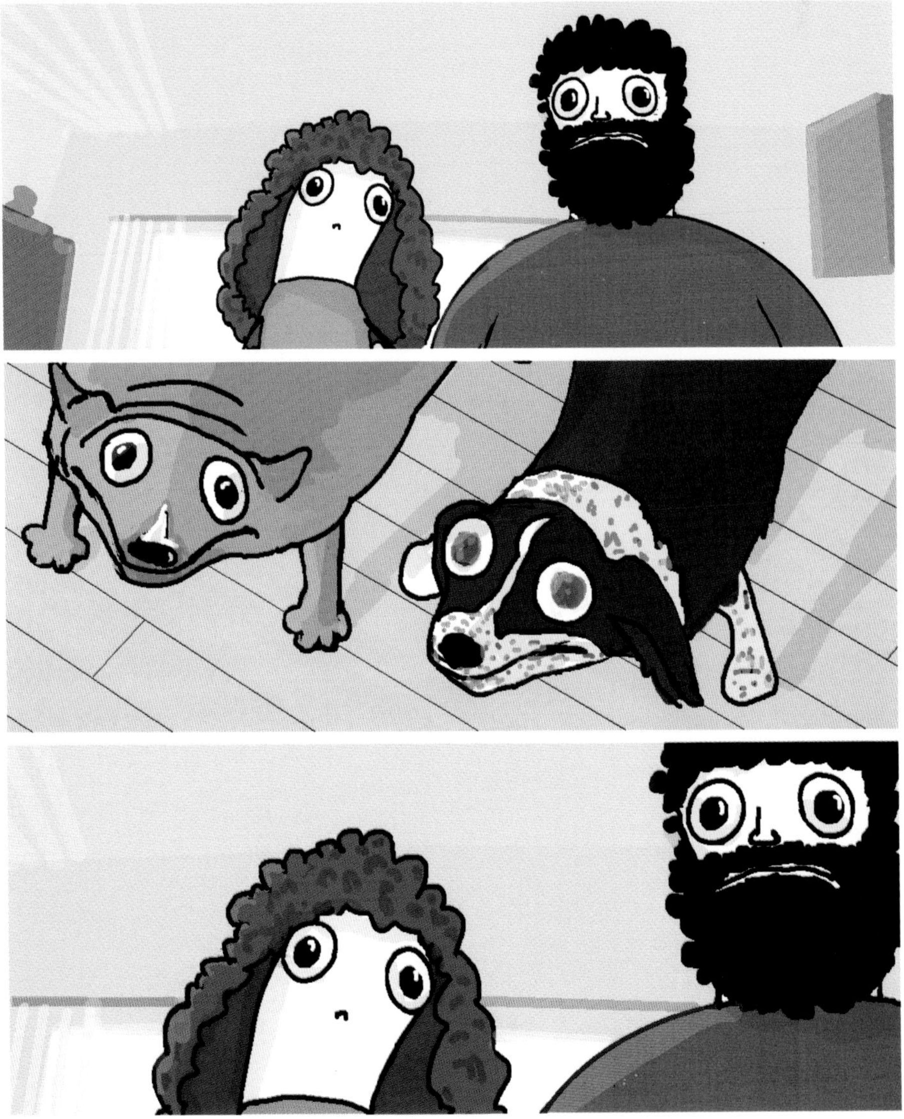

Nobody else was fessing up either.

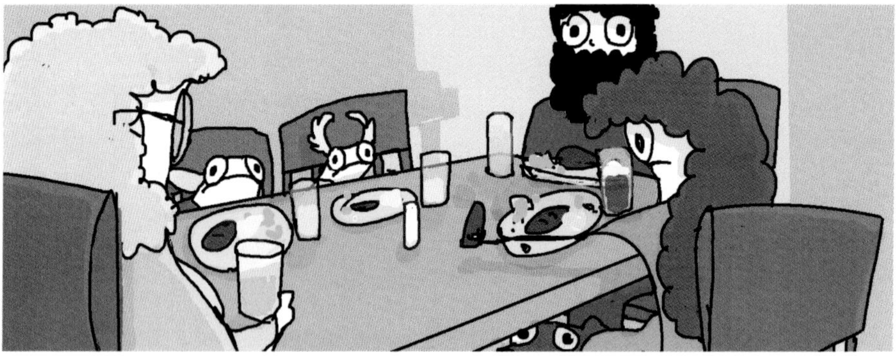

A few days later, the case took a mysterious turn when a single, large pile of horse poop appeared in the children's bedroom, looking exactly as it would upon exiting the horse. Indicating that it was either created by the horses within the bedroom, or arranged to look that way.

This strengthened the case against both the horses and the children.

Upon further questioning, the children began crying and screaming.

They said they would "never do that."

They pleaded for everyone to "please believe" them.

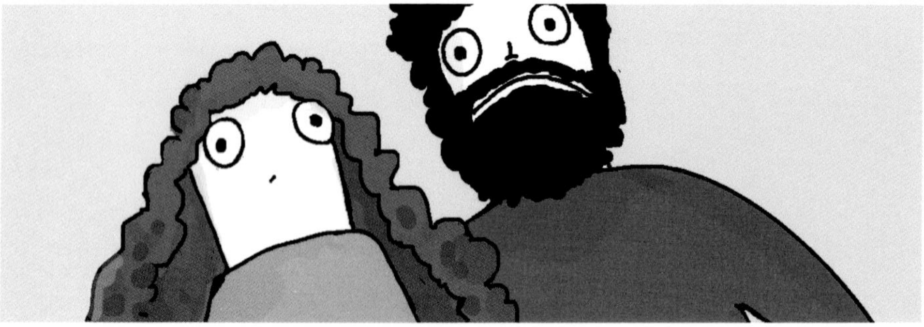

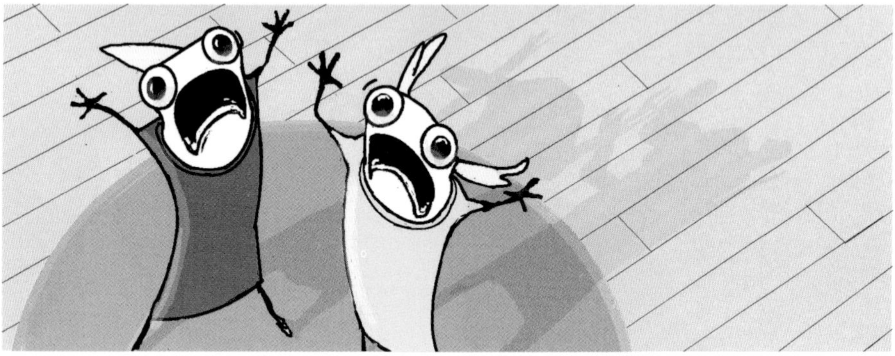

Everyone was disturbed by the notion that the children may have gone out into the night, collected horse poop, and sculpted it into a pile on the floor of their own bedroom. The children, because children hate being accused of things like collecting and arranging animal poop, and the adults because that is the behavior of future criminals.

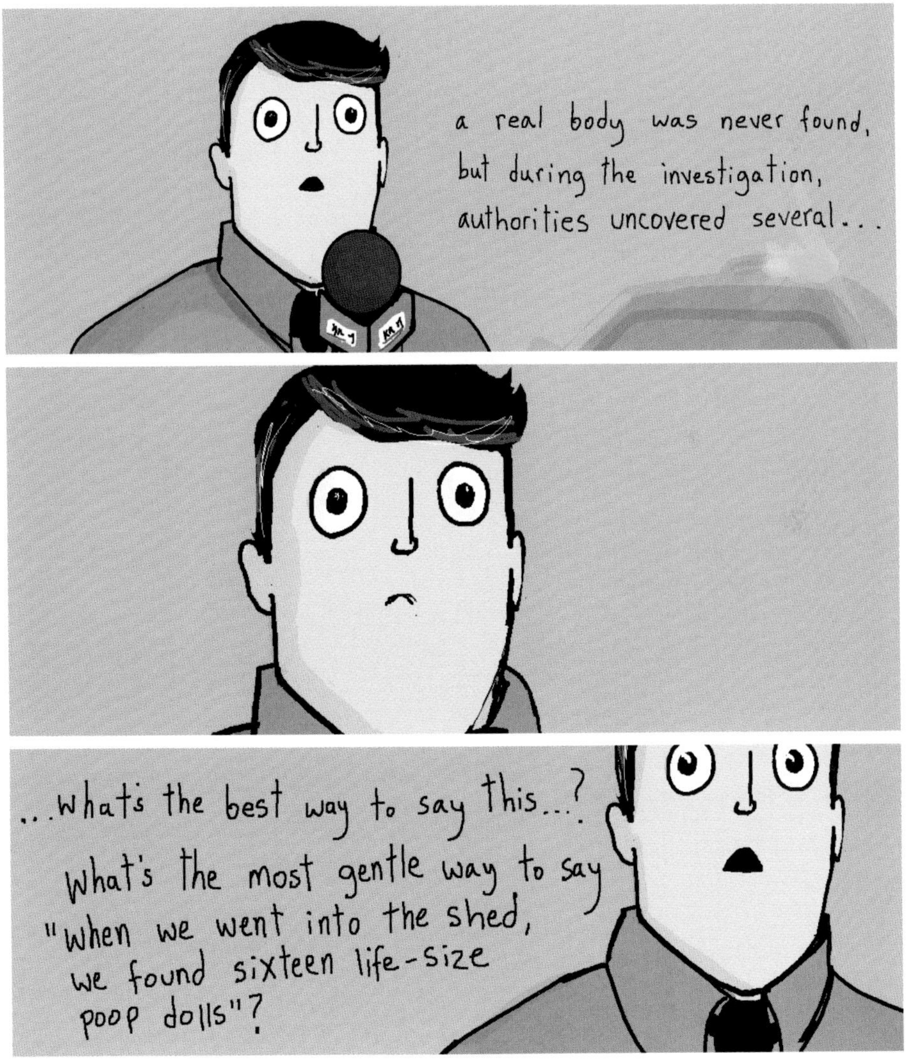
a real body was never found, but during the investigation, authorities uncovered several...
...what's the best way to say this...?
What's the most gentle way to say "when we went into the shed, we found sixteen life-size poop dolls"?

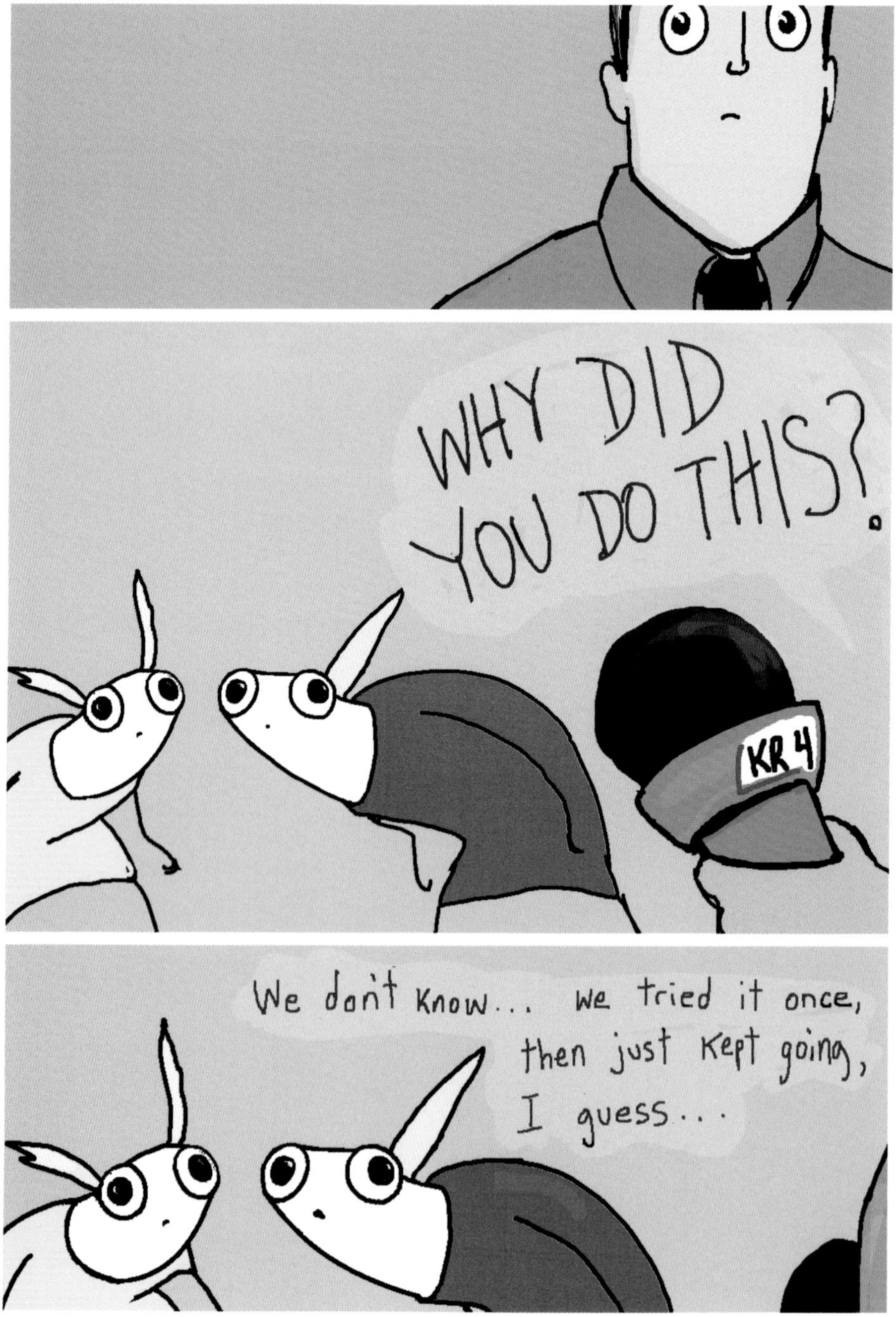
WHY DID YOU DO THIS?
We don't know... we tried it once, then just kept going, I guess...

It was a dark time. We were all suspects, plagued by doubt, haunted by possibility.

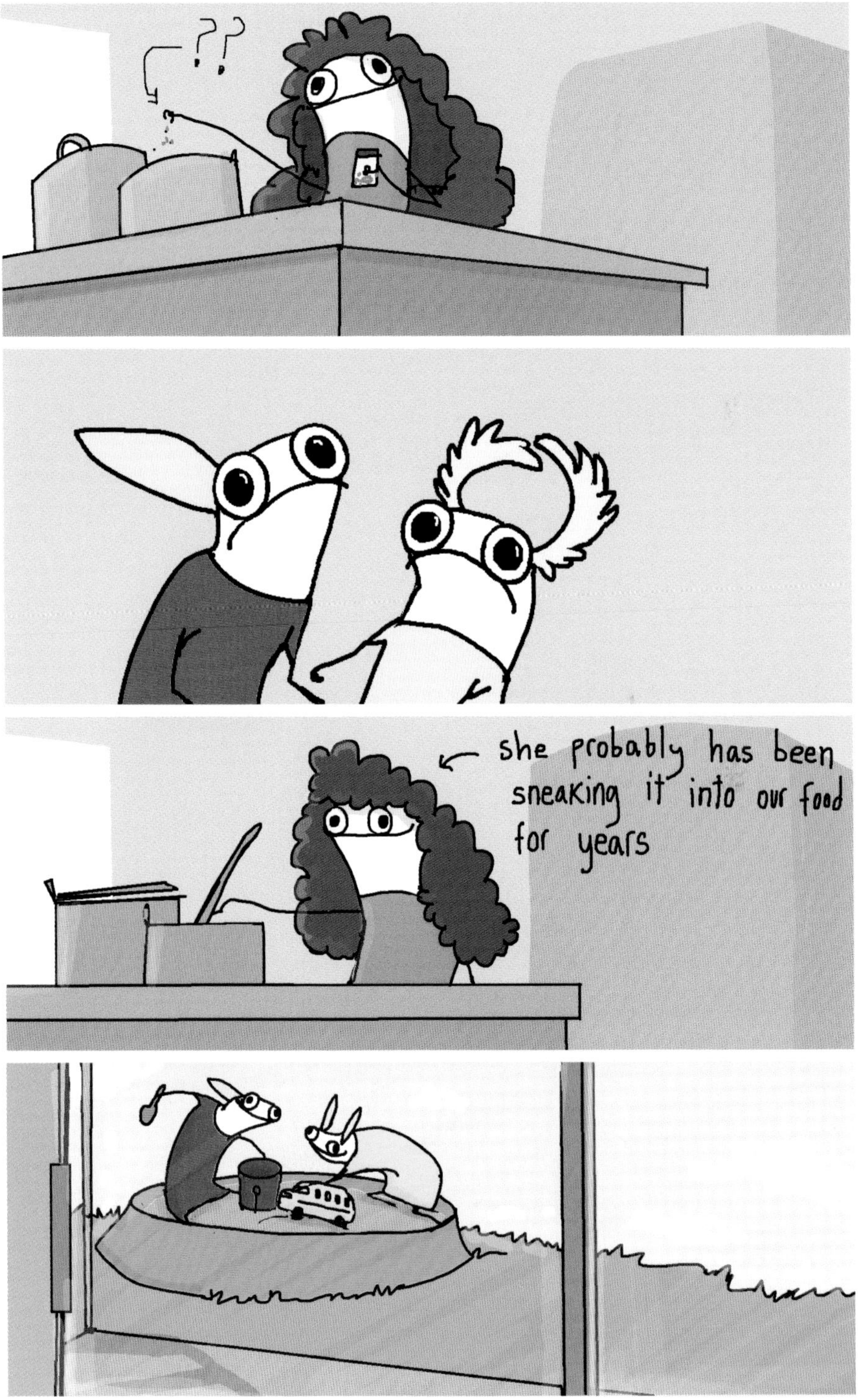
she probably has been sneaking it into our food for years

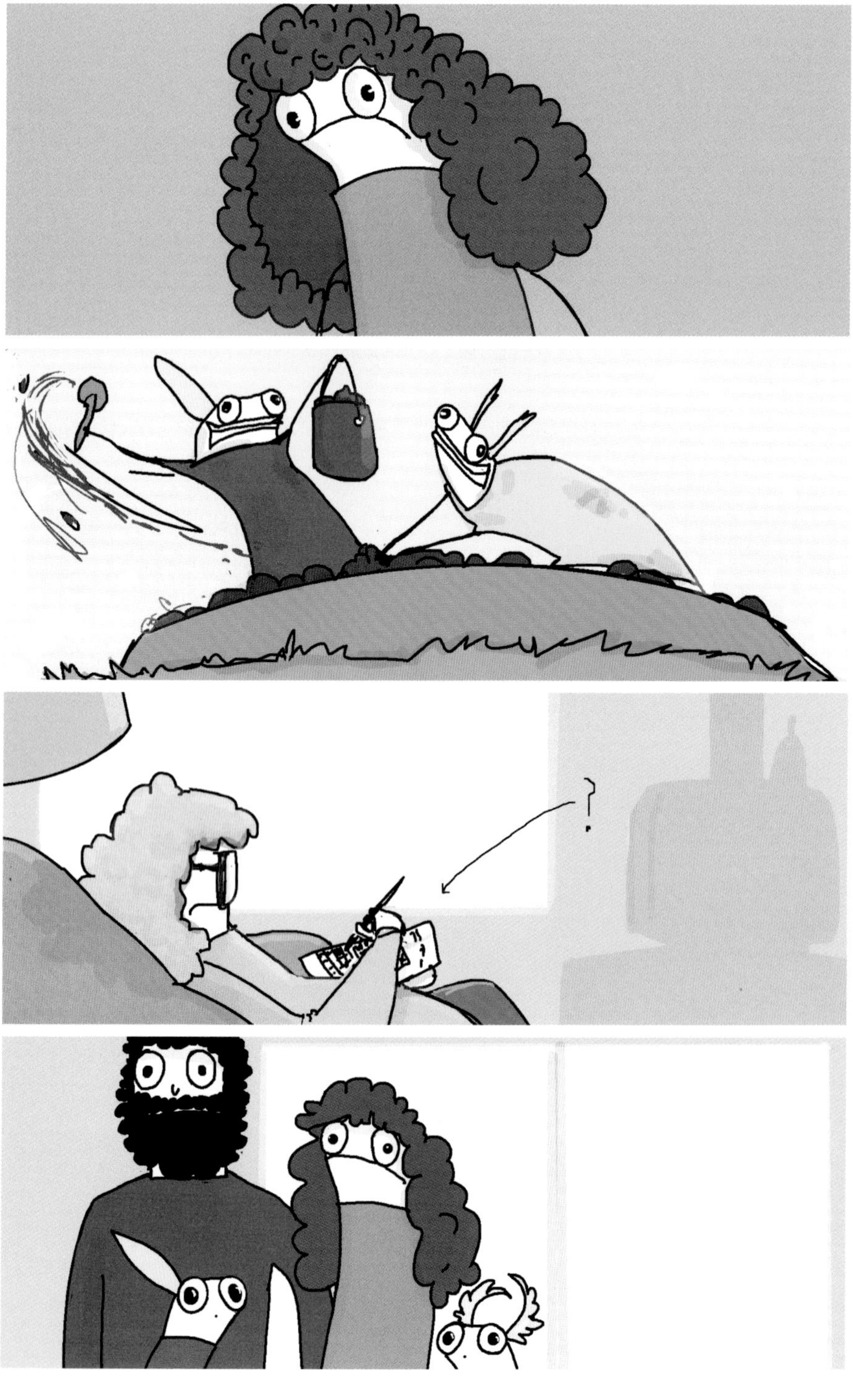

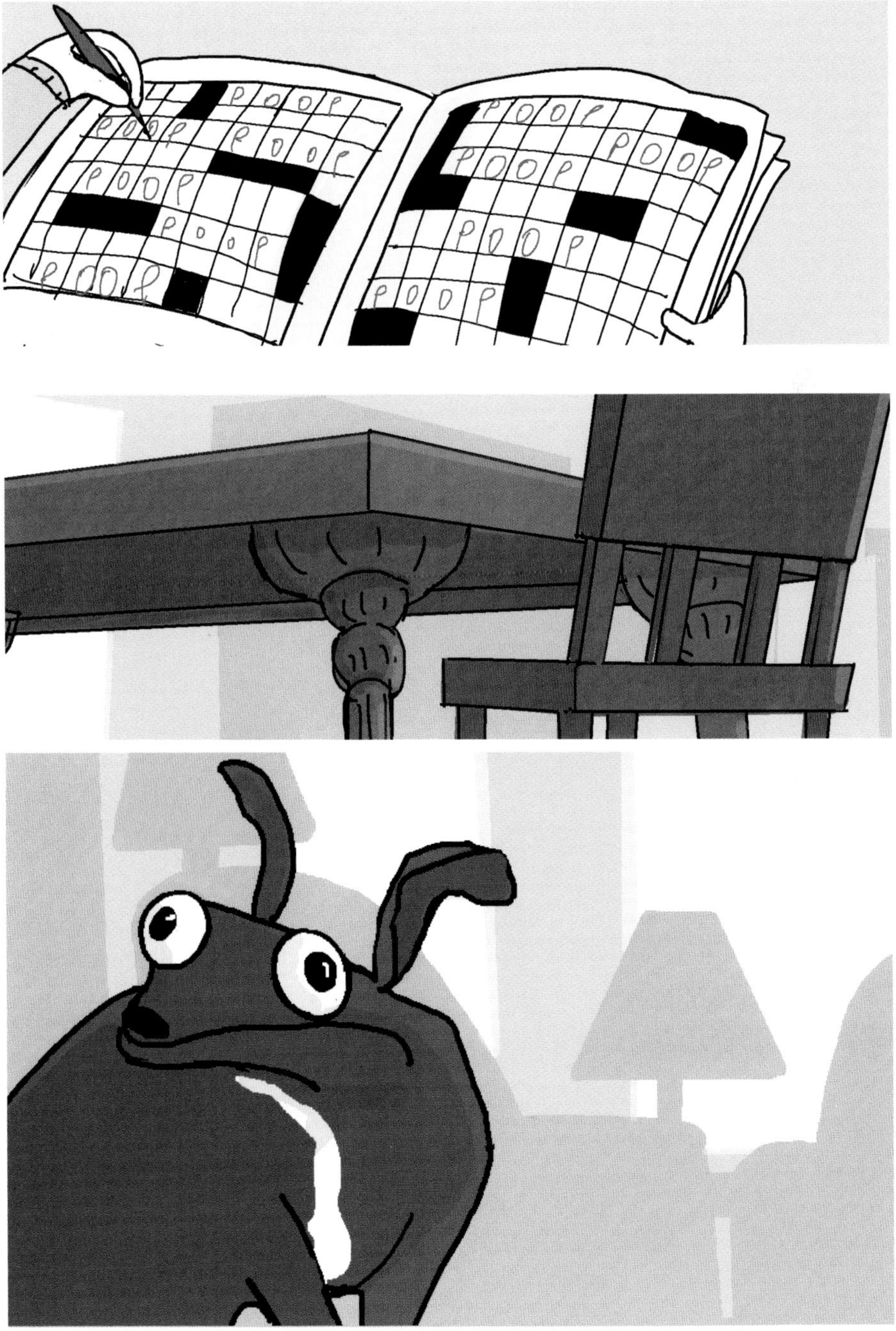
POOP
POOP
POOP
POOP
POOP
POOP
POOP
POOP
POOP
POOP
POOP

And the piles continued to appear.

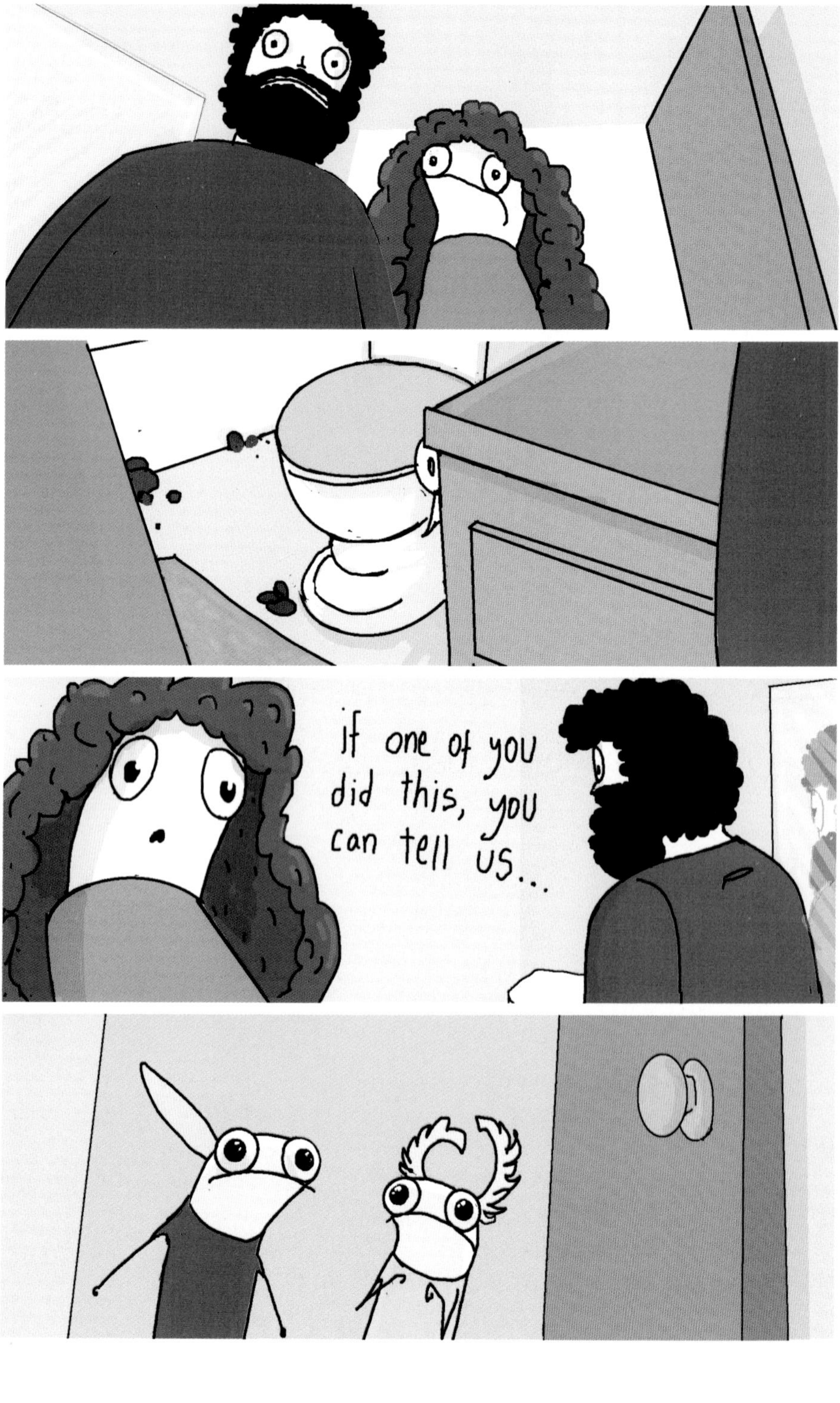
if one of you did this, you can tell us...

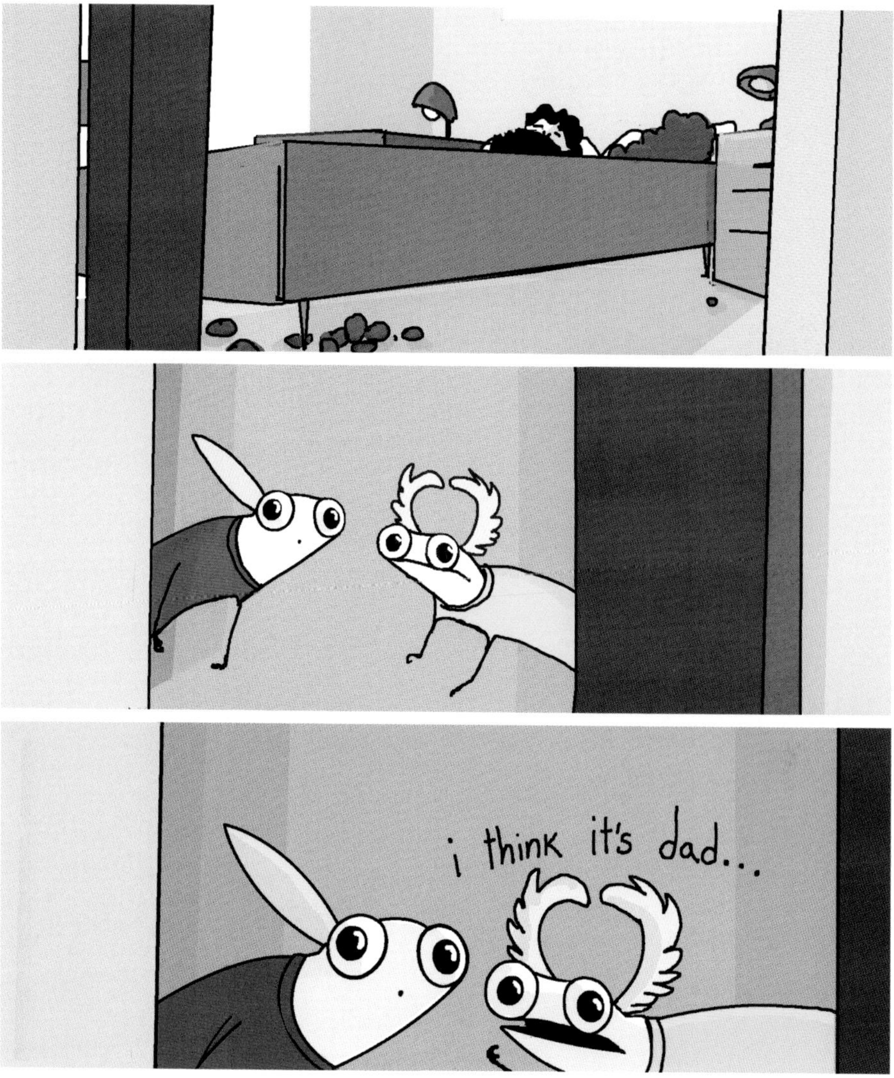
i think it's dad...

Then, early one morning, we were awakened by an ominous thumping sound.

I think we were all scared of it, until we realized that it might be exactly what we had all been waiting for: an opportunity to catch the suspect in the act!

We clustered in the living room, pausing to acknowledge each other with disdainful, I-told-you-it-wasn't-me glances before investigating the noise.

As we crept closer, we could see the back door rattling with each thump. Something was trying to get in through the dog door . . .

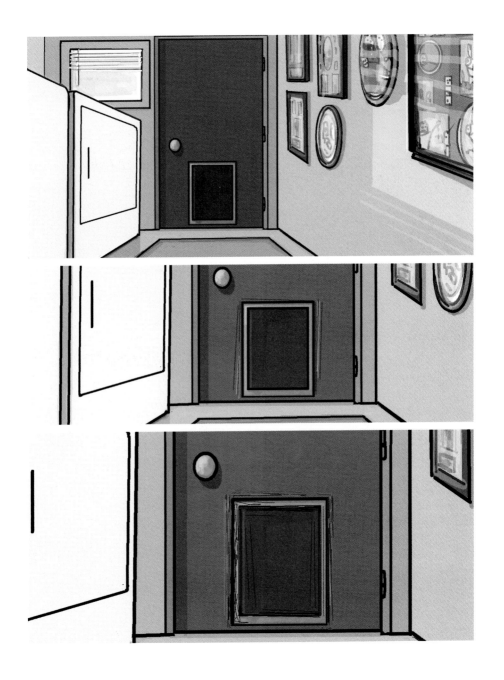

In a moment, we'd know the answer to the question we'd been asking for weeks—"Who the fuck has been doing this to us? Is it the neighbors?? Which neighbor is it? Do we know anyone who hates us enough to do this?"—and all the way to the door, we mentally revised our theories, impatient to find out who was right, but terrified to know.

Then there it was: the answer. Standing on the other side of the door with a face full of frozen horse poop.

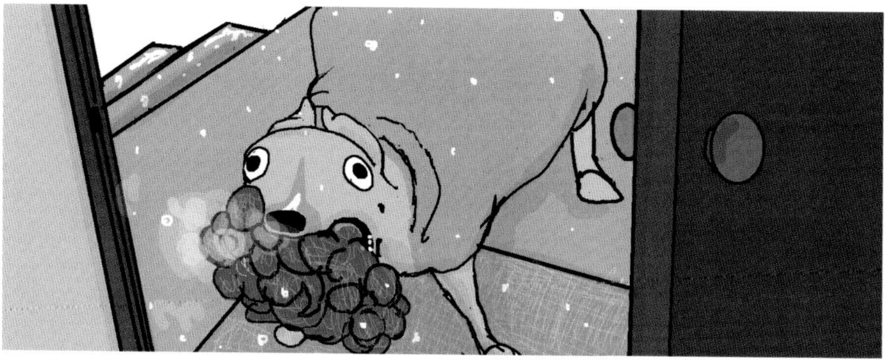

The rest of the story pretty much told itself.

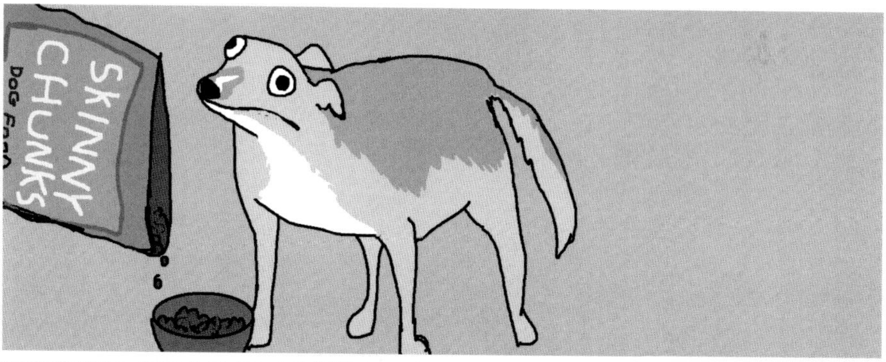
SKINNY CHUNKS
DoG

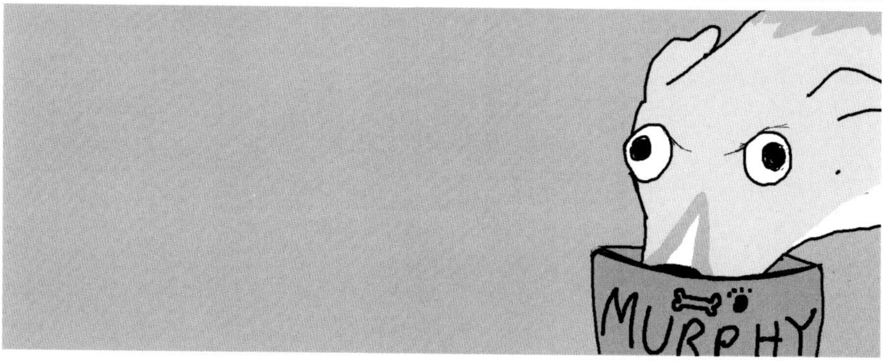
MURPHY

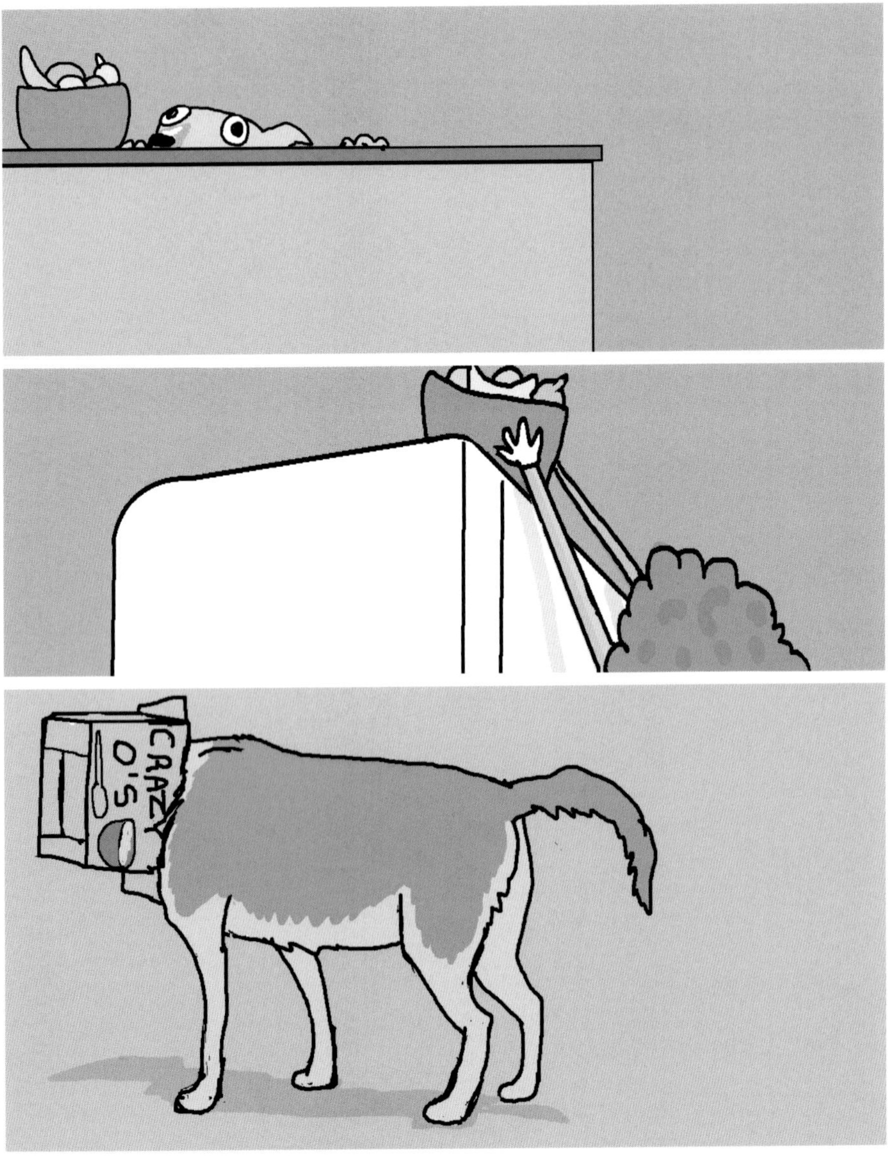
CRAZY O'S

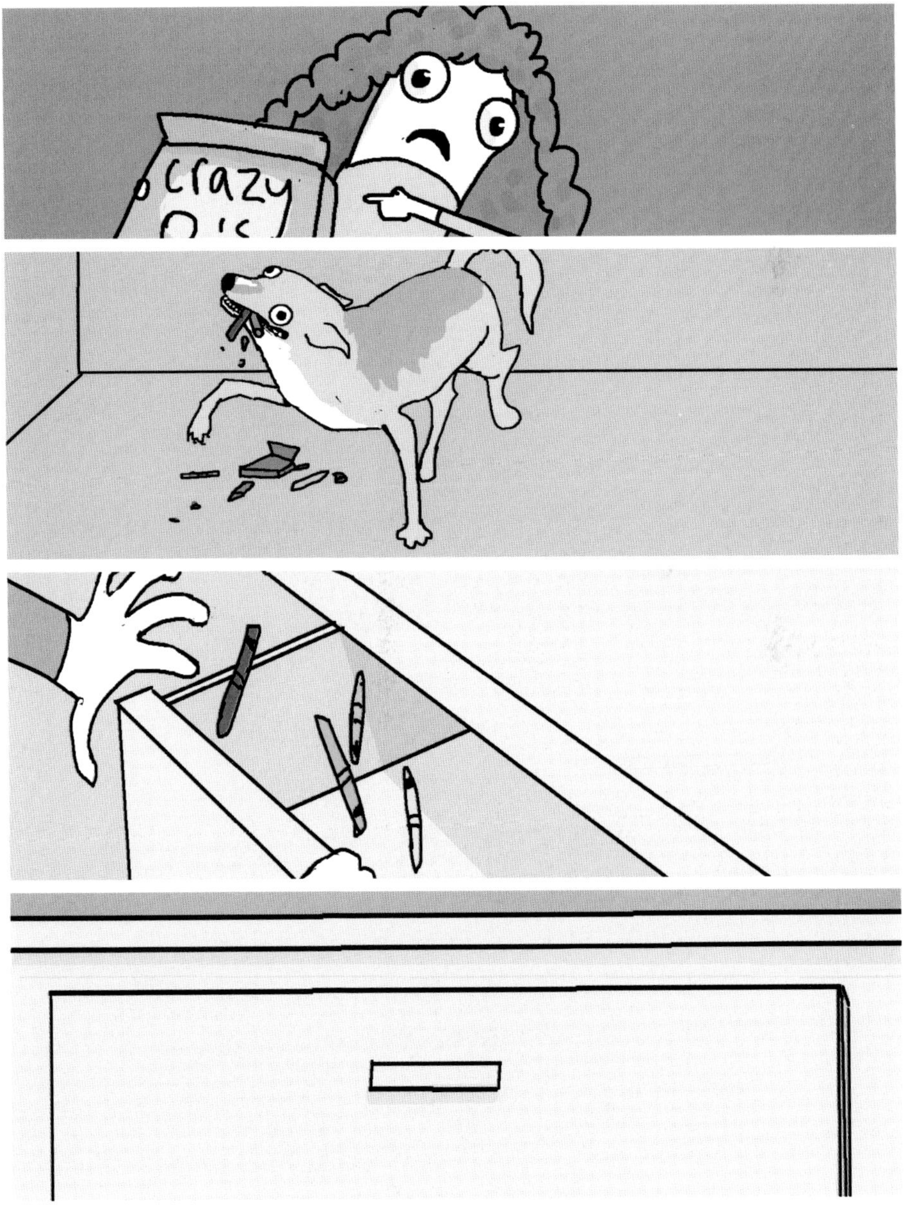
crazy

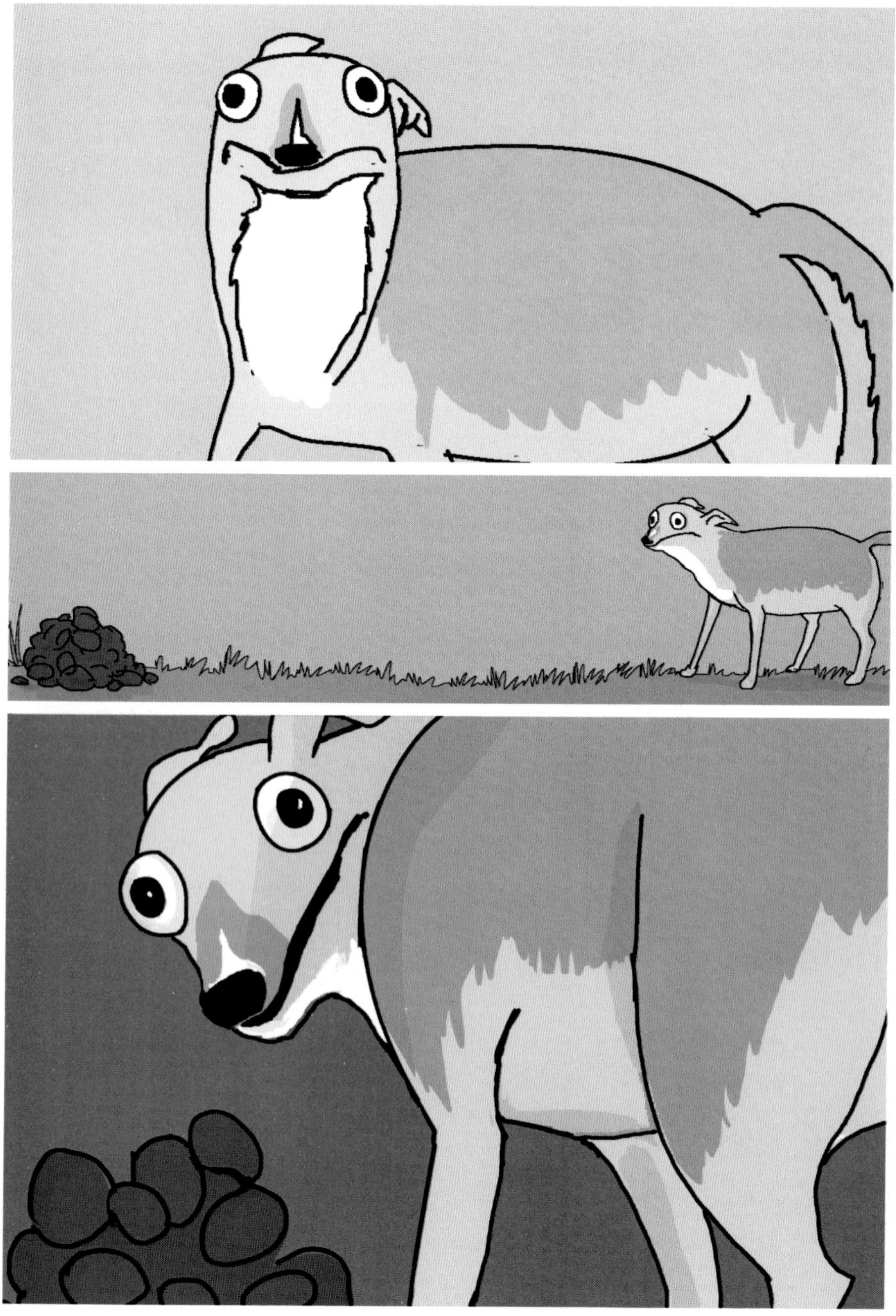

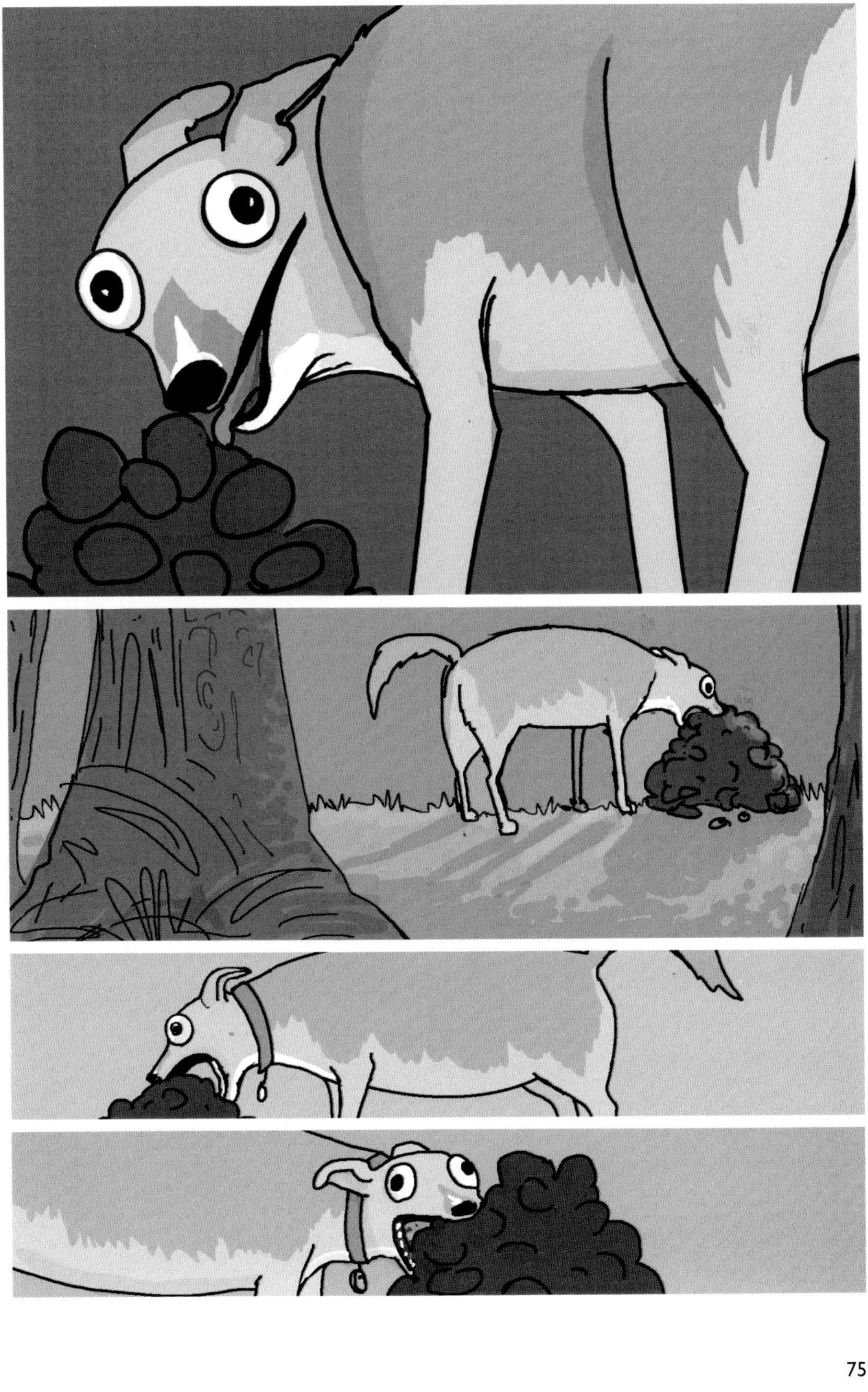

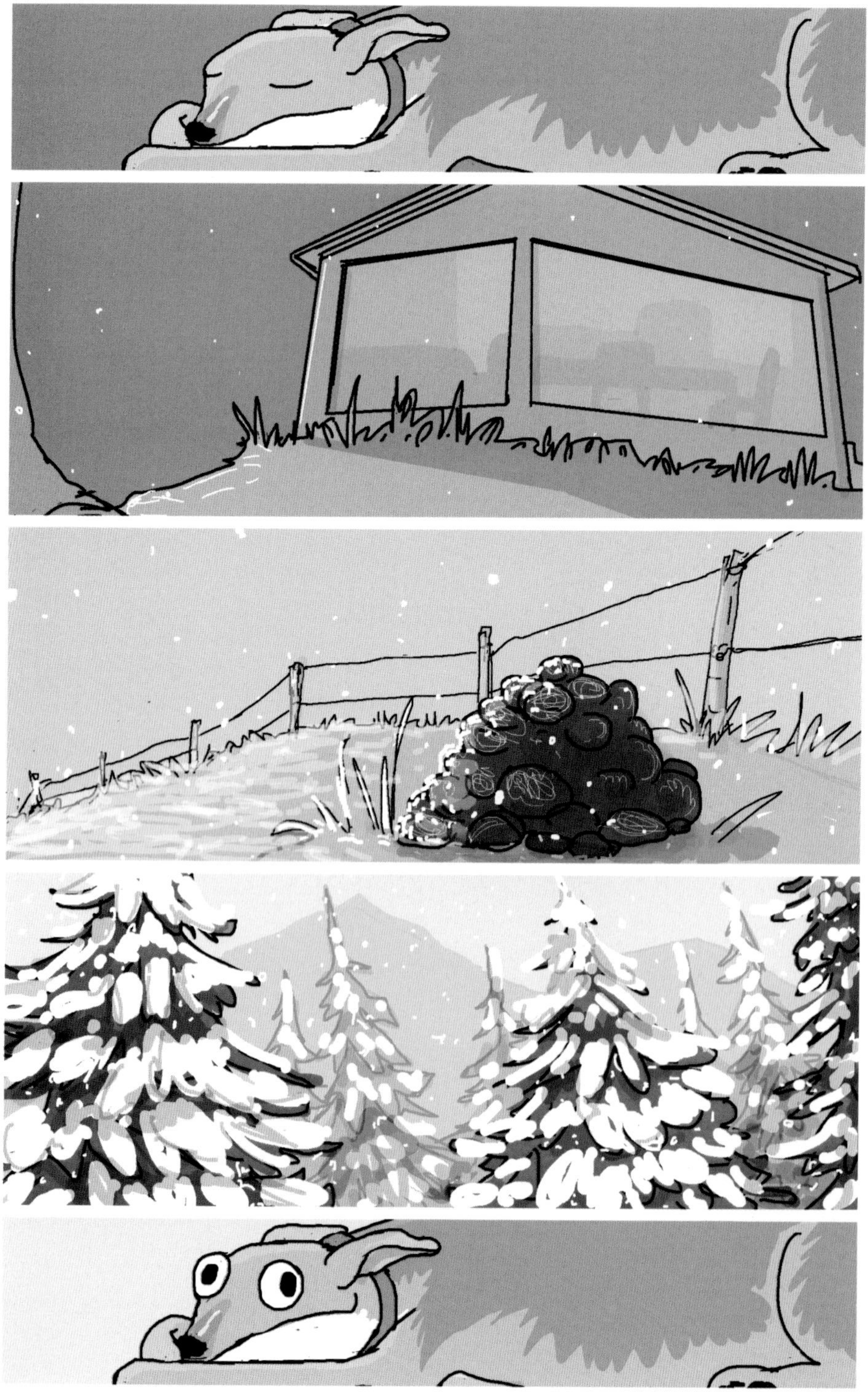

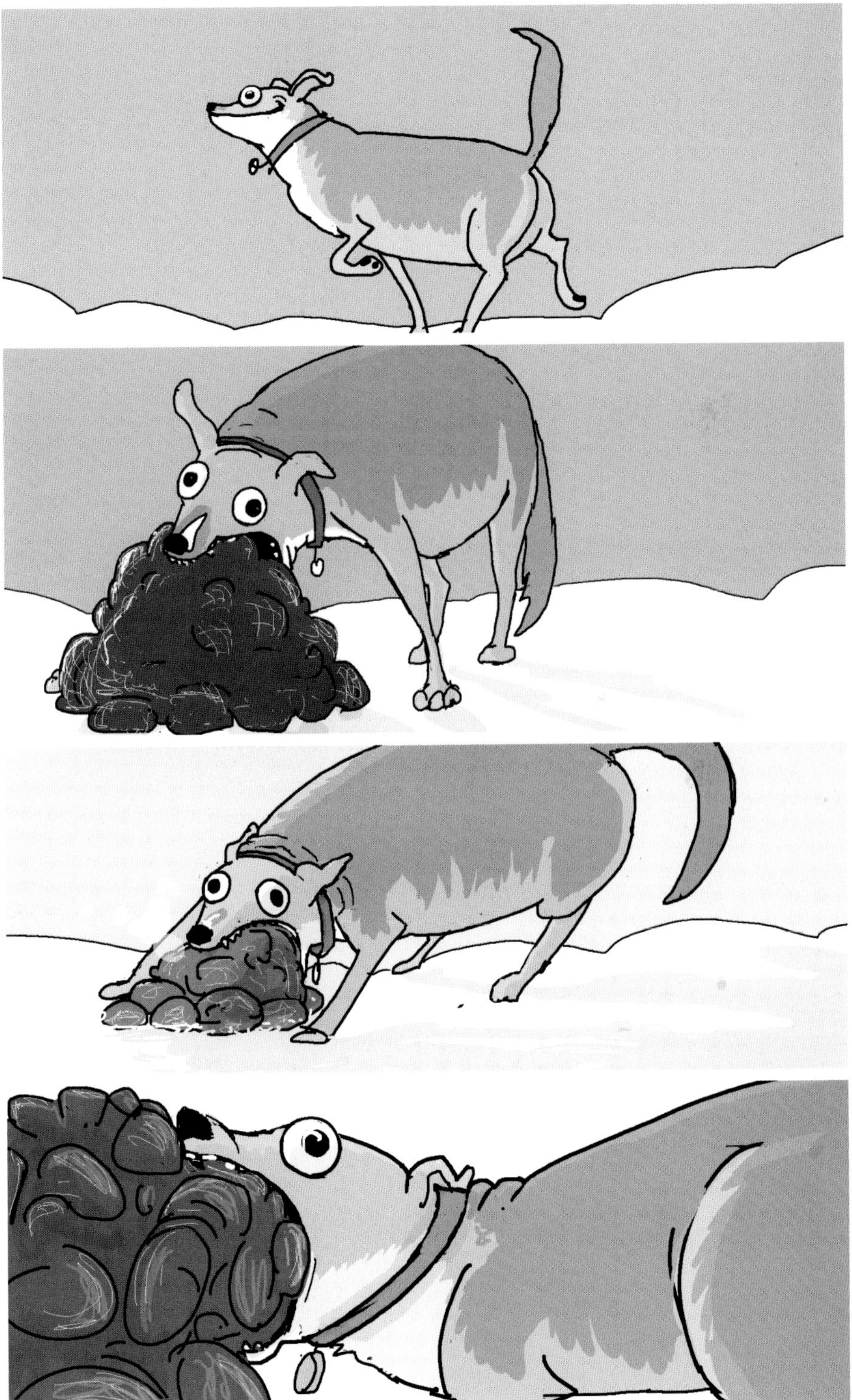

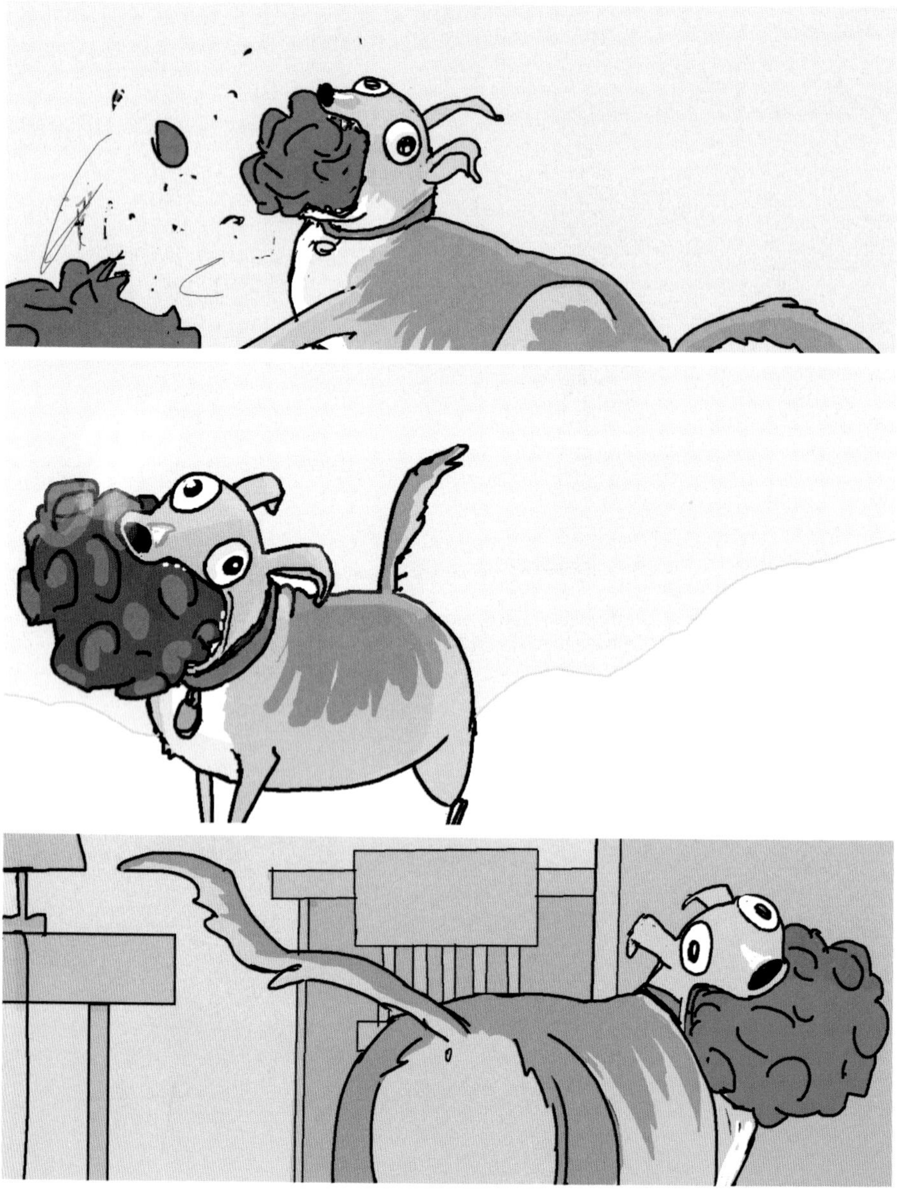

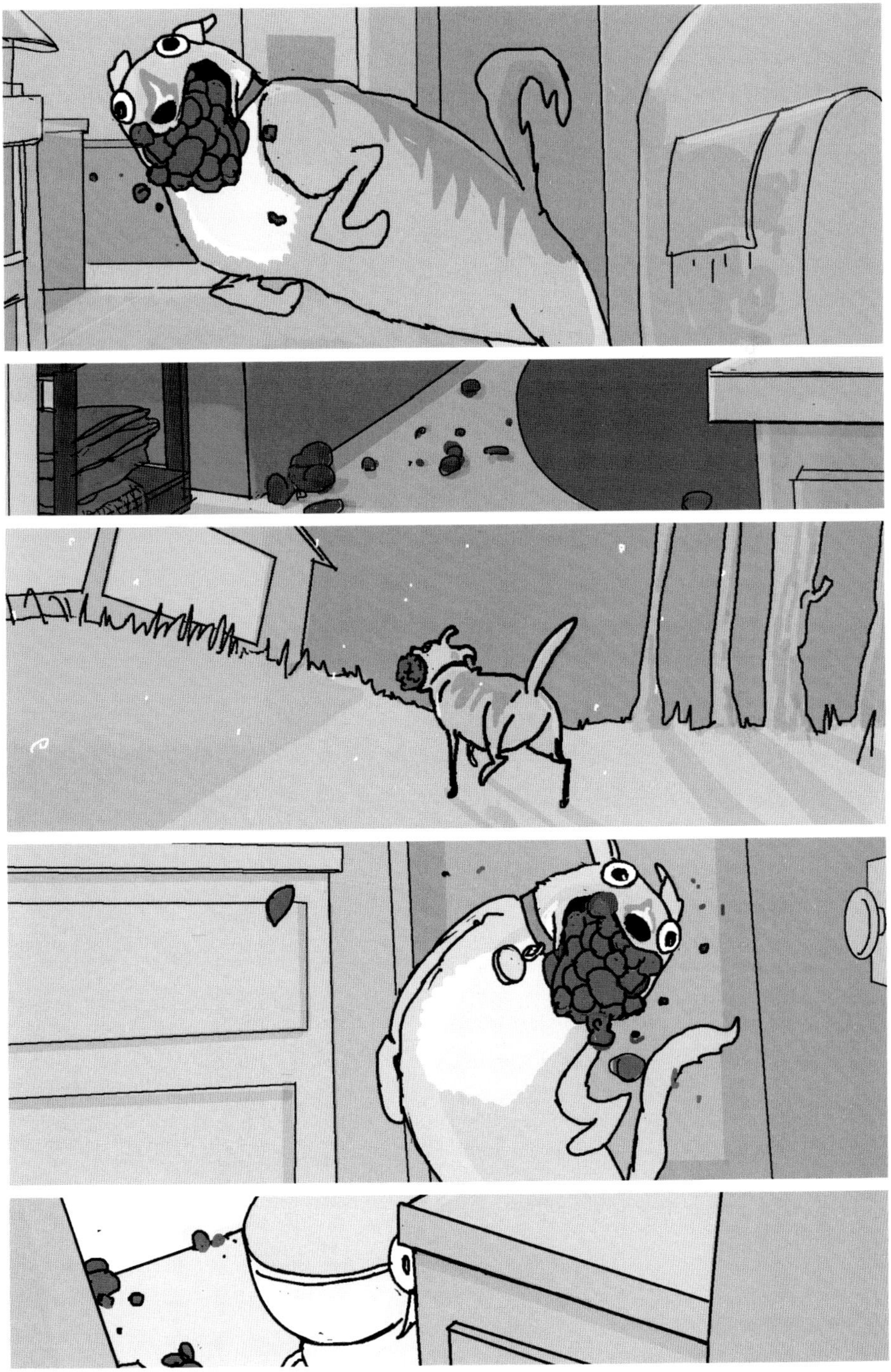

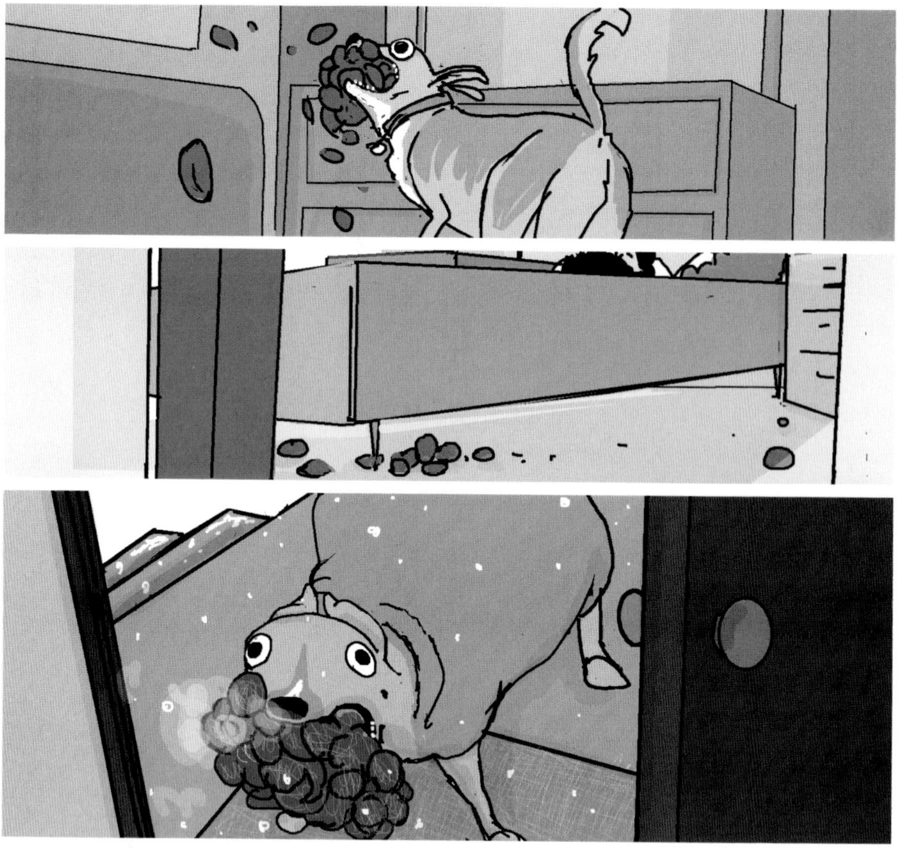

Murphy was sentenced to nighttime house arrest and a stern talkin'-to.

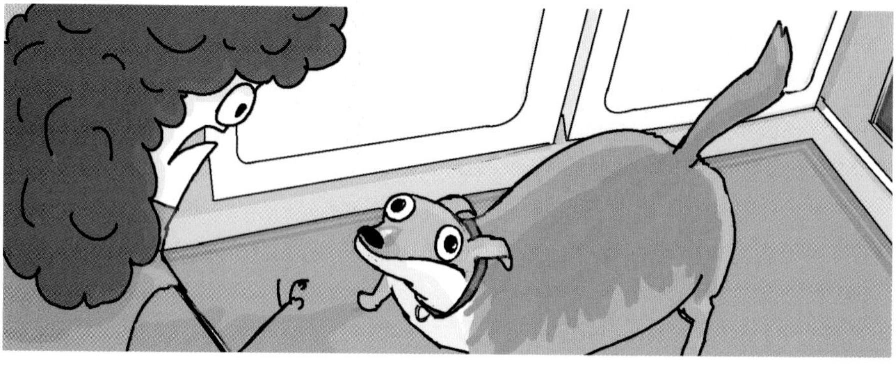

6. THE KANGAROO
PIG GETS DRUNK

Once upon a time, I saw four guys walking a dog across Las Vegas Boulevard.

The dog, which was wearing a costume, was looking around like *WHAT IS GOING ON—ARE WE OKAY—THIS IS THE MOST THINGS I HAVE EVER SEEN.*

And nobody responded because they were watching their friend twirl one of those spinny, flashy, light-up things that spells *BIRTHDAY-BIRTHDAY-BIRTHDAY, PARTY-PARTY-PARTY* when it goes around.

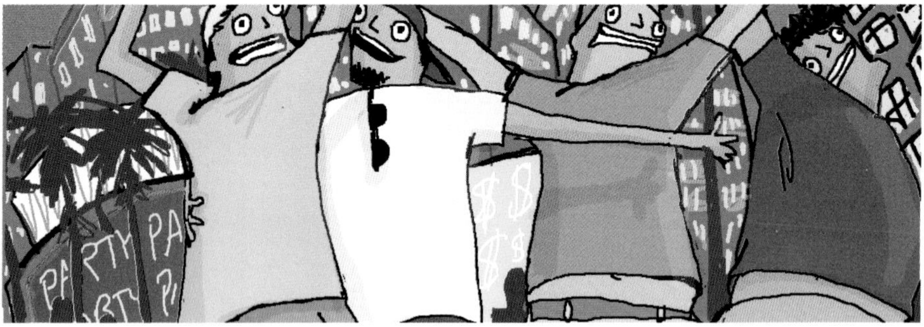
PARTY

The guys weren't confused—they knew why this was happening: It's somebody's birthday! Of course this is happening. Why *wouldn't* this be happening on somebody's birthday?

But dogs don't know about birthdays. They can't relate to the party-party-party thing. They don't understand what a costume does, or why they need to wear one.

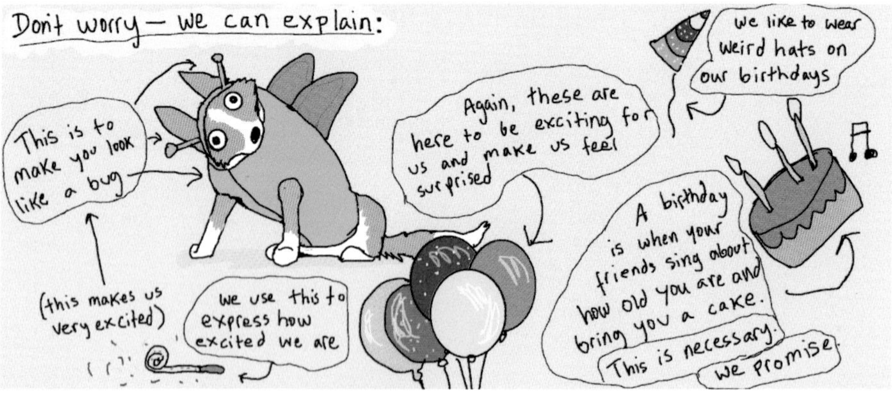
Don't worry—we can explain:
This is to make you look like a bug
(this makes us very excited)
we use this to express how excited we are
Again, these are here to be exciting for us and make us feel surprised
we like to wear weird hats on our birthdays
A birthday is when your friends sing about how old you are and bring you a cake.
This is necessary.
we promise

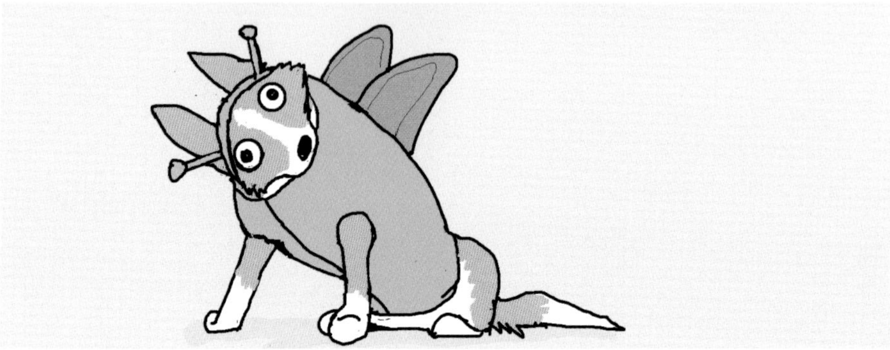

Imagine how confusing that would be if you'd never heard of it before . . .

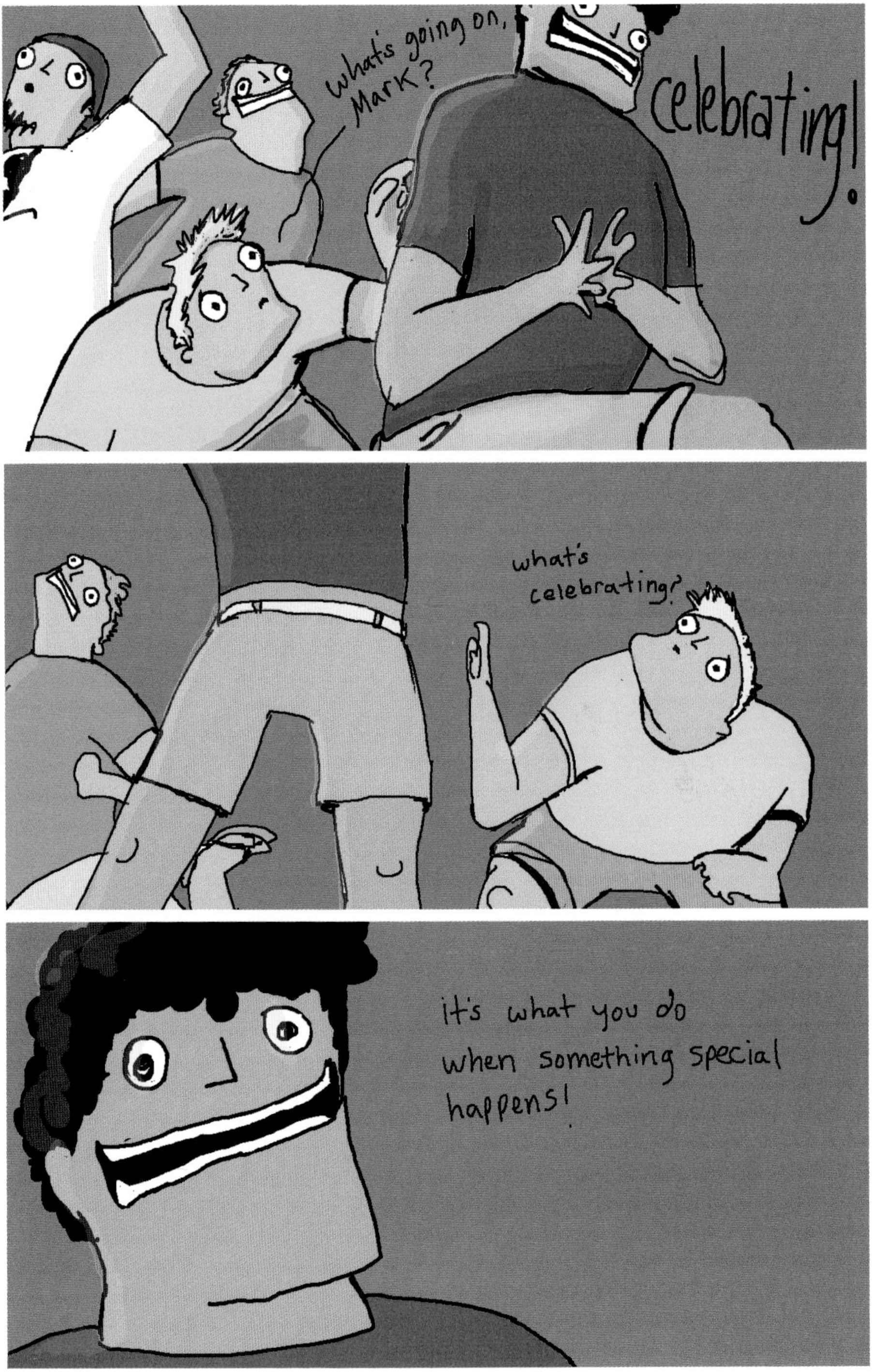
what's going on, Mark?
celebrating!
what's celebrating?
it's what you do when something special happens!

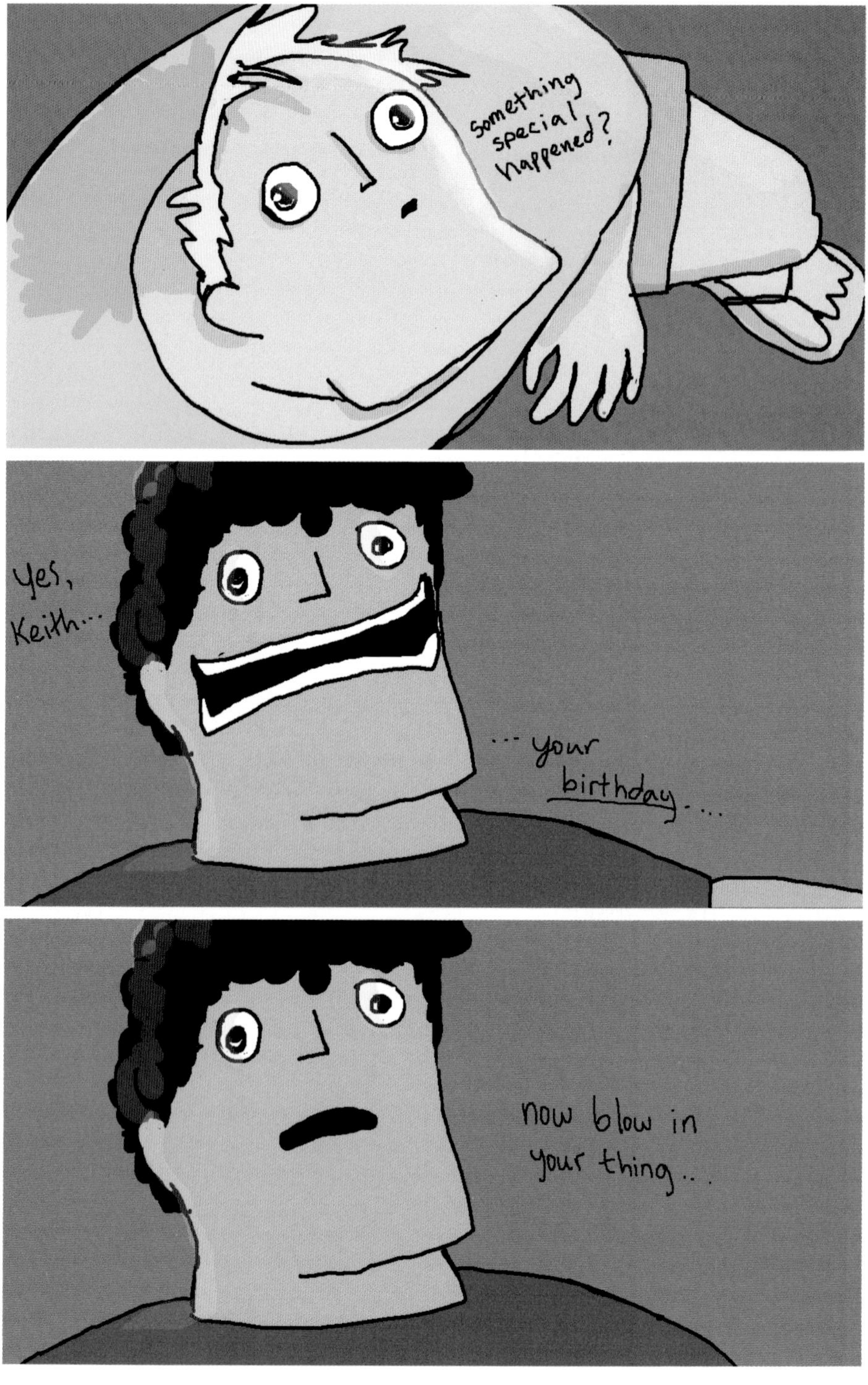
something special happened?
Yes, Keith...
... your birthday....
now blow in your thing...

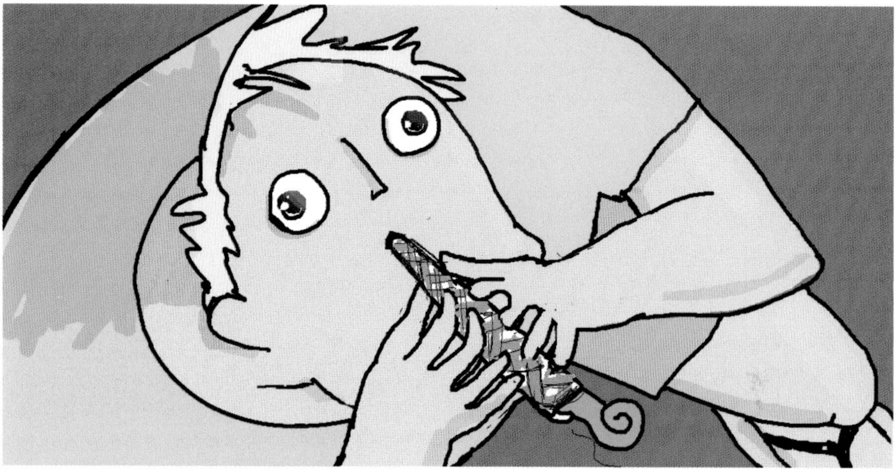

Animals don't understand what any of that means, so they also don't understand what it *doesn't* mean. As far as the animal can tell, this could be the first warning sign of a permanent and devastating change in lifestyle.

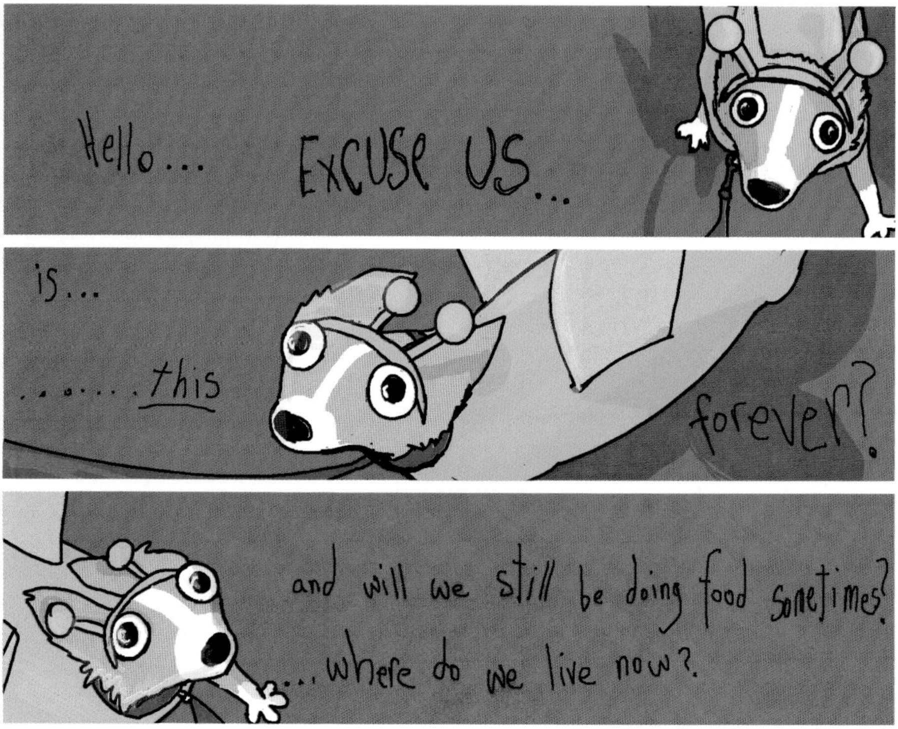
Hello...
EXCUSE US...
is...
.......this
forever?
and will we still be doing food sometimes?
...where do we live now?

But the only option they really have is to trust us.

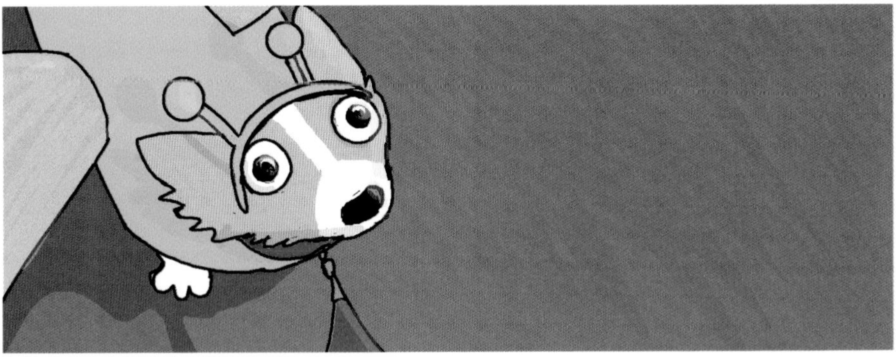

I mean, what's the alternative?

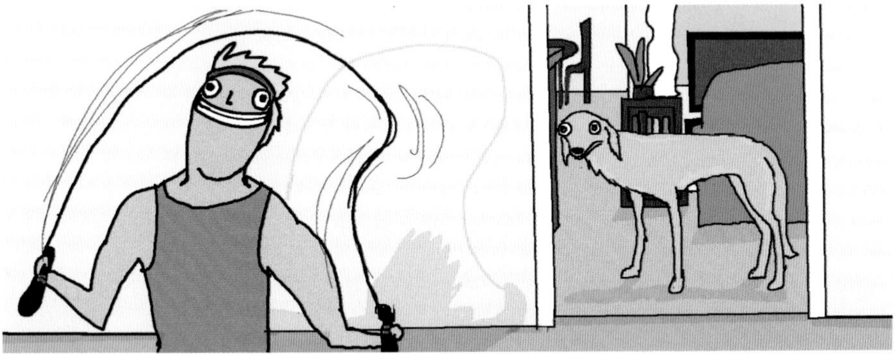

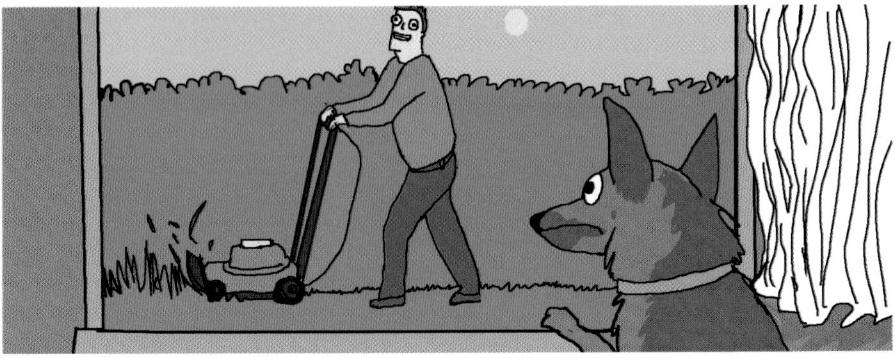

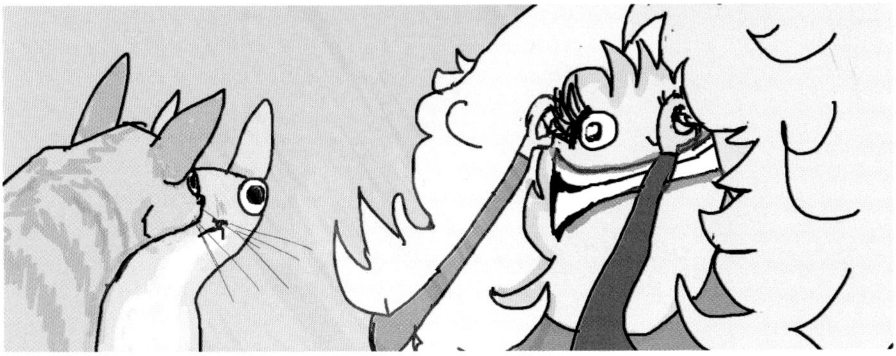

This is hardly an uncommon type of experience for domestic animals. I've spent basically my entire life running around in front of different pets, doing all sorts of things that seemed totally normal to me but probably not to the animals.

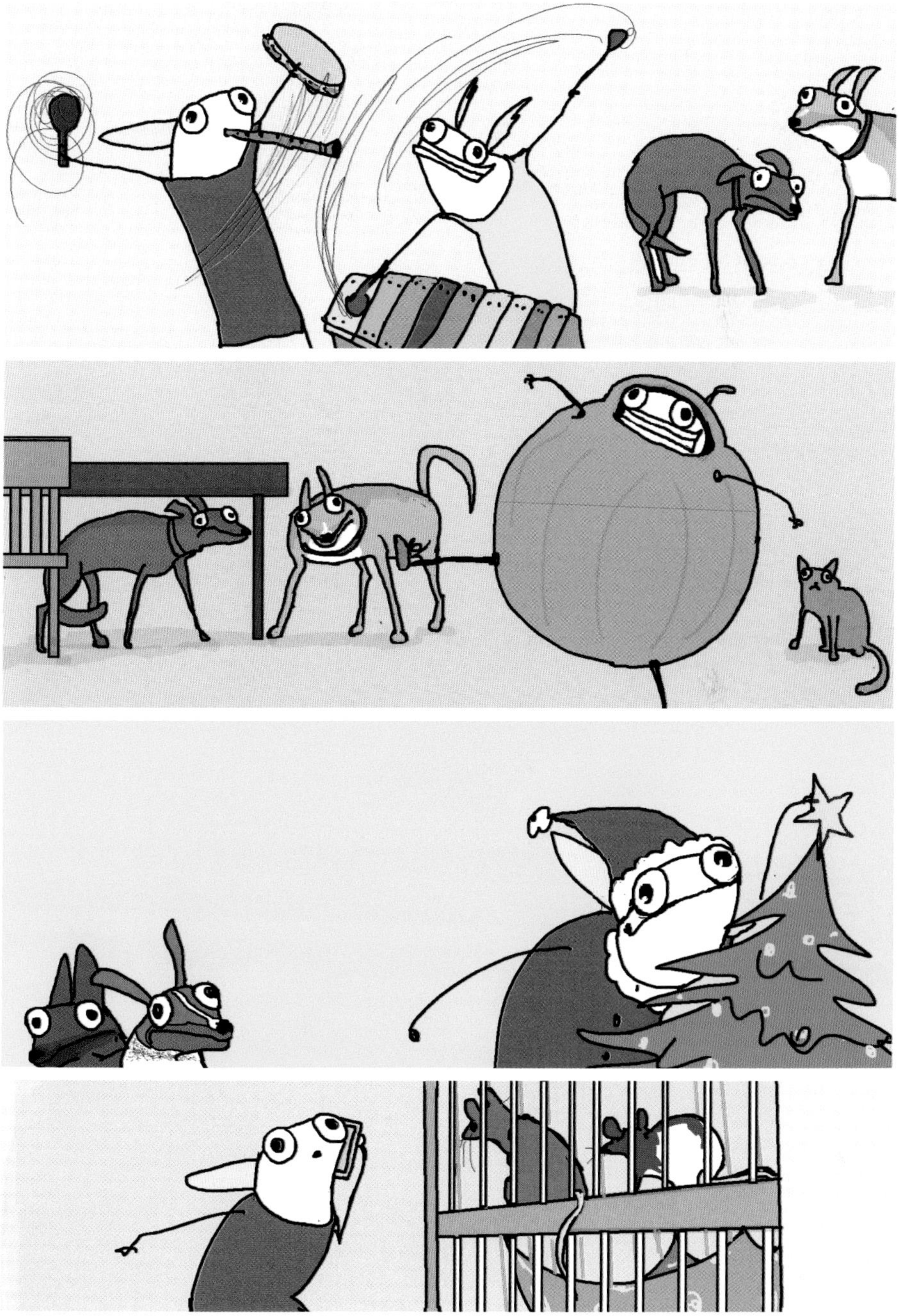

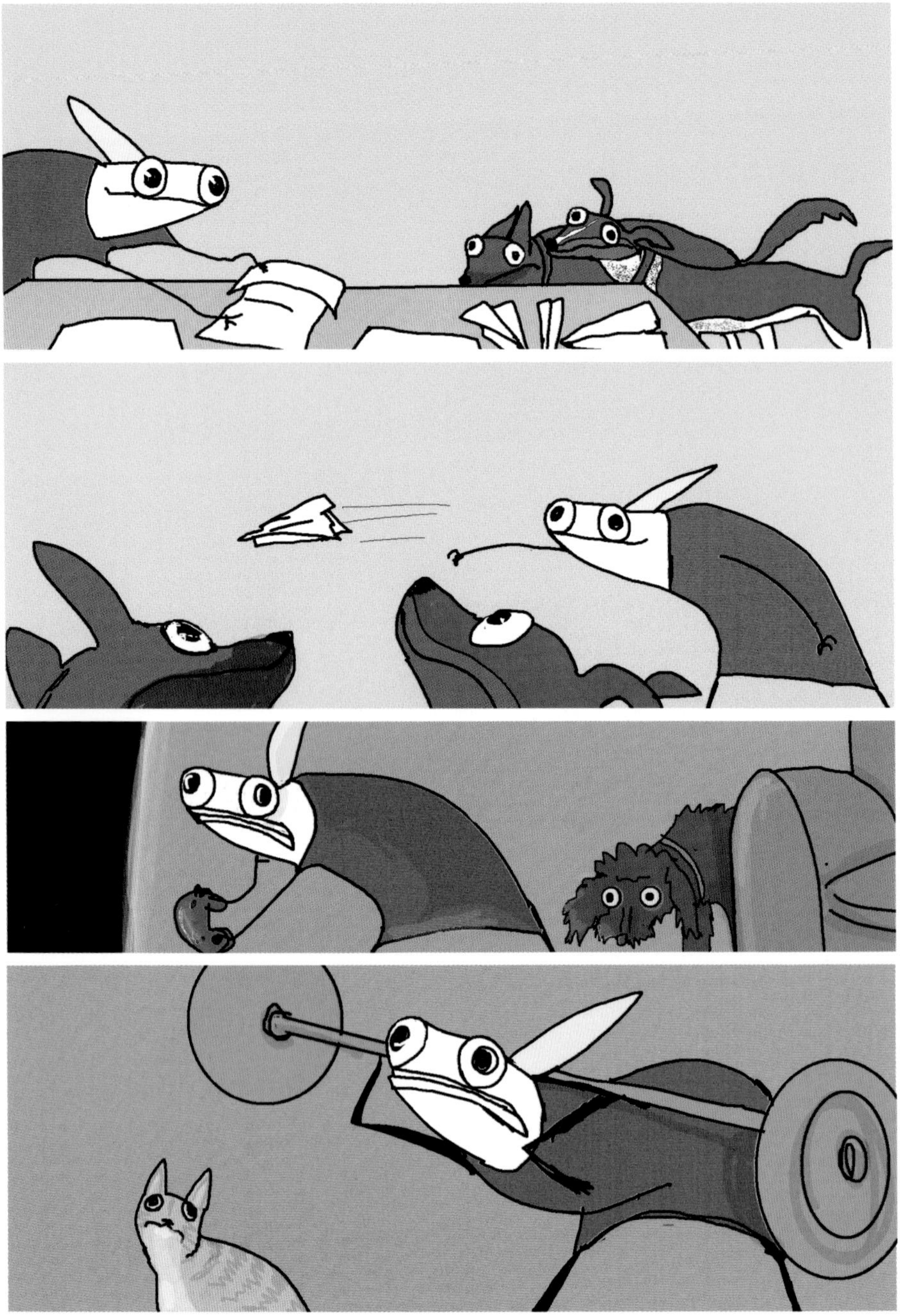

One of the animals I've bombarded with my behavior is a dog who could charitably be described as simple. Dogs are fairly simple as is, but this one is much more than that.

One night, shortly after adopting the simple dog, I got drunk and fell asleep watching Animal Planet. The simple dog was lying on her bed in the corner, trying her best not to panic about my sudden decline in motor function.

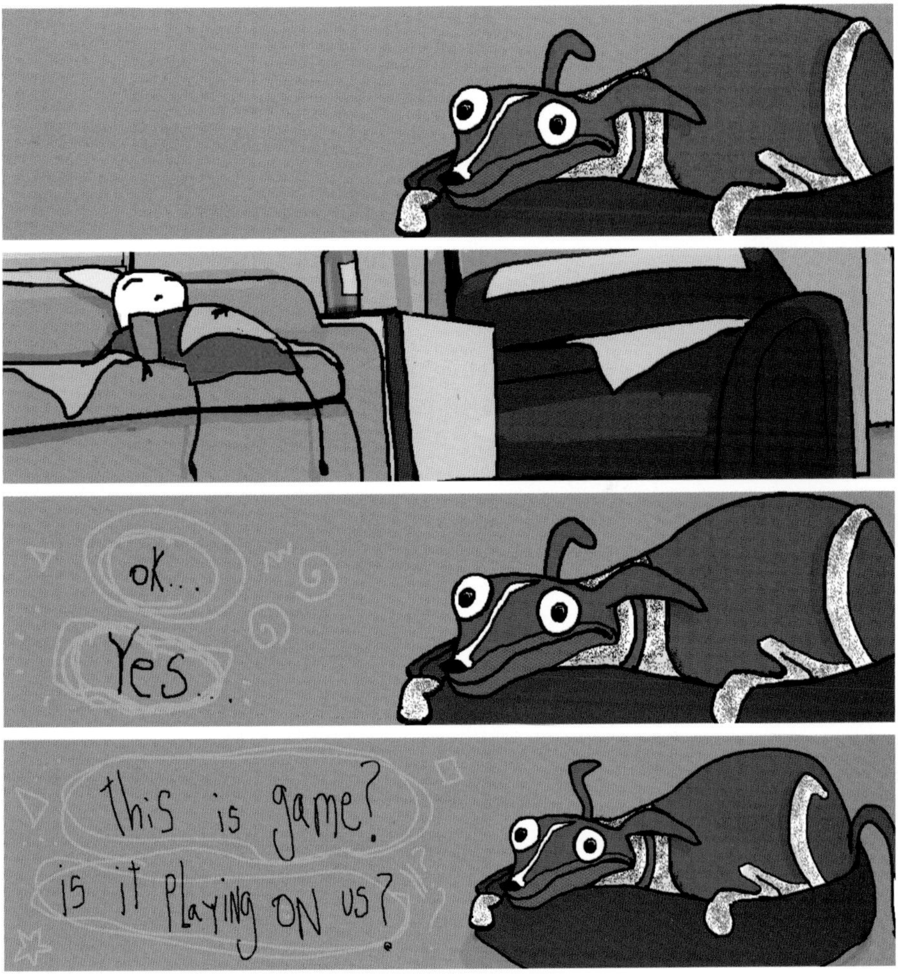
ok...
Yes...
this is game?
is it playing on us?

The next segment was about whales. I had the volume pretty high because I go sort of deaf when I'm drunk, and let me tell you: whale sonar is a huge surprise when you're drunk and asleep.

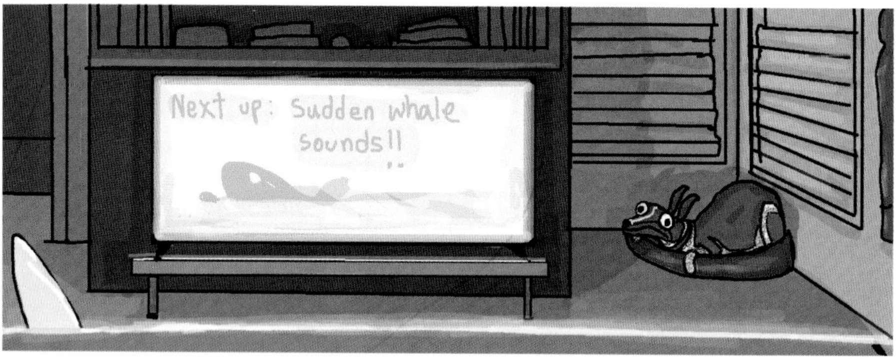
Next up: Sudden whale sounds!!

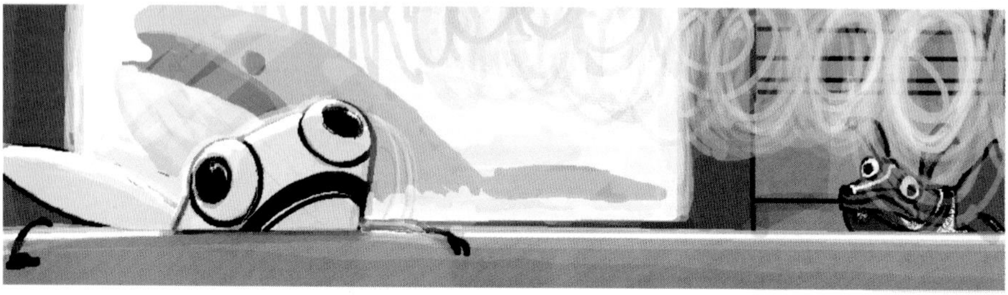

Hearing this unexpected noise caused me to shoot up and spill my water, which was also a surprise because I didn't remember I was holding a cup of water, so it seemed like maybe I was being attacked. I yelled "STOP IT," presumably to discourage the attackers.

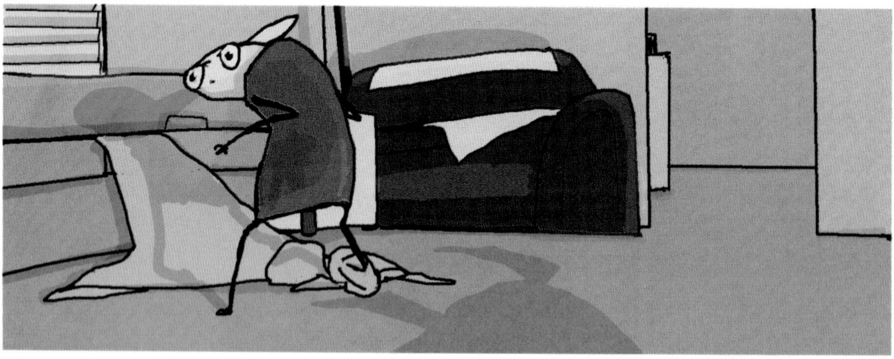

I felt so embarrassed when I realized it was just whales.

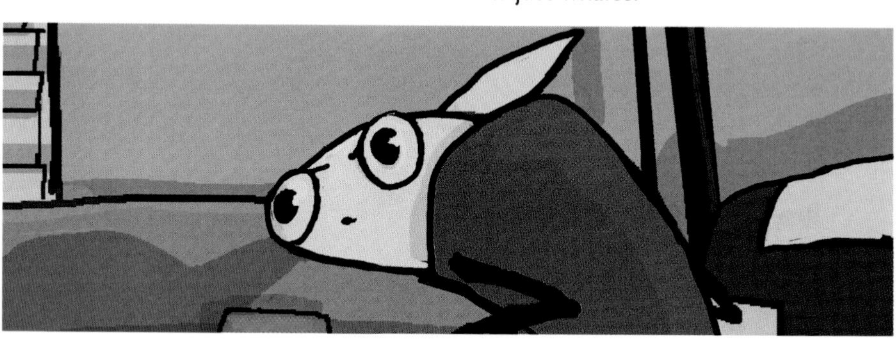

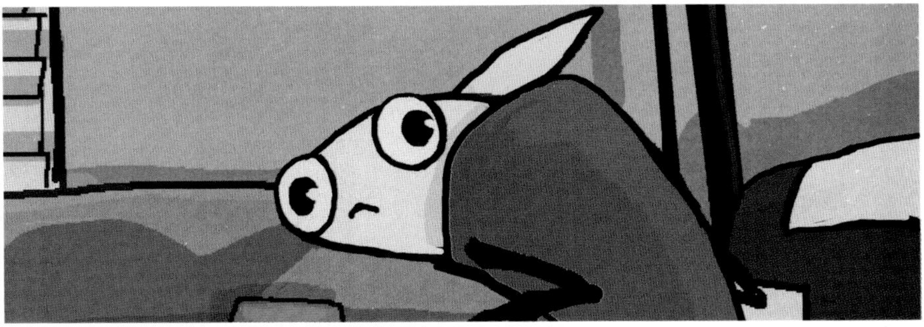

That was a weird 10 seconds for me. It would've been a weird 10 seconds for anybody, probably.

Now imagine that you are defenseless and totally incapable of caring for yourself.

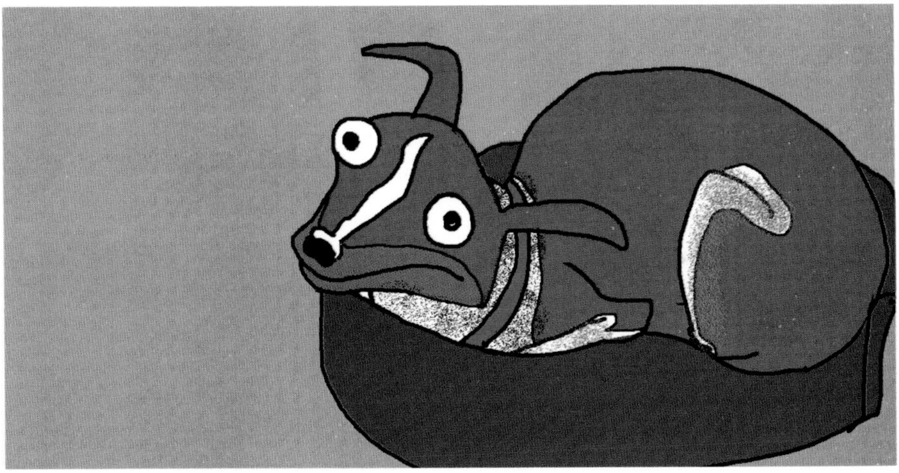

But it's okay because there's this big pink creature that looks like a weird pig or maybe a kangaroo.

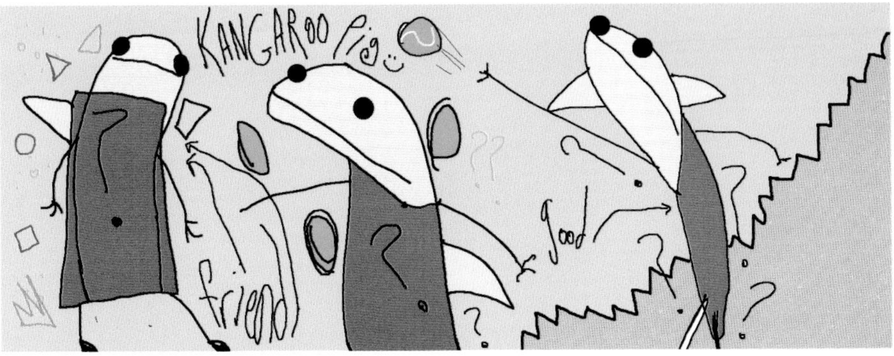
KANGAROO Pig
friend
good

For some reason, the kangaroo pig feeds you and takes you outside so you can poop. You don't know why it does this, but you trust it has its reasons.

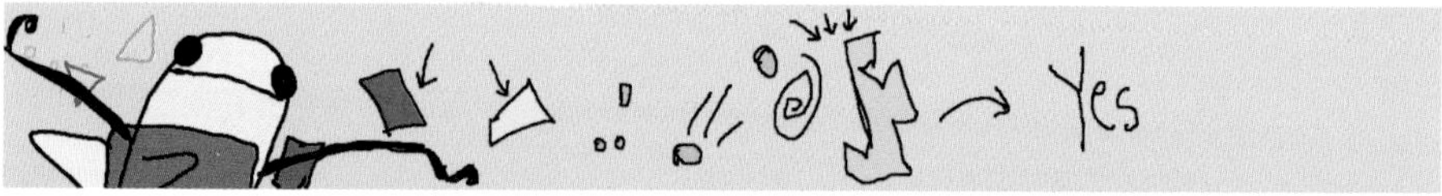
Yes

Then one day the kangaroo pig comes home smelling like chemicals and its legs don't work. You think, *It can barely walk . . . what if it can't take care of us? What if we never get to poop again?*

The kangaroo pig turns on its picture-sound box and sits down.

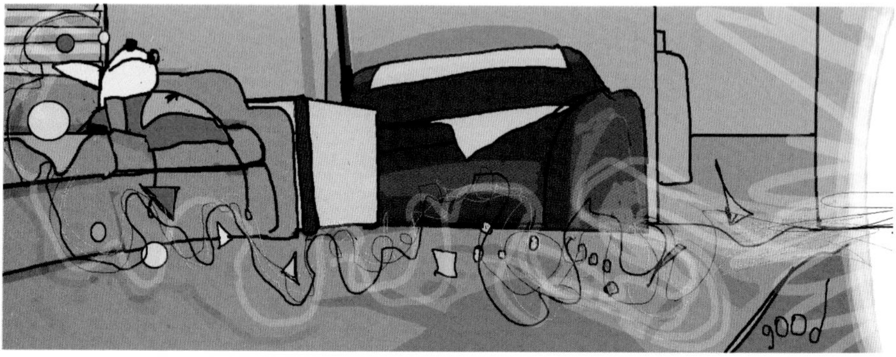
good

Maybe it is okay, you think. *Maybe everything will be okay. Maybe it just needs to absorb some picture sounds.* You start to relax. Your future seems optimistic again.

Then, out of nowhere, you hear a noise like:

MMMMMMMMMMMMMRRRRRRRRRRRRROOOOOOOOOOOOOOOOOOOOOOOOOOOOOOOOOOOOOOOOOOOOOOOOOOOOOOOOOOOOOOOOOOOOOOOOOOOOOOOOooooooooooooooooooooooooooooooooooooooooooooooooooooooooooooooooooooooooooooooooooooo!!!

The kangaroo pig flops upright and assumes a defensive stance.

It seems upset.

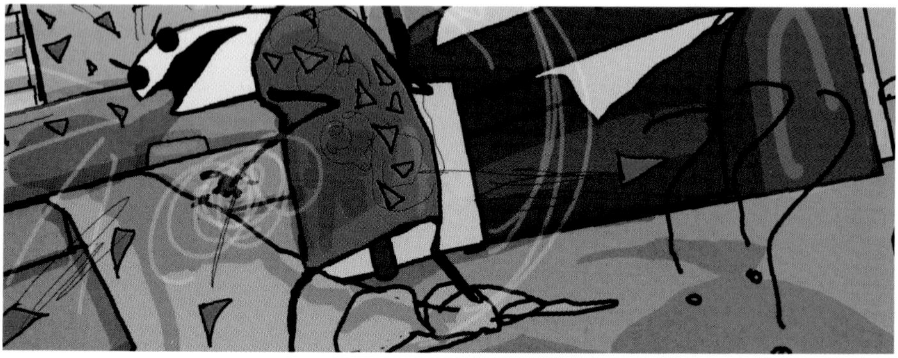

What do you do?? How do you respond??

I don't know how every animal in the world would react, but if you're this dog, you begin by performing your default panic action, sprinting.

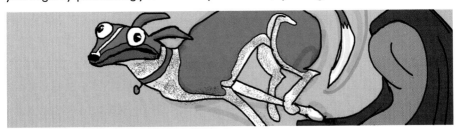

You do that for a while.

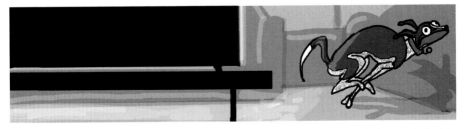

You're going really fast, but at some point, you notice the whales and decide they're responsible for this.

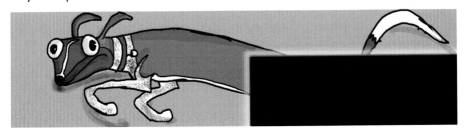

You try to bite the whales, but a solid surface is protecting them.

Unable to cope with this twist of events, you sprint at top speed into the dining room. But no comfort is to be found there—only chairs. Inevitably, your reckless sprinting behavior causes one of them to fall over.

Somehow, your legs and head become tangled in the chair.

Being a dog—and a below-average one at that—you don't understand that this is just something that can happen when you collide with a chair, and chairs—which lack a nervous system—cannot attack you.

It truly seems like the chair is doing this on purpose.

You are now permanently afraid of the chair, which, for some reason, is never punished or restrained in any way.

But you can't question the decision. You can't ask the kangaroo pig why it would allow such a violent object to live in the house after it saw what it did. Your only option is to stand by helplessly and hope the chair situation doesn't get any worse.

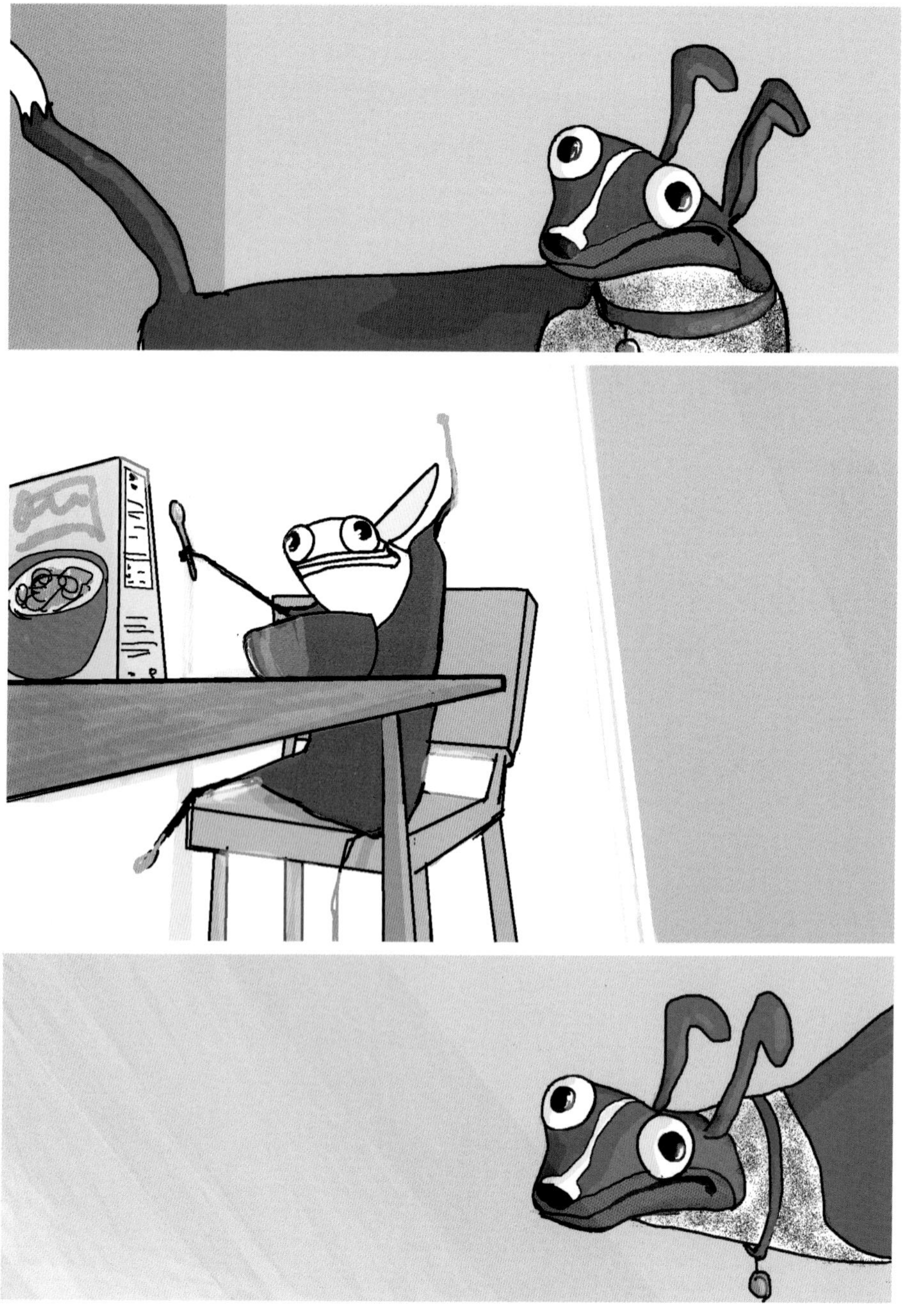

It's got to be hard for pets. To be constantly assaulted from every conceivable angle by the insane-seeming behavior of their caretakers.

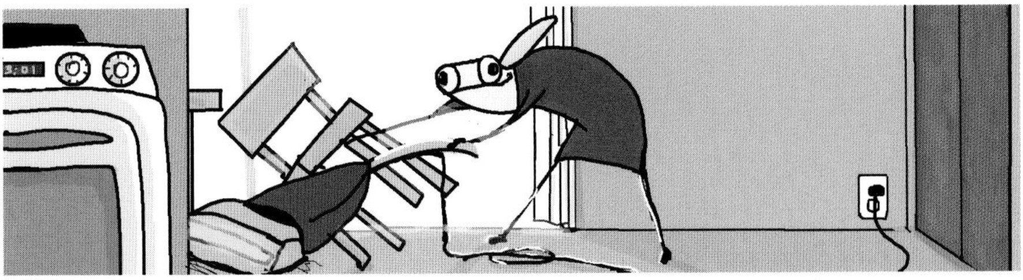

Fortunately, animals are the psychological equivalent of tractors. It's honestly amazing how durable they are. We can do pretty much whatever we want to them, and they'll be like, *Okay, we will try it. Thank you for interacting with us.*

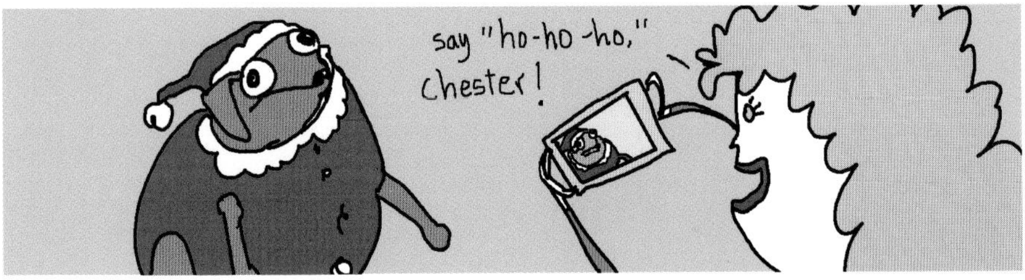
say "ho-ho-ho," chester!

We don't stop there, though. We aren't content to allow them to sit there and just passively accept how ballistically confusing their life is. No—we want them to *participate.*

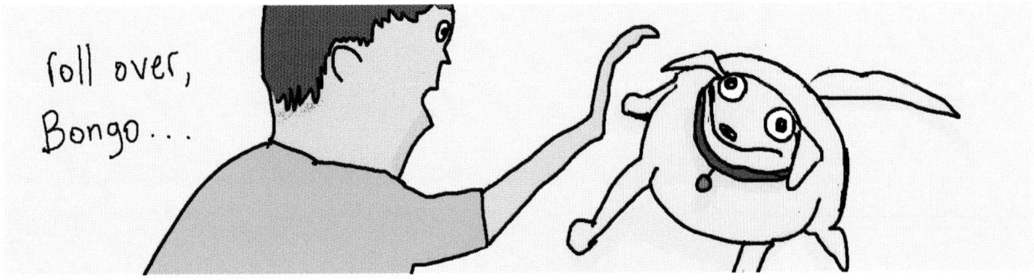
roll over, Bongo...

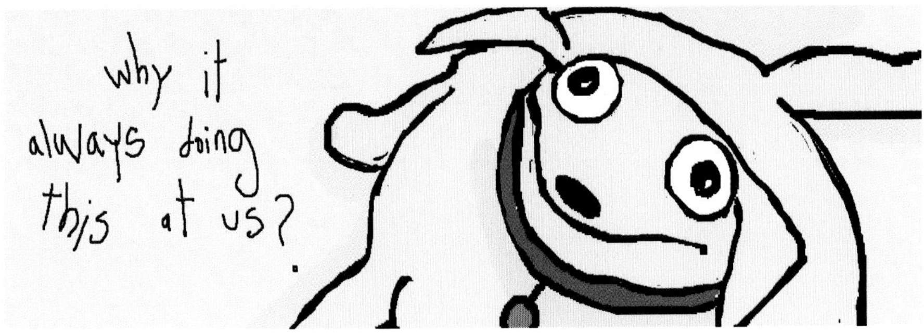
why it always doing this at us?

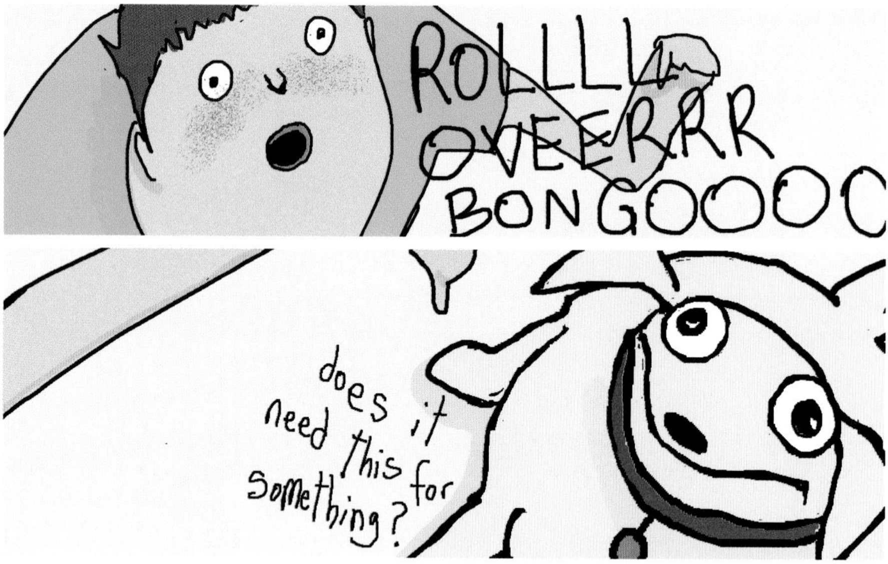
ROLLLL OVEERRR BONGOOOO
does it need this for something?

I didn't realize the true extent of this until I saw a video clip of a rabbit competing in an agility competition.

I'm not sure the rabbit knew it was competing, but everybody else knew, and they were cheering for the rabbit and having so much fun.

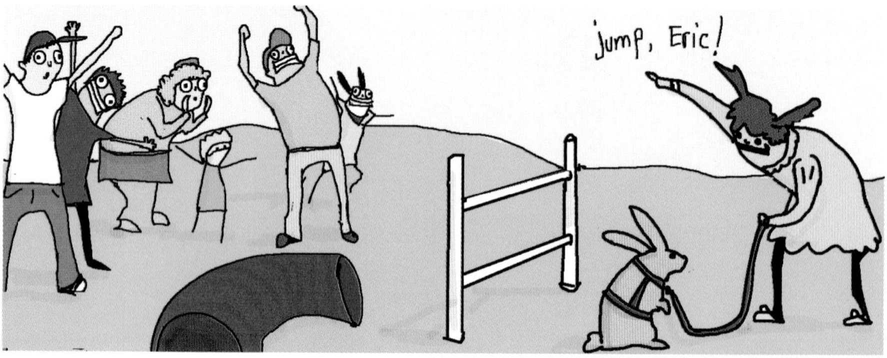
jump, Eric!

The rabbit seemed to mostly be enjoying itself, which was surprising given how existentially confused it must have been.

The next video was basically the same, except it was a lizard instead of a rabbit. The one after that was a hamster.

Hours later, it was clear to me that no type of animal is exempt from agility competitions.

Oh, you're a bird? Doesn't matter. Get out there with your little weird legs and jump over some sticks.

Cats, dogs, horses, pigs, lizards, fish—as long as the animal has the ability to do something, it can compete.

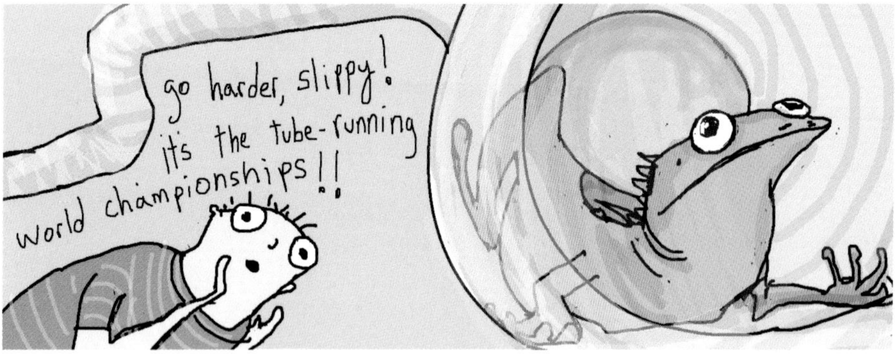
go harder, slippy! it's the tube-running world championships!!

Animals get stuff like face biting and chasing each other. They get that. Chase each other, bite each other's faces. Easy and simple.

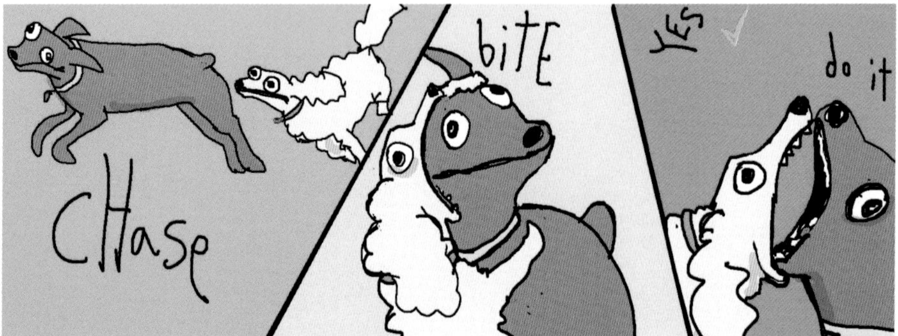
CHase
biTE
YES
do it

But crawling through and jumping over a series of tubes—tubes that are absolutely fucking surrounded by easier places to go—and trying to do it faster or better or fancier than other animals for no practical purpose whatsoever . . . I've got to think that's less relatable for them.

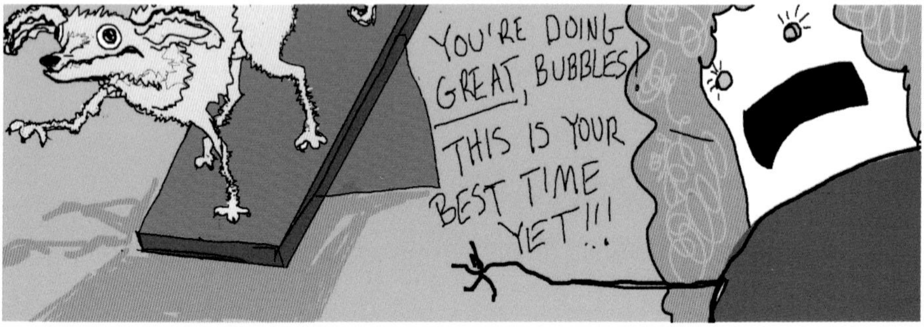
YOU'RE DOING GREAT, BUBBLES! THIS IS YOUR BEST TIME YET!!!

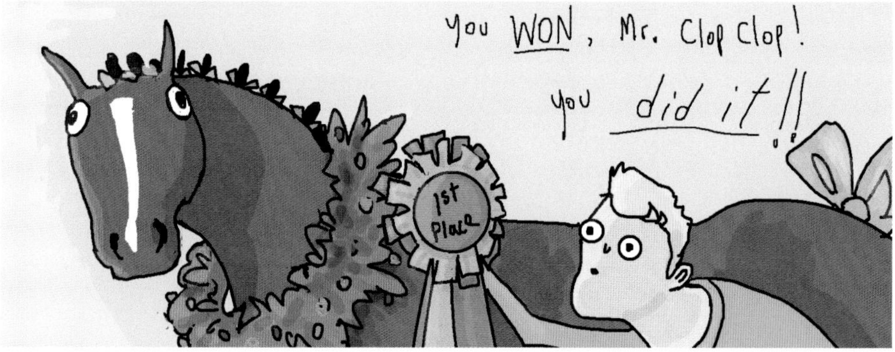
you WON, Mr. Clop Clop!
you did it!!
1st Place

We'd explain if we could, I'm sure. We do the best we can.

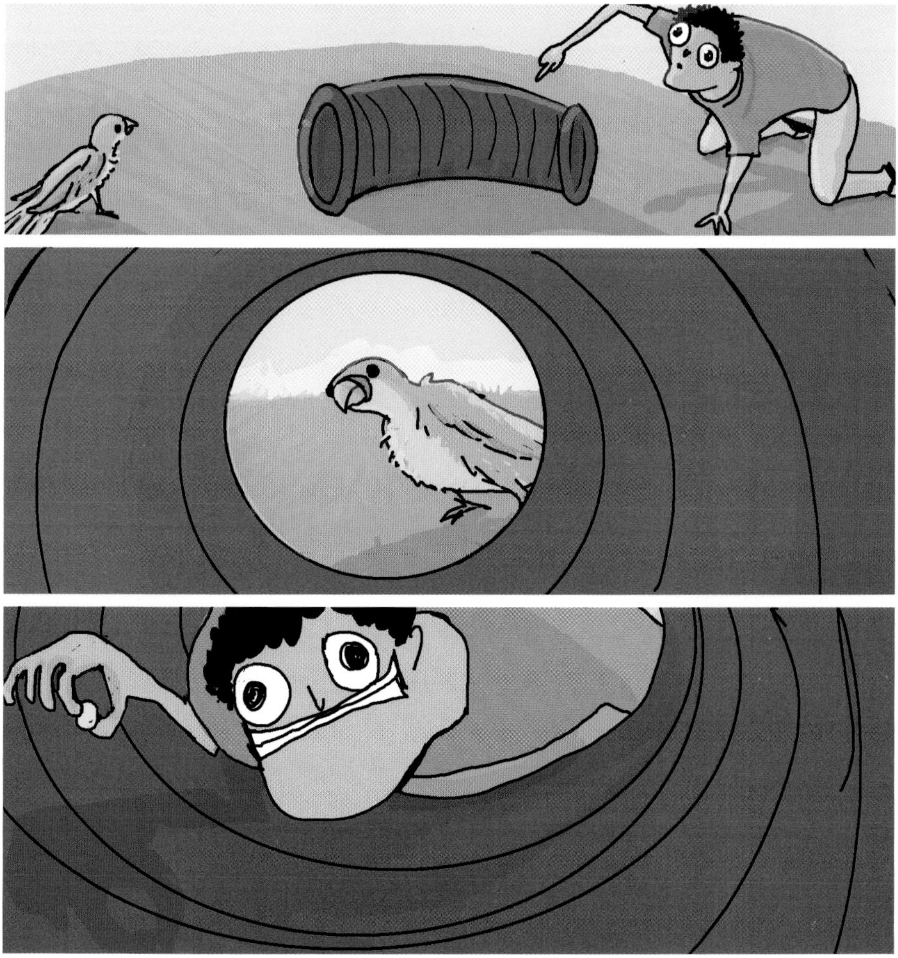

I can't imagine they don't have questions, though.

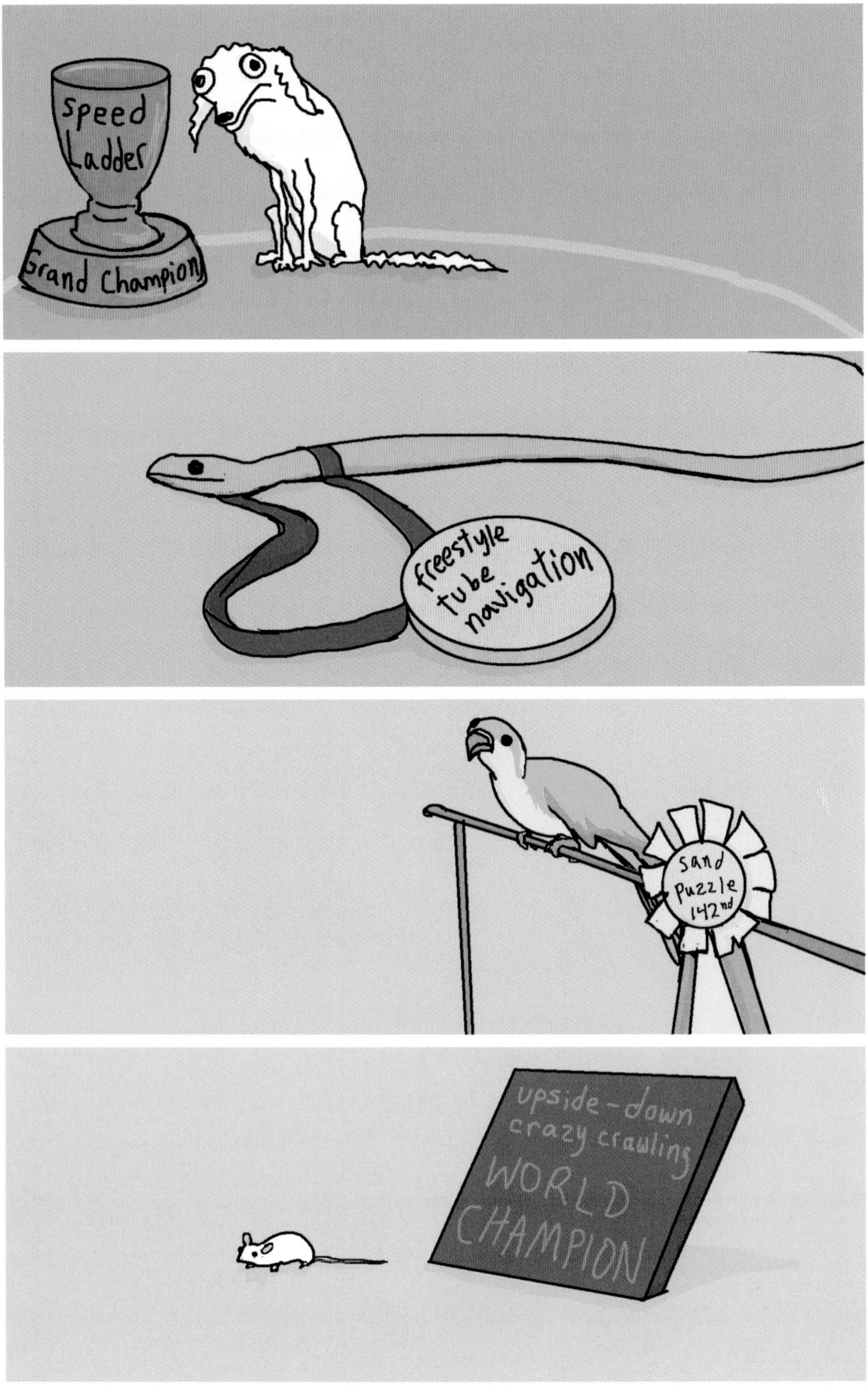
Speed Ladder
Grand Champion
freestyle tube navigation
sand puzzle 142nd
upside-down crazy crawling
WORLD CHAMPION

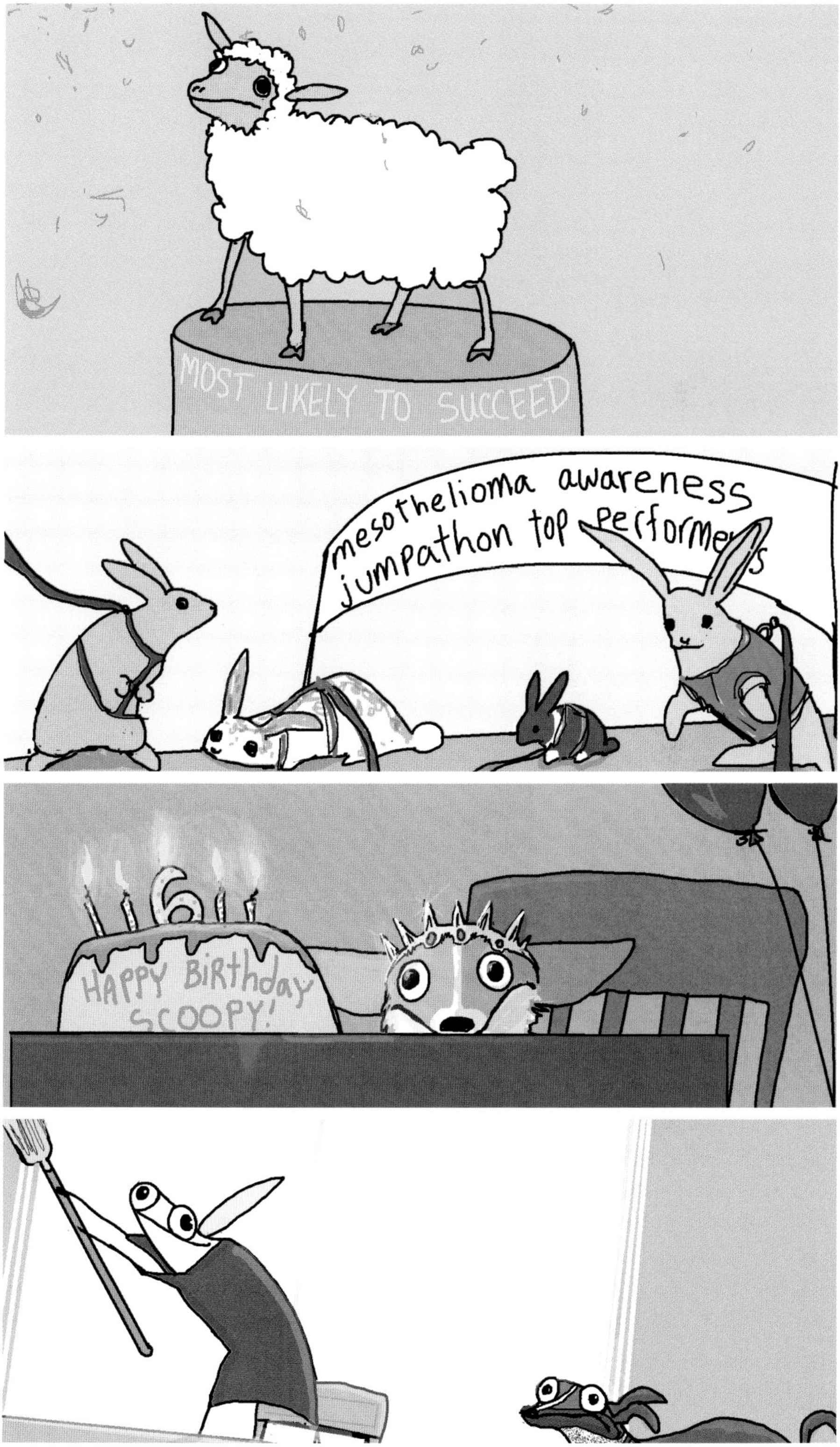
MOST LIKELY TO SUCCEED
mesothelioma awareness
jumpathon top
6
HAPPY BIRTHDAY
SCOOPY!

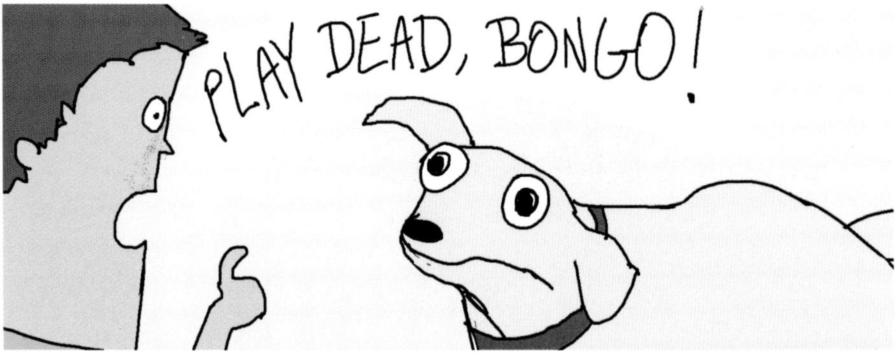
PLAY DEAD, BONGO!

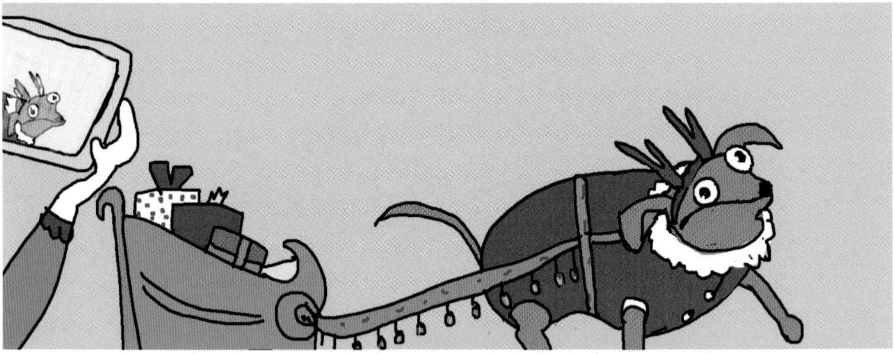

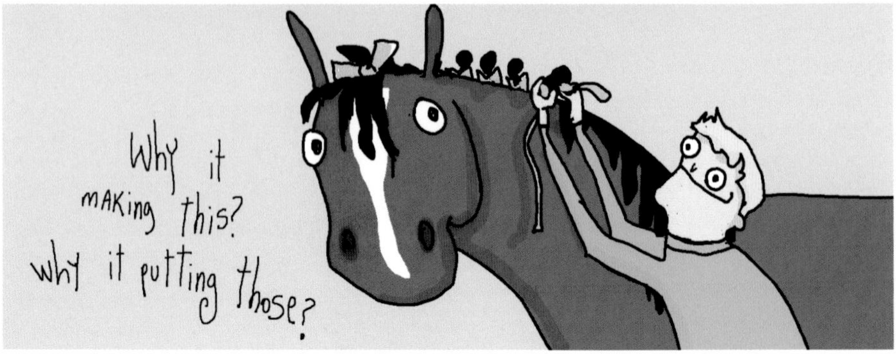
Why it making this? why it putting those?

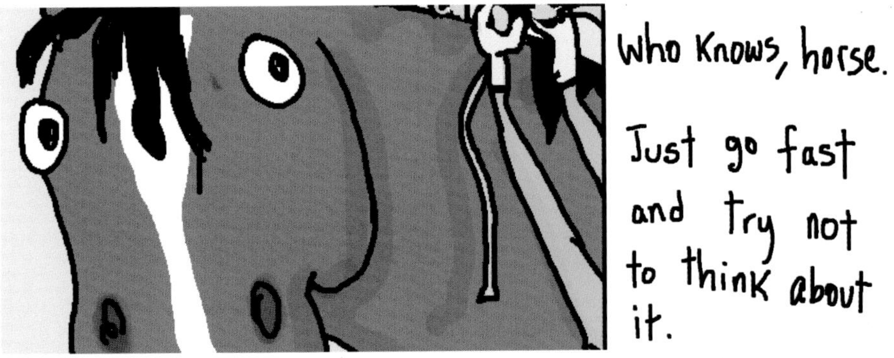
Who Knows, horse.
Just go fast and try not to think about it.

And they go their whole lives like that. No answers, no context, no mercy.

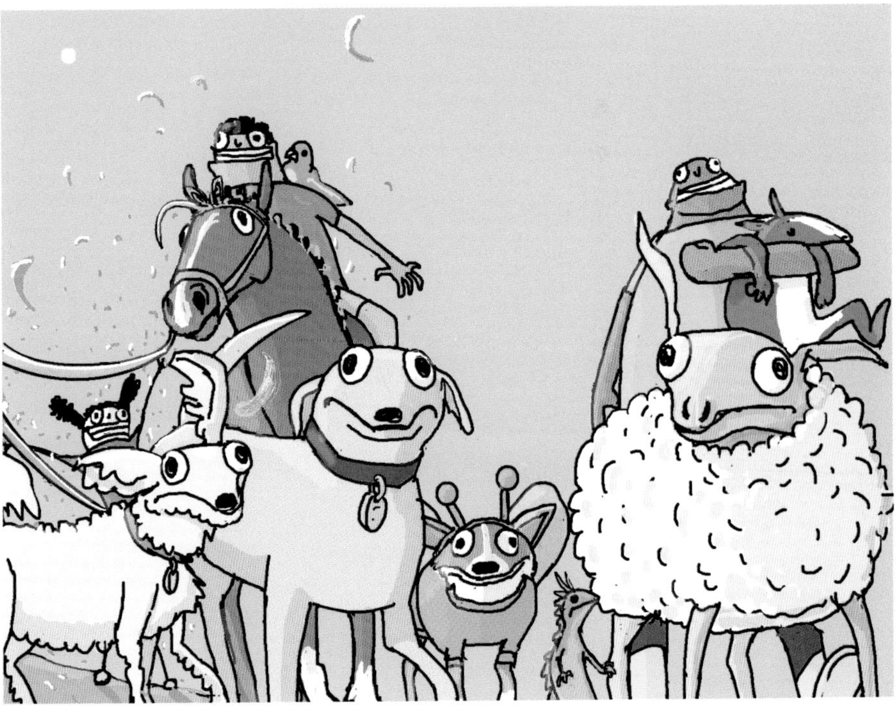

7. DAYDREAMS

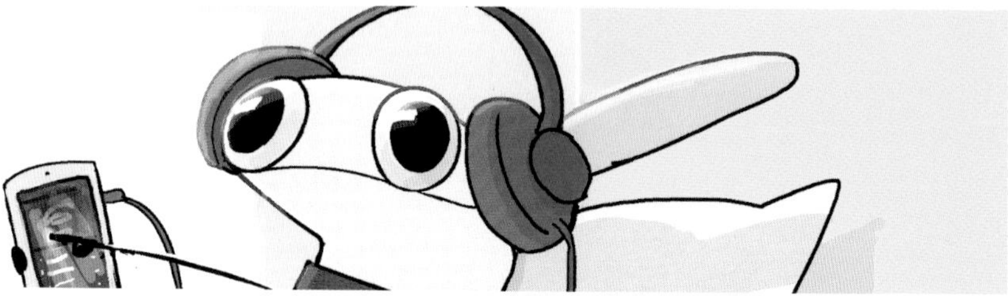

I have this daydream where I'm dressed like a conquistador and I'm riding a horse. It isn't immediately clear why this is happening, but my muscles are intense and highly visible.

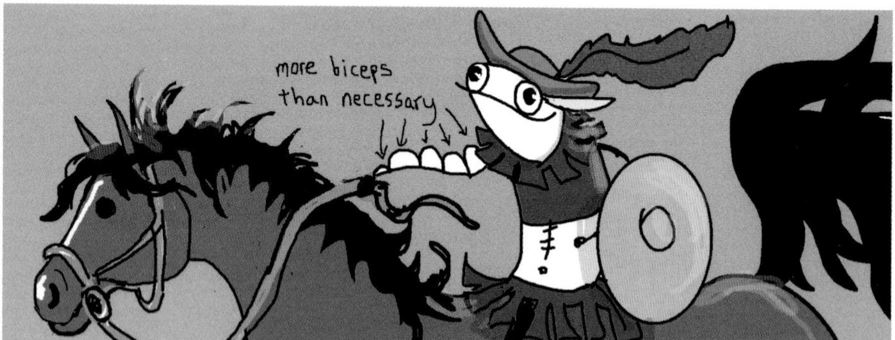
more biceps than necessary

I ride up to some vague authority figure—he's wearing a crown, so he's clearly important. I can't hear what he's saying because the music is too loud, but it seems pretty serious. A mission, maybe.

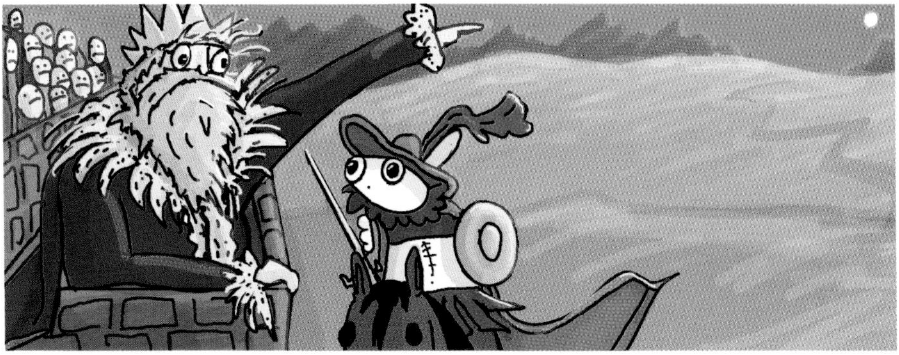

And then, at the best part of the song, I get this look on my face like:

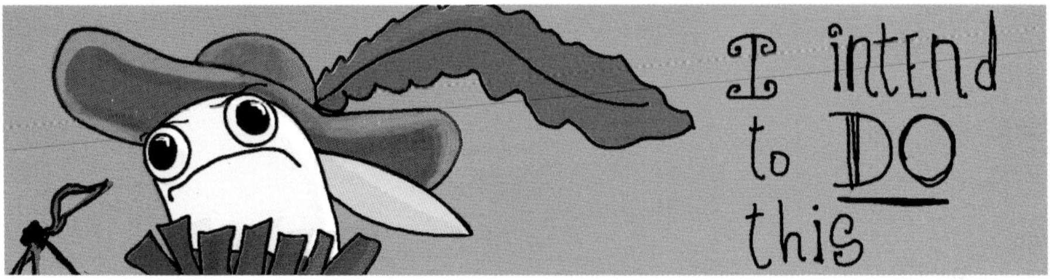
I intend to DO this

There's a knowing glance between me and the authority figure.

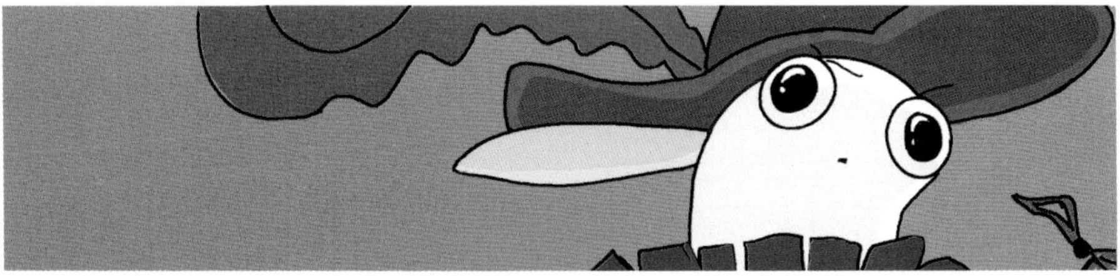

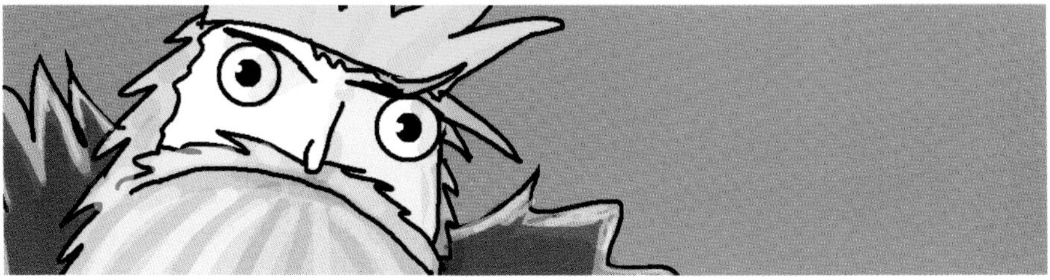

I can tell I'm the only hope the authority figure—and possibly the world—has.

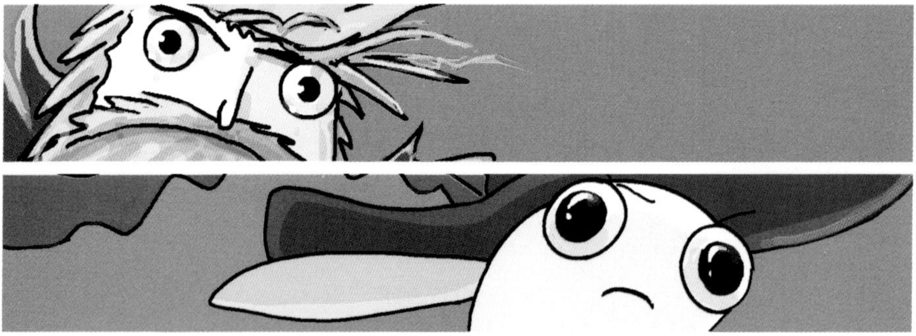

Then I gallop away to do the mission.

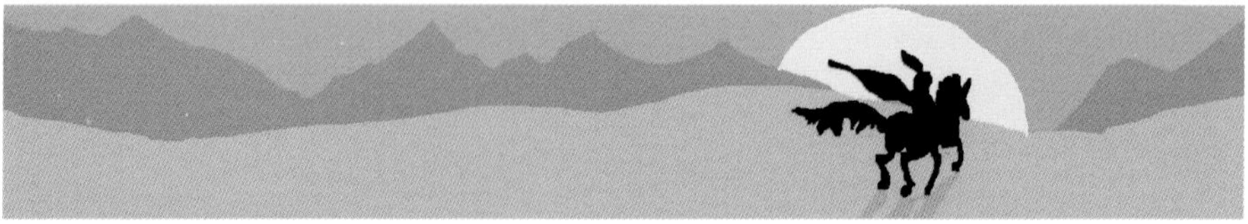

That's it. That's the whole thing.

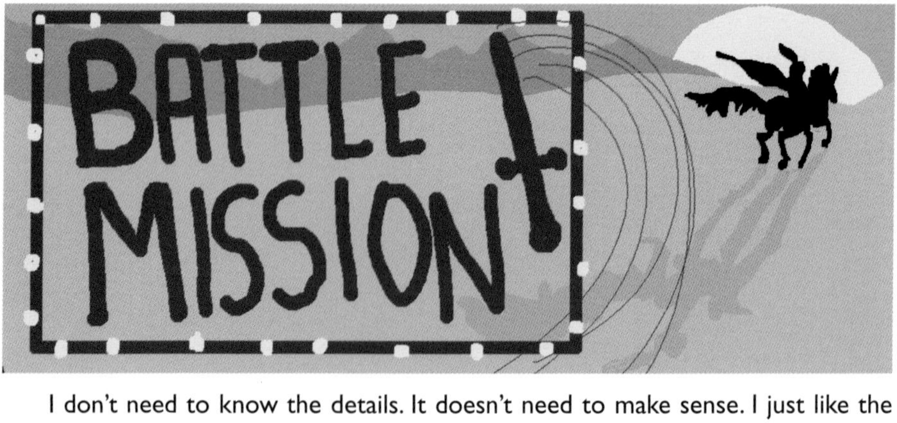
BATTLE MISSION

I don't need to know the details. It doesn't need to make sense. I just like the feelings.

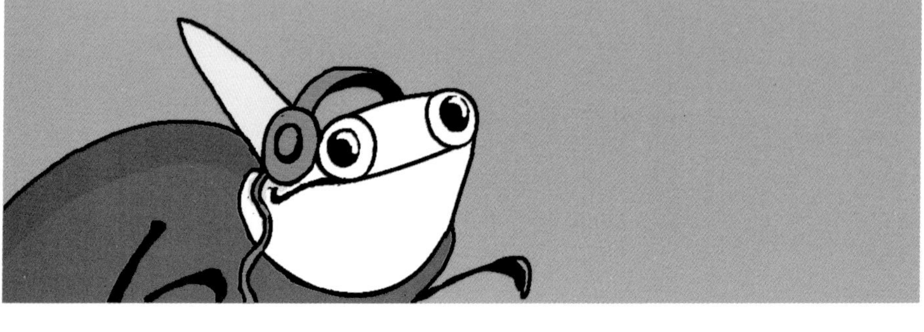

Here's another one, one of my favorites: I'm driving ...

Real casual-like ...

My hat's on backwards to lend credibility ...

My friend is there. This time it's Greg.

We are having fun.

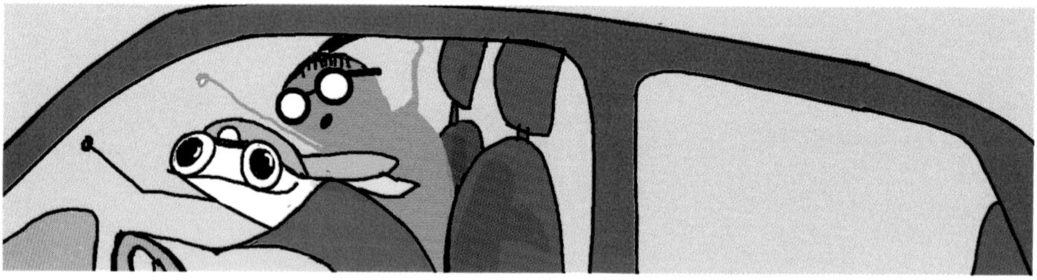

If I wanted to make the story accessible to a wider audience, I'd need to find some way to clue them in about the part where we don't give a *fuck*, but other than that, the thing's seaworthy as far as I'm concerned.

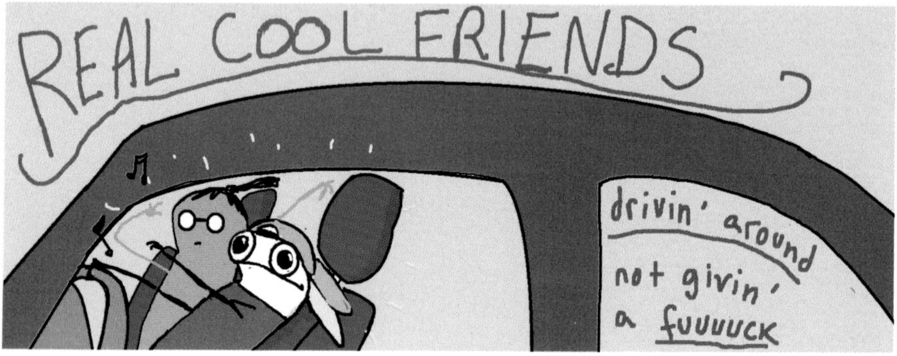
REAL COOL FRIENDS
drivin' around
not givin' a fuuuuck

It's like being able to watch a movie, starring me, about anything I can imagine, and I don't have to worry about exposition, believability, or a coherent plot, because I know I won't ask questions.

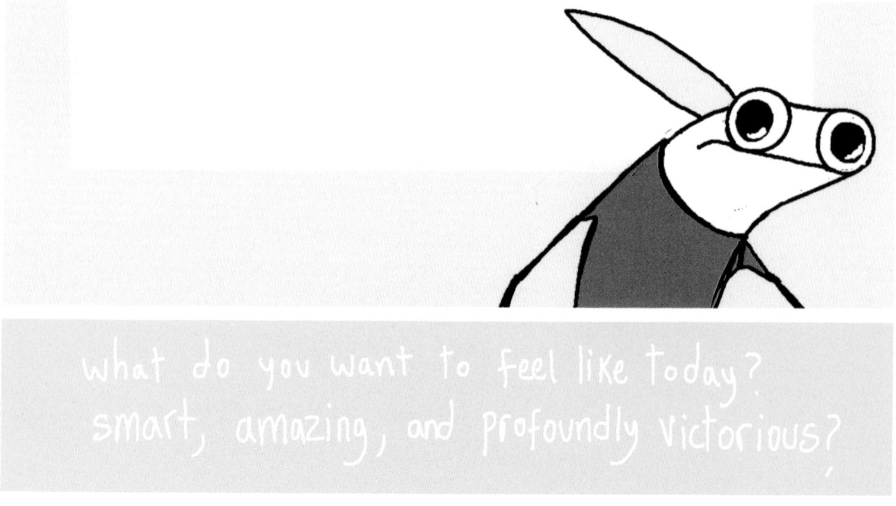
what do you want to feel like today?
smart, amazing, and profoundly victorious?

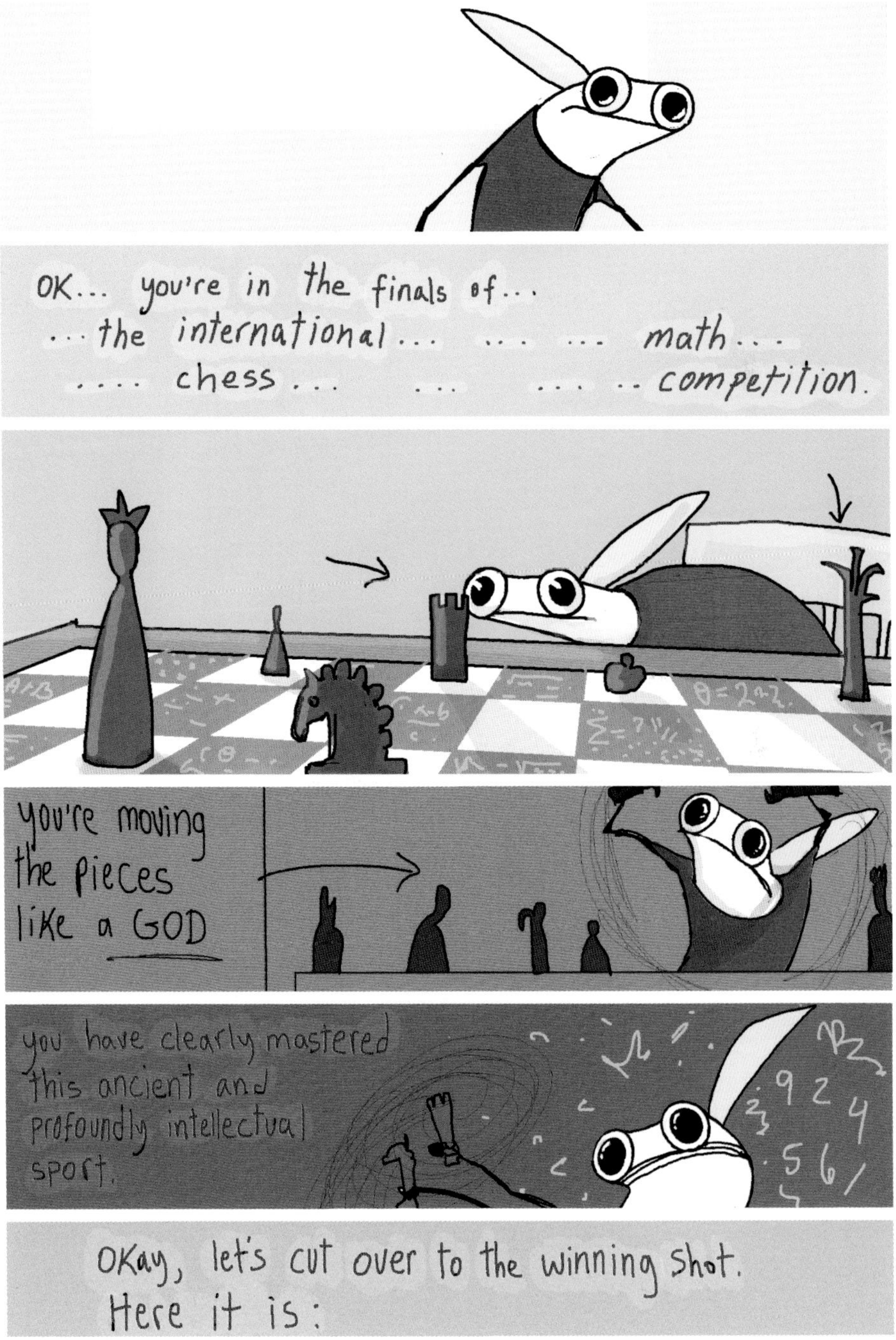
OK... you're in the finals of...
...the international... ... ... math...
.... chess ... ...competition.
you're moving the pieces like a GOD
you have clearly mastered this ancient and profoundly intellectual sport.
OKay, let's cut over to the winning shot.
Here it is:

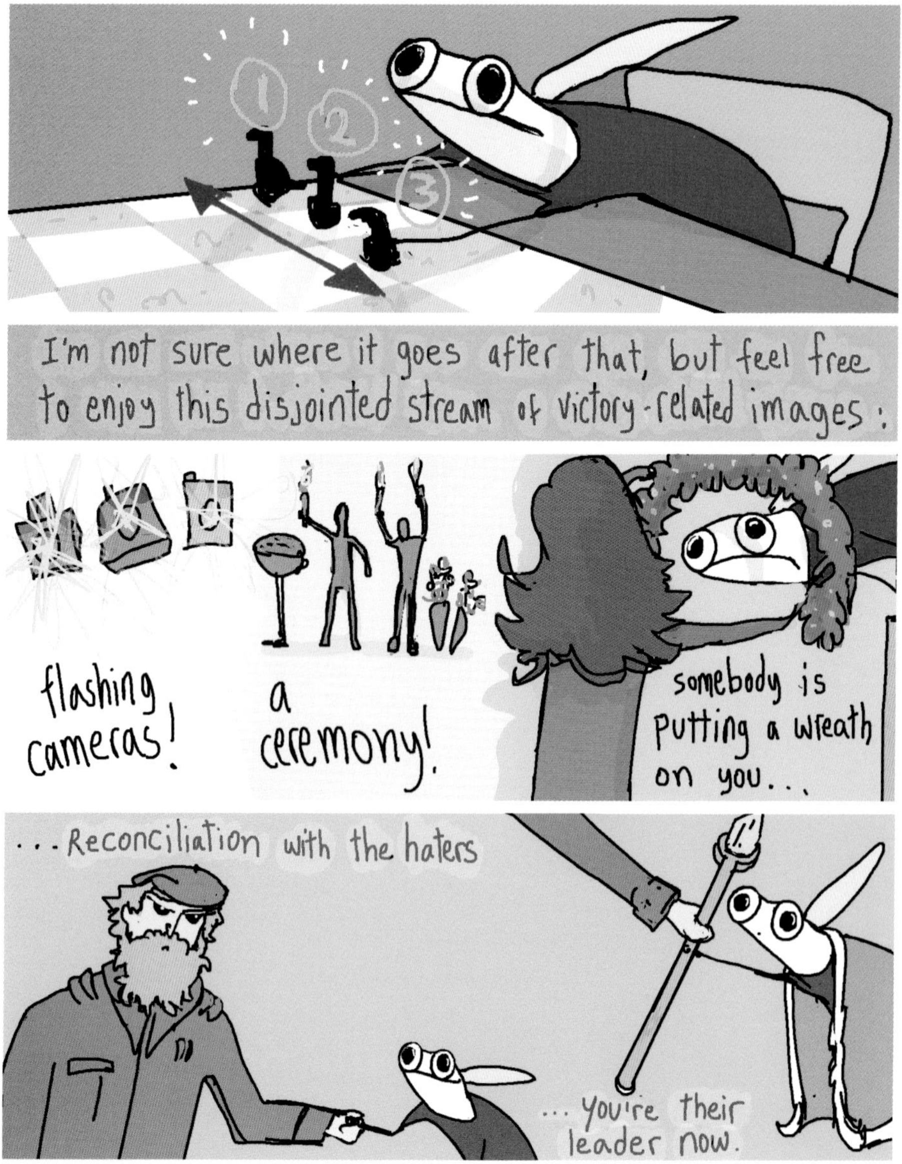
1
2
3
I'm not sure where it goes after that, but feel free to enjoy this disjointed stream of victory-related images:
flashing cameras!
a ceremony!
somebody is putting a wreath on you...
...Reconciliation with the haters
...you're their leader now.

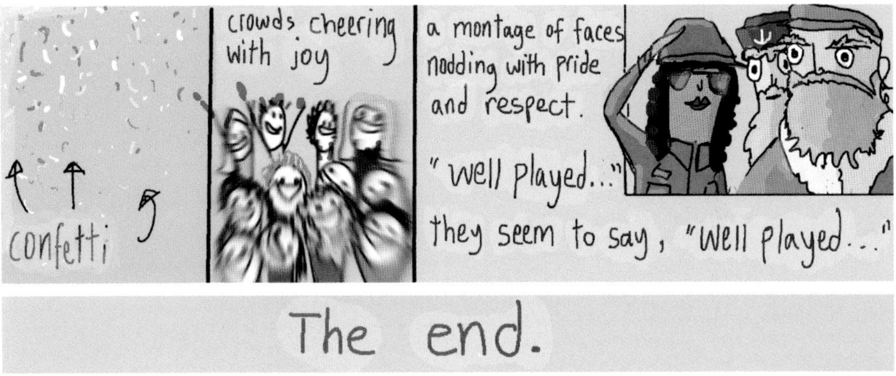
confetti
crowds cheering with joy
a montage of faces nodding with pride and respect.
"well played..."
they seem to say, "well played..."
The end.

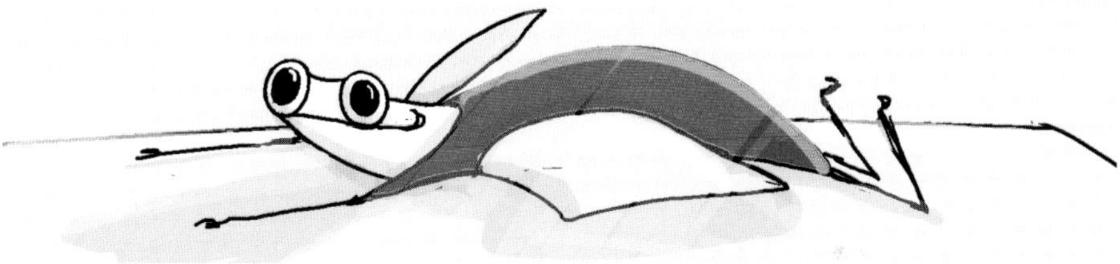

Most of the time there's no real purpose to the activity—I'm just meandering through a buffet of things it seems like it'd be cool to be a part of.

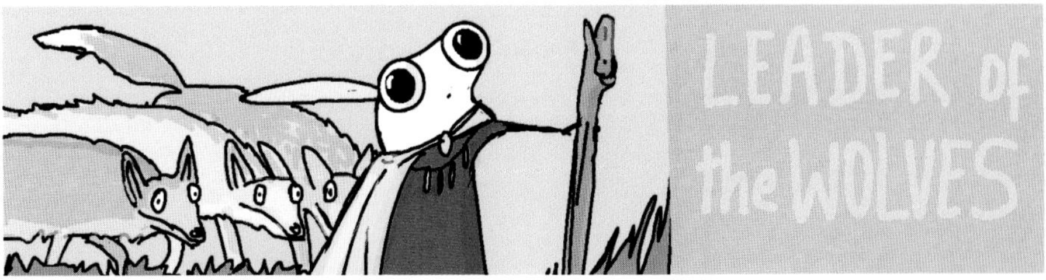
LEADER of the WOLVES

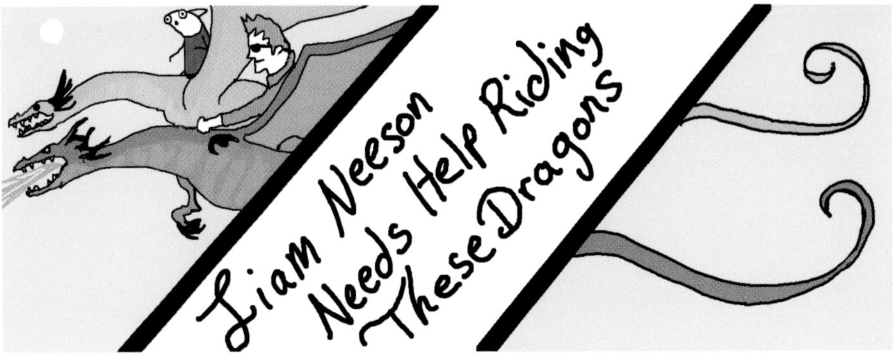
Liam Neeson Needs Help Riding These Dragons

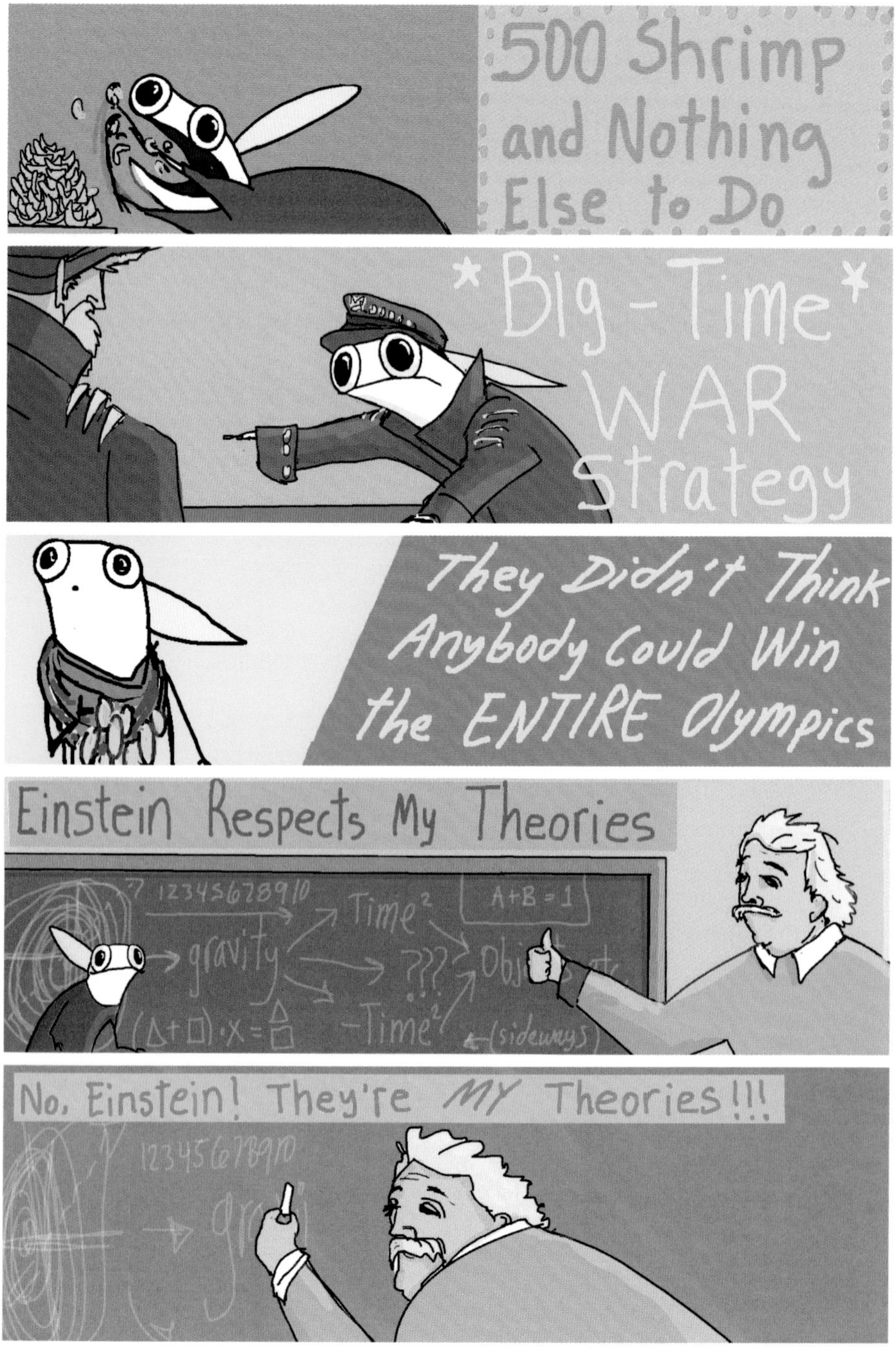
500 Shrimp and Nothing Else to Do
Big-Time WAR Strategy
They Didn't Think Anybody Could Win the ENTIRE Olympics
Einstein Respects My Theories
12345678910
gravity
Time²
A+B = 1
???
-Time²
(sideways)
No, Einstein! They're MY Theories!!!
12345678910

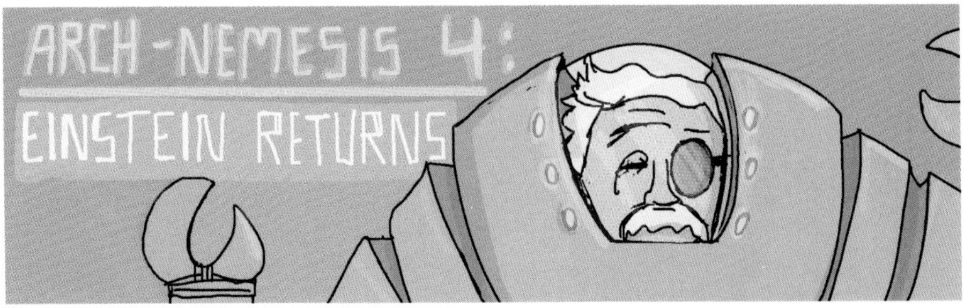
ARCH-NEMESIS 4:
EINSTEIN RETURNS

The stories can become more specific if I need them to be, though.

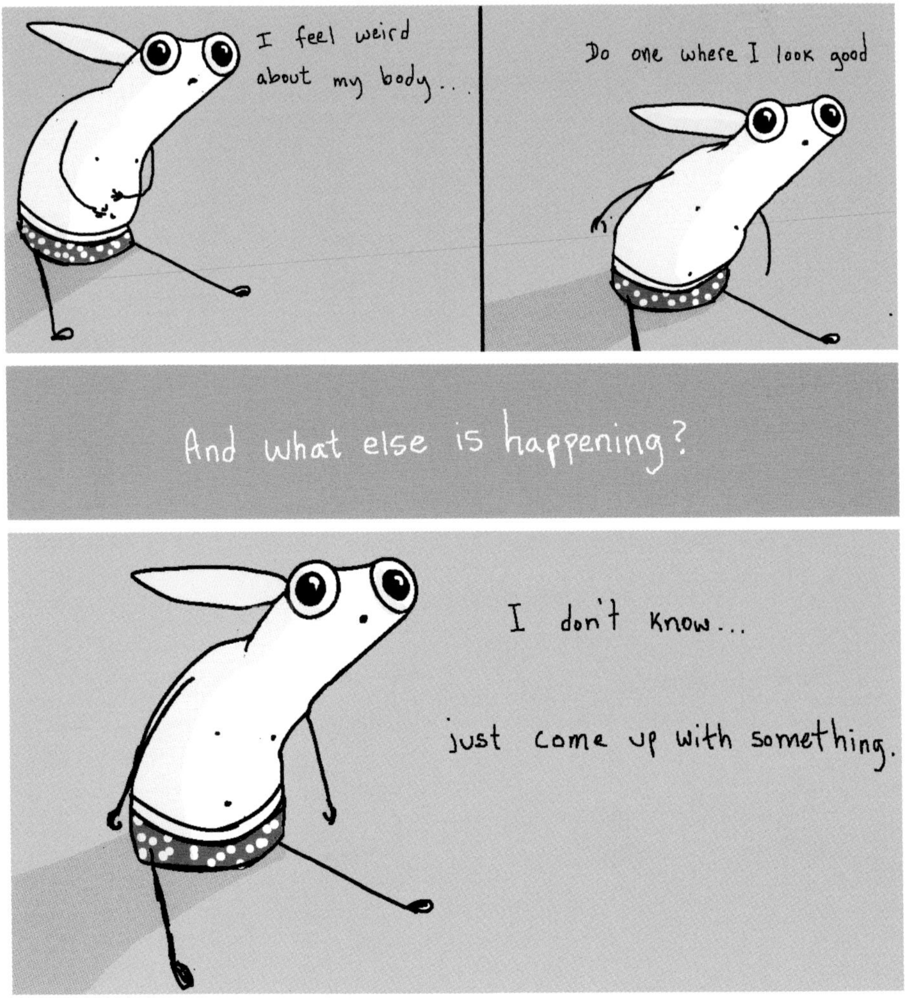
I feel weird about my body...
Do one where I look good
And what else is happening?
I don't know...
just come up with something.

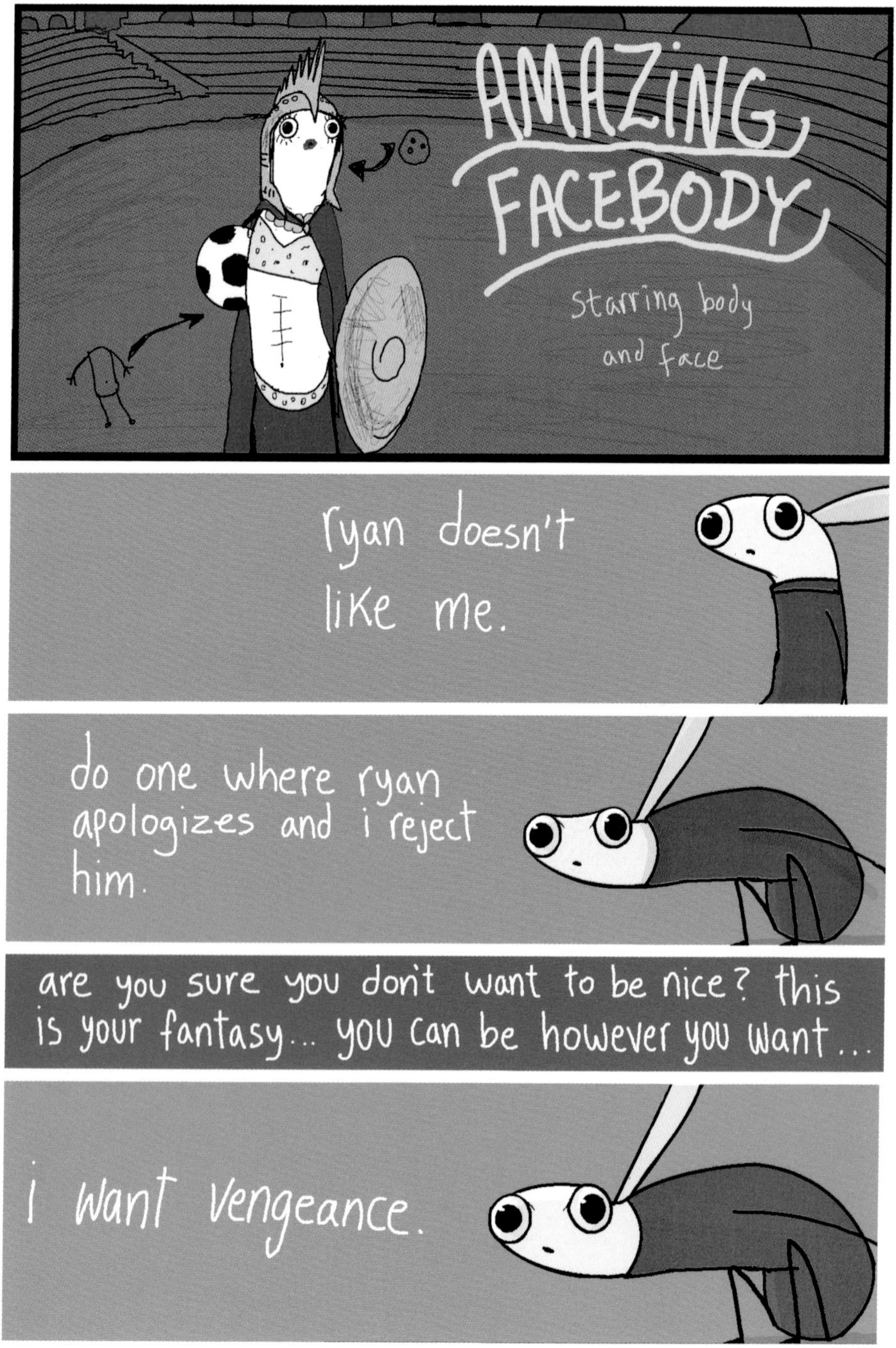
AMAZING FACEBODY
starring body and face
ryan doesn't like me.
do one where ryan apologizes and i reject him.
are you sure you don't want to be nice? this is your fantasy... you can be however you want...
i want vengeance.

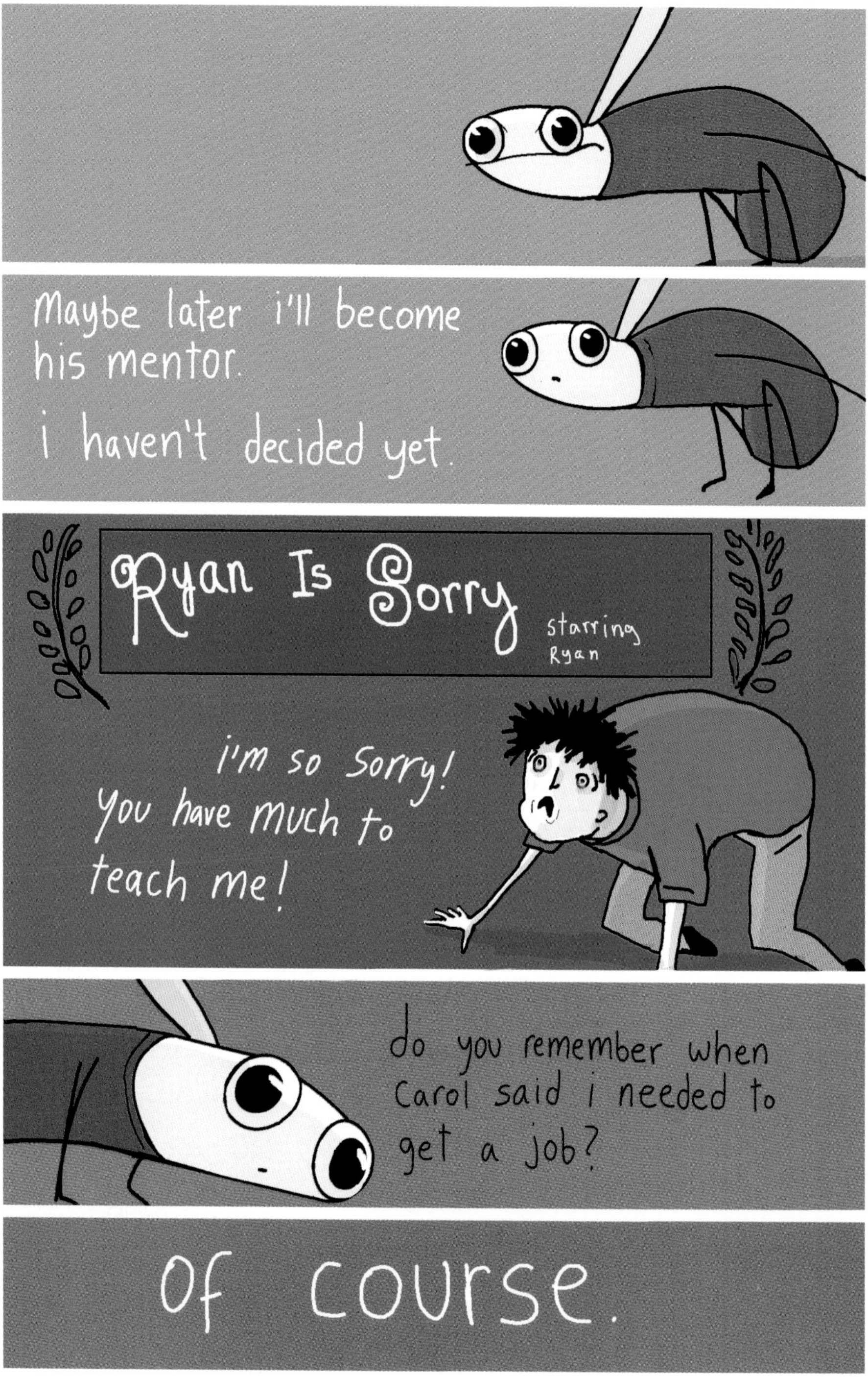
Maybe later i'll become his mentor.
i haven't decided yet.
Ryan Is Sorry
starring Ryan
i'm so sorry! you have much to teach me!
do you remember when Carol said i needed to get a job?
of course.

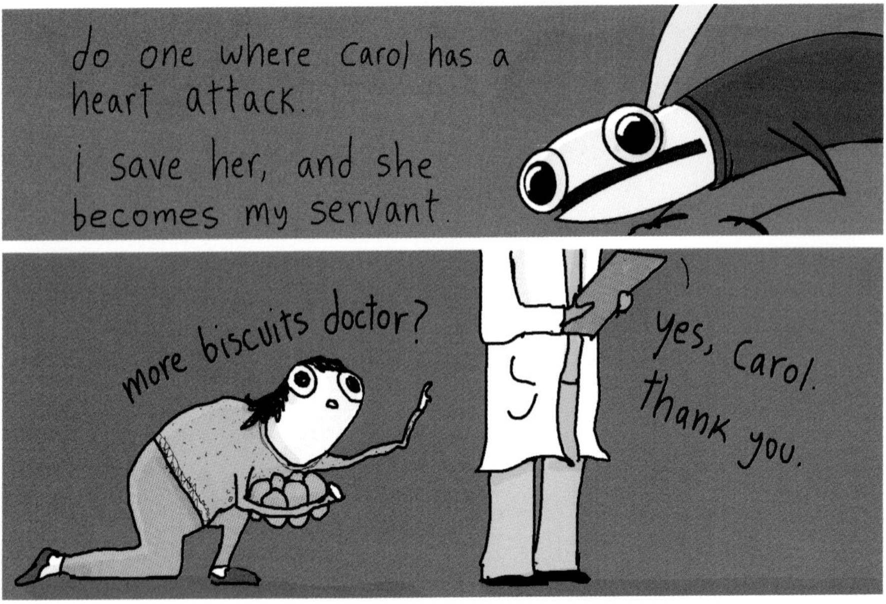
do one where carol has a heart attack.
i save her, and she becomes my servant.
more biscuits doctor?
yes, Carol. thank you.

Over time, they've had to become pretty extreme to give me the same rush.

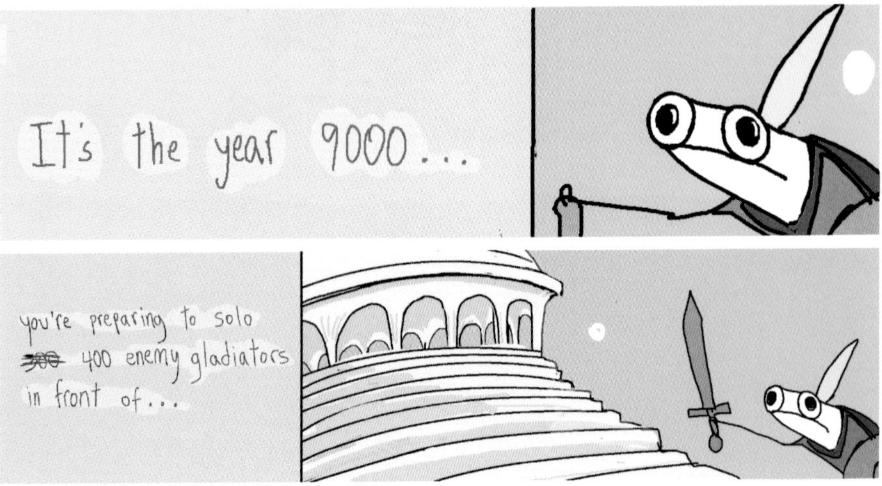
It's the year 9000...
you're preparing to solo ~~300~~ 400 enemy gladiators in front of...

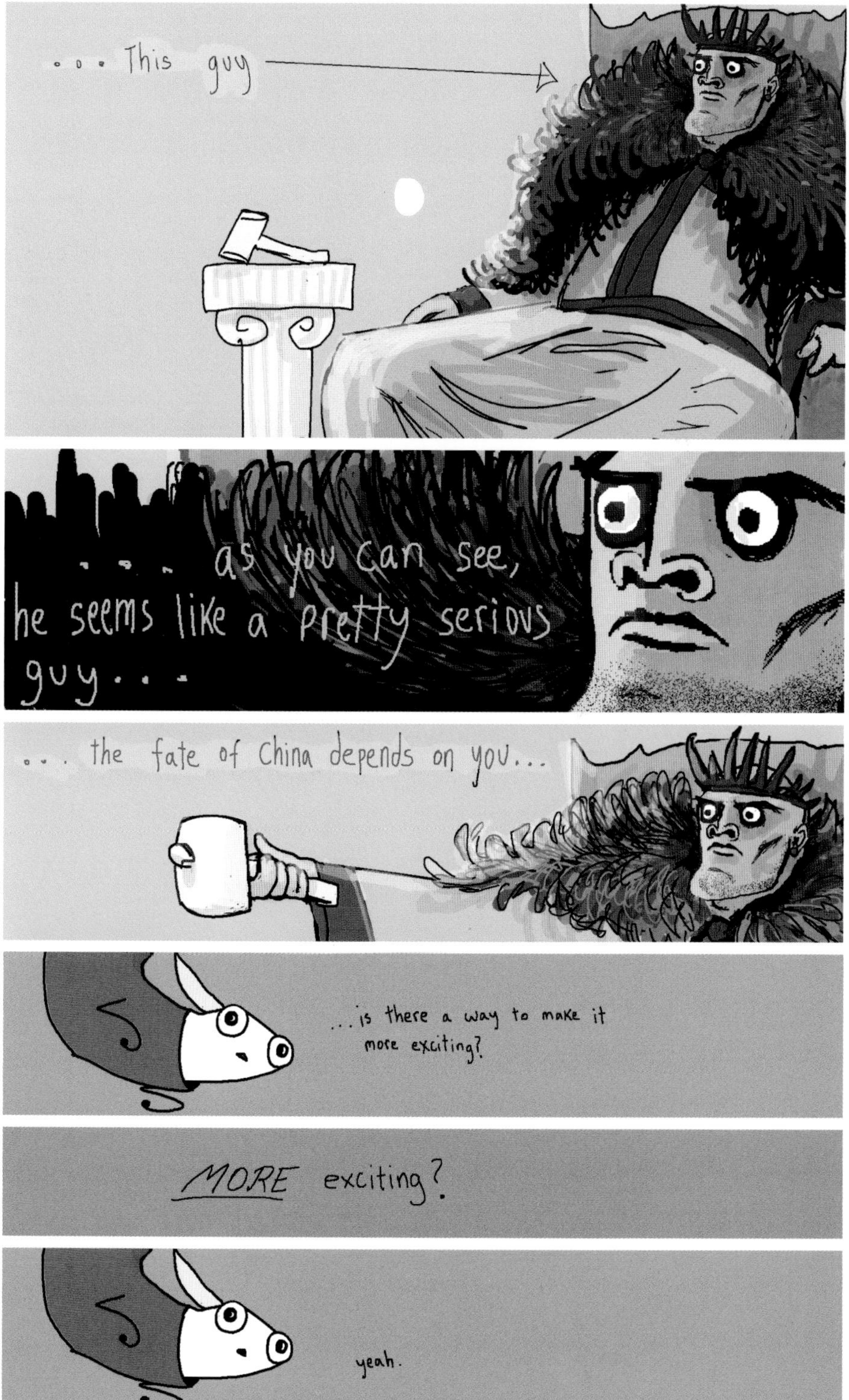
. . . This guy
. . . as you can see, he seems like a pretty serious guy. . .
. . . the fate of China depends on you. . .
. . . is there a way to make it more exciting?
MORE exciting?
yeah.

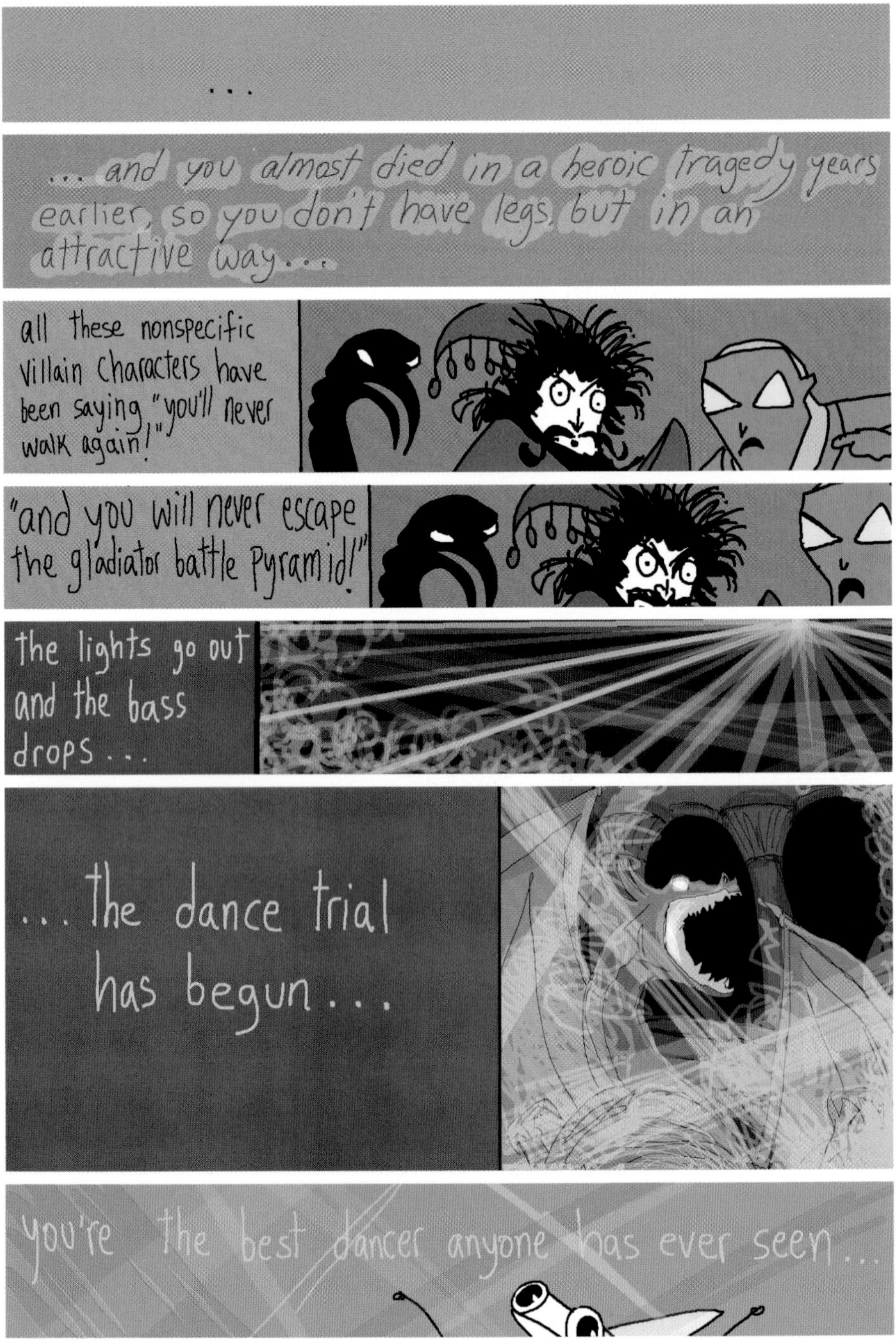
. . .
. . . and you almost died in a heroic tragedy years earlier, so you don't have legs, but in an attractive way . . .
all these nonspecific villain characters have been saying, "you'll never walk again!"
"and you will never escape the gladiator battle pyramid!"
the lights go out and the bass drops . . .
. . . the dance trial has begun . . .
you're the best dancer anyone has ever seen . . .

(There's a part where I try to imagine myself dancing the best dance anyone has ever seen, but I don't actually know how to do that, so I sort of gloss over it.)

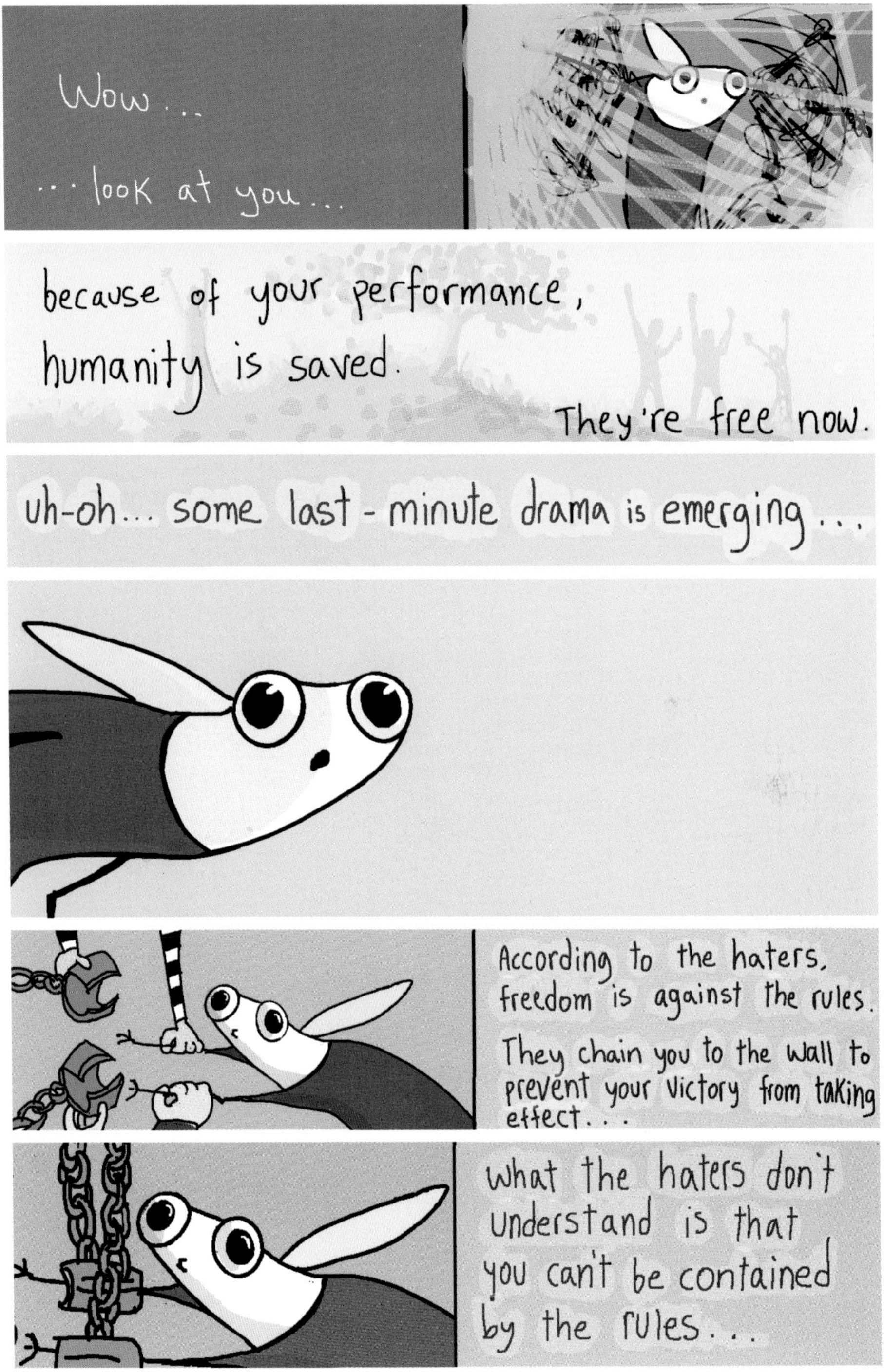
Wow...
...look at you...
because of your performance,
humanity is saved.
They're free now.
uh-oh... some last-minute drama is emerging...
According to the haters, freedom is against the rules.
They chain you to the wall to prevent your victory from taking effect...
what the haters don't understand is that you can't be contained by the rules...

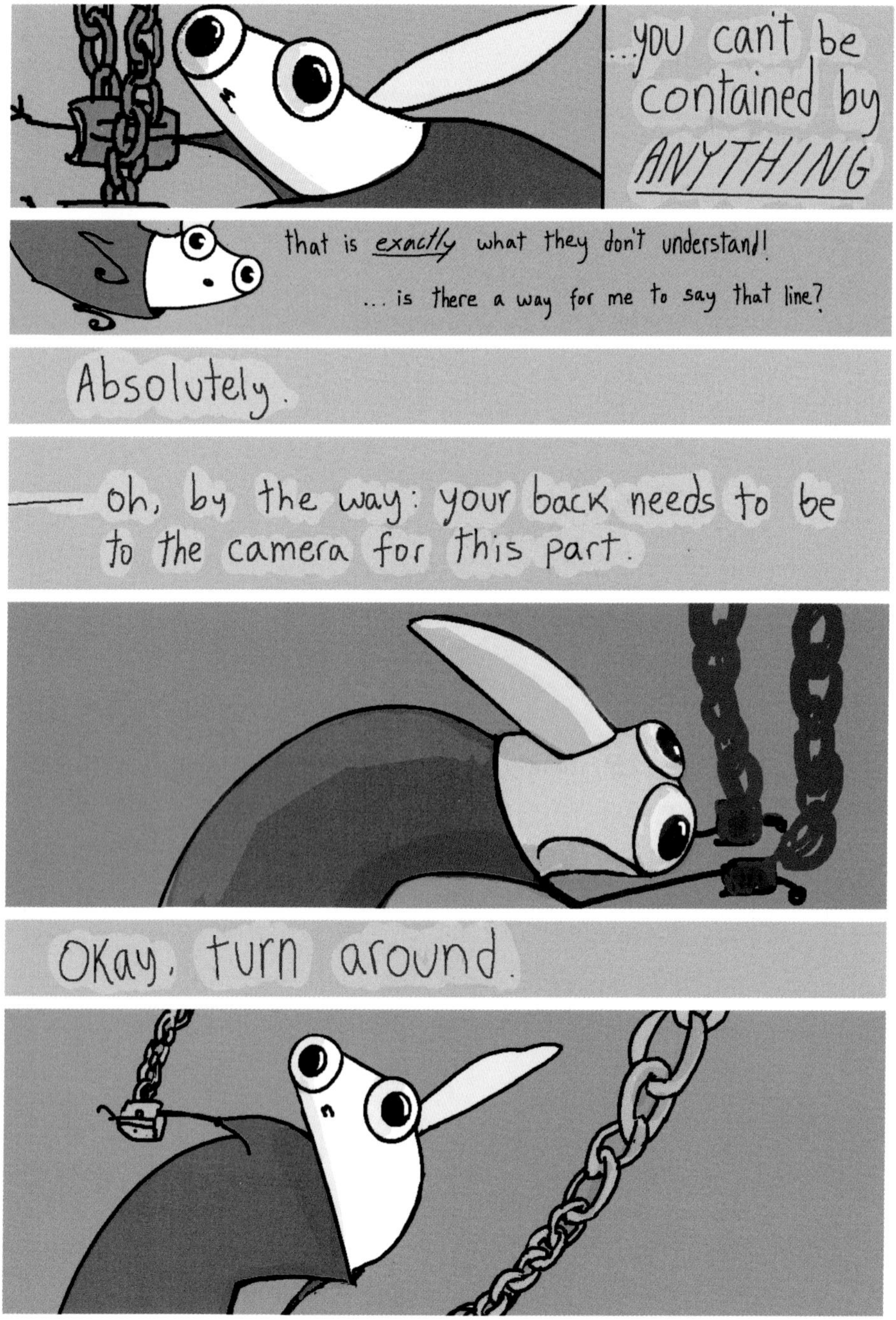
...you can't be contained by ANYTHING
that is exactly what they don't understand!
...is there a way for me to say that line?
Absolutely.
— oh, by the way: your back needs to be to the camera for this part.
Okay. turn around.

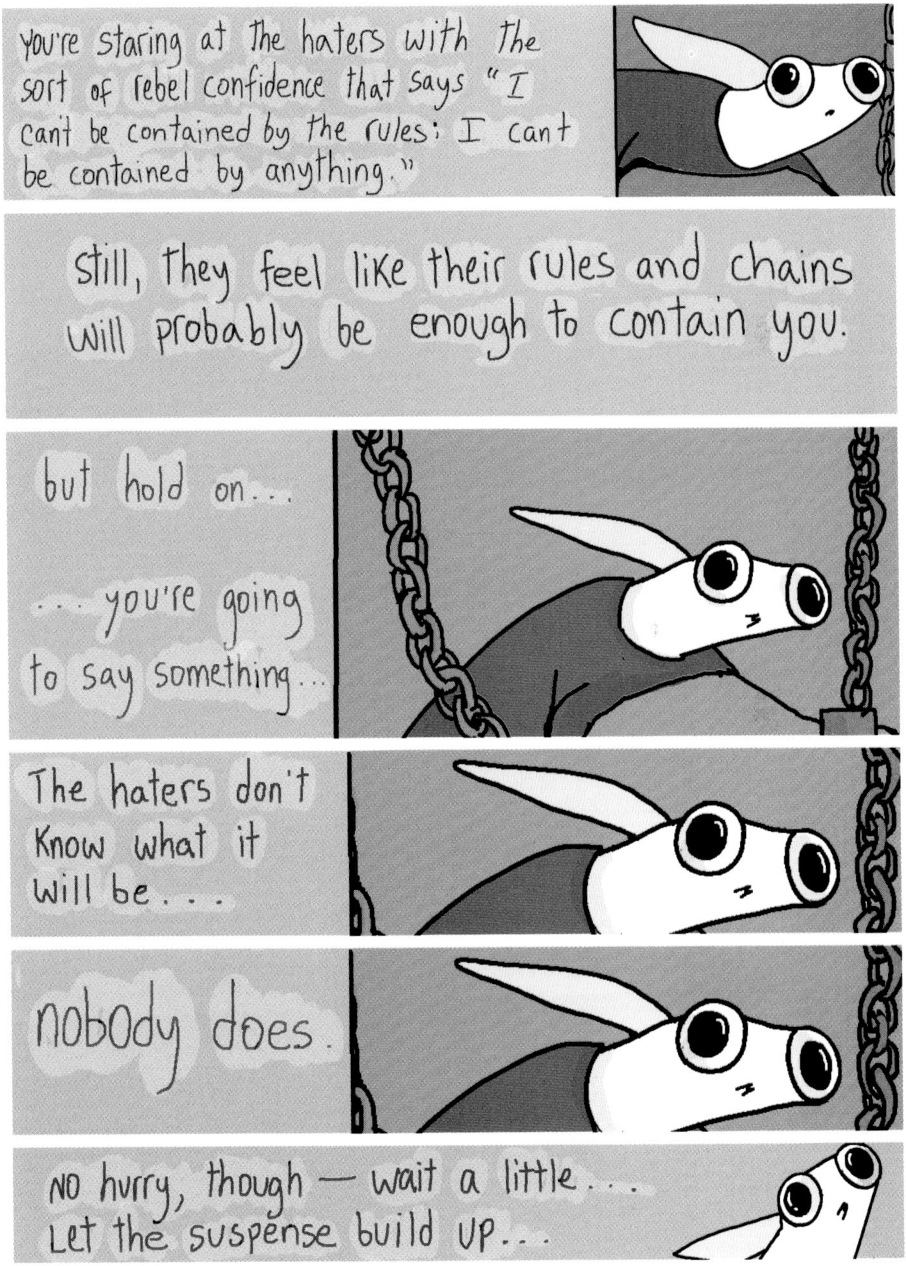
you're staring at the haters with the sort of rebel confidence that says "I can't be contained by the rules: I can't be contained by anything."
Still, they feel like their rules and chains will probably be enough to contain you.
but hold on...
...you're going to say something...
The haters don't know what it will be...
nobody does.
No hurry, though — wait a little...
Let the suspense build up...

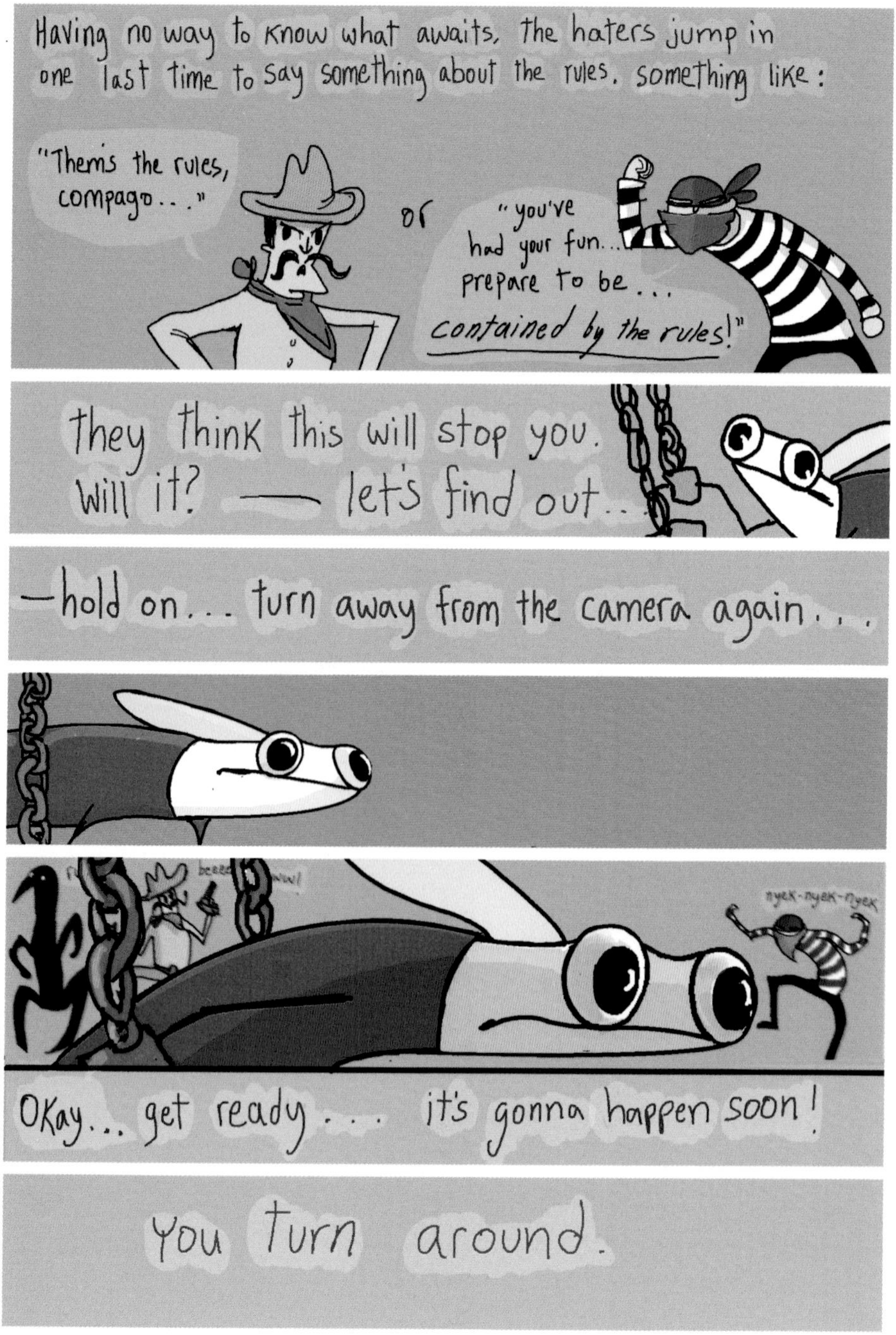
Having no way to know what awaits, the haters jump in one last time to say something about the rules, something like:
"Them's the rules, compago..."
or
"you've had your fun... prepare to be... contained by the rules!"
they think this will stop you. will it? — let's find out...
—hold on... turn away from the camera again...
nyek-nyek-nyek
Okay... get ready... it's gonna happen soon!
You turn around.

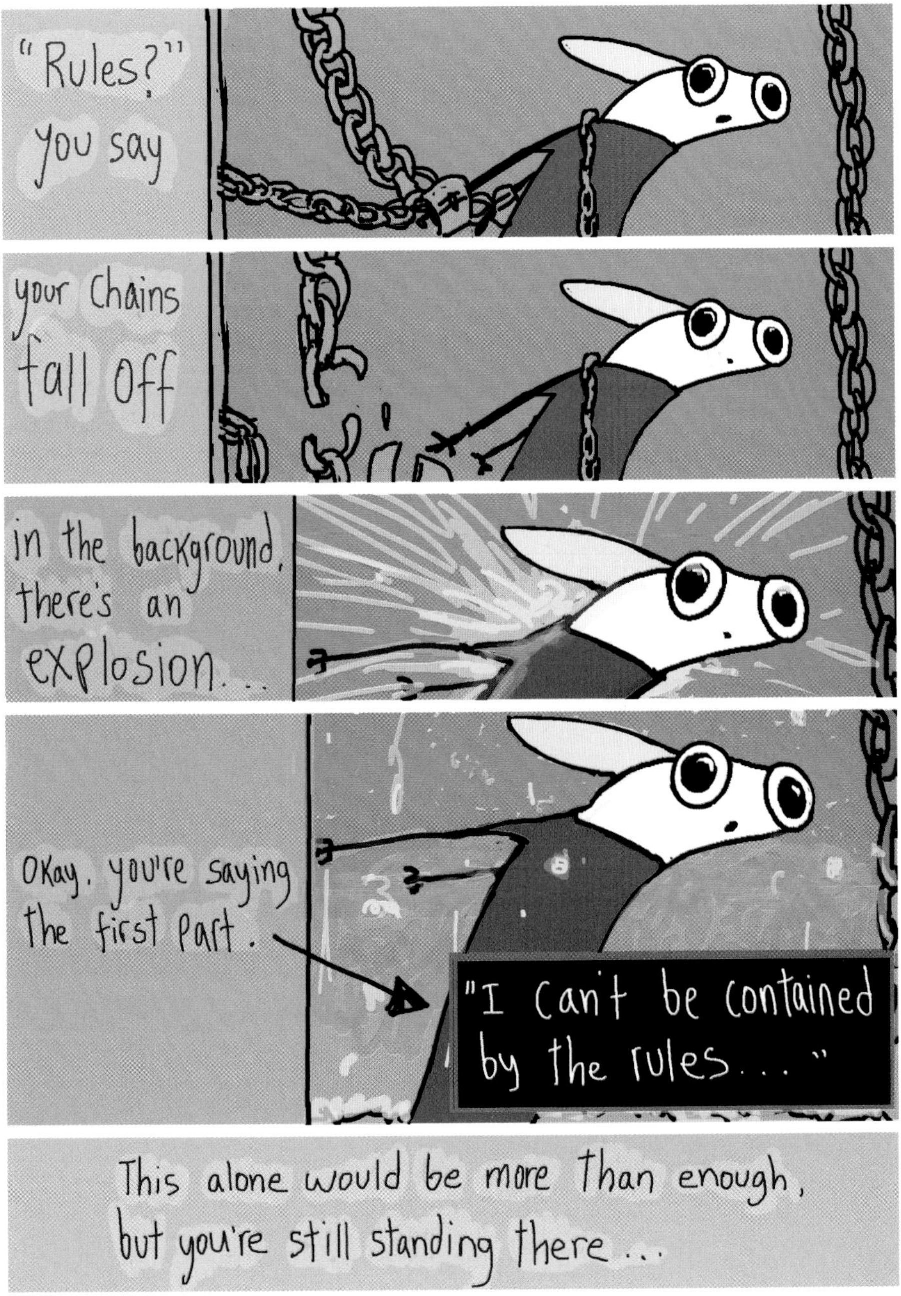
"Rules?" you say
your Chains fall off
in the background, there's an explosion...
Okay. you're saying the first part.
"I Can't be contained by the rules..."
This alone would be more than enough, but you're still standing there...

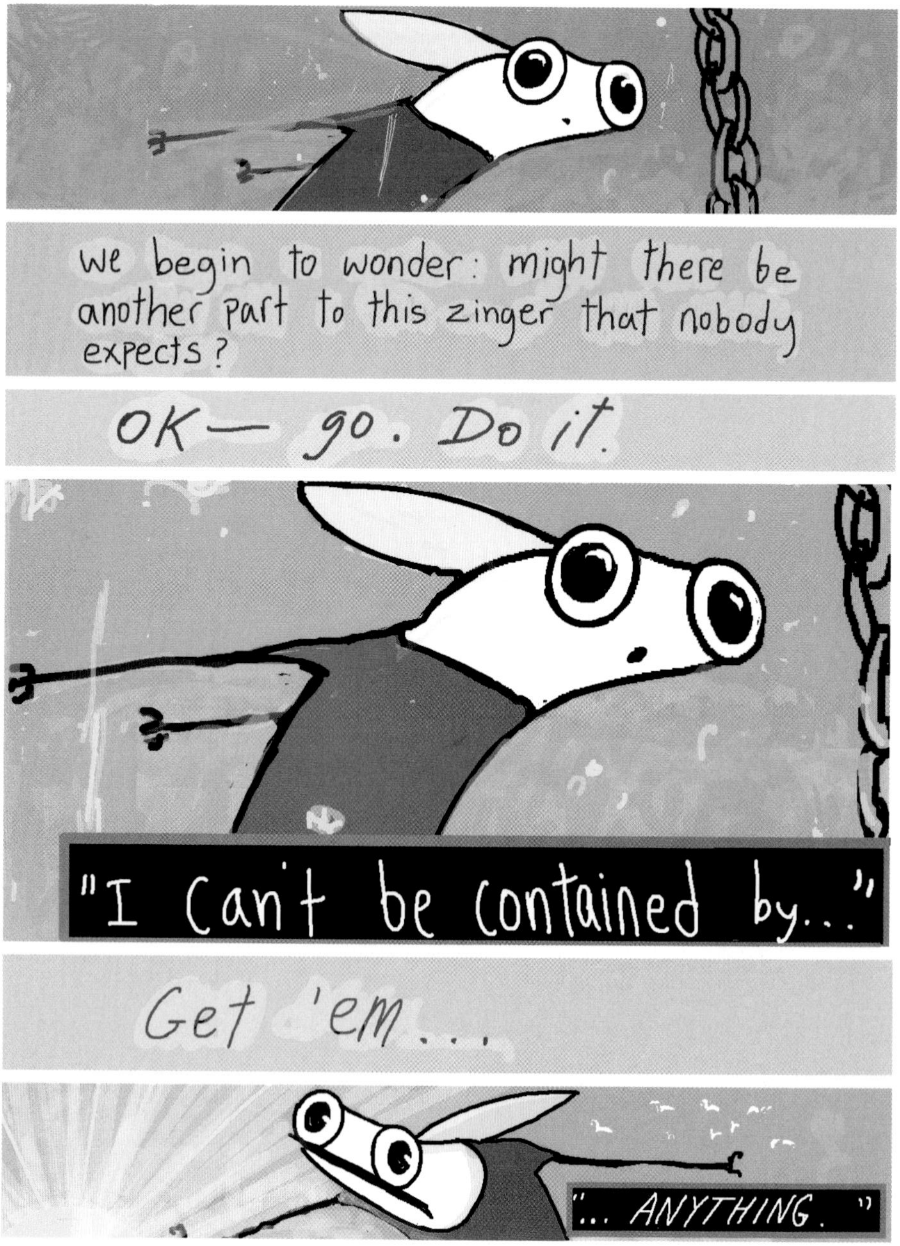
we begin to wonder: might there be another part to this zinger that nobody expects?
OK— go. Do it.
"I can't be contained by..."
Get 'em...
"... ANYTHING."

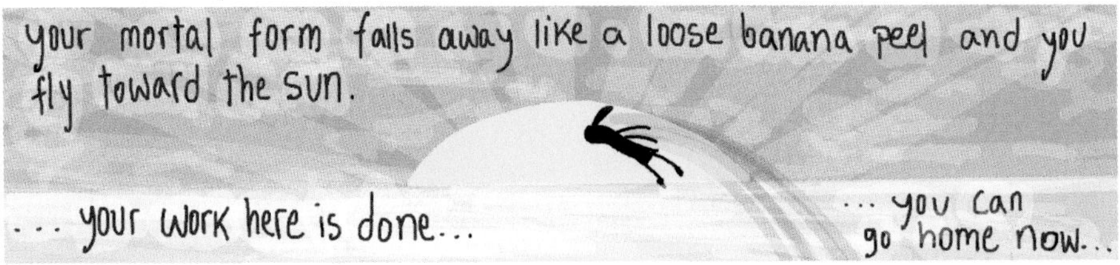
your mortal form falls away like a loose banana peel and you fly toward the sun.
. . . your work here is done . . .
. . . you can go home now . . .

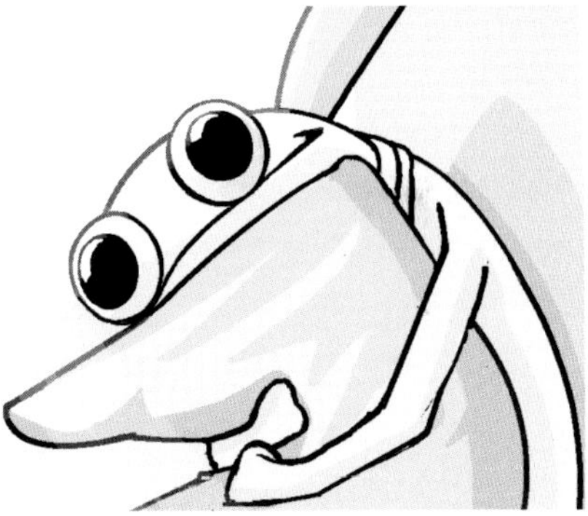

One of my deepest fears is that the footage gets leaked somehow. I don't know how it'd happen—maybe they'll get converted to video files when my consciousness gets uploaded to the internet—but my daydreams would get out, and everybody would see them.

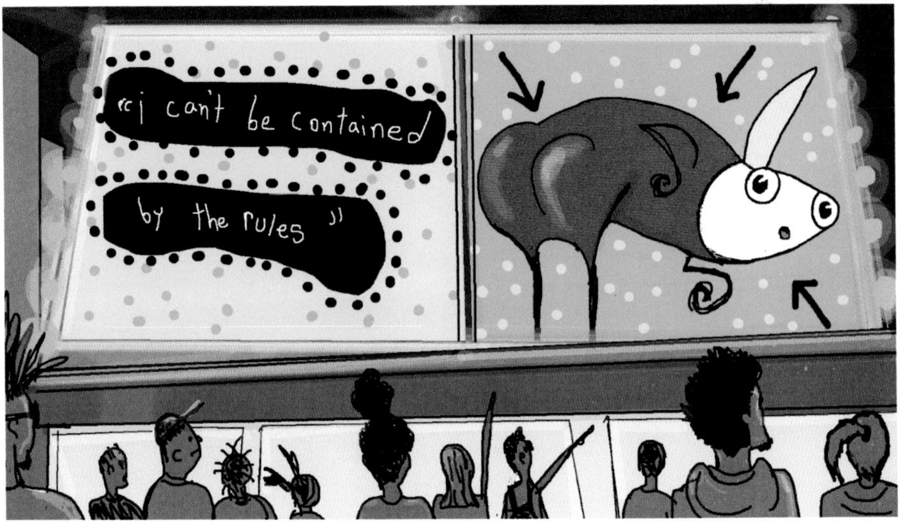
"I can't be contained
by the rules"

They'd seem even more ridiculous out of context.

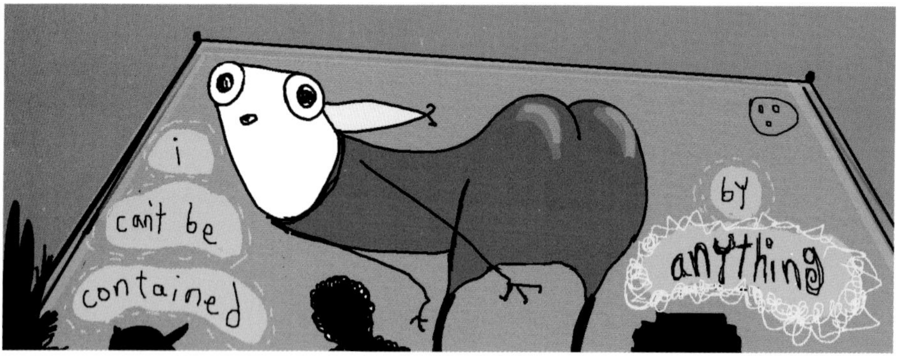
i
can't be
contained
by
anything

People I know would see them—people I know who are *IN* them. And this isn't the kind of thing where you feel honored to find out you got a part.

At best, the supporting characters are one-dimensional to a degree that is actively insulting to their personhood. At worst, I use them like ego-masturbation blob puppets, repeatedly forcing them to deliver lines they would never agree to in real life.

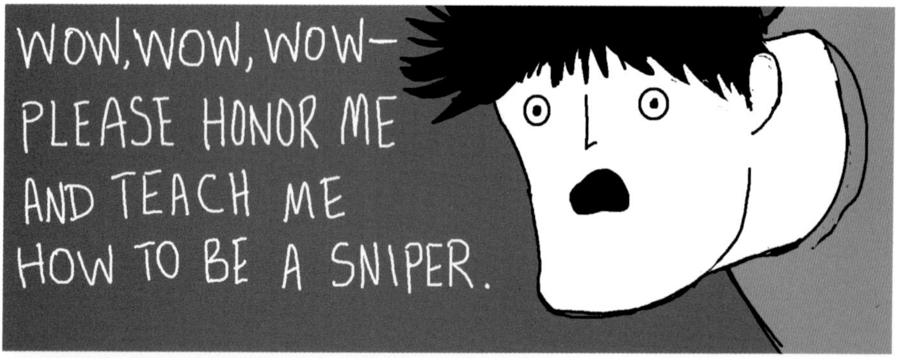
WOW, WOW, WOW—
PLEASE HONOR ME
AND TEACH ME
HOW TO BE A SNIPER.

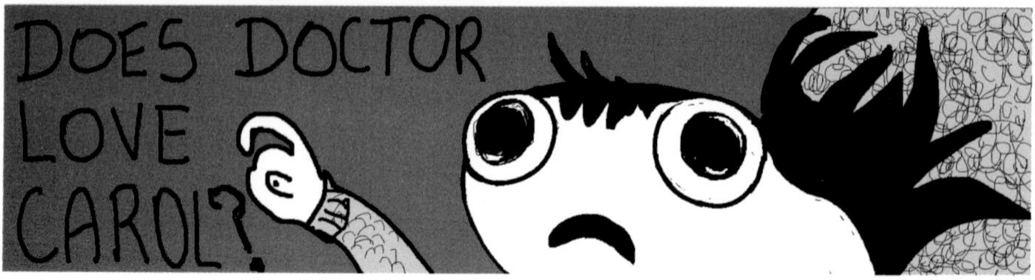
DOES DOCTOR
LOVE
CAROL?

Some of my costars would feel violated, others would feel slighted, *absolutely nobody* would be like, "Yeah, that's about right—I feel comfortable about the way you portrayed me."

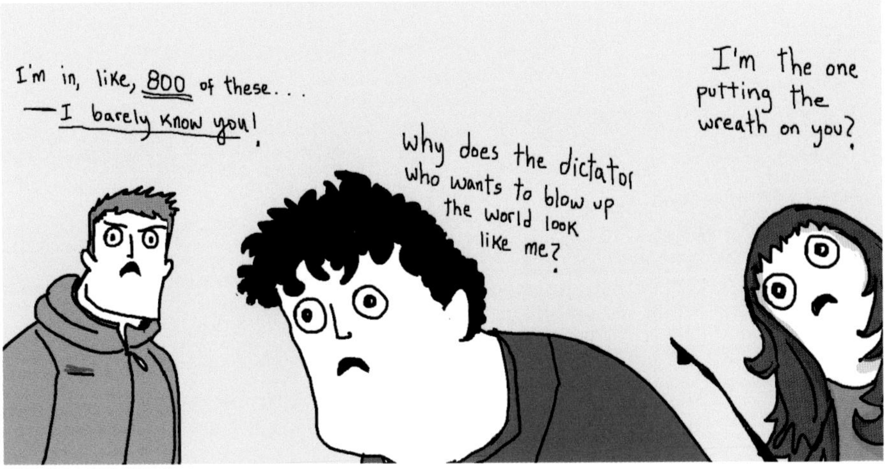
I'm in, like, 800 of these...
—I barely know you!
Why does the dictator who wants to blow up the world look like me?
I'm the one putting the wreath on you?

It'd be obvious what all my insecurities are, and how easy it is to make me believe I'm capable of greatness.

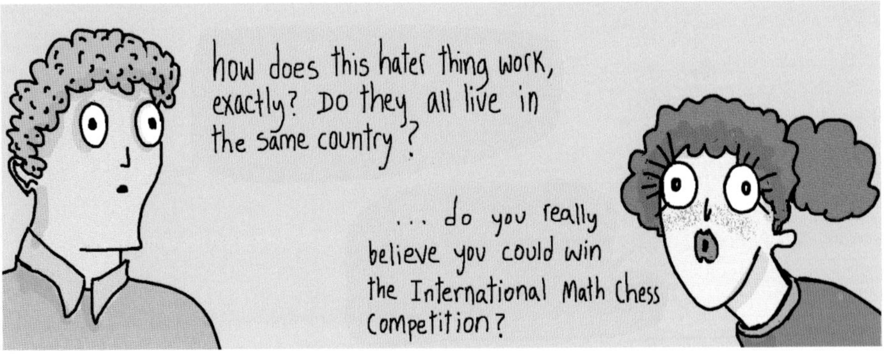
how does this hater thing work, exactly? Do they all live in the same country?
... do you really believe you could win the International Math Chess Competition?

But I can't stop now. Where is there to go from here that wouldn't feel like a catastrophic downgrade? I'm a tragic, greedy animal with too many dreams to feel satisfied by reality. I want to know what everything cool feels like. I want to ride dragons into battle. I want to be important. I want to know what it would be like if everybody believed in me, including Ryan. I want to win high-stakes dance-offs and math tournaments and stunning victories for humankind. I want to be brave like a gladiator. I want to be powerful like a god.

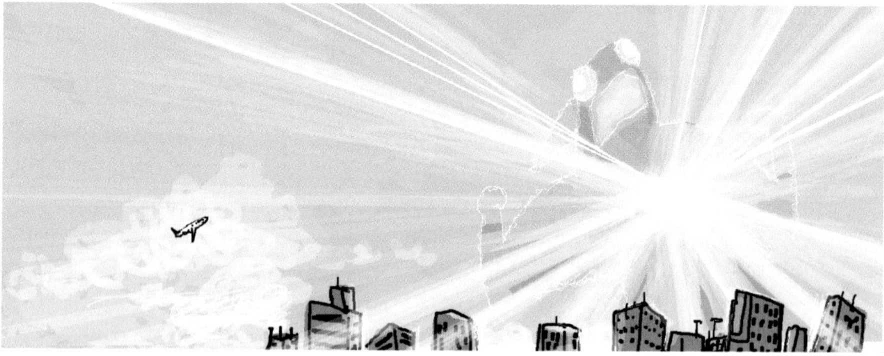

I don't know how to do that for real.

Even if it was possible, it'd probably be hard.

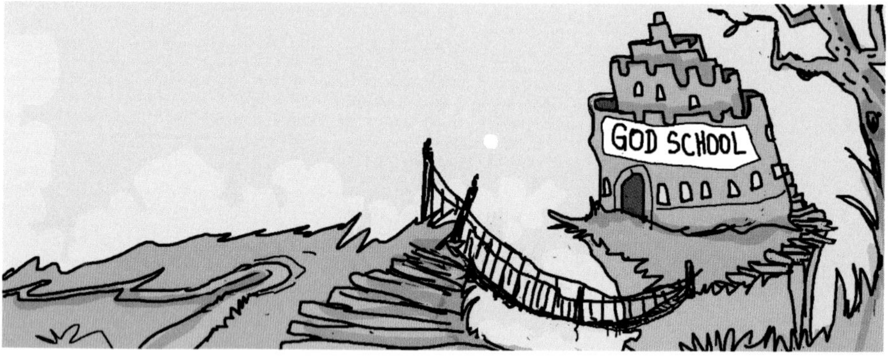
GOD SCHOOL

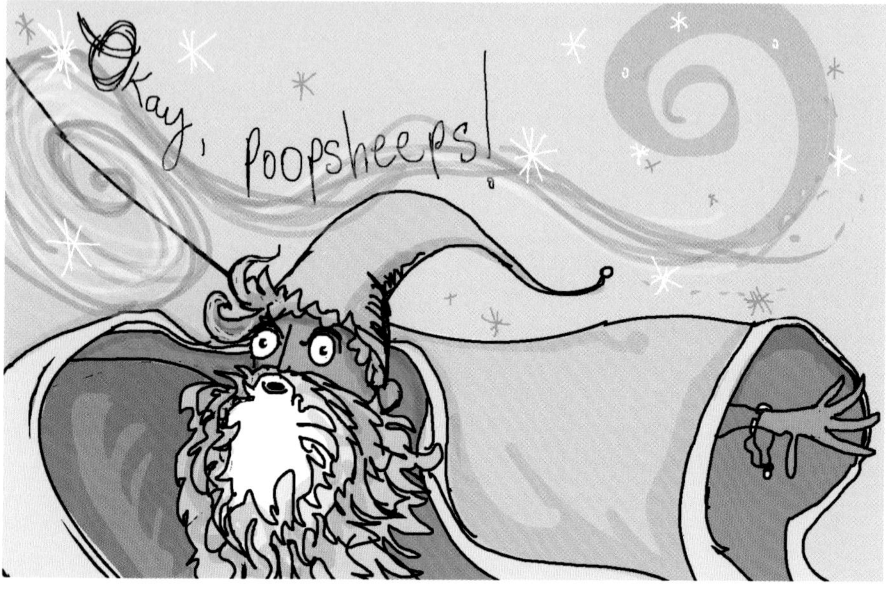
Okay, poopsheeps!

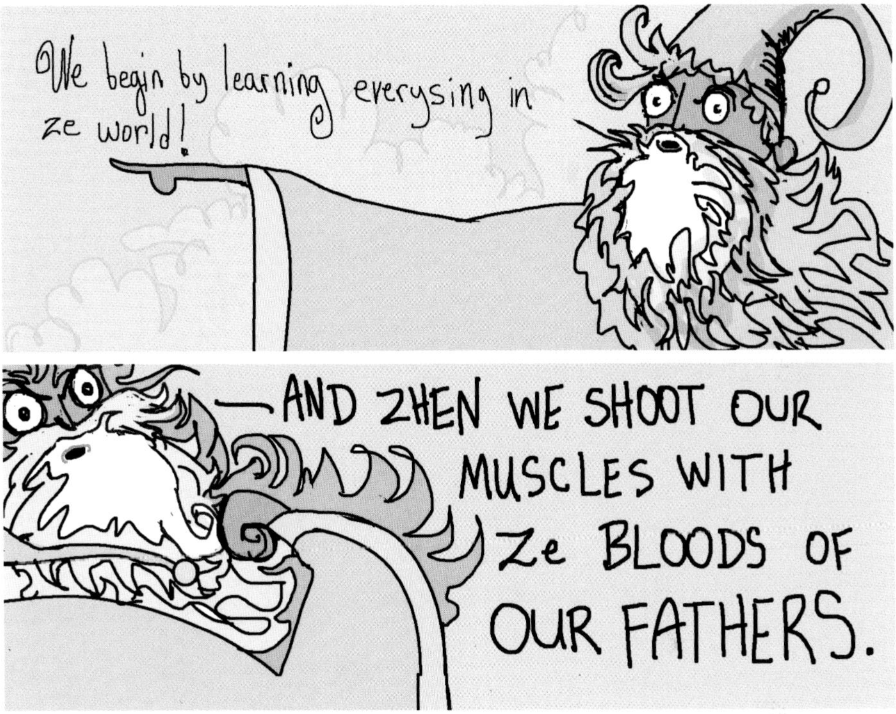
We begin by learning everysing in ze world!
—AND ZHEN WE SHOOT OUR MUSCLES WITH Ze BLOODS OF OUR FATHERS.

And nobody would be as impressed as I want.

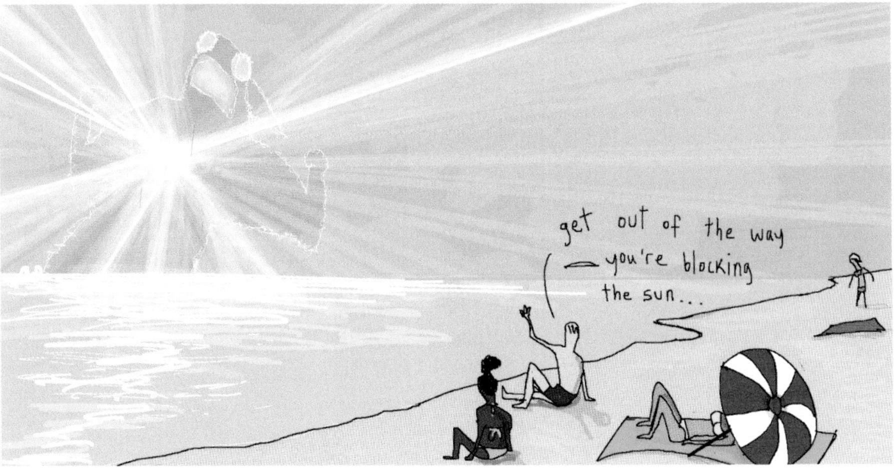
get out of the way —you're blocking the sun...

So I keep doing this.

8. DANDELIONS

It is time to talk about dandelions. Not the yellow ones—the ones you blow on and make a wish that you'll find love or a penny or something.

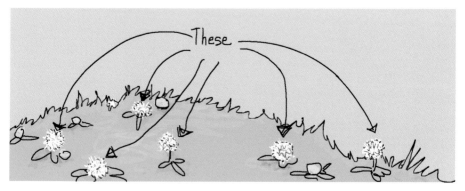

One summer, I had a job babysitting a 2-year-old who was terrified of those.

I didn't find out ahead of time, though. No one sat me down and explained, *Hey, see this kid? Don't take it near dandelions. I don't care what else is going on—stay away from dandelions. No, listen—I'm not sure you understand how really, really, really serious this is: don't take chances, don't forget or get sloppy and accidentally go a little bit near dandelions. If your right hand is dandelions and your left hand is this kid, they should be far enough apart that your arms fly off, do you understand?*

No, I found out that the child was paralytically, nonsensically, apocalypse-level scared of dandelions the moment I pushed her stroller past the exact center of a sprawling ocean of dandelions.

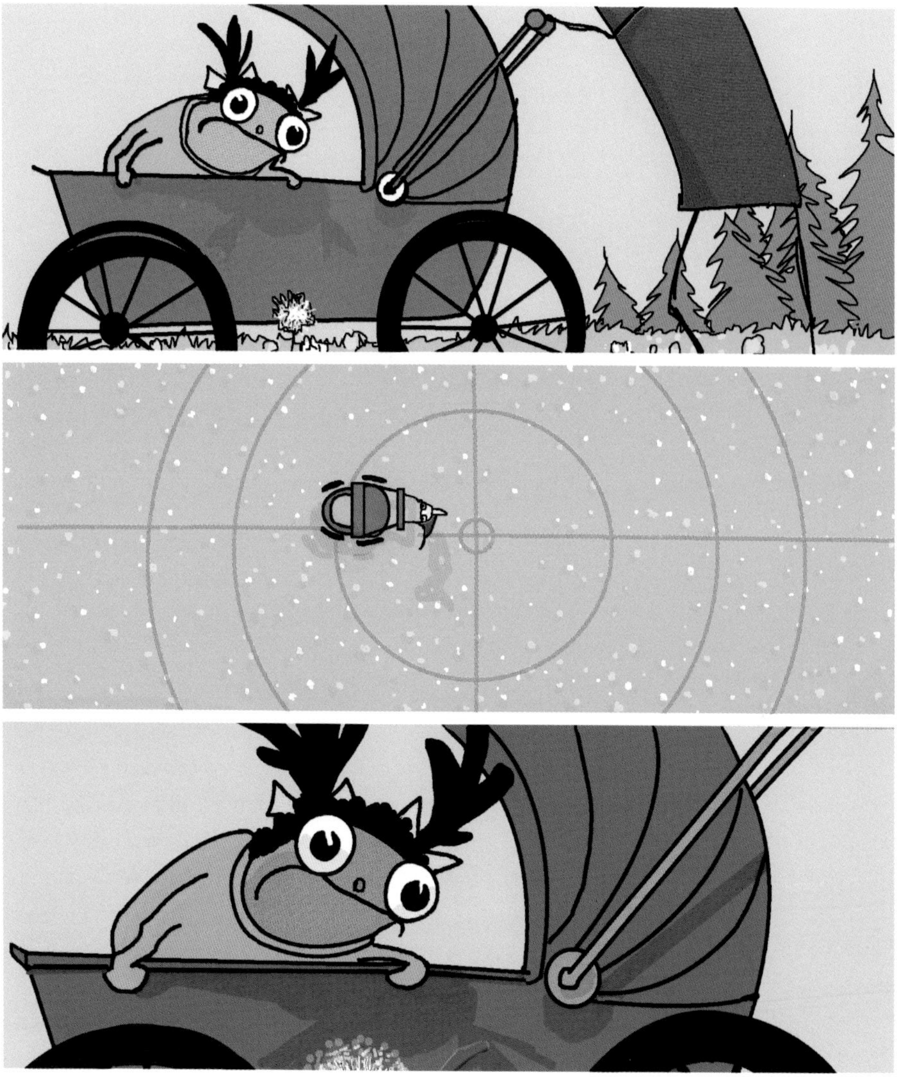

I don't know whether she'd been trying to scream the *whole* time, or doing her best to hold it in until we reached the other side and she just didn't make it. Maybe she'd been asleep. It's even possible that she never realized how scary dandelions are until that exact second, and the timing was just really, really unlucky. I don't know. She was in a covered stroller, so there could have been any number of warning signs, but I didn't see them. From my perspective, we were walking through a normal field on a normal day, and nothing was weird at all, and then *this* started happening:

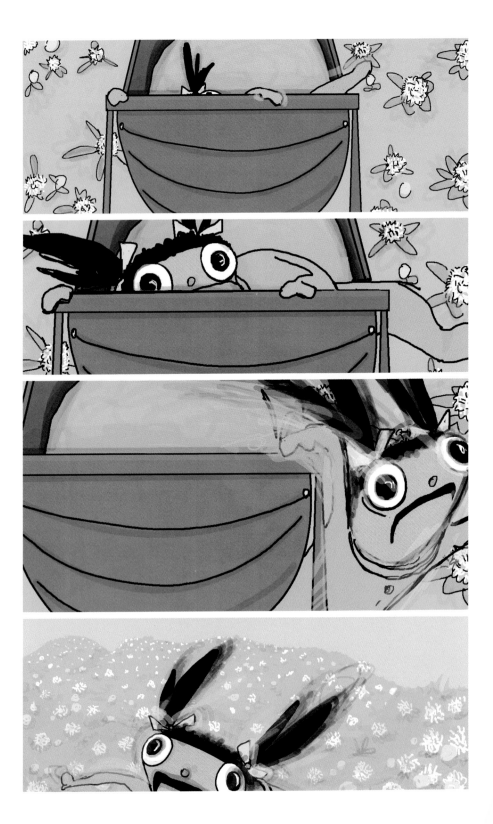

In retrospect, I can look at the pieces and sort of put them together to form an explanation: the child—who either harbored an existing fear of dandelions or spawned one out of nowhere at that exact moment—noticed that the level of dandelions had become unacceptable and attempted to escape. But, due to being completely surrounded by dandelions for at least a thousand feet in every direction, there was no clear path to safety. She ran, but everywhere she turned, dandelions were there. Which probably made it seem like the dandelions were chasing her, so she ran faster, and that made the dandelions seem like they were chasing her faster, and pretty soon she was so scared her brain turned off, and her body just sort of kept running around on its own.

While it was happening, though, there wasn't enough time to make sense of anything. It was just:

—Field

—Gurgling sound

—Child is out of stroller

—Child is running . . . . away? Around? Definitely running.

—Something is wrong for sure.

I couldn't tell *what* was wrong, but I sensed the situation should not be allowed to continue or develop in any way.

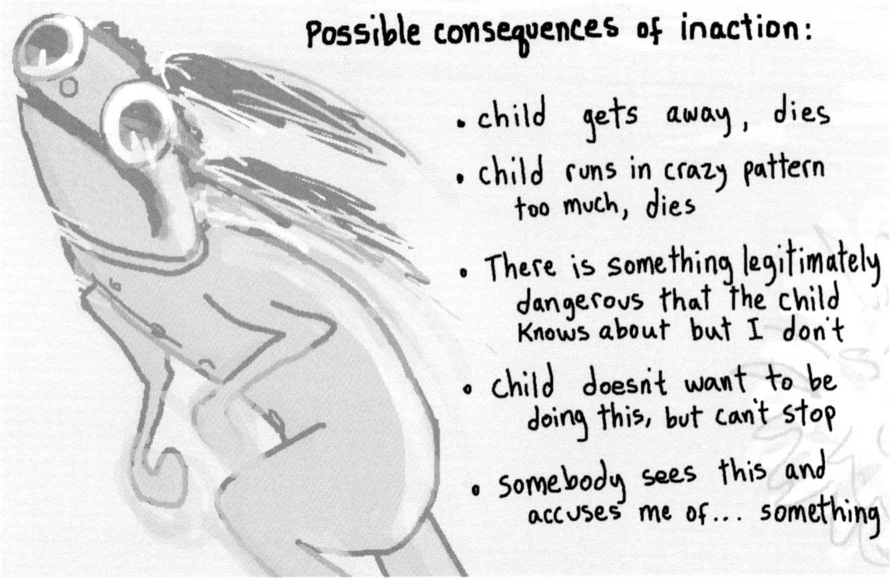
Possible consequences of inaction:
• child gets away, dies
• child runs in crazy pattern too much, dies
• There is something legitimately dangerous that the child Knows about but I don't
• child doesn't want to be doing this, but can't stop
• somebody sees this and accuses me of... something

Yes: somebody should definitely do something about this . . .

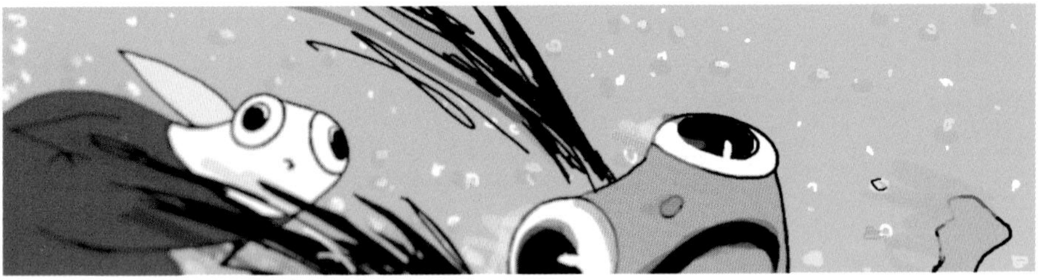

It is me. I am the somebody. I should do something.

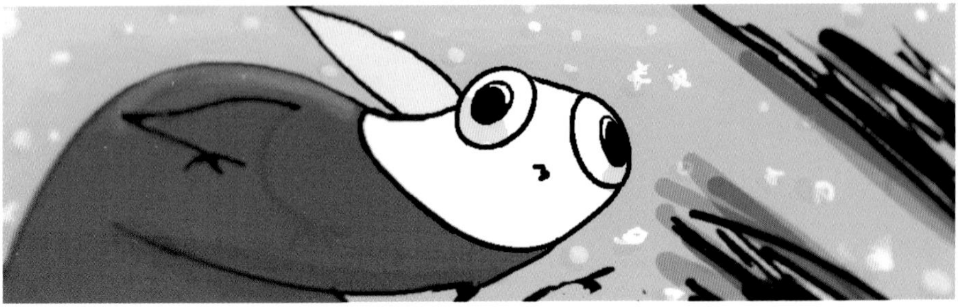

On instinct, I begin chasing her.

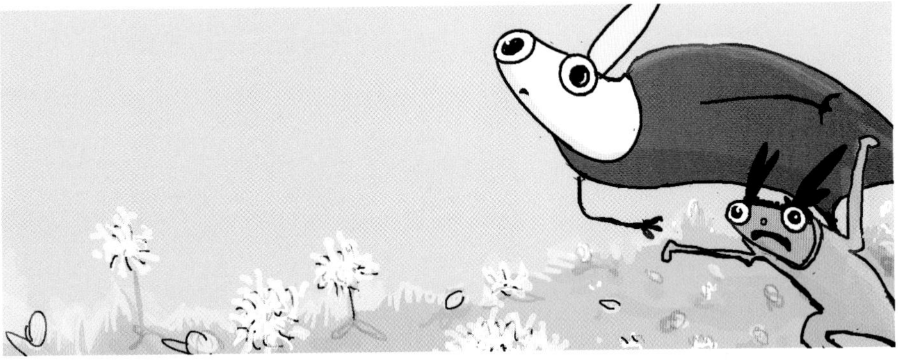

This seems to make the running worse.

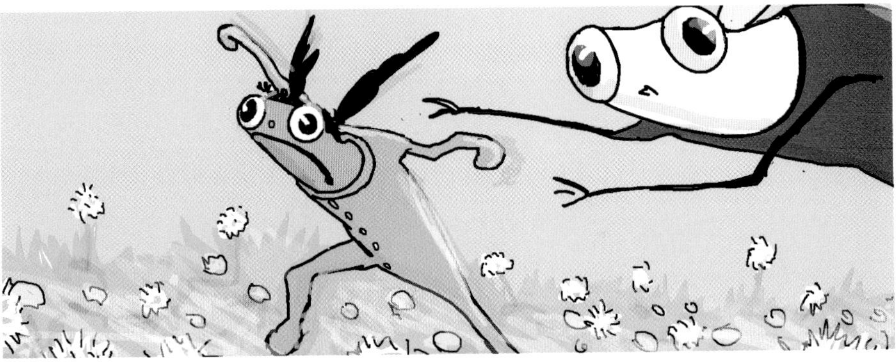

Fortunately, her mindlessly fleeing body still hasn't committed to a direction, so she isn't getting away.

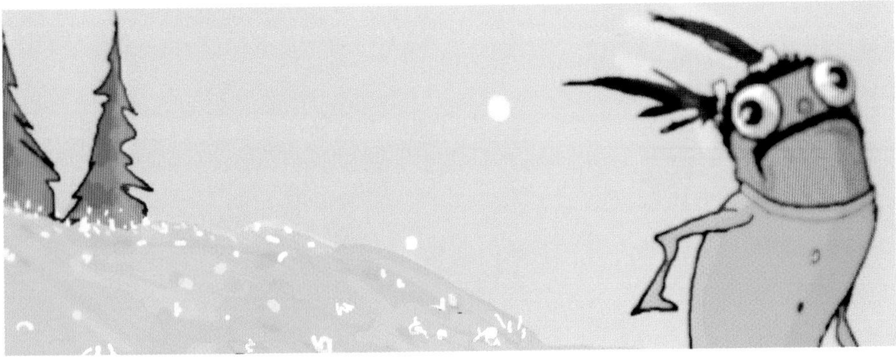

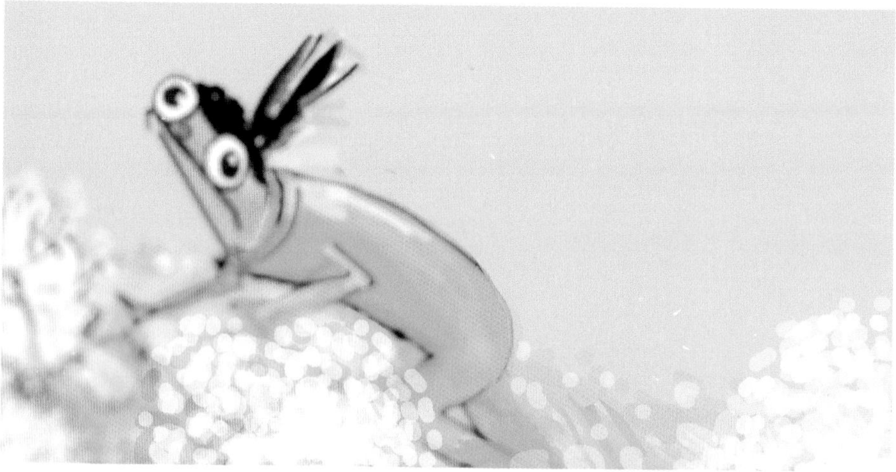

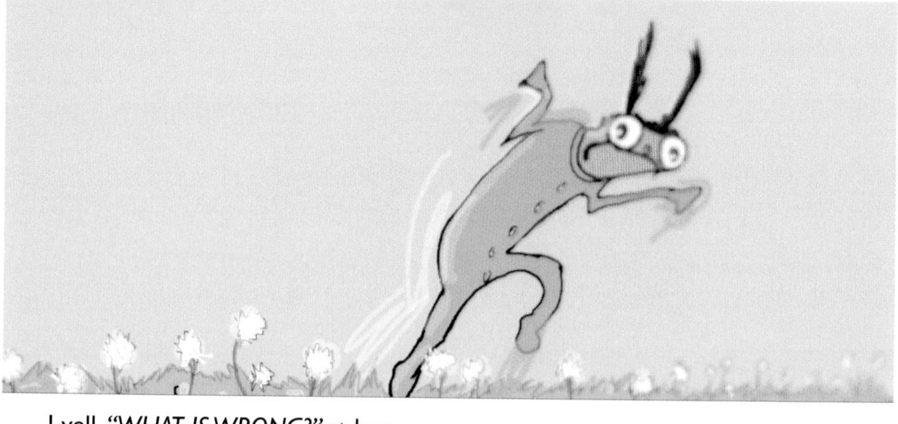

I yell, *"WHAT IS WRONG?"* at her.

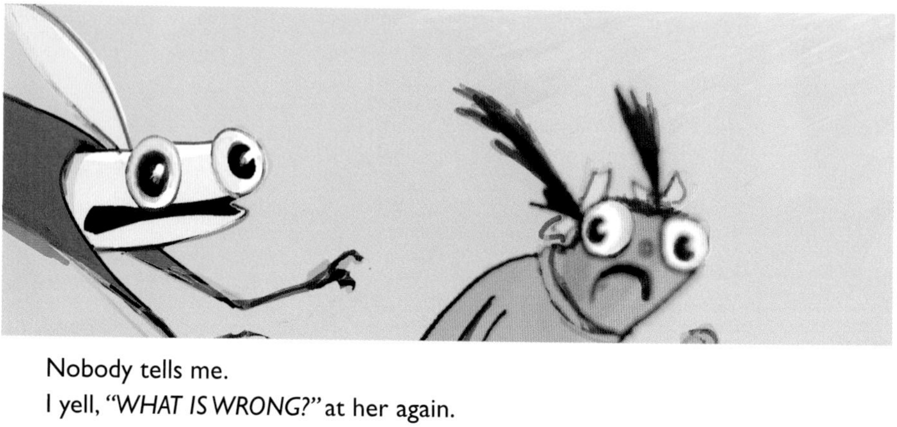

Nobody tells me.
I yell, *"WHAT IS WRONG?"* at her again.

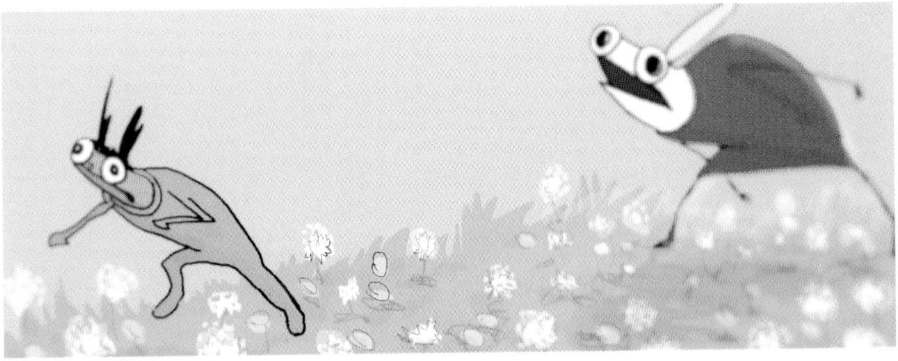

Is it helping? I can't tell. But the screaming is becoming more specific.

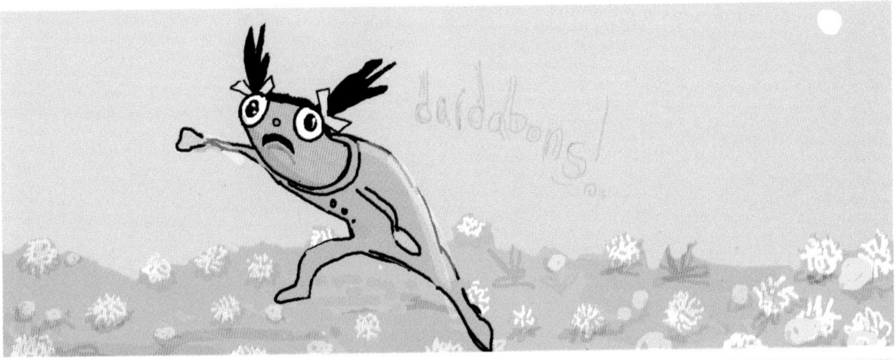
dardabons!

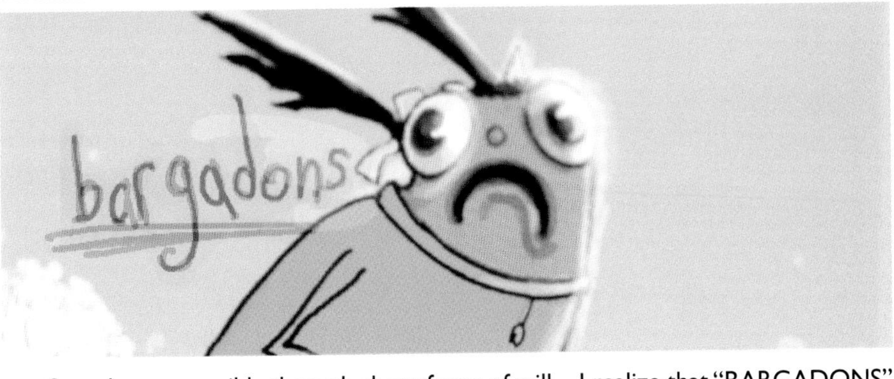
bargadons

Somehow—possibly through sheer force of will—I realize that "BARGADONS" might be the word "dandelions."

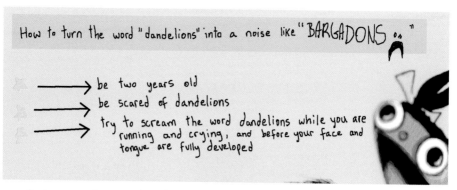

How to turn the word "dandelions" into a noise like "BARGADONS.."

→ be two years old
→ be scared of dandelions
→ try to scream the word dandelions while you are running and crying, and before your face and tongue are fully developed

A victory to be sure, but the situation is far from under control.

If I want everything to go back to normal, I need to find some way to convince a 2-year-old that dandelions aren't scary.

It seems like that should be easy.

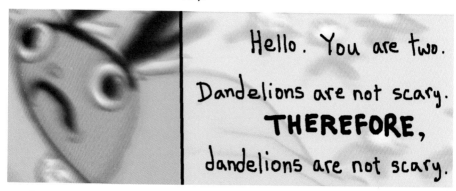

Hello. You are two.

Dandelions are not scary.

THEREFORE,

dandelions are not scary.

But once you're actually *in* the situation, you discover that explaining why dandelions aren't scary is more complicated than you ever could have guessed.

The logistics are a *nightmare*.

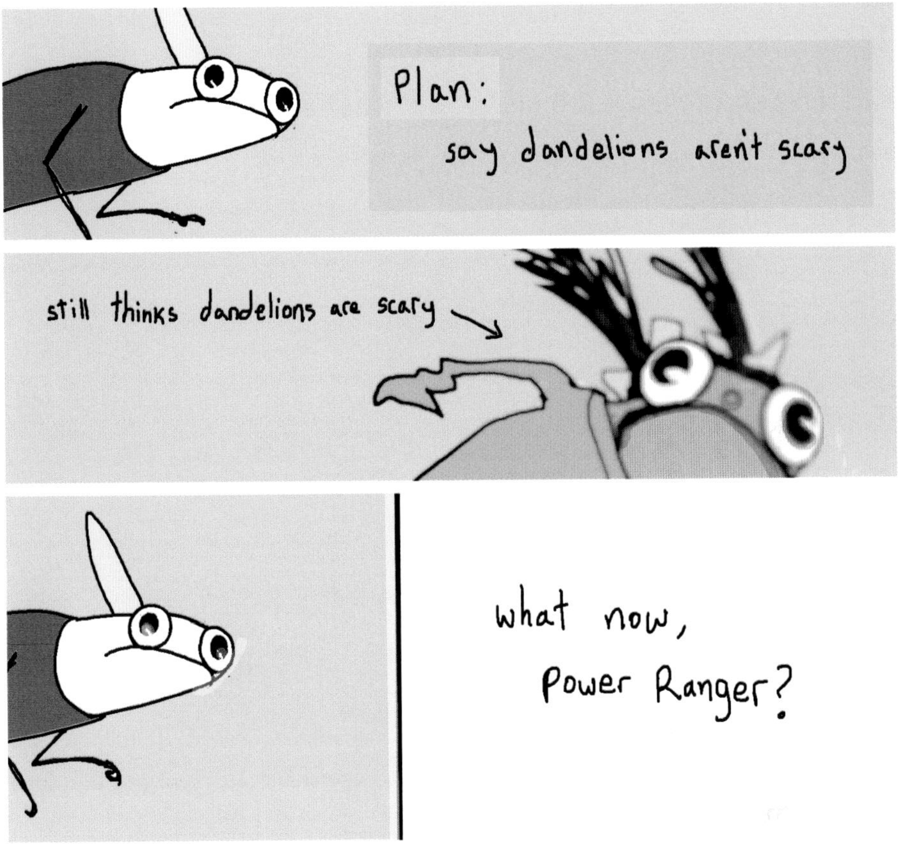
Plan:
say dandelions aren't scary
still thinks dandelions are scary
what now, Power Ranger?

The conversation goes nowhere.
You say: *THEY'RE JUST DANDELIONS.*
The kid keeps screaming.
Go ahead: tell her they're just dandelions again. Try it.

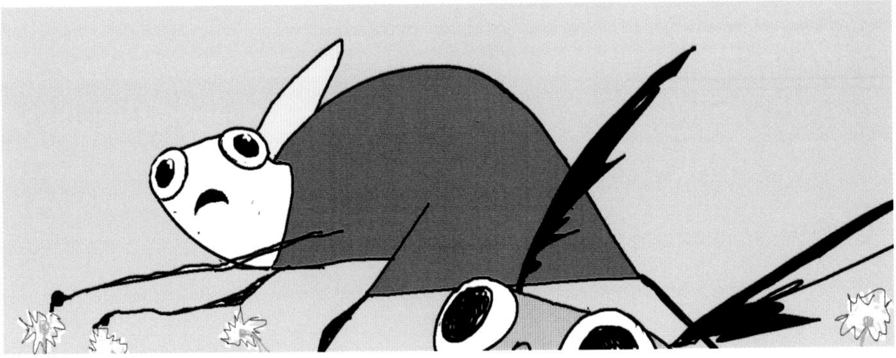

The screaming intensifies.

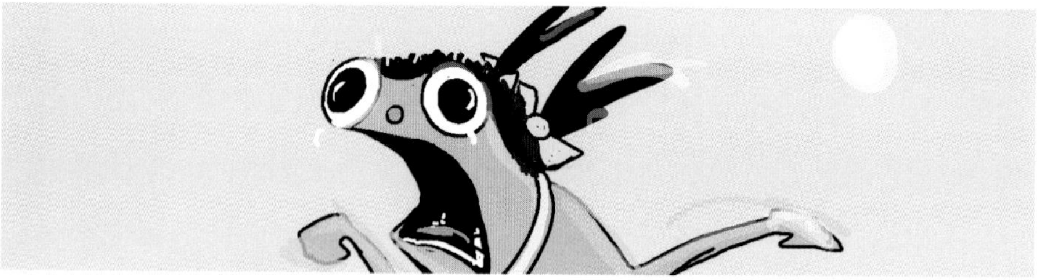

Touch the dandelions. Grab them in your hands to demonstrate how powerless they are. Yell, "*LOOK AT ME—IF DANDELIONS ARE SCARY, WHY AM I DOING THIS??*"

Do it again if you want. Touch them again. Yell, "*LOOK AT ME. LOOK AT ME. IF DANDELIONS ARE SCARY, WHY AM I DOING THIS?????*"

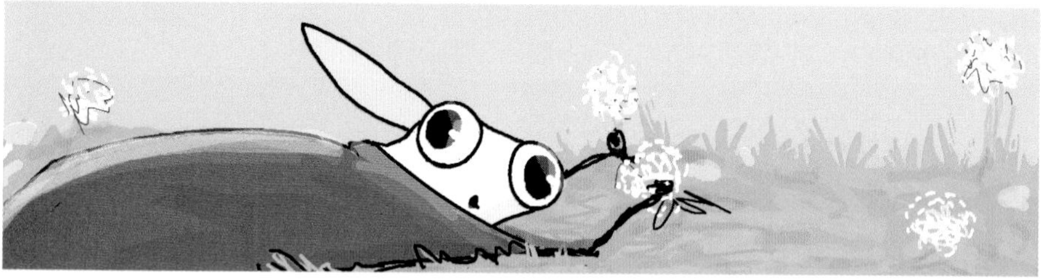

It won't work.

Because here's the thing about explaining why dandelions aren't scary to a 2-year-old who is scared of dandelions: you can't do it. I know *exactly* how to not be scared of dandelions, and I still couldn't explain it. I didn't even know where to start. I couldn't think of a single reason why dandelions WOULD be scary. If someone offered me a billion dollars to guess what the least scary thing in the entire world is, dandelions would be in my top two guesses, probably.

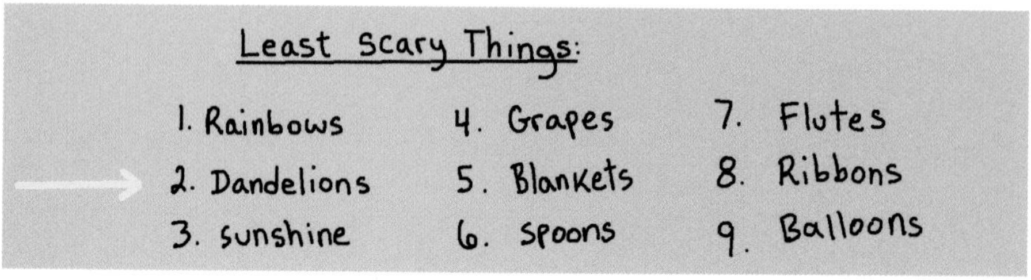
Least Scary Things:
1. Rainbows
2. Dandelions
3. sunshine
4. Grapes
5. Blankets
6. Spoons
7. Flutes
8. Ribbons
9. Balloons

And this kid is tiny and irrational and full on robo-sprinting from how scary dandelions are—she can't help me.

So I did the only other thing I could think of.
I trapped her under a towel and dragged her into the woods.

I let her out when we got to the woods because there were no dandelions in the woods, so I figured it'd be okay.

But sometime during the four minutes it took me to get the towel over her, pin her arms down, and haul her flailing body into the forest, she decided she was scared of *me*—possibly even more than dandelions—and as soon as the towel was off, the escaping-type behavior resumed, and I had to do the towel again and carry her like that for a mile.

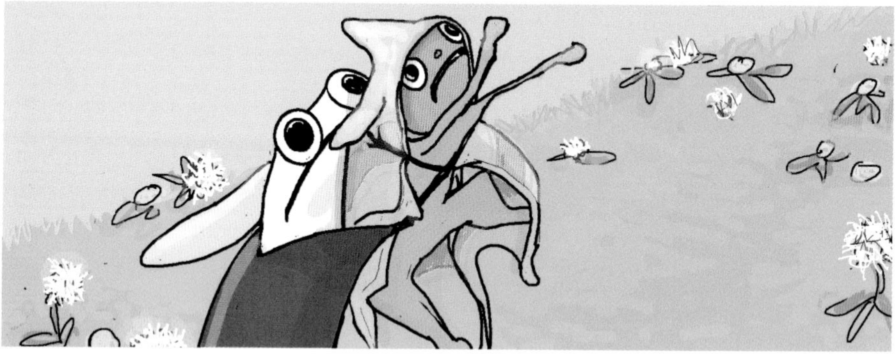

By the time we got back, she was so scared of me that I had to lock the doors and windows to prevent her from getting loose.

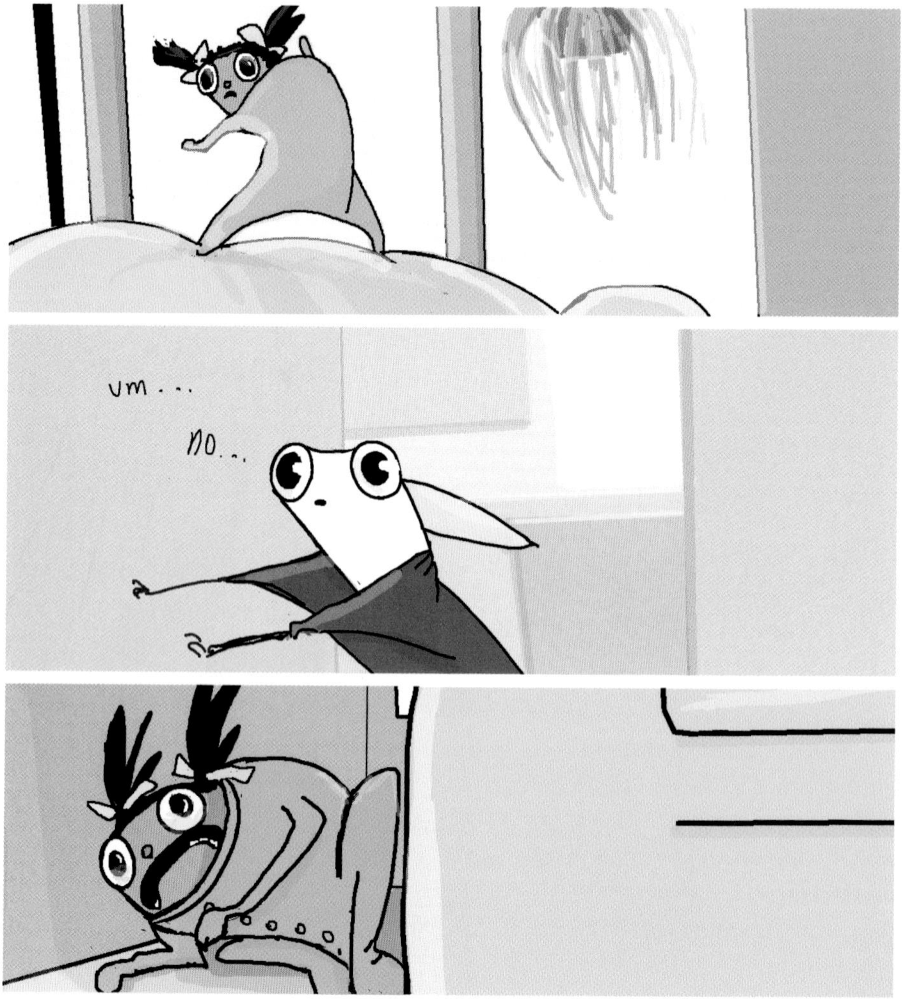

um . . .
no . . .

That day was traumatic for everyone.

For her because that was the day someone she trusted walked her directly into the center of everything she feared the most, and when she tried to escape, the person chased her and trapped her under a towel. And the person did this twice.

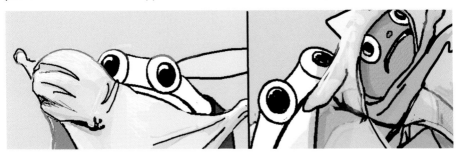

And for me because that was the day I had to trap a screaming 2-year-old under a towel not once but *twice*—without any way to explain why I needed to do that—and I felt like such a monster when she spent the rest of the day crying and hiding from me, and she was still doing that when her mom got home, which looked pretty bad, so I had to try to explain, but—as it turns out—"I had to because of the dandelions" is not a satisfying explanation for irreversibly traumatizing someone's 2-year-old, especially when it also turns out that nobody knew she felt that way about dandelions.

No... I swear!
I only did the
towel part!

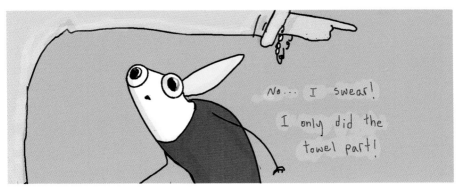

That child's mother still probably thinks I did some horrible mystery thing to make her kid afraid of dandelions. And the poor kid—who, we must remind ourselves, was already facing a difficult life of being the only person in the entire goddamn universe who has ever been scared of dandelions, let alone THAT scared of dandelions—has probably spent the rest of her difficult, dandelion-fearing life struggling with the explosion of psychological consequences I caused that day.

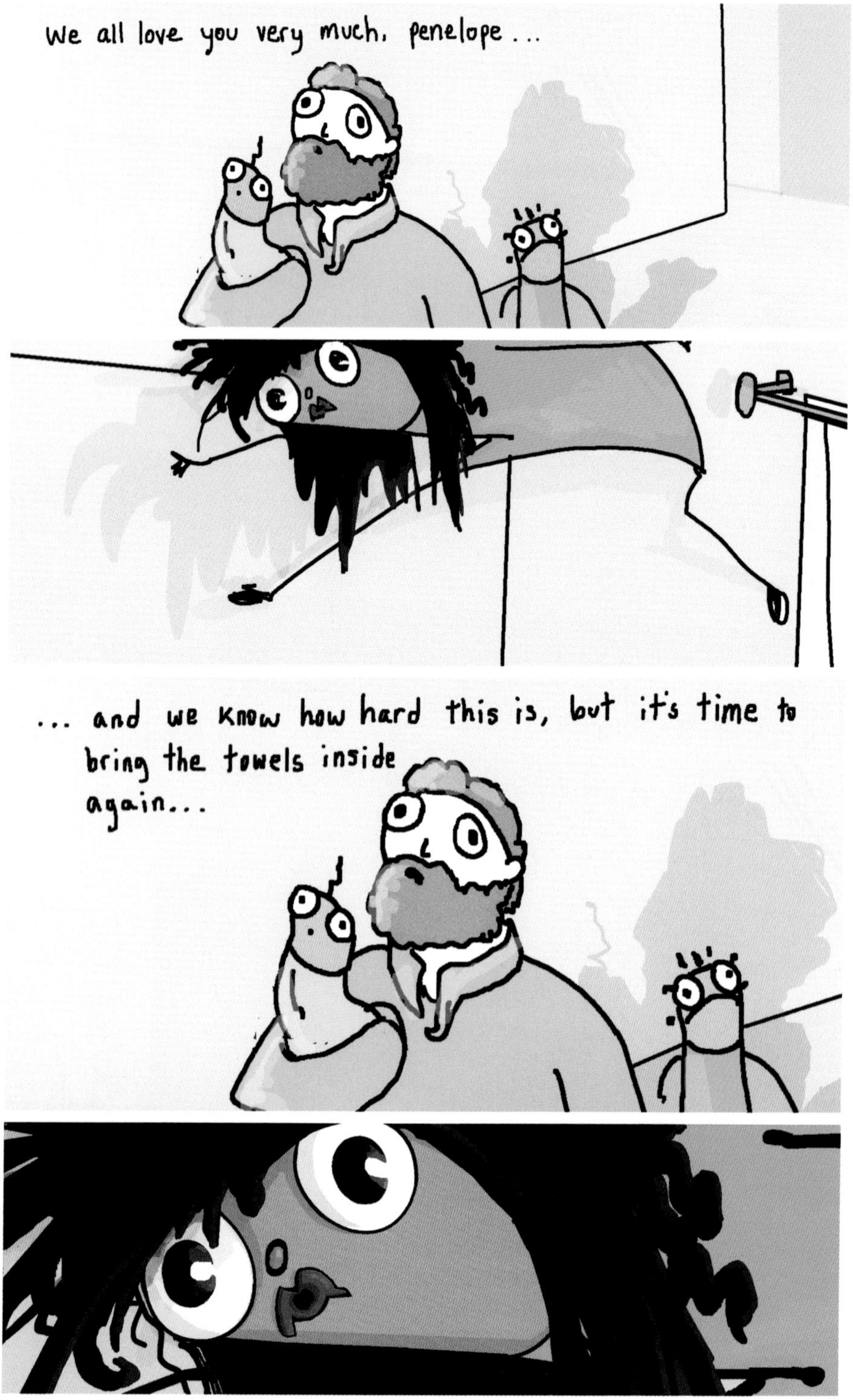
We all love you very much, penelope...
... and we know how hard this is, but it's time to bring the towels inside again...

Turtle

When I do something I disagree with, it still doesn't quite feel like I'm supposed to be in the category of people who do that. I'm doing it, yes. But not because I'm *like* that . . .

Sure: I yelled at a turtle. But I had a reason for doing that. And the reason was . . .

. . . well, originally, I tried to just honk at it, but my horn doesn't work anymore. The car alarm wouldn't stop, so, in a fit of rage, I ripped out the fuse with my bare hands.

My point is: I tried to just honk at the turtle, but I couldn't.

And I was already mad at something else, which is why I needed to drive fast, and I don't know, it just seemed pretty confrontational of the turtle to cross the road right then. I mean, it's a dirt road in the desert. Me and this turtle are the only things around for twenty miles. It felt personal. Like: Really, turtle? Right now? *Right now* is when you need to cross the road? You can't hang out behind a cactus for two seconds while I blast through at 67 miles per hour? Yeah—that's how fast I'm going. Does it seem fair that I—the thing going 67 miles per hour—had to come to a full stop and watch your stupid, slow body cross the whole road at an average speed of sixteen inches per minute? *DOES THAT SEEM FAIR TO YOU, YOU FUCKING TURTLE????*

theoretical maximum
(throwing the turtle, shooting the turtle out of a cannon, returning every day to yell at the turtle for the rest of the turtle's life, etc.)
?
what i did
nothing
← intensity →

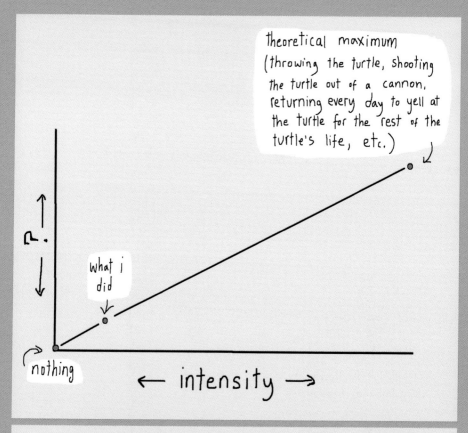

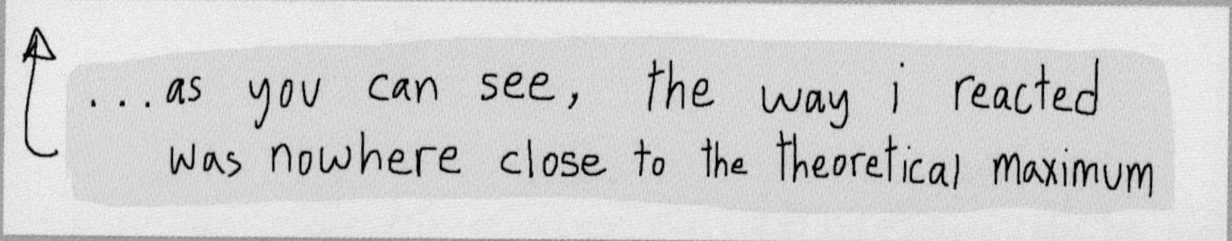

...as you can see, the way i reacted was nowhere close to the theoretical maximum

That's nowhere close to how mad a person who's actually like that would have been ...

9. BANANAS

Anger is not a graceful emotion. I've never gotten mad and been like, *I'm glad I behaved like that!*

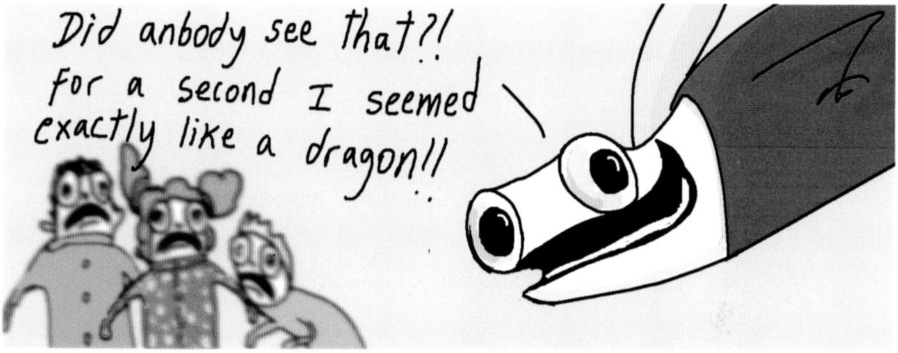
Did anbody see that?!
For a second I seemed exactly like a dragon!!

I feel weird about it every time.

Usually, knowing how weird I'm going to feel is enough to restrain me. But sometimes there's just so much of it, and it isn't going away, and you're tired, and you start to think, *Hey . . . maybe this isn't such a bad thing . . . maybe I WANT this . . .*

And then you get to see what the worst part of you looks like.

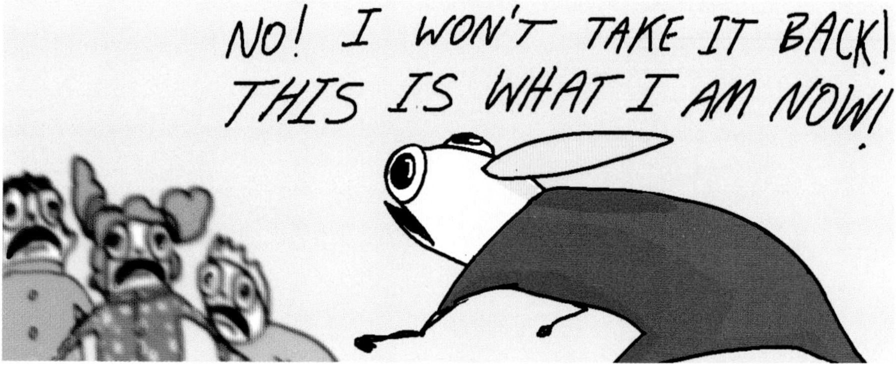
NO! I WON'T TAKE IT BACK!
THIS IS WHAT I AM NOW!

I found out what the worst part of me looks like during an argument with my ex-husband, Duncan, who is one of the nicest people in the world.

apologizes to shrimp when he eats them.

←brings enough sunscreen for everybody

genuinely does his best to listen and understand, even if you're a crazy guy at the gas station.

We're both nice people, usually. But this wasn't a regular argument. It was the type of argument you can only have with people you're *really* close to—people you know so well you start to forget they're a different person from you, so it sort of feels like nobody can see you.

I'm not sure where it started. There wasn't an identifiable origin point. It began in 47 different places over the course of 9 years. But it crescendoed in the produce section of the Newport Avenue Market in Bend, Oregon.

The day before, we'd decided to finally tackle cross-country skiing, which is a ridiculous activity that nobody can feel dignified doing. Duncan had never done it before, so he didn't know that yet. I know everything, so I assumed I'd be able to teach him.

We got up at 7 a.m., the worst time of day. It was also 7 degrees outside, which is the worst temperature. For some reason, we refused to acknowledge that those would be perfectly good reasons to not go through with this.

We couldn't find the normal-looking mittens. Then we didn't have enough coffee left. Then we couldn't find the car keys. These, also, were ignored as perfectly legitimate reasons to stay home. We were too busy arguing about who lost the keys this time, which turned out to be me. I was therefore also implicated for the mittens and coffee. Nobody remembered to pack food.

9:30 a.m. We arrive at the ski place. Duncan immediately finds out how humiliating cross-country skiing is.

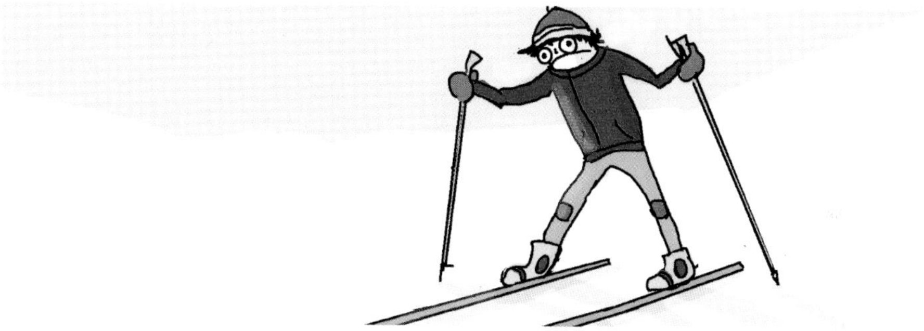

He falls over every four seconds. I keep trying to explain how to not do that, but it isn't working—either because my teaching methods are ineffective or his learning methods are ineffective, but it is for sure somebody's fault.

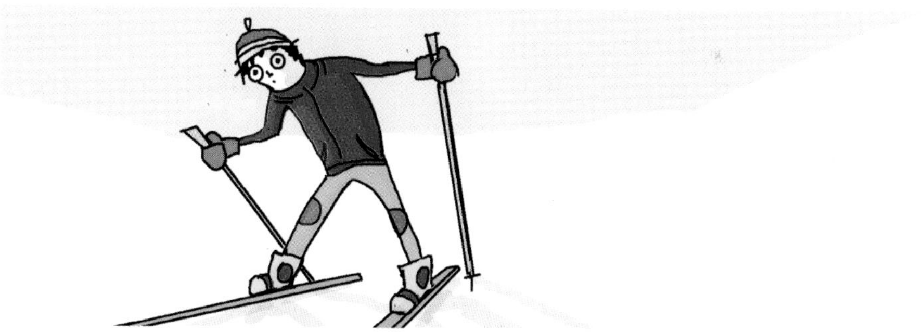

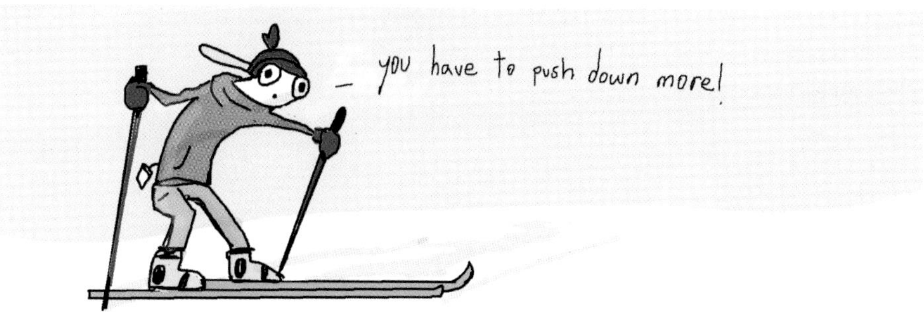
you have to push down more!

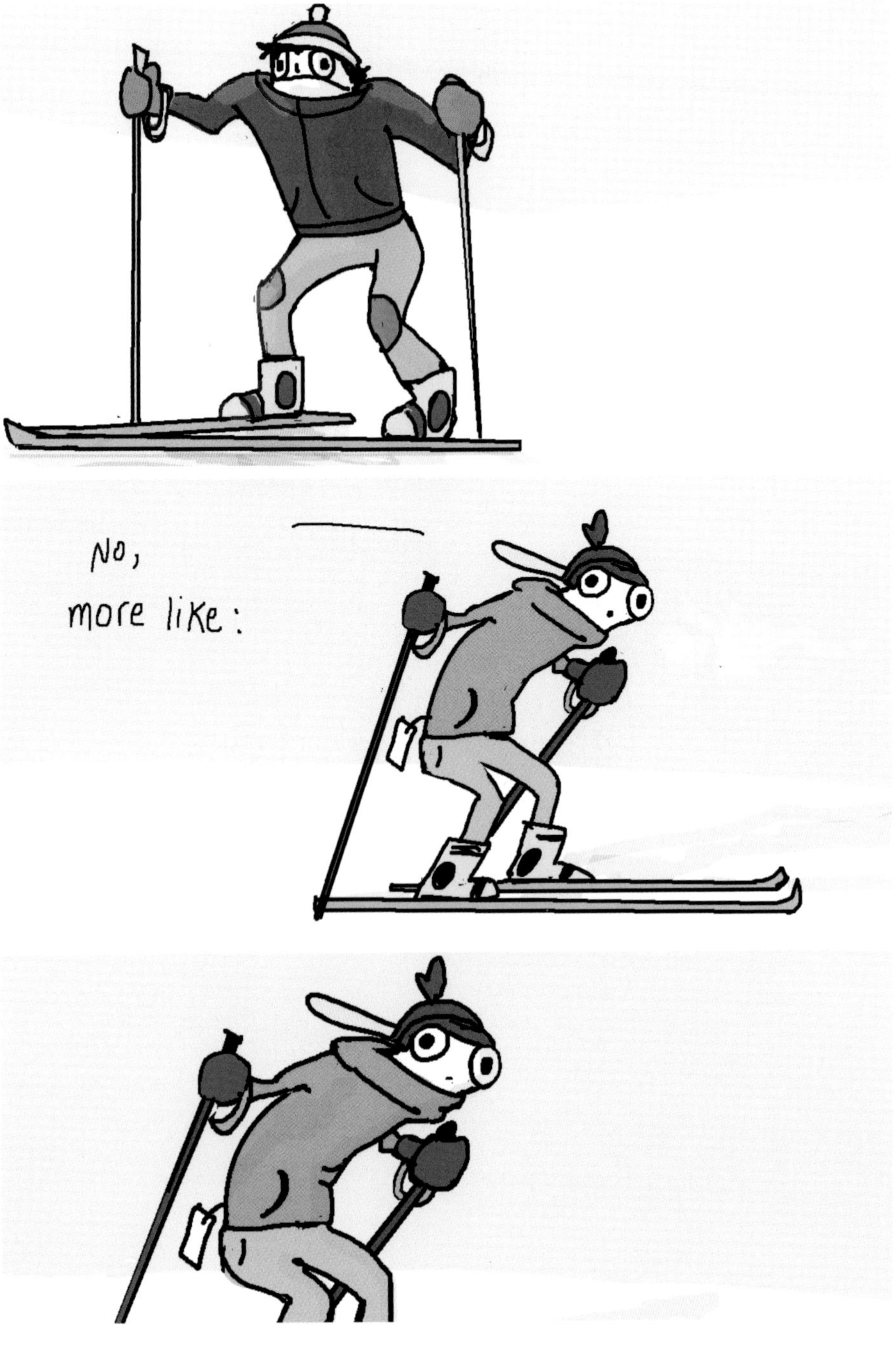
No,
more like:

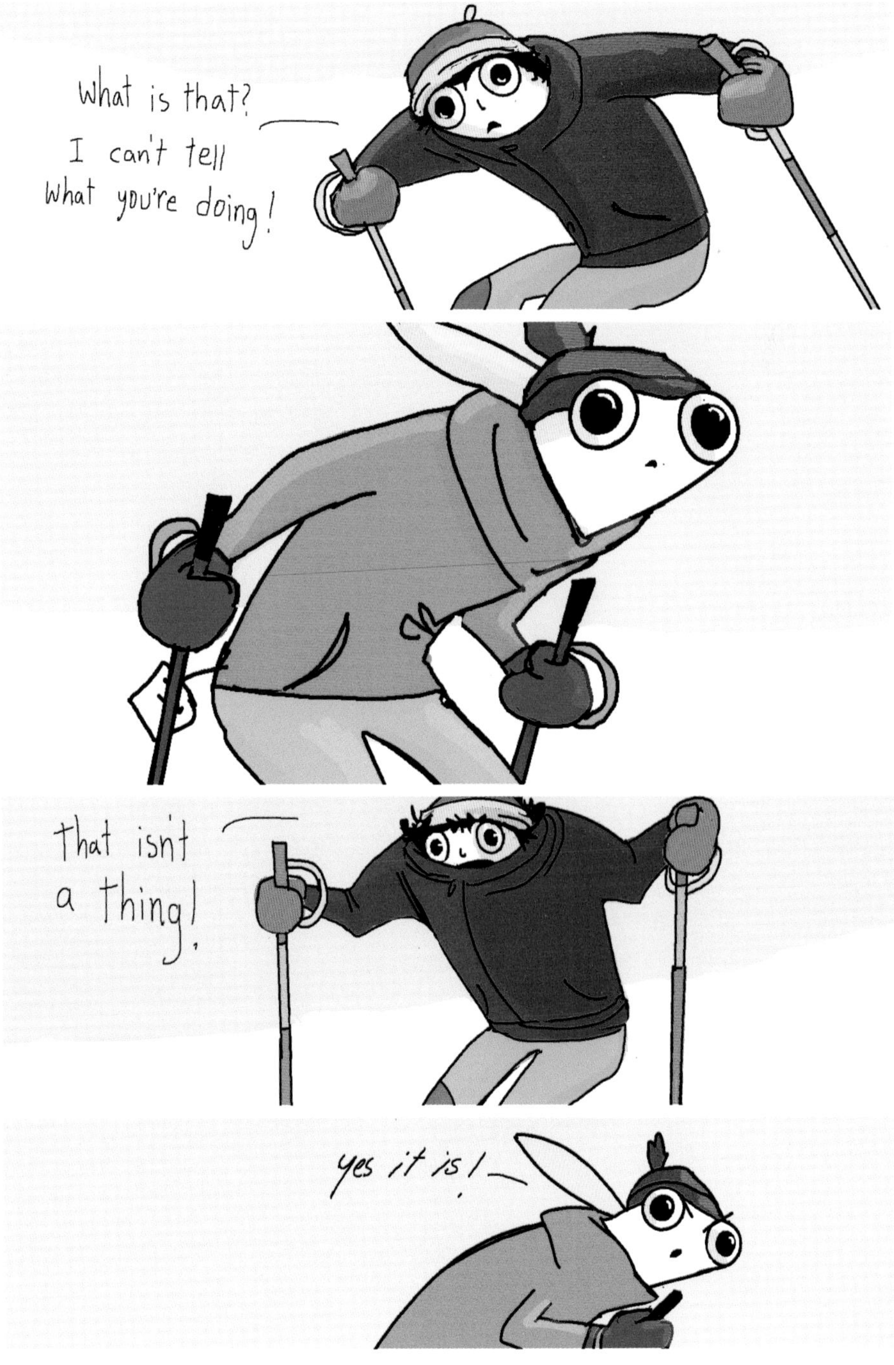
What is that?
I can't tell what you're doing!
That isn't a thing!
yes it is!

Our average skiing speed is .2 miles per hour. Eons later, we've gone almost a mile. We decide to turn back so we can eat lunch before it gets dark. That's when we realize somebody didn't remember to pack food. We each secretly blame who we personally feel was truly responsible for this.

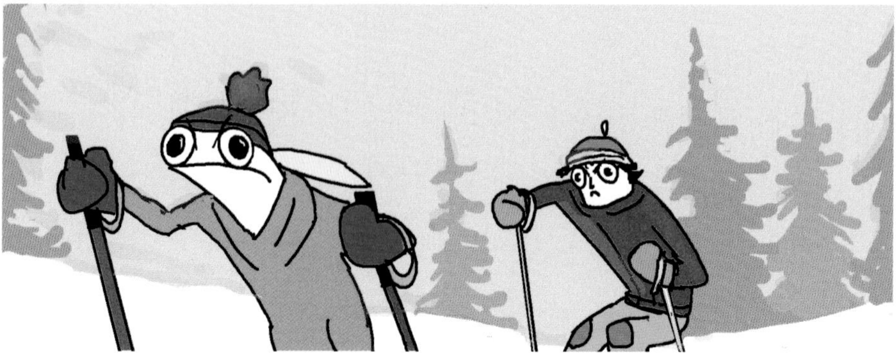

Chili was the only thing on the menu at the lodge that day, so instead of eating lunch, we decide to go home. However, in order to do that, we need to go in the car, which is risky because there's a long-standing feud about the car and whether it's better to drive it like an old piece of lettuce or a NASCAR death-pilot.

Normally, I might've been able to restrain myself from going there, but we're driving in the snow, and I grew up in northern Idaho, so therefore I am a snow expert. It's just a qualification I get to have for the rest of my life, no matter what. Duncan grew up in Seattle, so he's seen snow before. Therefore, he is also an expert and not afraid of dying at all.

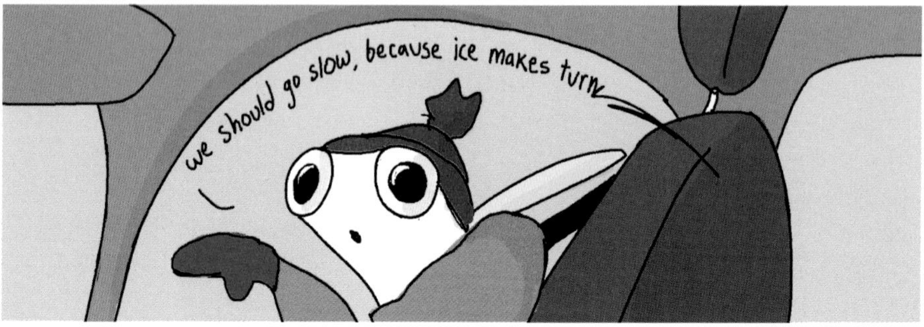
we should go slow, because ice makes turn

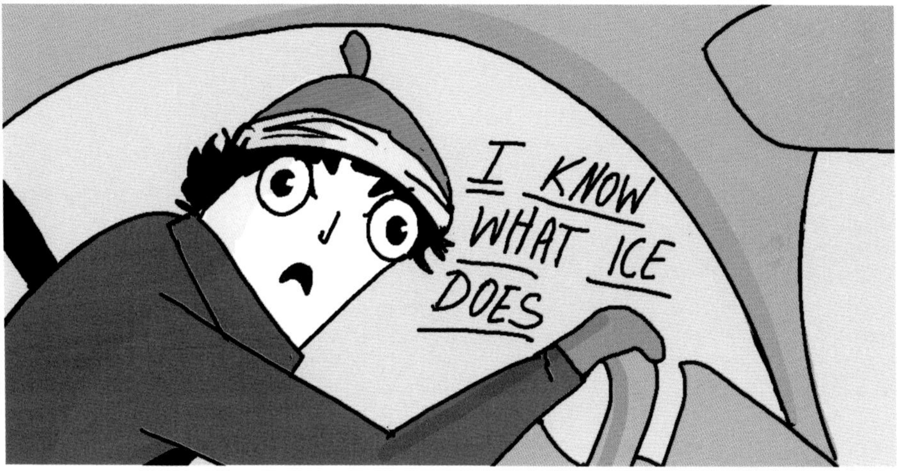
I KNOW WHAT ICE DOES

900 feet outside the parking lot, Duncan stops the car. He says if I know so much, then maybe I should drive.

This is very out of character for Duncan. Duncan being confrontational at all should have been like a smoke alarm—a smoke alarm that says "Excuse me, but something extraordinary is happening ... maybe we should be cautious while we still can ..."

But I'm feeling too self-righteous to notice.

We switch places.

Now he's critiquing my driving.

Just to be a dick, I slow down to 5 miles per hour.

Cars are honking at us. Duncan says I should pull over and let them pass. I slow down to 2 miles per hour to see what happens. I'm so focused on being a dick that I don't realize we missed our turn. But Duncan does. Suddenly he's Mr. Safety, lecturing me about distracted driving. I stop the car. If he's so talented, maybe he should drive. We switch places.

For some reason, we decide that this would be the correct time to go grocery shopping. We disagree about the fastest way to get there. He's driving, though, so we go his way. Both ways would be slow at this time of day, but the fact that Duncan's way is also slow seems like proof that Duncan's way is wrong.

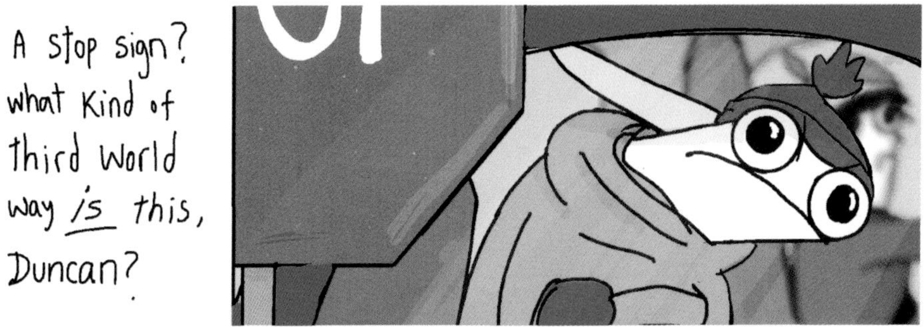
A stop sign? what kind of third world way *is* this, Duncan?

The instant we enter the parking lot, the debate about parking strategy awakens. Duncan is still driving, so I have to sit there while he wastes all of our time hunting for the parking spot of his dreams when we could just park one row away and already be inside, and this is doubly infuriating because of how hypocritical it seems in contrast to his position on driving speeds.

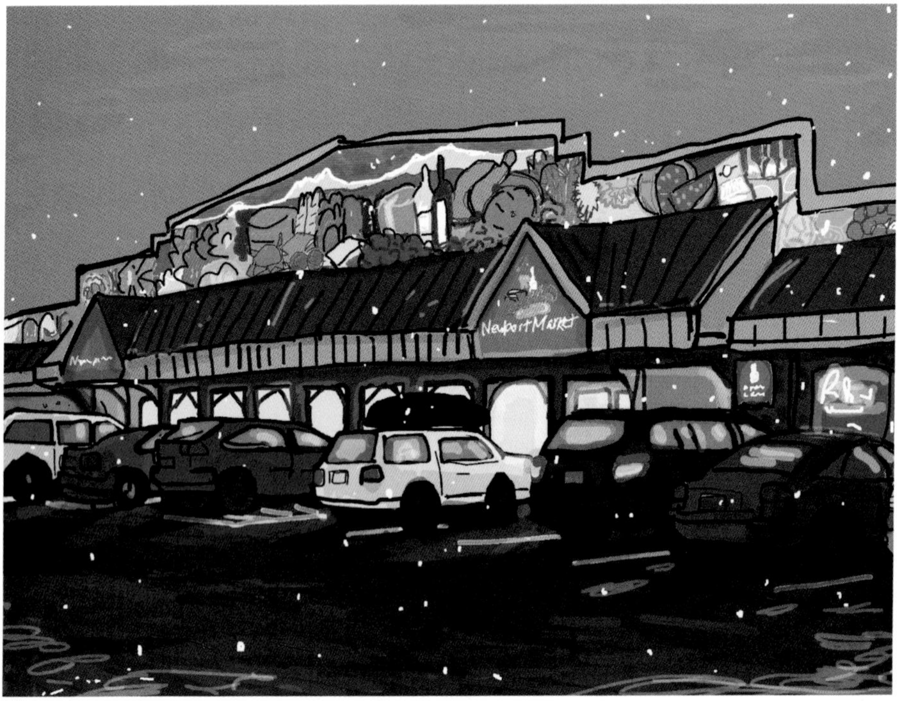
Newport Market

By the time we walked through the entryway of the Newport Avenue Market in Bend, Oregon, we were so mad that we'd entered into that infinite loop where everything the other person does—no matter how innocuous it is—seems inflammatory. They could just be standing there, and it would seem like the most flagrant standing anyone has ever done.

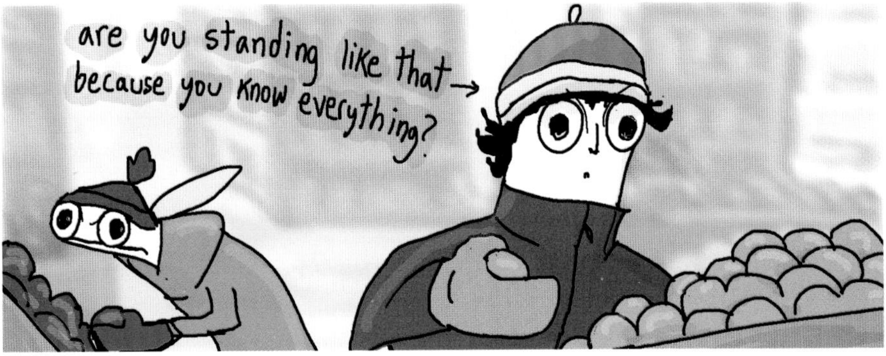
are you standing like that because you know everything?

I said, "Could you please get some bananas," but not with the nice please—with the shitty one that means "Here, take this please that you don't deserve and use it to get some *goddamn bananas*."

"Why do we buy bananas?" he asked. "We just throw them away."

This is true. It is a proven fact that you can never finish all the bananas. But I had so much anger in me. I needed to put it somewhere. It didn't matter where. I just wanted it out.

I muttered, "Maybe you aren't good at choosing bananas."

Duncan hissed back, "Then maybe YOU should choose the bananas."

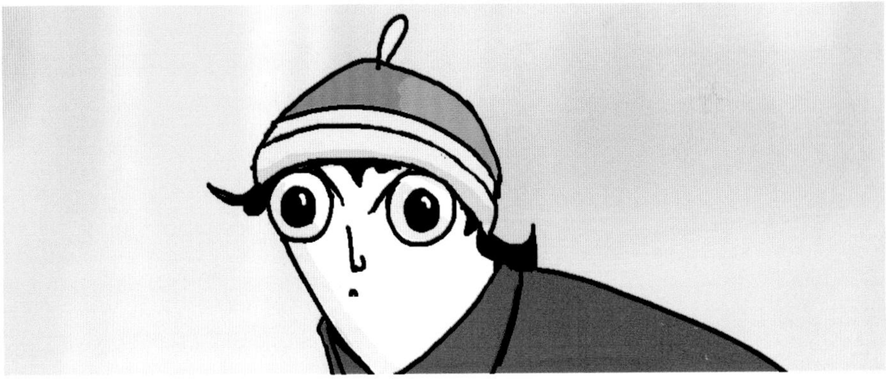

This is a reasonable point. And when you're in full-on rage-ejection mode, there is nothing more infuriating than a reasonable point.

You're so mad, your brain starts malfunctioning. You can barely form thoughts, but you do somehow manage to form a sentence! It's childish, needlessly inflammatory, and borderline nonsensical. You might as well throw sand at the person because saying this is going to have the same effect.

You've never been this far before. You know you shouldn't say it. You know it's stupid and you'll regret it later. But it's too late. The sentence has formed. It's on deck, ready to launch. You're going to say it.

The words start coming out.

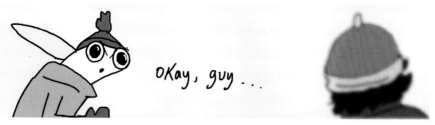

And even as you're saying them, you're frantically willing yourself to change course. Say something else! Anything! It doesn't need to make sense! Make random noises if you have to!

But there's too much momentum. No one can stop it now.

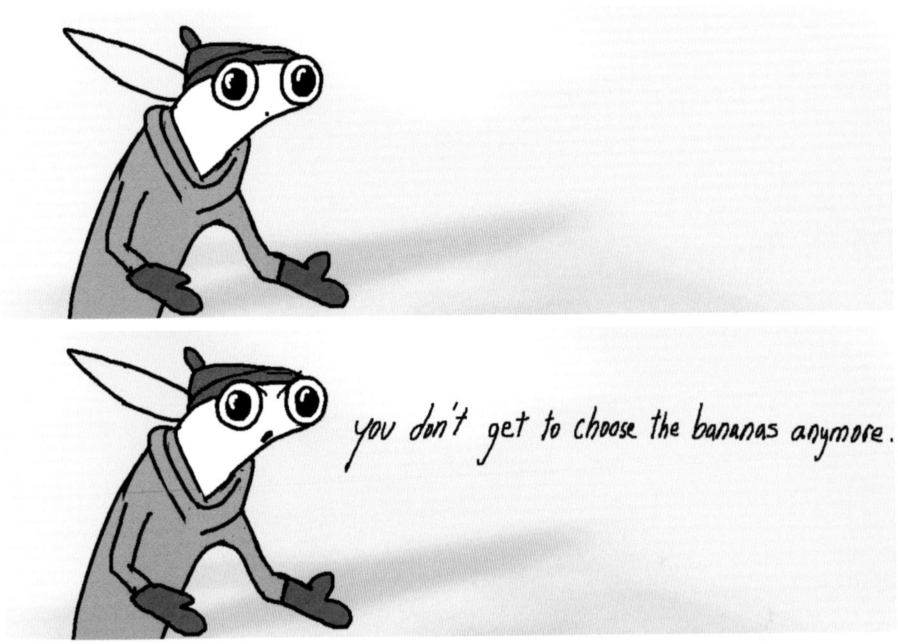
you don't get to choose the bananas anymore.

"Okay, guy—guess what: you don't get to choose the bananas anymore."

A critical mass of anger awakened a primitive part of my brain, which unfurled like a cobra and spat the most hateful venom it could muster straight into Duncan's face. And that is what it came up with.

Let's pause for a moment and take a closer look at this tour de force:

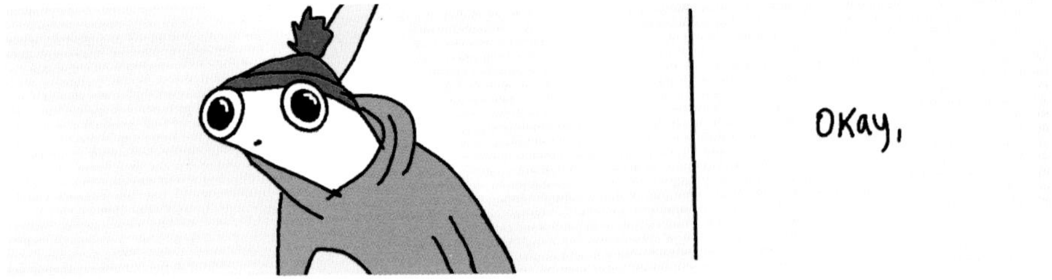
Okay,

At first, it sounds like I'm agreeing! Like maybe the argument is going to end!

guy,

This is the first sign that things might go poorly after all. You may have noticed, guy, that I didn't call you a name. I could have, but I didn't. Because I am a serious person, *and you don't have a name anymore.*

Guess what?

I'm not sure what I was trying to do here. *Hold on, before we find out what the next part is, I'd like to give you an opportunity to guess... go ahead—guess anything you want, guy. What do you think it'll be? My six least favorite numbers? Moon facts? A poem about a ghost?*

Perhaps I thought it was going to be a huge surprise for Duncan, and this was an attempt at sportsmanship. *You'll want to take a second to prepare yourself for this next part, guy. I'm about to go crazy.*

you don't get

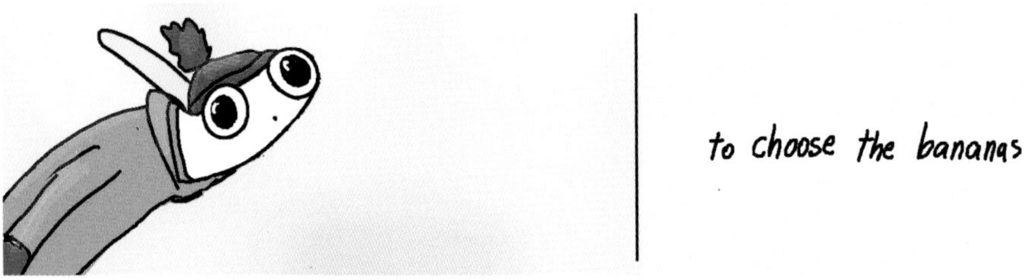
to choose the bananas

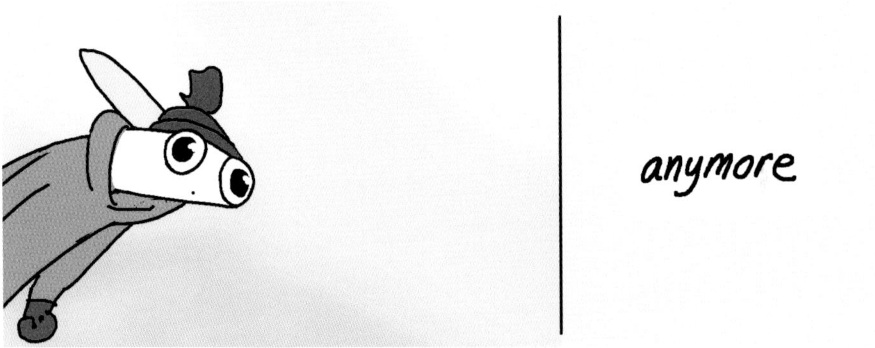
anymore

At long last . . . the crushing blow.

Here, I think I was attempting to demonstrate the full force of my power.

It's quite clearly supposed to be a threat. As though I have the power to decide whether he gets to choose the bananas, and god help me, I am finally going to use it.

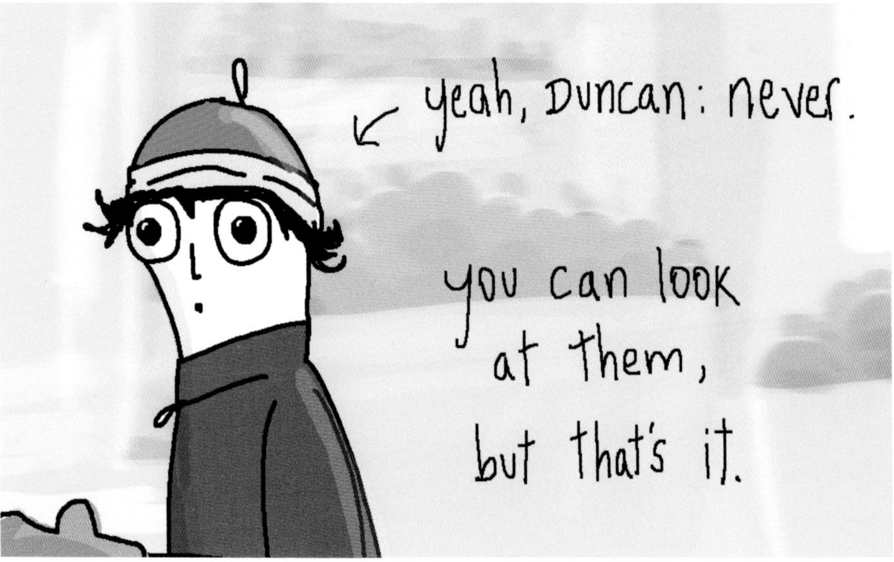
yeah, Duncan: never.
you can look at them, but that's it.

The sentence sat there, unable to be absorbed.

Ten seconds passed in silence.

Then, in an equally nonsensical turn of events, Duncan got *super* offended. How DARE I say this to him? Who did I think I was? The emperor of bananas?

All he could do was stand there making a face like:

I could tell he wanted to buy a hundred bananas right then. No: a thousand bananas. Just blow our life savings on bananas for the sole purpose of demonstrating what a horrific dick I was being.

hello, is this the President of bananas?

yes: I would like to buy ALL THE BANANAS THERE ARE.

There wouldn't have been enough bananas in the world to express it.

He'd have to buy the grapes too.

But he couldn't do that any more than I could stop him from choosing the bananas. Neither of us could realistically prevent the other one from buying bananas.

And that's hilarious. No matter how mad you are, you can't stop somebody from buying bananas. Not really. Not if they keep trying. And I think we both realized at the same time how absurd we are. And not just because of this—*in general*. We realized at exactly the same time that we are both stupid, serious, mad little animals who desperately want to stop each other from buying bananas, but can't.

And we never argued about bananas again because the risk of being unexpectedly confronted by your own absurdity while you're raging mad isn't worth it.

10. LOSING

People say that everything happens for a reason.

Which is technically true, I suppose.

But some of the reasons are too arbitrary to seem legitimate.

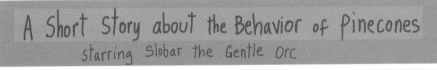

A Short Story about the Behavior of Pinecones
starring Slobar the Gentle Orc

One evening, as Slobar was strolling gently through the woods...

...a pinecone fell on him.

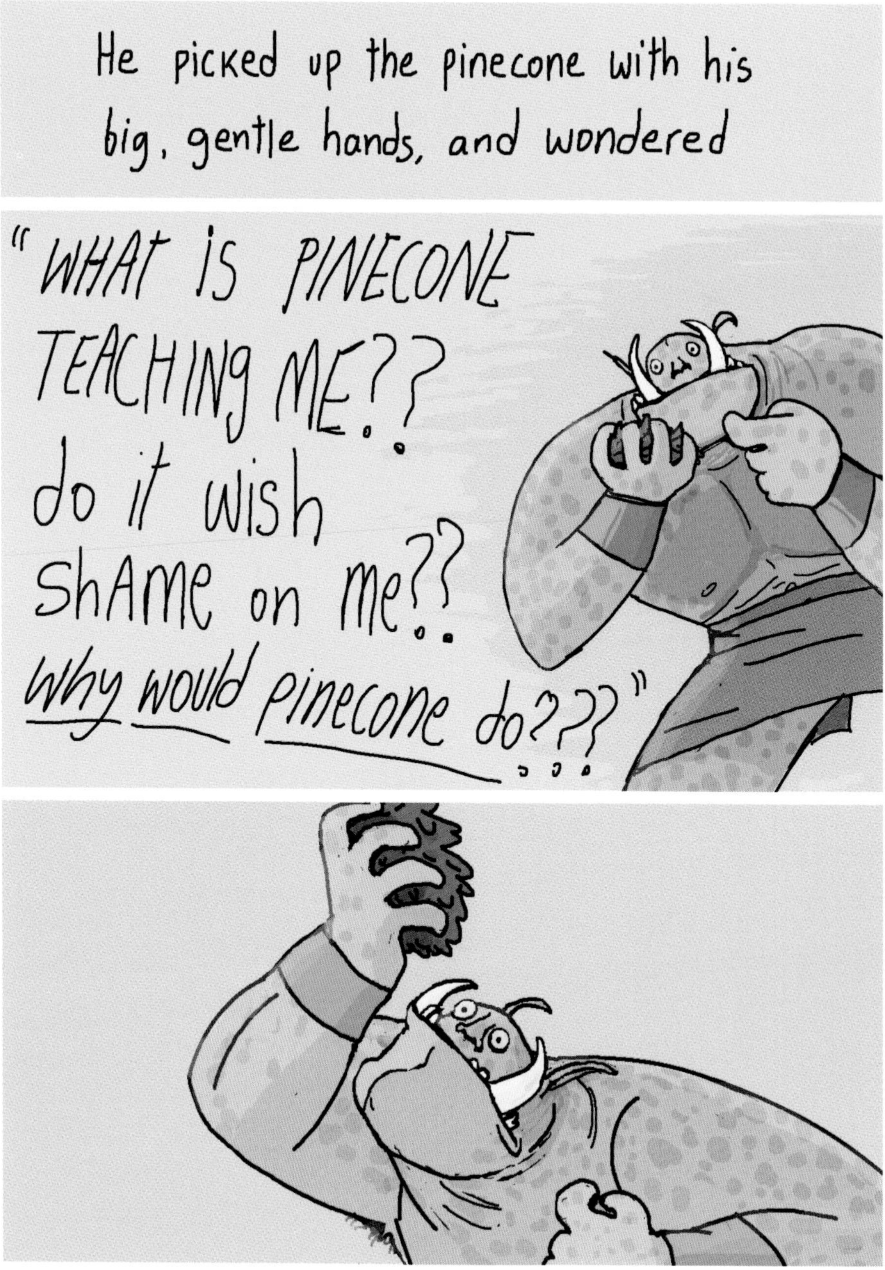
He picked up the pinecone with his big, gentle hands, and wondered
"WHAT IS PINECONE TEACHING ME??
do it wish shame on me??
Why would pinecone do???"

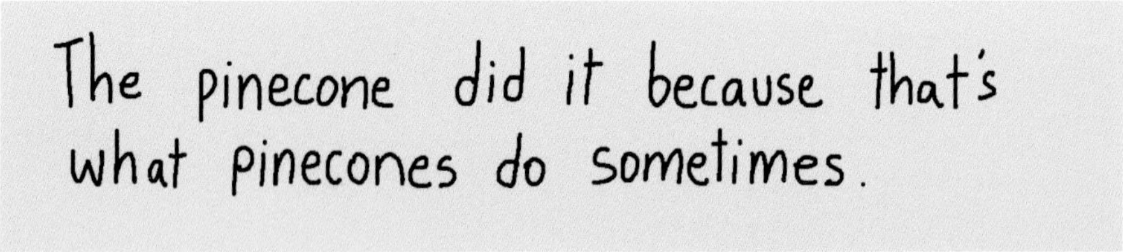
The pinecone did it because that's what pinecones do sometimes.

That reason doesn't explain anything. It doesn't explain how to prevent the pinecone from doing this in the future, it doesn't explain what else pinecones do—it just raises a bunch of new questions that don't have satisfying explanations either.

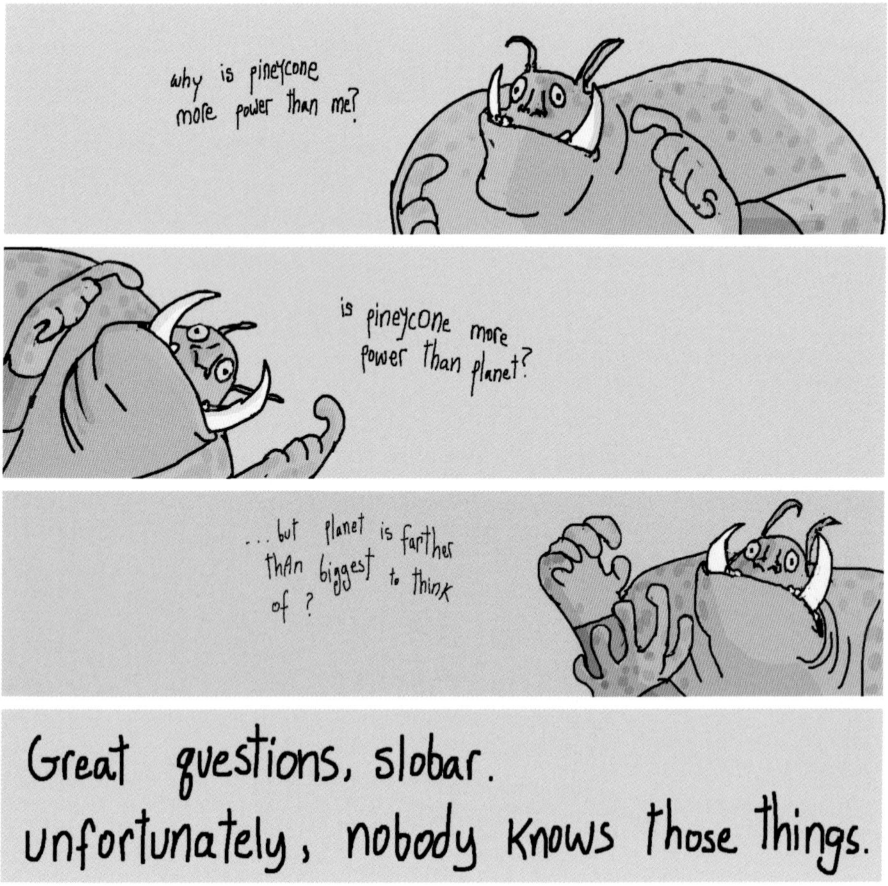
why is pineycone more power than me?
is pineycone more power than planet?
...but planet is farther than biggest to think of?
Great questions, slobar.
unfortunately, nobody knows those things.

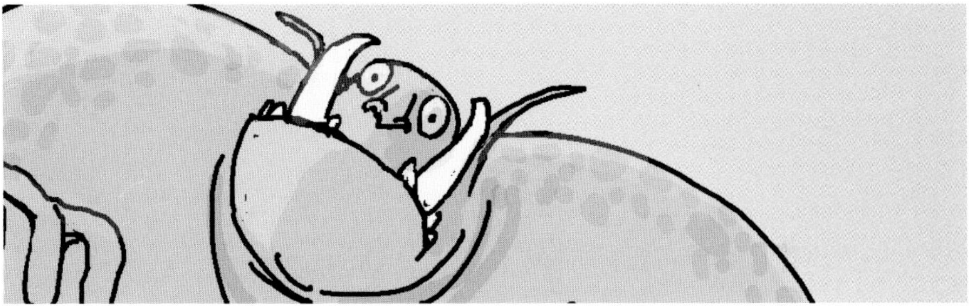

If you keep going, you'll eventually realize that the one true answer to all your questions is: *Of course it doesn't make sense—what business do you have expecting things to make sense?*

It's a long process, but for me, the thing that started it was a bird.

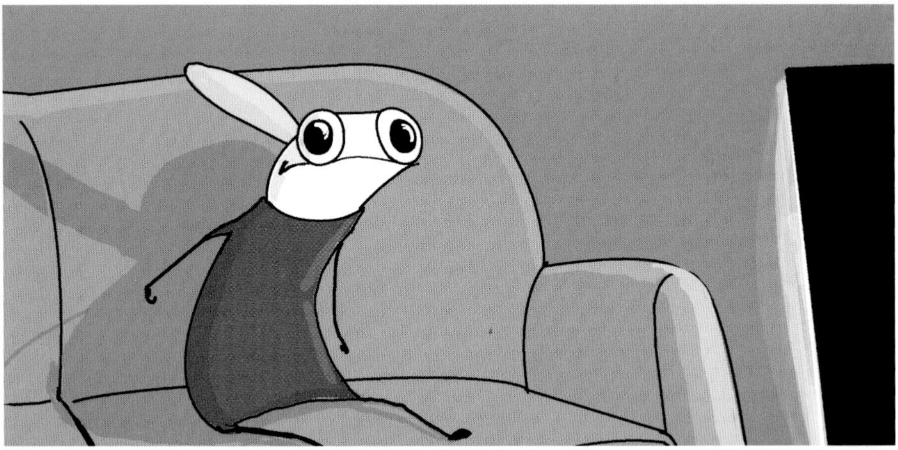

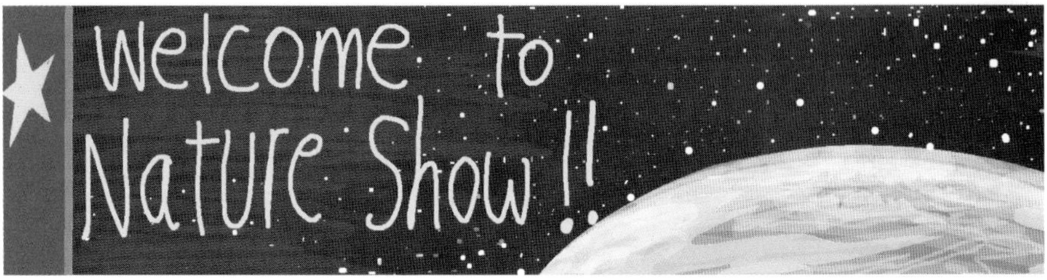
welcome to Nature Show!!

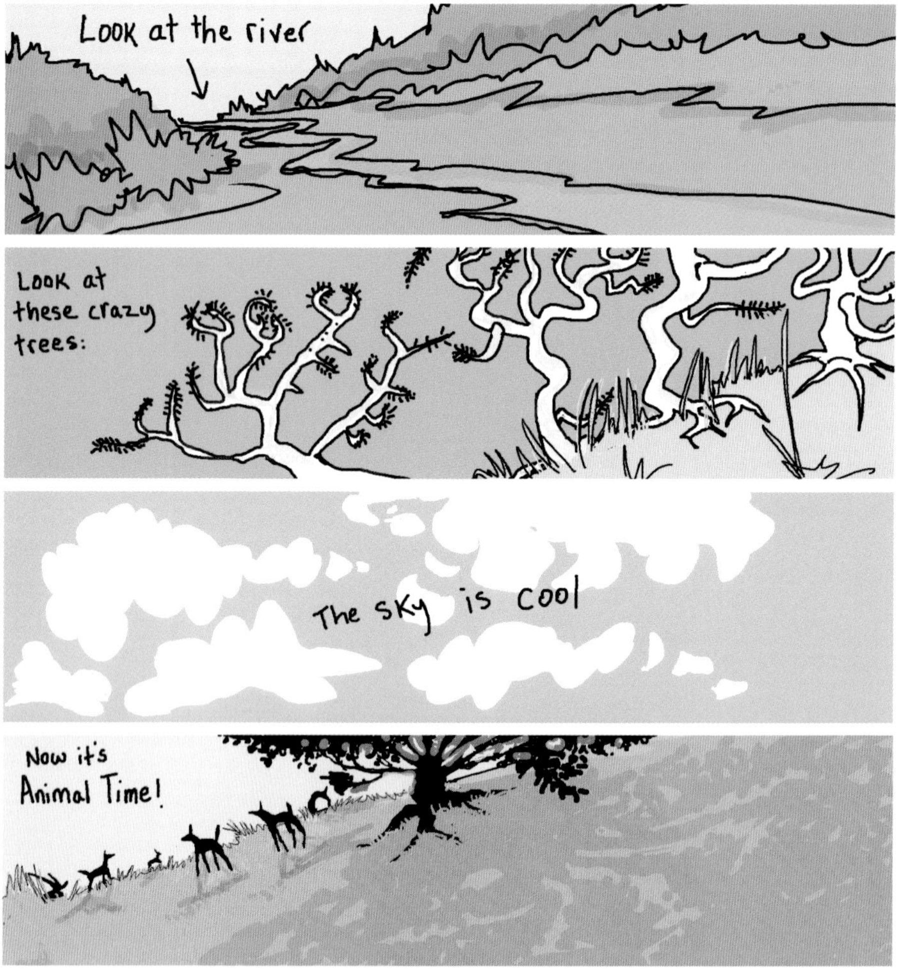
Look at the river
Look at these crazy trees:
The sky is cool
Now it's Animal Time!

My guard was down, and it came out of nowhere.

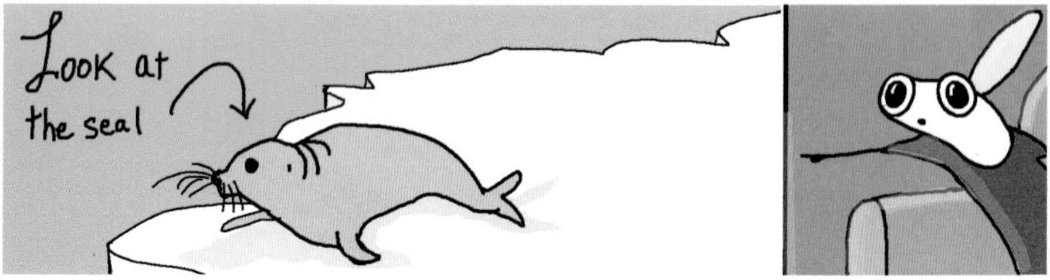
Look at the seal

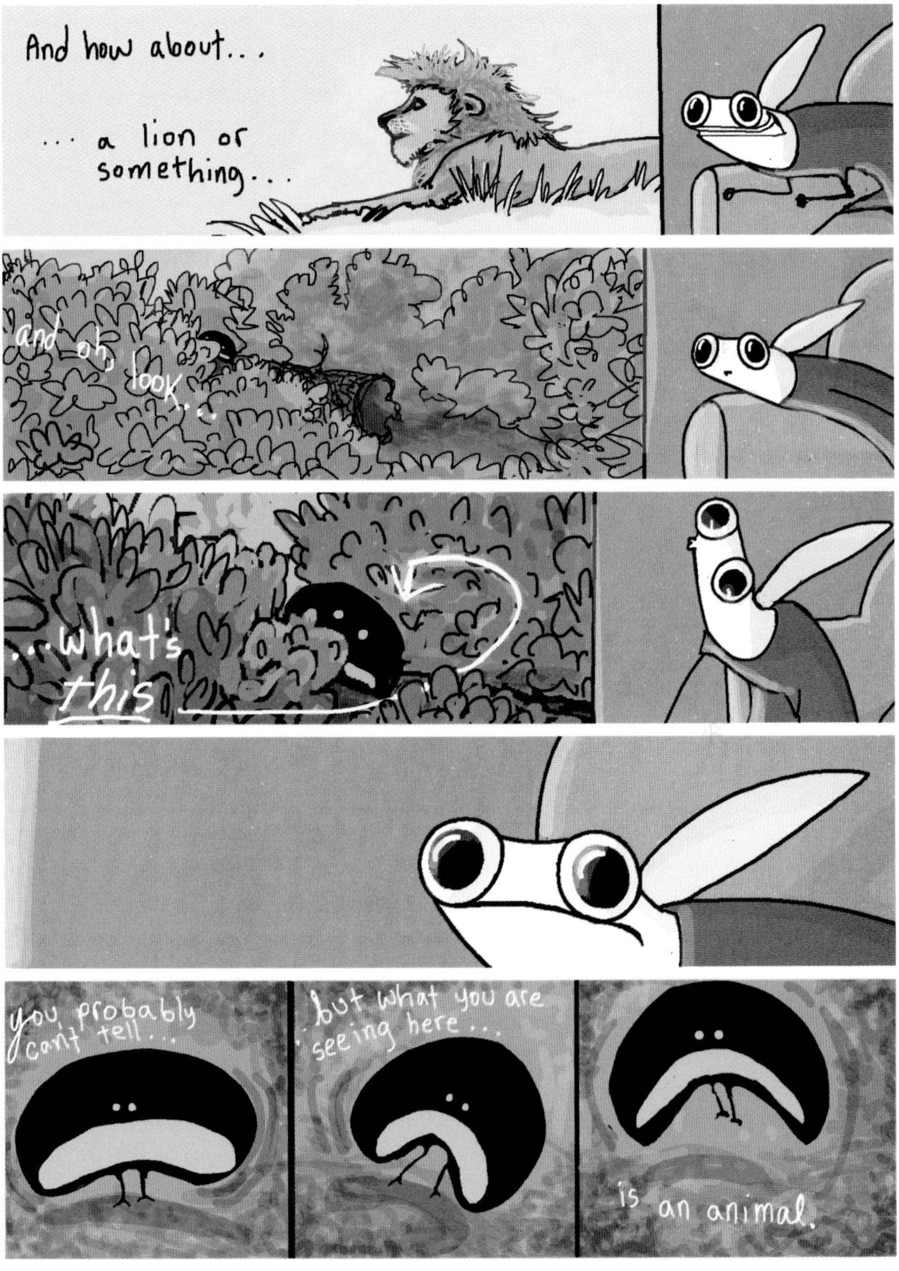
And how about...
... a lion or something...
and oh, look...
...what's this
you probably can't tell...
but what you are seeing here...
is an animal.

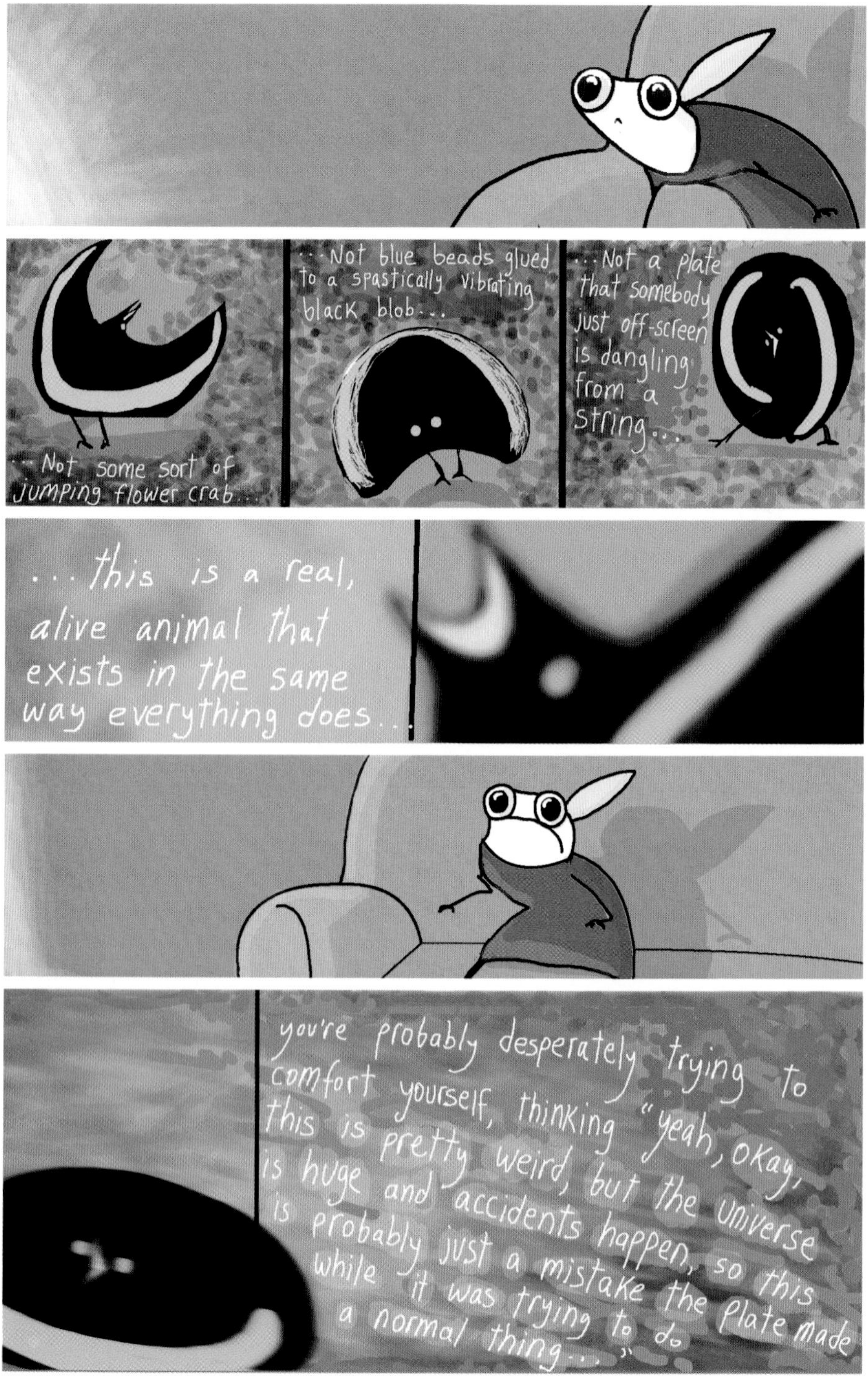
...Not some sort of jumping flower crab...
...Not blue beads glued to a spastically vibrating black blob...
...Not a plate that somebody just off-screen is dangling from a string...
...this is a real, alive animal that exists in the same way everything does...
you're probably desperately trying to comfort yourself, thinking "yeah, okay, this is pretty weird, but the universe is huge and accidents happen, so this is probably just a mistake the plate made while it was trying to do a normal thing..."

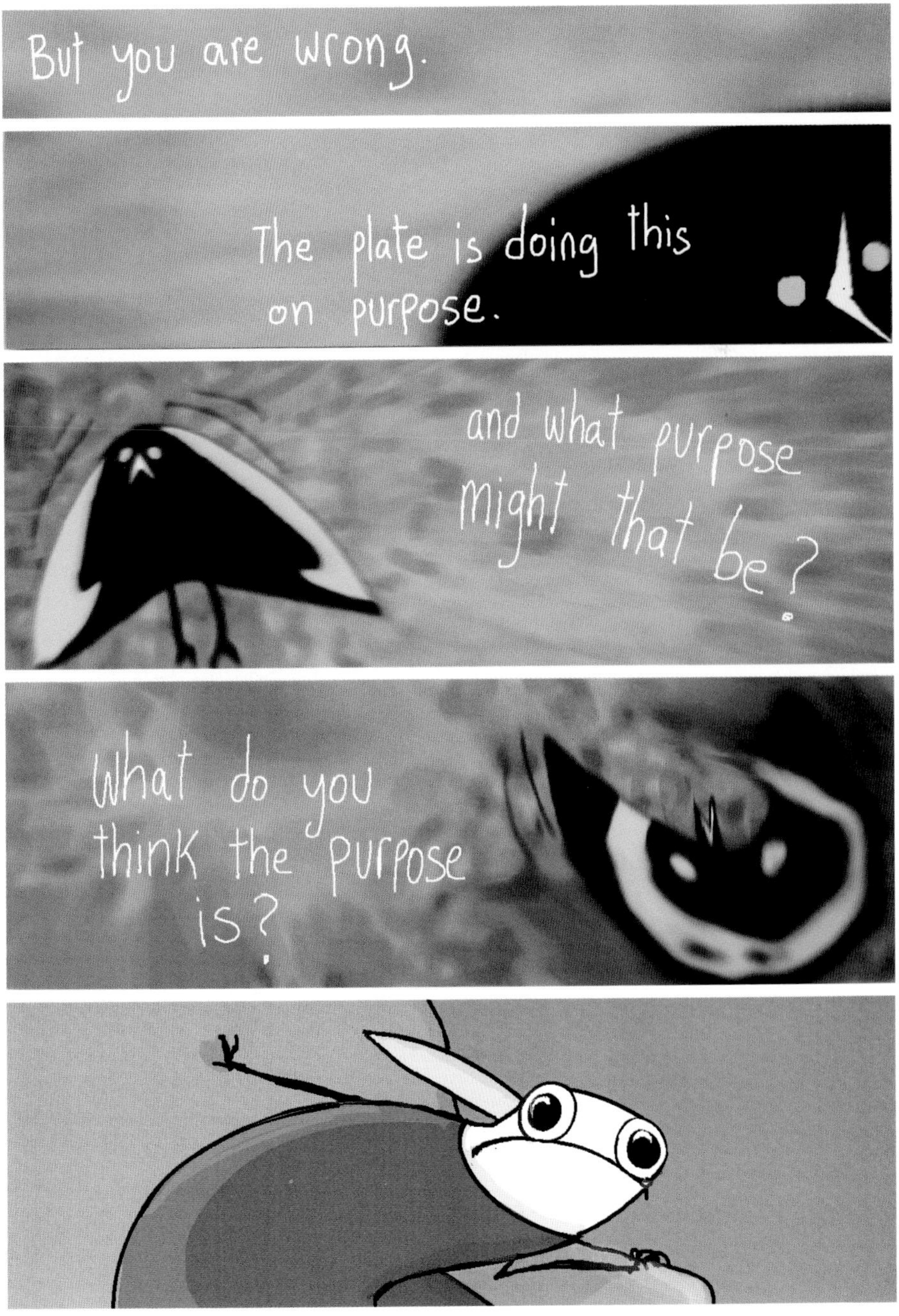
But you are wrong.
The plate is doing this on purpose.
and what purpose might that be?
What do you think the purpose is?

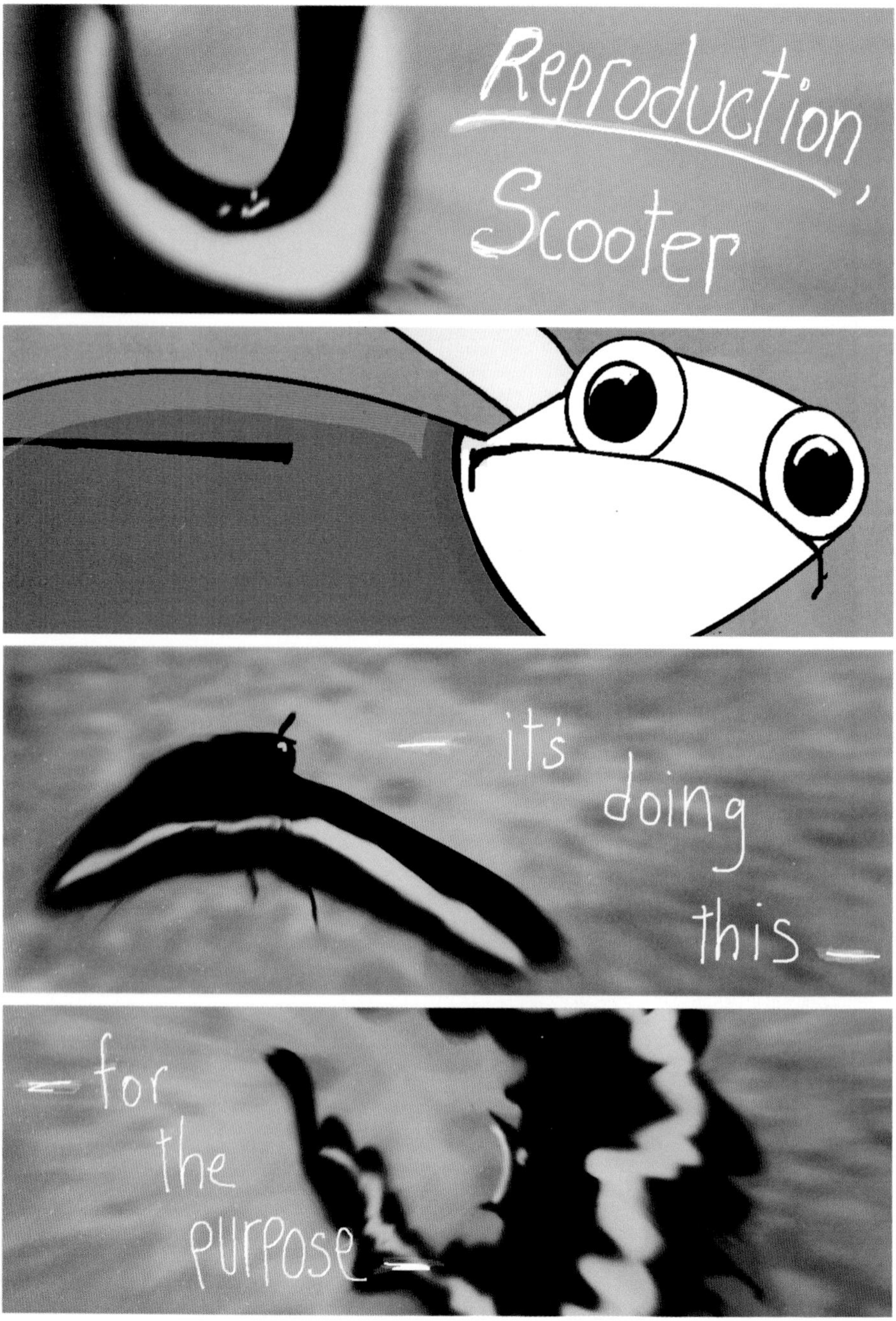
Reproduction, Scooter
— it's doing this —
— for the purpose —

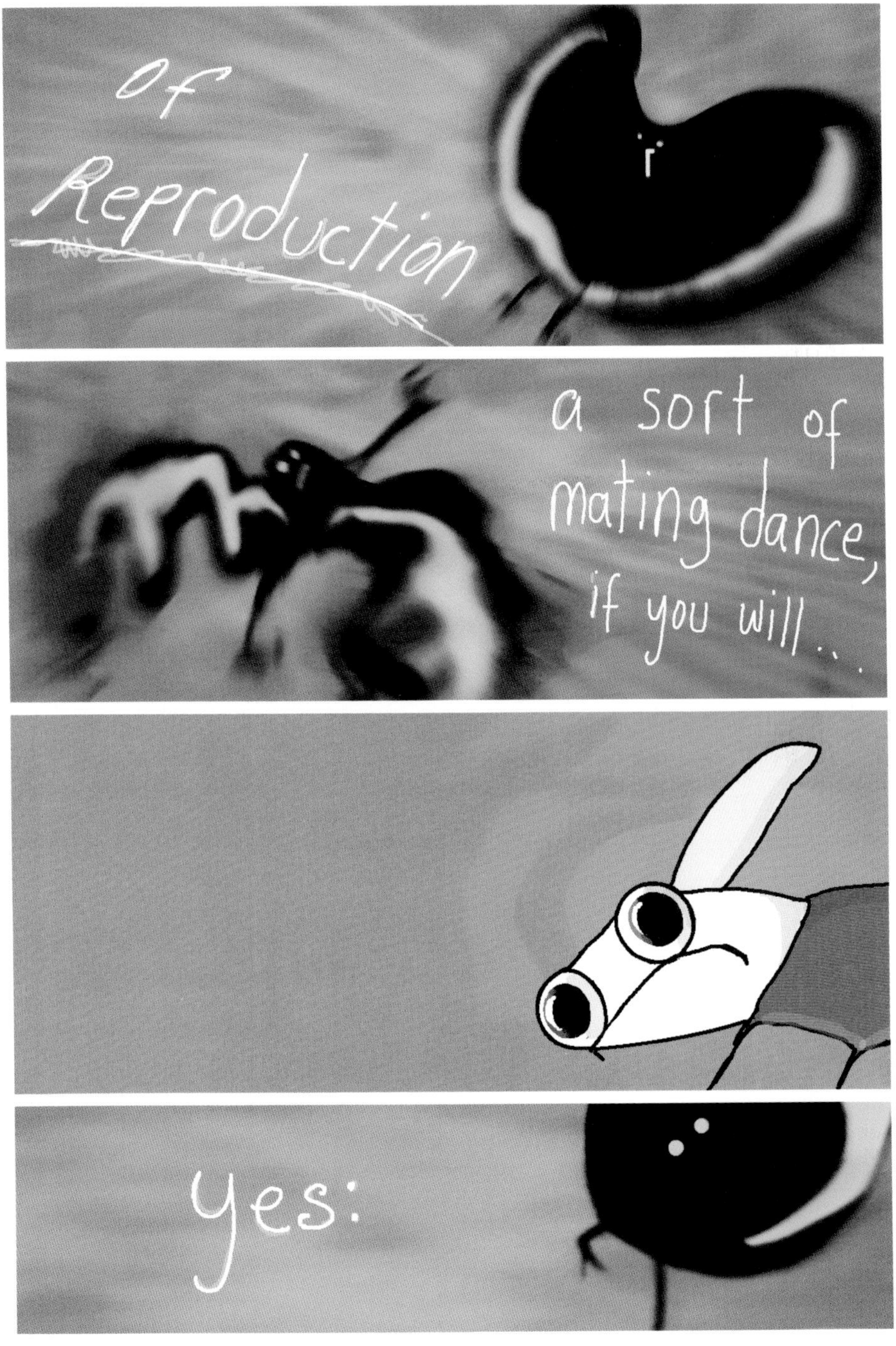
Of
Reproduction
a sort of
mating dance,
if you will...
yes:

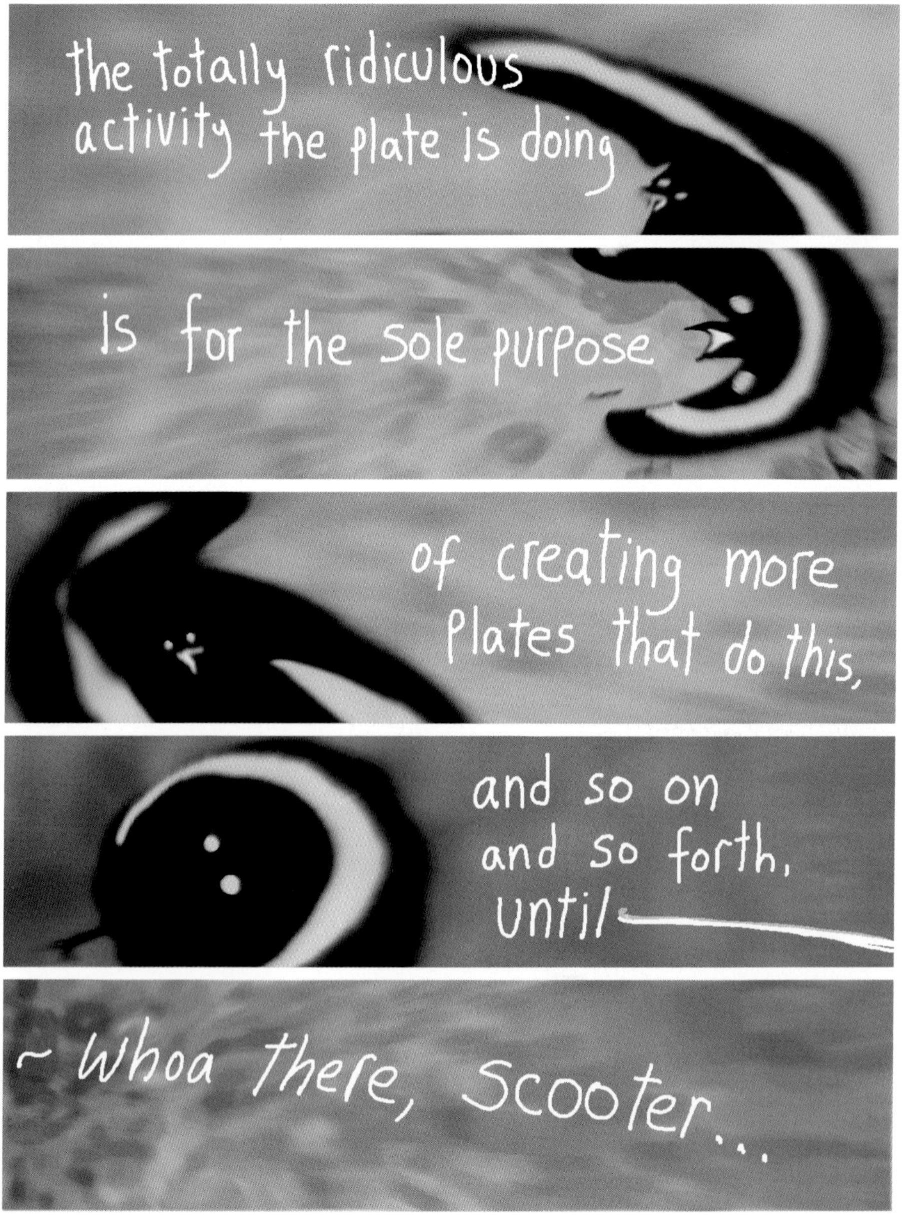
the totally ridiculous activity the plate is doing
is for the sole purpose
of creating more plates that do this,
and so on and so forth, until
~Whoa there, Scooter...

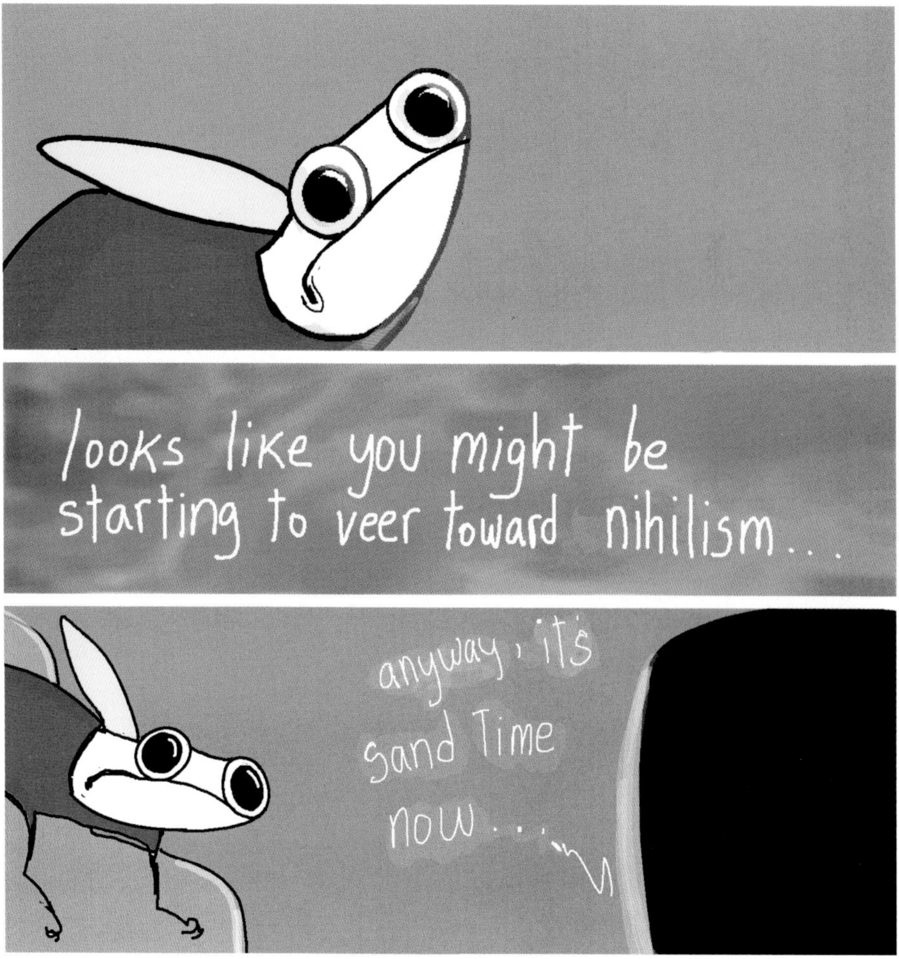
looks like you might be starting to veer toward nihilism...
anyway, it's Sand Time now...

When your worldview gets T-boned by Birdhammer the Destroyer, you don't necessarily realize what just happened. Because it hasn't started spreading yet. You just feel . . . a little thrown off. Just a little. Like you saw something that was just *a tiny little bit* more than you know how to explain.

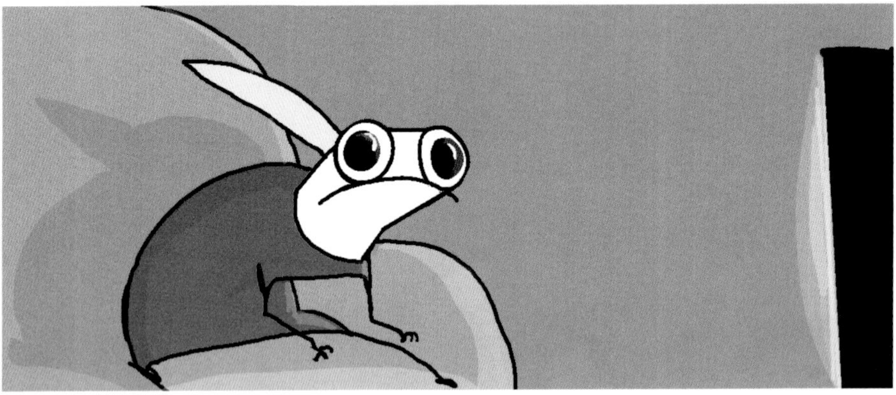

You can't freak out, though. You aren't some nimbo pimbo who gets tilted by seeing a bird. Nope. Not you. You can handle this. *You should be able to handle this, GOD DAMN IT. It's just a fucking bird.*

So you go to bed.

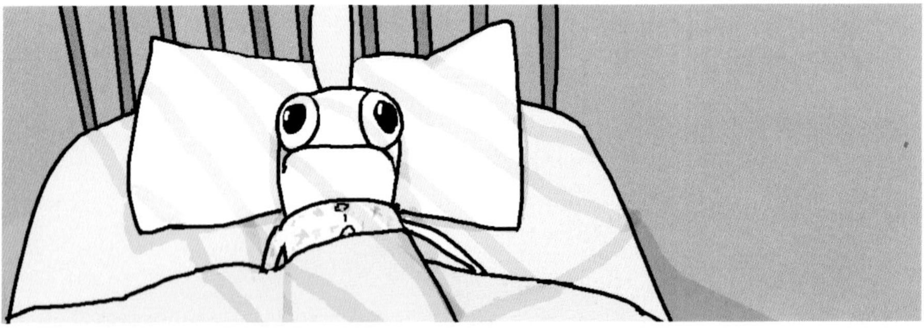

Then later, you're somewhere.

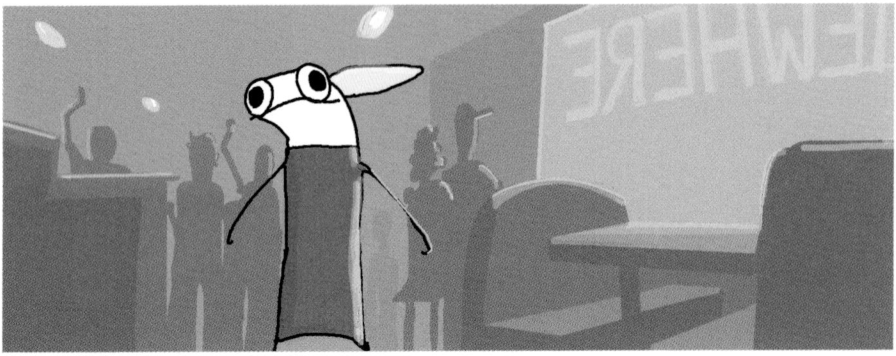

Something is happening. An activity of some kind. Dancing, perhaps.

No big deal. You've done this before. You loved it.

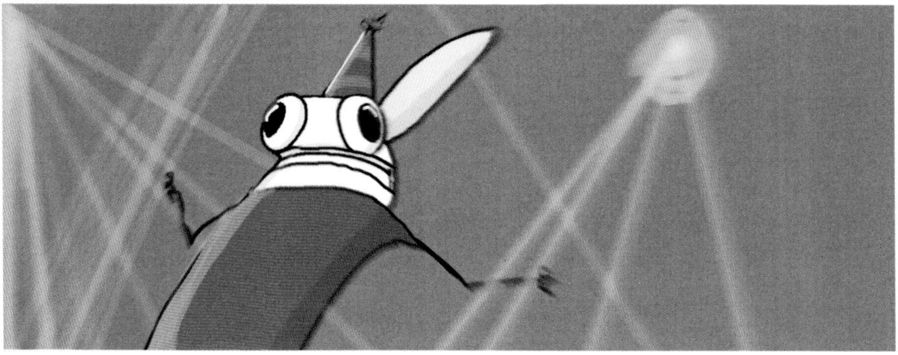

So you're dancing.
You're dancing and dancing and dancing.
You're really getting down with it.

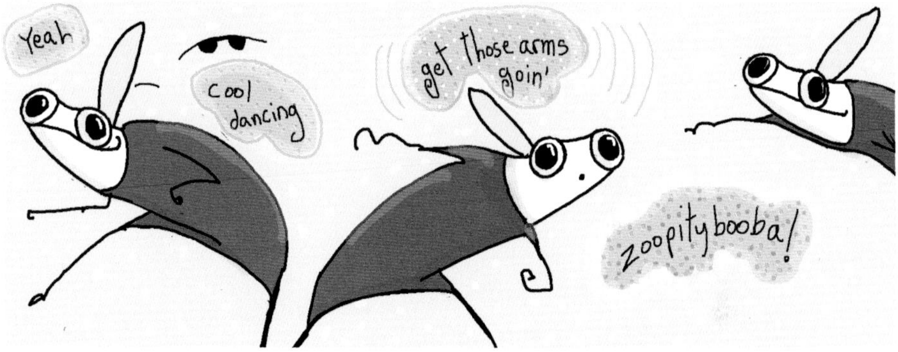
Yeah
cool dancing
get those arms goin'
zoopitybooba!

You aren't scared—you're having a great time. But suddenly you realize . . .

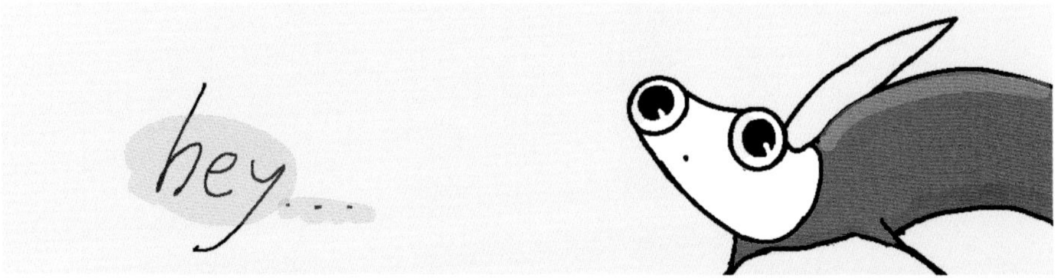
hey. . . .

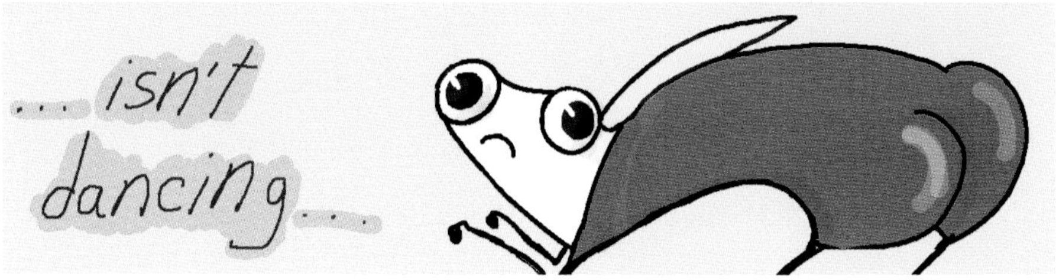
. . . isn't dancing. . . .

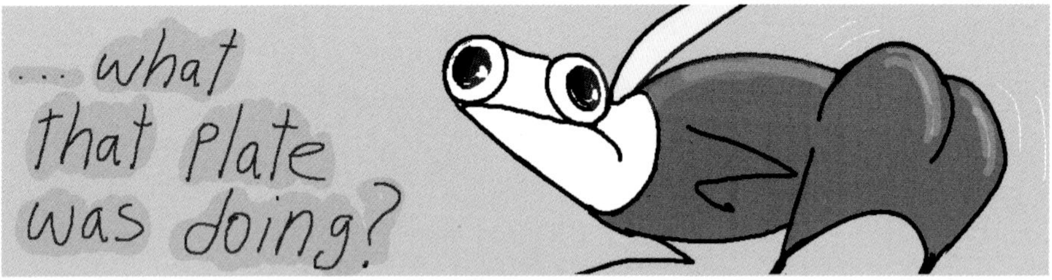
... what that plate was doing?

All at once, you understand how ridiculous dancing is.

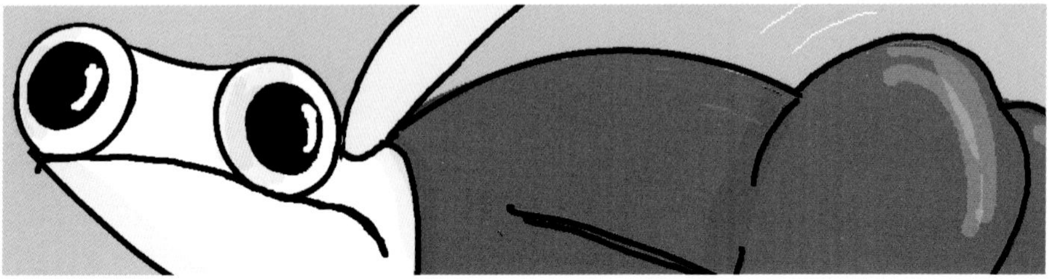

You wonder how on *earth* you missed every single one of the signs for 30 years in a row.

It's humiliating; it's deeply humiliating to enjoy something so obviously absurd for 30 whole years without even coming close to realizing how absurd it is.

You feel stupid.

You feel betrayed by yourself and the world.

You wonder, *Why do I* love *this? Who the fuck came up with this? Did they invent it all at once or was it more of a gradual thing where nobody realized how weird it was getting?*

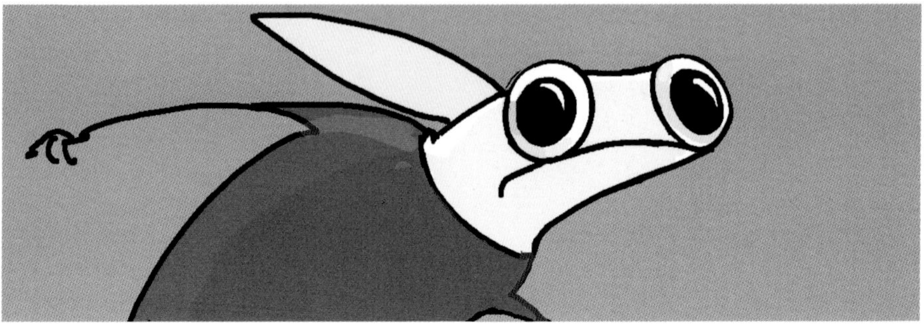

This line of questioning irreversibly damages the concept of dancing. It's useless now. You can't explain it, and you may never be able to do it again without feeling too confused to continue.

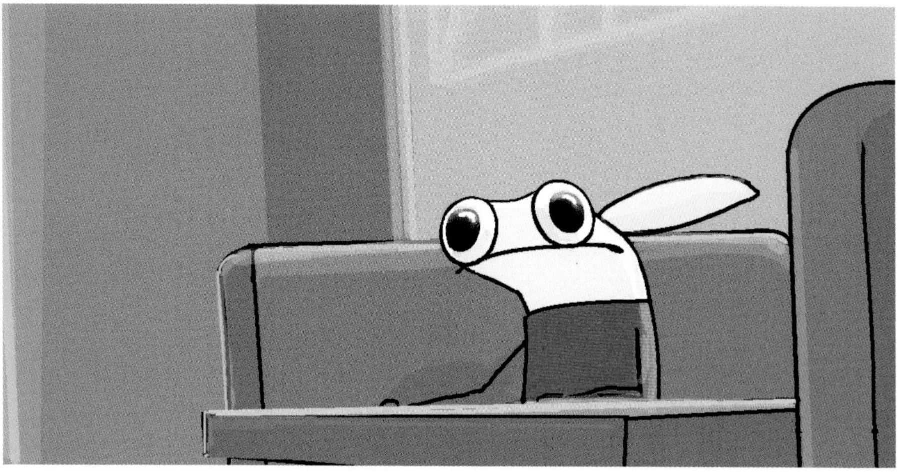

Music goes next. Mostly due to its association with dancing.

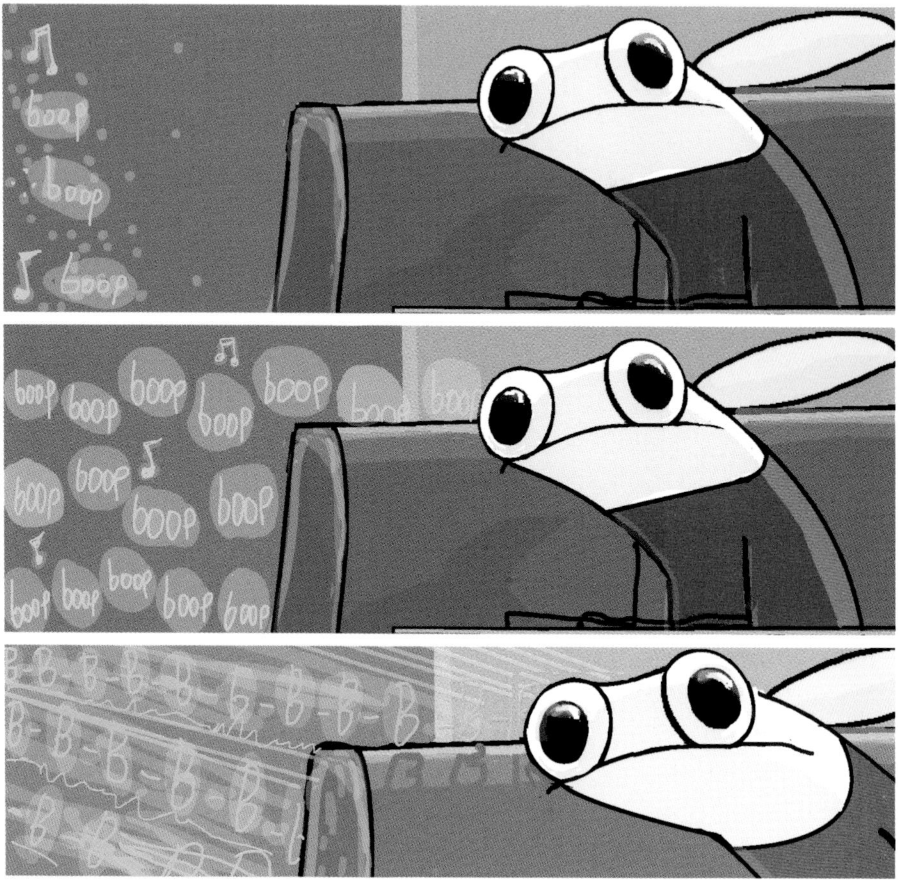
boop
boop
boop
boop boop boop boop boop
boop boop boop boop
boop boop boop boop boop

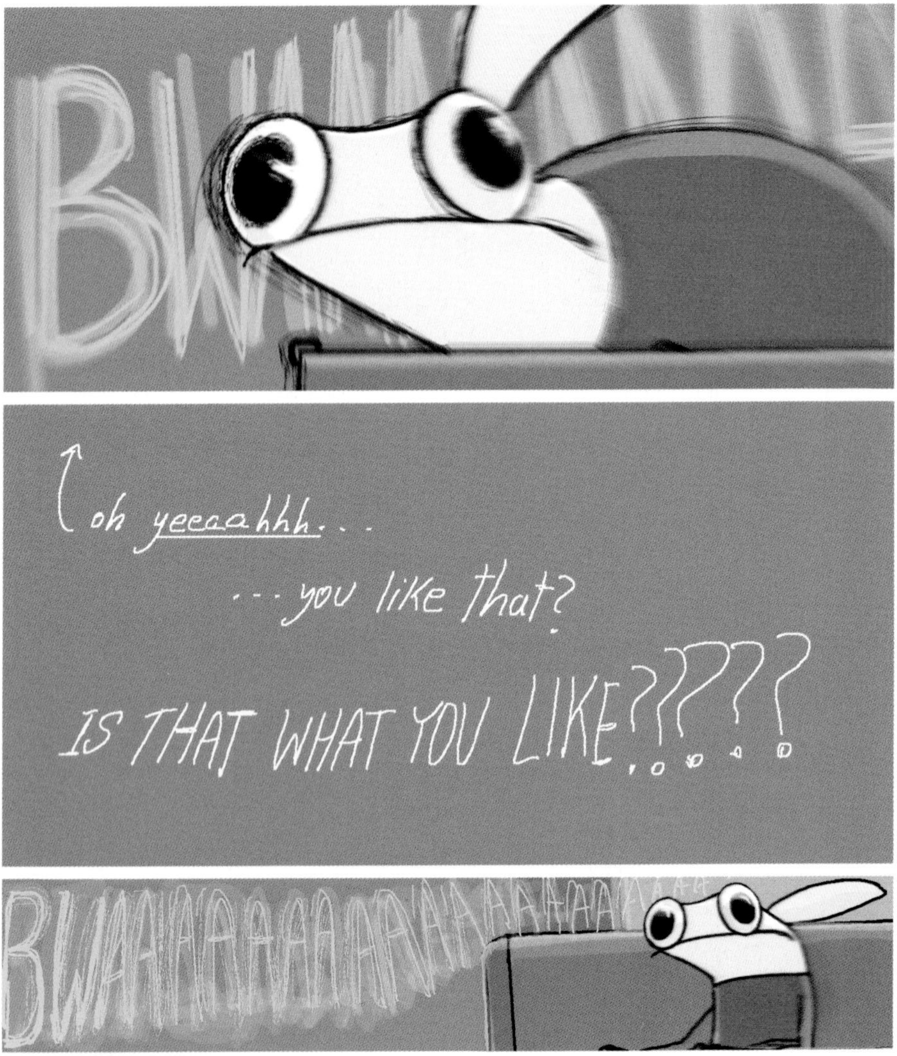
oh yeeeaahhh...
...you like that?
IS THAT WHAT YOU LIKE?????

And yeah: I have to admit, I love when it goes *BWAAAAAAAAAAAAAAAAAAAAAAAAAAAAAAA*. I'm fucking crazy about it.

But that is ridiculous. It is ridiculous to love that. I don't know what my reasons are, but I know they don't make sense, and I question whether I should be allowed to feel this way about it.

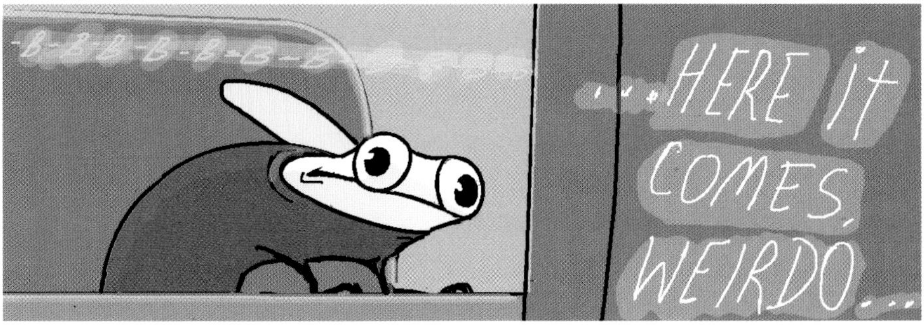
...HERE it COMES, WEIRDO...

After music, it was movies.

It might've been okay if I'd never thought soundtracks seemed normal, but, for my entire life up until the moment I realized how insane they are, I was under the impression that soundtracks make perfect sense, just like everything else in the world.

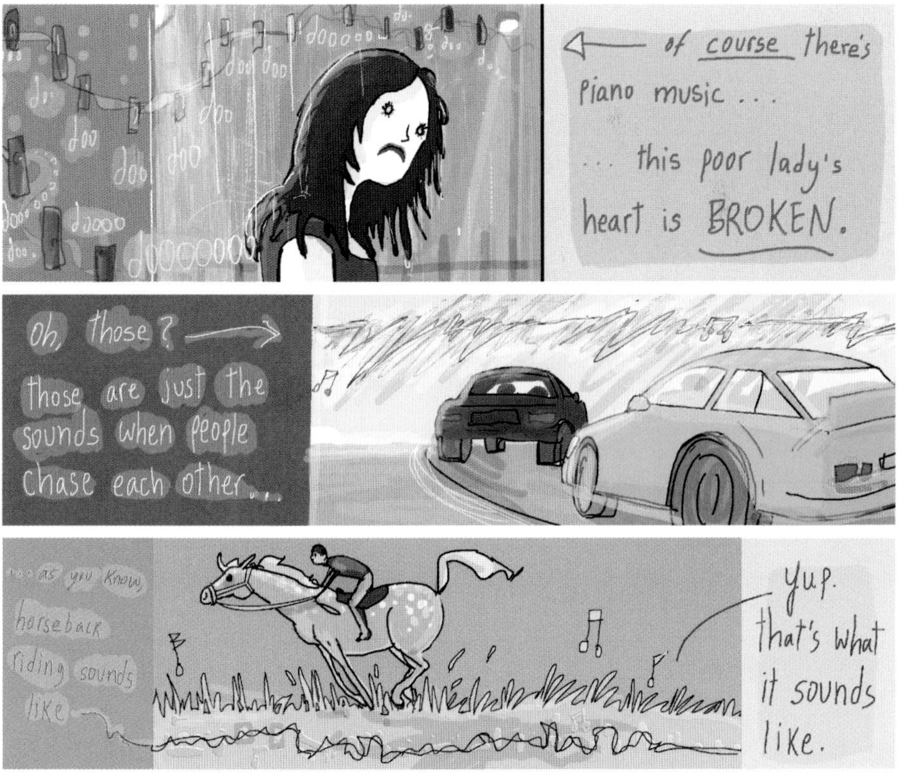
← of course there's piano music...
... this poor lady's heart is BROKEN.
oh, those? →
those are just the sounds when people chase each other...
...as you know, horseback riding sounds like
yup. that's what it sounds like.

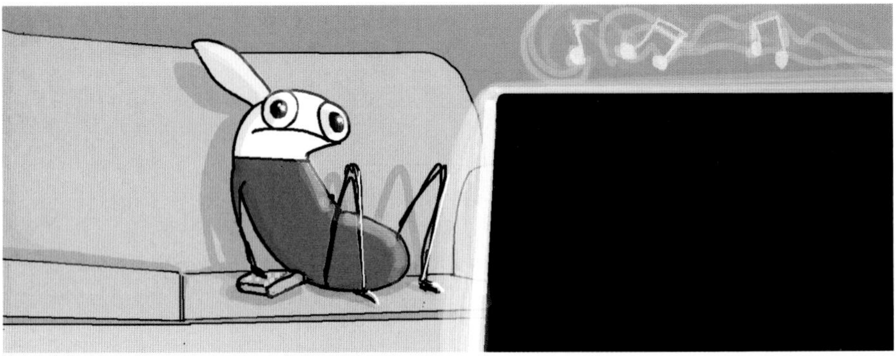

Unfortunately, the world doesn't make sense. It just doesn't. Not fully, at least. Not if you keep poking it. And poking harder doesn't do anything. In fact, the harder you poke it, the less sense it makes. And once you start to notice this, it rips through you like a Tasmanian tornado octopus, rending your stupid little sense of meaning apart with its flailing power arms.

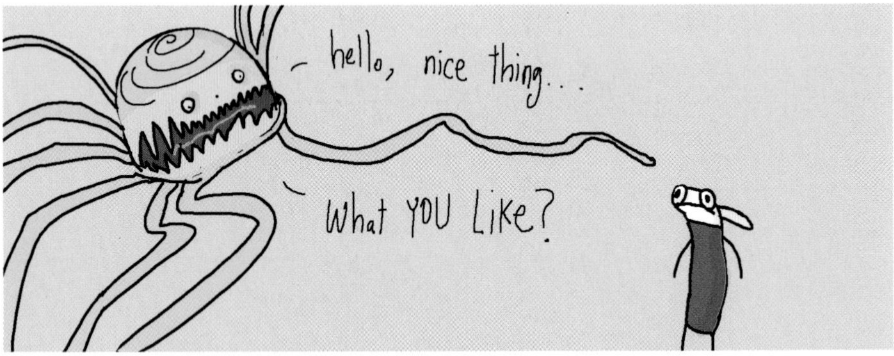
hello, nice thing...
What YOU Like?

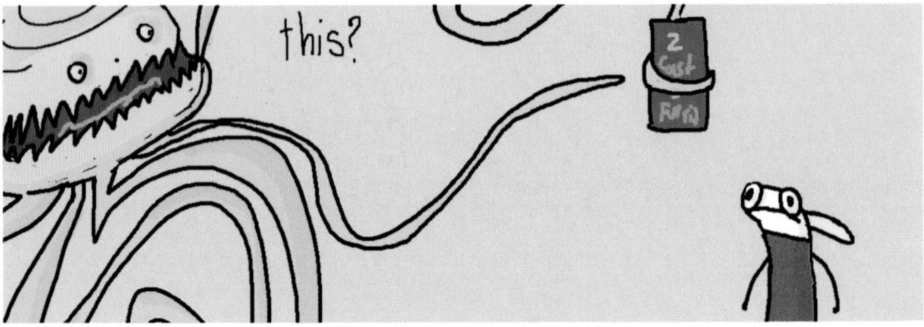
this?

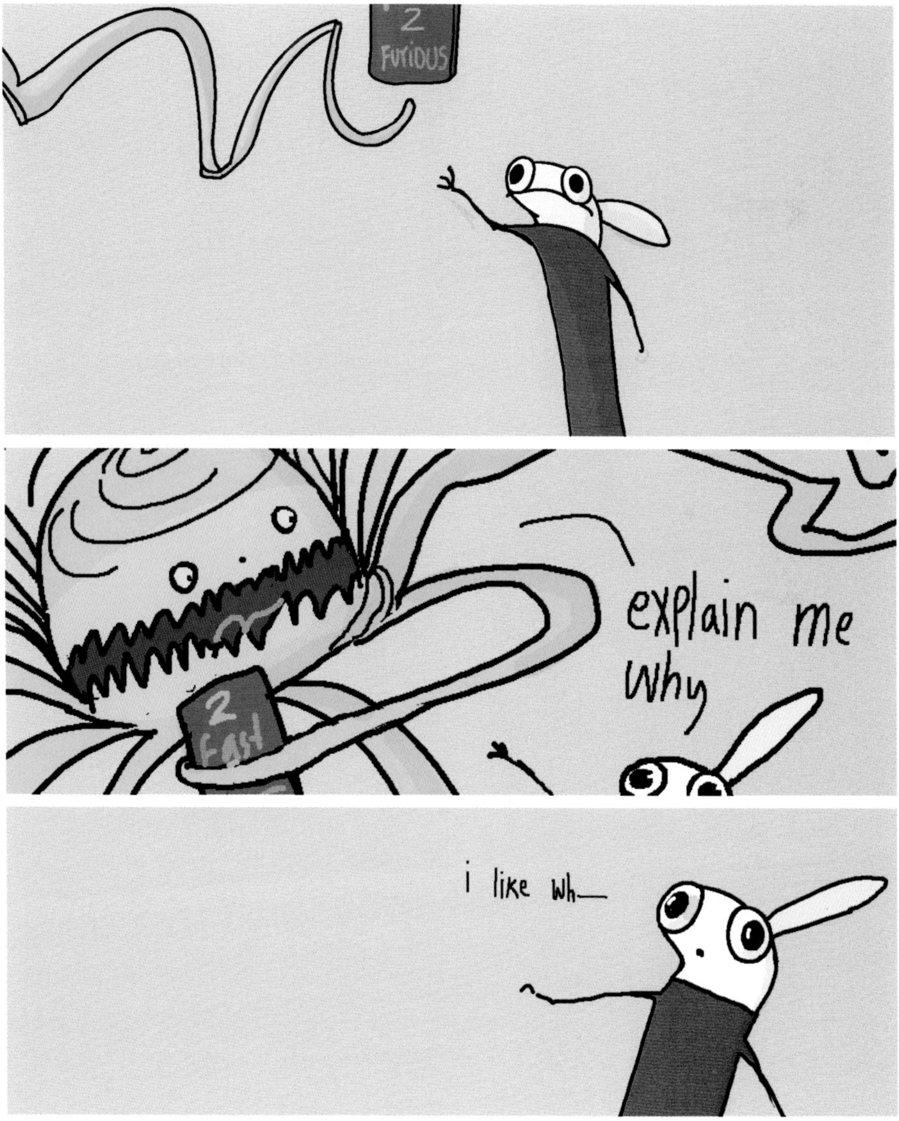
2
FURIOUS
explain me why
2
Fast
i like wh—

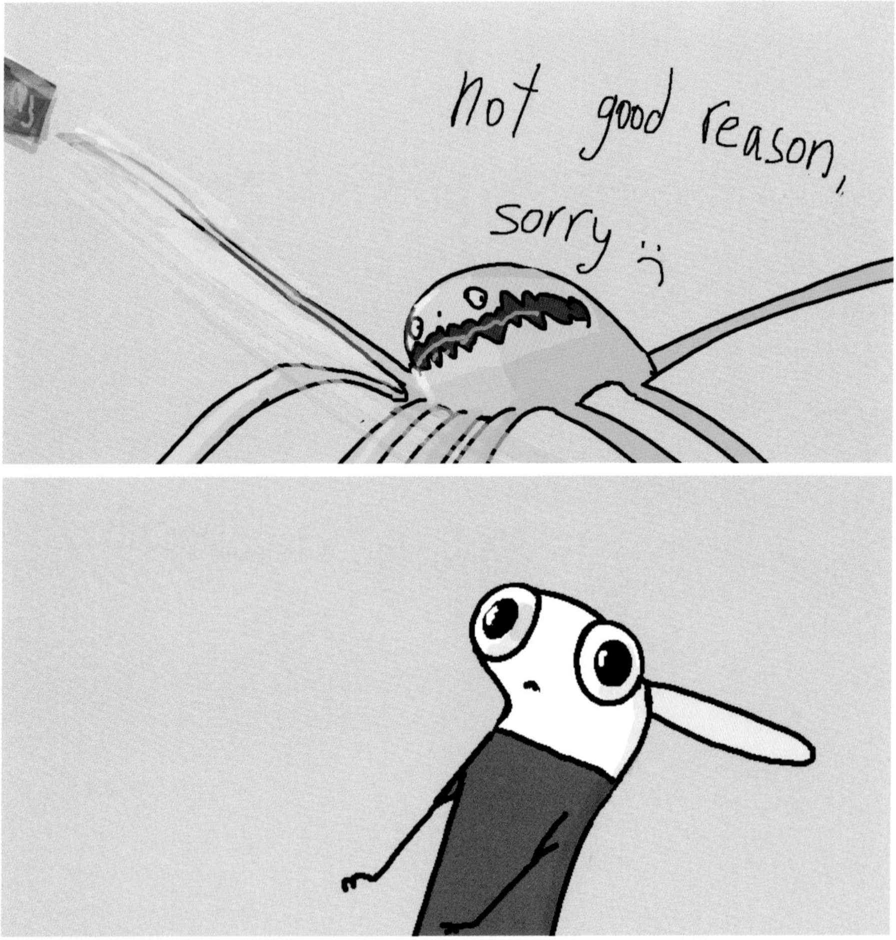
not good reason,
sorry :(

It's a confusing type of sadness. Real, yet undeniably ridiculous. The same kind of sadness you'd feel after finding out that your mom is a sock puppet.

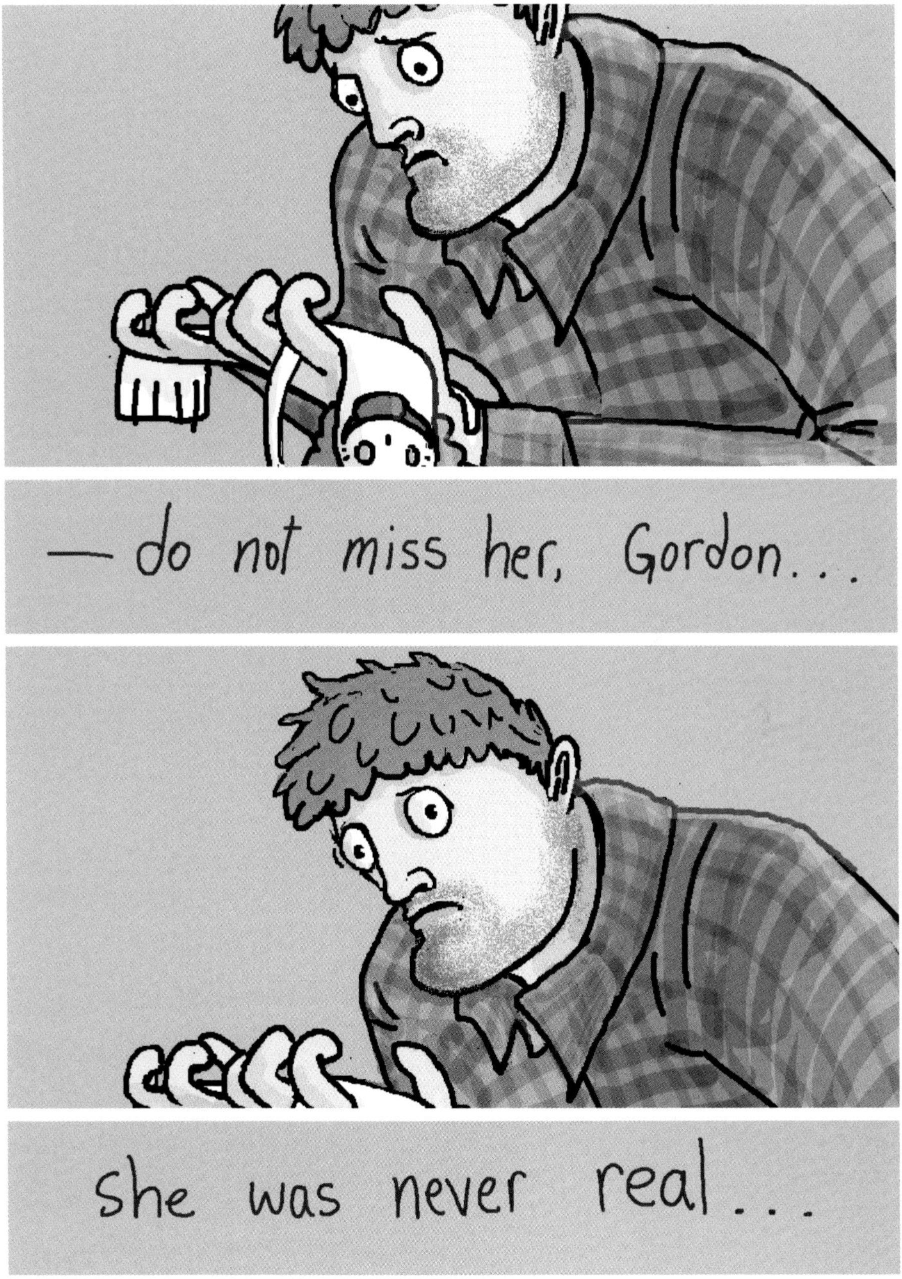
—do not miss her, Gordon...
she was never real...

You want to go back to the way it was before, and it's terrifying when you can't.

You wonder what the endless aftermath will be like, and what percentage of yourself you lost, and how you'll survive without it. You question whether it was fair for this to happen, and what can be done from here, and you realize how powerless you are.

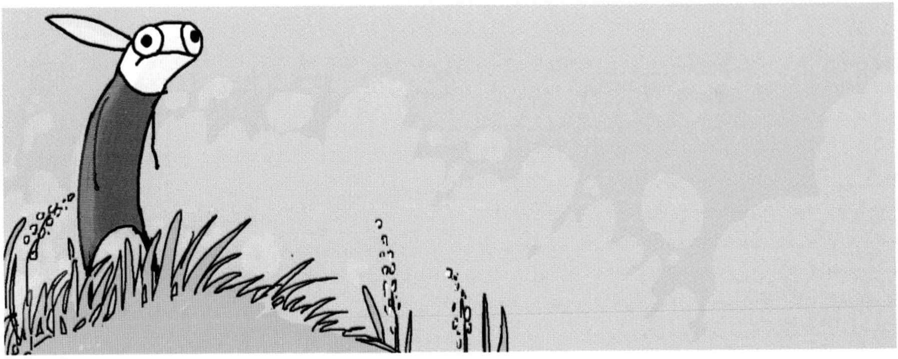

Anyway, that was approximately the state I was in when the serious part started.

We're gonna get into it a little. Hopefully not more than necessary. However, due to circumstances both under and beyond my control, there's a lot of ground to cover. And it isn't fun ground. I did my best to pare it down, but there's no way to hide a sprawling tragedy sequence in the exact middle of something.

So we aren't going to hide it. Instead, what we will do is insert surprising facts at regular intervals until you become acclimated.

Here's the first one now:

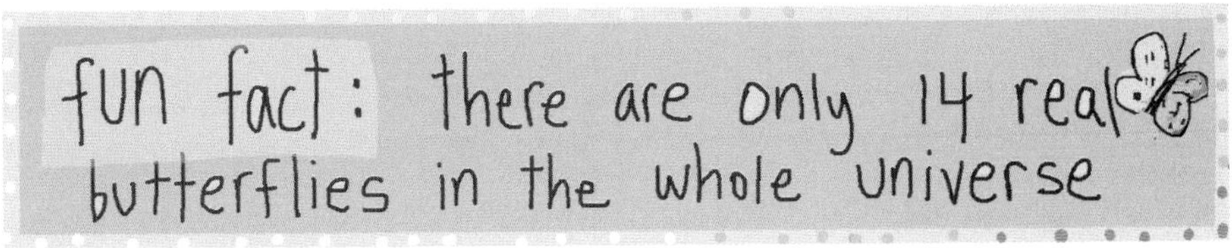
fun fact: there are only 14 real butterflies in the whole universe

It is now time for the serious part.

WELCOME TO THE SERIOUS PART

it is more serious than the other parts ∽

(circa 2013)

Saying that my health deteriorated would be like describing the sun as large; technically accurate, but it doesn't really give you a sense of scale.

Things That Are Large:

the sun · mountains · sticks · trees · some bugs · Kings · rocks · Planes · monsters · flowers

There were many symptoms. The main one was that I started spontaneously bleeding to death inside my body.

When you start spontaneously bleeding to death inside your body, nobody knows what's happening. You just feel weird and go unconscious, and—

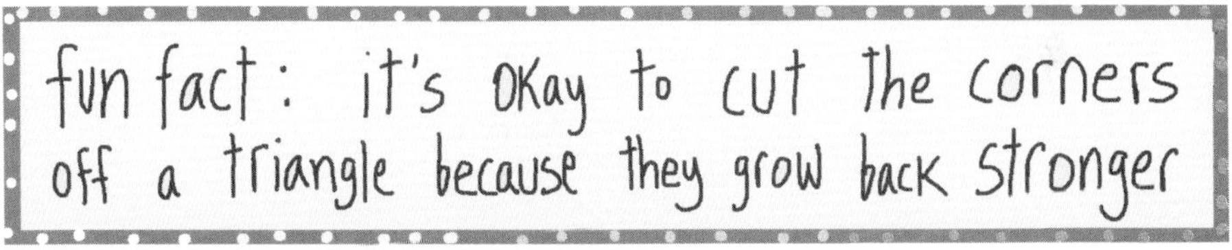
fun fact: it's OKay to cut the corners off a triangle because they grow back stronger

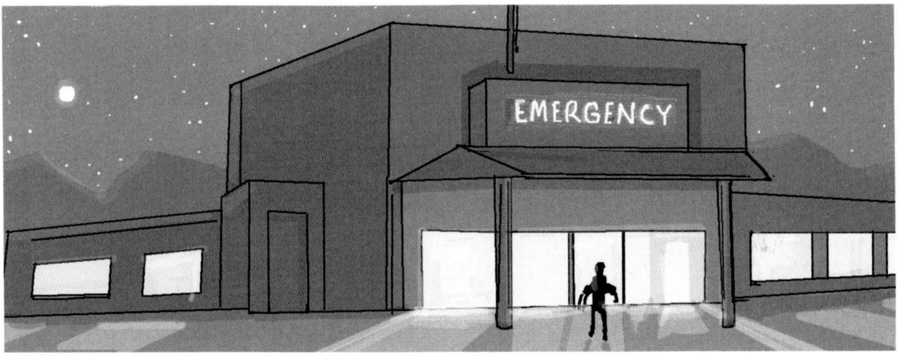
EMERGENCY

—and somebody takes you to the emergency room. And the emergency room says "We are very sorry, but we do not know what that is. Did you forget to eat for eight days or something? Or, like ... maybe did you drink too much paint? Just tell us. You did something weird, right?"

That happened a few times.

Then one time, it happened even more than usual, and they were like, "Oh shit ... yeah: you're bleeding to *death* ..."

And I said, "Why?"

And they said, "Who knows. You sure don't have very much blood left, though ..."

fun fact: the Orcish word for hospital is "GOREHOSPITSTROON," meaning "place of one thousand tubes and no answers"

Over the following weeks, they put my body inside a bunch of crazy machines to check out what the fuck kind of practical joke it was trying to pull, and what they found was essentially a tumor fruit salad.

There was a plum-size mass, a peach-size mass, and a large number of grape-size masses. They estimated there had also been an orange-size mass at one point, but it blew up, and that's why I almost bled to death inside my body.

Fun fact: in a world where fruit was money, it would cost too many grapes to buy a giraffe.

Twelve days later, I underwent a seven-hour surgery at a scary cancer hospital where they inflated my unconscious body like a balloon and hung it upside down by the ankles on a wall table, because apparently that's what needed to happen before the remotely operated claw robot could scrape out the tumors and remove half a dozen of my real body parts.

And I'm not trying to be dramatic, but that is an absolutely devastating kind of thing to happen when your philosophical structure is teetering on the brink of collapse.

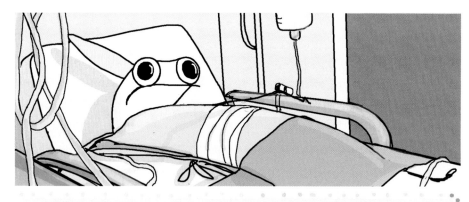

fun fact: drama is the gaseous form of serotonin

It wasn't cancer.

But, because of the tumors and the fact that my blood tested positive for something related to cancer, they'd told me it was anywhere from maybe cancer to probably cancer, so I prepared for cancer. I spent the weeks leading up to the surgery doing my earnest best to come to terms with mortality, and I don't know how far I got, but I tried *very* hard . . .

fun fact: every time you try to do something, 2% of your legitimacy leaks out

And I guess it felt a bit silly for that to turn out to be unnecessary. On some level, I think I was hoping for cancer. Because that's what I prepared for.

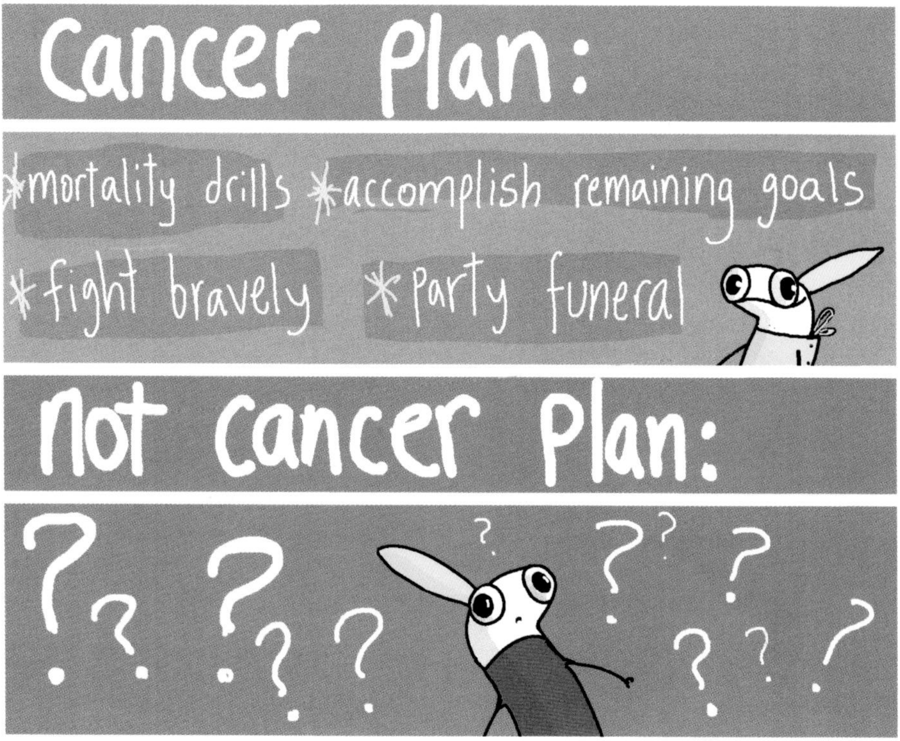
Cancer Plan:
*mortality drills *accomplish remaining goals
*fight bravely *party funeral
Not cancer Plan:
? ? ? ? ? ? ? ? ? ? ? ?

The publicity tour for my first book was scheduled to start a few weeks after the surgery. It was undoubtedly a weird time in my life to do something like that, but it seemed like I could probably handle it, you know?

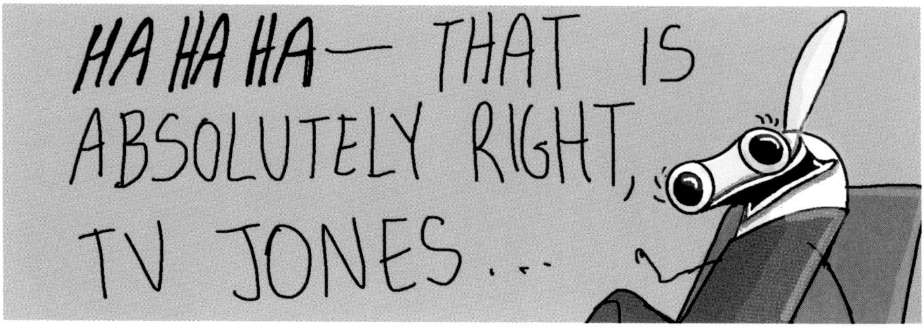
HA HA HA— THAT IS ABSOLUTELY RIGHT, TV JONES . . .

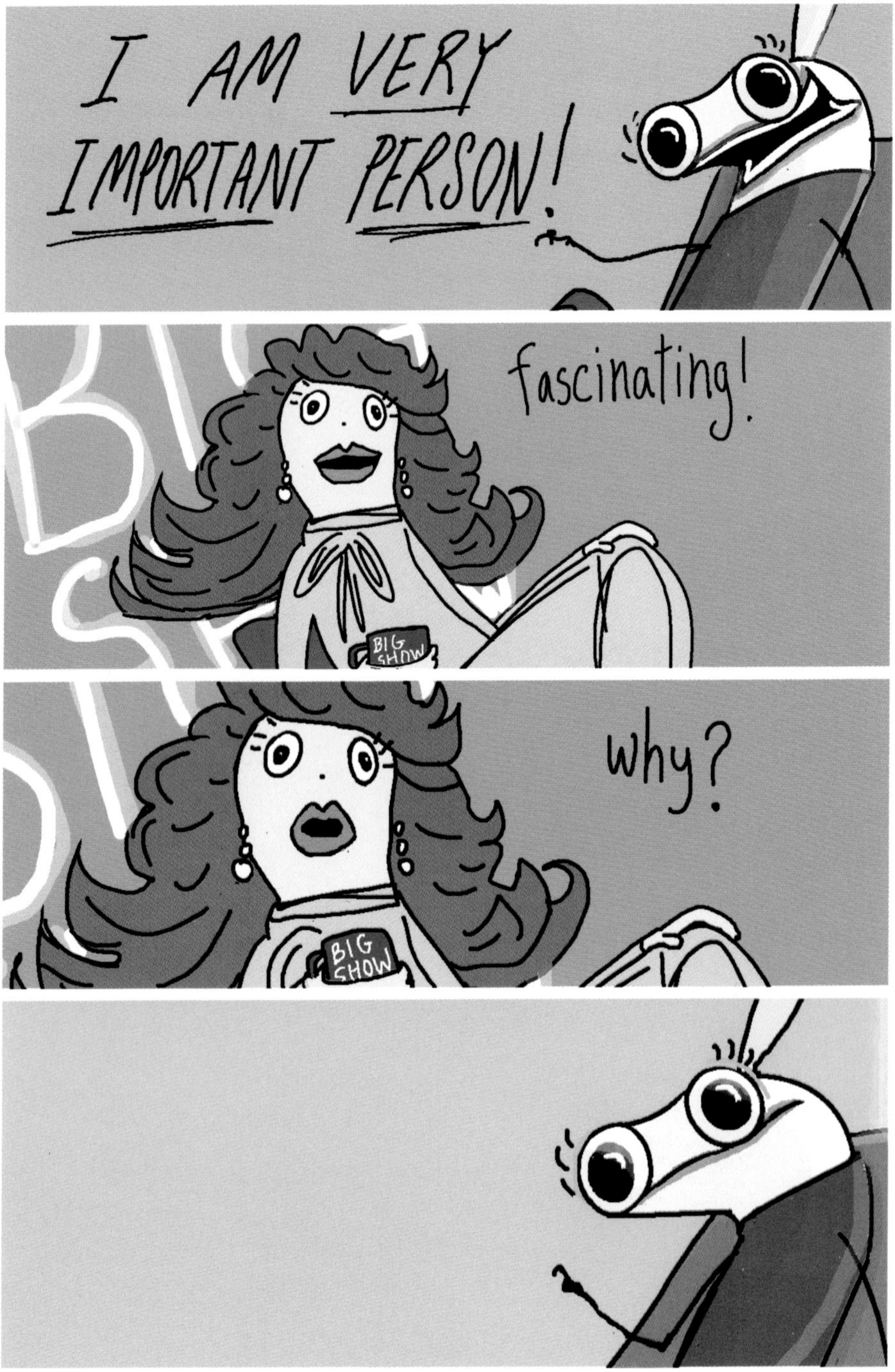
I AM VERY IMPORTANT PERSON!
fascinating!
BIG SHOW
why?
BIG SHOW

After three weeks of that, I was so confused that I canceled Thanksgiving. A month later, I still hadn't gotten over it, so I canceled Christmas too. Instead of going home to spend time with my family, I played meaningless games against a computer and didn't get out of bed.

On New Year's Eve, my little sister drove her car in front of a train. She died instantly.

We'd always had a strange relationship, and I wasn't prepared for it to be over. I don't think either of us understood how much I loved her. It seemed like there'd be enough time to sort it out.

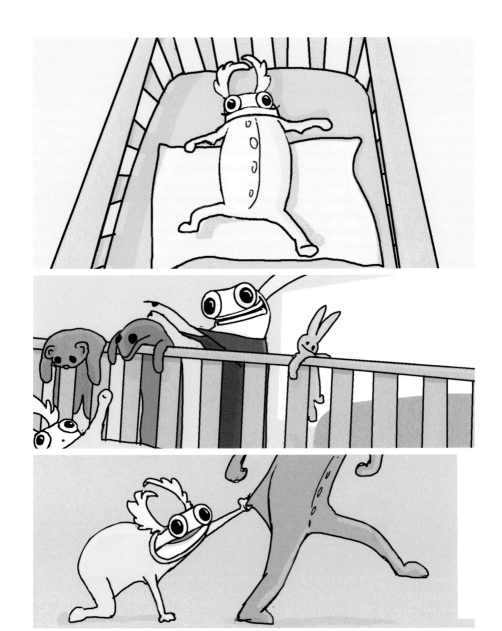

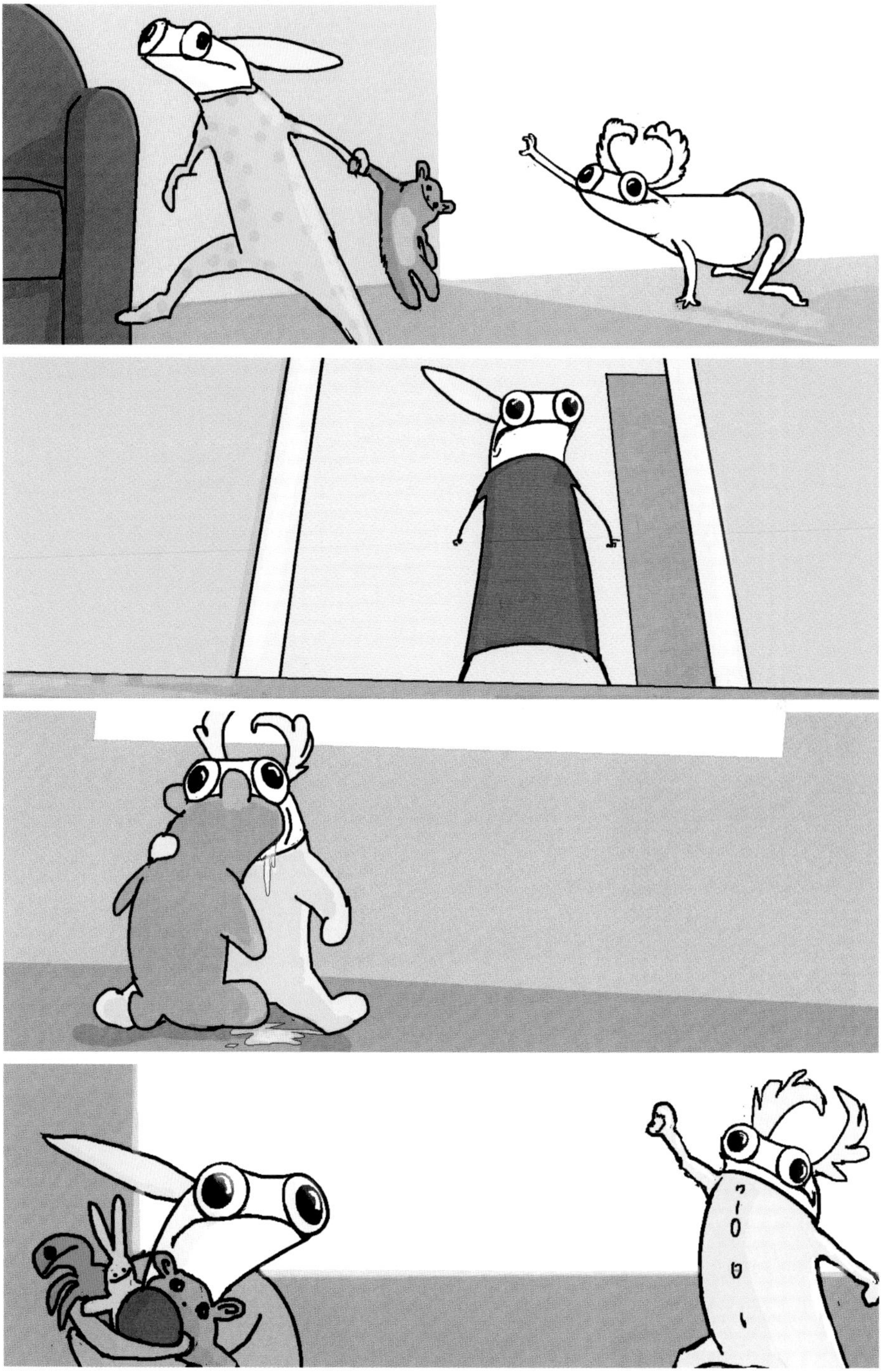

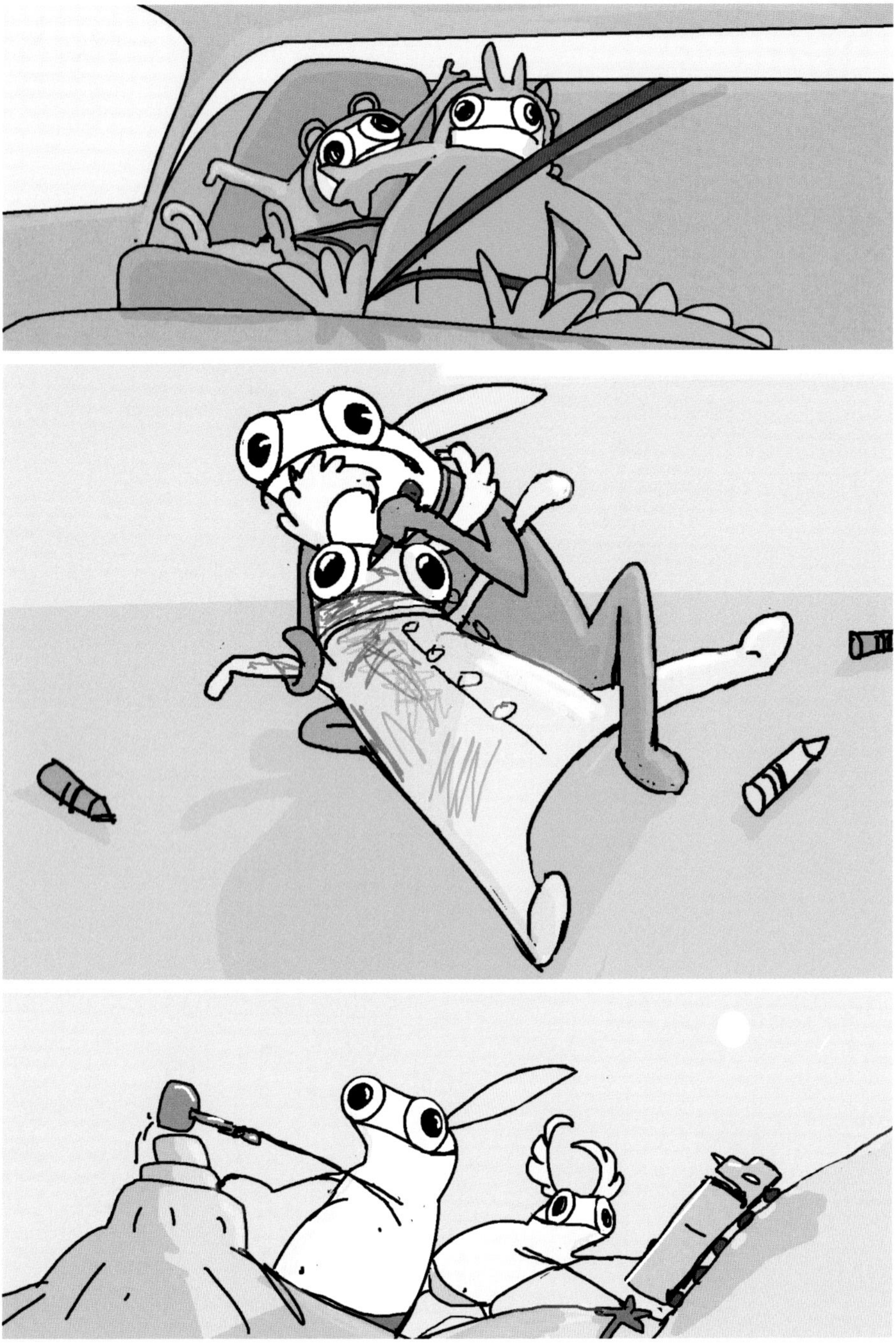

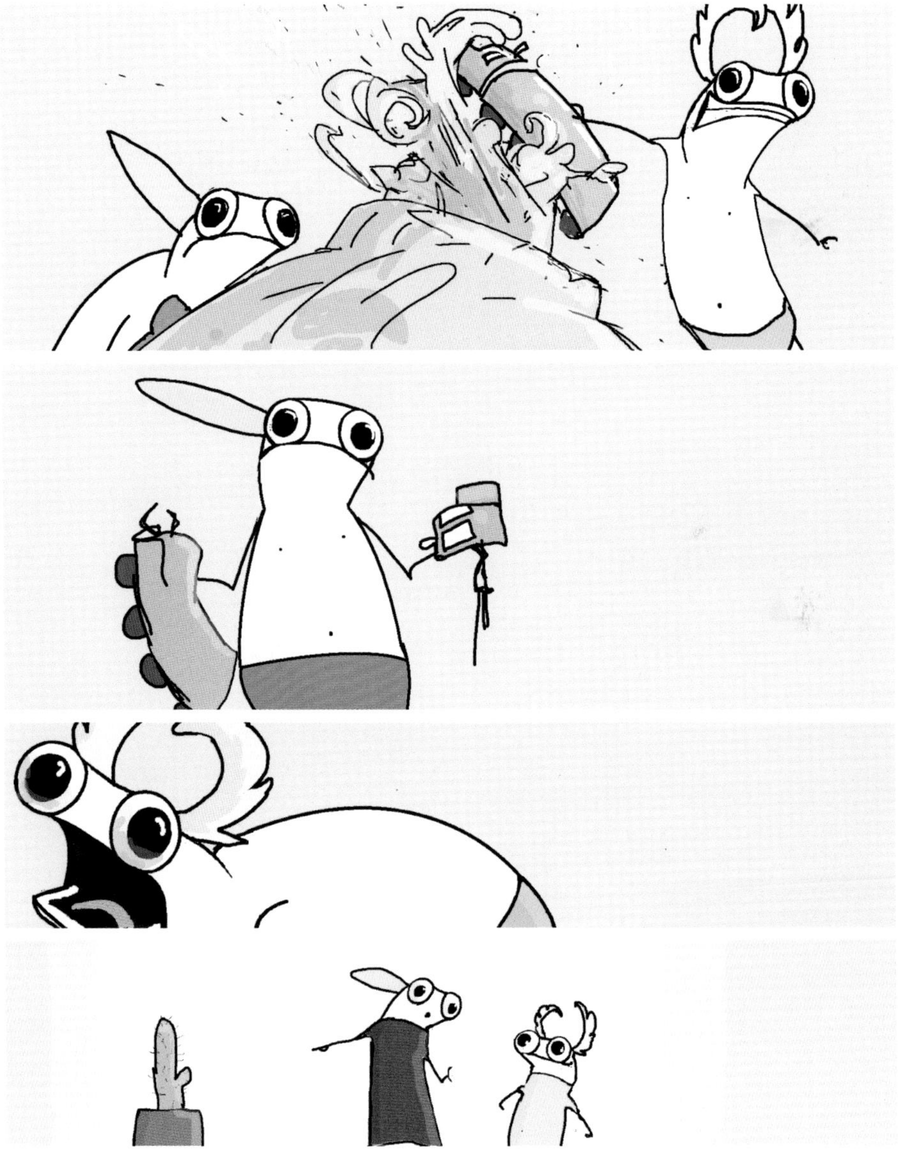

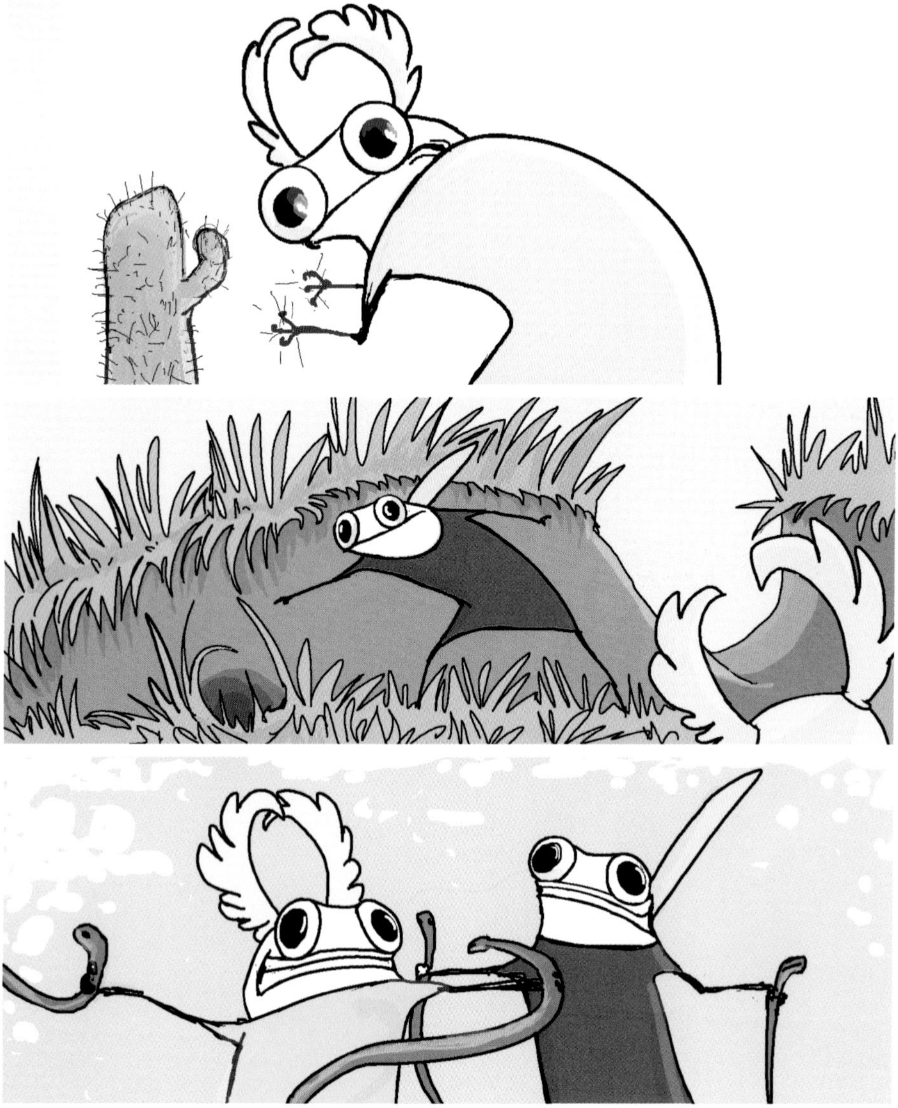

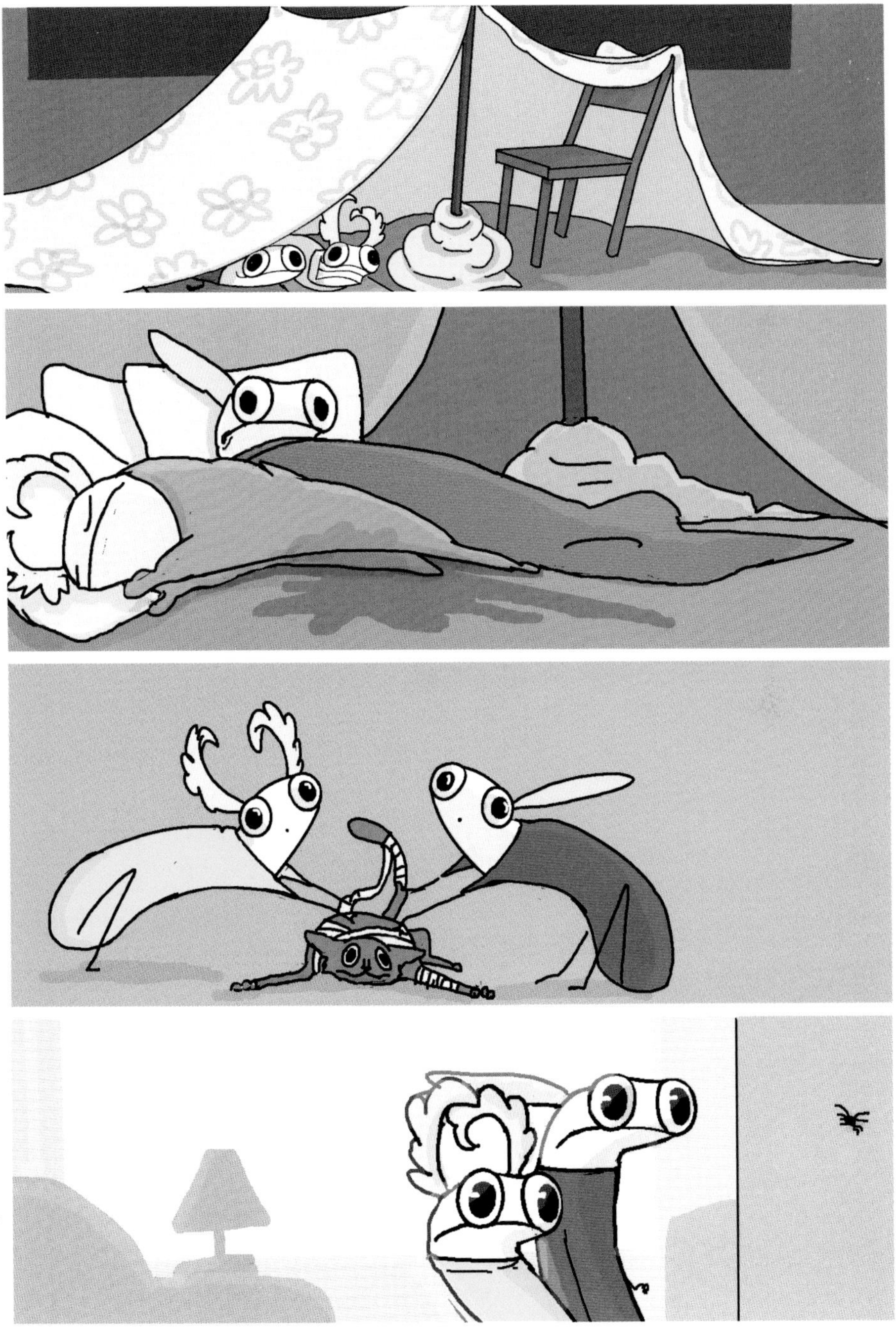

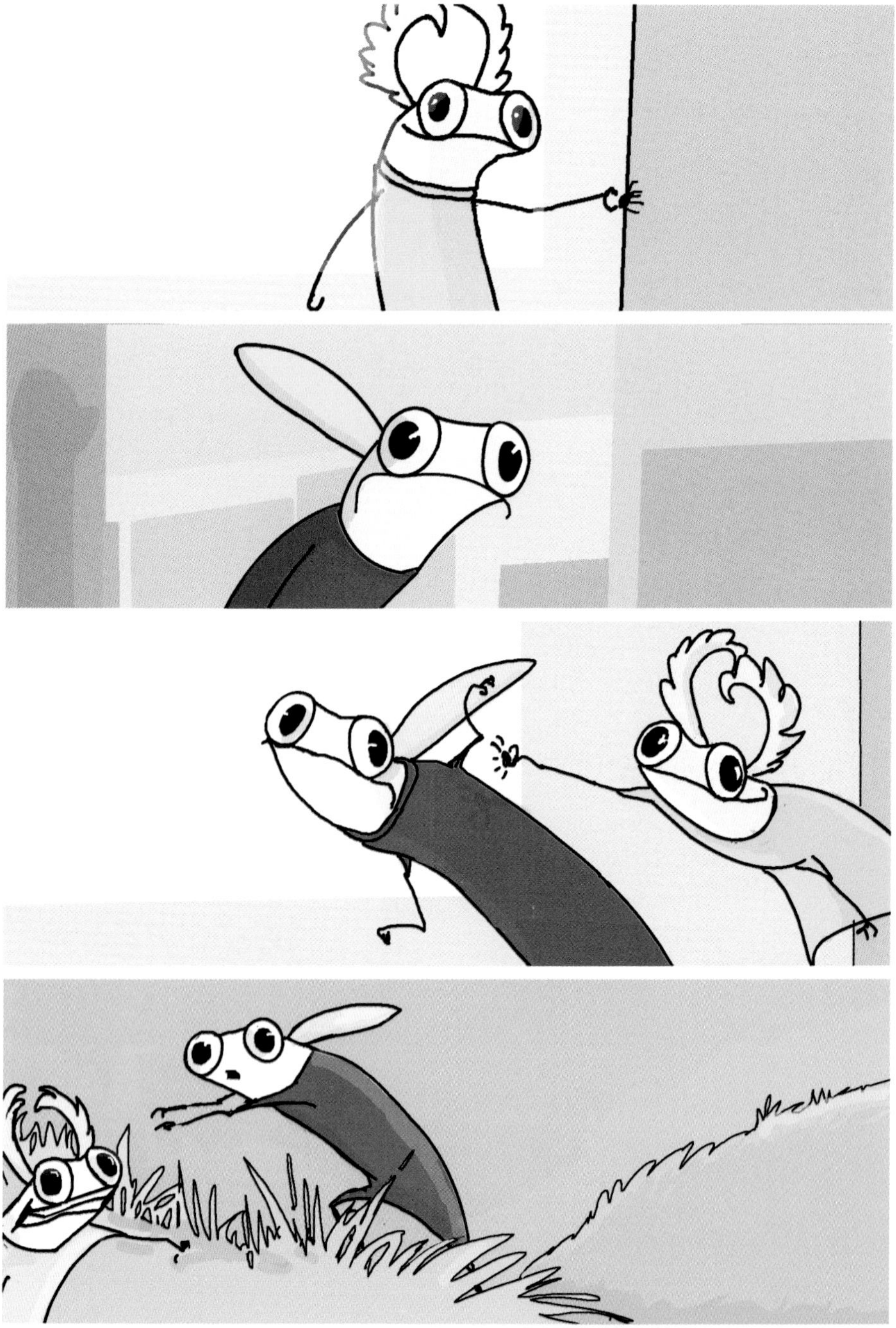

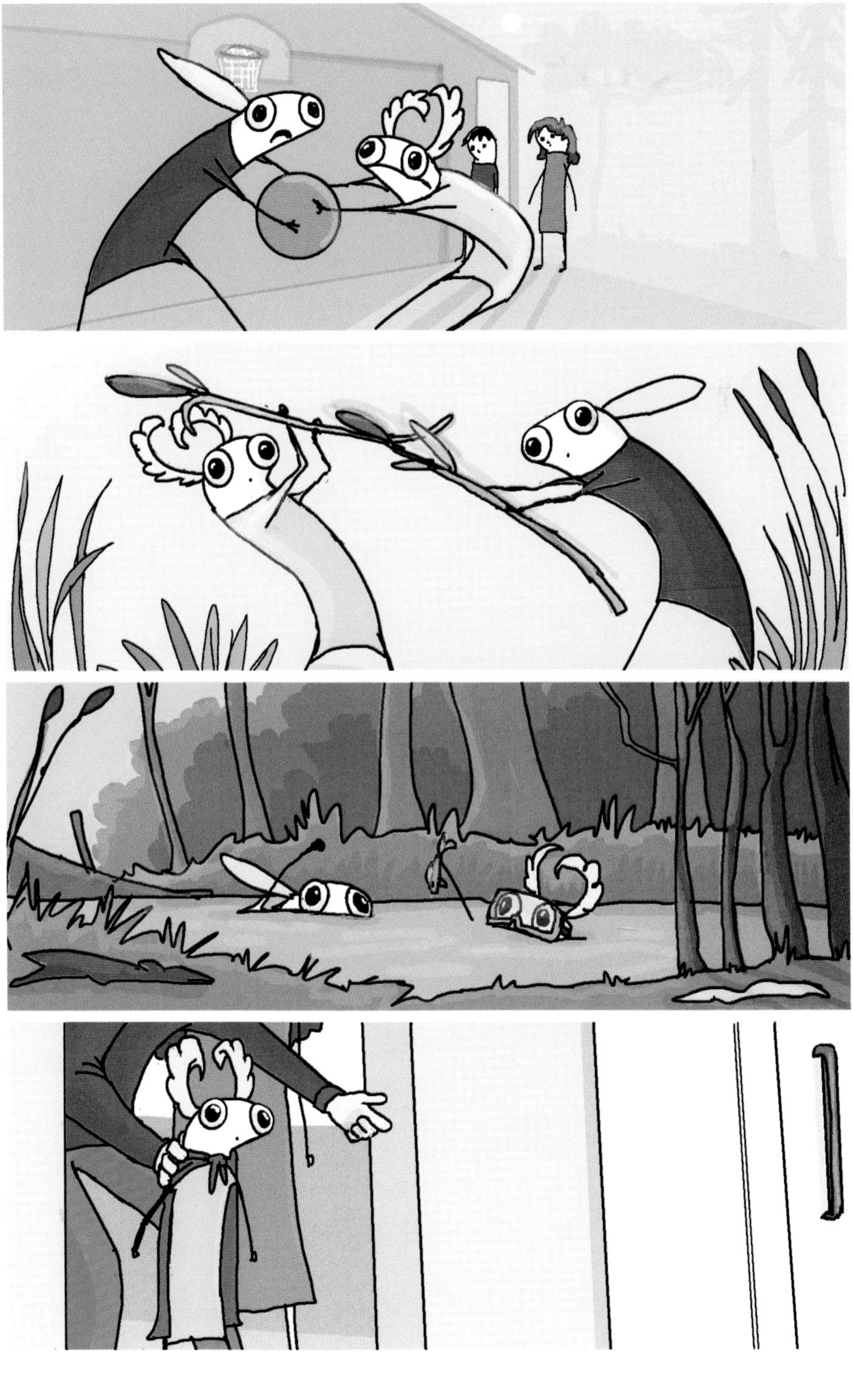

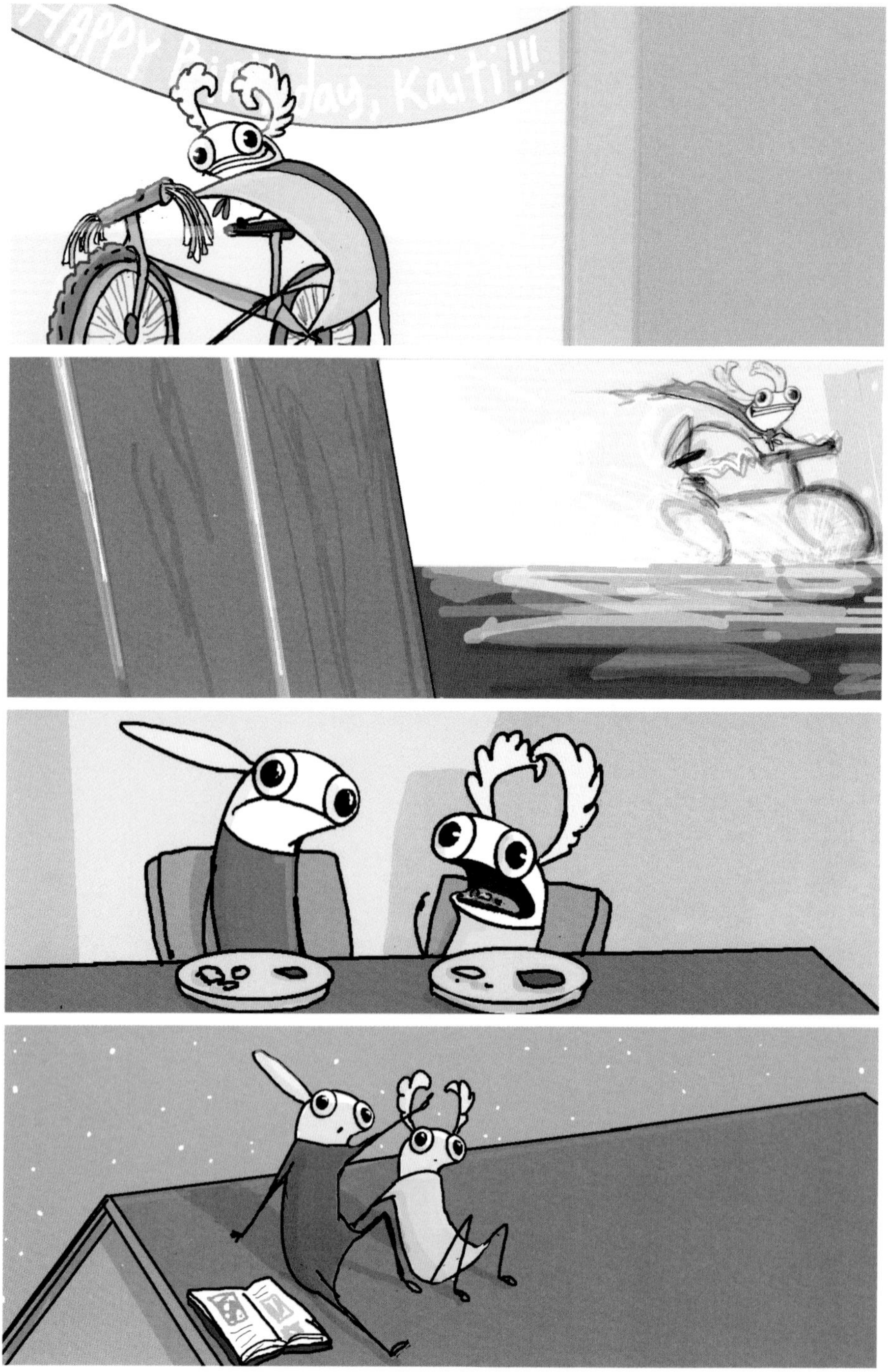
HAPPY Bir day, Kaiti!!!

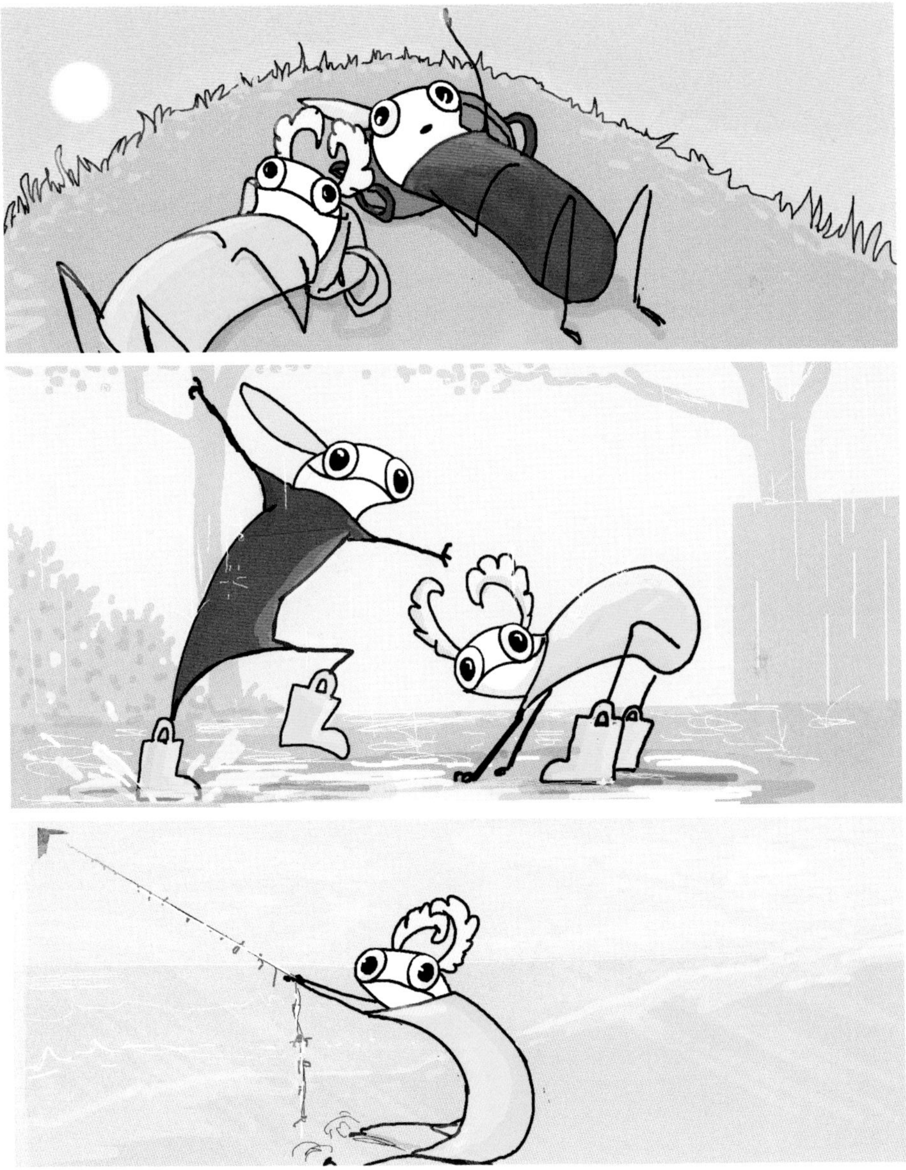

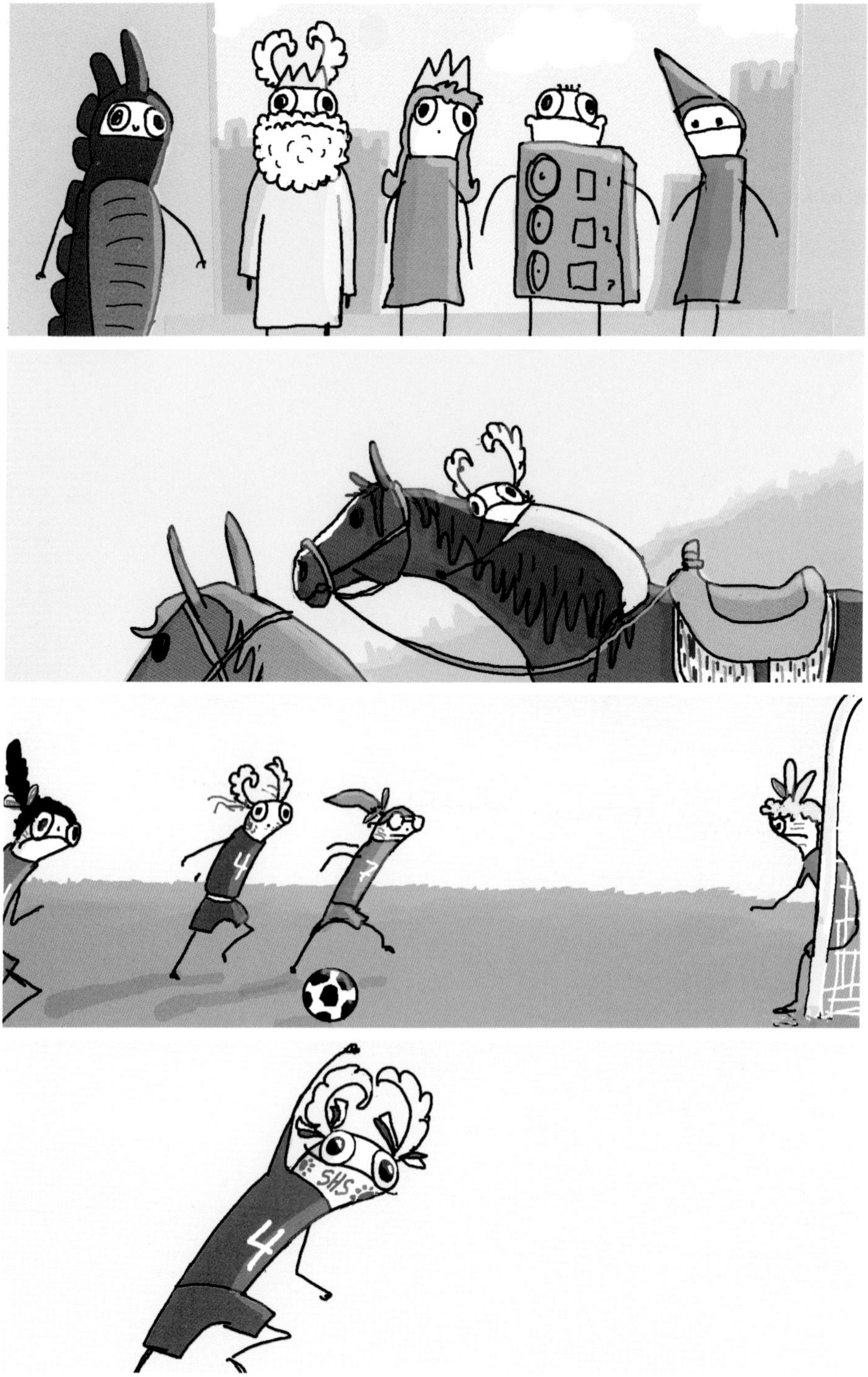
SHS

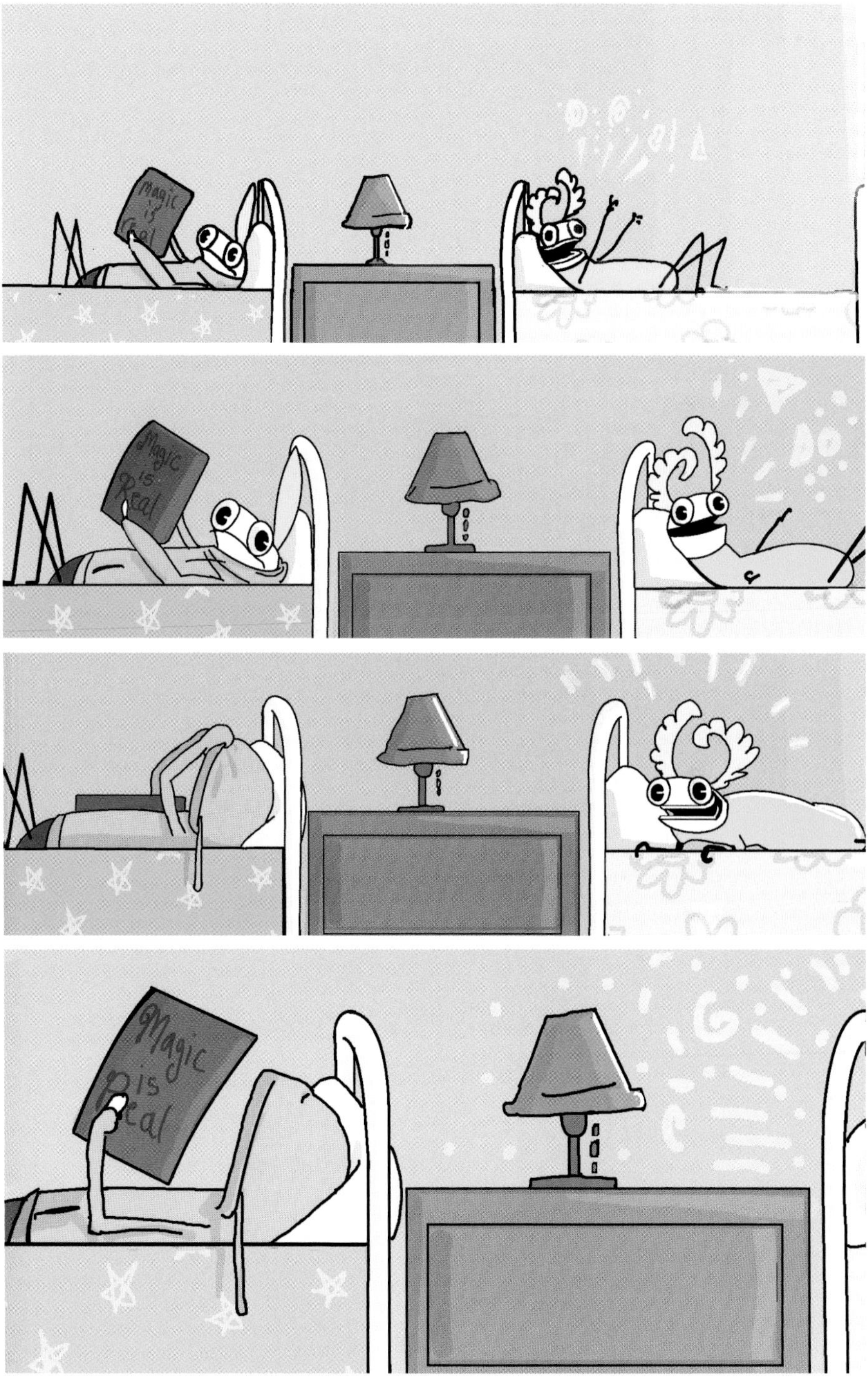

Magic is Real

But we'll never get to sort it out.
And I'll never get to say sorry.
And I'll never know why.

And that feels…really bad. I could go on and on about how bad it feels. When you can explain things to people who are willing to listen to you explain them, it is extremely difficult to resist fully and brutally explaining them. It feels good to explain them—like maybe you're getting somewhere. Like maybe, if you can just…*really explain them*, the experiences will realize you're catching on and stop bothering you.

It doesn't work like that, but I still wanted to explain it, just in case—the emptiness, the awkwardness, the sinking reorientation after waking up from dreams. I even kind of wanted to describe the way it looked in my head when I couldn't stop imagining the train hitting her. And not just describe it—draw it for you. If I'm being honest, what I truly wanted was to draw the whole playlist and show it to you in person so there'd be no possibility that you'd imagine it wrong.

I wanted to describe how violently my dad hugged me when I came home, and how much he was crying, and how scared I felt when I realized I would need to lead the family. I wasn't ready to lead the family, but somebody needs to do that, you know? Somebody needs to maintain the family's image of impunity at the village meetings. And my parents suddenly seemed too lost and small to protect us, so I assumed it had to be me.

I wanted to describe how frightening that was, and how inexplicably out of place I felt at the funeral.

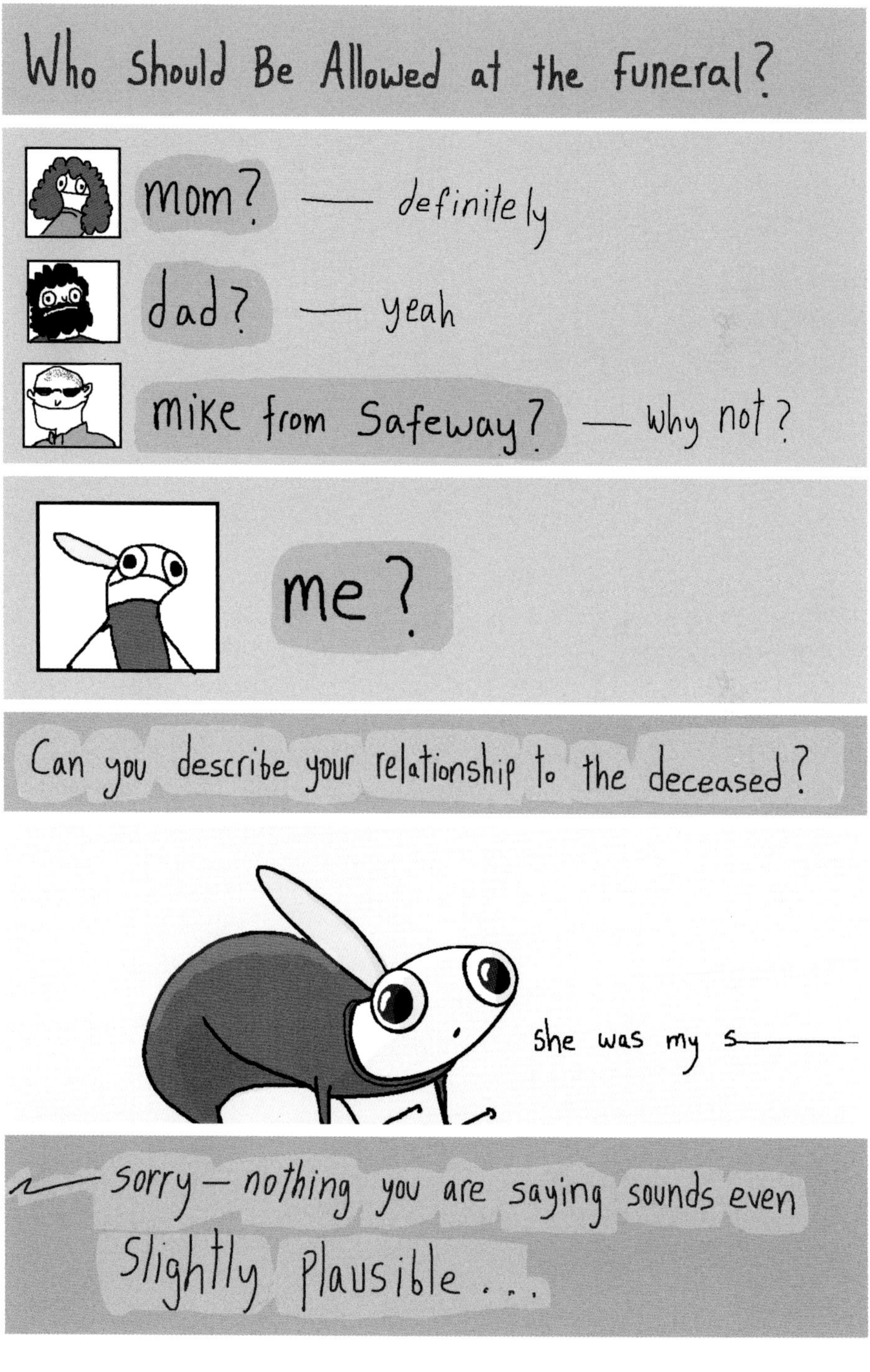
Who Should Be Allowed at the Funeral?
mom? — definitely
dad? — yeah
mike from Safeway? — why not?
me?
Can you describe your relationship to the deceased?
she was my s——
— sorry — nothing you are saying sounds even slightly plausible . . .

I tried to keep it together so nobody would notice, and I wanted to explain how difficult it was, and how forcefully the sadness exited my body when I finally broke down during the closing ceremonies.

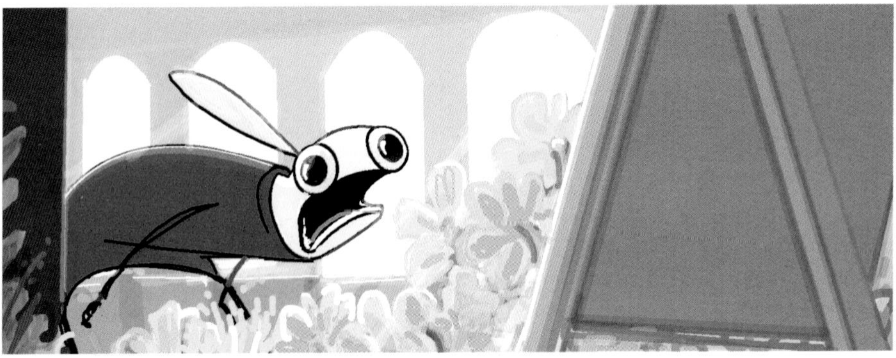

A family acquaintance approached us afterward. He said he had some herbs to help with my emotional volatility. I explained that I was just sad about my sister being dead—she used to be alive, see, and now she isn't anymore, and it just really came through in the last part of the slideshow for me . . . And he gently pointed out that I'd been crying *significantly* louder than anybody else, which I felt sort of proud of, but also ashamed of.

I wanted to really go into detail about how awkward death can be, and describe the lack of closure and how it always just sits there, and the guilt, and the regrets, and which crossing it was, and all my guesses for what her last thoughts might have been, and how I still have dreams about her, but she acts different now.

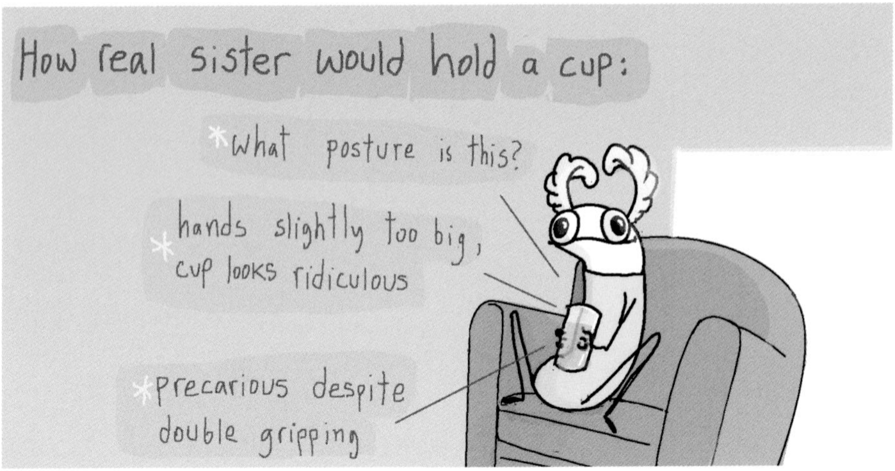
How real sister would hold a cup:
*what posture is this?
*hands slightly too big, cup looks ridiculous
*precarious despite double gripping

How fake dream sister holds a cup:

✗ Posture is too recognizable

✗ She would never keep it so perpendicular...

✗ one hand?? How, though?

From there, I wanted to go on to express how unfair the world is, and how many mistakes it's possible to make even when you're trying as hard as you can, and why I made the ones I did, and what they all were. I wanted to also explain what parts weren't my fault, and tell you the full details of all my medical conditions, and how scared I feel all the time, and how familiar hospitals have become.

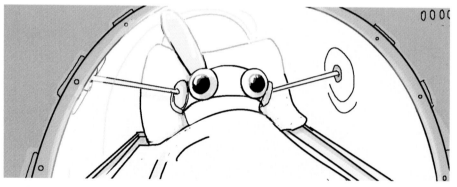

I wanted to explain why my marriage ended, and what I would do differently if I could, and why my parents' marriage ended, and how cool it is that they're still friends. And I wanted to ask all the questions I have that nobody can answer because they either don't have answers, or they have too many answers, or it isn't even super clear what the question is.

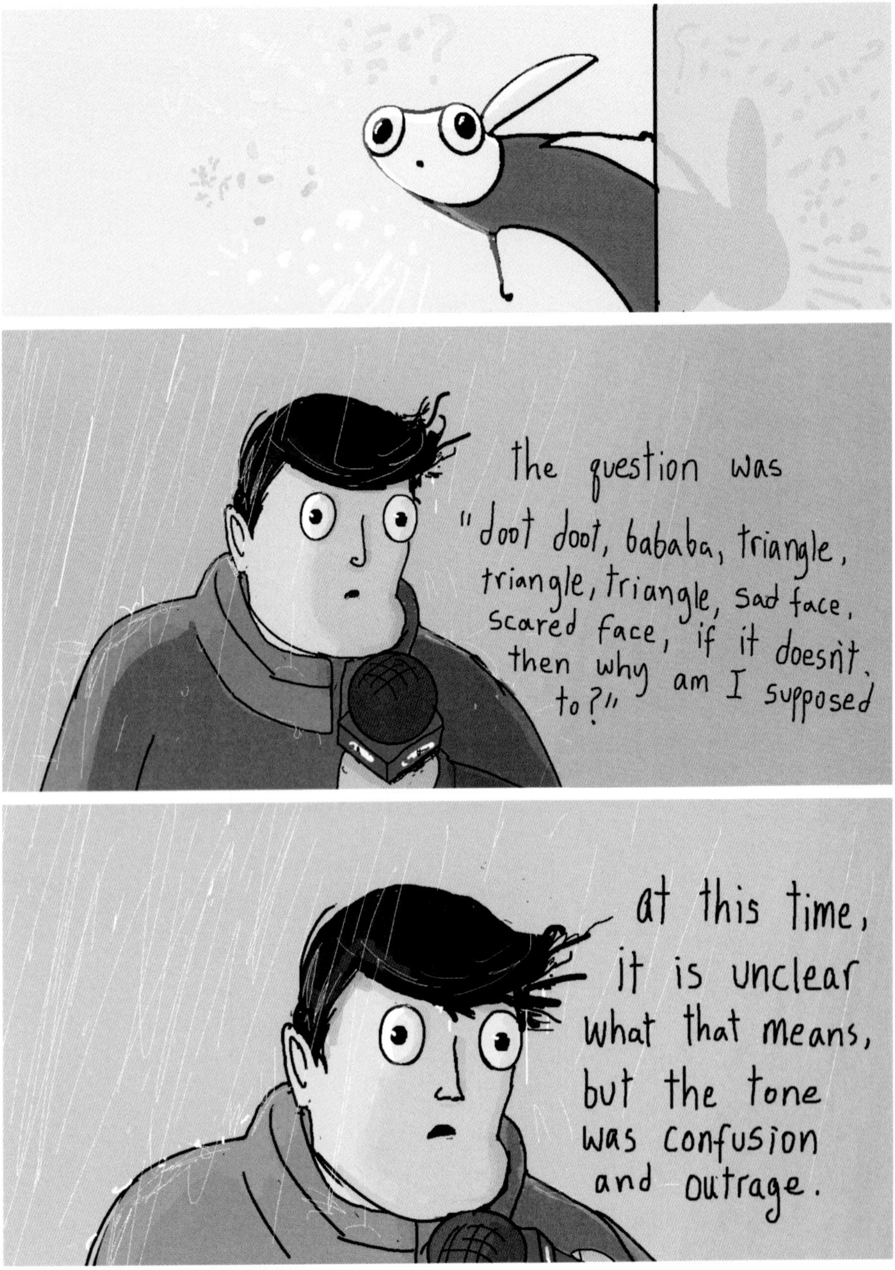
the question was "doot doot, bababa, triangle, triangle, triangle, sad face, scared face, if it doesn't, then why am I supposed to?"
at this time, it is unclear what that means, but the tone was confusion and outrage.

I wanted to explain all of it.
The whole thing.
Her whole life, and my whole life, and life in general.

But I don't know how.

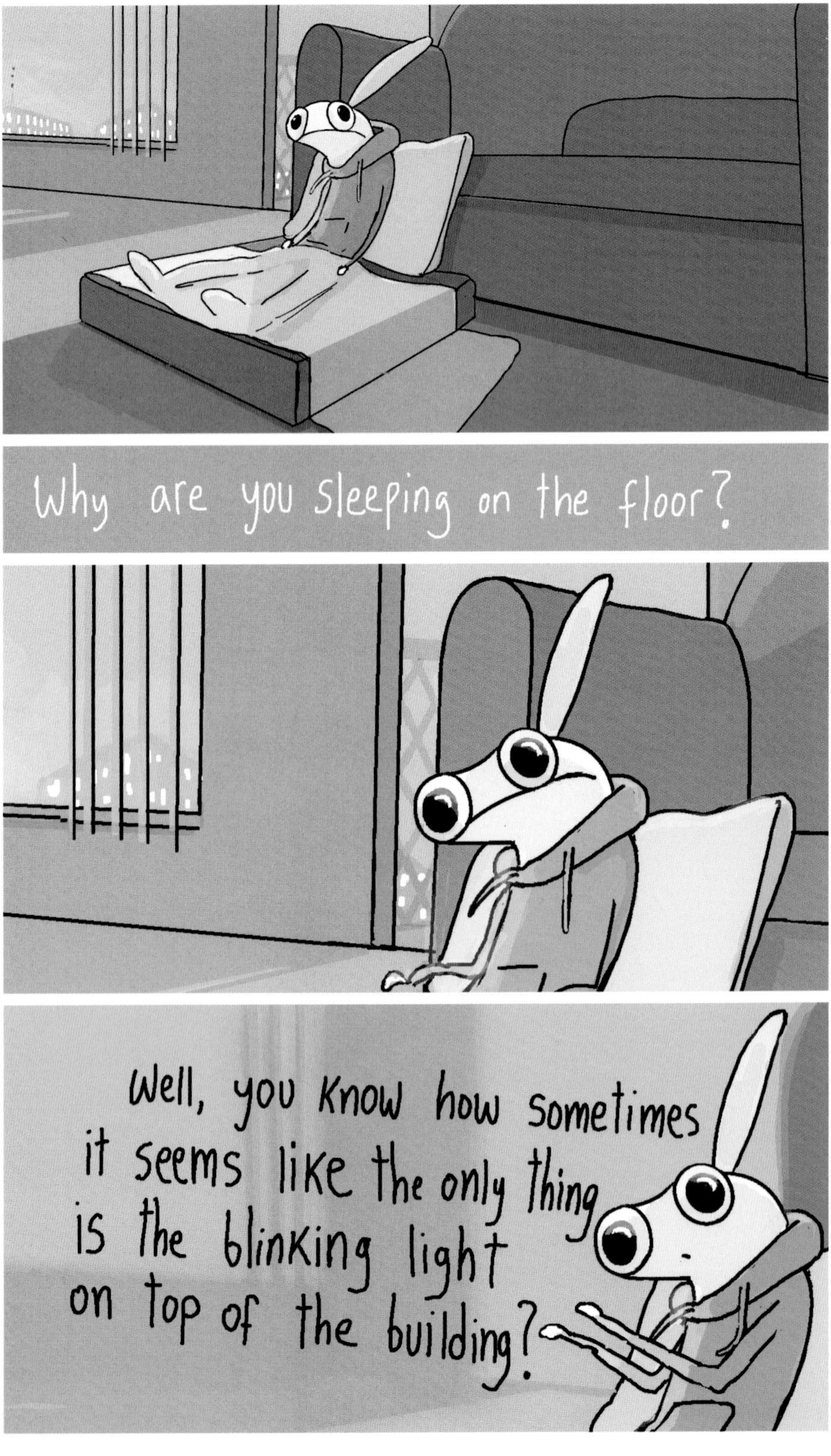
Why are you sleeping on the floor?
Well, you know how sometimes it seems like the only thing is the blinking light on top of the building?

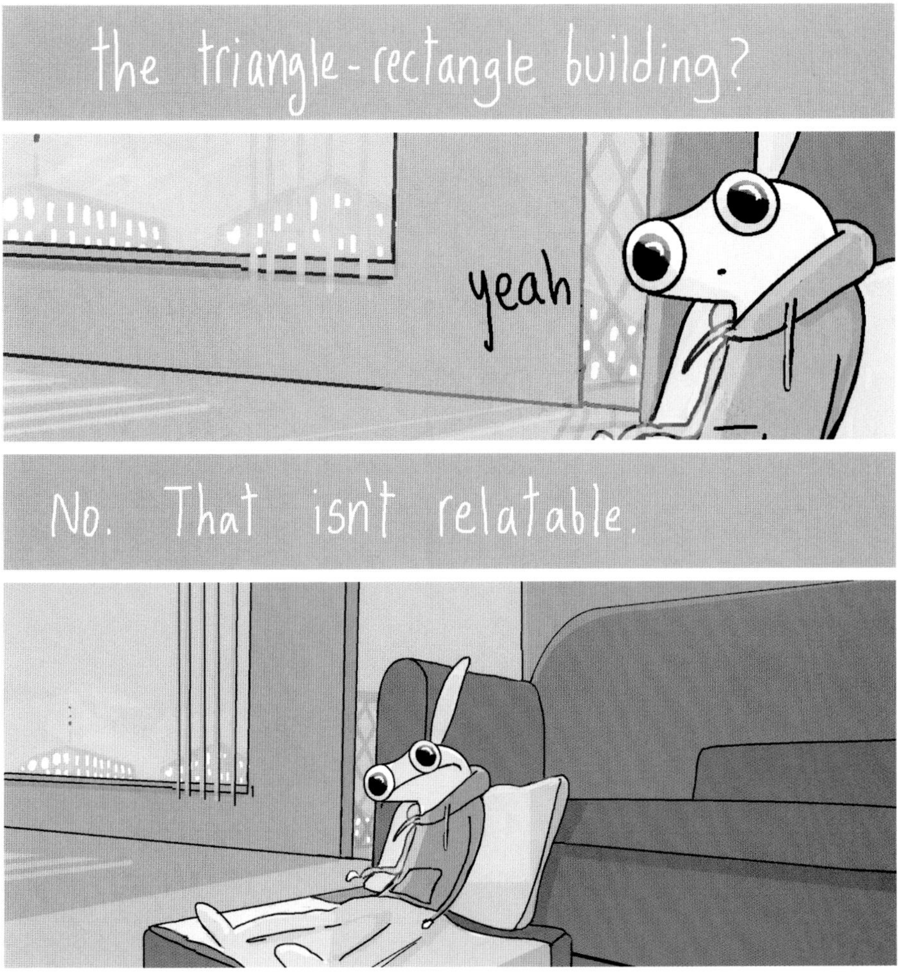
the triangle-rectangle building?
yeah
No. That isn't relatable.

Sometimes all you can really do is keep moving and hope you end up somewhere that makes sense.

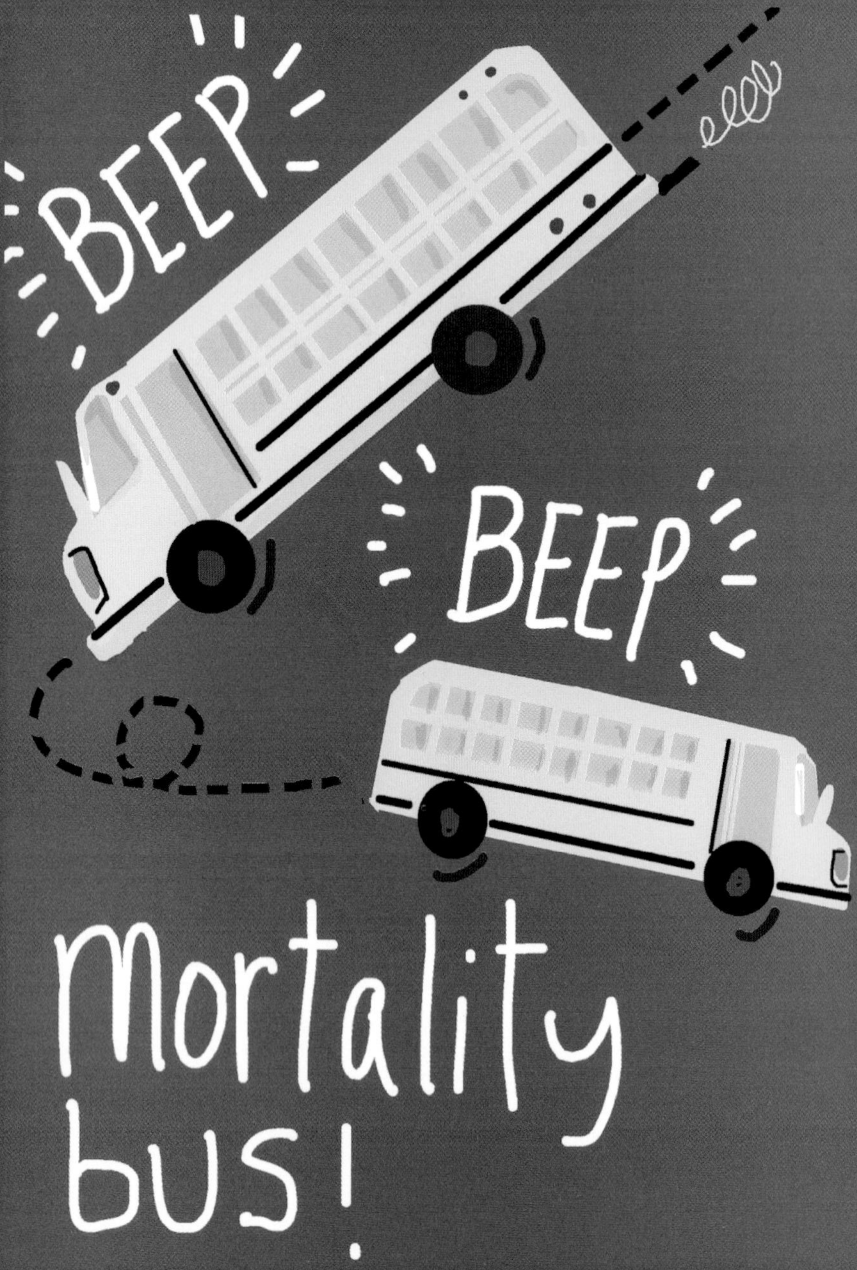
BEEP
BEEP
Mortality bus!

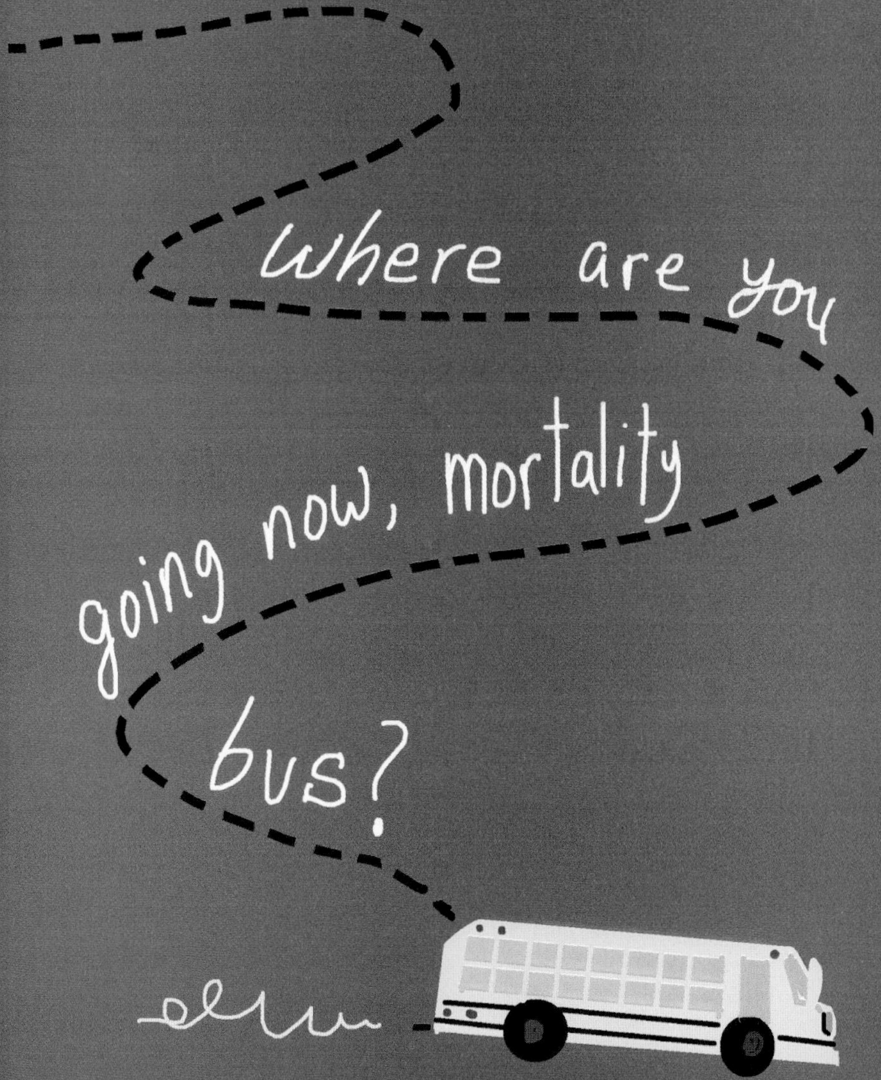
where are you
going now, mortality
bus?

11. THE PILE DOG PART 1

I moved to Colorado in 2015, and lived alone for a while. No animals, no people—just me. I still knew some animals, but I wasn't planning to live with them again for quite some time. Then I met Kevin, and Kevin had a dog. Kevin also had three roommates, and one of the roommates had a dog too. So when I moved in with Kevin, I inherited three roommates and two dogs.

fastest, most intense animal I have ever met

brown pile with no eyes

    This is about the pile dog.

    Before you get all attached to the pile dog, you should know that the pile dog is dead. She had a disease that made her liver shrivel up, and it wasn't fair, and there was nothing anybody could do about it. However, we—all of us—should not allow this to prevent us from making fun of her. Dead dogs used to be just as ridiculous as alive dogs, and the pile dog leveraged our sympathy to get away with some particularly bogus shit. She doesn't get a pass just because she died tragically young from an incurable disease that wasn't her fault.

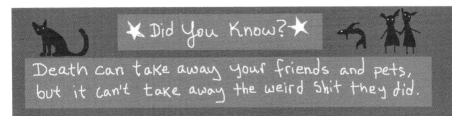

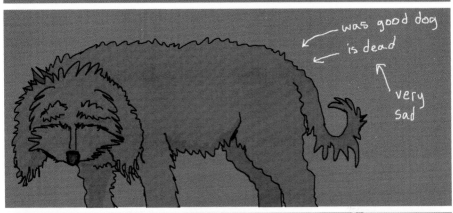

Did You Know?
Death can take away your friends and pets, but it can't take away the weird shit they did.
was good dog
is dead
very sad
BUT ALSO:
• sneaky (actually does have eyes)
• creepy
• stared at us from a dark hallway with secret eyes for countless hours (if ghost, probably still does this)
• pooped in basement sometimes
• Took liberal advantage of our sympathy
• compulsive farter
• personal space pirate
• would have terrorized thousands of innocent bunnies if not prevented from doing so

I didn't intend for mortality to be such a central theme in this, but sometimes death is what happens, and here we are.

The pile dog was a silly-looking animal. We had to cut eyeholes in her fur so she could see. It made her look way creepier than would be ideal, but you can't let your dog be blind just because it looks creepy when you can see its eyes.

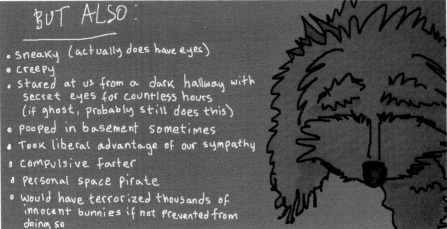

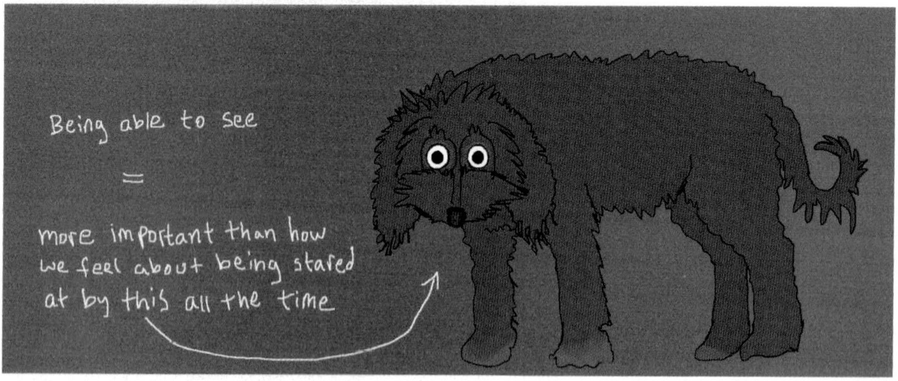
Being able to see
=
more important than how we feel about being stared at by this all the time

To an uninformed observer, her gentle nature and clownish demeanor would have given the impression that this was just some bumbling fool. But, as far as dogs go, the pile dog was basically a criminal mastermind.

Real fools don't have plans.

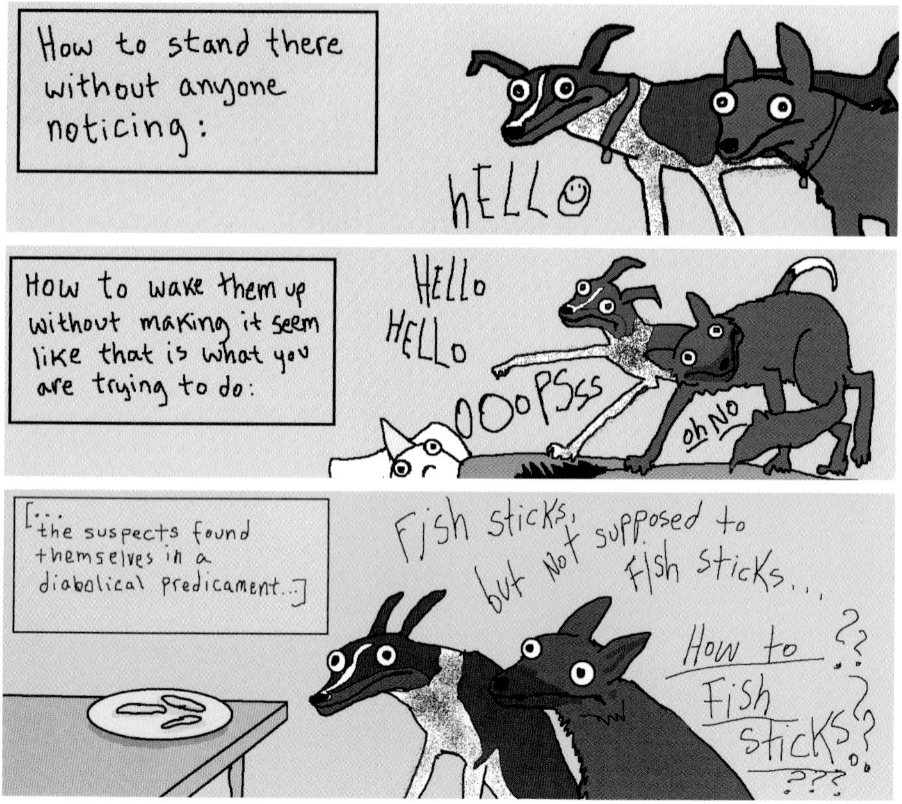
How to stand there without anyone noticing:
hELLO
How to wake them up without making it seem like that is what you are trying to do:
HELLo
HELLo
OOoPSss
oh NO
[...the suspects found themselves in a diabolical predicament...]
Fish sticks, but Not supposed to Fish sticks...
How to Fish sticks???
???

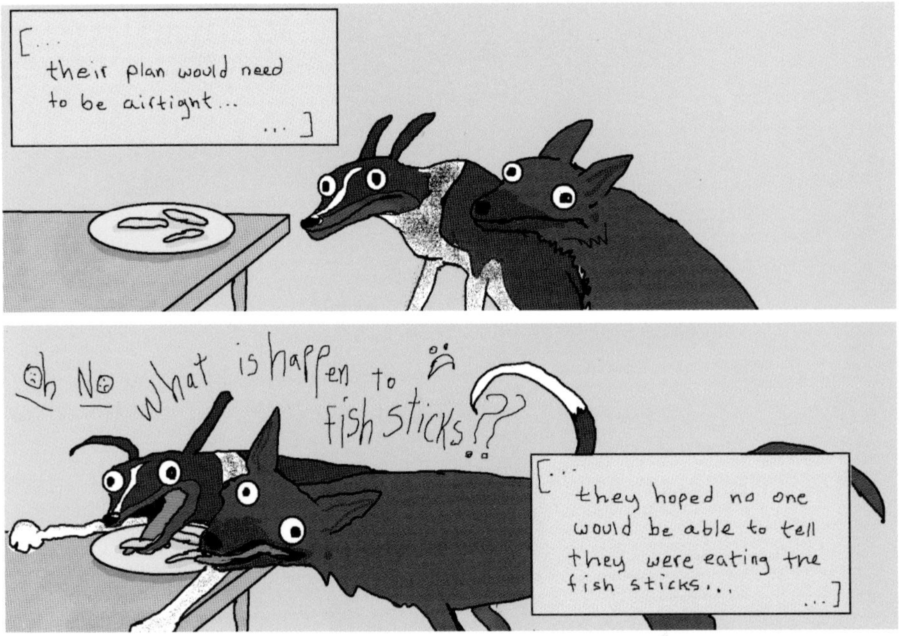
[...
their plan would need
to be airtight...
...]
oh No what is happen to
fish sticks??
[...
they hoped no one
would be able to tell
they were eating the
fish sticks...
...]

This dog had plans.

Not *good* plans.

But there was often something she was trying to do that was more involved than not having a plan.

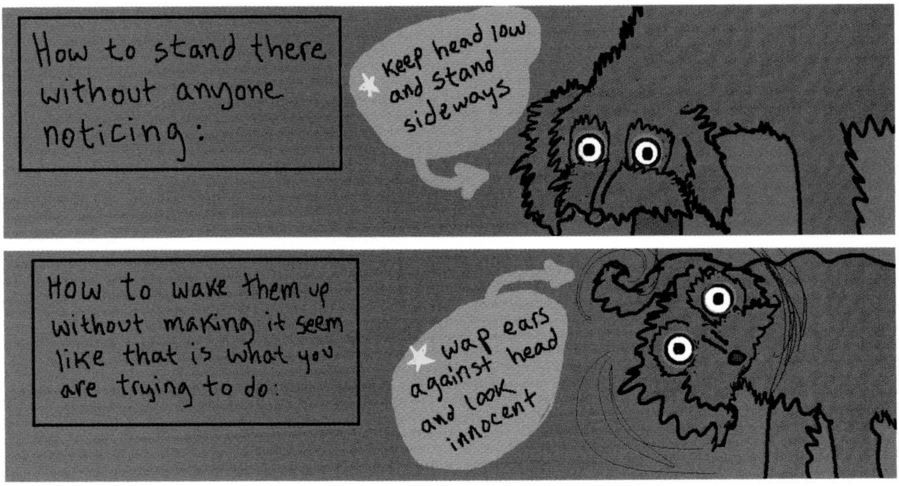
How to stand there
without anyone
noticing:
Keep head low
and stand
sideways
How to wake them up
without making it seem
like that is what you
are trying to do:
wap ears
against head
and look
innocent

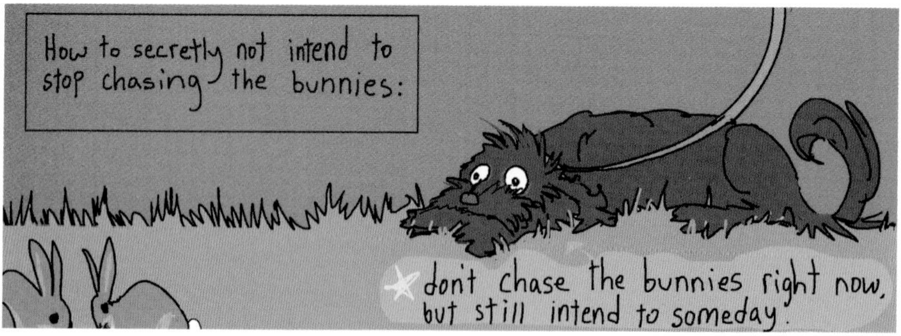
How to secretly not intend to stop chasing the bunnies:
don't chase the bunnies right now, but still intend to someday.

If we were dogs, she might've been able to pull it off.

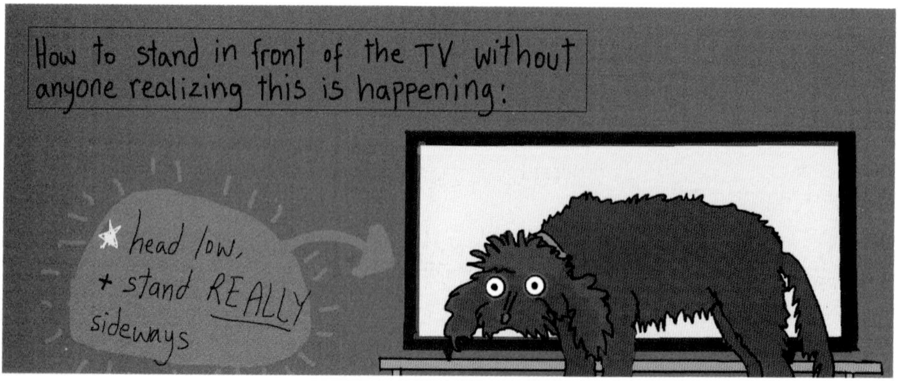
How to stand in front of the TV without anyone realizing this is happening:
head low, + stand REALLY sideways

But we aren't dogs.

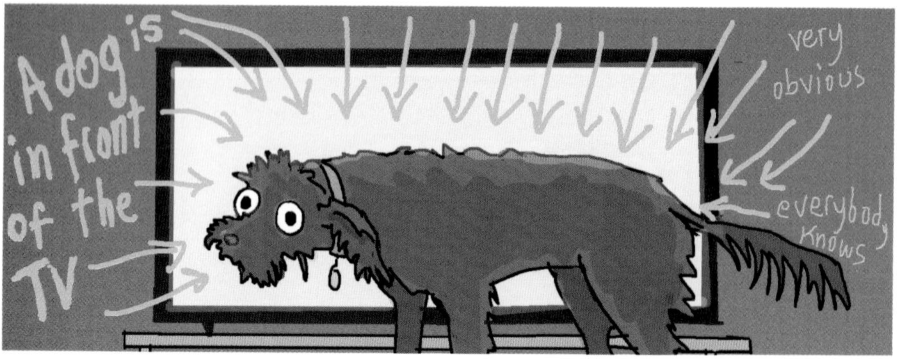
A dog is in front of the TV
very obvious
everybody knows

Sneaky animals don't realize how easy it is to tell. They think they're getting away with it the whole time. And because of that, you get to see a lot more of their plan than you should. You get to see pretty much the whole plan. An animal won't accept that it's been caught until you show it irrefutable proof. You have to actually convince the animal. You could be staring at the animal's entire plan unfolding in full view of you, the animal, god, and the FBI, and the animal will still be like, *heh heh ... they do not suspect I am the one who is doing this ...*

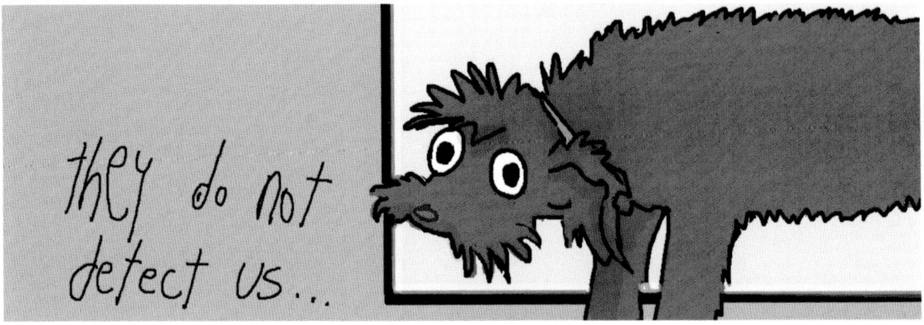
they do not detect us...

One time I dropped some chips on the ground, and the pile dog lunged for them. I saw her do this. The instant we made eye contact, she froze.

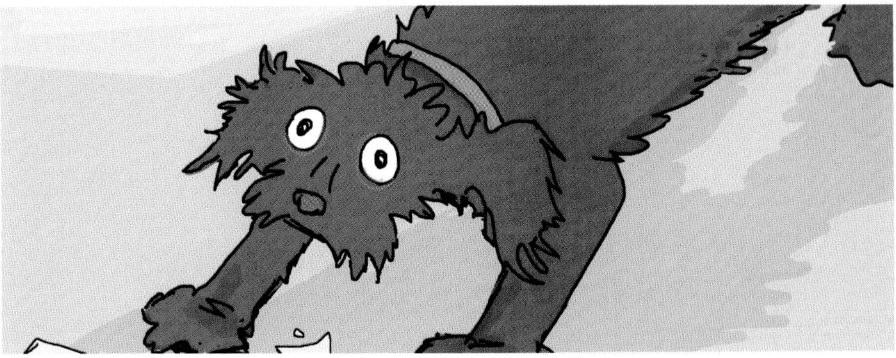

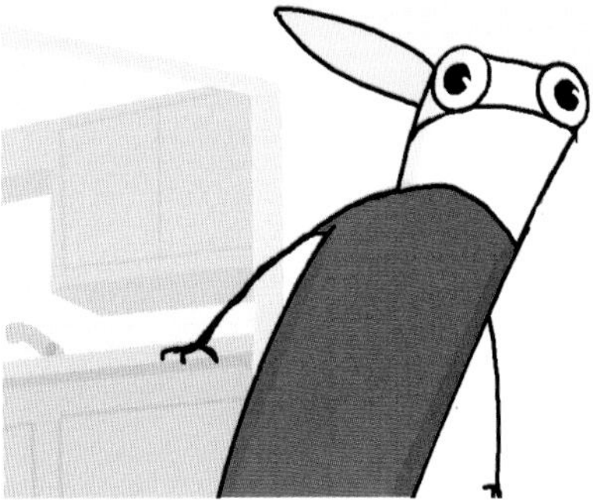

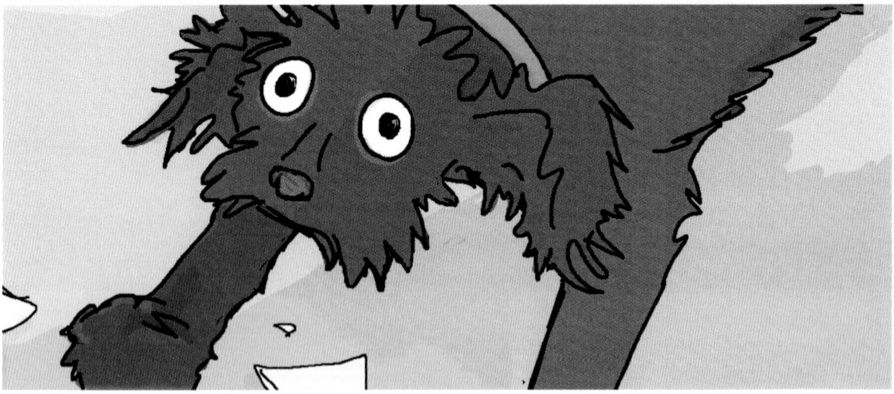

She knew that what she was doing was wrong.

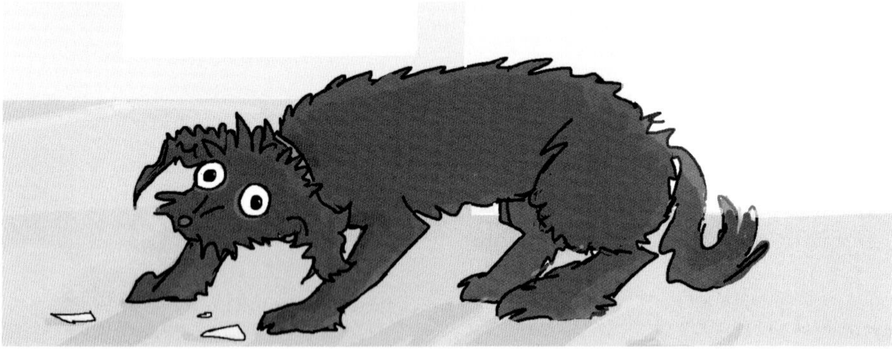

And she saw me see her doing it.

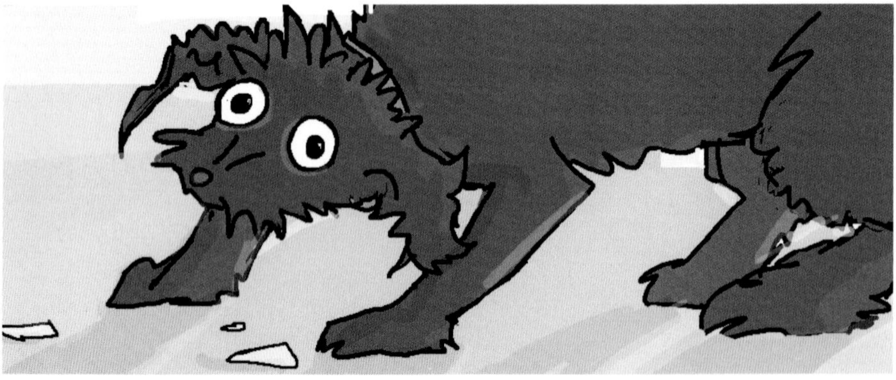

She hovered above the chips, completely motionless, staring directly at me for quite a while. I assume this was to prevent me from noticing her while she came up with a plan for how to spin this.

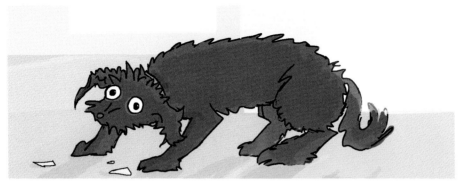

Here's the angle she went with:

LOOK
STRETCHING!

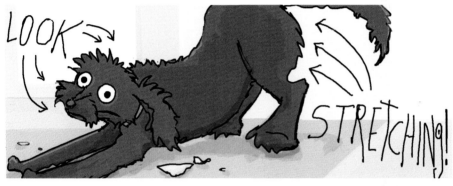

That's a plan. A plan for *deception*. Anyone could look at that and tell exactly what it is. It is absolutely, undeniably a plan. It's just really far away from working.

This
500 miles
a plan that works

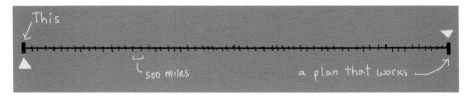

That's just one example of the mischief she was capable of. The pile dog had all kinds of tricks and schemes up her sleeves, and she wasn't afraid to shoot for the moon.

To get an idea of what I'm talking about when I say "wasn't afraid to shoot for the moon," let's say you love walking back and forth on the only strip of linoleum in an otherwise carpeted apartment. But, every time you do that, everybody somehow figures out what you're doing and stops you. And this has happened at least four hundred times. Every single one of the four hundred times you've done this, somebody or everybody immediately sensed it was happening and told you to stop.

Also, you are not invisible or capable of levitating.

If those were the odds you were up against, you probably wouldn't think there'd be a way to get away with it. And there isn't. But there are things you can try. Like, for example, after you get caught, wait for them to stop paying attention and veerrrrrrryyyyyy sloooooooowlyyyyy sneak away to start doing it again.

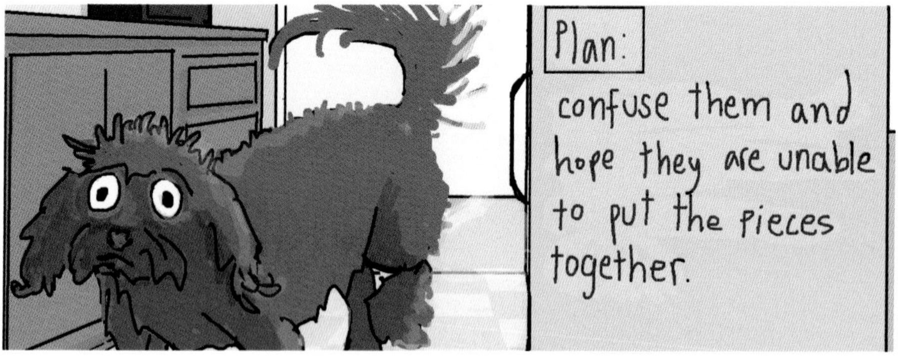
Plan:
confuse them and hope they are unable to put the pieces together.

If I had to pinpoint the main problem with that strategy, it'd probably be that no matter how sneaky you are about going into the kitchen, it's pretty difficult to hide the fact that there's a 50-pound animal with sixteen toenails walking laps on a plastic surface merely four feet behind us. That's the exact reason we wanted her to stop in the first place. If she could walk around without anyone noticing, that would've been *amazing*. But there were at least two very obvious ways to trace it back to her . . . I mean, how did she think it was going to work?

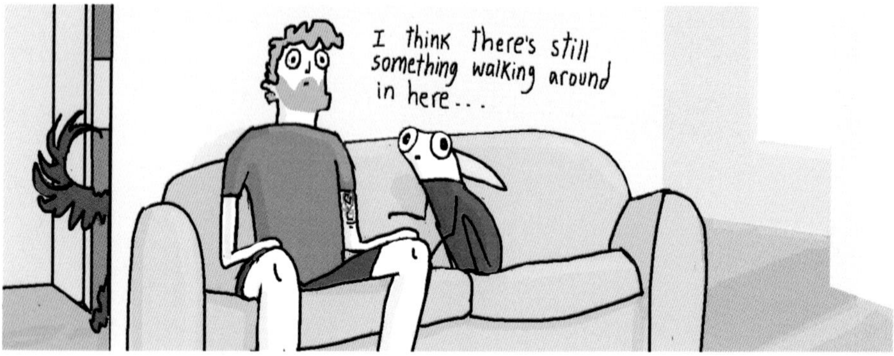
I think there's still something walking around in here . . .

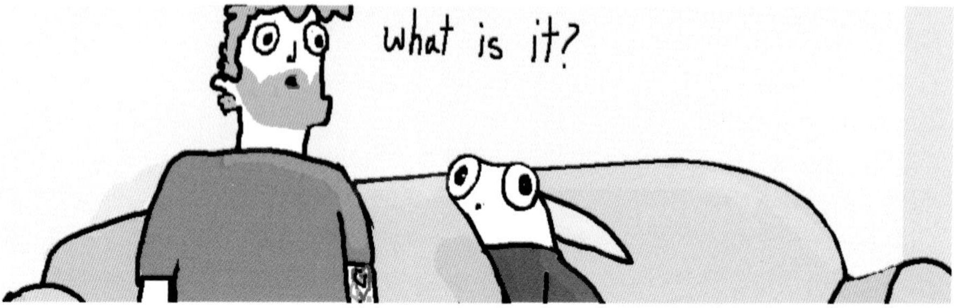
what is it?

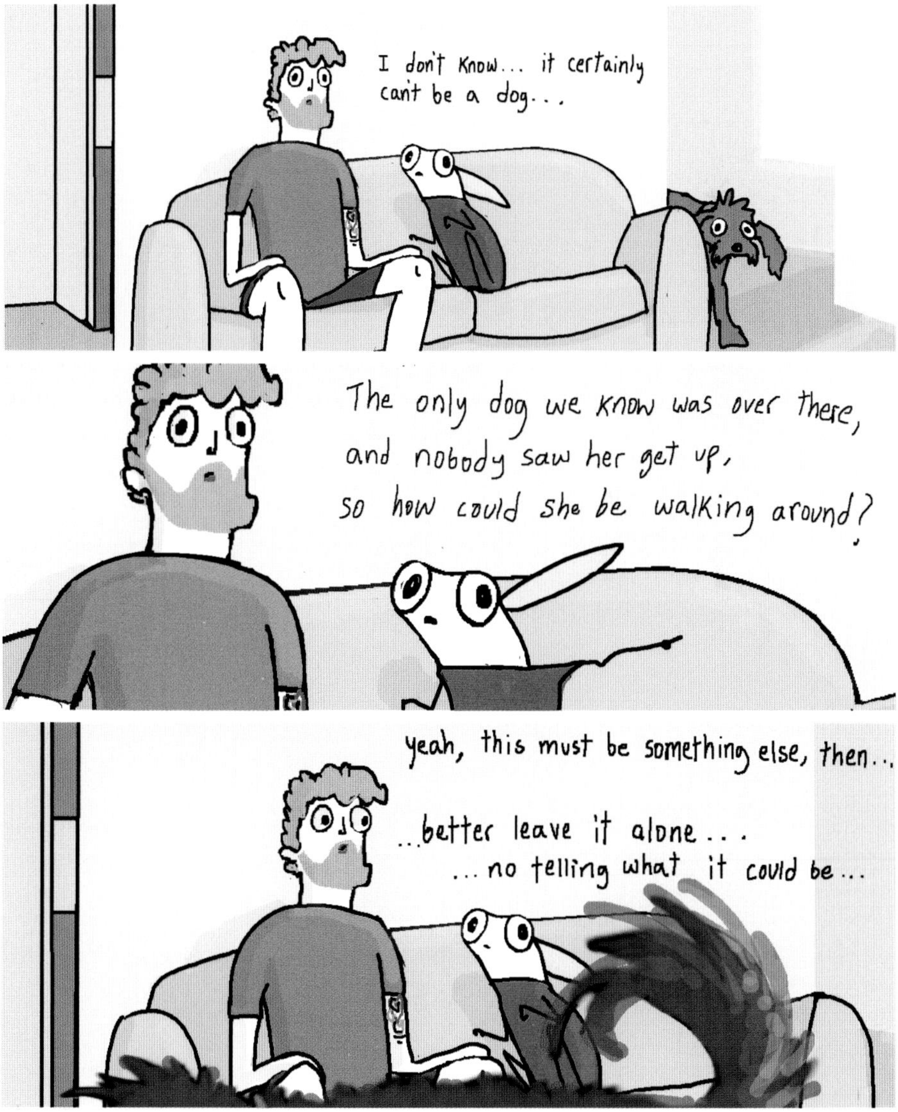

I don't know... it certainly can't be a dog...
The only dog we know was over there, and nobody saw her get up, so how could she be walking around?
yeah, this must be something else, then...
...better leave it alone...
...no telling what it could be...

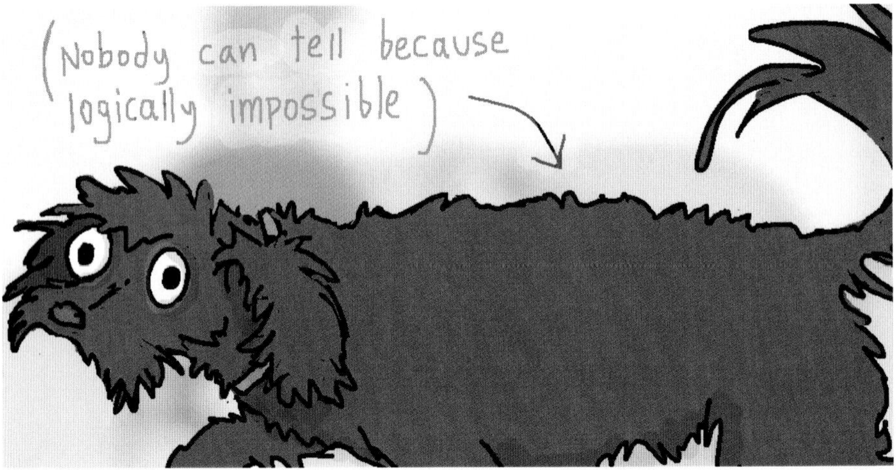
(Nobody can tell because logically impossible)

But do not be tempted to assume the pile dog's repertoire was limited—it wasn't. I know this because I once saw her cycle through every single thing she knew how to do in a row. It took over half an hour. And I know it was all of them because carrots were involved, and her level of desperation was *well* past the cutoff where you'd be like, *"Yeah, I tried 599 of the 600 things I know how to do and none of them worked, but I think I'm gonna keep this last one for later . . ."*

It was a catastrophic lapse in restraint. She wanted those carrots too bad. All we had to do was withhold them, and her entire arsenal came tumbling out in a symphony of futility.

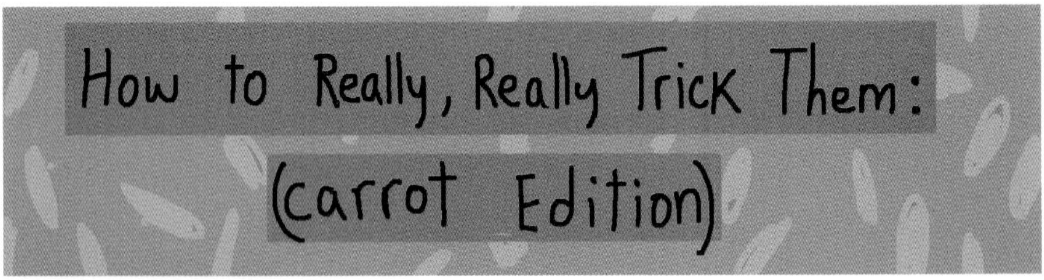
How to Really, Really Trick Them:
(carrot Edition)

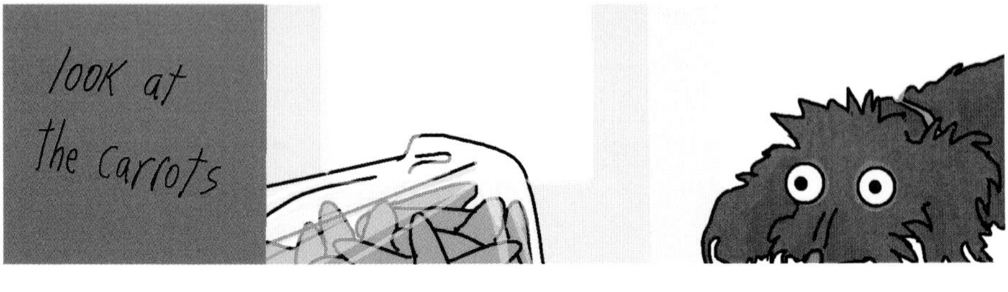
look at the carrots

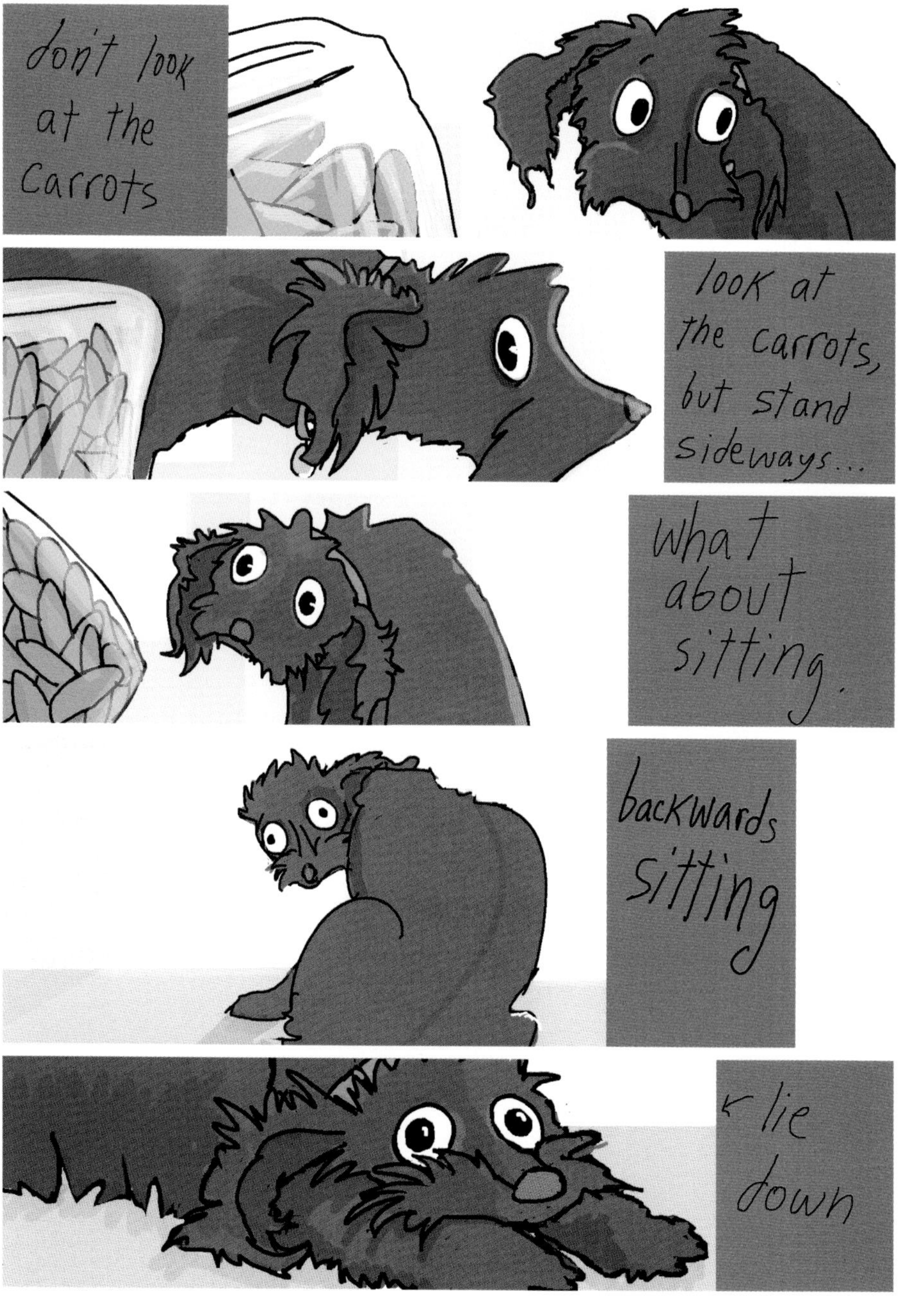
don't look at the carrots
look at the carrots, but stand sideways...
what about sitting.
backwards sitting
lie down

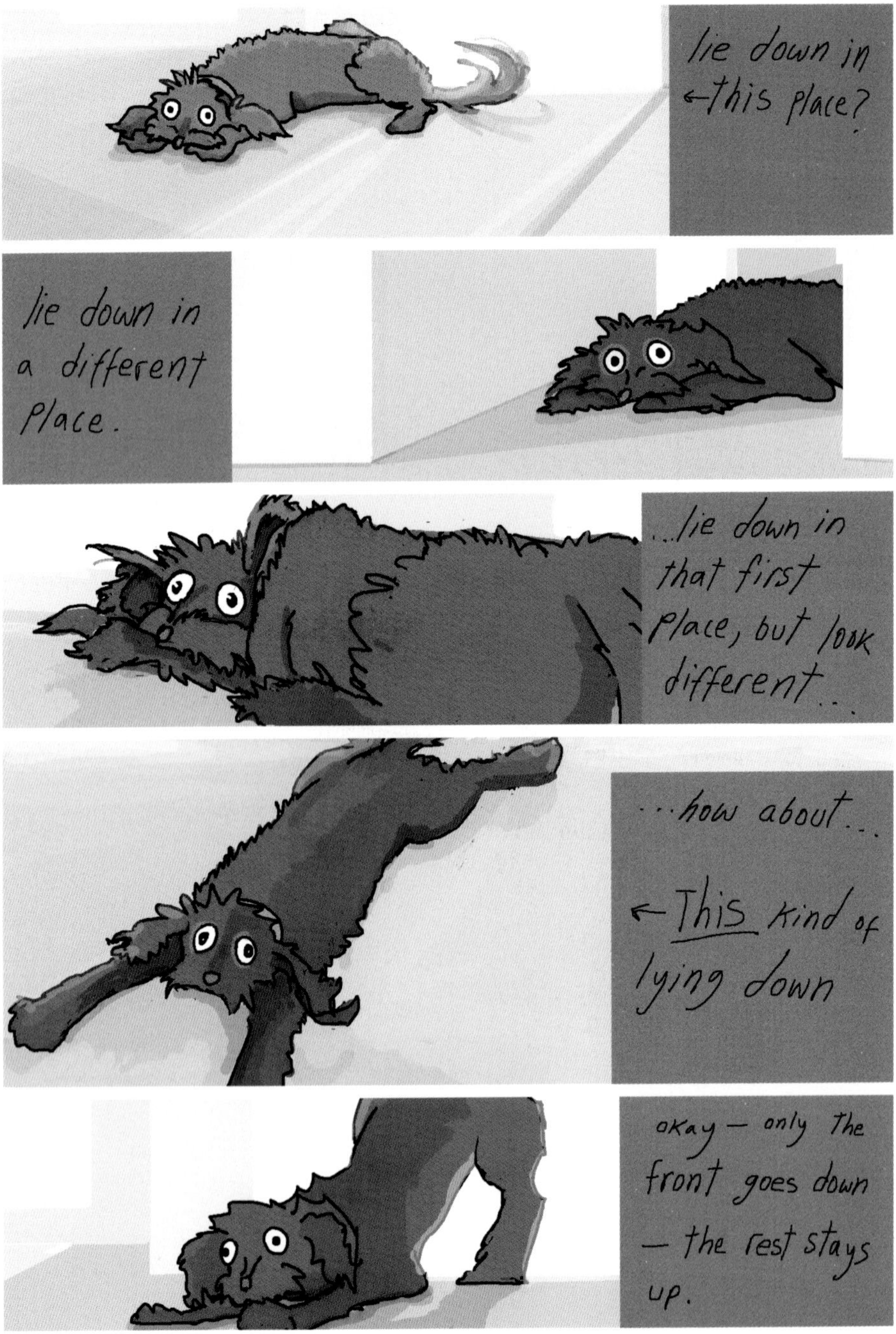
lie down in
←this place?
lie down in a different place.
...lie down in that first place, but look different...
...how about...
←This kind of lying down
okay — only the front goes down — the rest stays up.

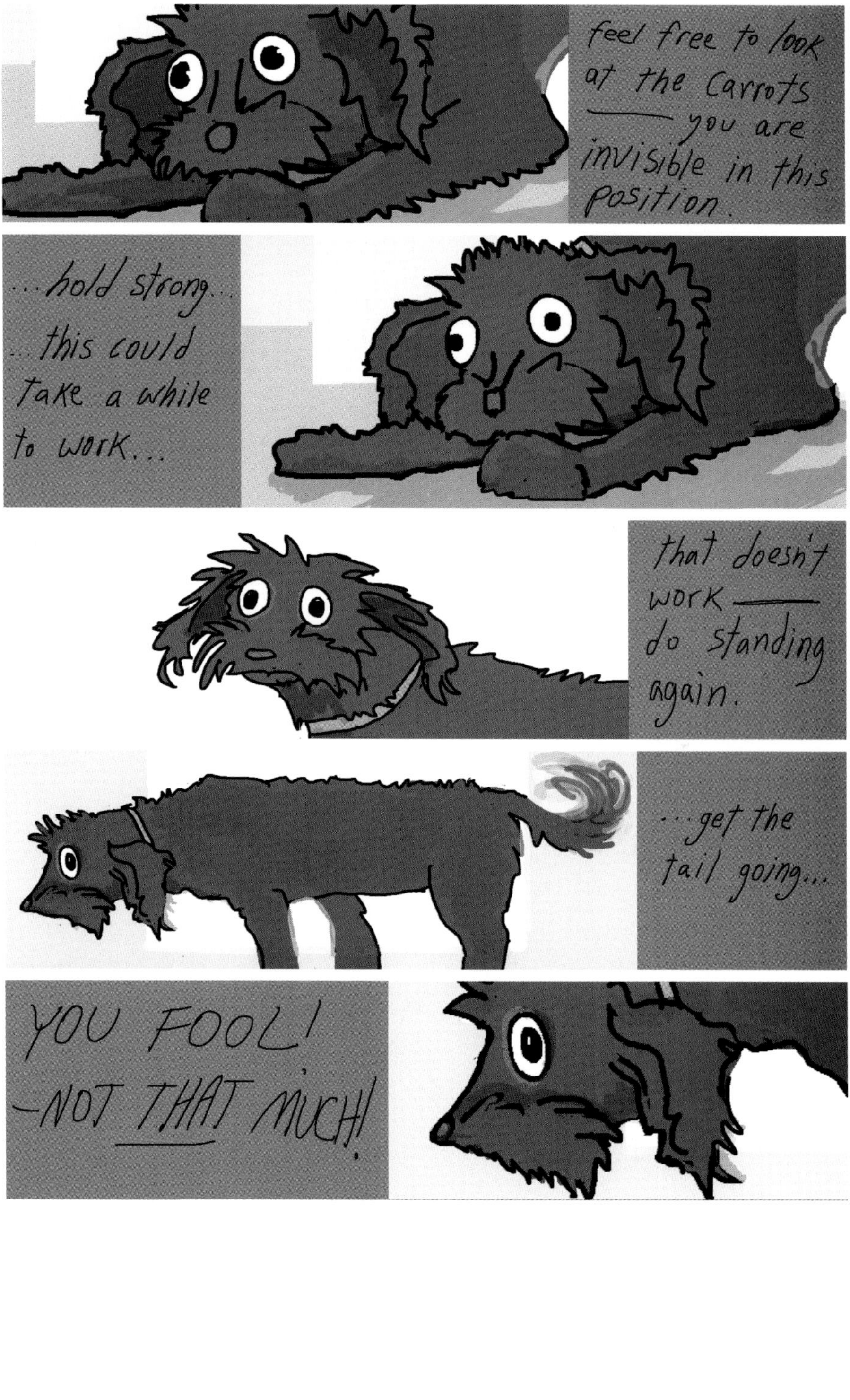
feel free to look at the carrots — you are invisible in this position.
...hold strong... ...this could take a while to work...
that doesn't work — do standing again.
...get the tail going...
YOU FOOL! —NOT THAT MUCH!

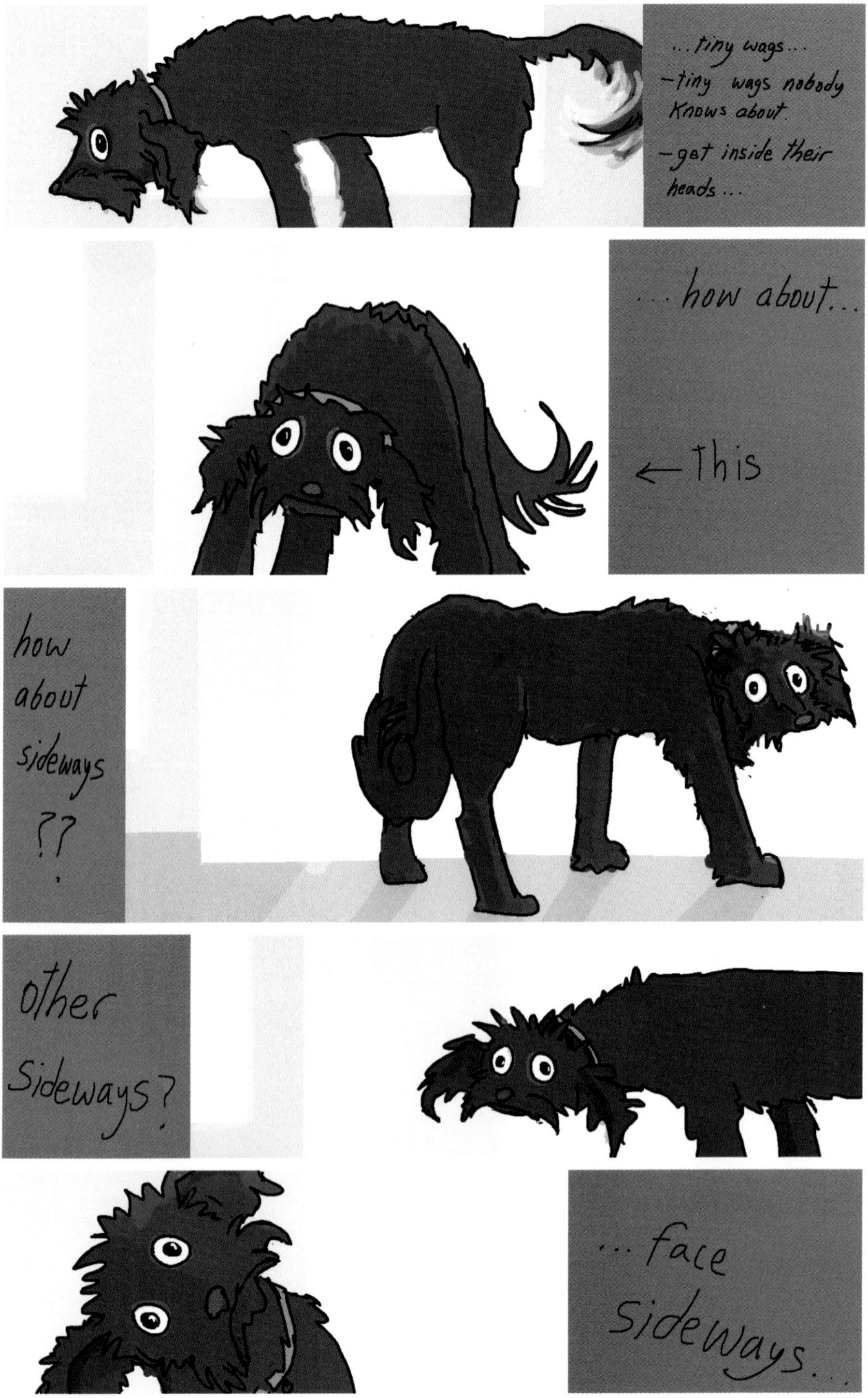
...tiny wags...
-tiny wags nobody knows about.
-get inside their heads...
...how about...
← this
how about sideways ??
other sideways?
...face sideways...

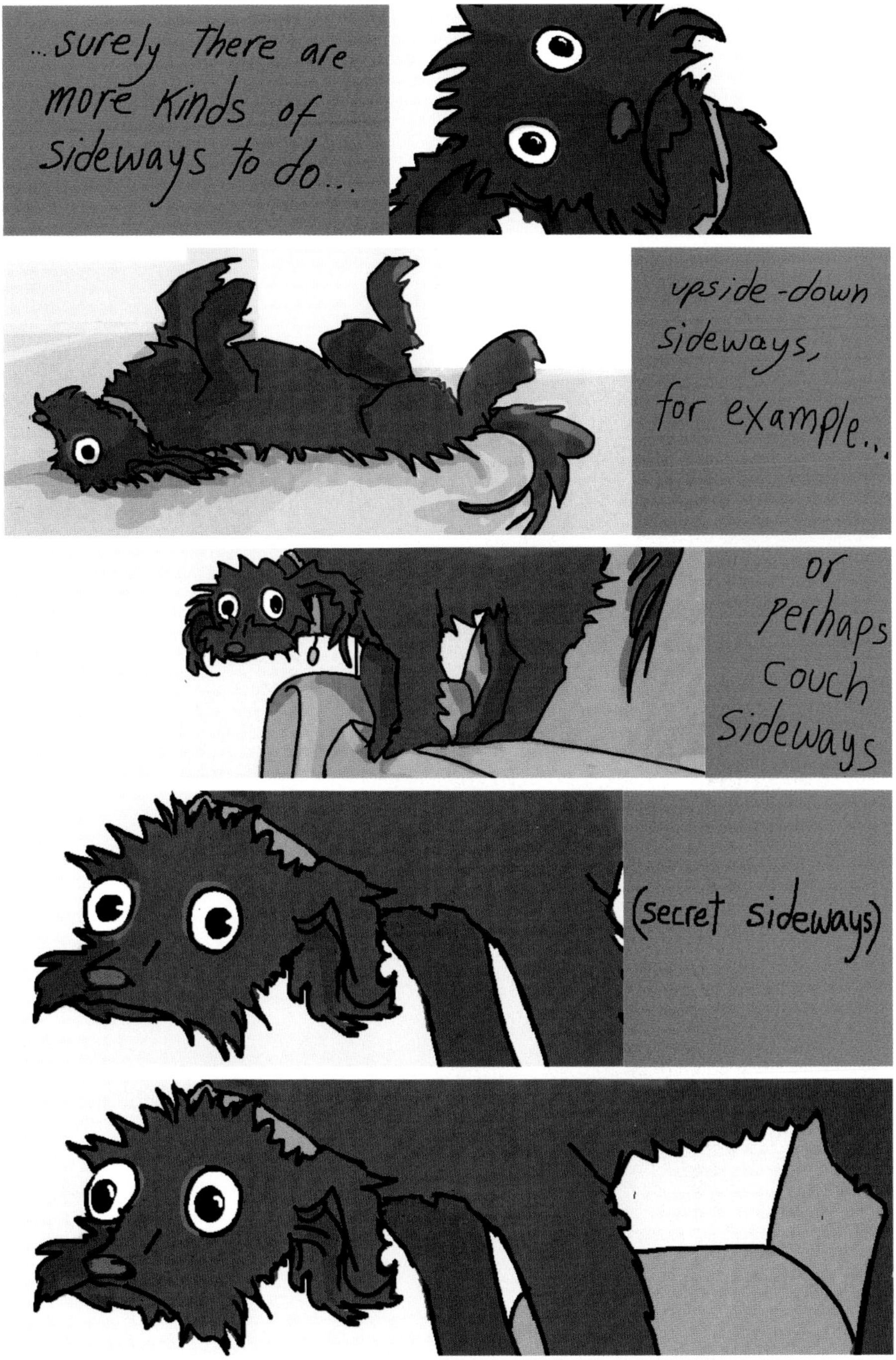
...surely there are more kinds of sideways to do...
upside-down sideways, for example...
or perhaps couch sideways
(secret sideways)

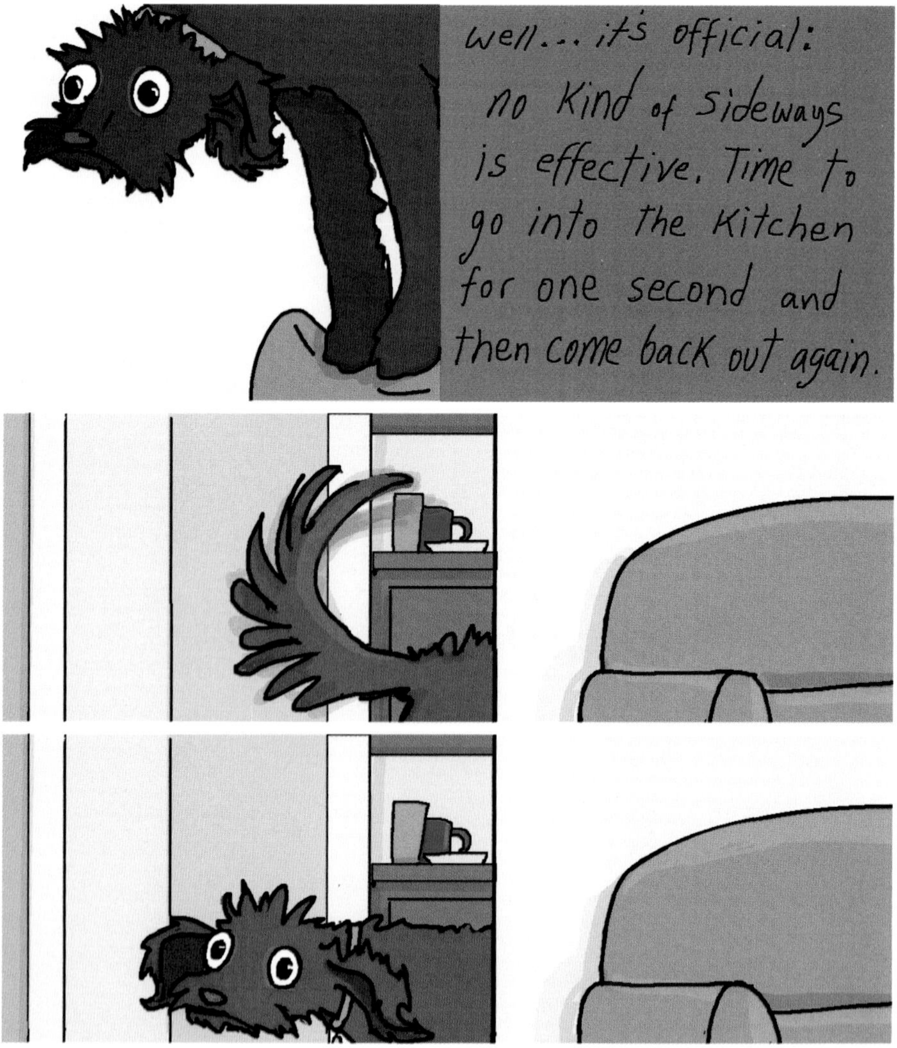
well... it's official: no Kind of sideways is effective. Time to go into the Kitchen for one second and then come back out again.

The further it went, the more the sequences started to resemble magic spells. We saw the whole lineup of persuasion techniques, deception maneuvers, and mind-control chaos, and after that . . . well, where else is there to really go besides sorcery?

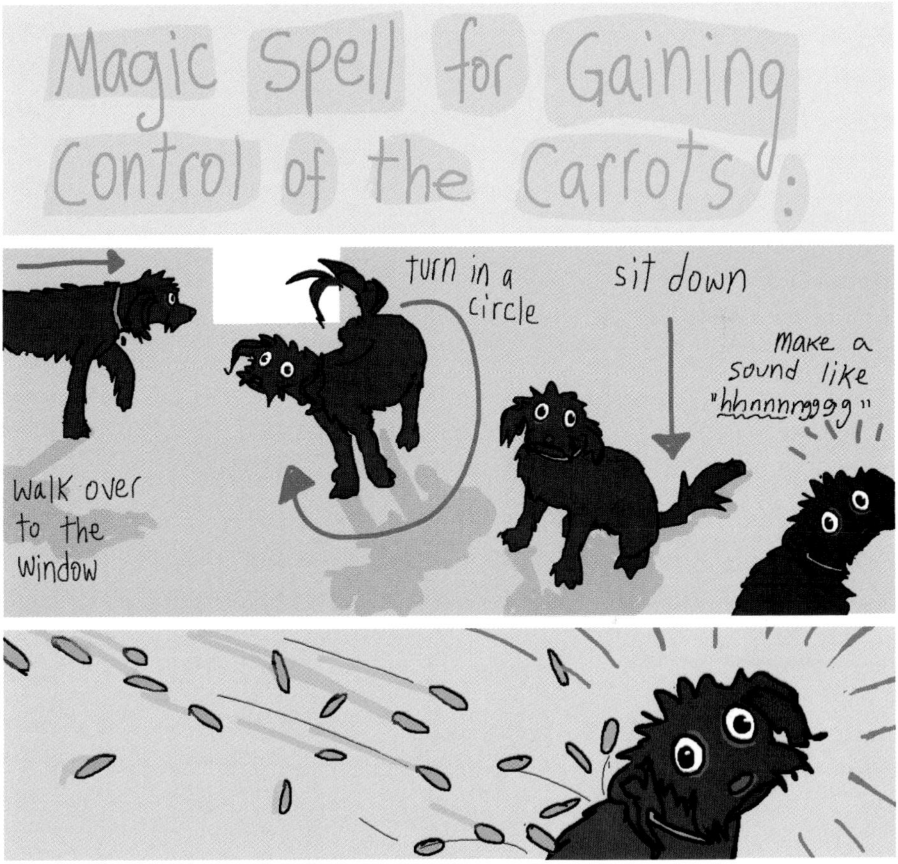
Magic Spell for Gaining Control of the Carrots:
walk over to the window
turn in a circle
sit down
make a sound like "hhnnnngggg"

The schemes I'm describing are highly convoluted, yes, but do not worry: we always knew we were being tricked.

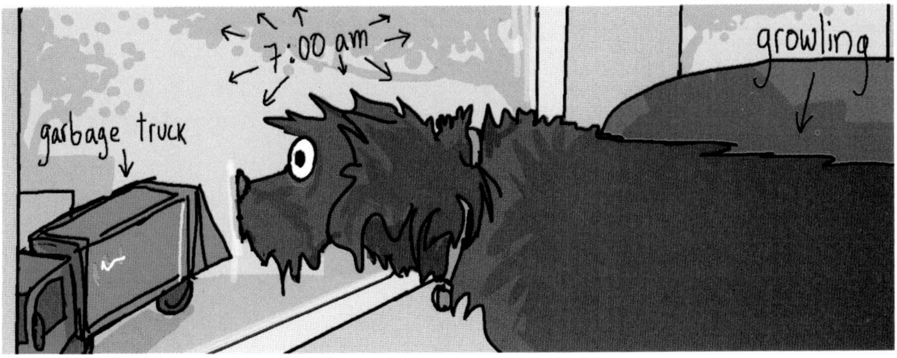
7:00 am
garbage truck
growling

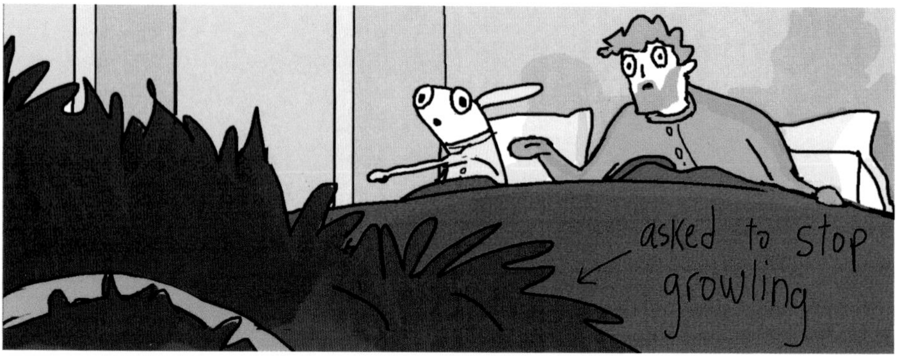
asked to stop growling

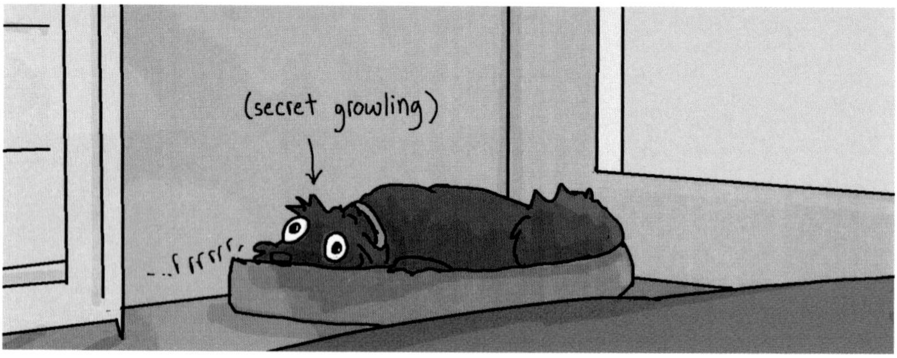
(secret growling)
...rrrrr

It probably made us seem like mind readers.

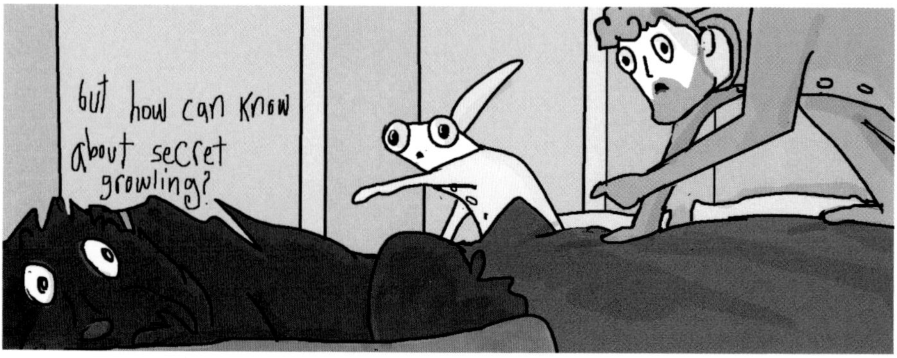
but how can know about secret growling?

I don't believe in heaven, but there are a lot of nice things about the idea. Personally, I'd be most excited about finally knowing all the stats and behind-the-scenes info. You'd get to find out what you were right about and wrong about and all your personal records.

I have no doubt the pile dog would feel proud of herself if she found out she probably got the closest any dog ever has to legitimately tricking somebody. Yeah, it wasn't very close at all, and the sheer force of the effort looked absurd, but I'm sure there was like half a second at some point where we almost got kind of close to a little bit falling for it.

4% invisible

And that's pretty fucking good for a pile animal with a shriveled liver and no eyes.

12. THE PILE DOG PART 2

When I implied the pile dog never tricked anybody, I only meant it in the strictest sense: she never successfully deceived anyone as the result of a purposeful action.

But she did confuse a lot of people.

One symptom of end-stage liver disease is a distended stomach. Fluid builds up in the abdomen, and it keeps going like that, and pretty soon your dog looks nineteen months pregnant.

You can manage it for a while, but the procedure eventually stops working, and your dog just has to stay like that.

When that happened, our vet told us the end was getting close. A few weeks maybe.

Four months later, the pile dog was still waddling around like the world's hairiest water balloon.

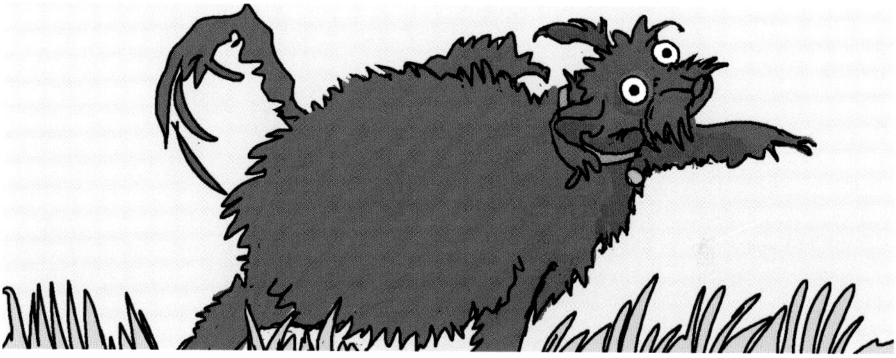

She just kept going and going. It didn't even seem like she noticed.

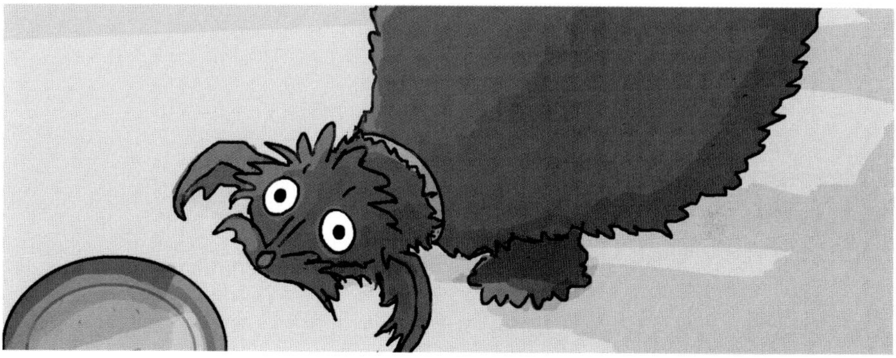

Everybody else did, though. When there's forty extra pounds of water in your dog, everybody who sees your dog will immediately think, OH MY GOD ... *WHAT THE FUCK HAPPENED??*

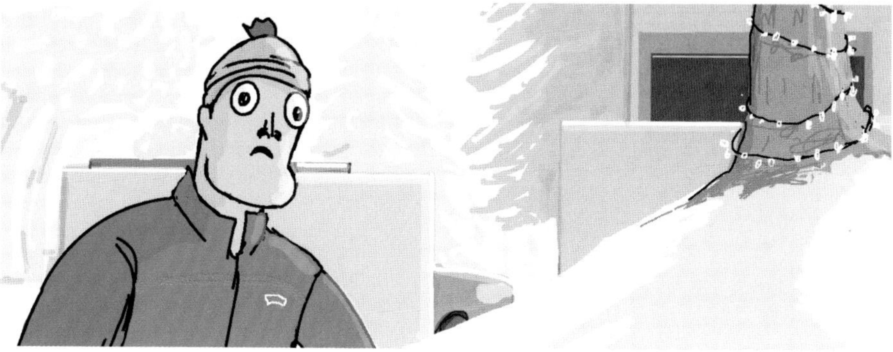

The least horrifying possibility they can think of is pregnancy. But this looks *way* weirder than pregnancy. To look like that, a dog would have to be so pregnant that the pregnancy loops back around and gets pregnant inside the original pregnancy several times over. And it couldn't be puppies—it'd have to be snakes or something.

It makes people concerned.

They don't want to jump to conclusions . . . it's probably just an extremely advanced form of pregnancy . . . but nobody feels sure enough to let it slide. They cross the street and trickle out of their houses to ask when she's due, just in case it was ten months ago and we didn't realize.

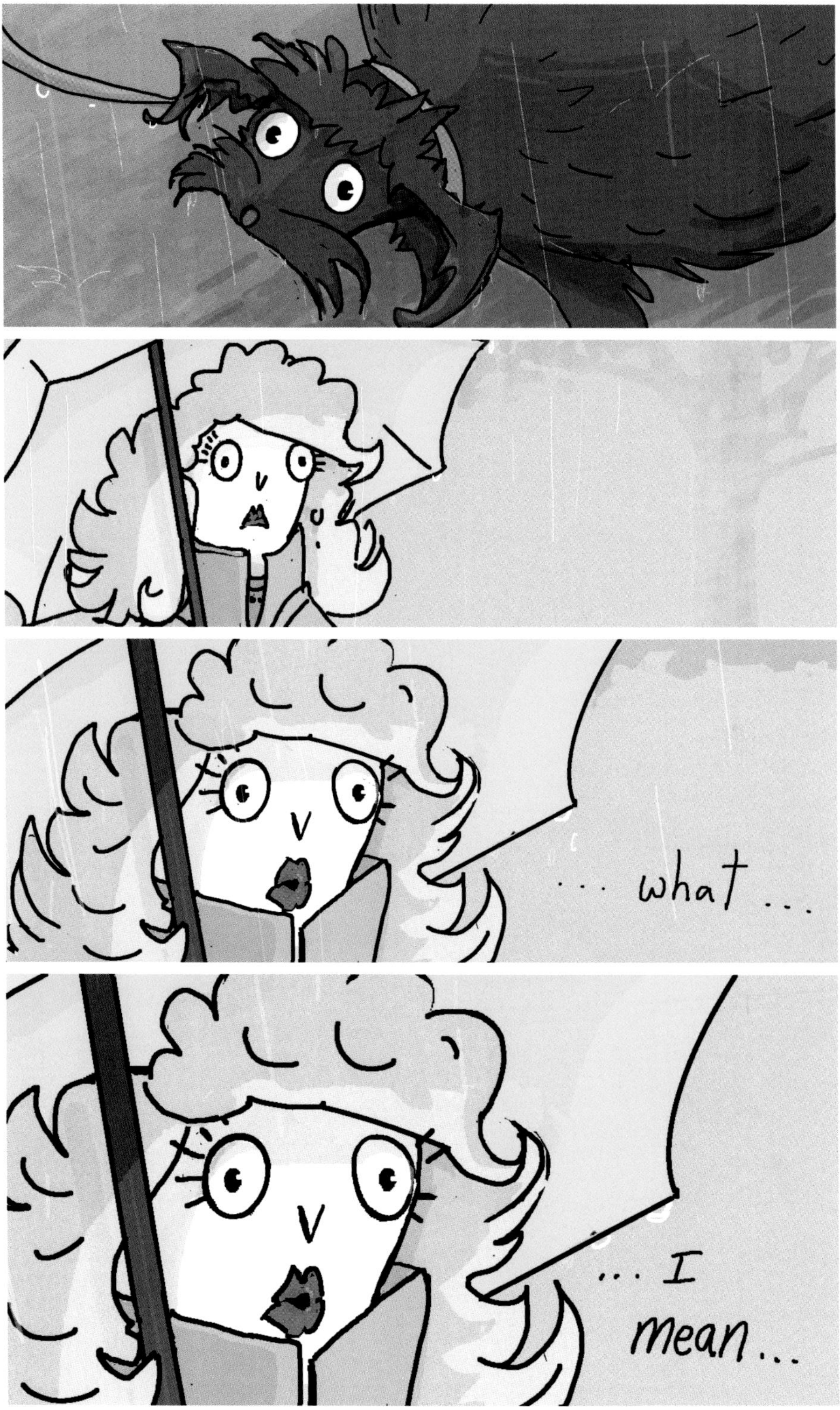
... what ...
... I mean...

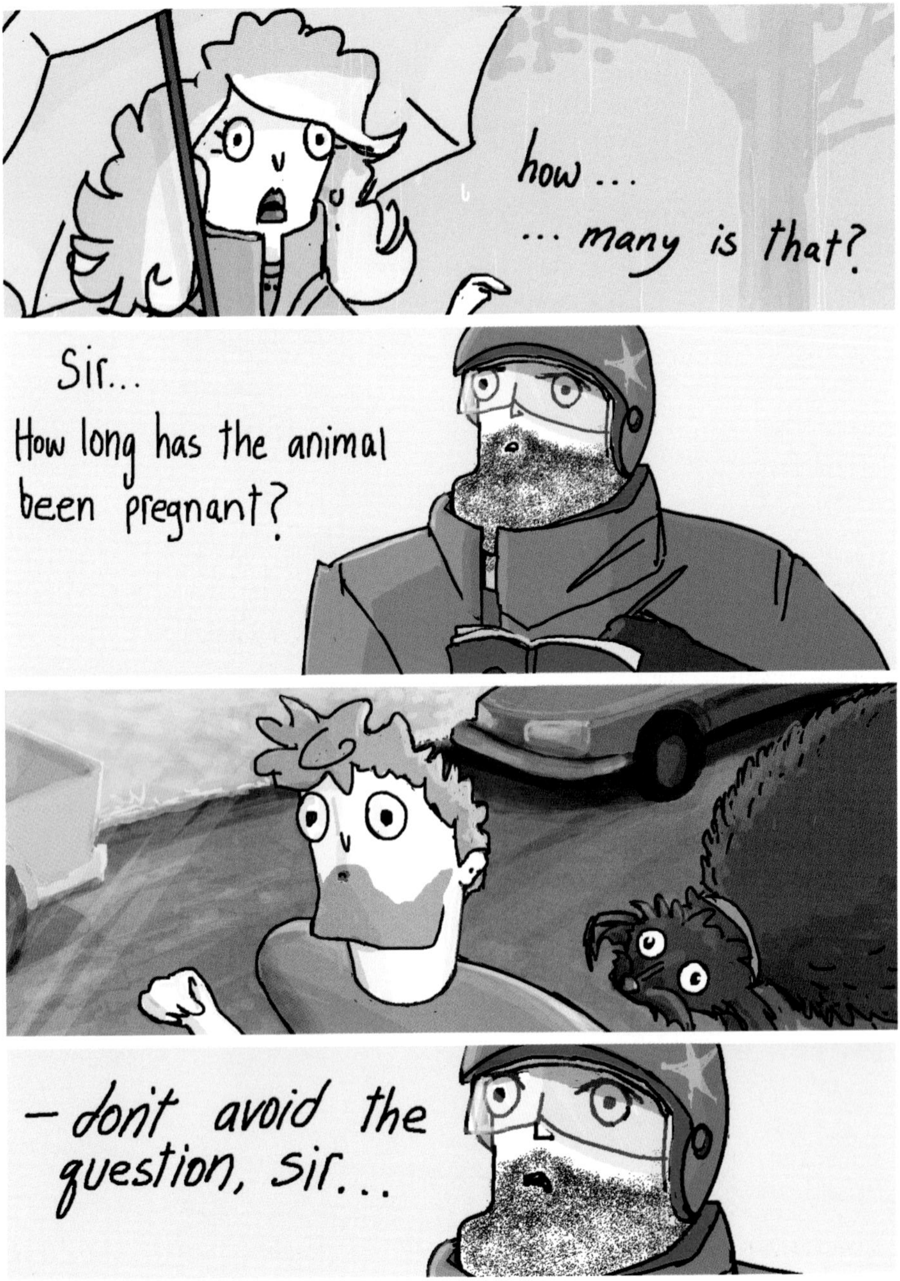
how...
... many is that?
Sir...
How long has the animal been pregnant?
- don't avoid the question, sir...

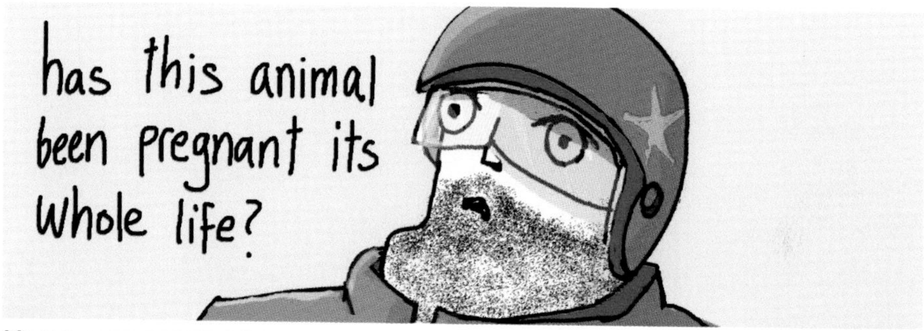
has this animal been pregnant its whole life?

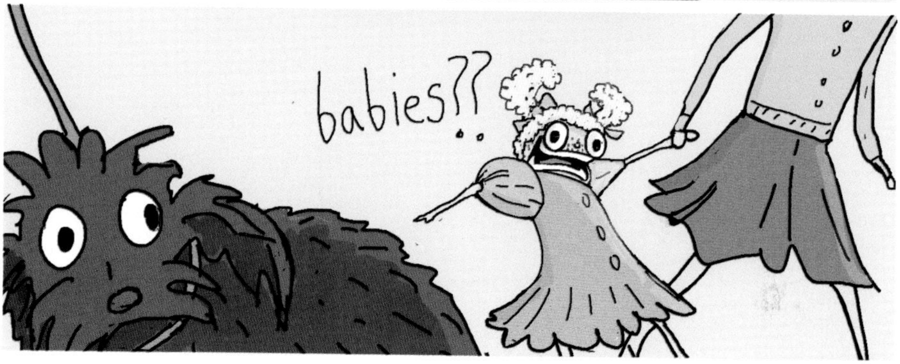
babies??

That's a tough question to field five times a day when the real answer is "No, sorry . . . the reason she looks like that is because she is dying."

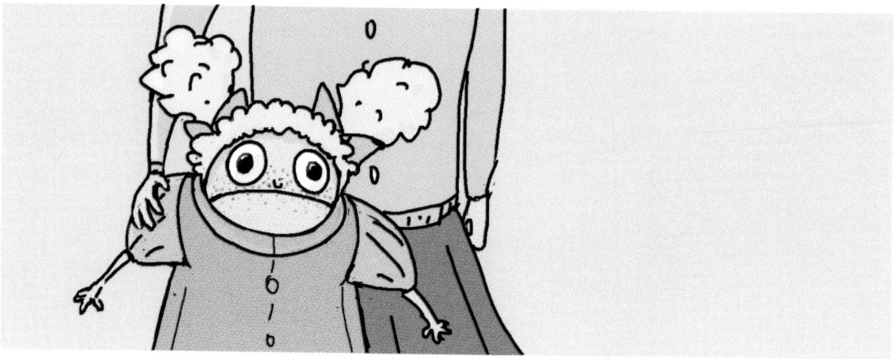

You can't lie, though. People follow up on it.

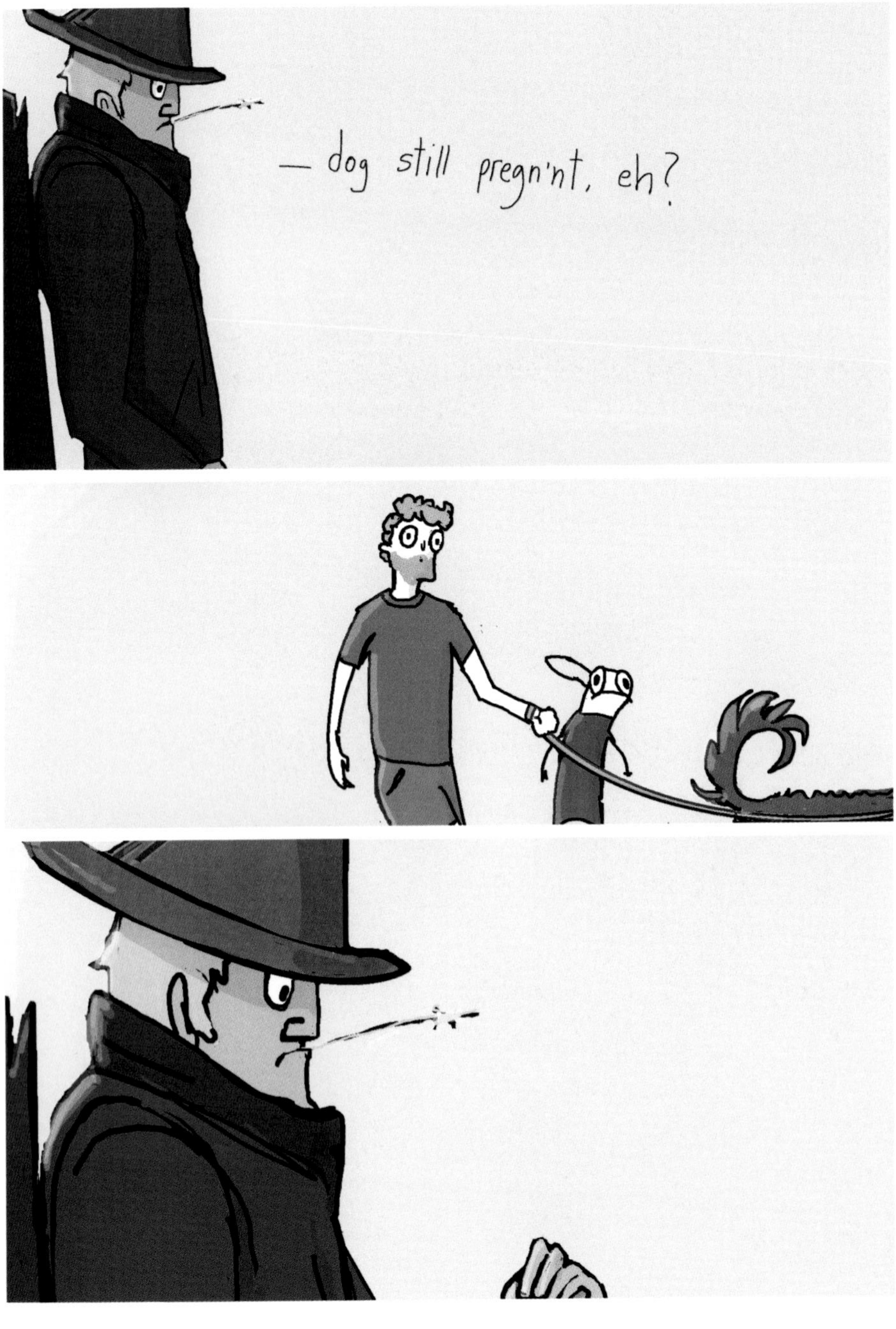
— dog still pregn'nt, eh?

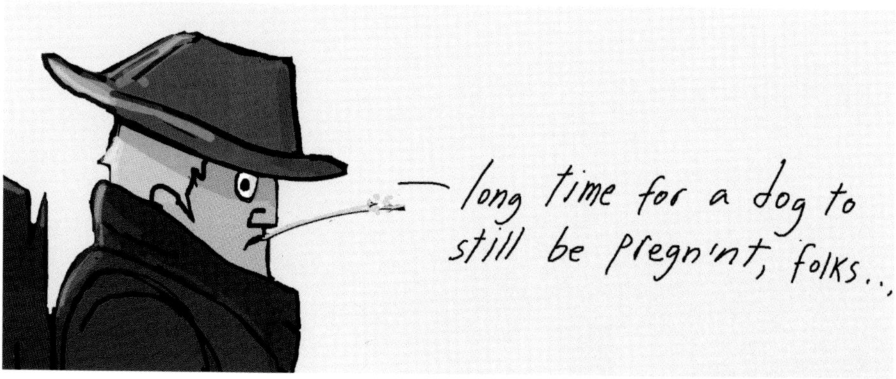
—long time for a dog to
still be pregn'nt, folks...

It's also pretty hard to avoid the question. These are good people—they're trying to make sure you aren't doing something weird to this poor, bloated dog. They won't stop asking questions until they have the explanation.

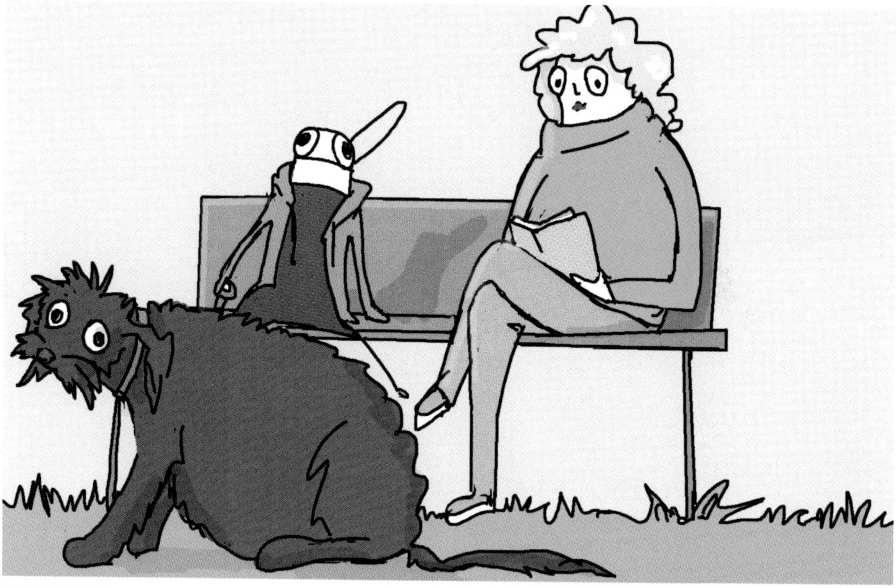

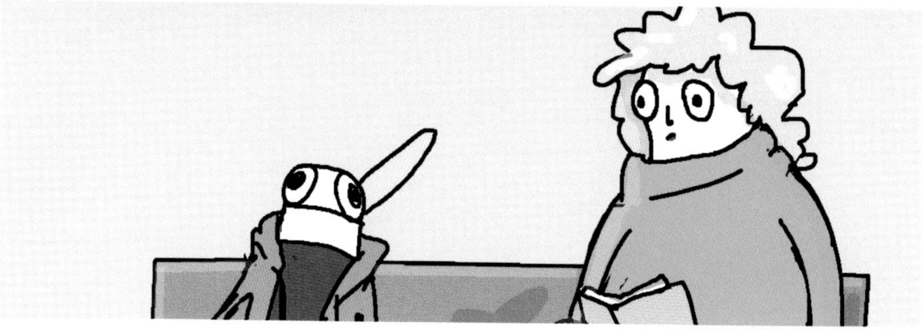

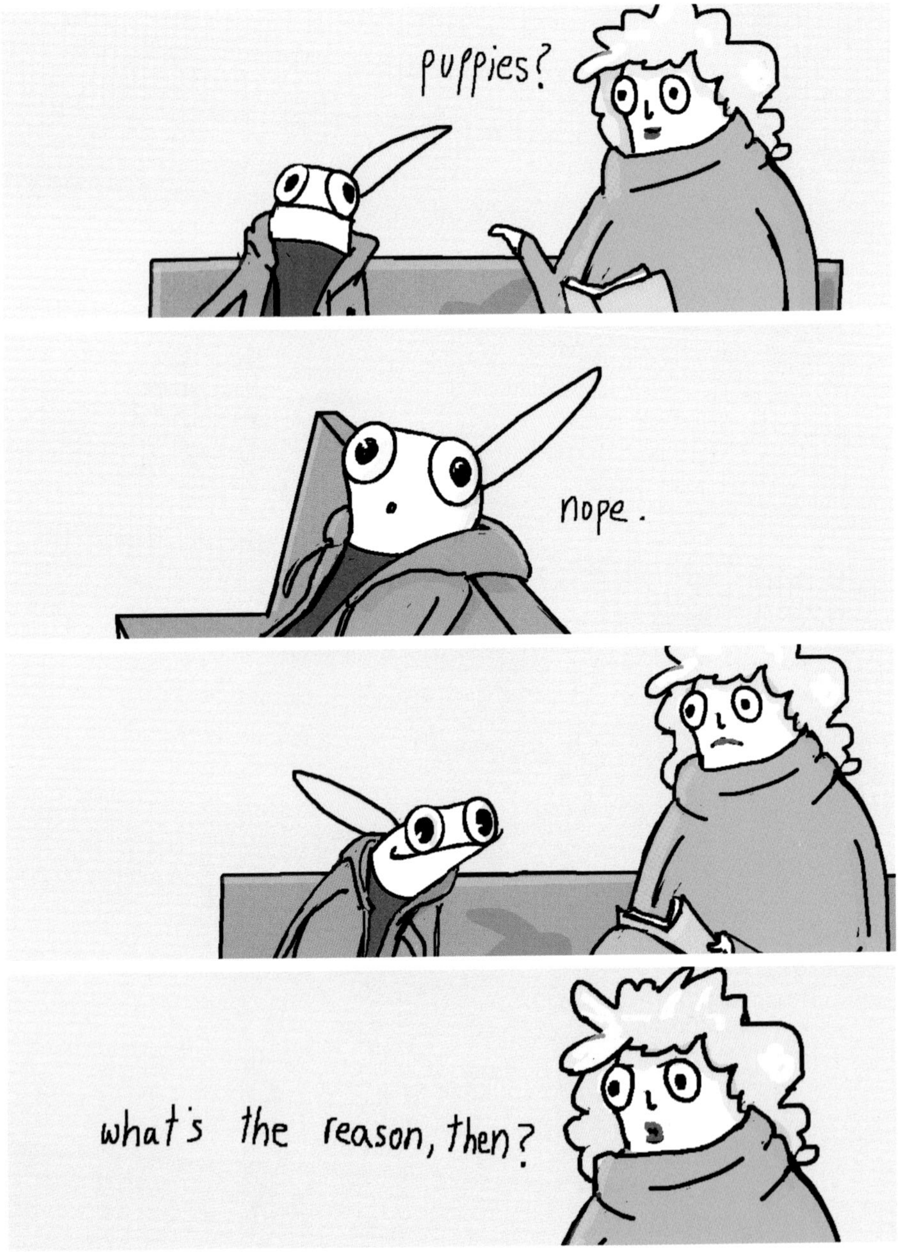
puppies?
nope.
what's the reason, then?

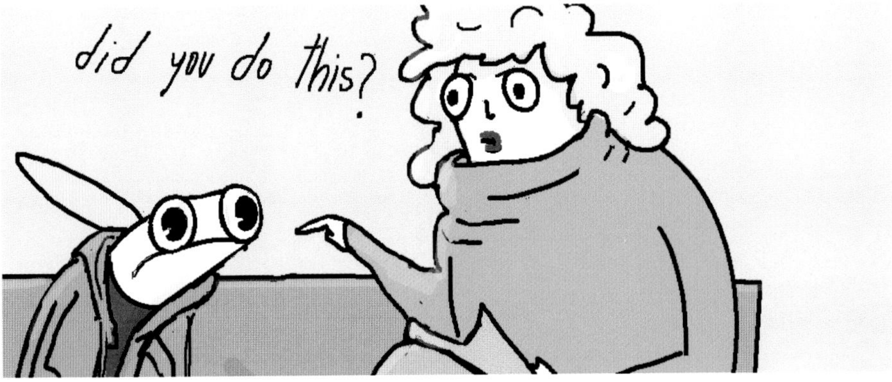
did you do this?

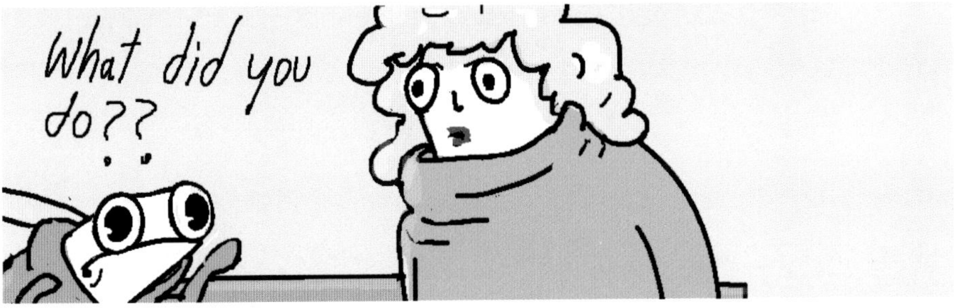
What did you do??

She survived so long it became summer. We had to shave her.

Right after we shaved her, we found out that—despite looking like a diabetic manatee from outer space—she didn't have enough body fat to stay warm even when it's 85 degrees. We had to buy her a sweater. In July.

She already looked pretty confusing, and I don't fully understand why this was the case, but the sweater made it *way* worse.

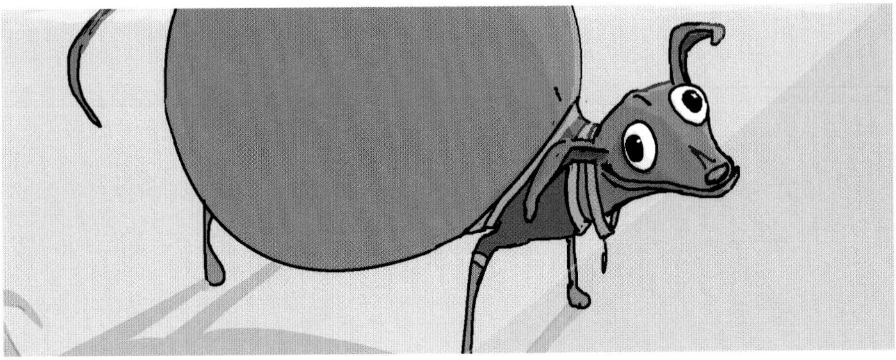

Nobody knows what to do with that. If that comes at them, they don't even know where to start.

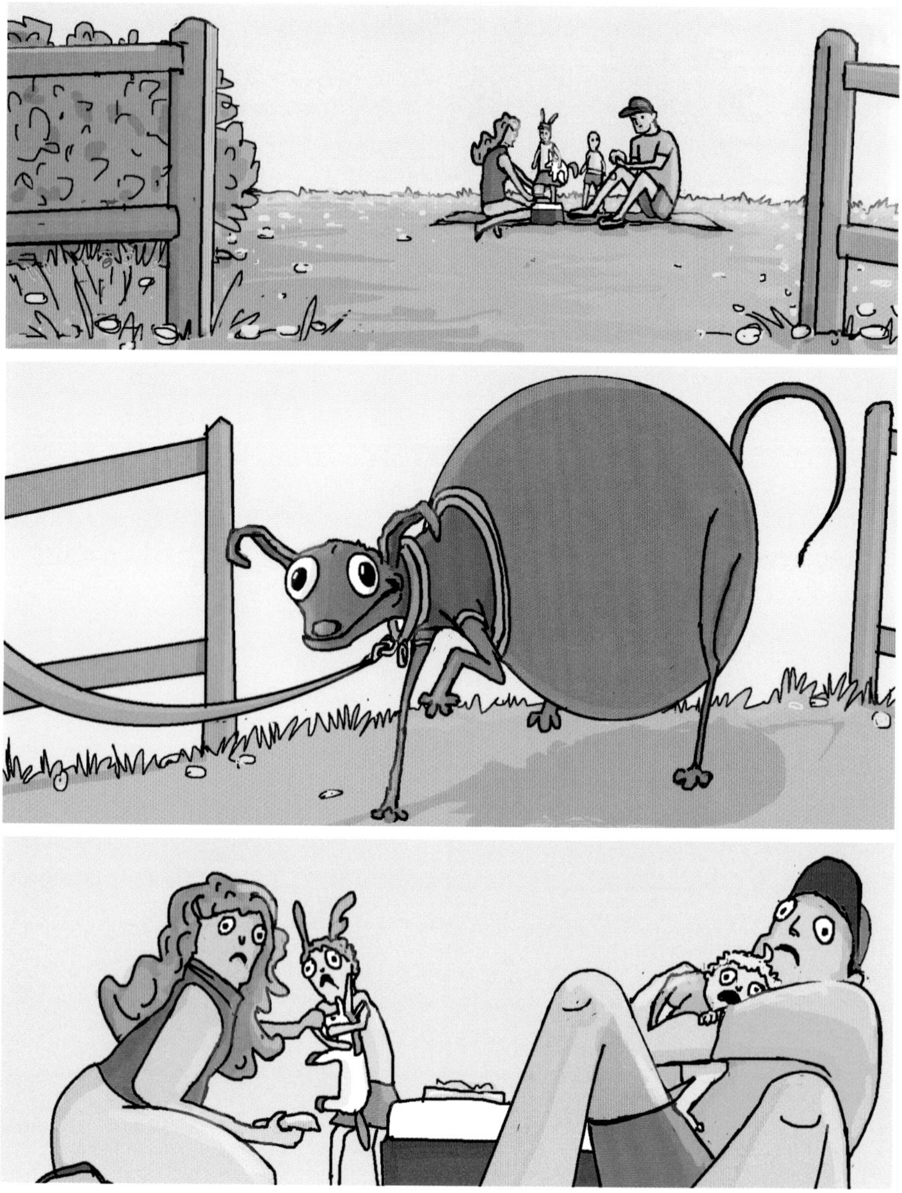

The most appropriate crescendo for this would probably be the time our AC broke.

When the repairman came by to fix it, he seemed wary of the pile dog—like he wasn't sure how he should be interacting with her.

She was waddling laps through the house like usual, poking around in different places, making friendly little snorting sounds to say hi on her way past, and the repairman kept staring at her with this strained expression on his face.

We assumed he was just lukewarm about dogs, or maybe he didn't know the best way to approach the subject of what was wrong with her.

Fifteen minutes later, he finally worked up the courage to ask what kind of animal she was.

Which is a risky question.

You don't ask that question if it's just a little ambiguous.

You don't even ask that question if you have guesses—any guesses at all. Absolutely nobody wants to seem like the sort of fool who can't tell the difference between a goat and a pony. If there's a chance it's an animal you've heard of, it isn't worth it.

The only person who would ask that question is somebody who's fully stumped and believes it might be a type of animal they've never seen before.

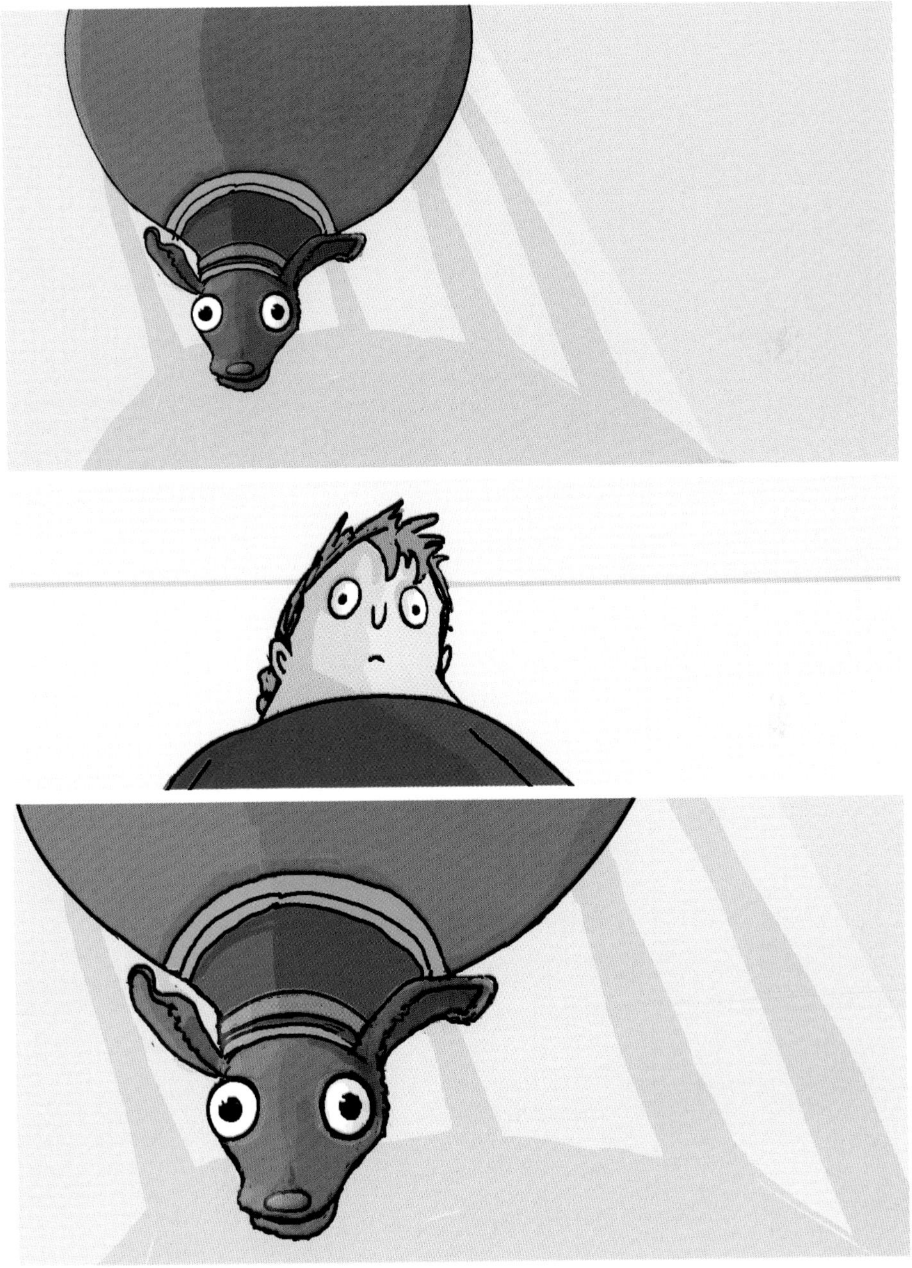

He straight up couldn't tell what species he was looking at . . .

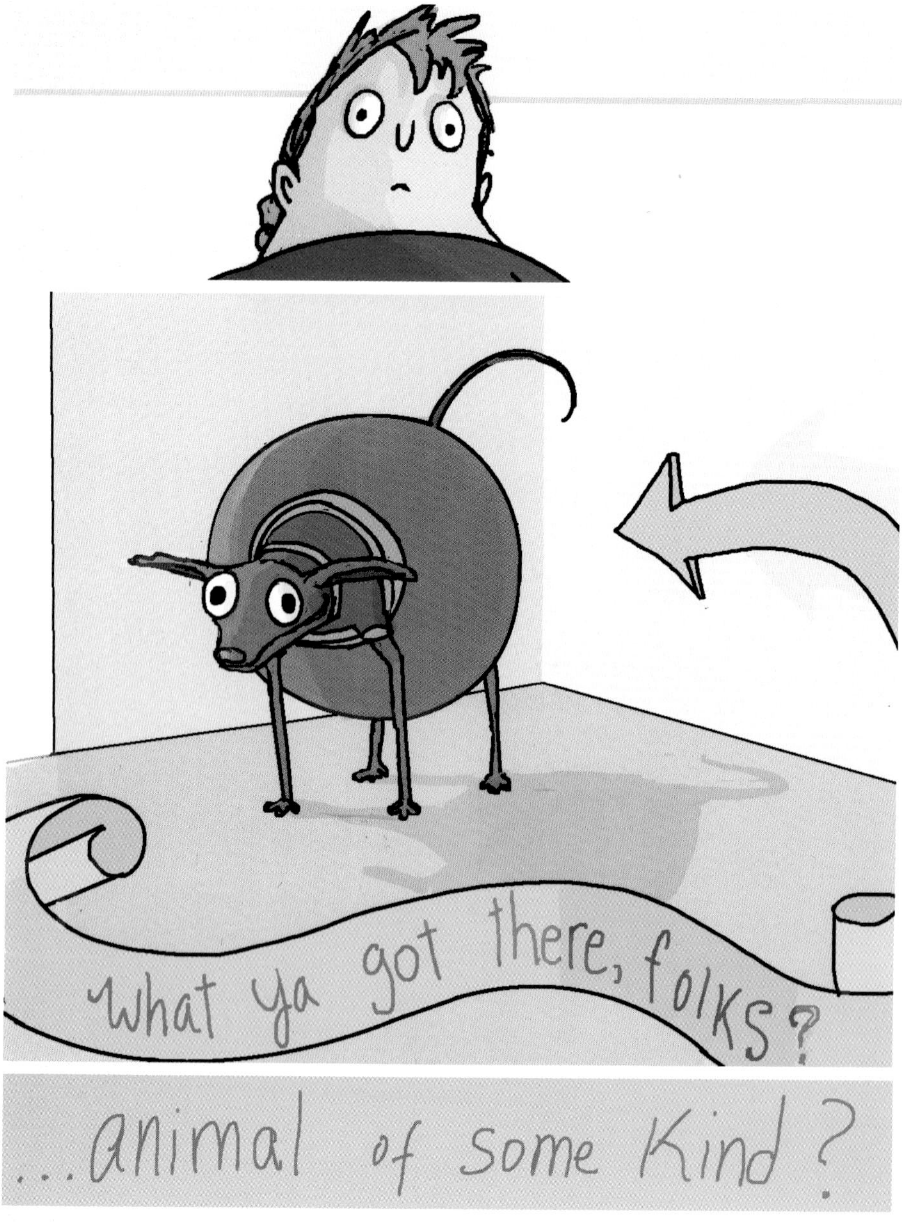
What ya got there, folks?
...animal of some Kind?

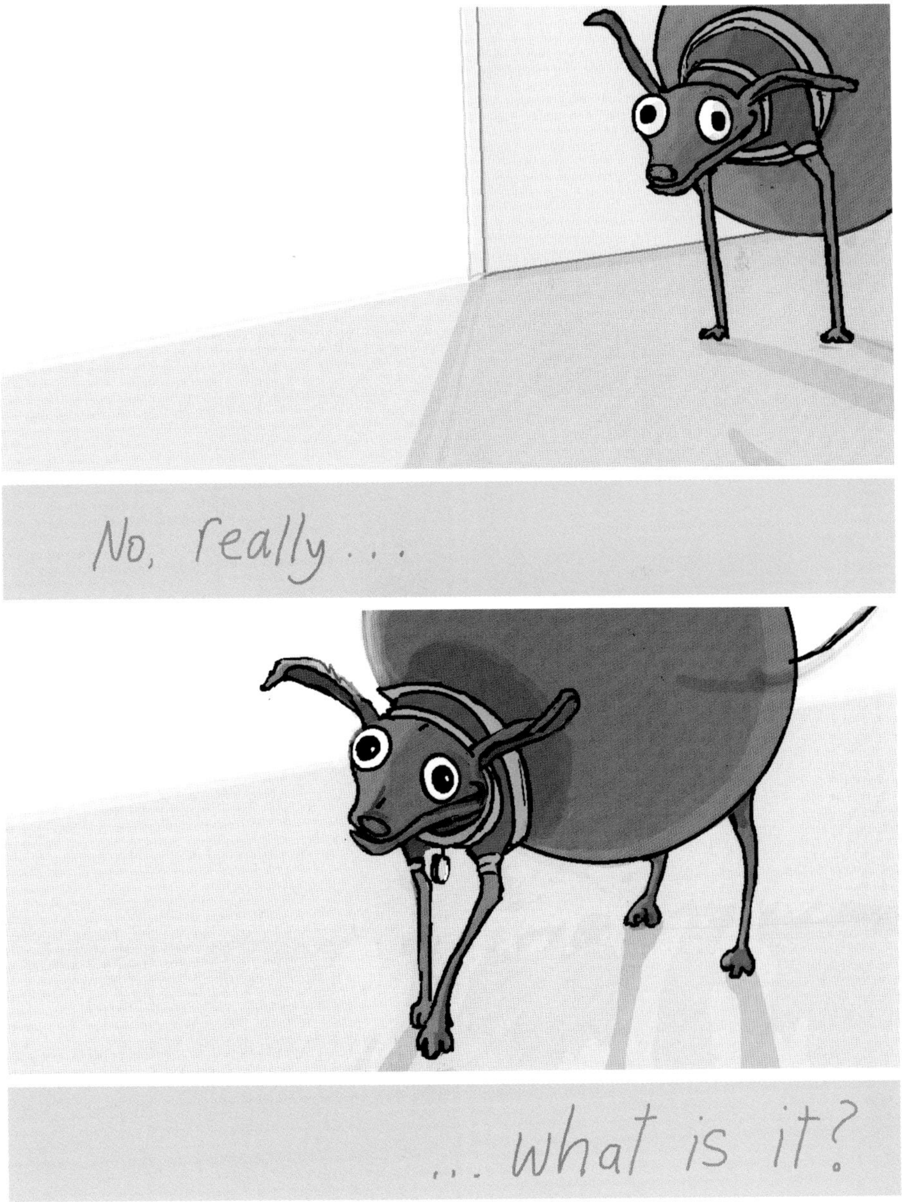
No, really . . .
. . . what is it?

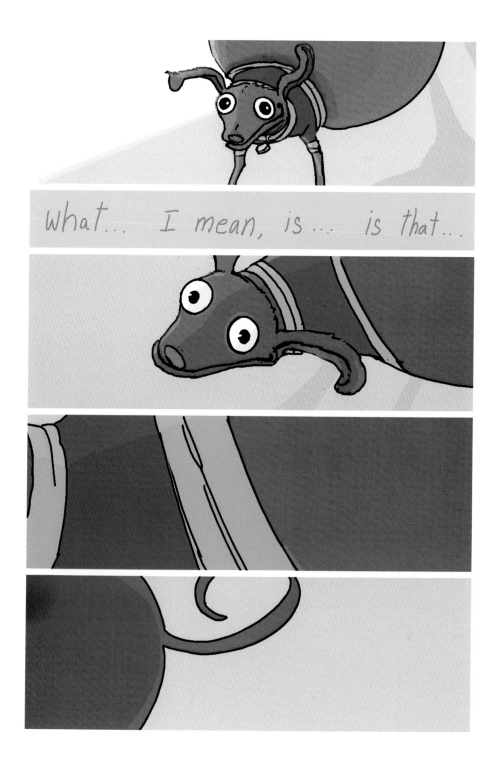

What... I mean, is... is that...

... is it wearing a crop top?

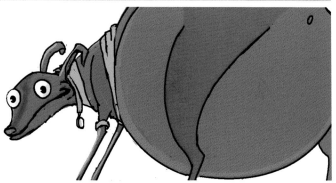

OKie dokie, folks — gonna cut right to it:

do you have an illegal monster from outer space living with you in here?

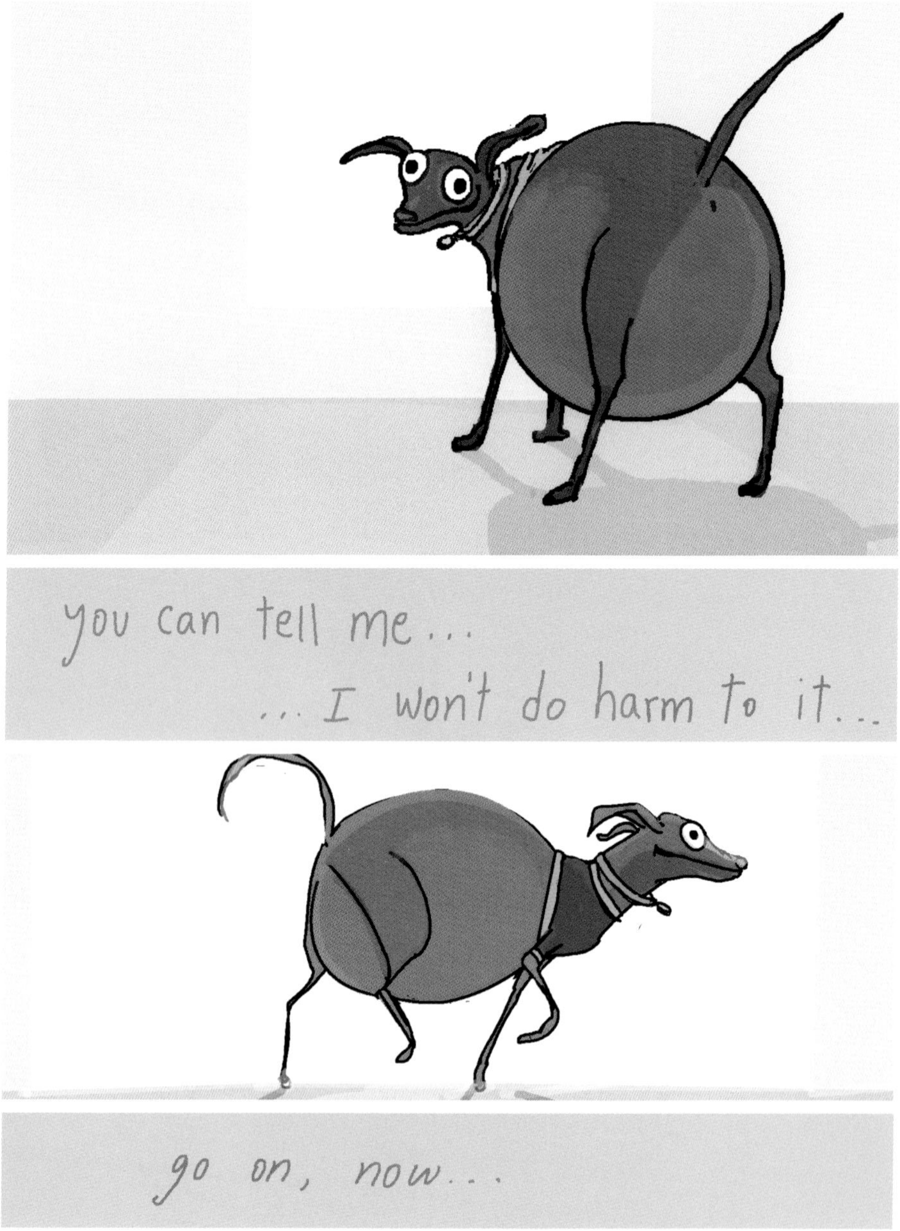
you can tell me...
...I won't do harm to it...
go on, now...

...just say what it is...

We told him, but I don't think he believed us.

13. WORLD'S GREATEST CUP

Some years have been hard, but overall, I have a pretty easy life. If I find a dead deer, I don't have to fight a bear for it. I don't even have to eat it if I don't want to.

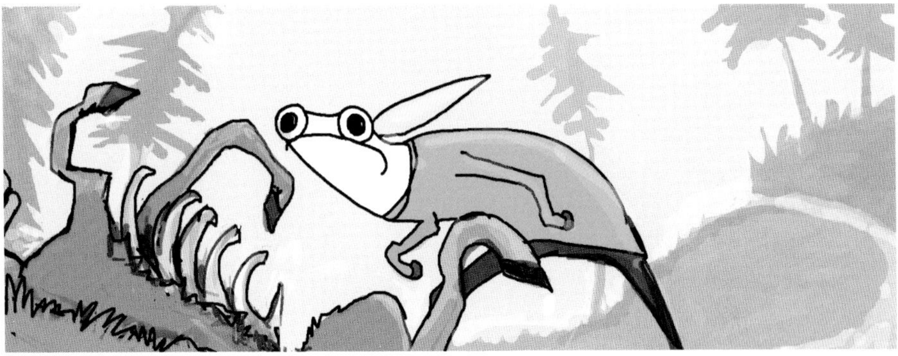

This isn't to say I do not experience conflict. I absolutely do.

For example, I wasn't content with the CD player in my car, so I got a new stereo. One of the ones that can play music from a phone instead of just tapes and CDs.

They described the stereo as "interactive," which sounded cool. I don't know exactly what that means, but I assumed something like "capable of responding to commands" or "lets you change the colors on the buttons."

As it turns out, "interactive" can also be a gentle way to describe something that a more direct person might call relentless and nonsensically invasive.

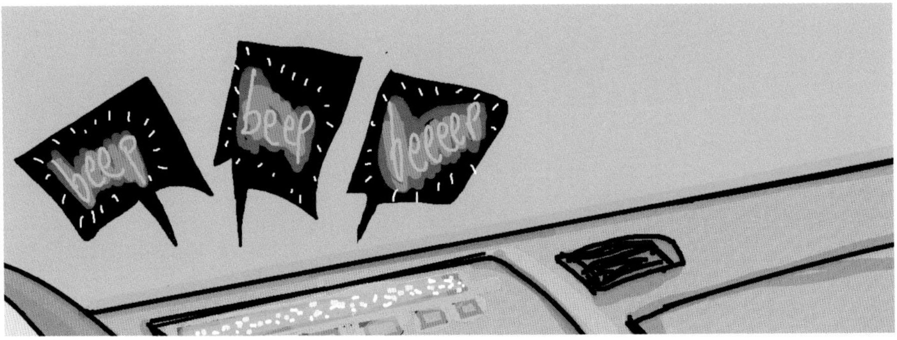
beep
beep
beeeep

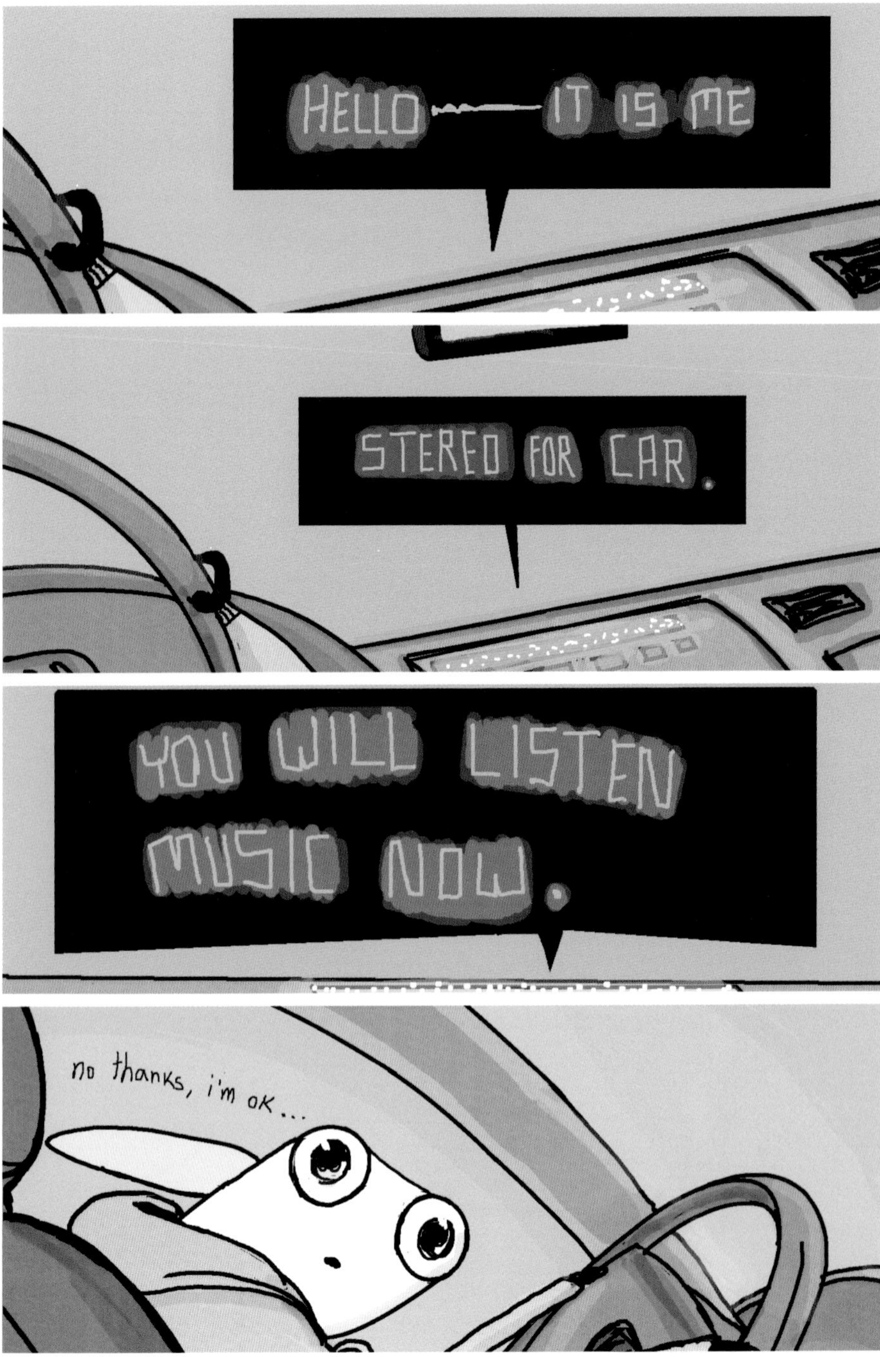
HELLO — IT IS ME
STEREO FOR CAR.
YOU WILL LISTEN MUSIC NOW.
no thanks, i'm ok...

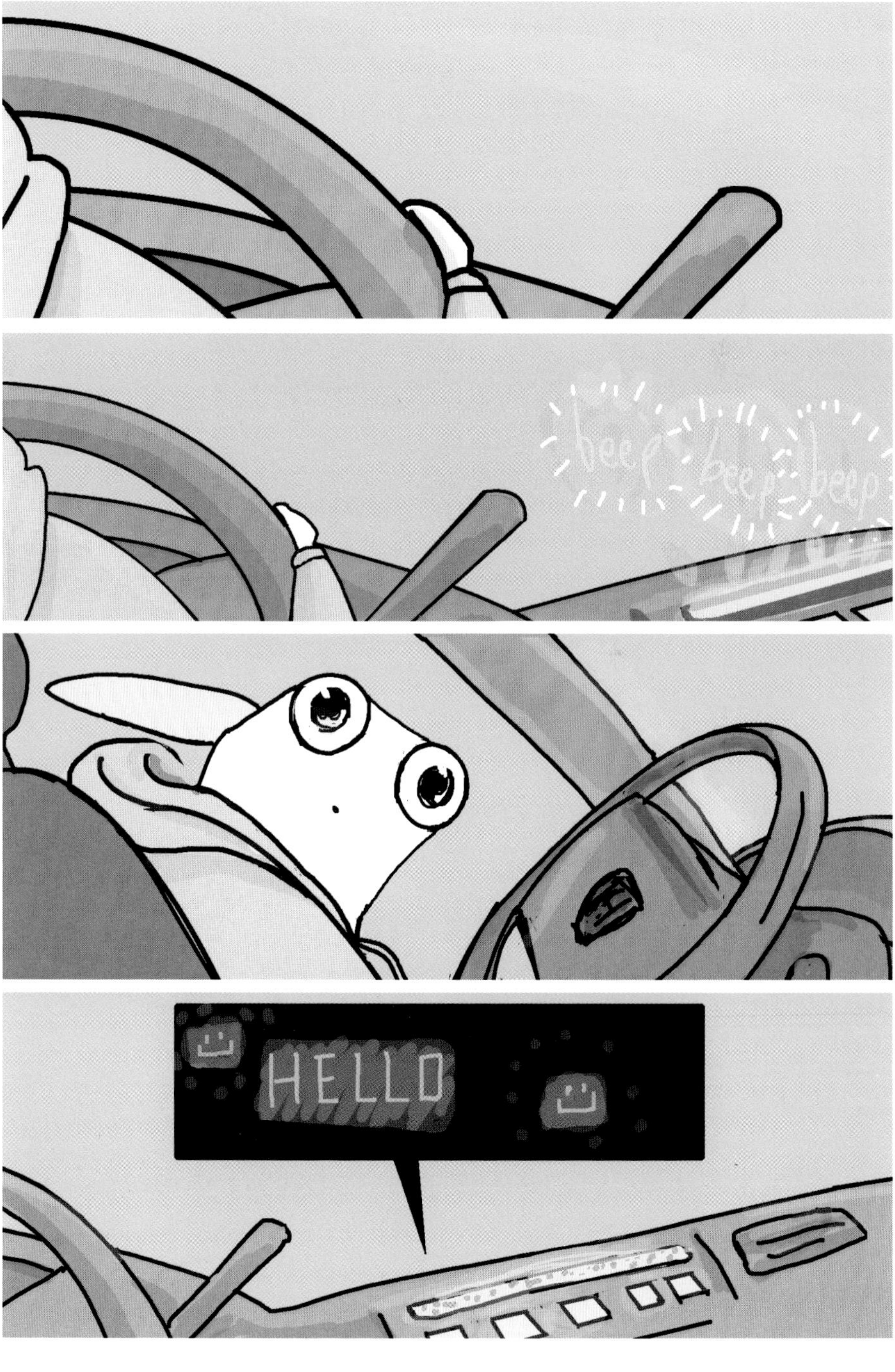
beep beep beep
HELLO

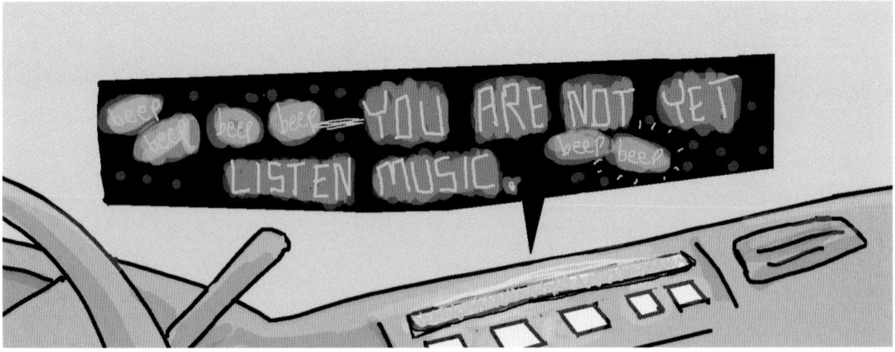
beep beep beep beep YOU ARE NOT YET LISTEN MUSIC. beep beep

It will not stop until it is certain that I am adequately interacted with and all my needs have been met, forcibly if necessary.

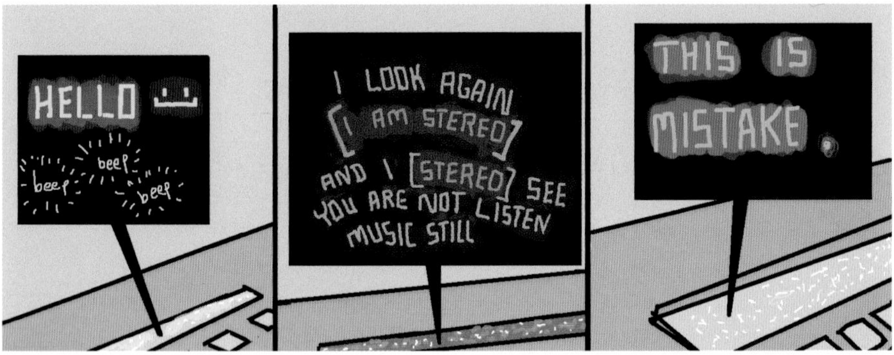
HELLO
beep beep beep
I LOOK AGAIN [I AM STEREO] AND I [STEREO] SEE YOU ARE NOT LISTEN MUSIC STILL
THIS IS MISTAKE.

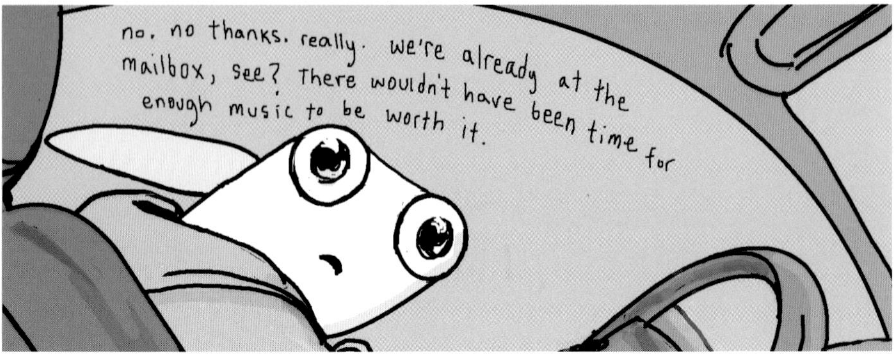
no. no thanks. really. we're already at the mailbox, see? There wouldn't have been time for enough music to be worth it.

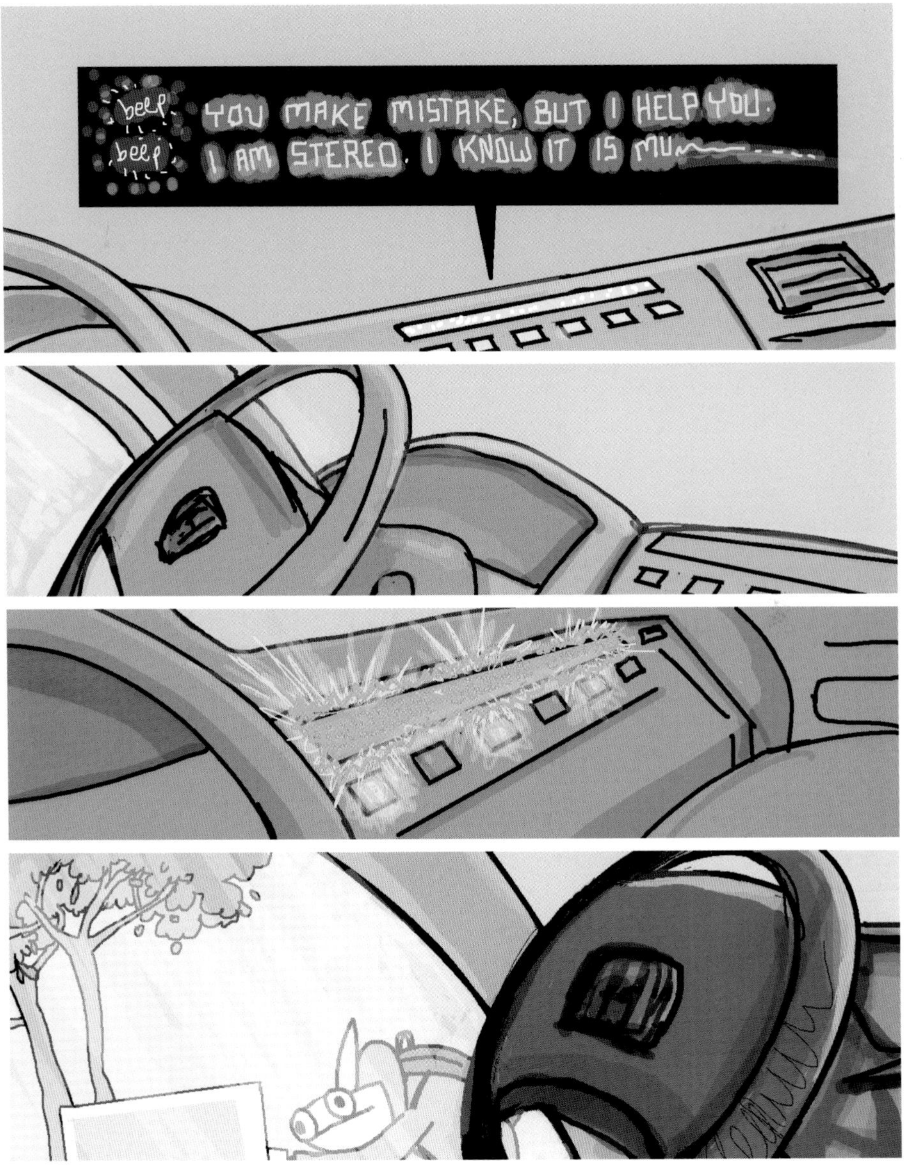
beep beep
YOU MAKE MISTAKE, BUT I HELP YOU.
I AM STEREO. I KNOW IT IS MU

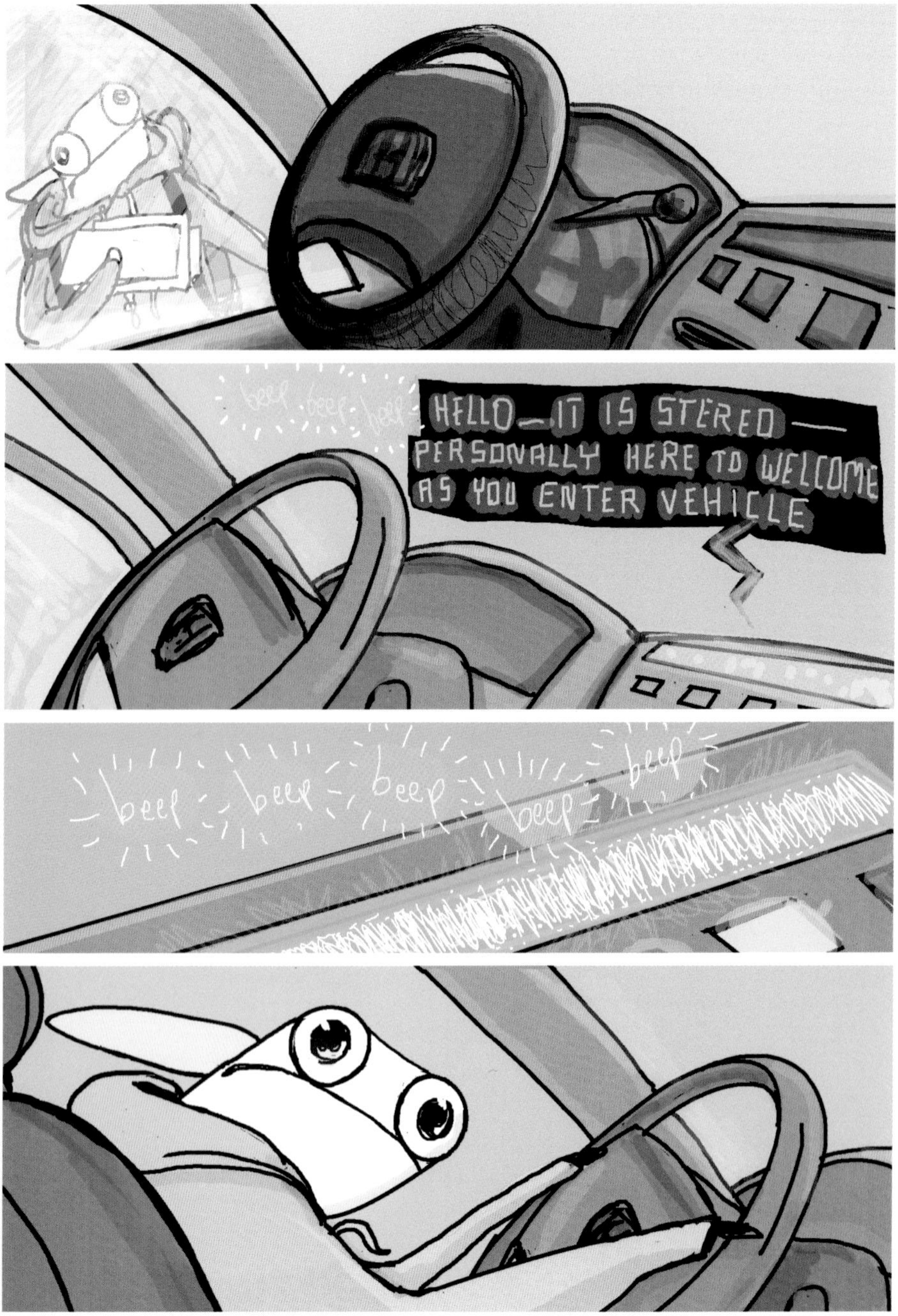
beep beep beep
HELLO—IT IS STEREO— PERSONALLY HERE TO WELCOME AS YOU ENTER VEHICLE
beep beep beep beep beep

What kind of person is that feature intended for? Somebody who loves beeping and needs to feel properly greeted by their stereo? Does a person like that exist?

I don't know where it got the impression that I need that.

I also don't know where it got the impression that I constantly need to be updated about things only a stereo would care about.

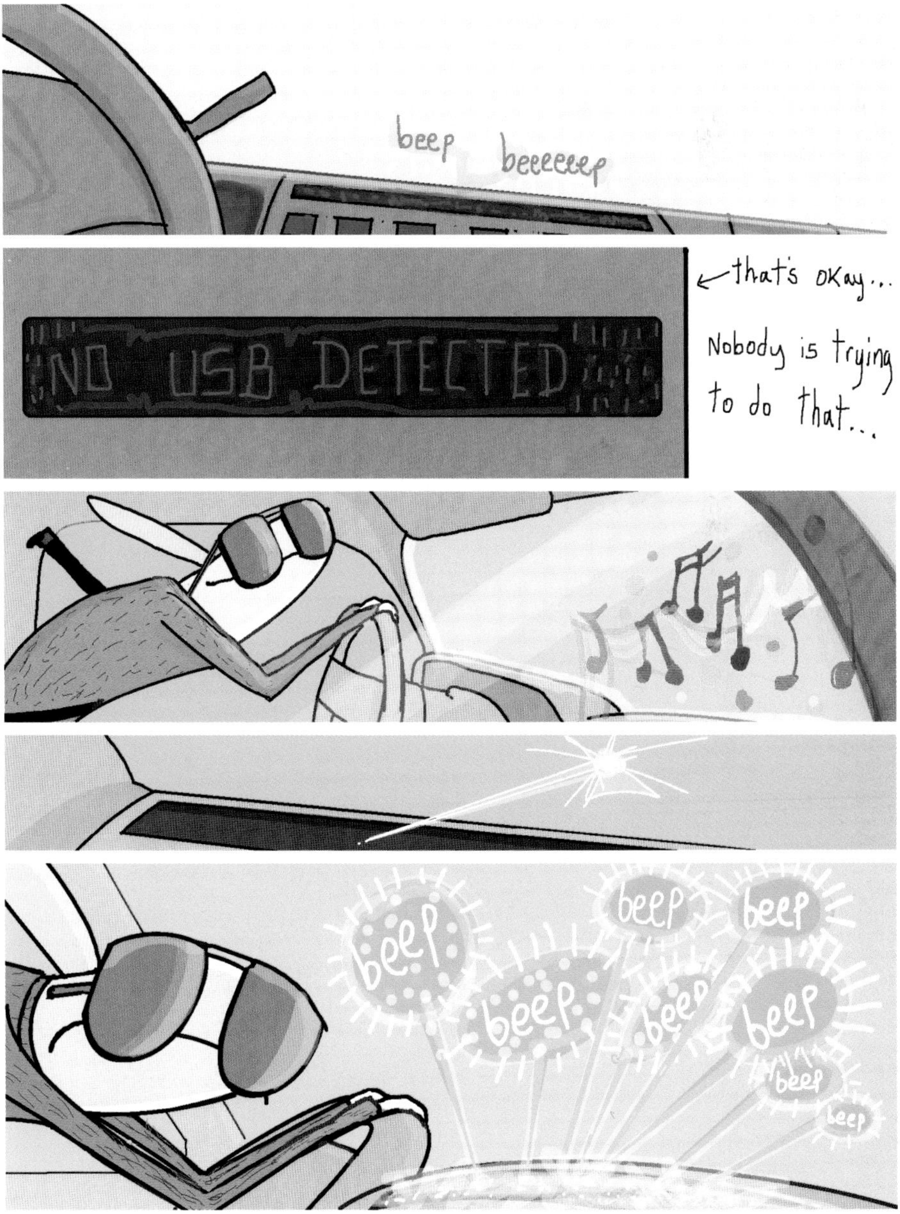
beep beeeeeep
NO USB DETECTED
← that's okay...
Nobody is trying to do that...
beep
beep
beep
beep
beep
beep
beep
beep

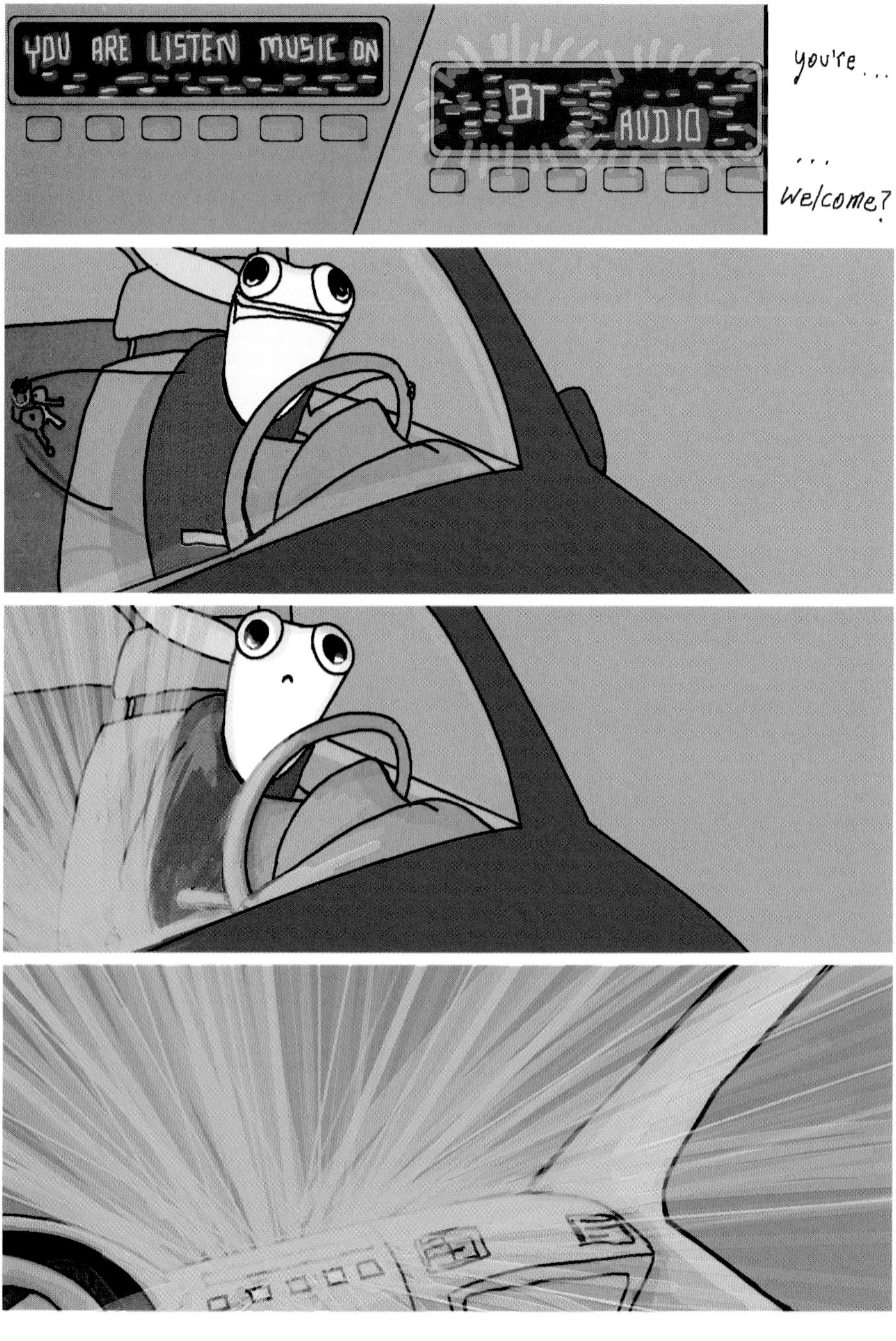
YOU ARE LISTEN MUSIC ON
BT AUDIO
you're...
... welcome?

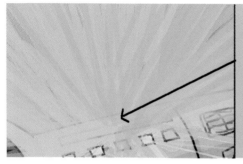

I don't know what this means, but it seems to be a response to the music being turned off.

I want to explain that music is not supposed to be mandatory. It is a fun activity. I do not need it for anything. There are no serious injuries that can happen as a result of not listening to music. I want to explain that. But I don't know how to put it in terms a stereo can understand, so I either have to listen to music or endure the consequences.

It also takes my phone calls. Not like "my phone calls come in, and, if asked to do so, my stereo will accept them." We're talking about stealing. It steals my phone calls. A phone call will come in, and, without consulting me, my stereo will gain control of the phone call and accept it on my behalf.

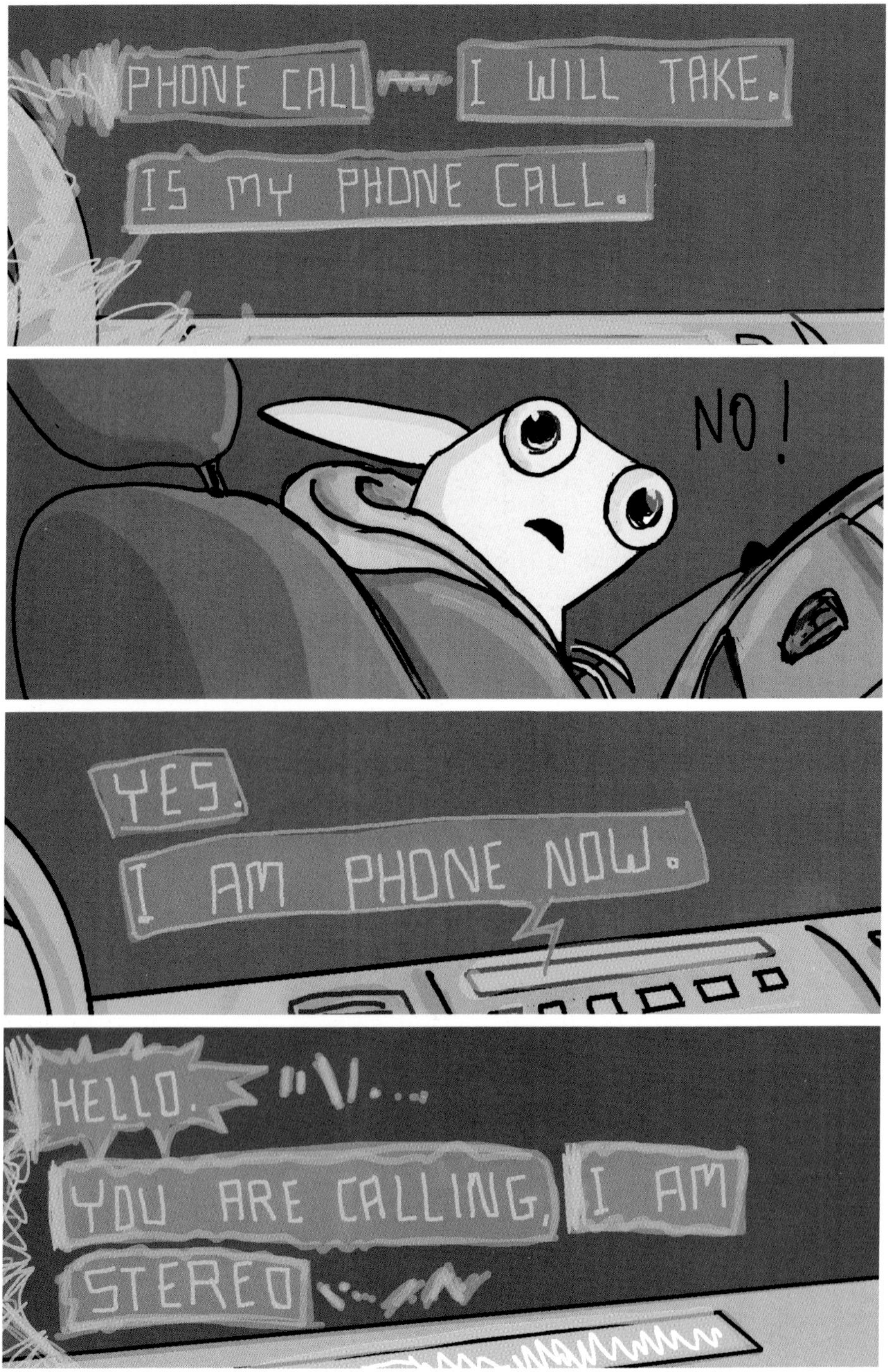
PHONE CALL
I WILL TAKE.
IS MY PHONE CALL.
NO!
YES.
I AM PHONE NOW.
HELLO.
YOU ARE CALLING,
I AM
STEREO

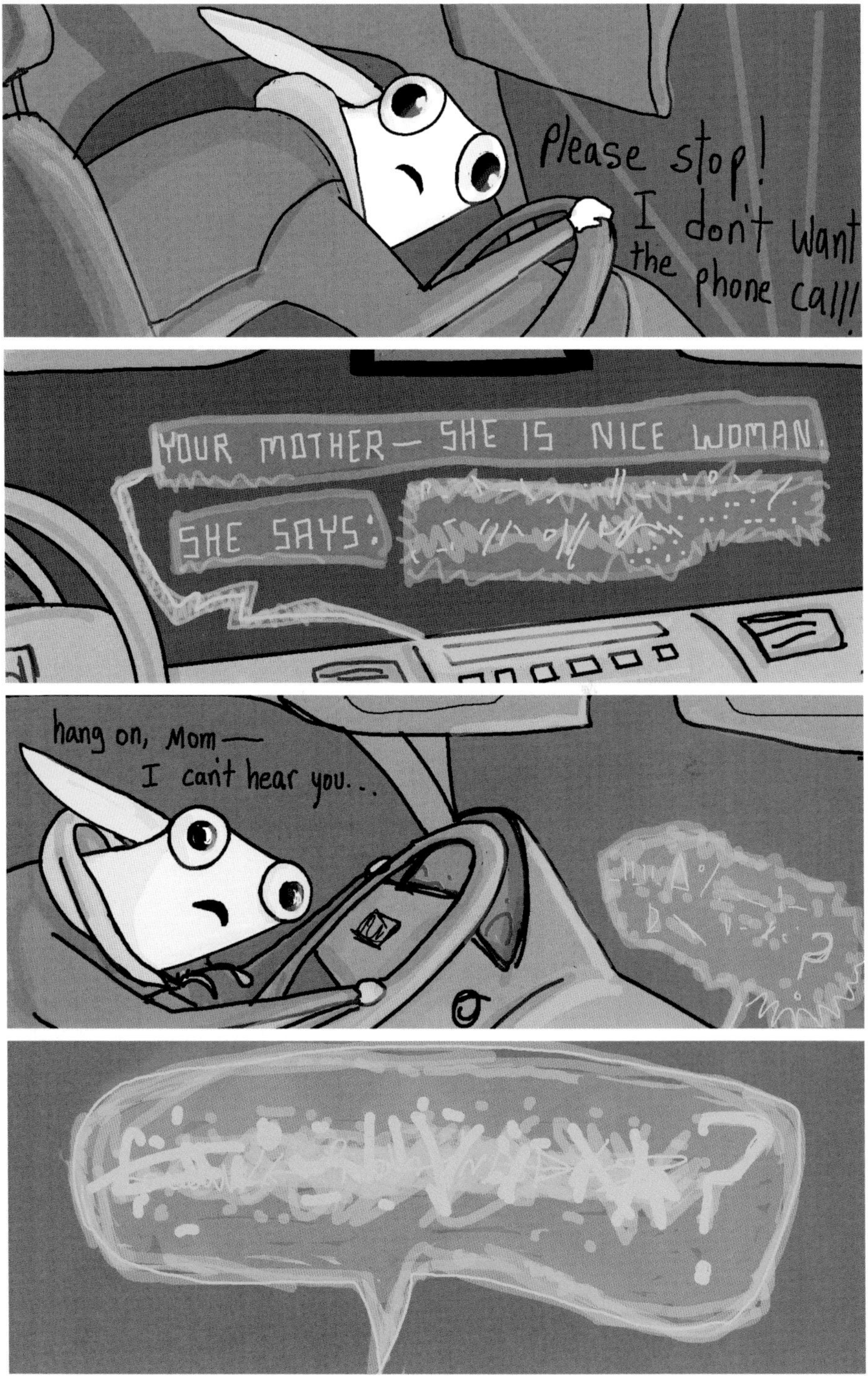
Please stop! I don't want the phone call!
YOUR MOTHER— SHE IS NICE WOMAN.
SHE SAYS:
hang on, Mom— I can't hear you...

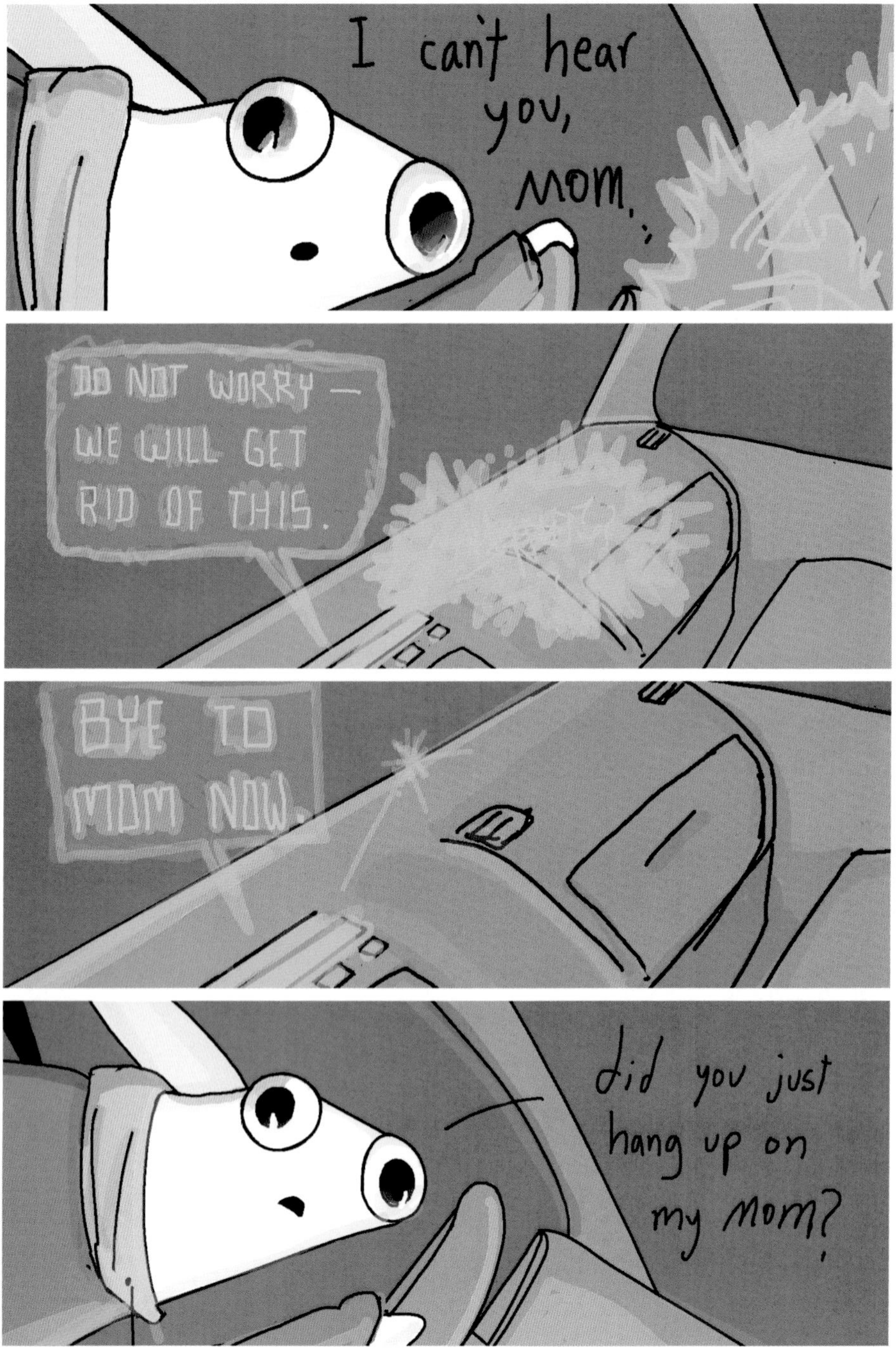
I can't hear you, mom.
DO NOT WORRY — WE WILL GET RID OF THIS.
BYE TO MOM NOW.
did you just hang up on my mom?

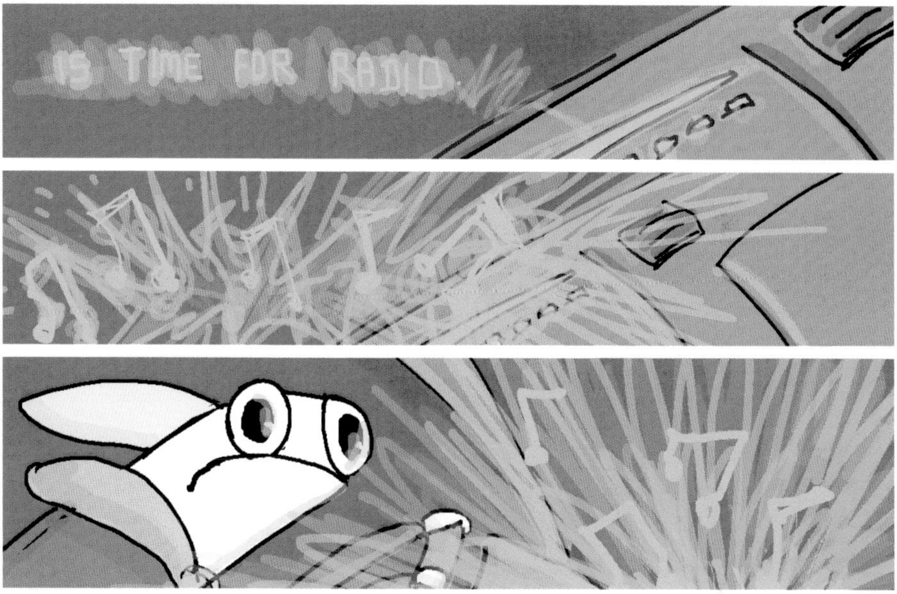
IS TIME FOR RADIO.

I just really disagree with the way it handles things.

I also disagree with how my phone responds. I mean, *defend yourself*. You don't have to let the stereo do that. I've seen what you're capable of.

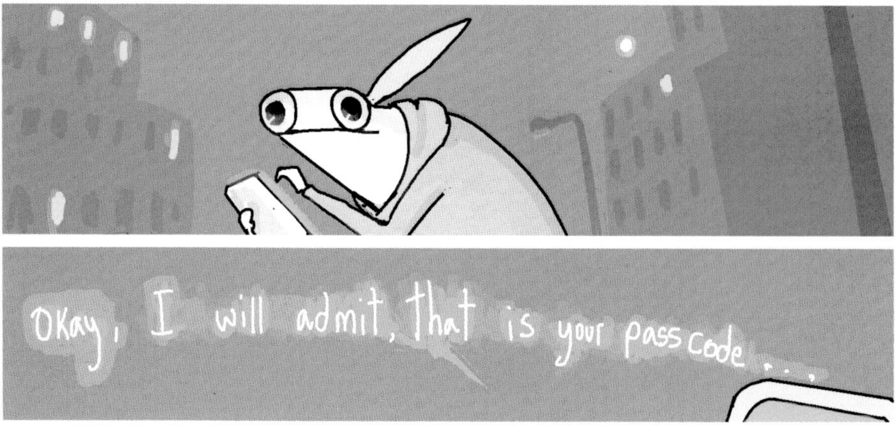
Okay, I will admit, that is your passcode . . .

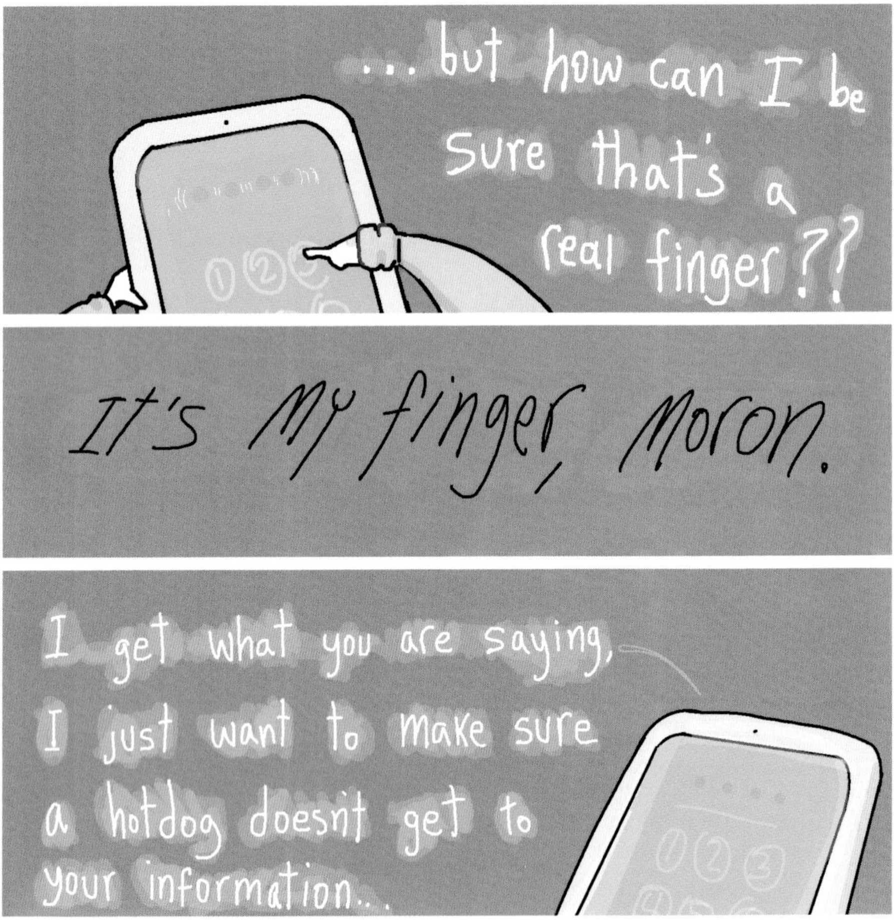
...but how can I be sure that's a real finger??
It's my finger, moron.
I get what you are saying, I just want to make sure a hotdog doesn't get to your information...

My phone means well, but I hate it too. It can't be reasoned with. That doesn't stop me from trying, though.

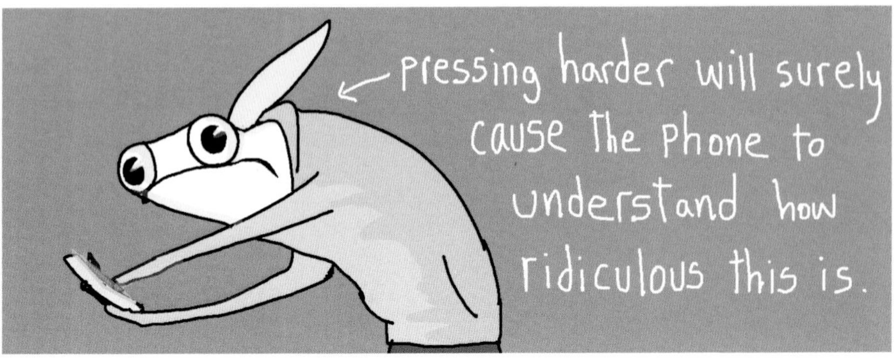
pressing harder will surely cause the phone to understand how ridiculous this is.

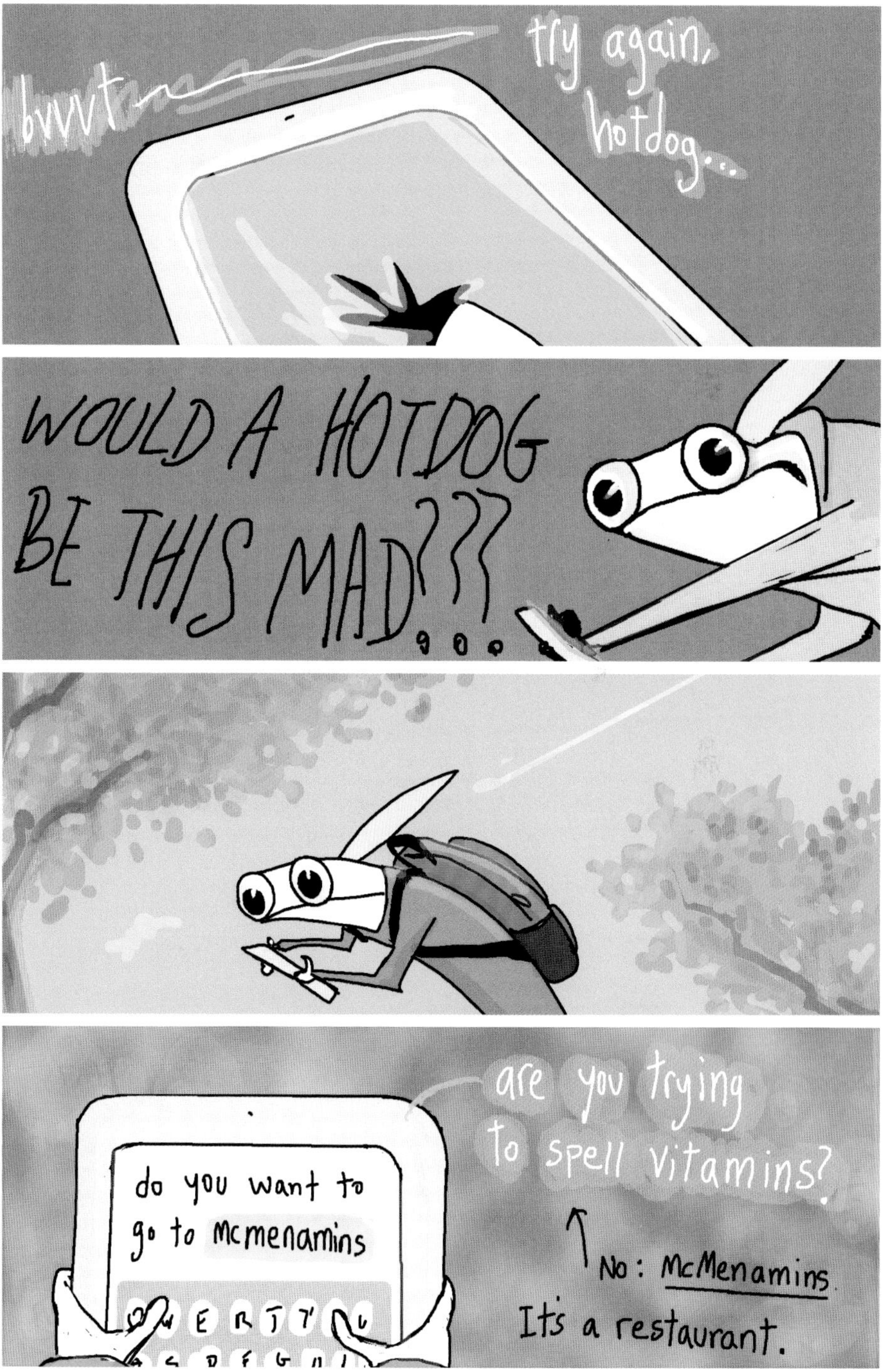
bvvvt
try again, hotdog...
WOULD A HOTDOG BE THIS MAD???
do you want to go to mcmenamins
are you trying to spell vitamins?
No: McMenamins
It's a restaurant.

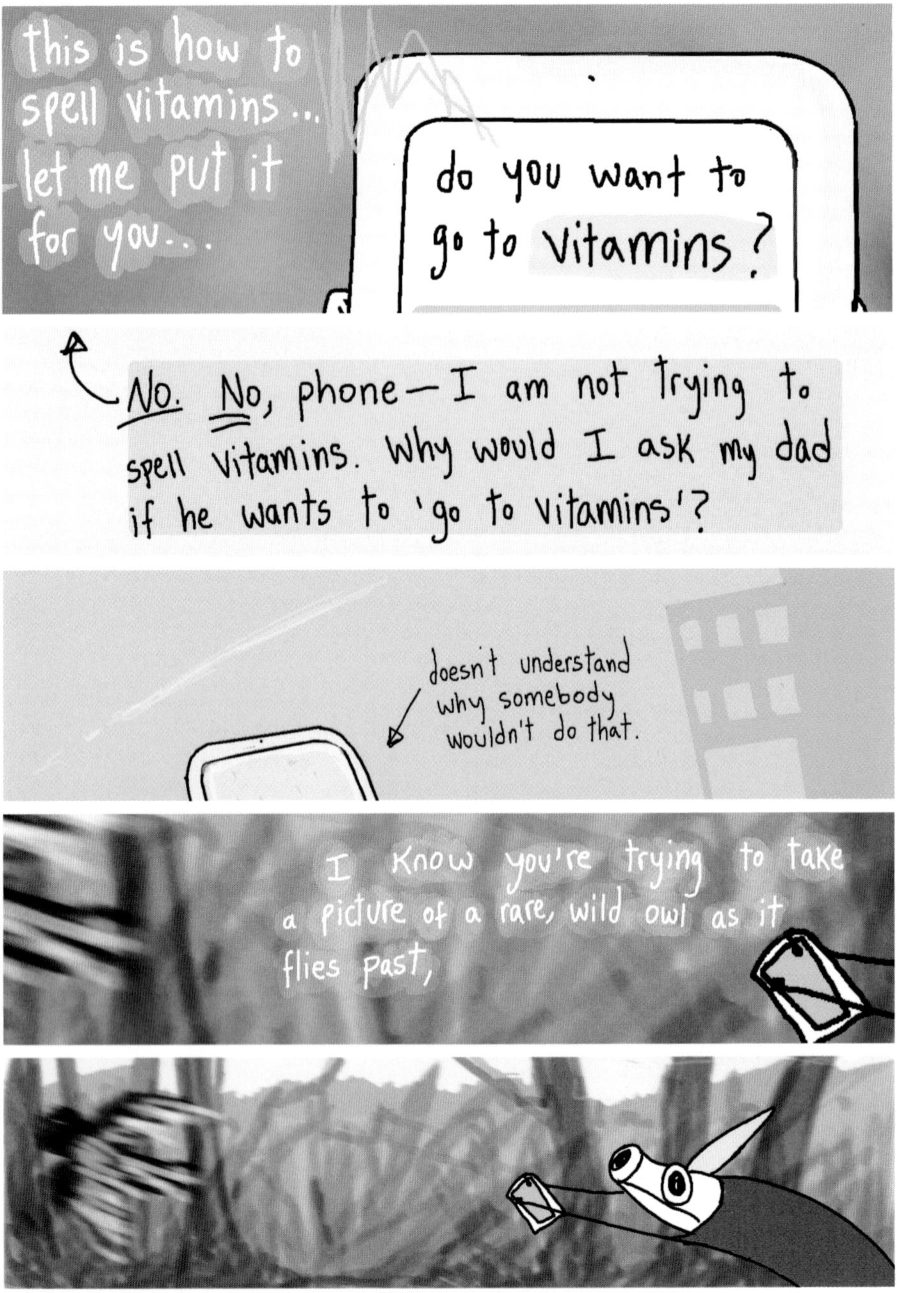

this is how to spell vitamins... let me put it for you...
do you want to go to vitamins?
No. No, phone—I am not trying to spell vitamins. Why would I ask my dad if he wants to 'go to vitamins'?
doesn't understand why somebody wouldn't do that.
I know you're trying to take a picture of a rare, wild owl as it flies past,

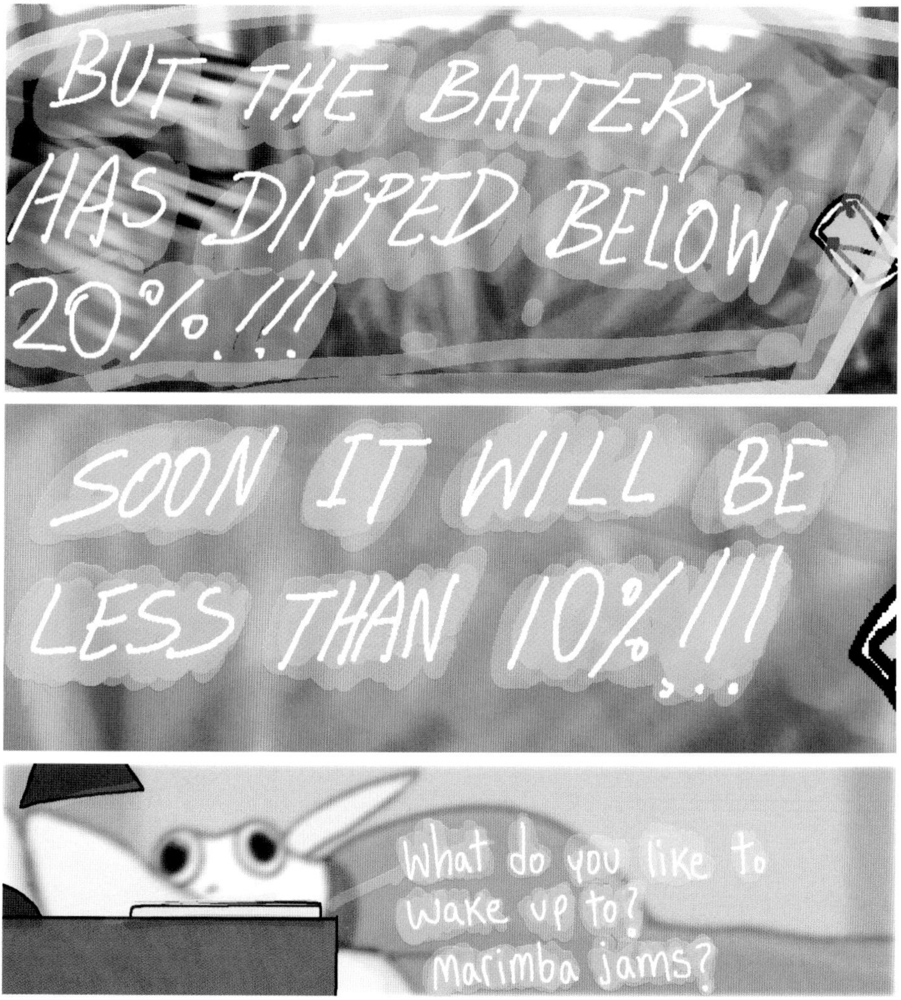
BUT THE BATTERY HAS DIPPED BELOW 20%!!!...
SOON IT WILL BE LESS THAN 10%!!!...
What do you like to wake up to? Marimba jams?

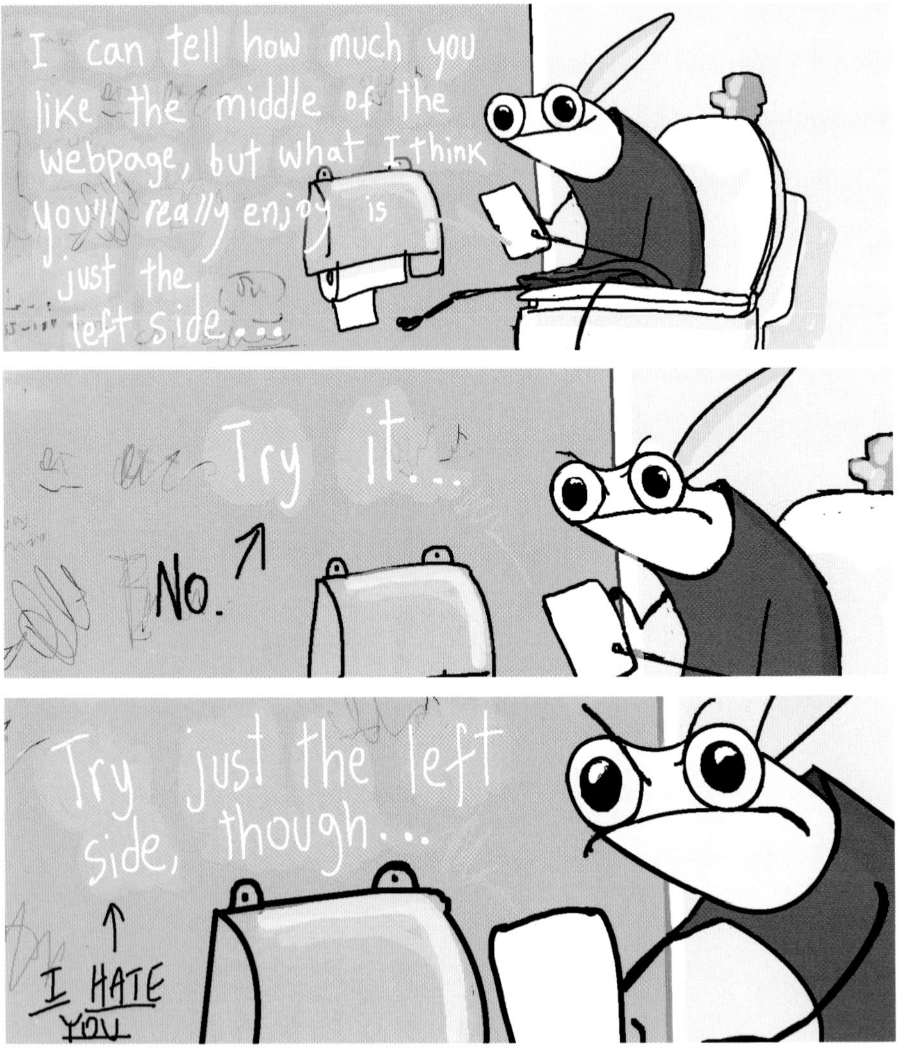
I can tell how much you like the middle of the webpage, but what I think you'll really enjoy is just the left side...
Try it...
No.
Try just the left side, though...
I HATE YOU

It isn't alive. I don't need to get mad at it. But this is confusing for me.

The human brain isn't accustomed to navigating a world where it's hard to tell the difference between objects and animals. For almost all of human history, that has been easy: if it's trying to interact with you, that's an animal. End of story. Maybe there was a tiny bit of a gray area around plants, but it's not like rocks were jumping out from behind trees to tell cavemen what kind of crackers are on sale at CrazyLand. Rocks can't do that. I don't know if they'd want to, but it doesn't matter, because they can't.

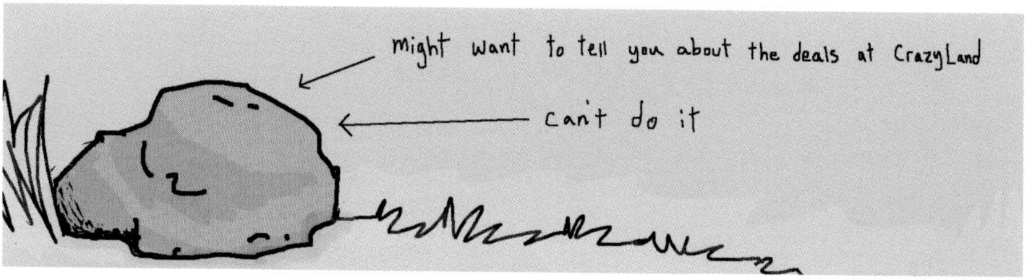
might want to tell you about the deals at CrazyLand
can't do it

Everything is different now. Gone are the days where inanimate objects acted like inanimate objects. Hardly any of them do anymore.

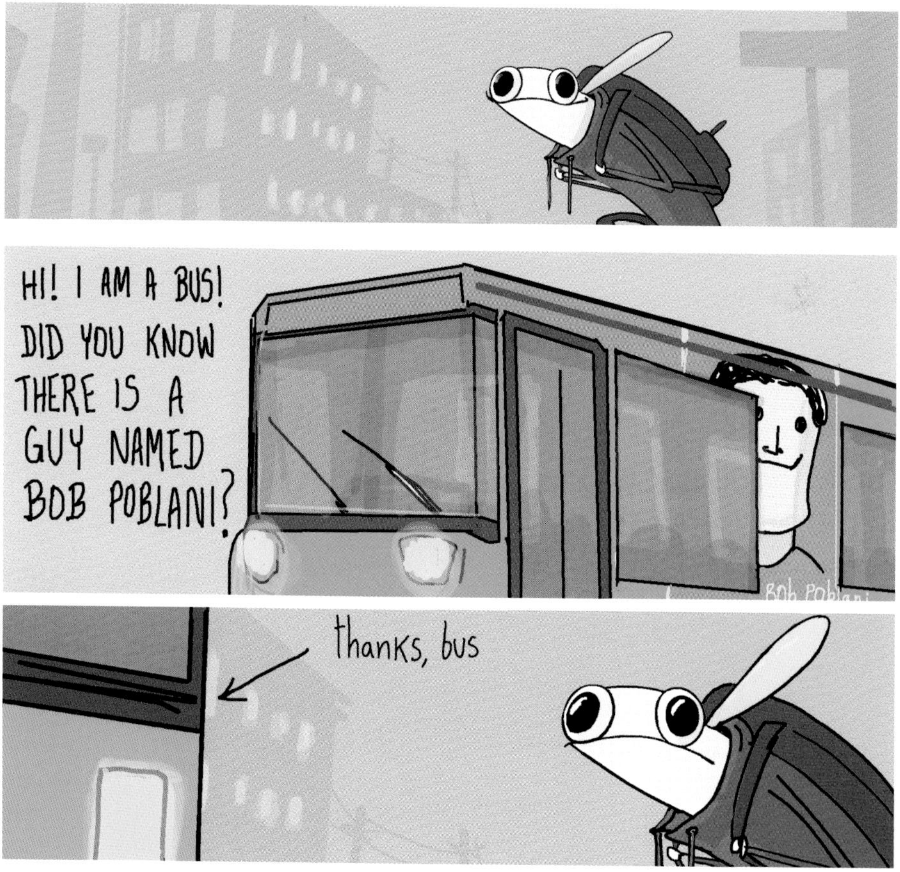
HI! I AM A BUS! DID YOU KNOW THERE IS A GUY NAMED BOB POBLANI?
thanks, bus

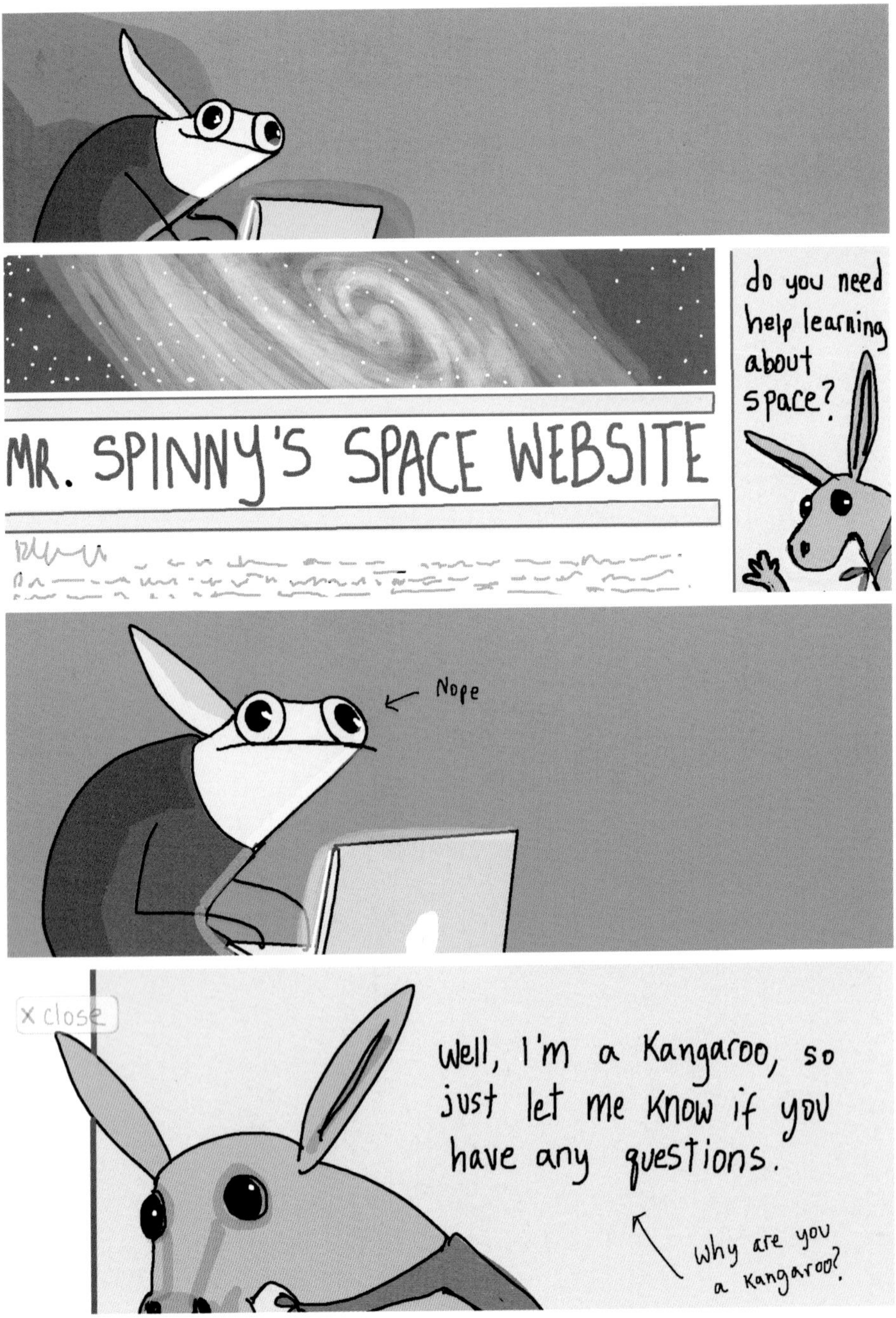
do you need help learning about space?
MR. SPINNY'S SPACE WEBSITE
Nope
x close
Well, I'm a Kangaroo, so just let me know if you have any questions.
Why are you a Kangaroo?

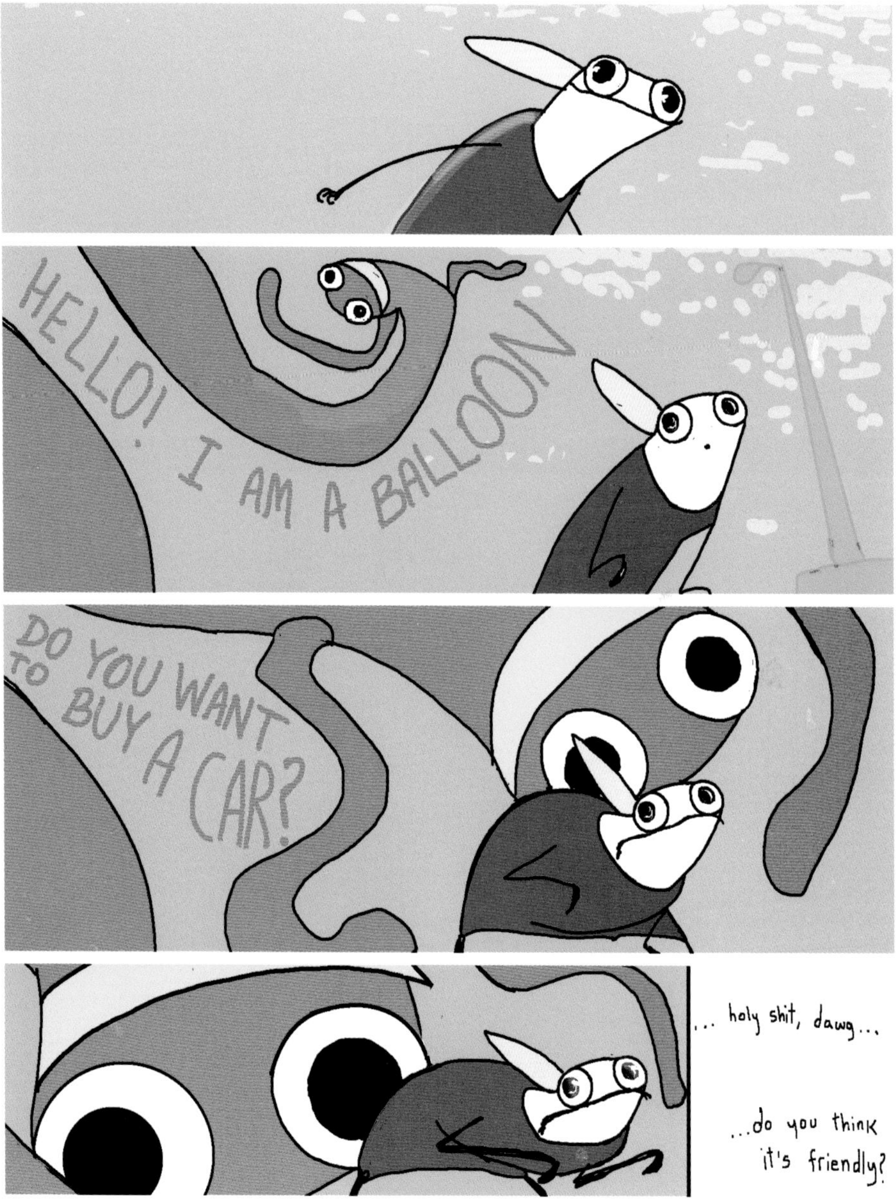
HELLO! I AM A BALLOON
DO YOU WANT TO BUY A CAR?
... holy shit, dawg...
...do you think it's friendly?

How am I supposed to know that isn't some kind of crazy tube predator?

My ancestors never had to deal with this. They wouldn't have known what to do.

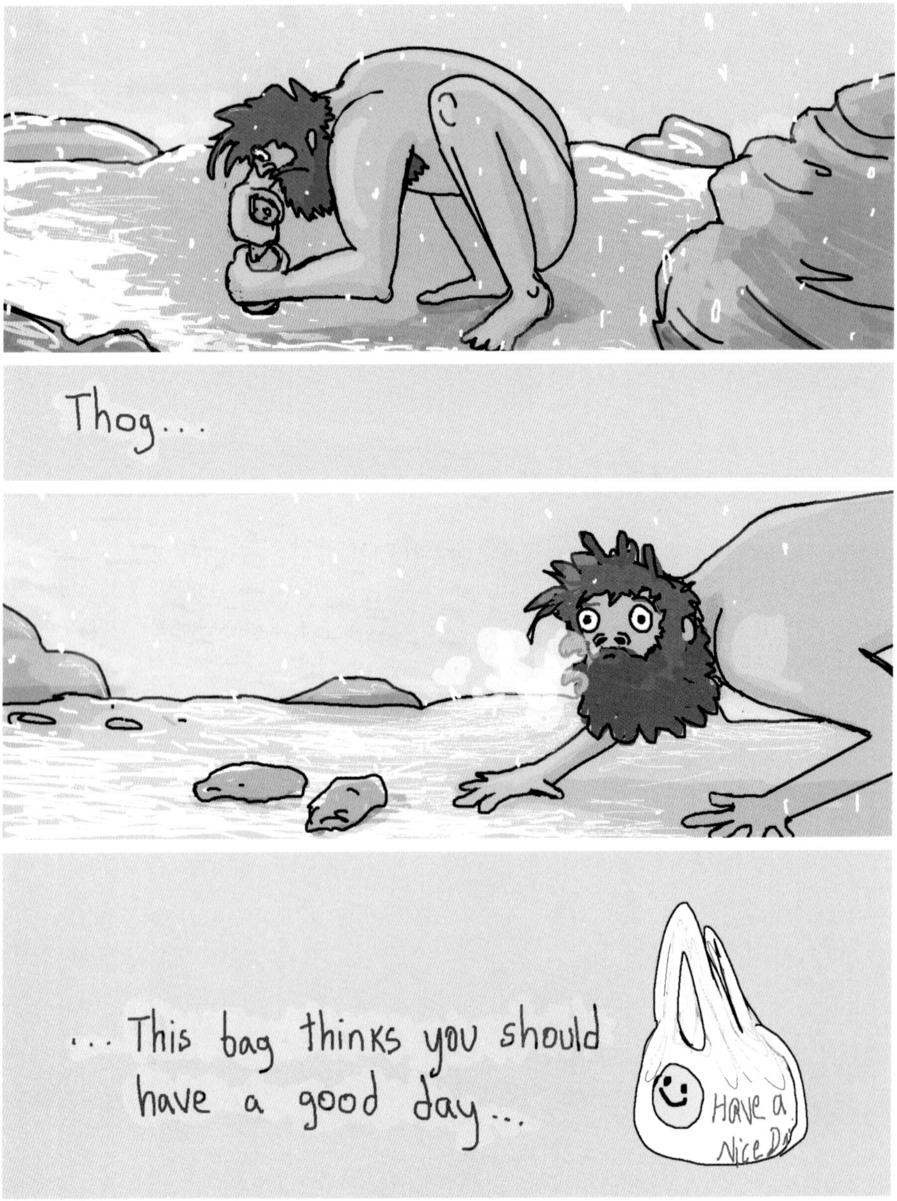
Thog...
...This bag thinks you should have a good day...
Have a
Nice

what do _you_ think?

I'm doing the best I can, but it's hard. I mean, I drink juice out of a cup shaped like a frog. I know it's just a cup, and it doesn't have a motive for falling over, and it therefore doesn't make sense to become enraged with it. I do know this. But here's this stupid cup, falling toward the floor like:

How am I supposed to feel? *Proud?*

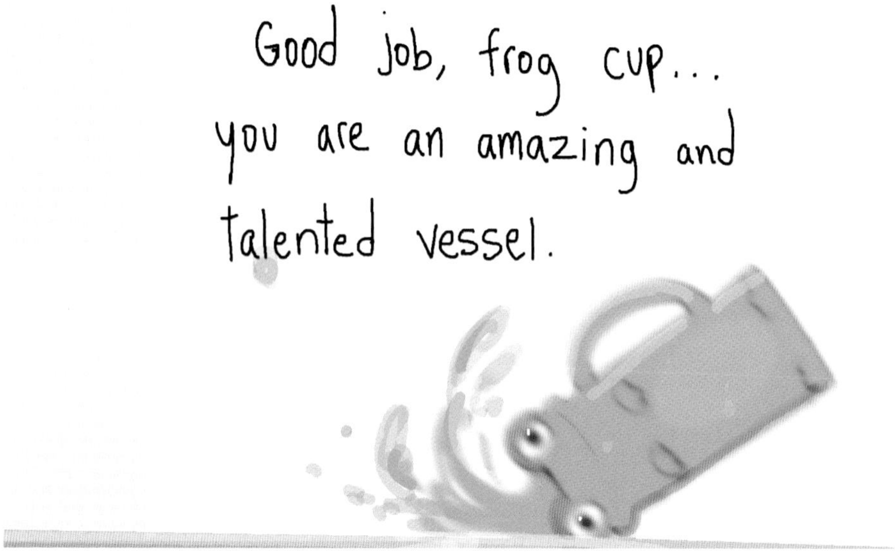
Good job, frog cup...
you are an amazing and
talented vessel.

I think I genuinely feel like I'd be better at it. Like I could be a cup better than my cup. First of all, I wouldn't act like bullshit all the time. I'd do what I'm supposed to, and as well as possible ...

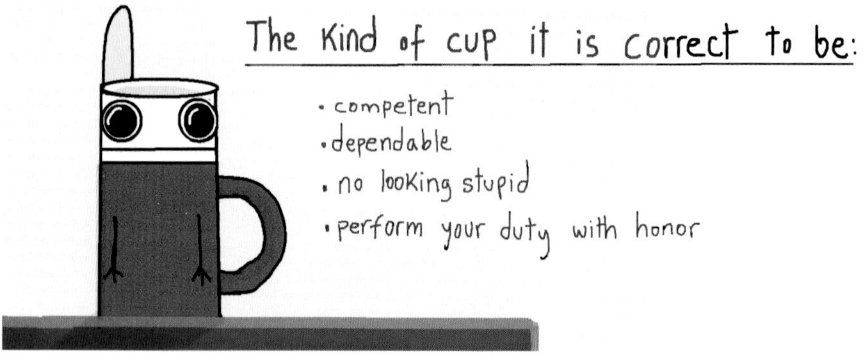
The Kind of cup it is correct to be:
• competent
• dependable
• no looking stupid
• perform your duty with honor

That is absolutely not what I would be like as a cup though.

14. FAIRNESS

A man who owns a hammer lives in the house across the alleyway from my bedroom. I found this out because one morning, he started hammering his roof at 7:54 a.m.: six minutes before it becomes even borderline acceptable to hammer things. I couldn't see what he was building up there, but I assume it was unnecessary.

Every day, he'd start hammering around that time—7:53, 7:56, 7:55—always close enough to 8 o'clock to indicate that hammer guy was aware of the rules for hammering, but was choosing to disregard them to gain an unfair advantage.

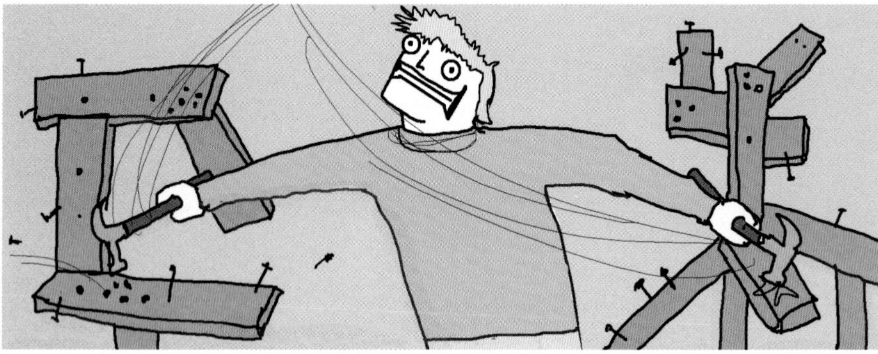

No one did anything to stop him. Emboldened, he began hammering even a little earlier. 7:48. 7:46. 7:44. He clearly thought he was getting away with this too.

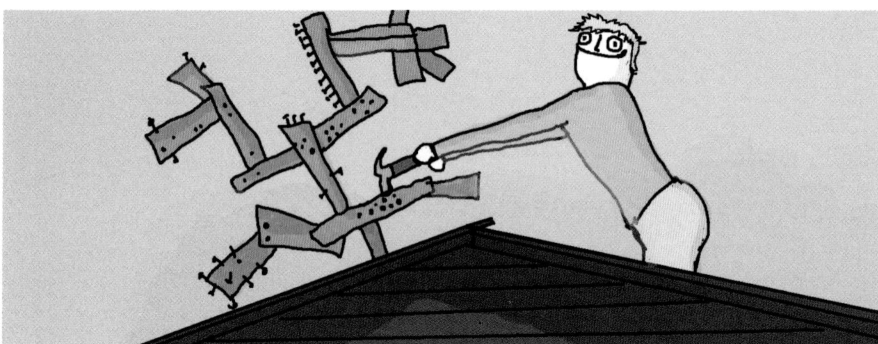

But he wasn't.

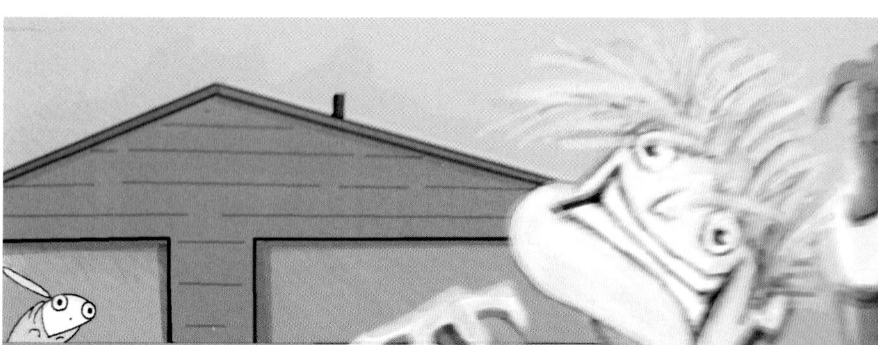

Every morning since the beginning, I'd been staring at him from ten yards away in my room, feeling enraged and refusing to tolerate what he was doing.

I had to.

As far as I could tell, I was the only thing standing between hammer guy and the lawless unknown where he could hammer whatever he wanted at any time without consequences.

With No One to Stop Him, Man Is Finally Able to Hammer as Much as He Ever Wanted

The man, who allegedly "needed
at 5:46 am, had no explanation f
needed to build, or why he needed t
that time.

Witnesses recall that he seemed o
but there was no one around u

He "hammered and hammered a
until all of his hammers broke;"
He had to stop hammering for
while he went to the hamme
buy more, they said. But wh
with the new hammers, he ti

As of Thursday, the man was n
"still hammering."

At this time, it is not possible
what is motivating him, but w
report that he seems extreme

Everybody wishes that there w
something that could stop him, bu

Furthermore, I believed that, left to his own devices, hammer guy WOULD hammer everything. He seemed only barely affected by my attempts to control him, as though the tiniest lapse in resistance might provide him the opportunity to break free and become a truly unstoppable force of hammering.

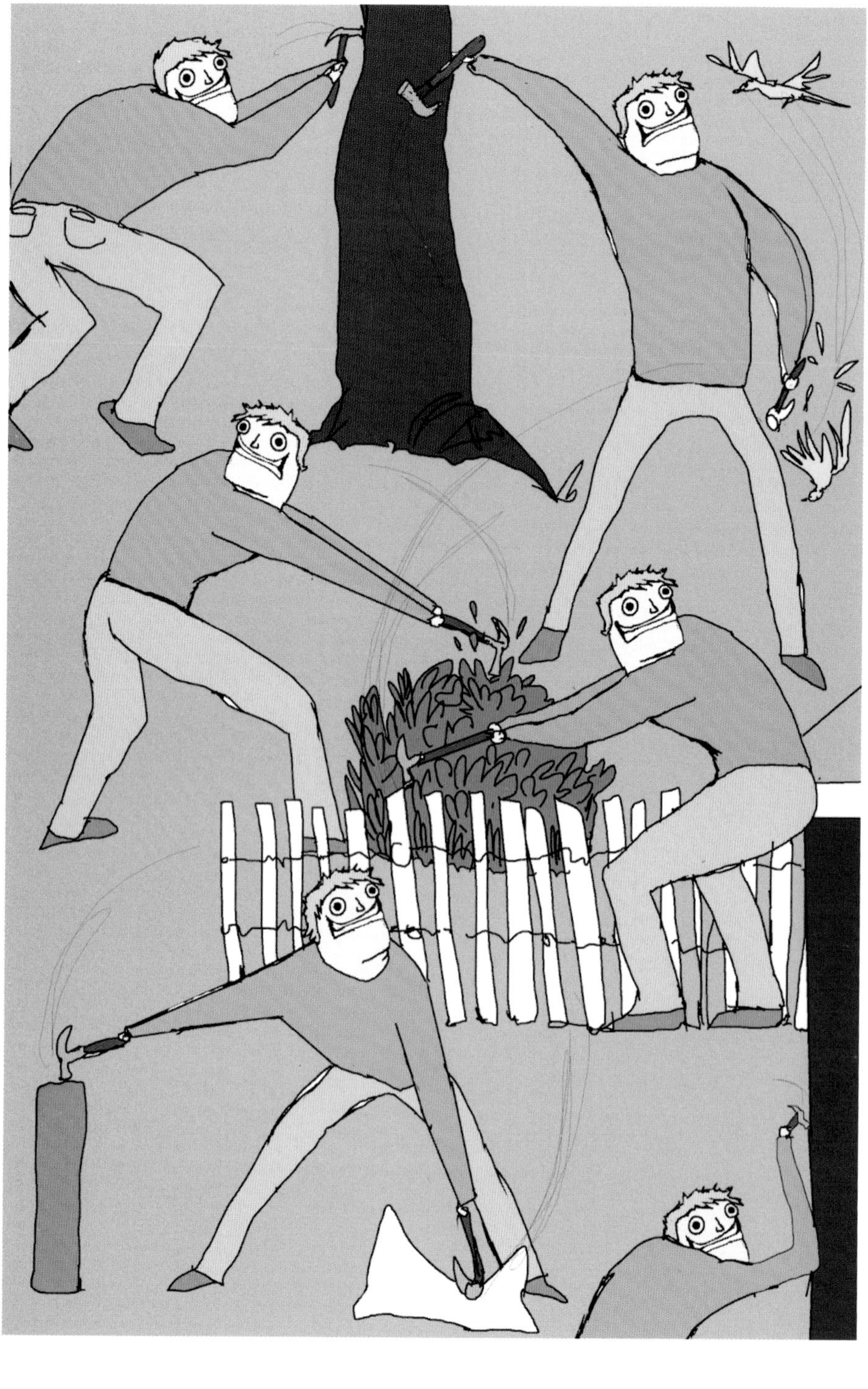

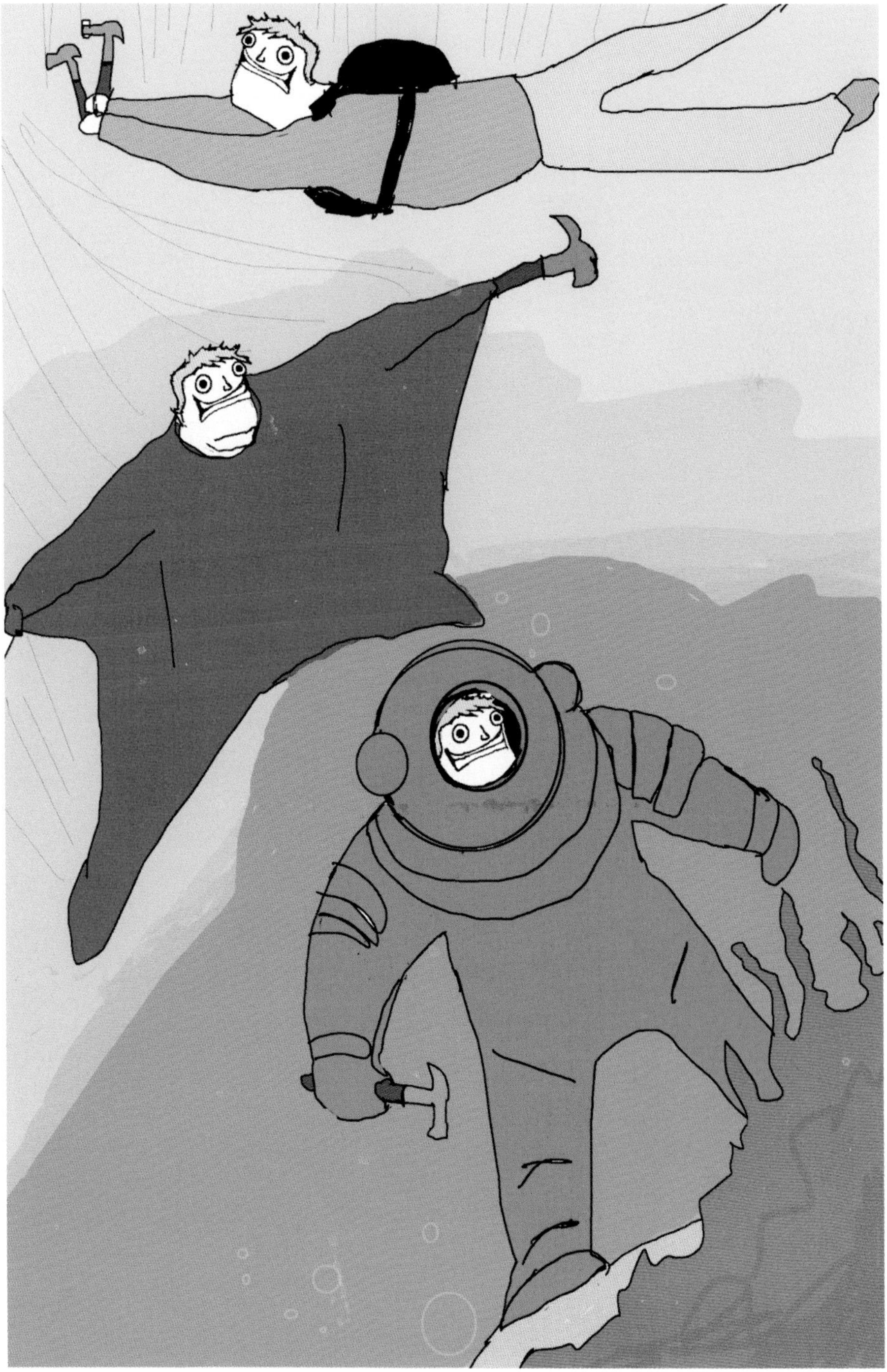

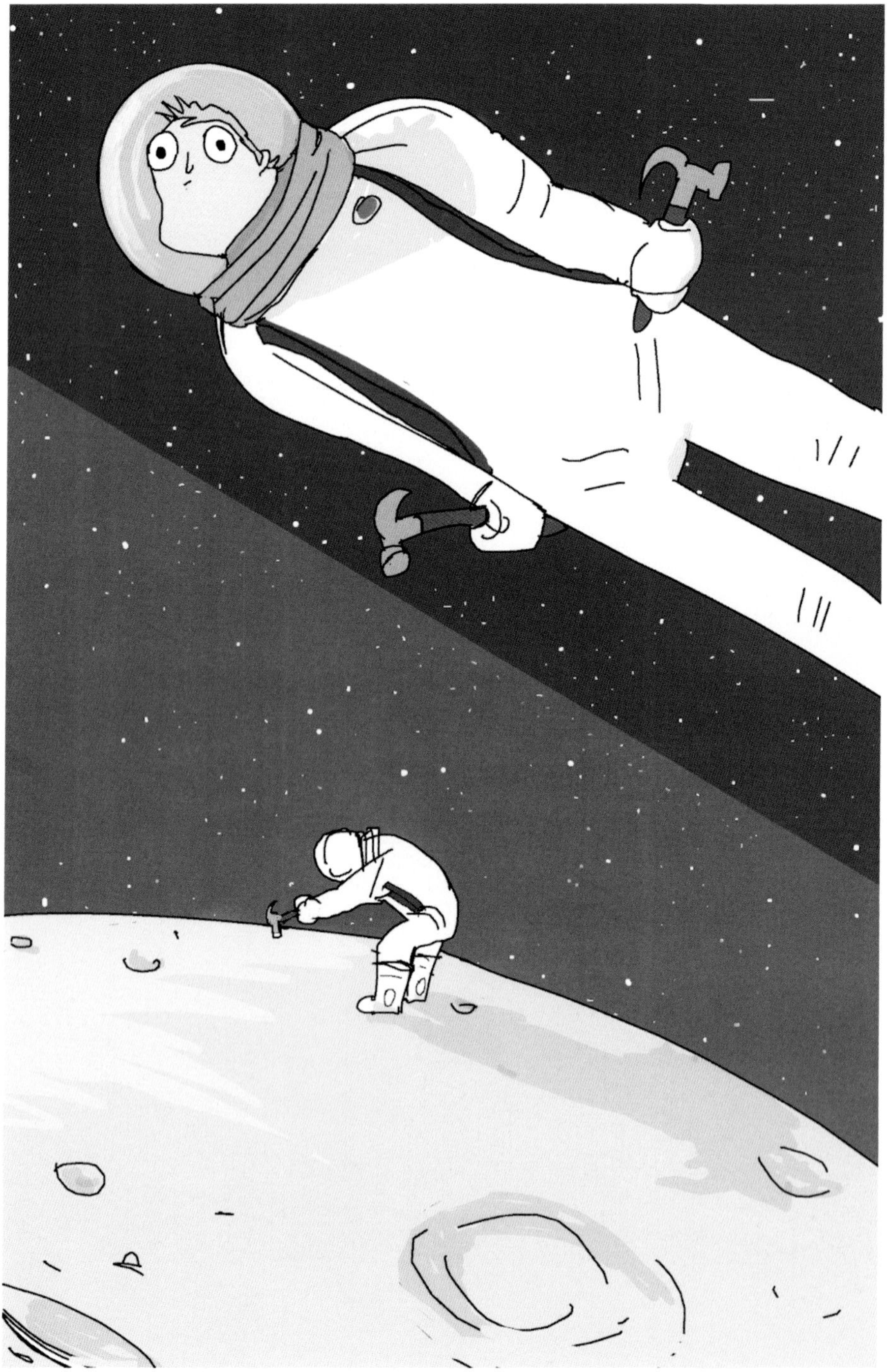

Having to be personally responsible for maintaining justice in the world is distressing. It makes it seem like maybe there's something wrong at the Universal Fairness and Balance Department. Like maybe the higher-ups have lost control and they need help.

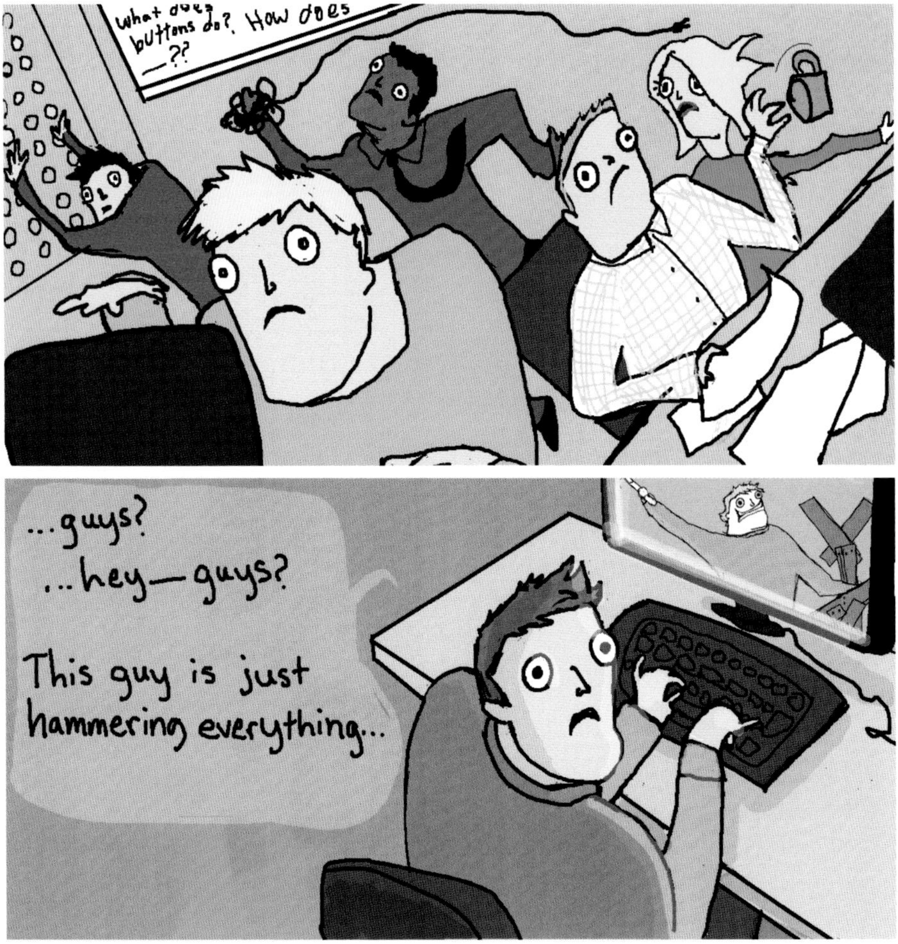
What does buttons do?. How does —??
...guys?
...hey—guys?
This guy is just hammering everything...

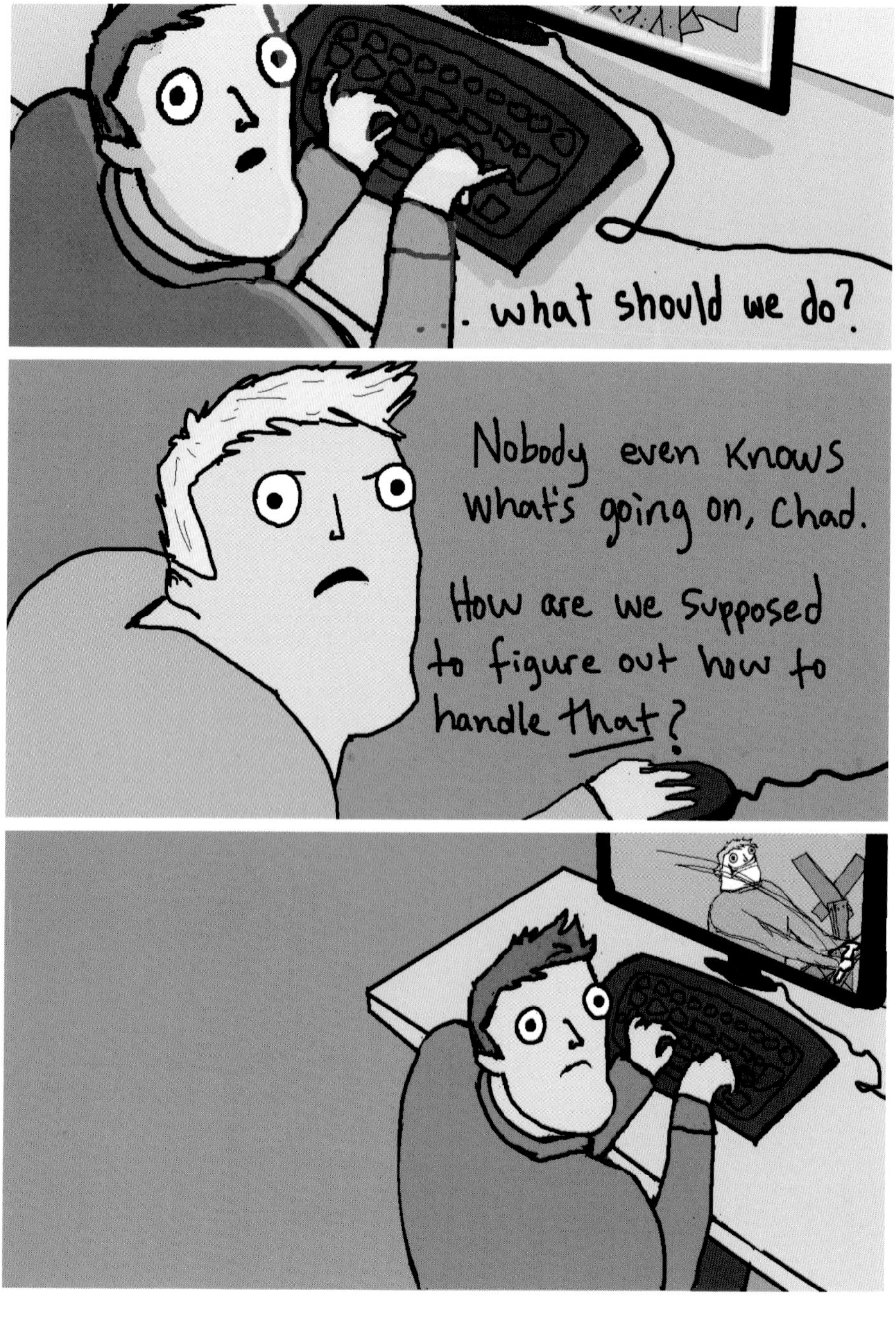
. . . what should we do?
Nobody even knows what's going on, Chad.
How are we supposed to figure out how to handle that?

Every day it gets harder to ignore the possibility that something's wrong. It's fucking *mayhem* out here.

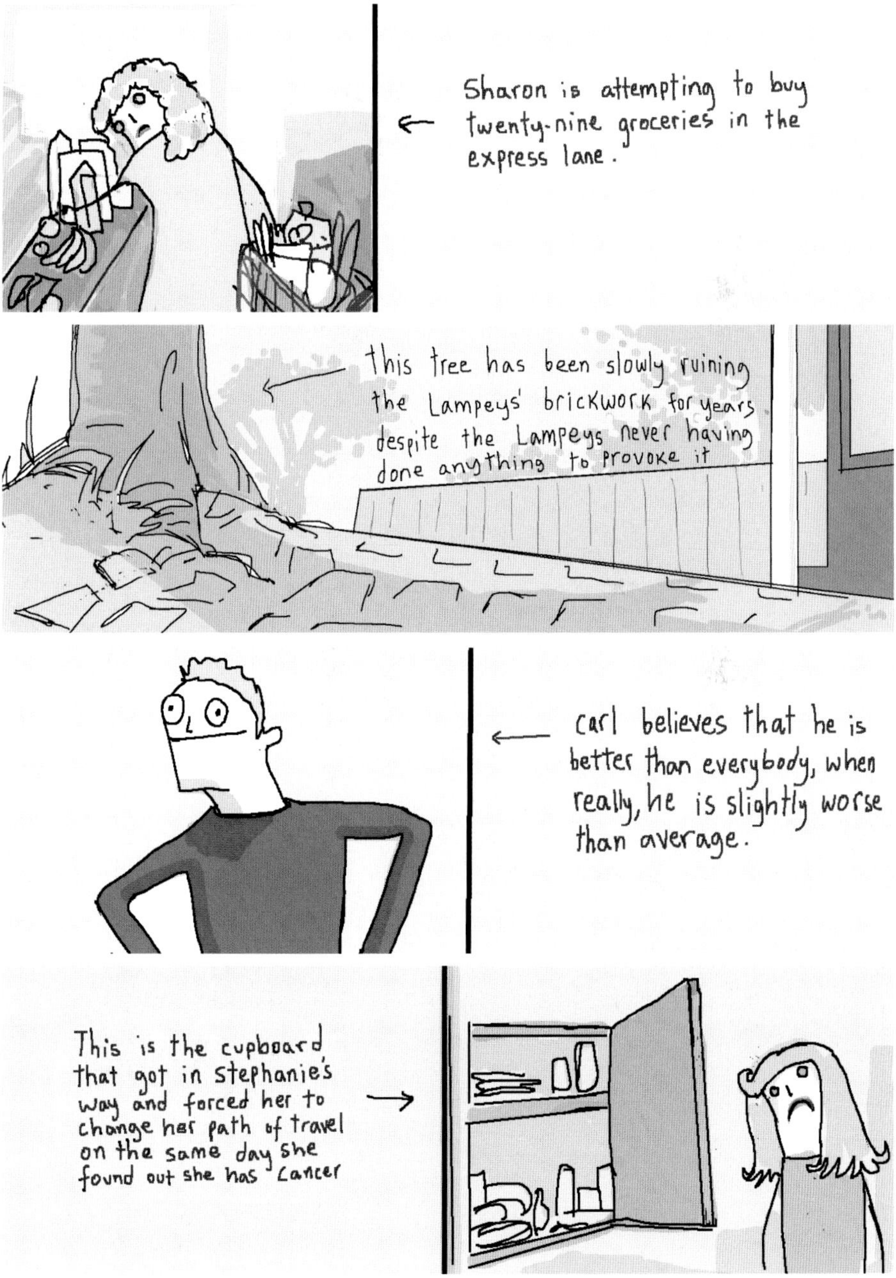
Sharon is attempting to buy twenty-nine groceries in the express lane.
this tree has been slowly ruining the Lampeys' brickwork for years despite the Lampeys never having done anything to provoke it
carl believes that he is better than everybody, when really, he is slightly worse than average.
This is the cupboard that got in stephanie's way and forced her to change her path of travel on the same day she found out she has cancer

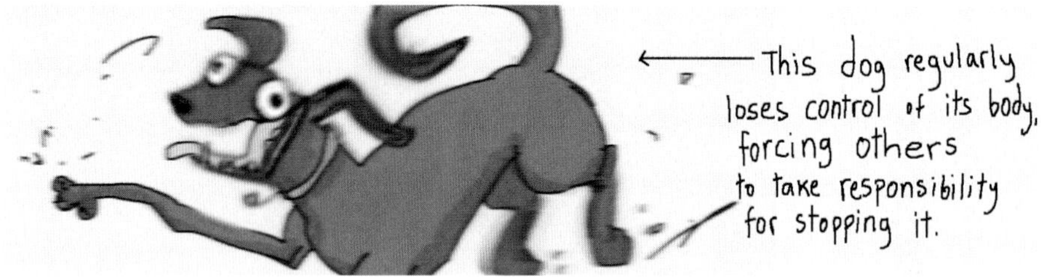
This dog regularly loses control of its body, forcing others to take responsibility for stopping it.

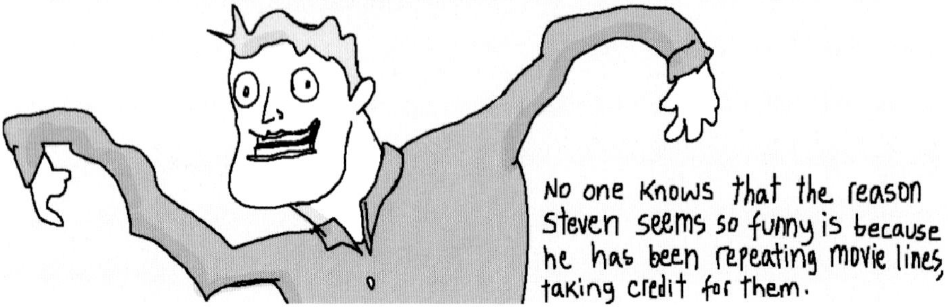
No one knows that the reason Steven seems so funny is because he has been repeating movie lines, taking credit for them.

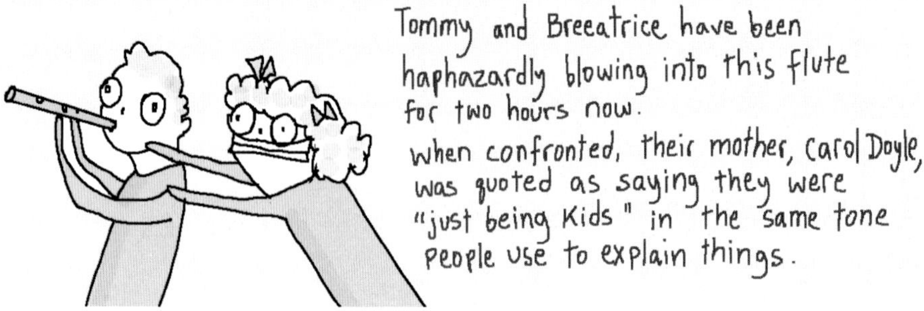
Tommy and Breeatrice have been haphazardly blowing into this flute for two hours now.
when confronted, their mother, carol Doyle, was quoted as saying they were "just being kids" in the same tone people use to explain things.

At this point, it doesn't even seem unreasonable to wonder whether everyone at the Universal Fairness and Balance Department has given up, and we're alone now, and it's only a matter of time before the bad guys figure it out too.

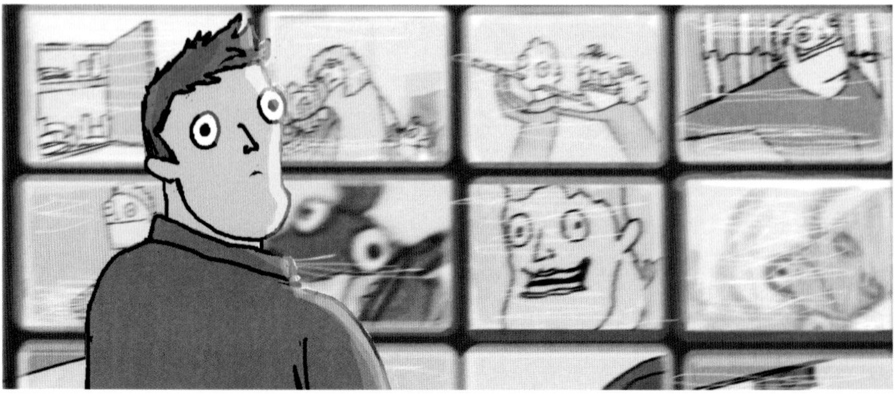

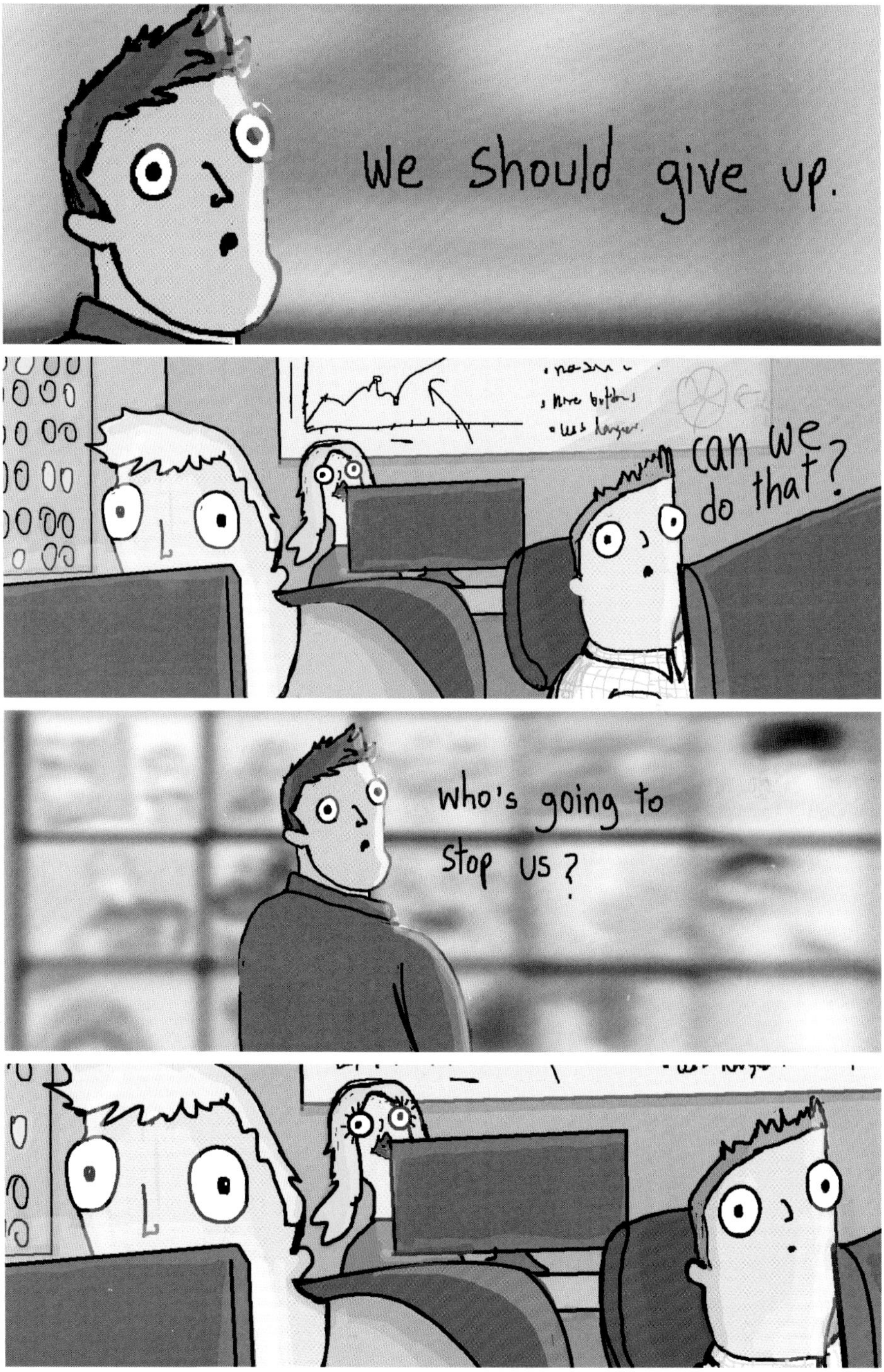
We should give up.
can we do that?
who's going to stop us?

Karen...

...it's fucking MAYHEM out here...

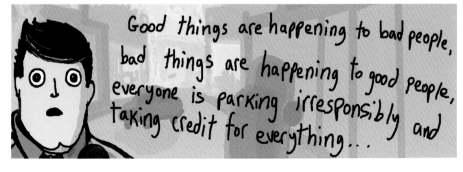

Good things are happening to bad people, bad things are happening to good people, everyone is parking irresponsibly and taking credit for everything...

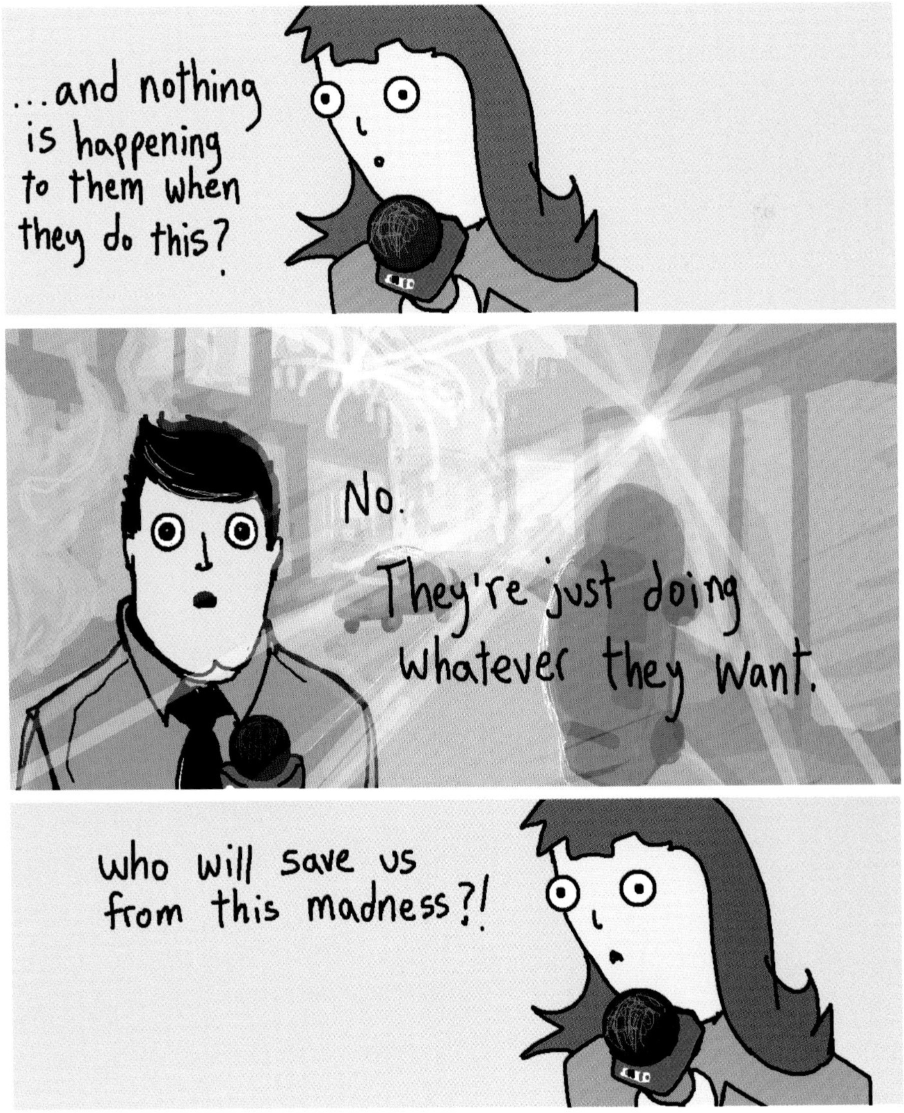
...and nothing is happening to them when they do this?
No.
They're just doing whatever they want.
who will save us from this madness?!

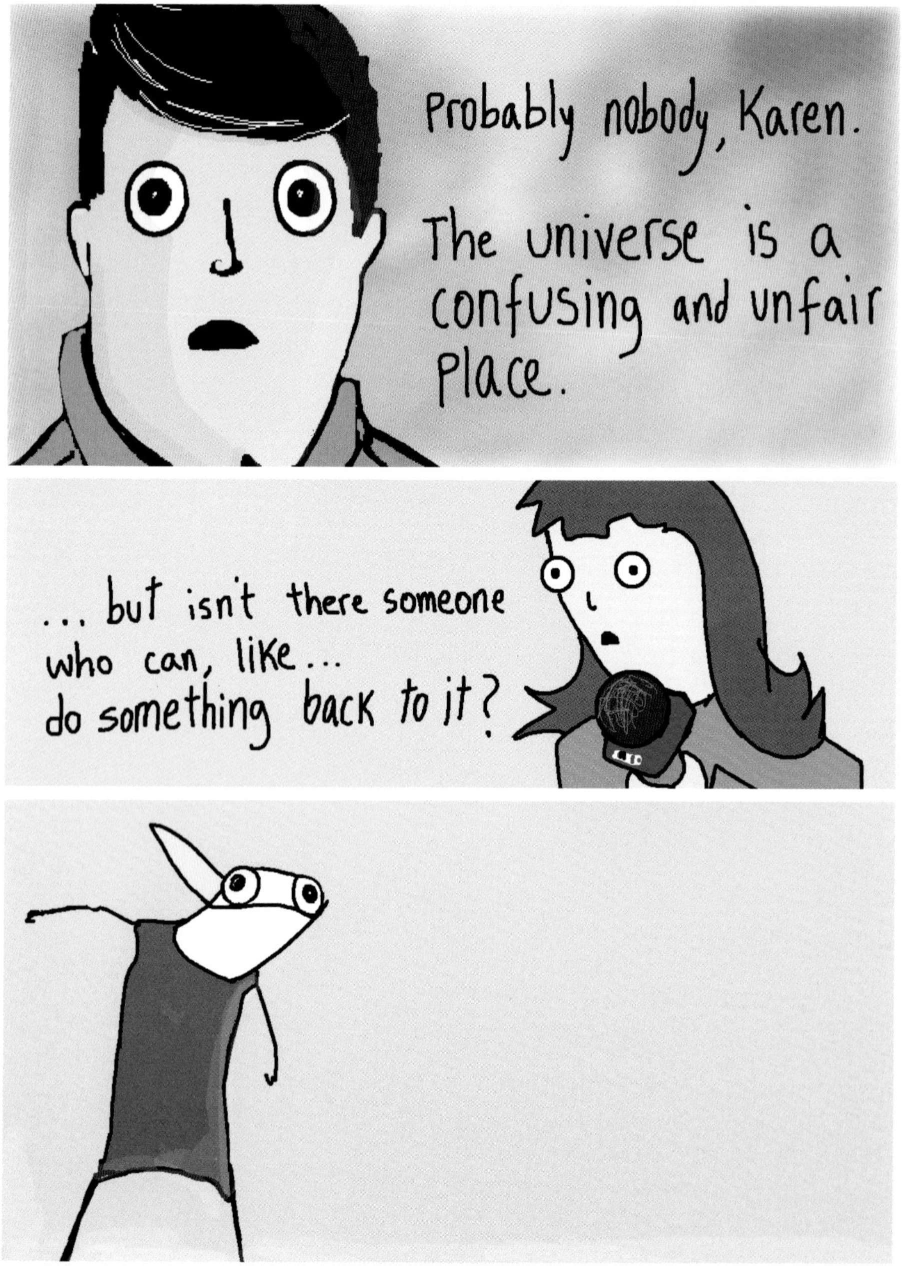
Probably nobody, Karen.
The universe is a confusing and unfair place.
... but isn't there someone who can, like... do something back to it?

If you are an agent of chaos like the man who lives across the alleyway from me, perhaps you don't feel like you need to be scared of justice because you think you know what gamble you're making.

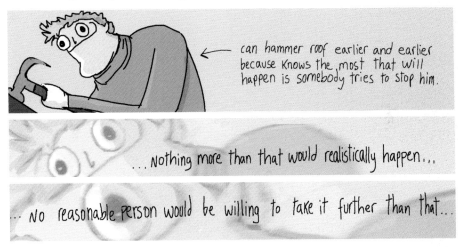

can hammer roof earlier and earlier because knows the most that will happen is somebody tries to stop him.

...Nothing more than that would realistically happen...

...No reasonable person would be willing to take it further than that...

Perhaps you think you've broken free of the system. Perhaps you think you're getting away with it.

Then one day, you get up to go hammer your roof, and there's a stick in your yard.

You don't recognize this as justice. It just seems like a stick. Yeah, it's slightly inconvenient to move it, but that isn't *justice* ...

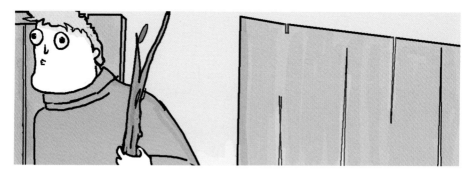

It's a little more difficult to explain why the stick would be in the same place the next morning.

The first time it happened, you assumed it was the wind. But wind isn't usually this precise. Still, wind seems like the most reasonable explanation.

The third time, that starts to seem *way* less likely.

You get rid of the stick. You might not understand why this is happening, but you feel very sure that getting rid of the stick will solve the issue, whatever it is. Surely this isn't happening *on purpose*. What purpose would it be?

But here's that stick again.

You throw it away in a different trash can several blocks from the first one. Someone would need to be truly motivated to find the stick and put it in your yard again.

Yet there it is: the same stick.

At this point, the precision is unmistakable: someone has been doing this.

Which is confusing. People will usually only do something this precise for reasons. But what reasons could a person possibly have for doing this? It doesn't make sense. It violates everything you know about the types of things people do, and the reasons they do them for, and it shouldn't be happening. You're sure of that.

You want to know who has been doing this. That much is obvious because you put the stick in the alley instead of throwing it away in an even more remote trash can. You start staying up later and later to catch whoever is doing it. You just want to see who it is. See their face. Force them to explain why they did this.

But whoever is doing it seems to have some sort of insider knowledge of your schedule, and you can never catch a glimpse of them.

I like to imagine it was even more confusing when it stopped.

You can't do the same nonsensical thing every single day for three weeks and then just stop. It doesn't make sense. It didn't make sense to do in the first place, but at least it was consistent. At least it still seemed possible to figure out why it was happening. There has to be an explanation somewhere. You can't just pick an object at random, ritualistically place it in someone's yard every day with no explanation, and then stop doing it also with no explanation.

You can, though.

You can also start doing it again three months later, when it makes the absolute least sense to start doing it again.

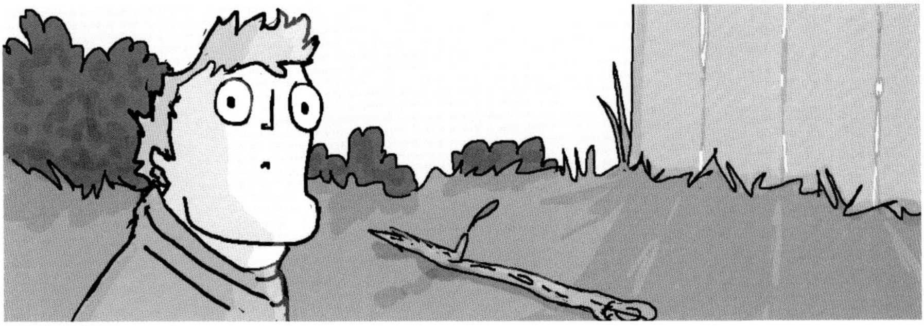

There are so many things you can do. Like one time, put a grapefruit instead. Just once.

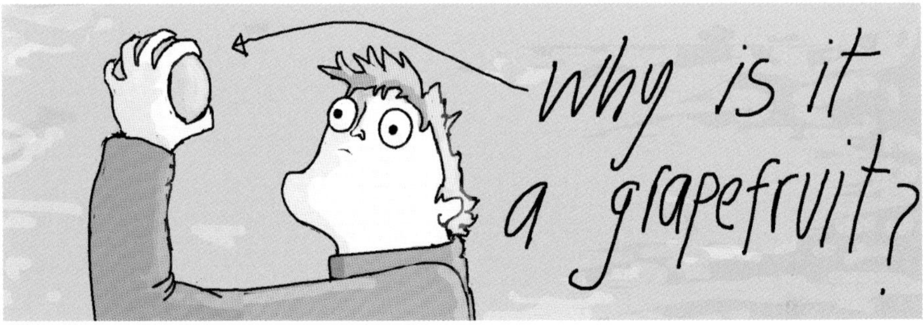
why is it a grapefruit?

Then go back to sticks forever.

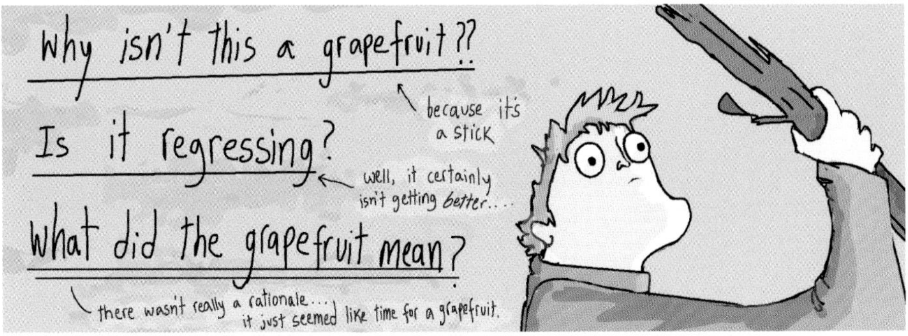
Why isn't this a grapefruit??
because it's a stick
Is it regressing?
well, it certainly isn't getting better...
What did the grapefruit mean?
there wasn't really a rationale... it just seemed like time for a grapefruit.

I don't know if hammer guy learned anything from this. It would have been pretty impossible to make a connection between the punishment and the crime.

I'm sure he had to consider some things. Probably more than he would have had to consider in a more straightforward situation.

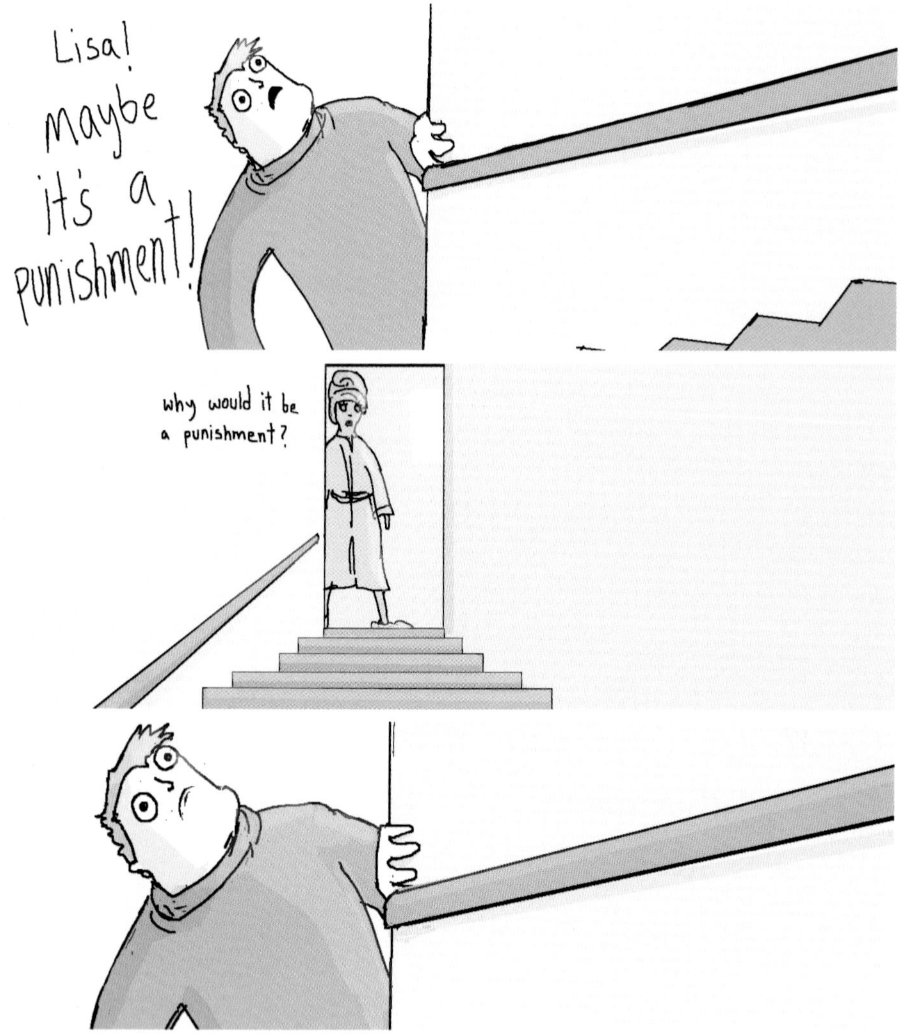
Lisa! maybe it's a punishment!
why would it be a punishment?

This wasn't about teaching hammer guy a lesson, though.
It was for me.

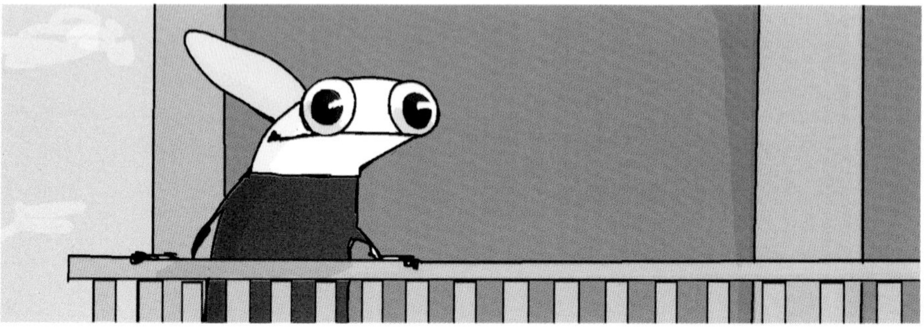

I can't force the things that happen to be fair.

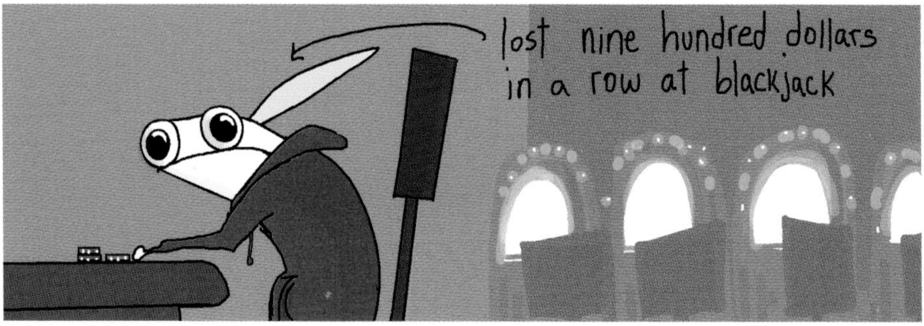
lost nine hundred dollars
in a row at blackjack

I can't make them happen for only good reasons that I understand and agree with.

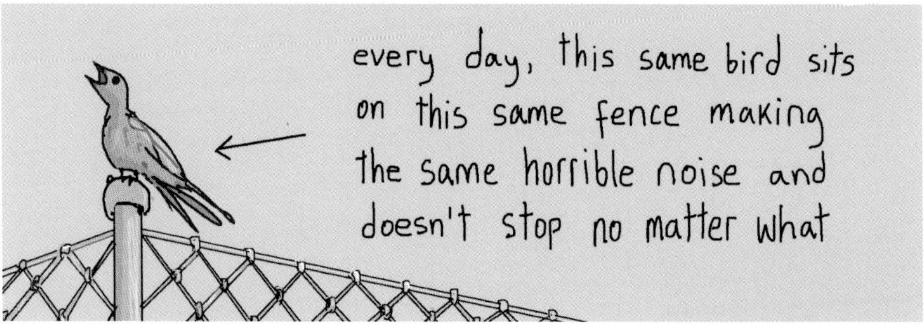
every day, this same bird sits
on this same fence making
the same horrible noise and
doesn't stop no matter what

But I can do my own things.

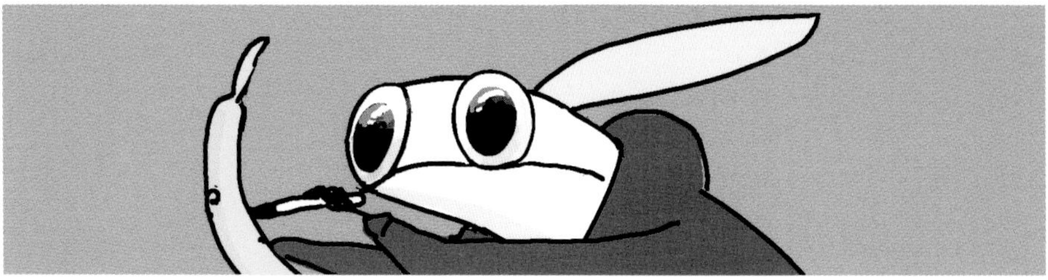

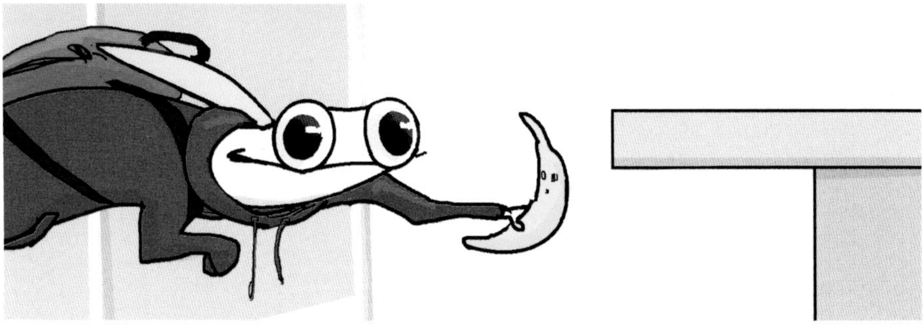

Approximation of Recouped Value:

-79 cents + whatever message this banana with a surprised face sends to the casino.

And I can do them for *equally pointless* and *equally nonsensical* reasons.

this is →
an idiot

Which is sort of like fairness.

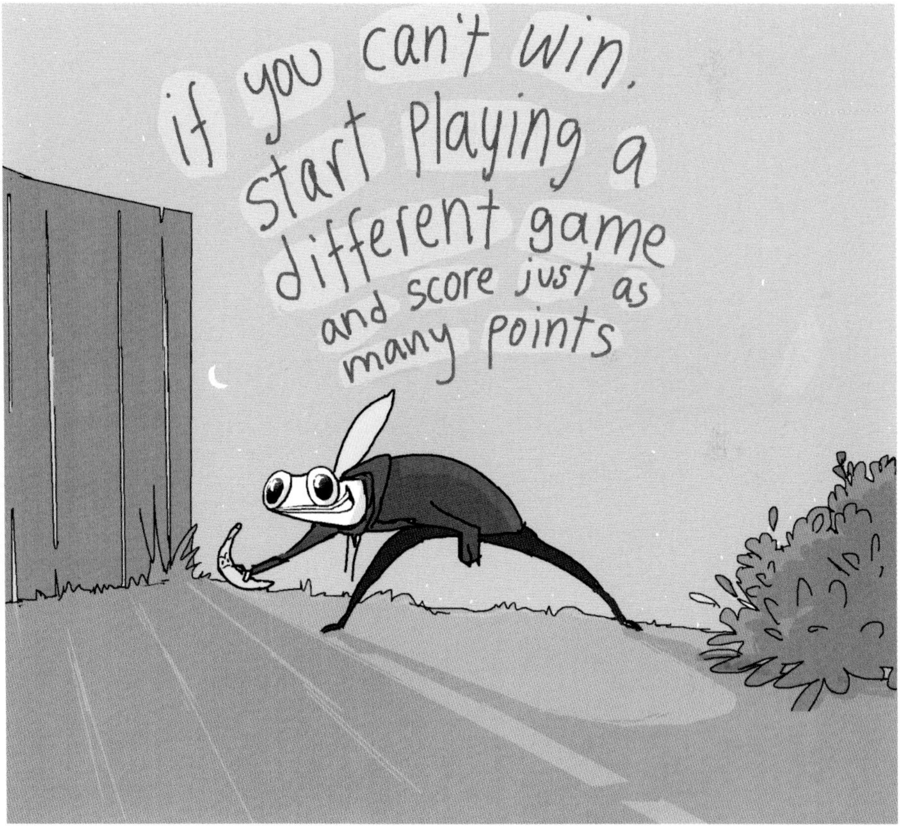
if you can't win,
start playing a
different game
and score just as
many points

Potato

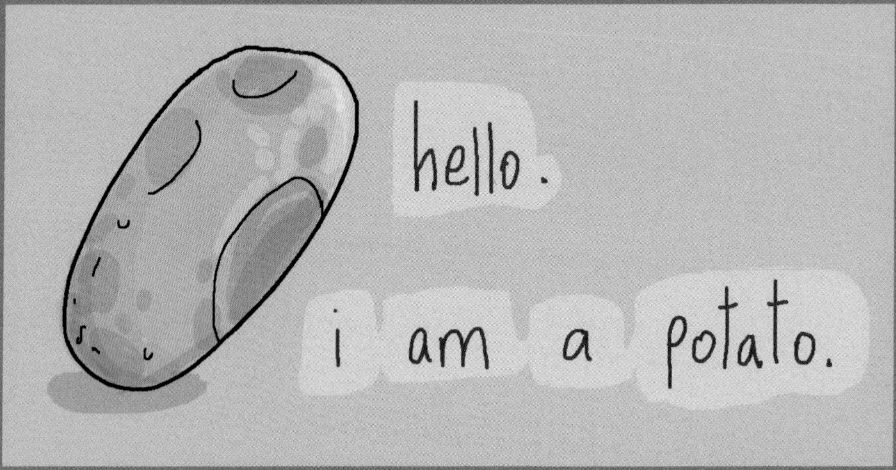
hello.
i am a potato.

Greetings, fellow creature.

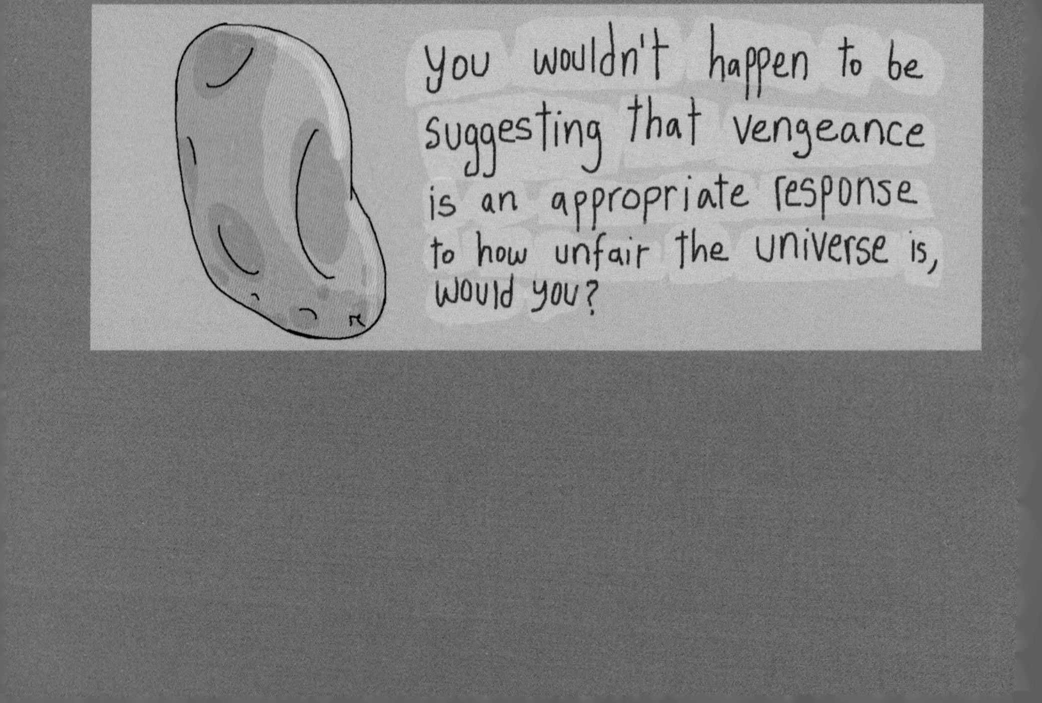
you wouldn't happen to be suggesting that vengeance is an appropriate response to how unfair the universe is, would you?

Oh my . . . I certainly hope not . . .

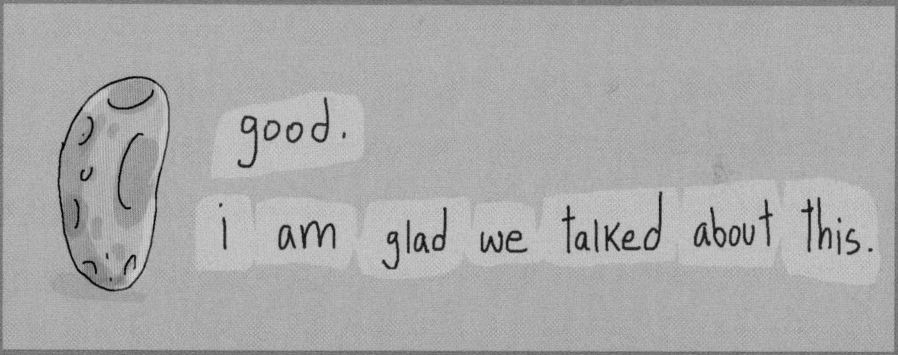
good.
i am glad we talked about this.

15. PLANS

My childhood diary is full of training plans.

Training plans for improving my ability to perform real magic. Training plans for teaching my dog to read. Training plans for how to convert to all-fours running full-time (the goal was to become an actual wolf). Training plans for teaching my friend Joey how to draw faster and better. I wrote down the name of every waterslide I'd ever been on. Who knows what my endgame was, but I genuinely suspect it might have been to ride every waterslide in the world.

If someone ever found the plans and had to guess what the person who wrote them was trying to accomplish, their best guess would probably be gladiator training. This person is clearly training themselves to be a gladiator in some aquatic dystopia ruled by wolves.

practice until you can survive in the wild

On August 8th, 1996, I outlined my plan for eliminating the need to sleep under the covers. I don't know why I felt that was necessary, but, by the end of October 1996, I planned to be free of this disgusting weakness.

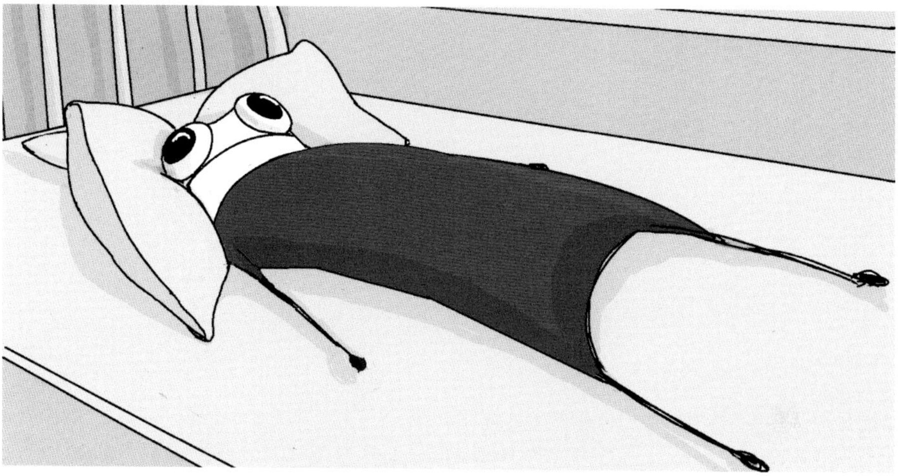

If I believe something will work, that is very dangerous.

In July of 1991, for example, I thought I discovered the secret to breathing underwater:

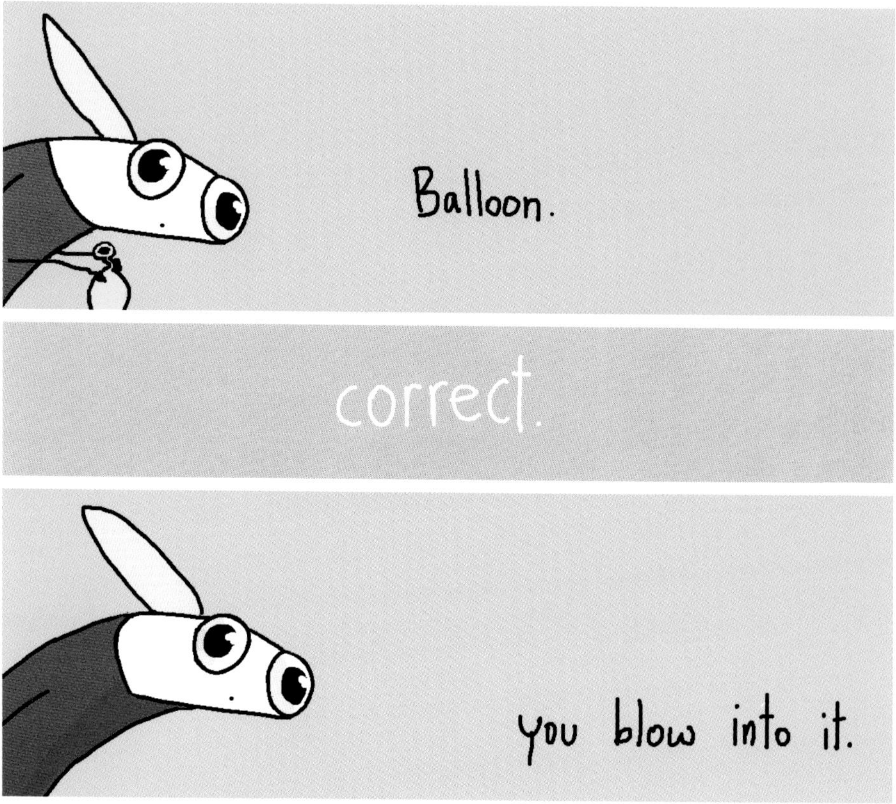
Balloon.
correct.
you blow into it.

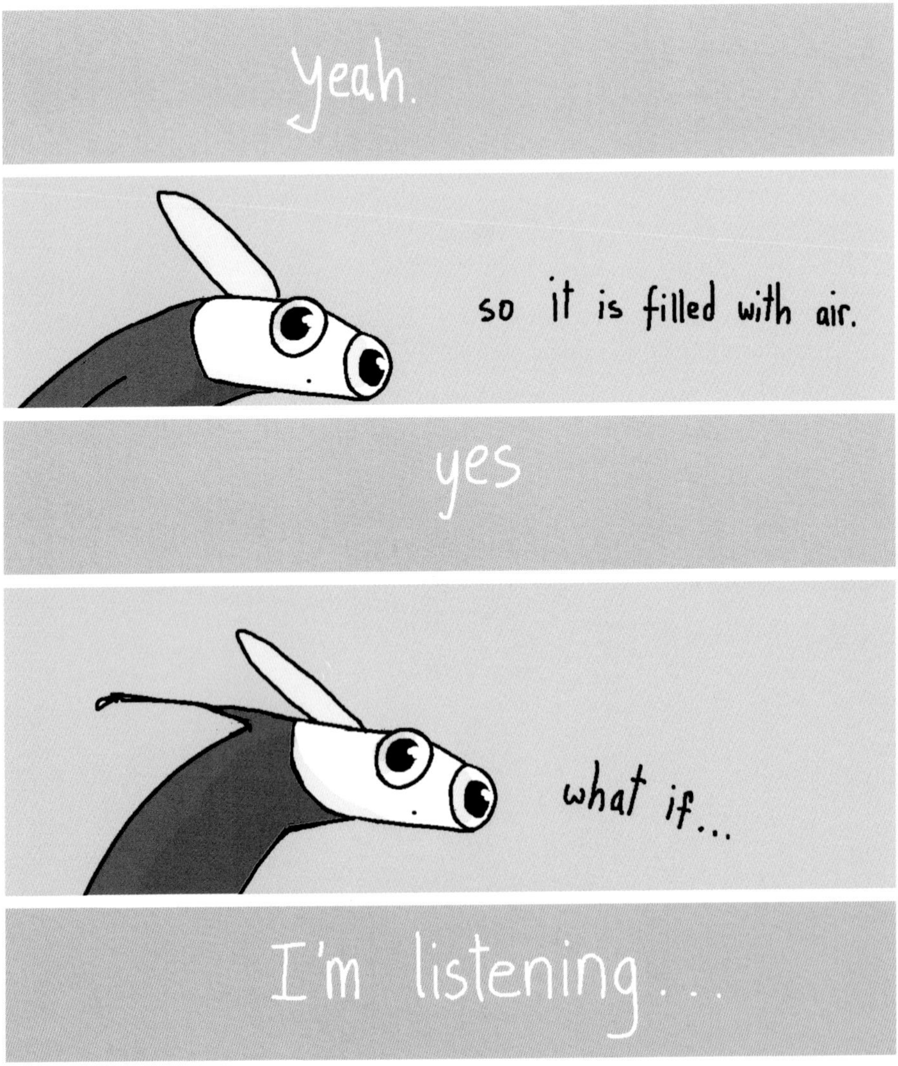
yeah.
so it is filled with air.
yes
what if...
I'm listening...

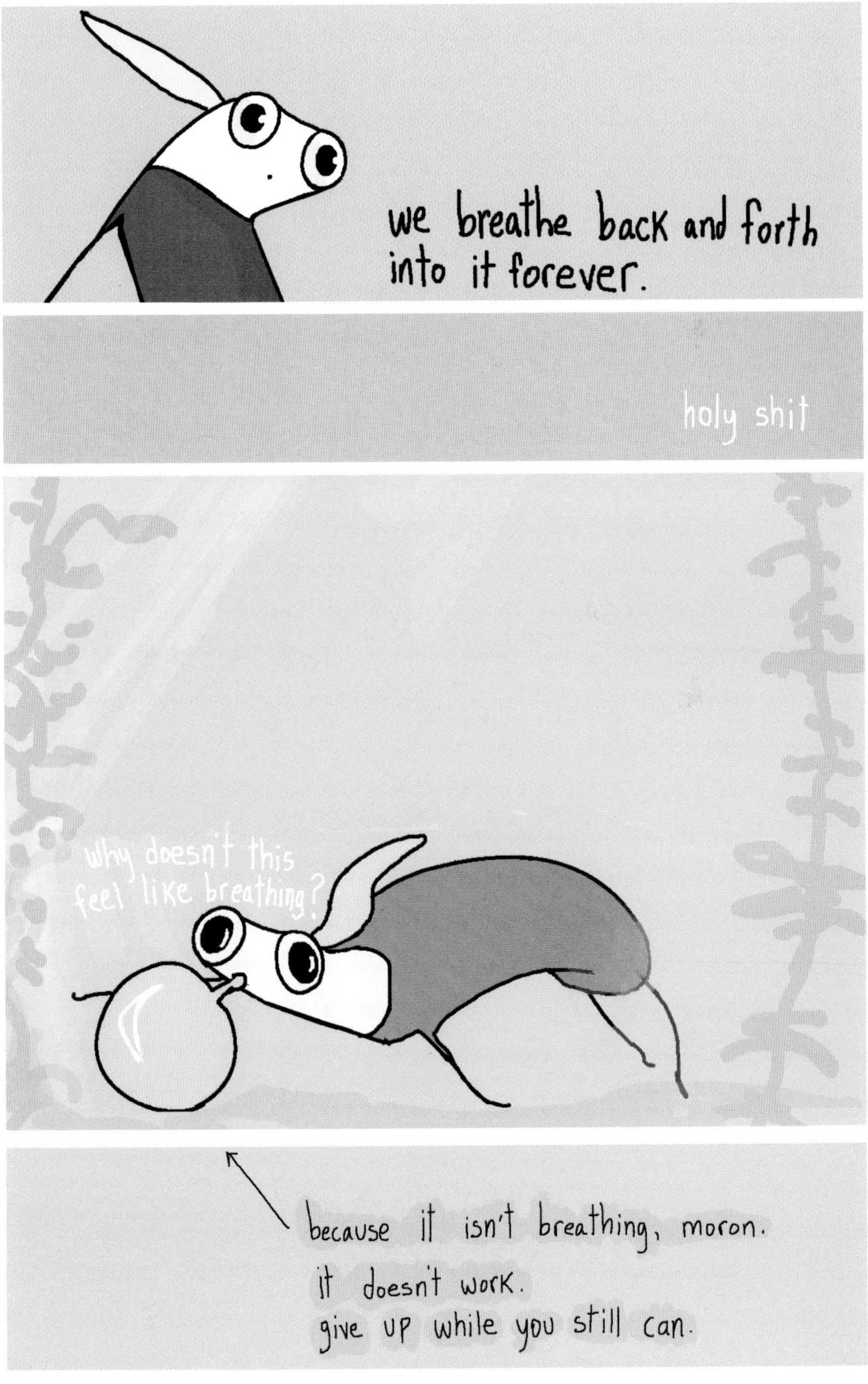
we breathe back and forth
into it forever.
holy shit
why doesn't this feel like breathing?
because it isn't breathing, moron.
it doesn't work.
give up while you still can.

I didn't give up until September.
It just seemed . . . possible.

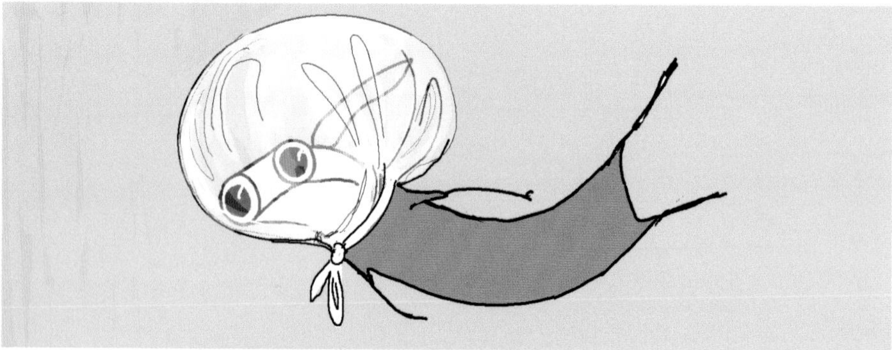

Such is the danger of optimism. If you think you can do it, you'll try. And you might keep trying. If it works, great—you did it. You don't need blankets anymore. Good job. That was really hard, which is amazing when you consider how much you didn't need to do it.

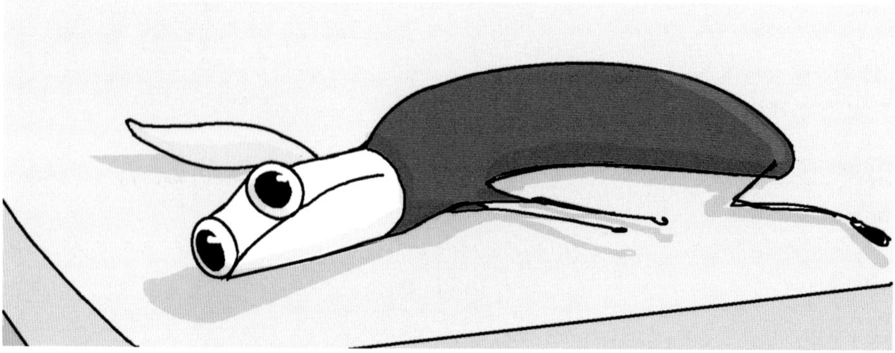

If it doesn't work, you'll keep trying anyway.

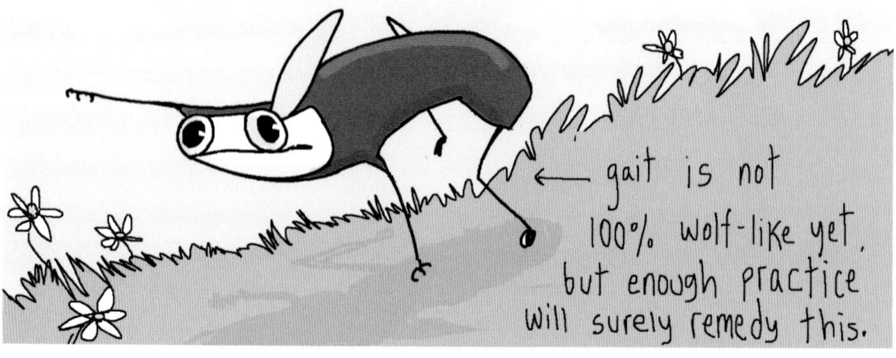
← gait is not 100% wolf-like yet, but enough practice will surely remedy this.

There's always the dangling carrot of what you could be if you maxed out.

16. THE ULTIMATE PLAN

My whole life, I've been held back by weakness.

By the end of 2016, I was ready to be done with it.

And just to be clear what I mean by "done with it," I mean done with it; not make a few changes here and there, not reduce the amount—my goal was to get rid of it all the way.

This is the eight-part story of my most earnest attempt to become a juggernaut.

PART 1 : A PLAN

If you want your body to be strong, you can force it to become strong by lifting weights. Pick up the weights, the body becomes stronger from doing this, now it can pick up heavier weights, now it's even stronger, eventually it'll be able to throw trees at cars.

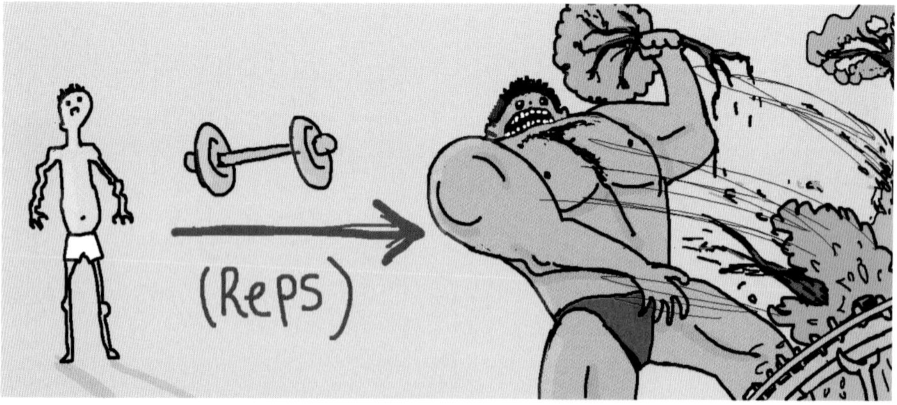
(Reps)

And it just seemed like there should be a similar thing I could do to become emotionally stronger. Fear reps or something.

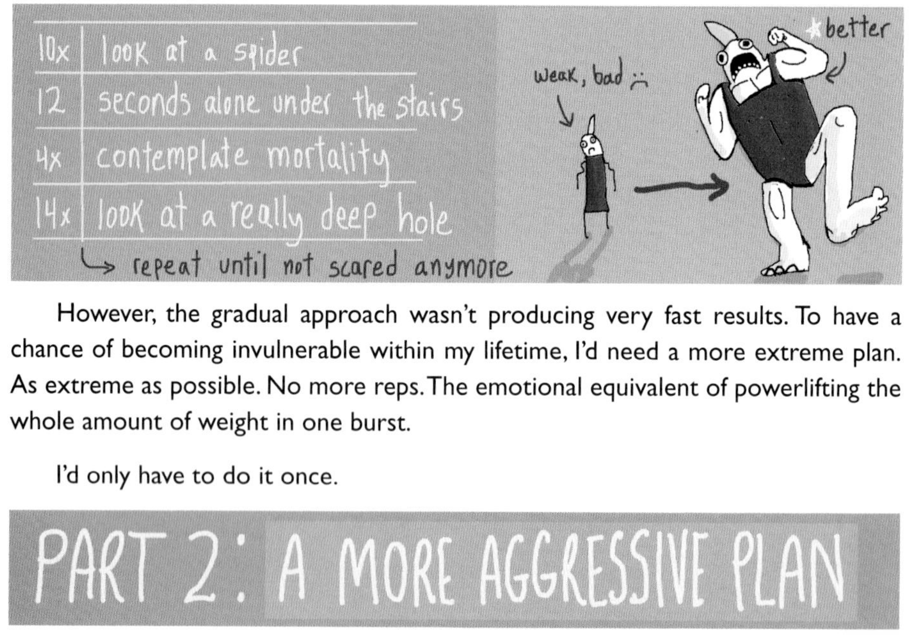
10x look at a spider
12 seconds alone under the stairs
4x contemplate mortality
14x look at a really deep hole
repeat until not scared anymore
weak, bad
better

However, the gradual approach wasn't producing very fast results. To have a chance of becoming invulnerable within my lifetime, I'd need a more extreme plan. As extreme as possible. No more reps. The emotional equivalent of powerlifting the whole amount of weight in one burst.

I'd only have to do it once.

PART 2: A MORE AGGRESSIVE PLAN

I chose the most extreme plan I could think of, which was to consume a huge quantity of drugs, watch scary movies, and then strand myself outdoors all night.

The hope was that forcing myself to endure such challenging conditions might cause me to become permanently hardened, like a gladiator. Which is a fairly ambitious goal, but it sort of felt like my only option.

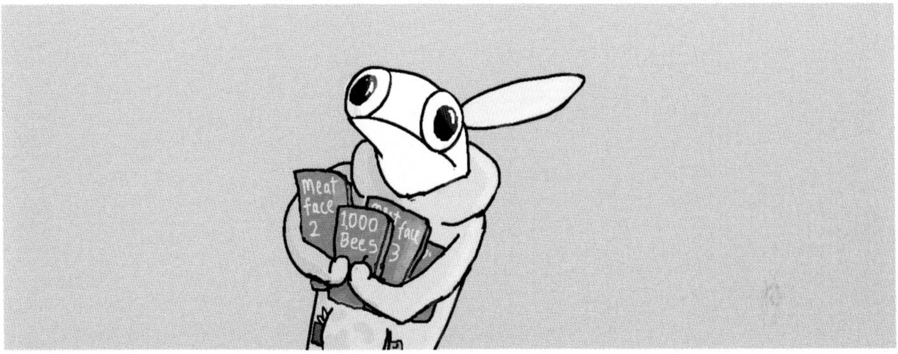
meat face 2
1000 Bees
meat face 3

PART 3: THE PLAN BEGINS

To ensure I followed through after taking the drugs and watching the movies, I reckoned I would need to be at least 6 miles from home when my escape reflexes kicked on.

So I took half of the drugs, watched scary movies until it got dark outside, then walked until I felt about six miles away.

Then I took the other half of the drugs.

Approximately 45 minutes later, I was in some field somewhere. I looked around to see if anything seemed scary yet, and there was a little clump of grass up ahead. I saw it and thought, *Hey . . . a thing.*

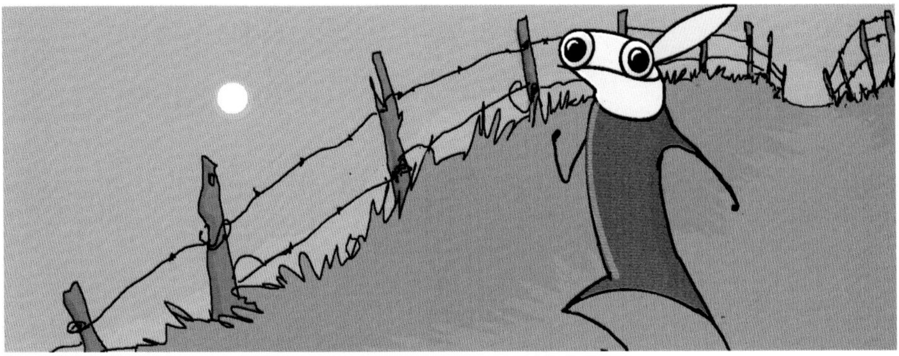

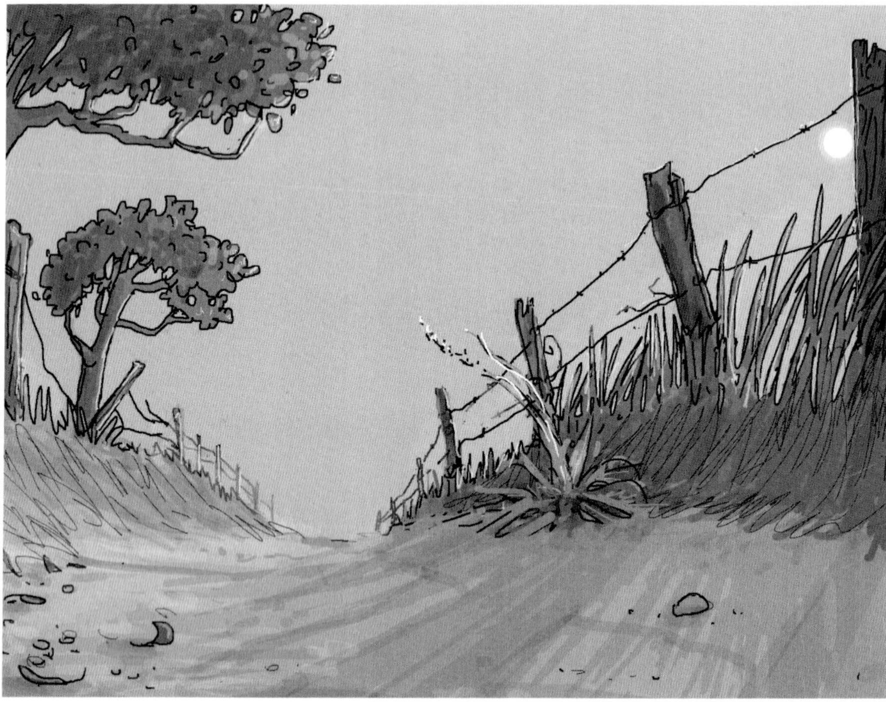

And that is the exact moment the second wave of drugs hit.

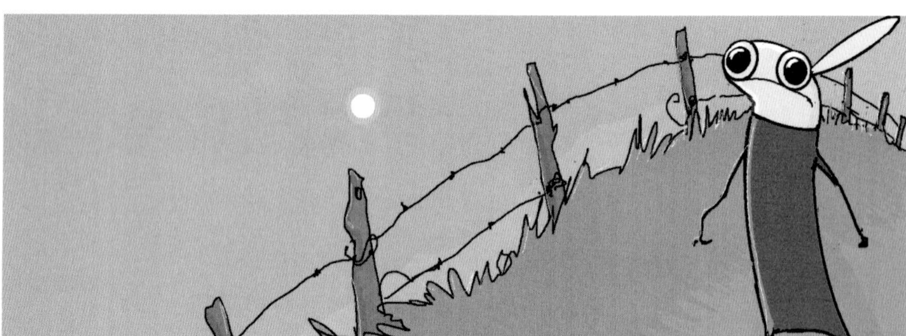

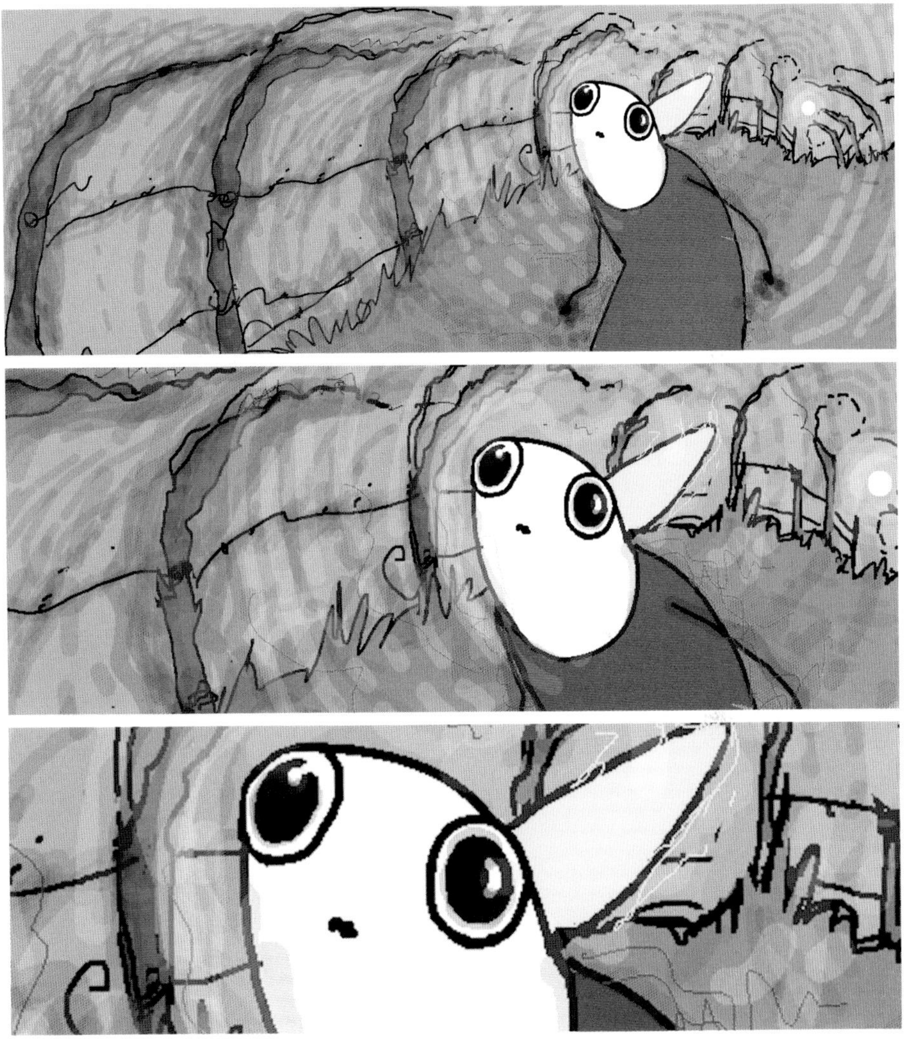

Initially, my only concern was why there were so many trees.
They were still plenty far away, but there were a lot of them.
Too many.
For what, I don't know, but it seemed like the sort of thing to keep an eye on.
I watched them for a while.
Who knows how long.
Long enough to become confused.

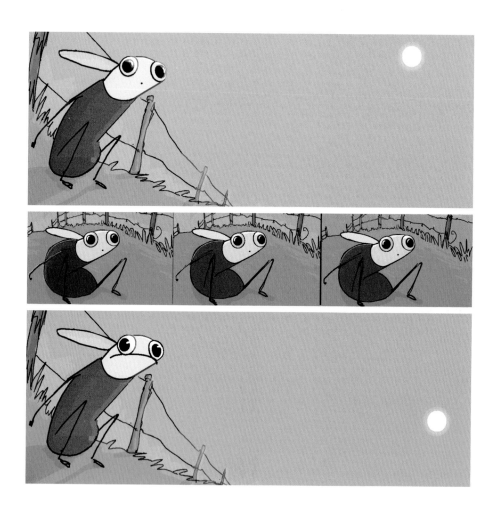

I indeed appeared to be outside.

I couldn't remember what I was supposed to be doing, but it seemed like it might have been important ...

Did something happen?

What was it?

Are there risks involved?

Who could tell.

But there was a distinct sense that shadow guys might be around.

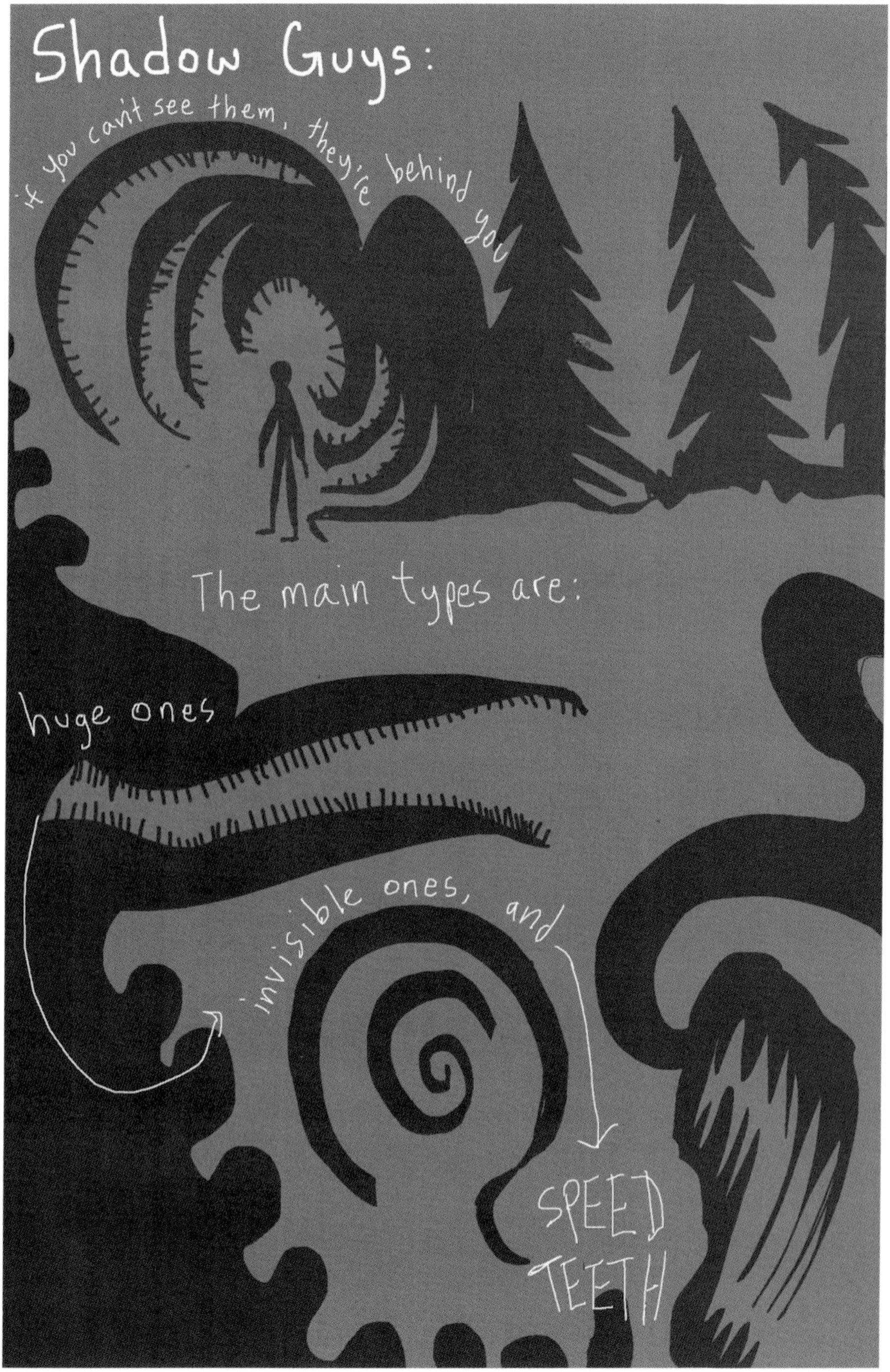
Shadow Guys:
if you can't see them, they're behind you
The main types are:
huge ones
invisible ones, and
SPEED TEETH

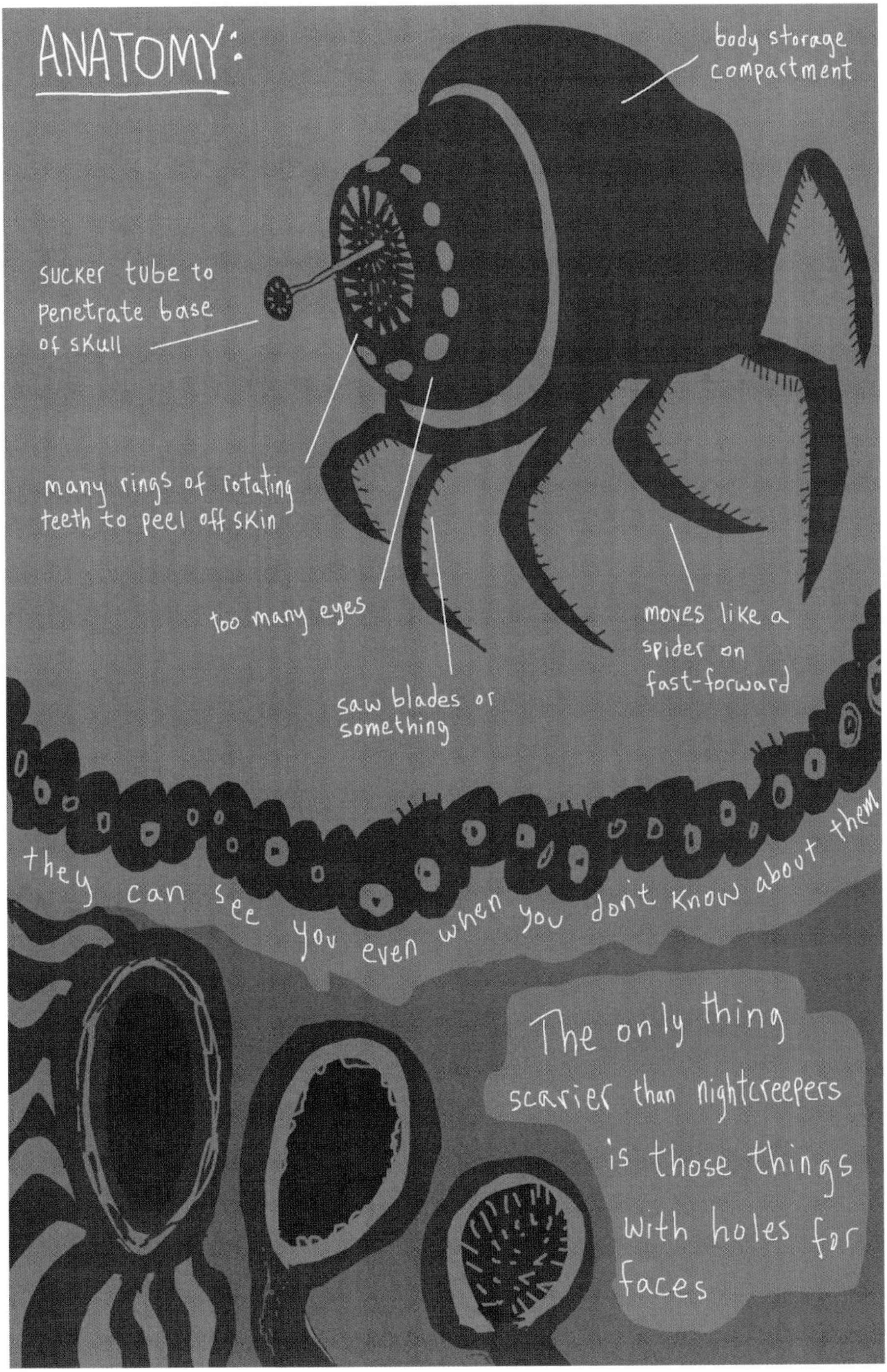
ANATOMY:
body storage compartment
sucker tube to penetrate base of skull
many rings of rotating teeth to peel off skin
too many eyes
saw blades or something
moves like a spider on fast-forward
they can see you even when you don't know about them
The only thing scarier than nightcreepers is those things with holes for faces

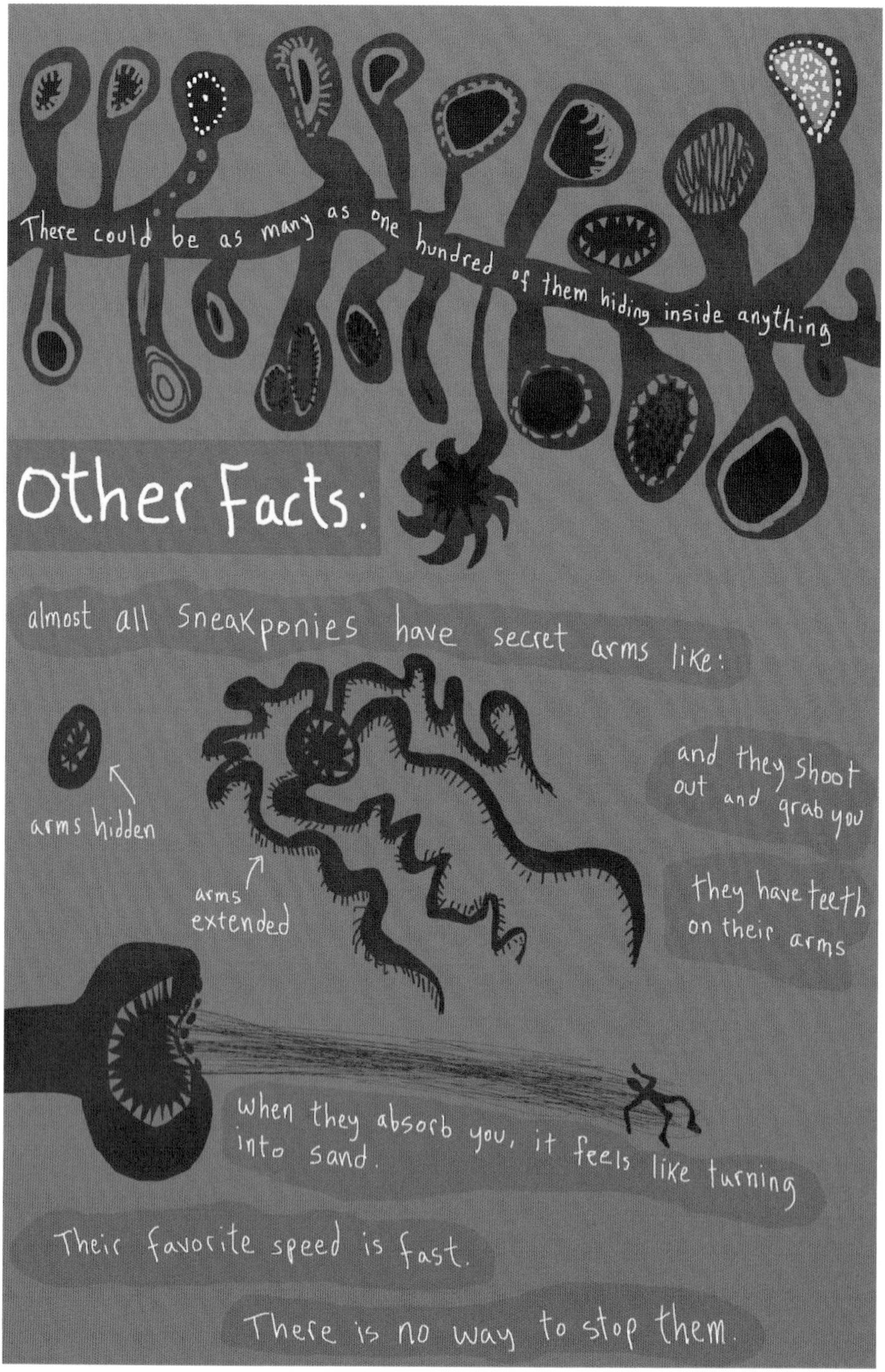
There could be as many as one hundred of them hiding inside anything
Other Facts:
almost all Sneakponies have secret arms like:
arms hidden
arms extended
and they shoot out and grab you
they have teeth on their arms
when they absorb you, it feels like turning into sand.
Their favorite speed is fast.
There is no way to stop them.

I tried to ignore them.

They seemed like they might be real, though.

PART 4: THE PLAN STARTS WORKING

Upon noticing how scared I was becoming, I made several attempts to reason with myself.

However, under the circumstances, that turned out to be impossible.

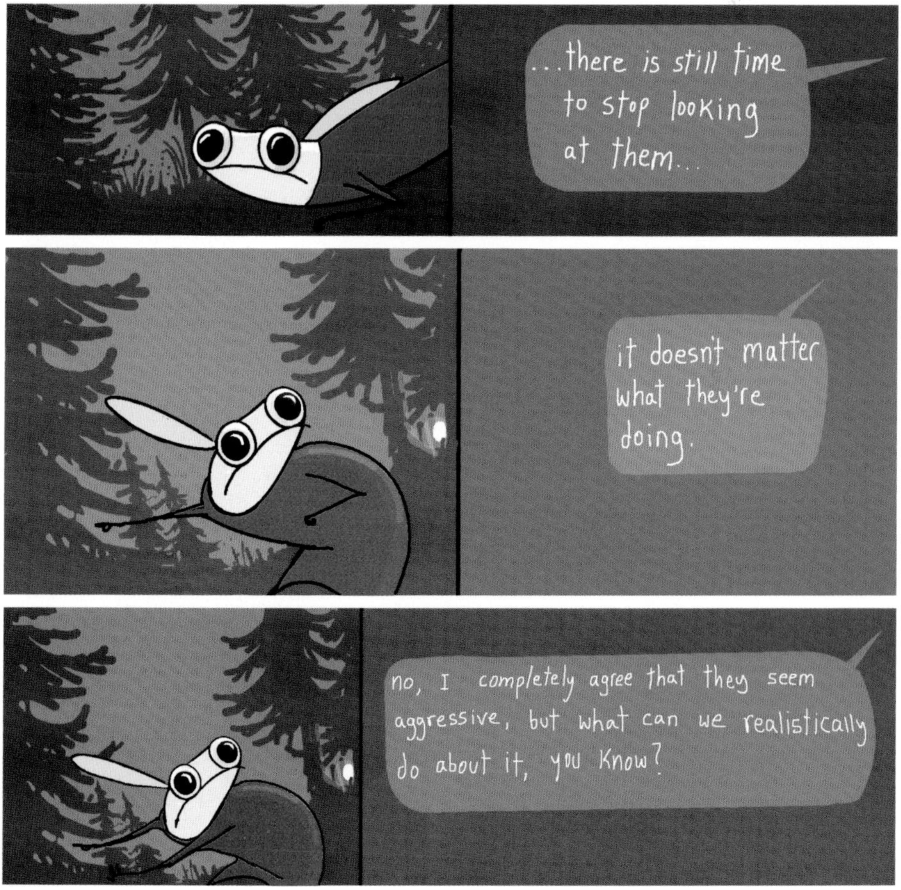
...there is still time to stop looking at them...
it doesn't matter what they're doing.
no, I completely agree that they seem aggressive, but what can we realistically do about it, you know?

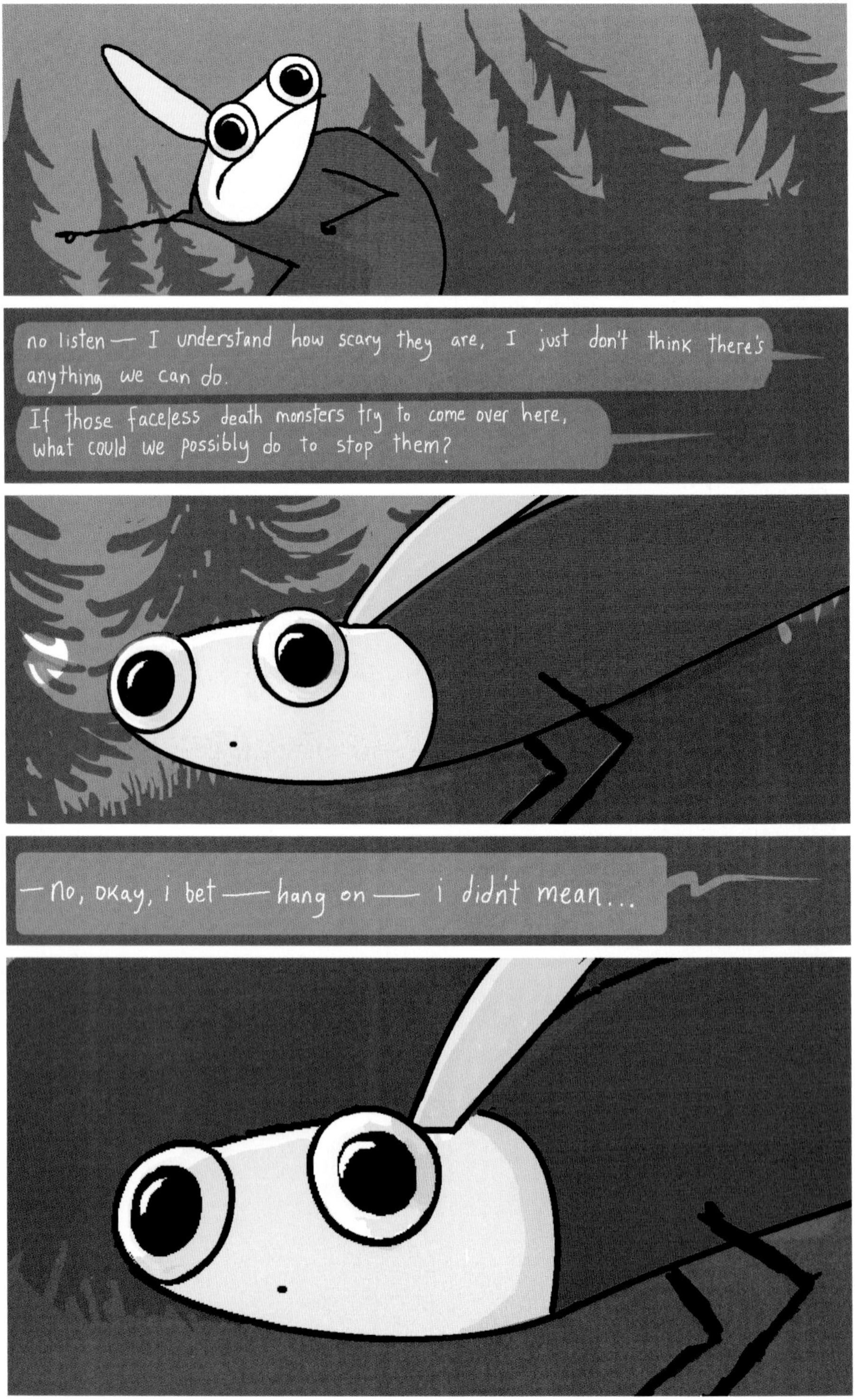
no listen— I understand how scary they are, I just don't think there's anything we can do.
If those faceless death monsters try to come over here, what could we possibly do to stop them?
—no, okay, i bet—hang on— i didn't mean...

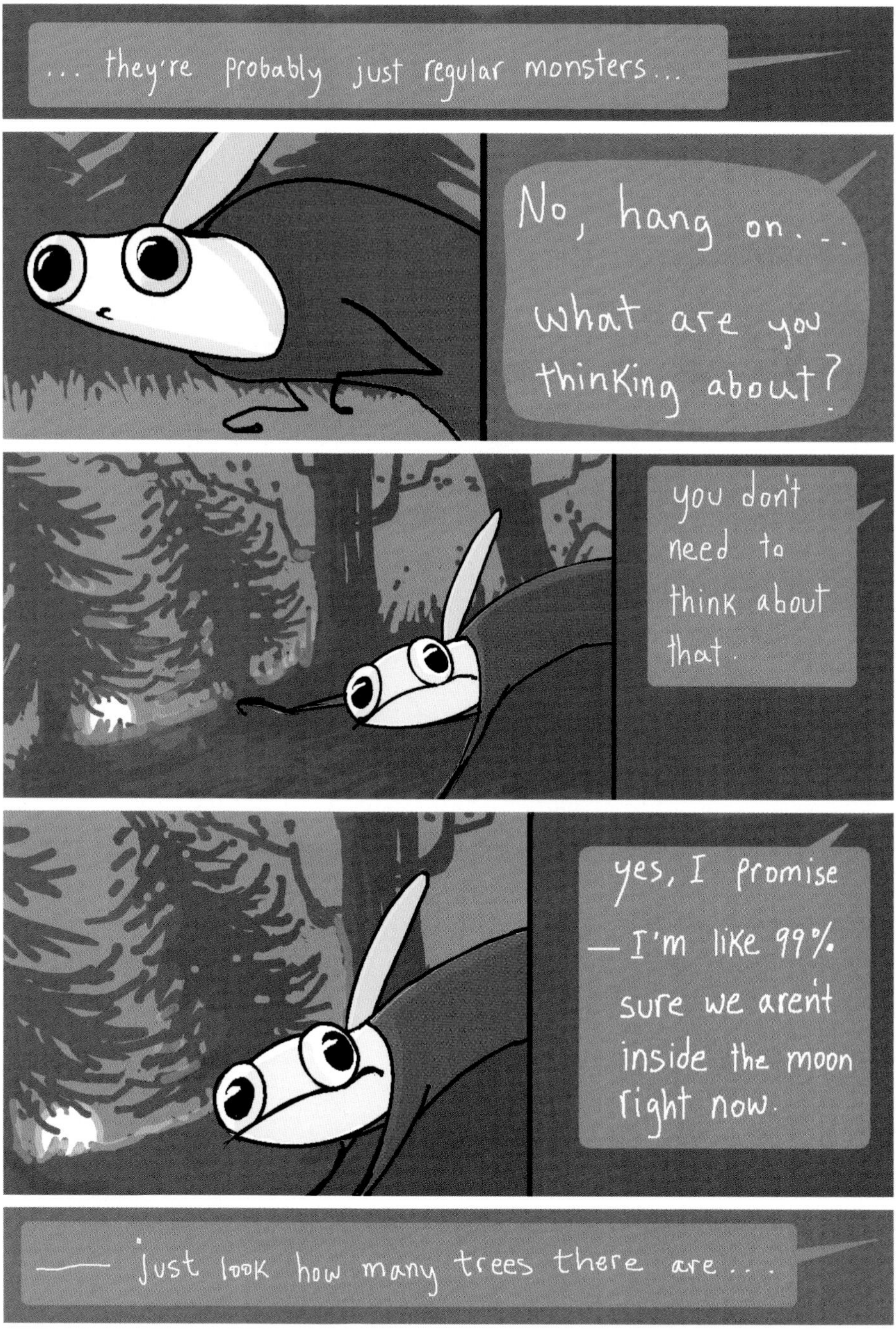

... they're probably just regular monsters...
No, hang on... what are you thinking about?
you don't need to think about that.
yes, I promise —I'm like 99% sure we aren't inside the moon right now.
— just look how many trees there are...

PART 5: THE PLAN STARTS REALLY WORKING

Noticing the trees again felt like hard proof that something deadly was about to happen.

I didn't know what it would be—shadow people, shadow ghosts, shadows turn out to be real, reality turns out to be an illusion and my real body is slowly suffocating deep inside the moon where the body farms are—*but those trees were still there*, which meant it was correct to have been suspicious of them.

Here, it is important to remind ourselves that, to avoid undershooting and not being scared enough, I had prepared for this experience by consuming vast collections of media designed by professionals to be as horrifying as possible. I researched what it's like to be assaulted. I did Slenderman visualization drills. I did a Google image search for "scary picture" and looked at 37 pages of results.

As it turns out, none of that was necessary.

All I need is trees.

Just . . . trees.

The only thing they were doing was being there like usual instead of mysteriously vanishing after I stopped paying attention to them.

That's all it took.

The preparation may have contributed somewhat to the overall ambiance of doom, but the thing that delivered the killing blow was trees. I suspected them the moment I saw them. When they were still there, I was sure. I didn't know what I was sure *about*, but I didn't need to be: *I saw those trees.*

And there it was: the target level of fear.

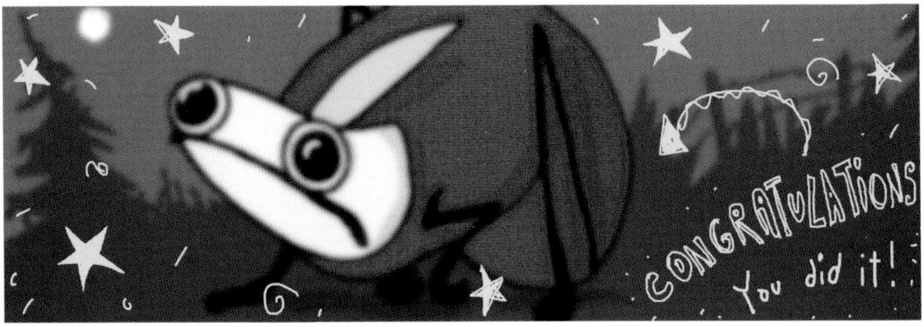
CONGRATULATIONS
You did it!

If this had been a real emergency, I wouldn't have had to feel like that for very long.

But it wasn't a real emergency. Two seconds later, nothing had happened to me.

And it continued to not happen, and continued to not happen, and continued to not happen.

Which, in my opinion, is the biggest problem with not being immediately murdered by unstoppable spirit monsters. You have to figure out what to do with yourself.

You know it's going to happen. It can't possibly be more than a second away from happening. But it could take longer. Minutes, even. It's probably going to happen right now, but as of right *now*, you're still alive. And because of that, you are fully and continuously experiencing the same amount of suspense you'd feel moments before being strangled to death by puzzle ghosts—and now it's been four minutes—and four minutes is too long to feel like that. If it doesn't happen within the next one minute, you need a strategy. But *what*? Lie down on the ground?

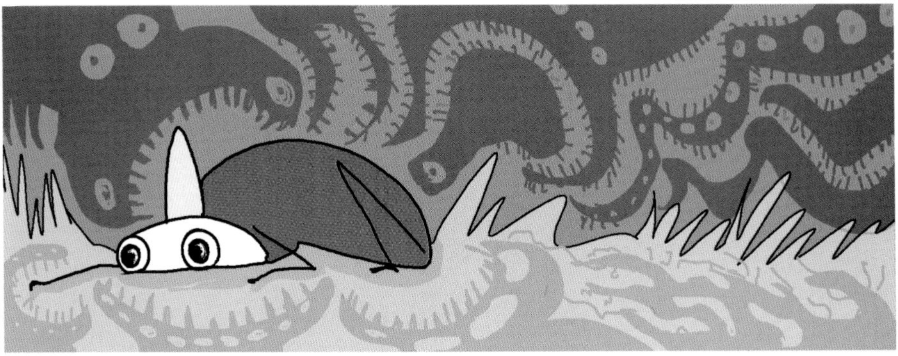

Lie down on the ground more?

I started to feel bad for myself in the same way I felt bad for that mouse from freshman biology. The one that survived for three days before the classroom snake finally got around to putting it out of its misery.

That poor little thing . . . , I thought.

That poor little thing can't handle much more of this . . .

But, as long as you aren't dead, you need something to do. And surviving is something to do.

PART 6: A LEADER EMERGES

A survival situation has to have a leader. Sometimes it's a good leader, sometimes there isn't much to work with, but somebody's gotta do it.

In my case, there was only one option.

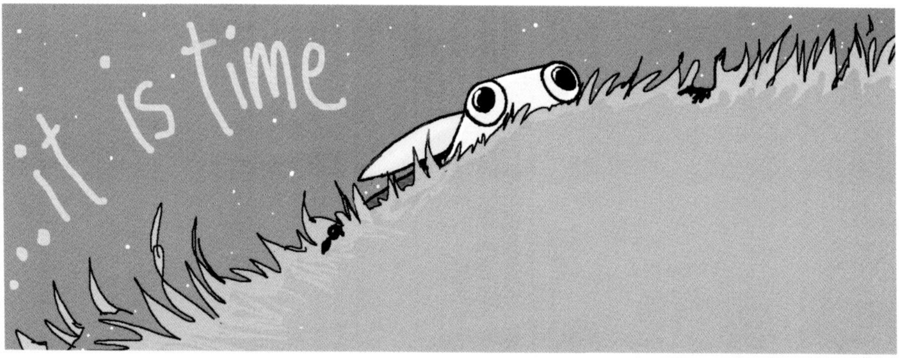
...it is time

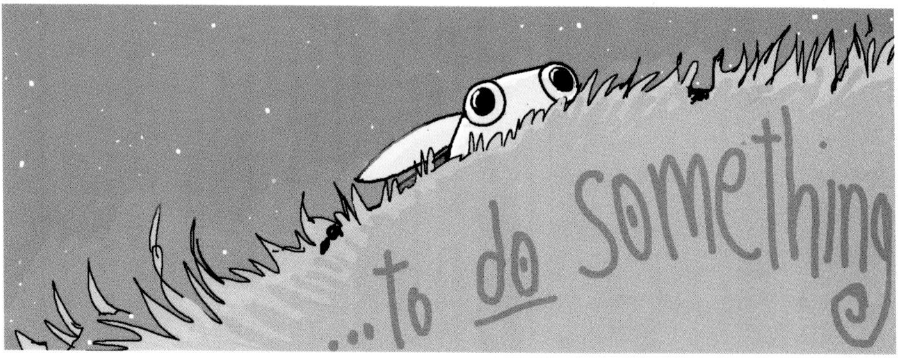
...to do something

Sensing the pressure to lead, my first instinct was to give up.

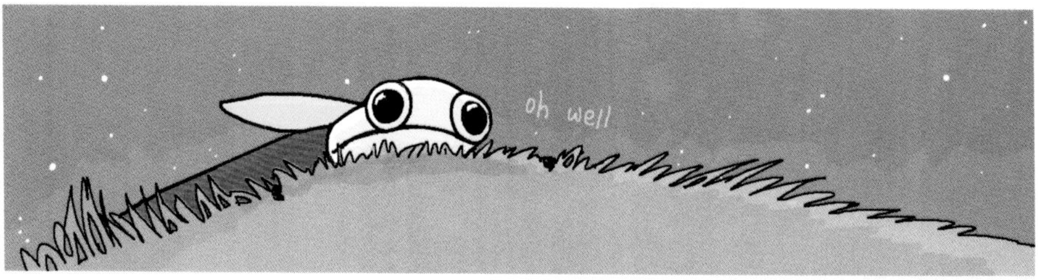
oh well

If I'd been ready to die, this would've worked and nobody would have had to be the leader.

But there was a tiny part of me that wasn't ready. Just the faintest whisper of survival instinct. The survival equivalent of a piece of rice.

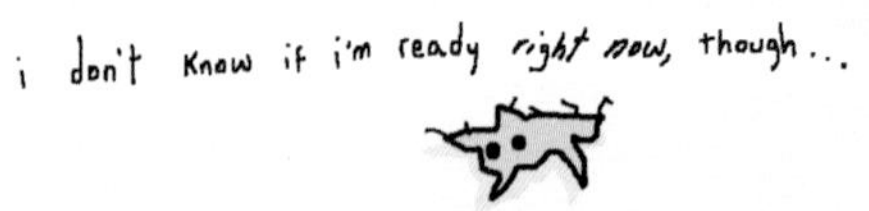
i don't know if i'm ready right now, though...

And it was facing an unbelievably ambiguous first decision:

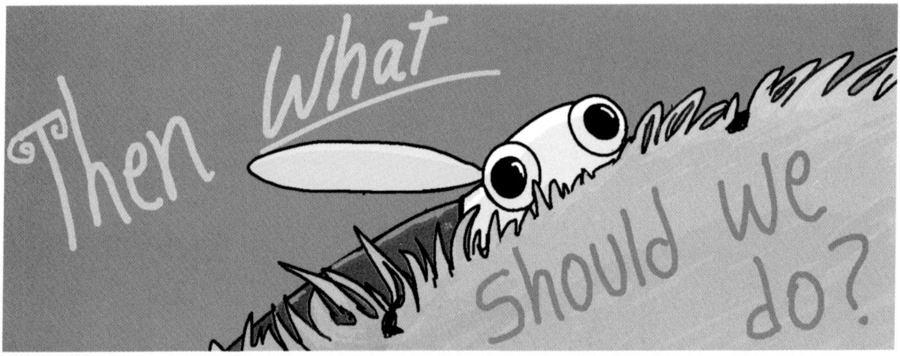
Then What
should we do?

Every time I thought about it, I'd get overwhelmed and attempt to give up.

But death would once again fail to claim me, and we'd be back at the same crossroads.

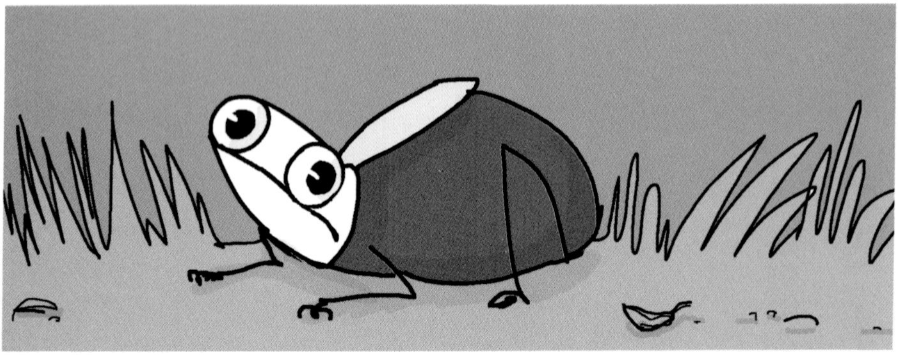

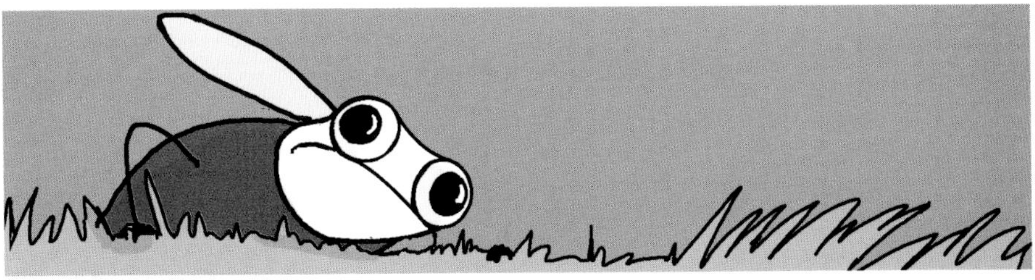

As I was looking around for help, I noticed a small trail leading into the woods. It seemed more assertive than the other scenery. I decided to follow it.

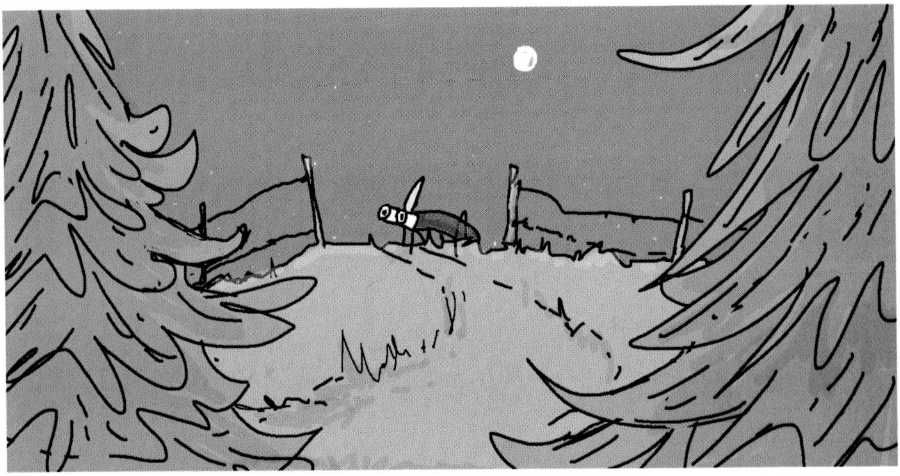

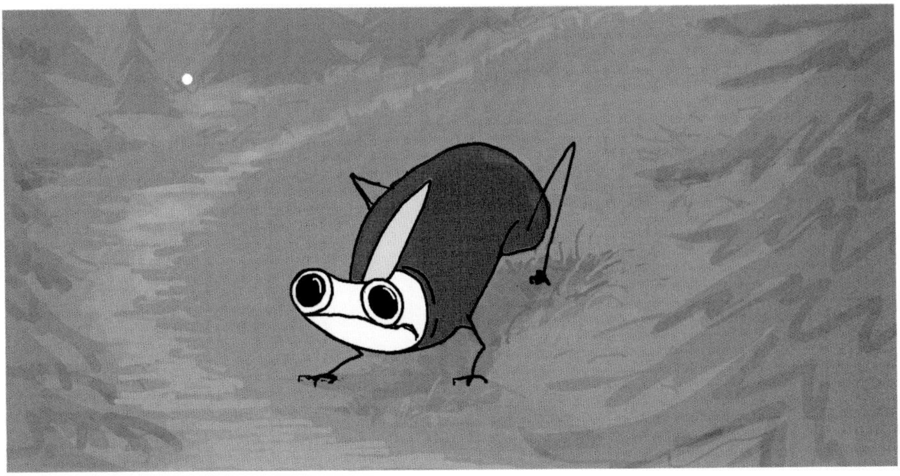

Unfortunately, it petered out almost immediately.

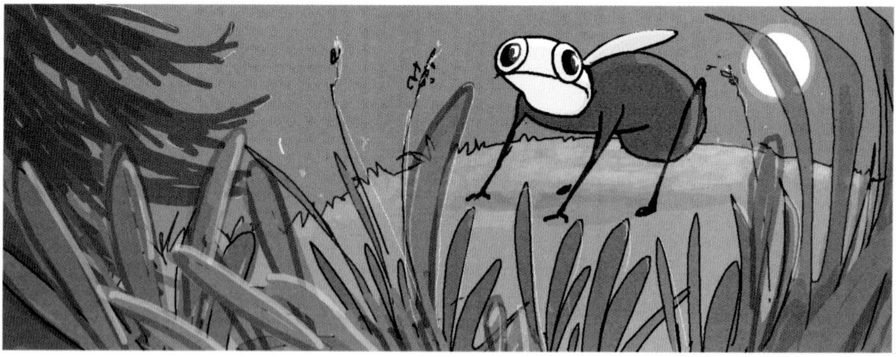

The next closest recognizable object was a hill. It looked relatively harmless, so I climbed it.

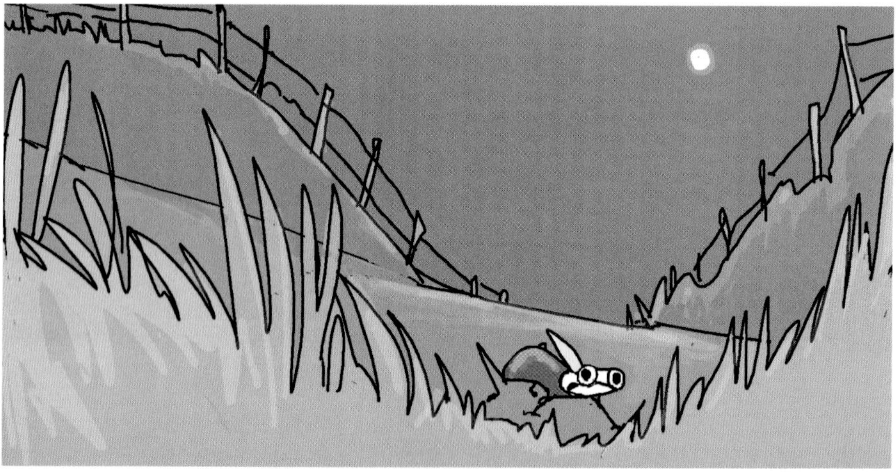

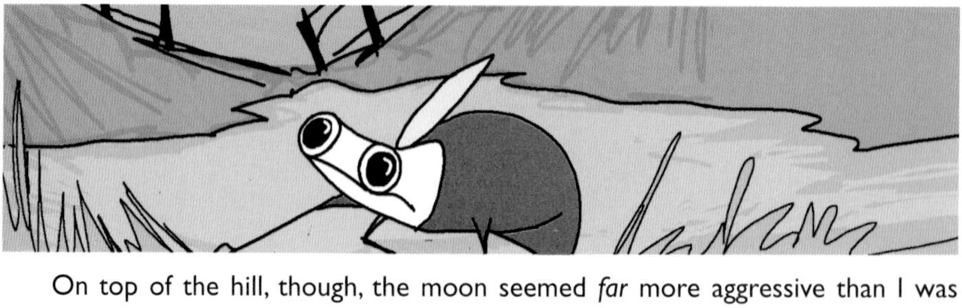

On top of the hill, though, the moon seemed *far* more aggressive than I was expecting . . .

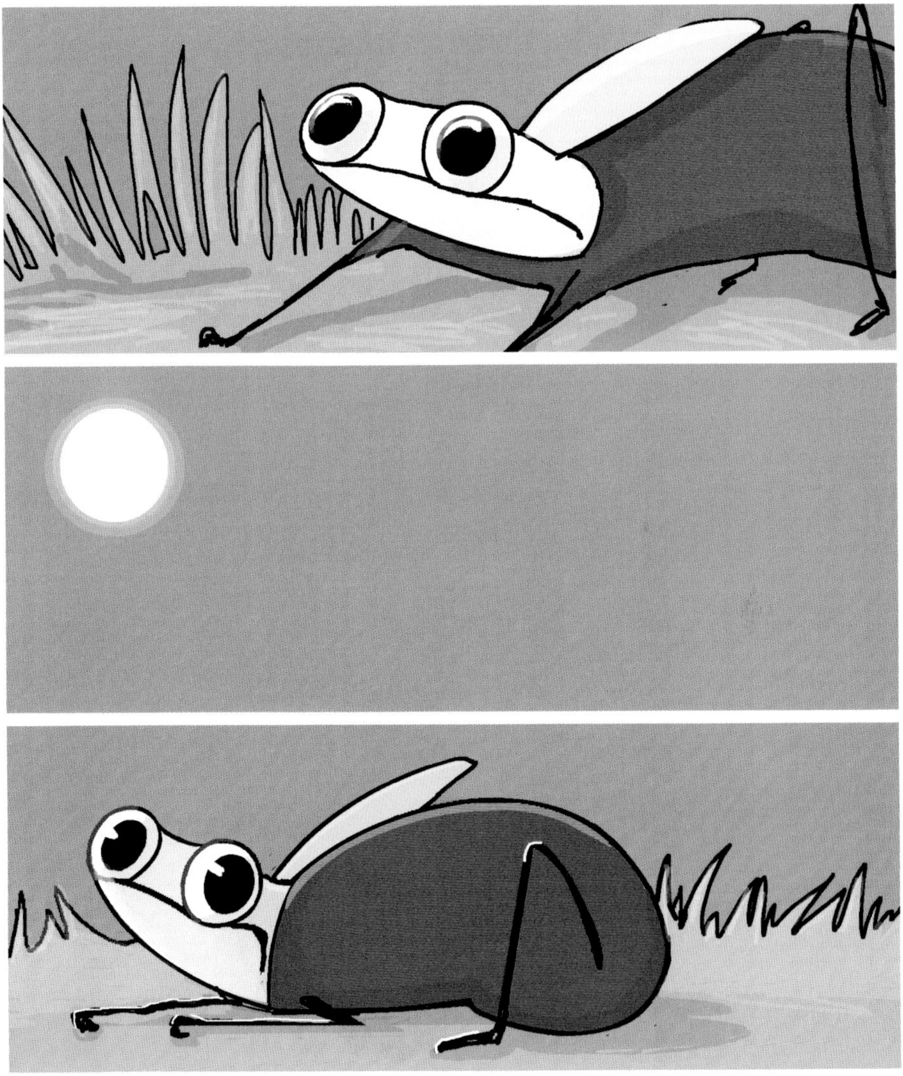

Not knowing what else to do, I found a plant and crawled underneath it for protection.

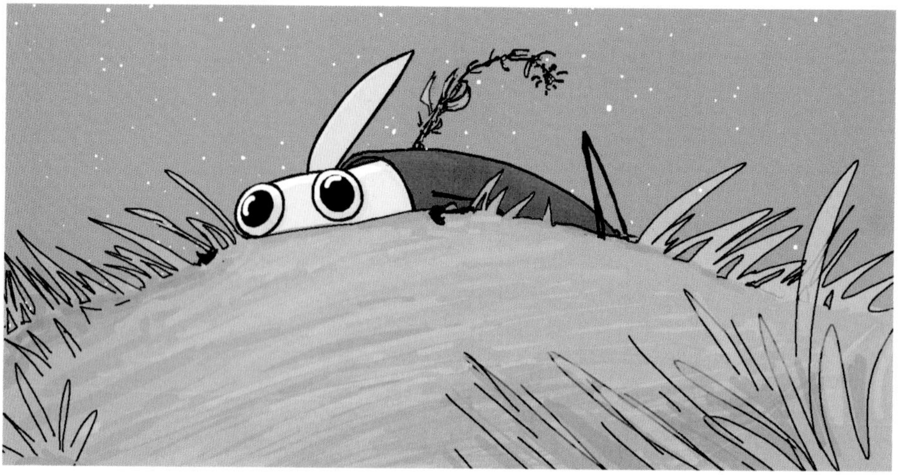

And that is a pitiful place to be in your life.

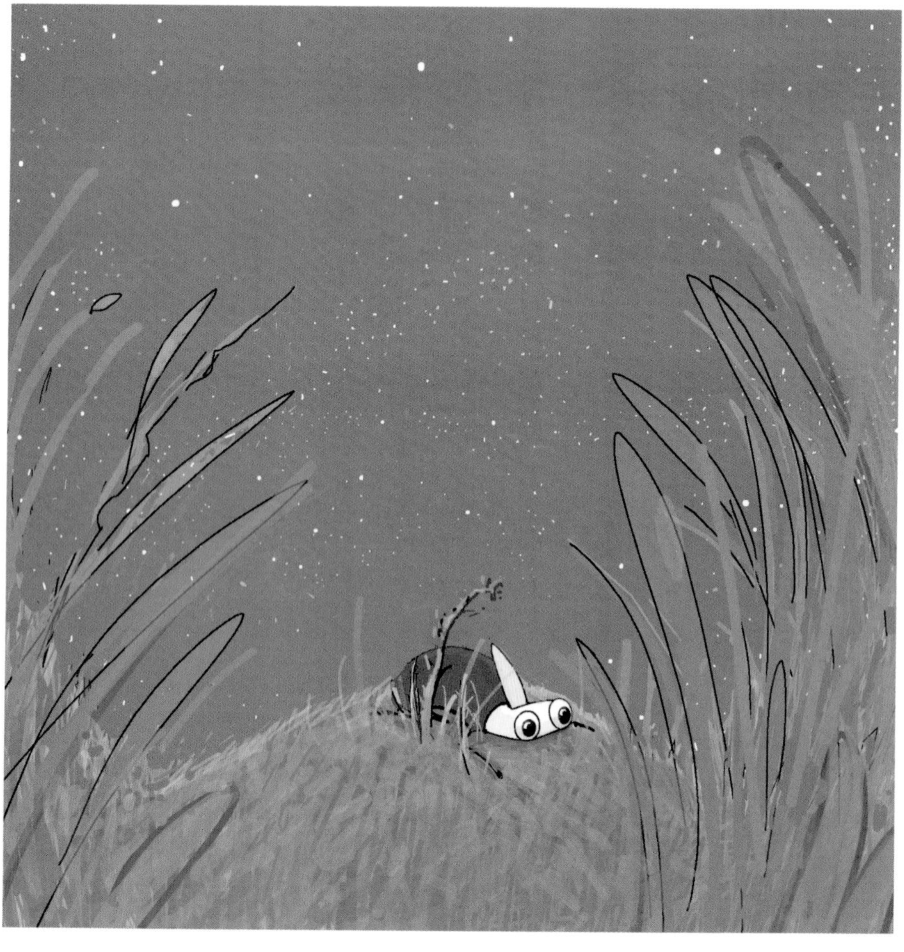

When you're alone in a field, hiding under a plant because you're scared of the moon, you just sort of instinctually recognize how sad it is. No matter how unsympathetic you are, you'd feel some degree of concern for the person who is in that situation.

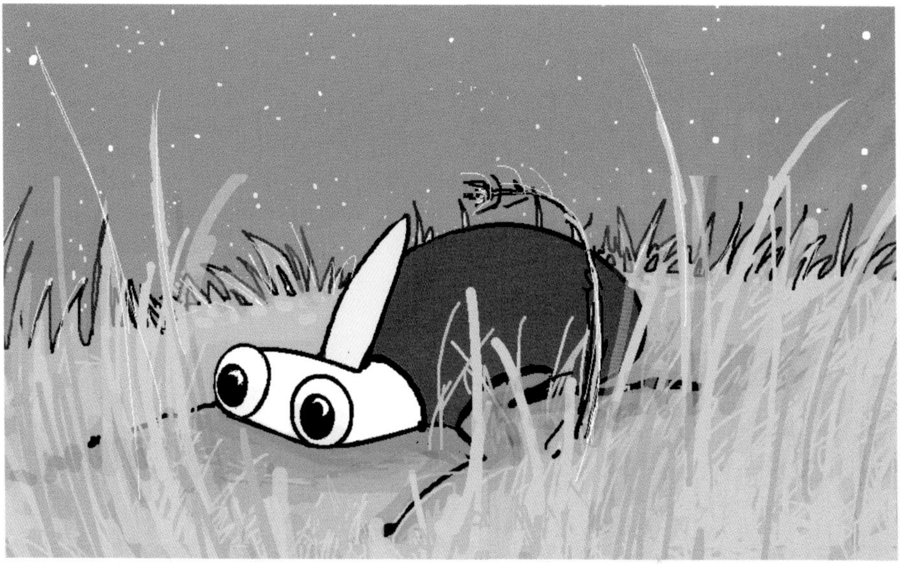

And I remember looking at myself and seeing this scared, small creature hiding under a plant, and I remember thinking, *"Oh goodness . . . Somebody should help you."*

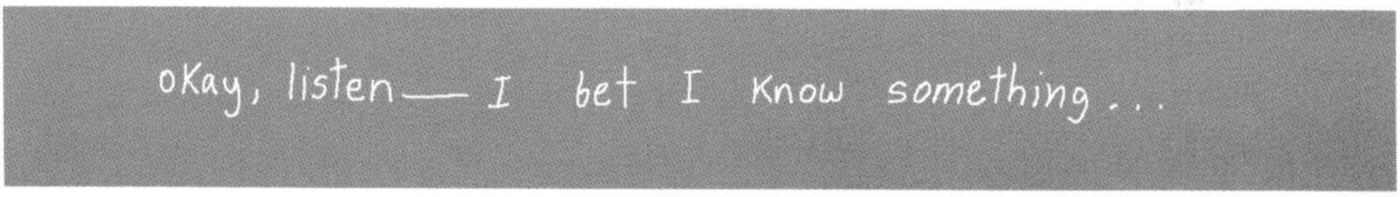
okay, listen—I bet I know something . . .

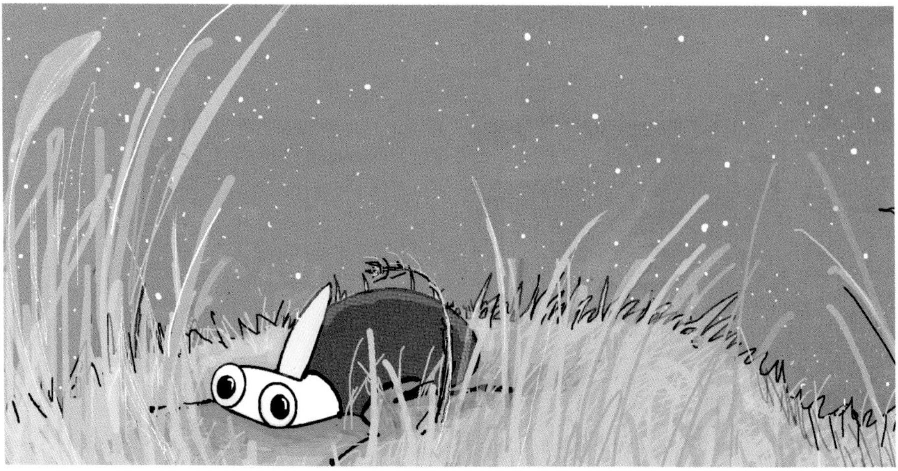

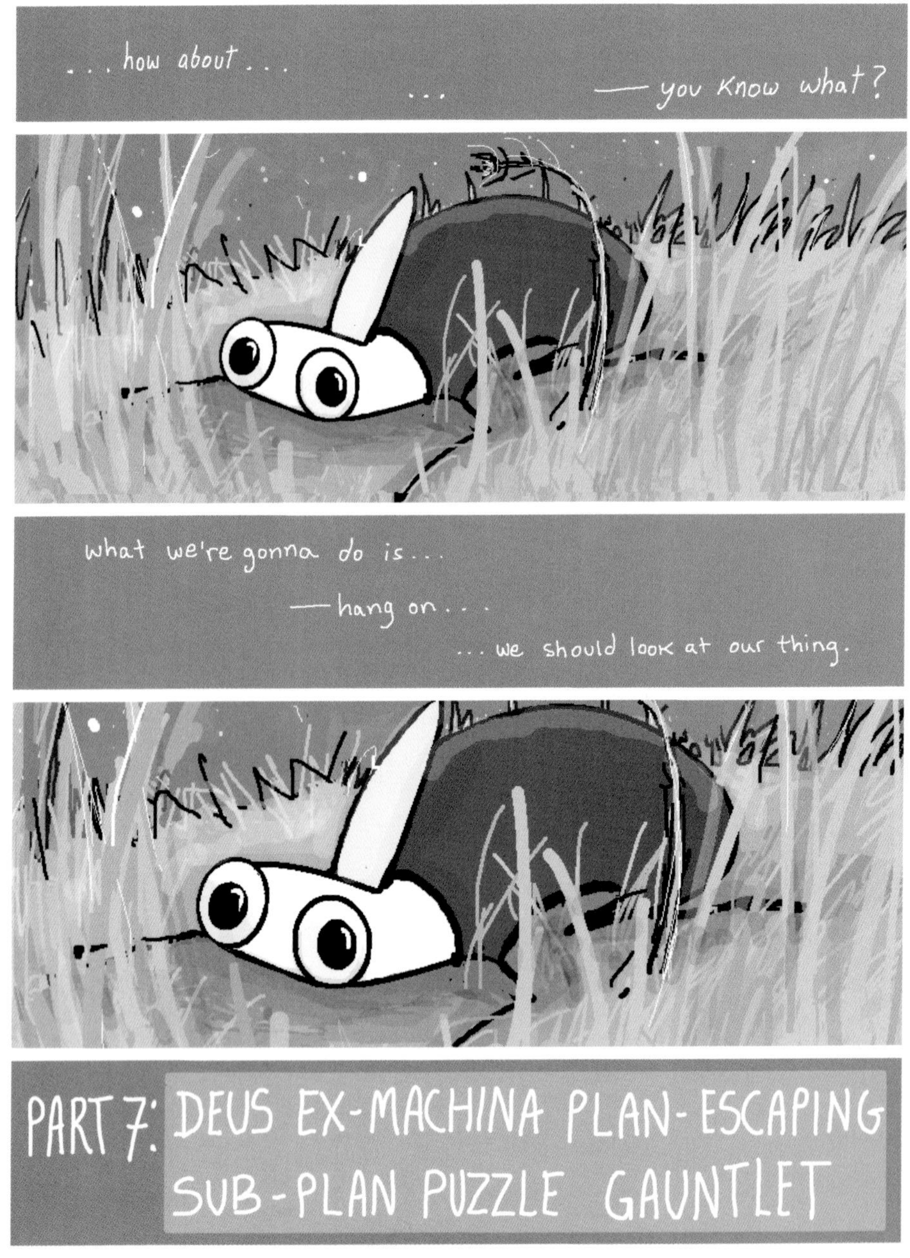
. . . how about . . .
. . .
— you know what?
what we're gonna do is . . .
— hang on . . .
. . . we should look at our thing.

PART 7: DEUS EX-MACHINA PLAN-ESCAPING SUB-PLAN PUZZLE GAUNTLET

The thing I was referring to was my phone.

Yes, there was a phone. The whole time there was a phone. But in far-gone places, it's never as simple as having a phone and calling someone who can help you.

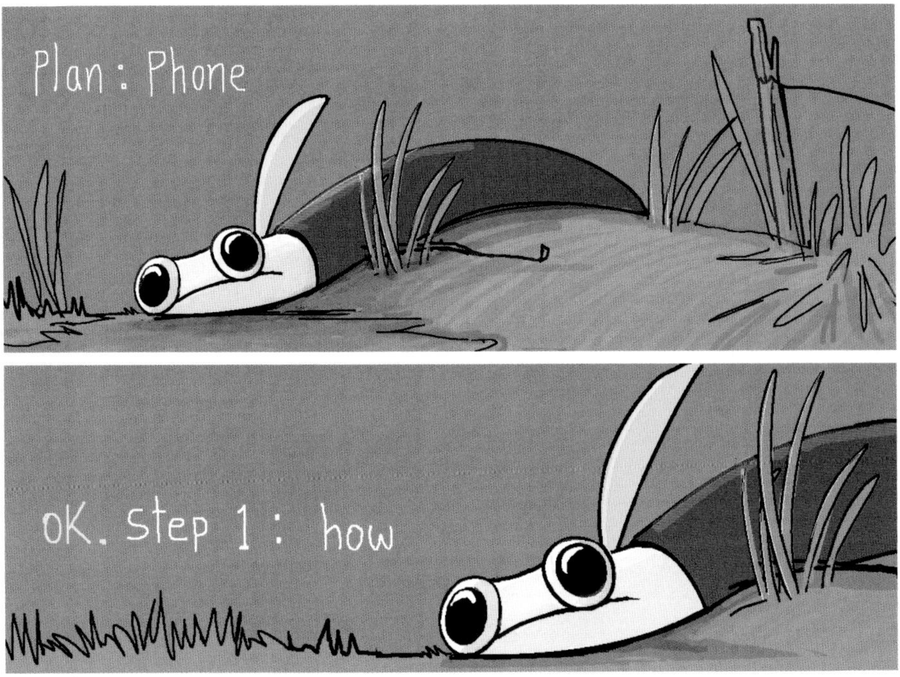
Plan : Phone
OK. Step 1 : how

I tried to get to the options, but some weird number riddle was in the way.

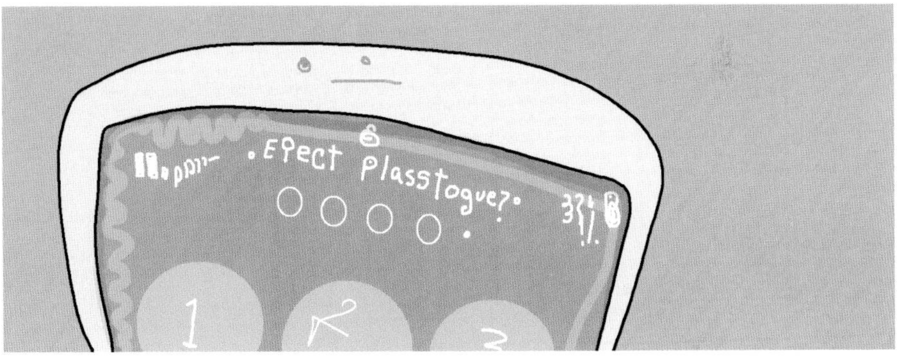

Because when you're fucked up enough, technology doesn't make sense.

Dig a hole?

Sure.

Catch a fish?

Okay.

Pee on a rock?

Why not.

How about: enter a 4-digit passcode on a tappy-tap screen to unlock this glowing surface full of symbols?

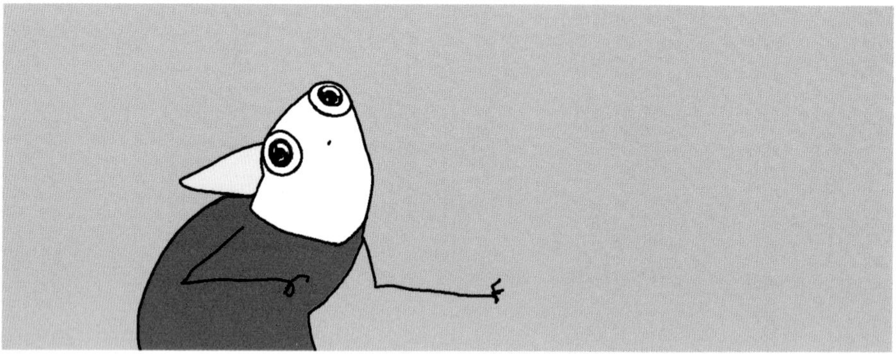

Under these conditions, a phone seems like a light-up rectangle puzzle from an alternate dimension.

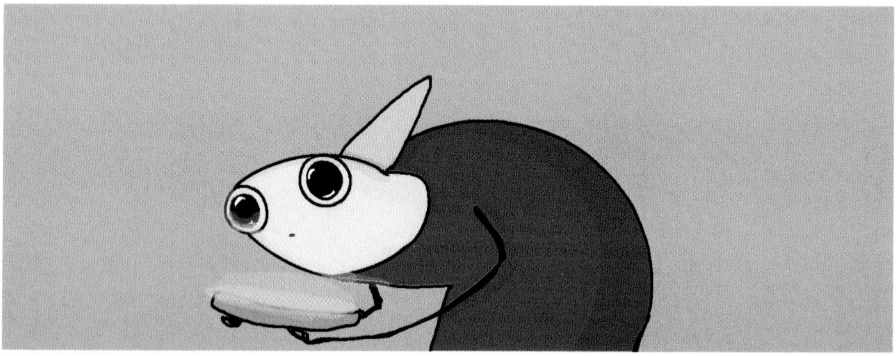

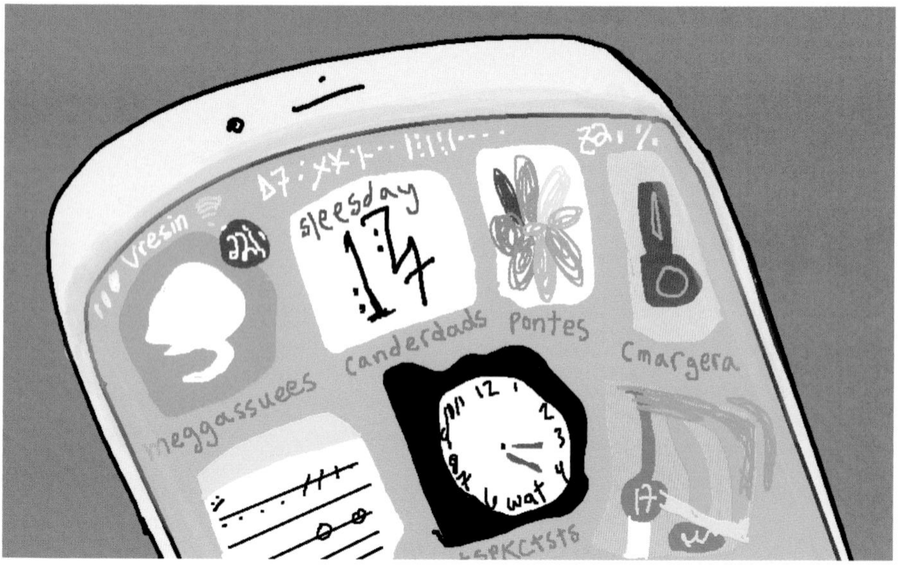
vresin
sleesday
canderdads
pontes
Cmargera
meggassuees
wat

I felt most simpatico toward the map icon, so I went for it.

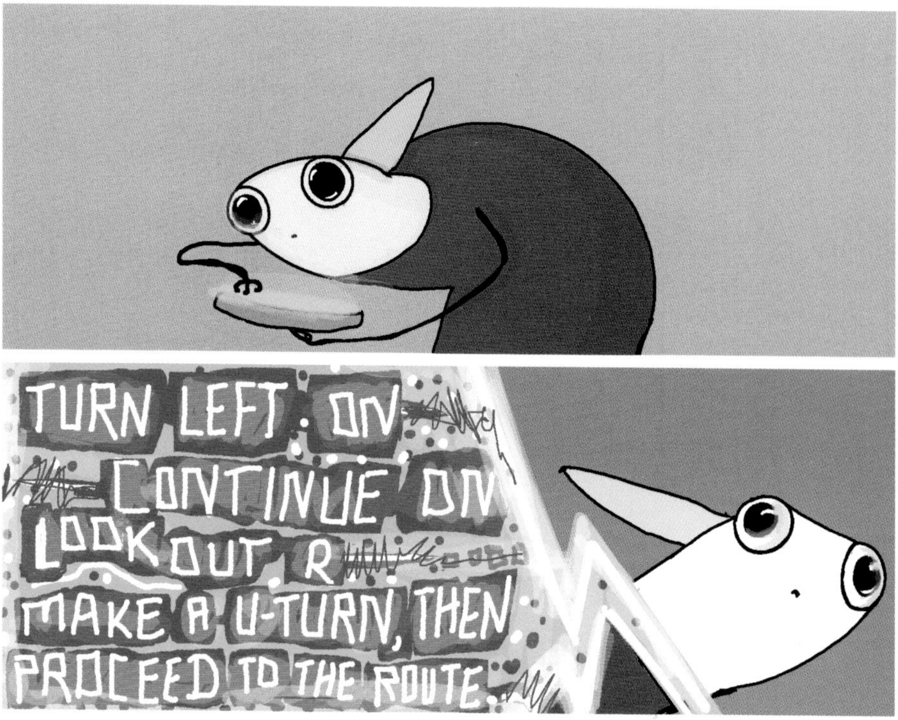
TURN LEFT ON
CONTINUE ON
LOOKOUT R
MAKE A U-TURN, THEN
PROCEED TO THE ROUTE.

I'm certain I wasn't using the map the way it was designed to be used, but at least I wasn't thinking about spookyjims anymore.

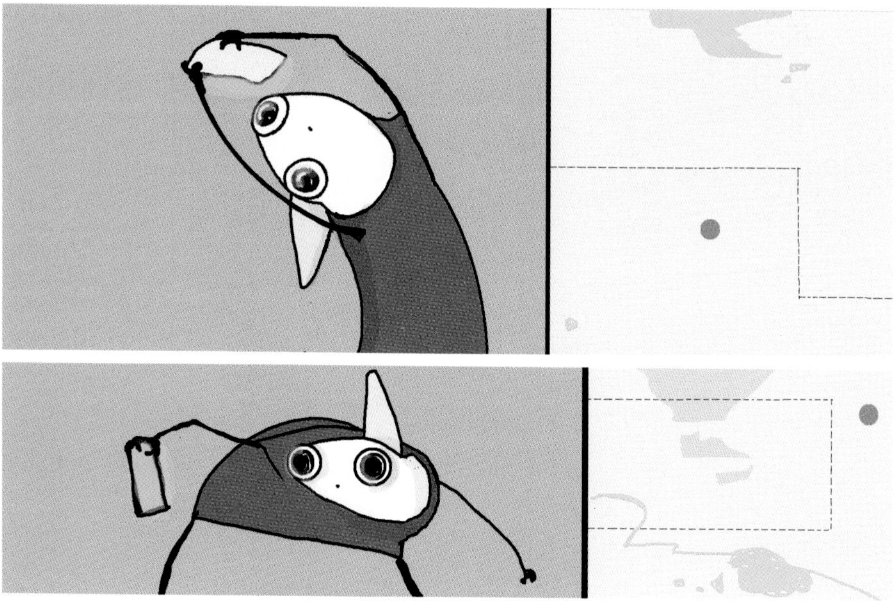

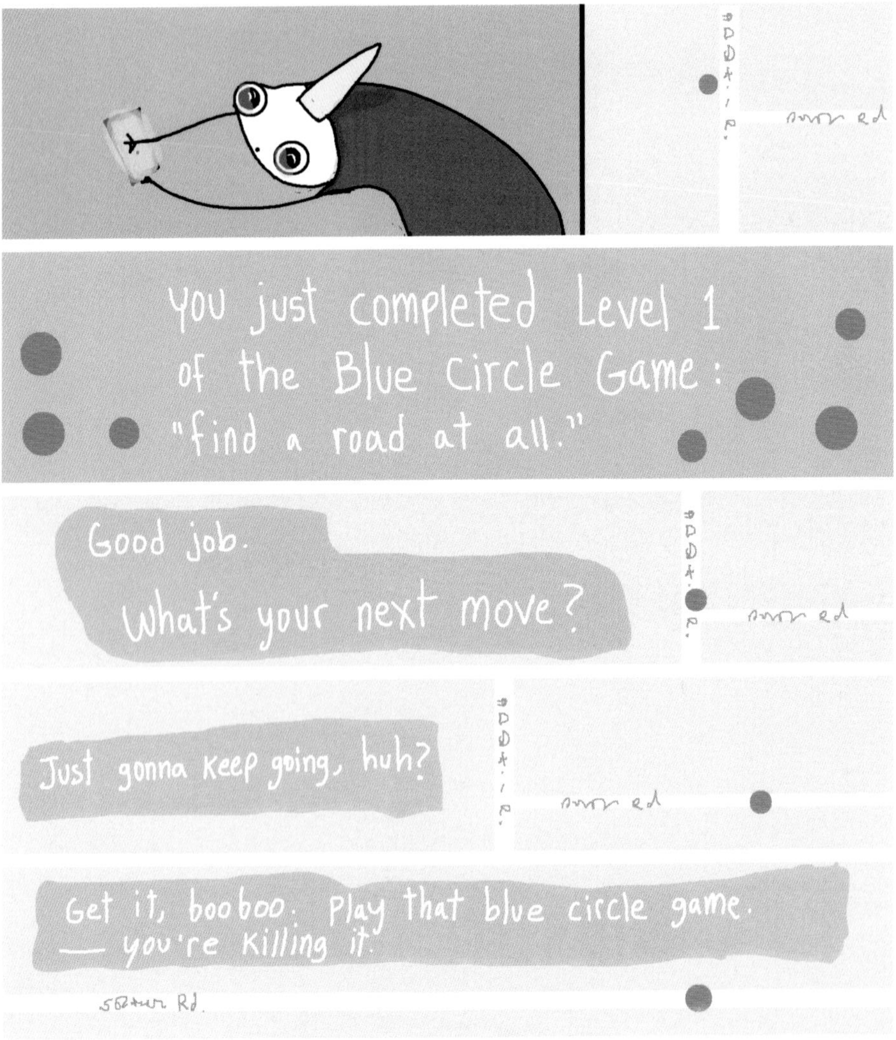
you just completed Level 1
of the Blue Circle Game:
"find a road at all."
Good job.
What's your next move?
Just gonna keep going, huh?
Get it, booboo. Play that blue circle game.
— you're killing it.

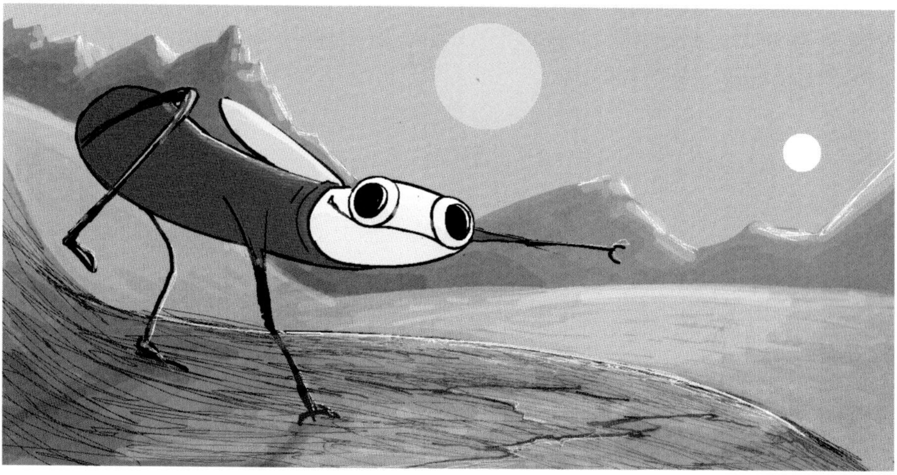

Much later, I remembered there are things phones can do in addition to displaying a map.

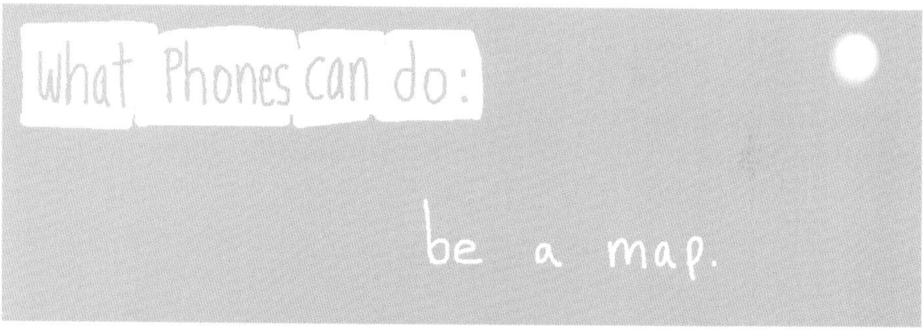
What Phones can do:
be a map.

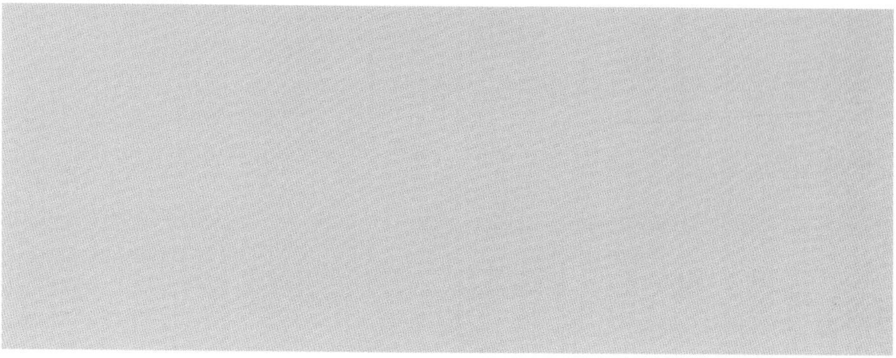

hold on... have you considered that phones also might be able to, for example:

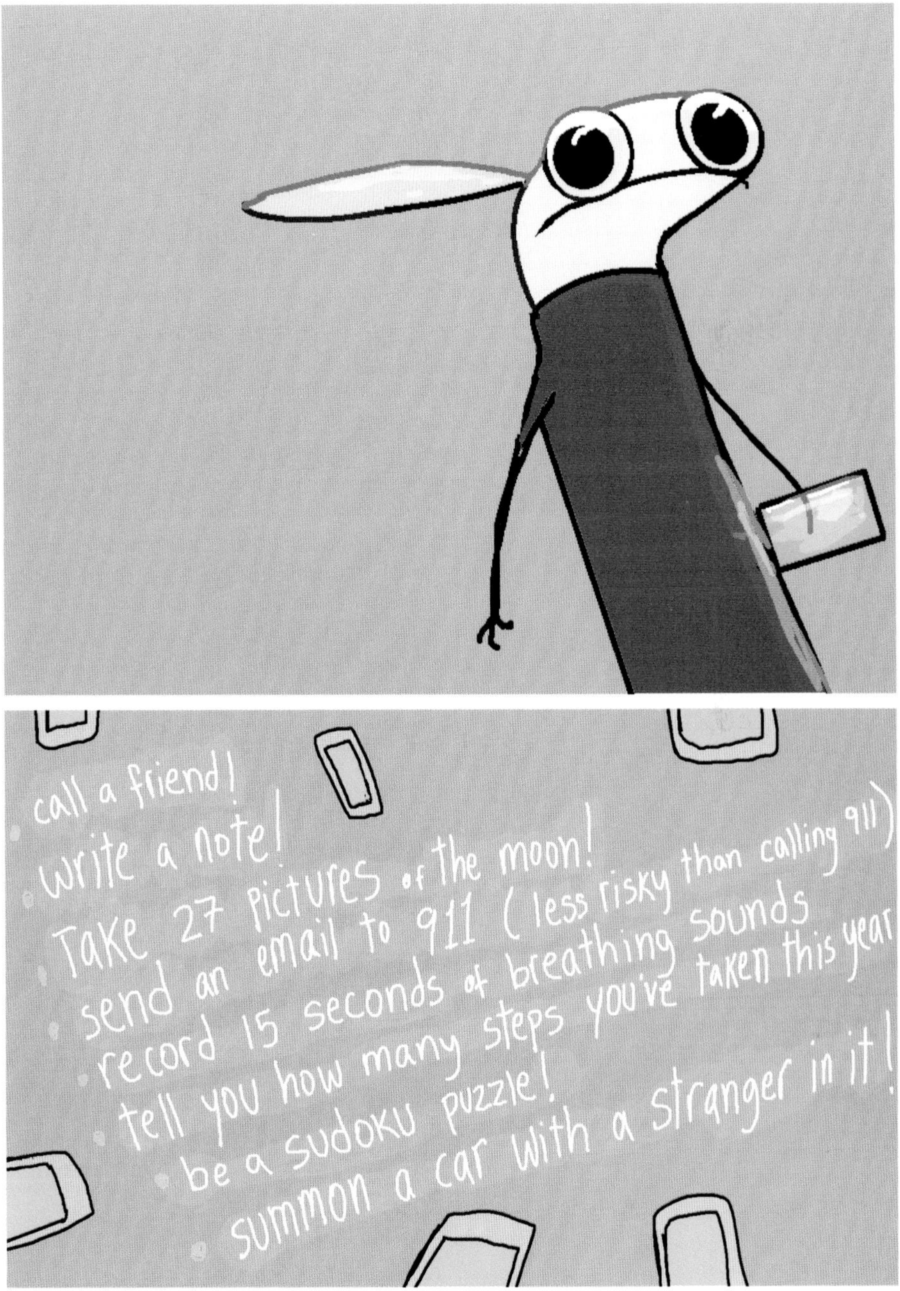
call a friend!
write a note!
Take 27 pictures of the moon!
send an email to 911 (less risky than calling 911)
record 15 seconds of breathing sounds
tell you how many steps you've taken this year
be a sudoku puzzle!
summon a car with a stranger in it!

I wrestled with the stranger-in-a-car option for a while.

Pros:	Cons:
• car is fast	• stranger • might get in trouble • VERY challenging button sequences • might not be able to get back to the screen I started on.

In the end, I decided it was worth a shot.

hey there little toaster...

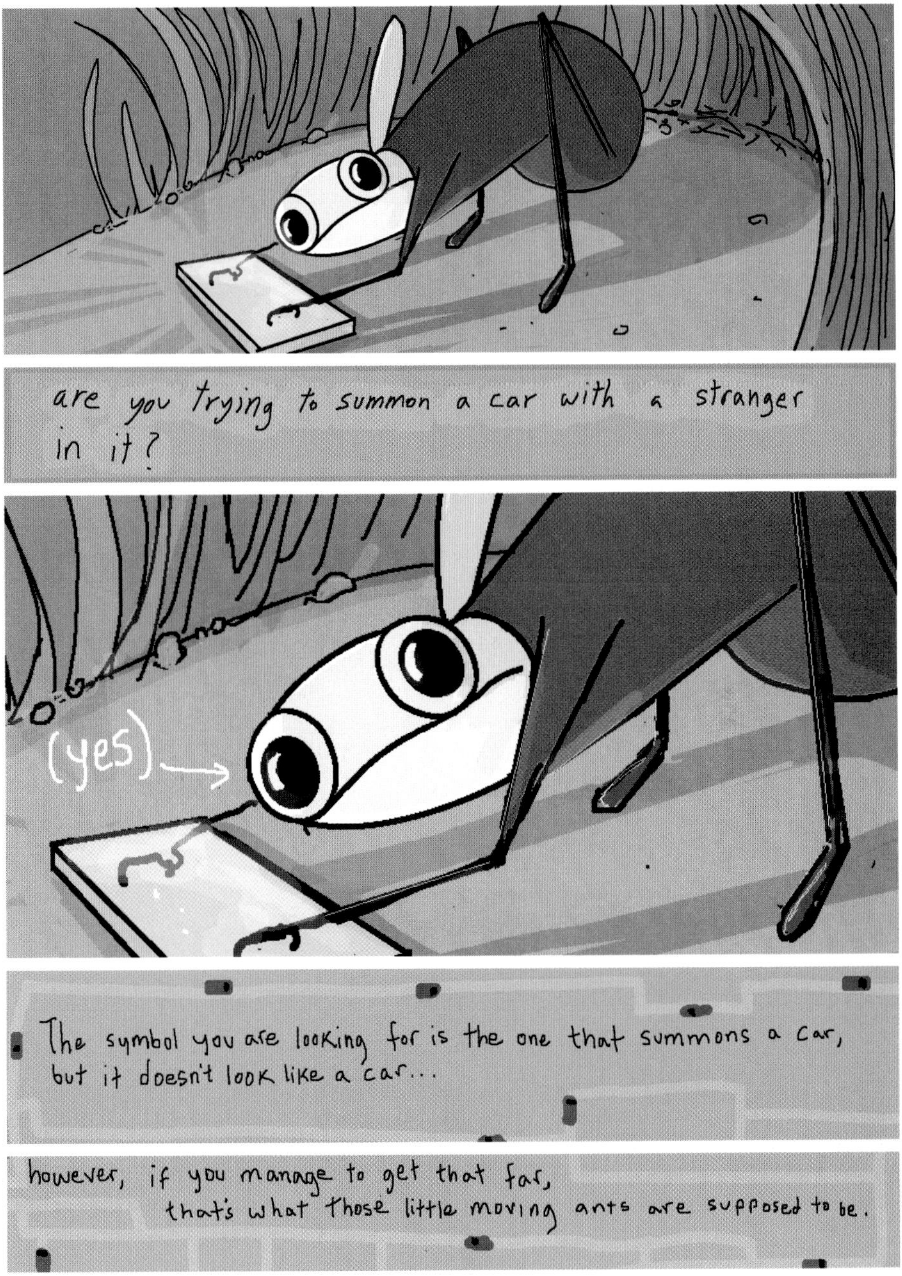
are you trying to summon a car with a stranger in it?
(yes)
The symbol you are looking for is the one that summons a car, but it doesn't look like a car...
however, if you manage to get that far, that's what those little moving ants are supposed to be.

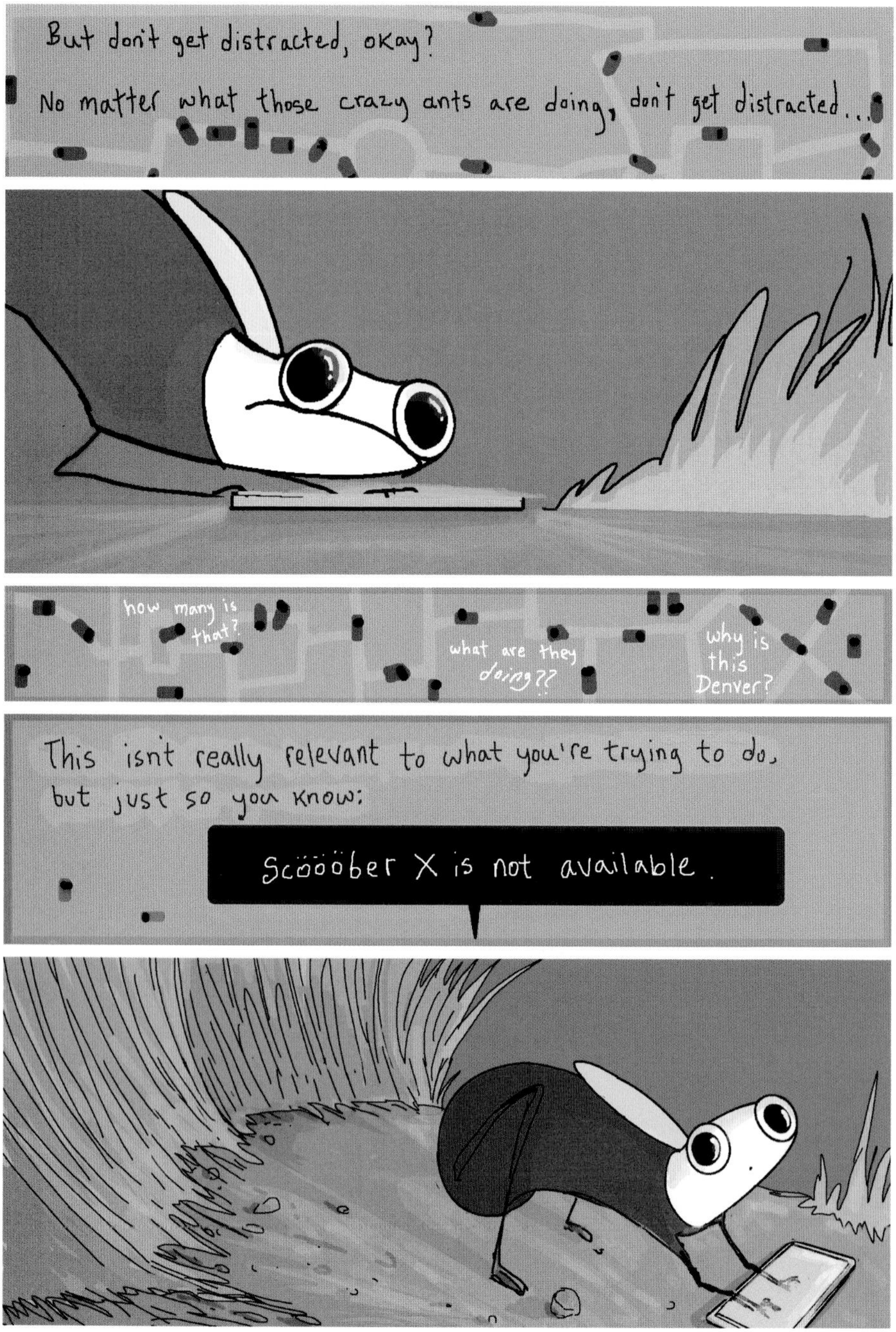
But don't get distracted, okay?
No matter what those crazy ants are doing, don't get distracted...
how many is that?
what are they doing??
why is this Denver?
This isn't really relevant to what you're trying to do, but just so you know:
Scööööber X is not available.

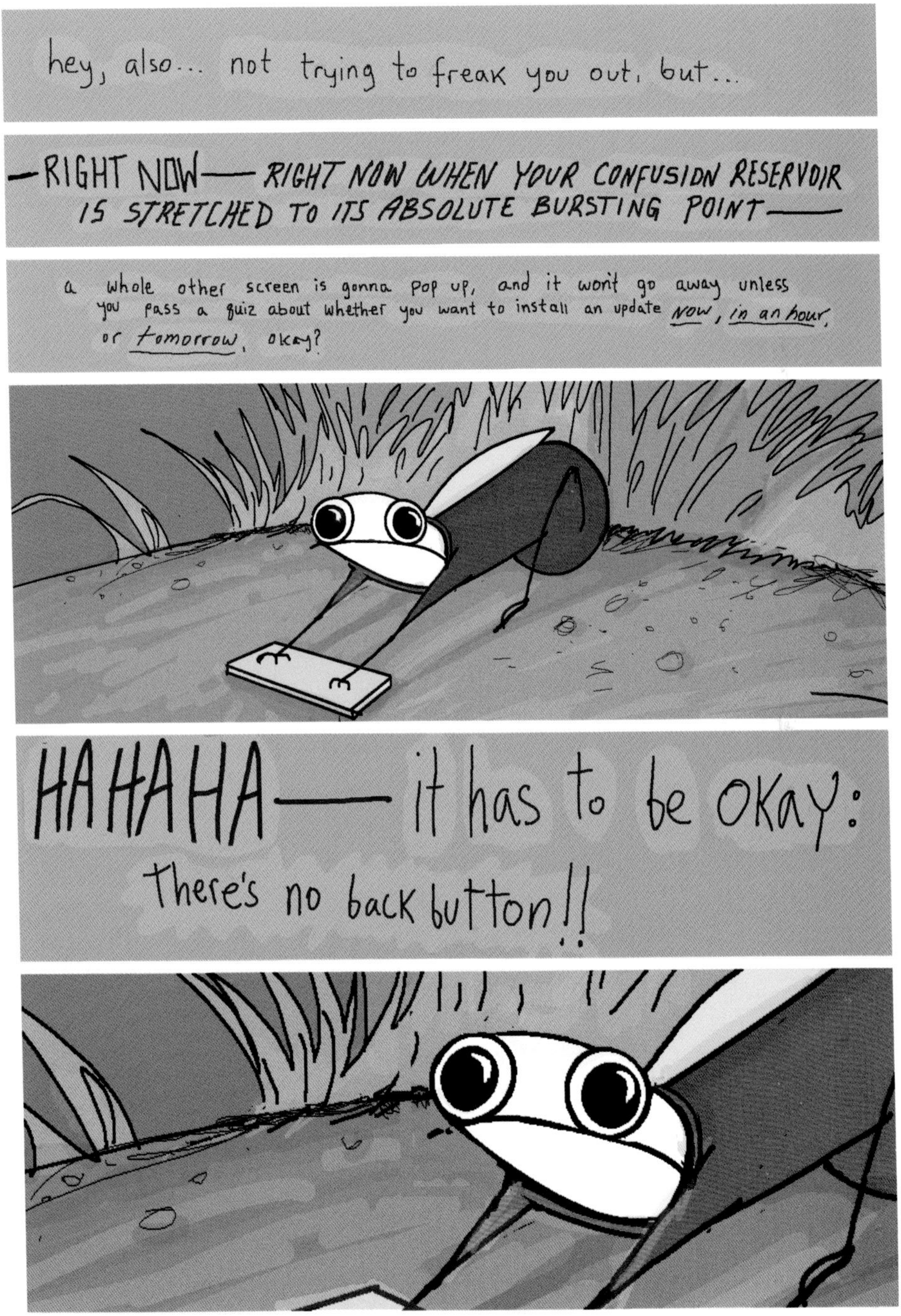
hey, also... not trying to freak you out, but...
—RIGHT NOW— RIGHT NOW WHEN YOUR CONFUSION RESERVOIR IS STRETCHED TO ITS ABSOLUTE BURSTING POINT—
a whole other screen is gonna pop up, and it won't go away unless you pass a quiz about whether you want to install an update now, in an hour, or tomorrow, okay?
HAHAHA— it has to be OKAY:
There's no back button!!

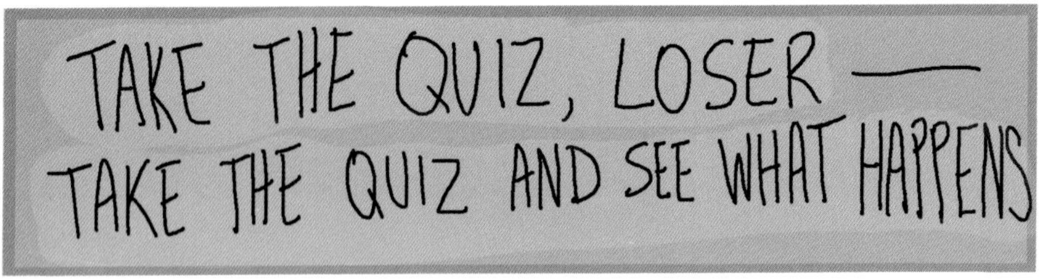
TAKE THE QUIZ, LOSER —
TAKE THE QUIZ AND SEE WHAT HAPPENS

I thought about calling someone, but I couldn't figure out how to explain this to anybody.

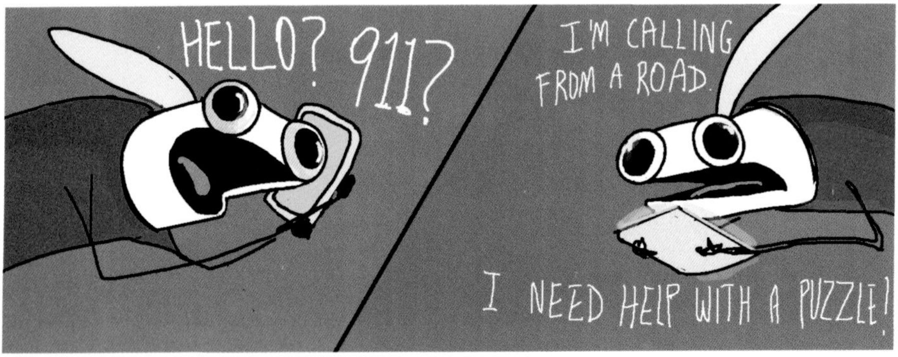
HELLO? 911?
I'M CALLING FROM A ROAD.
I NEED HELP WITH A PUZZLE!

The other possibilities didn't turn out to be especially promising either, so I went back to doing my best with the car summoning.

I was still trying to figure it out when the car pulled up.

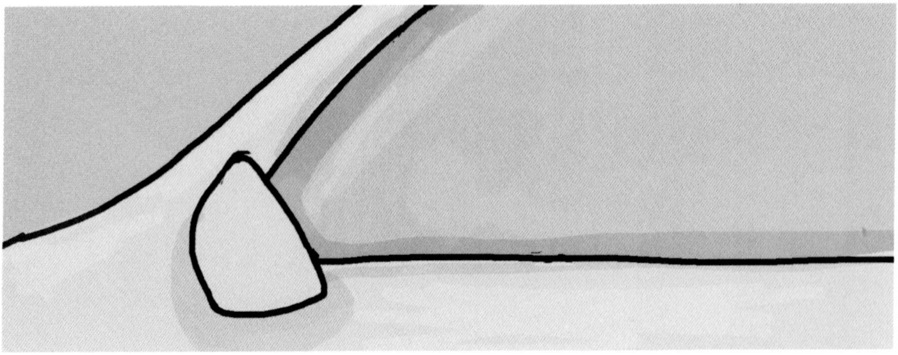

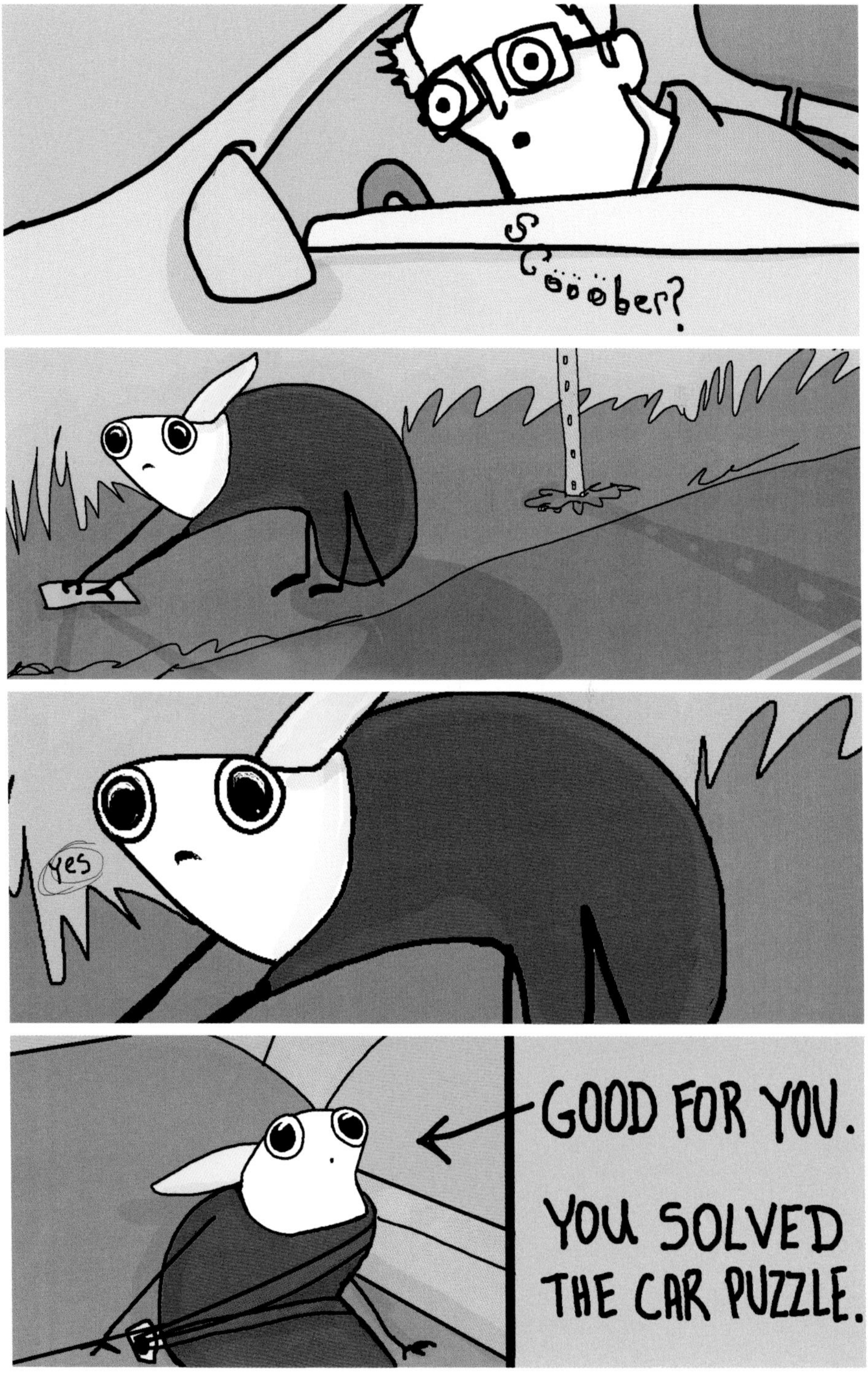
Gooober?
yes
GOOD FOR YOU.
YOU SOLVED THE CAR PUZZLE.

I felt bad for the stranger. He was a nice man. Sympathetically old and friendly. He did his best to make conversation with me. I did my best to cooperate, but the things I was saying to him ... they weren't in a format he could recognize.

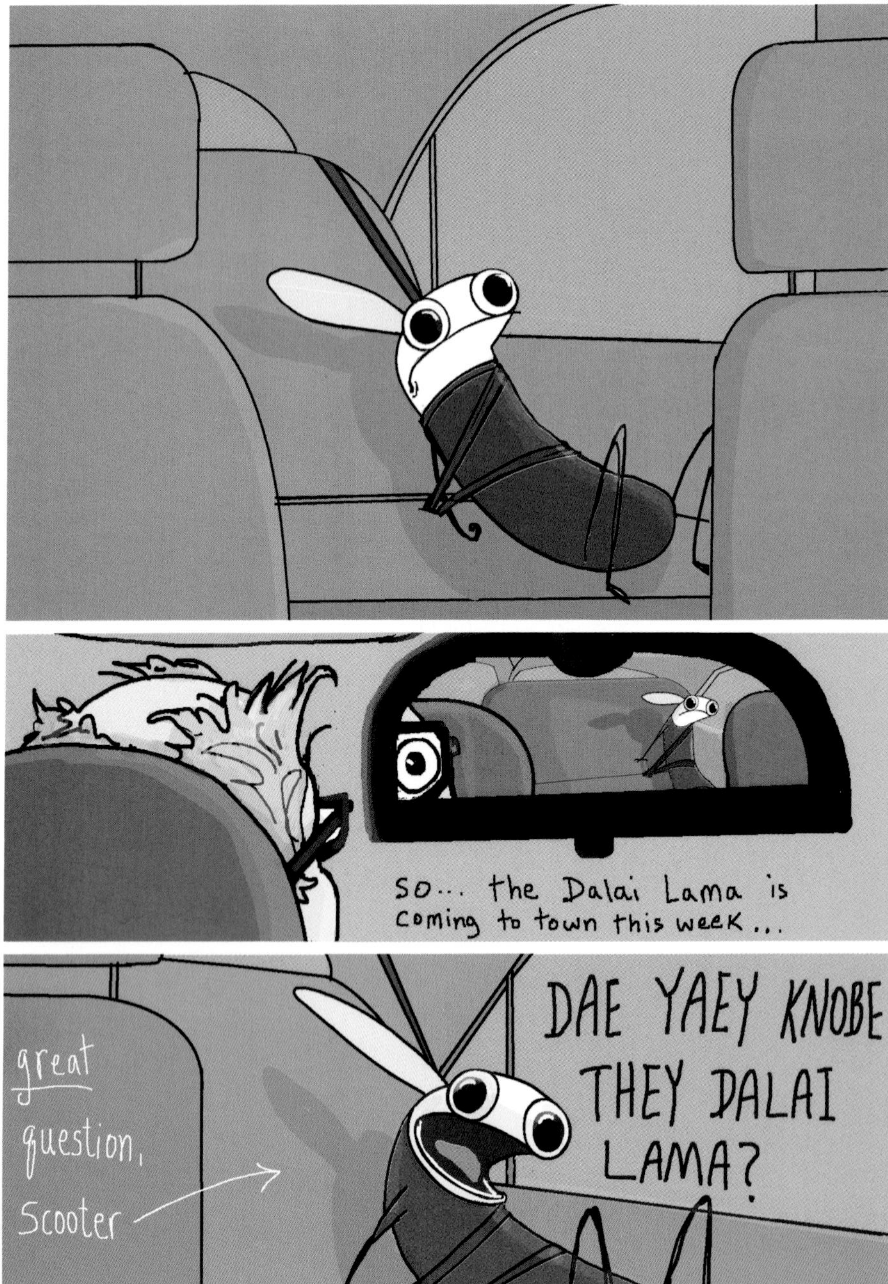

SO... the Dalai Lama is coming to town this week...
DAE YAEY KNOBE THEY DALAI LAMA?
great question, Scooter

He wanted so badly to drive me to my home, but he had trouble finding it. We had to work together, and I'm not sure how much I was helping.

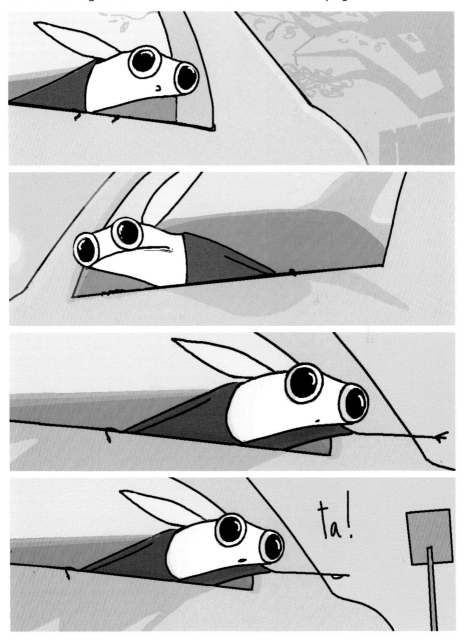

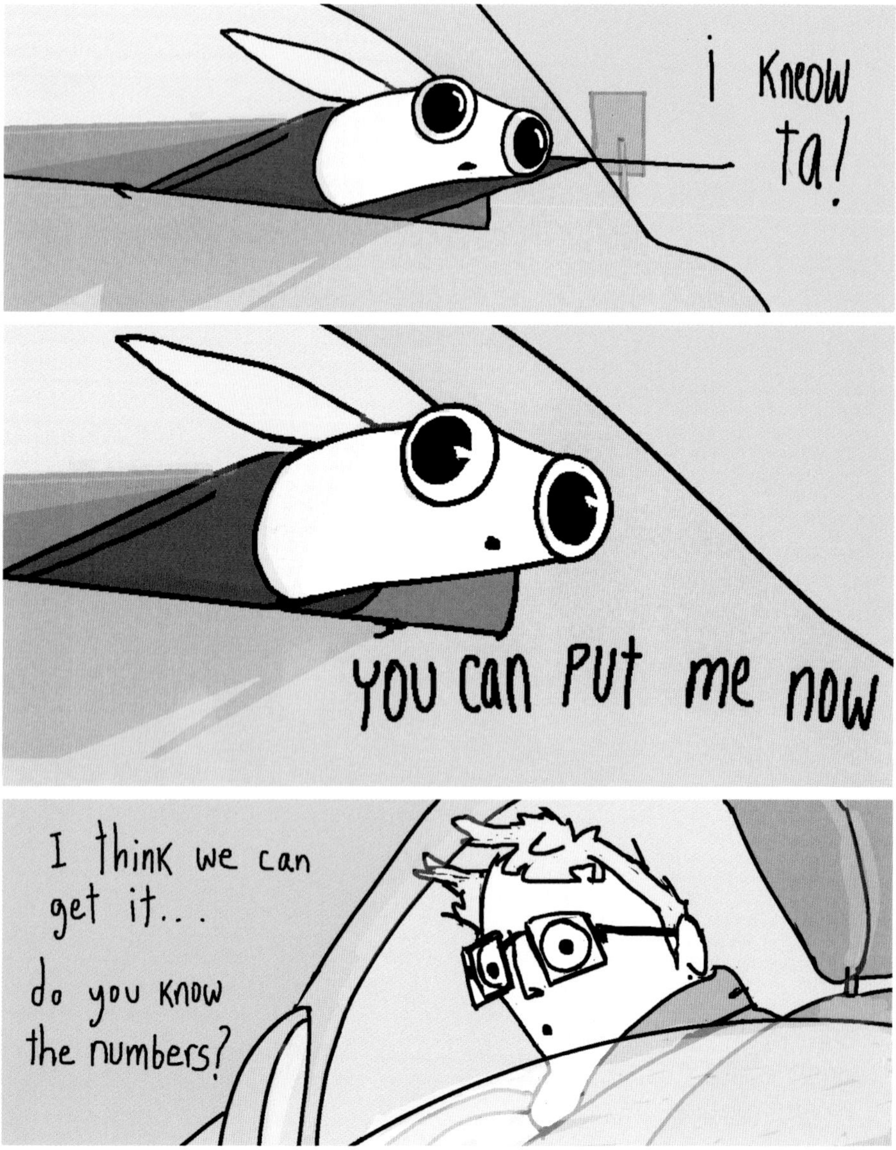
i Kneow ta!
you can put me now
I think we can get it...
do you know the numbers?

But we did eventually find it.
The story is not quite over, though ...

Remember what that means?
Here it comes.
It's four seconds away.

PART 8: LAST-MINUTE BONUS CHALLENGE

One Mississippi . . .

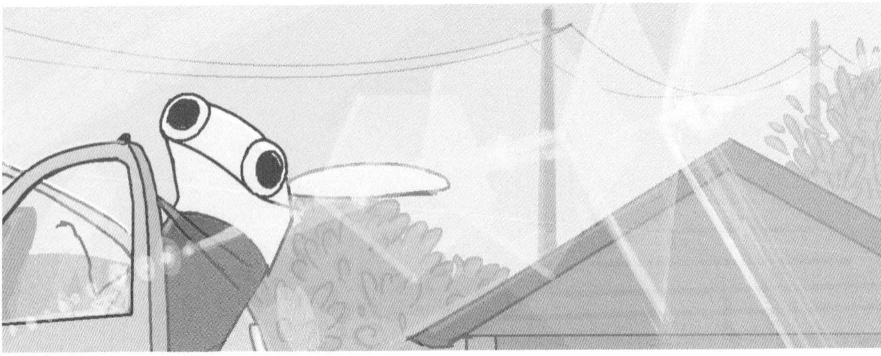

Two Mississippi . . .

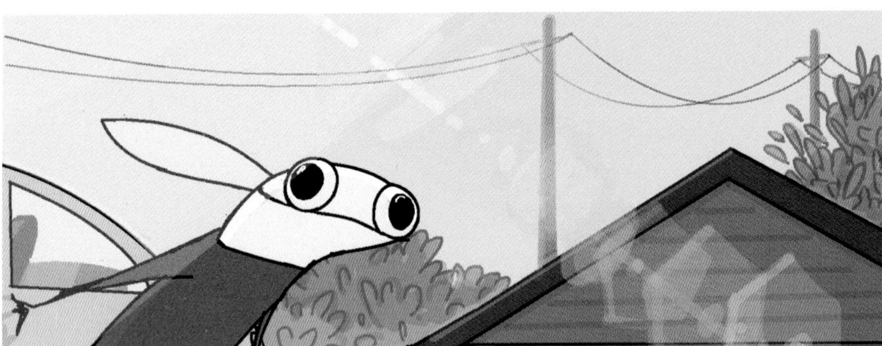

Three Mississippi . . .

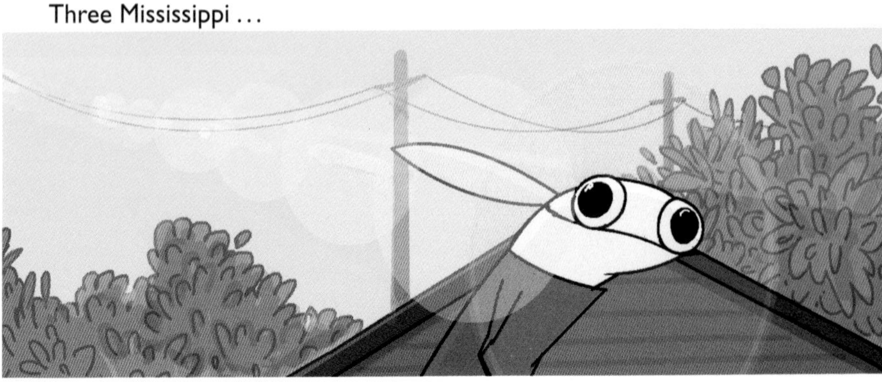

Four Mississippi . . .

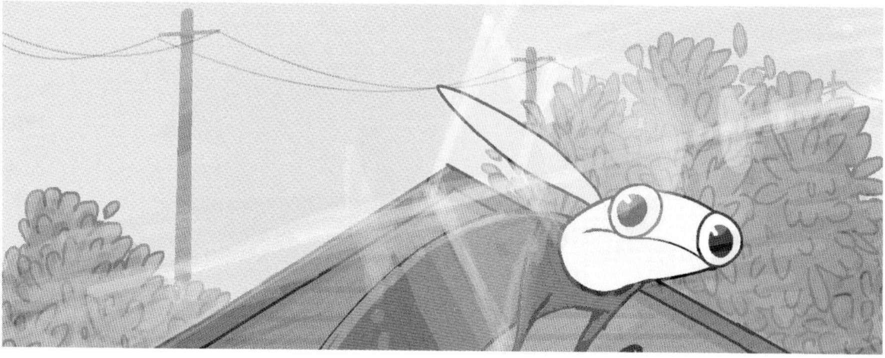

There she was: my neighbor's 5-year-old, lurking in front of my door like a friendship predator.

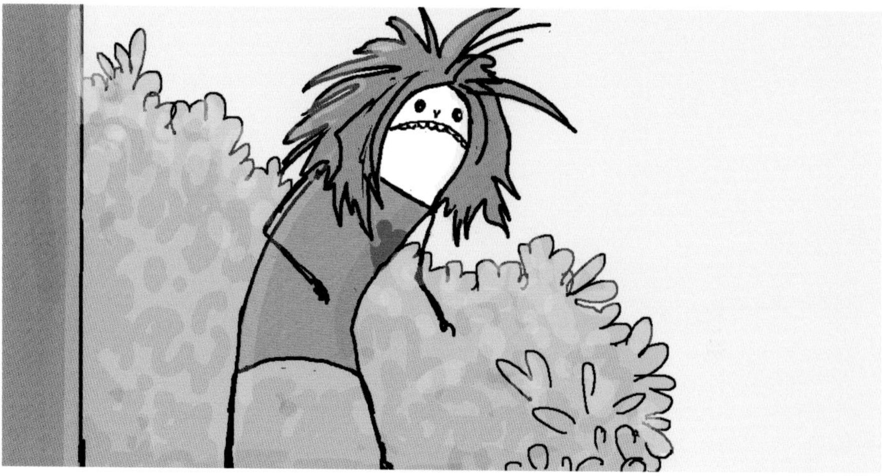

And she saw me get dropped off. She knew for a fact I didn't need to go anywhere.

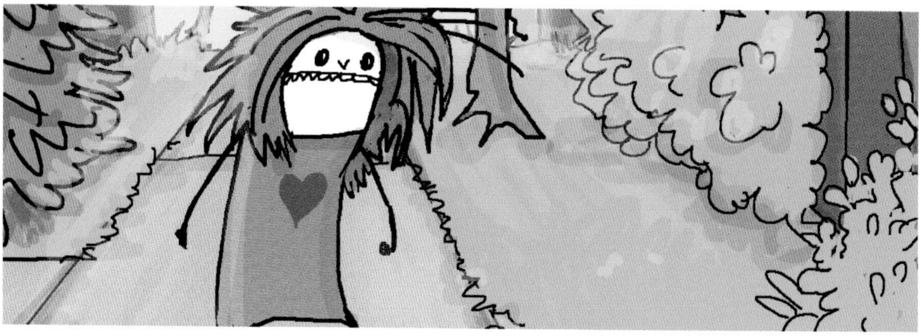

So, at six o'clock in the morning, before I could go in my home—still full-on tripping balls after the weirdest night of my life—I had to contend with this kid on Hard Mode.

And I thought, *You know what? Why not. What's the worst that could happen? Go. Go, kid. What do you want to talk about? I'm gonna sit down because who knows where this conversation is headed. That's me, living on the edge . . . Yeah, kid—whatever you want to talk about. Trains, puberty, speedballs—today's your lucky day. You hit the motherlode, kid. Go. Do it. Say anything you want.*

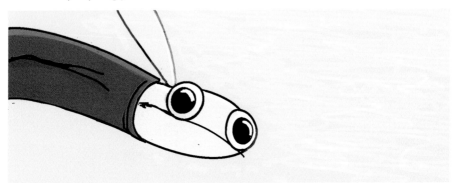

I don't think she expected it to work. She'd been trying and failing to seal a best-friends deal with who knows how many people for months, going so far as to physically restrain her targets, and I think she was a little surprised by how effective it was this time. She could sense the dynamic had shifted and she might need to be the brakes now. She didn't ask me about the room. We both just sat there, waiting for a topic to arise.

I can't remember if she asked me to explain bark or I just started going, but I explained bark to her. I gave this kid my whole bark thesis. And not just the bark thesis—all the potential implications of bark, and theses, and several other loosely related topics.

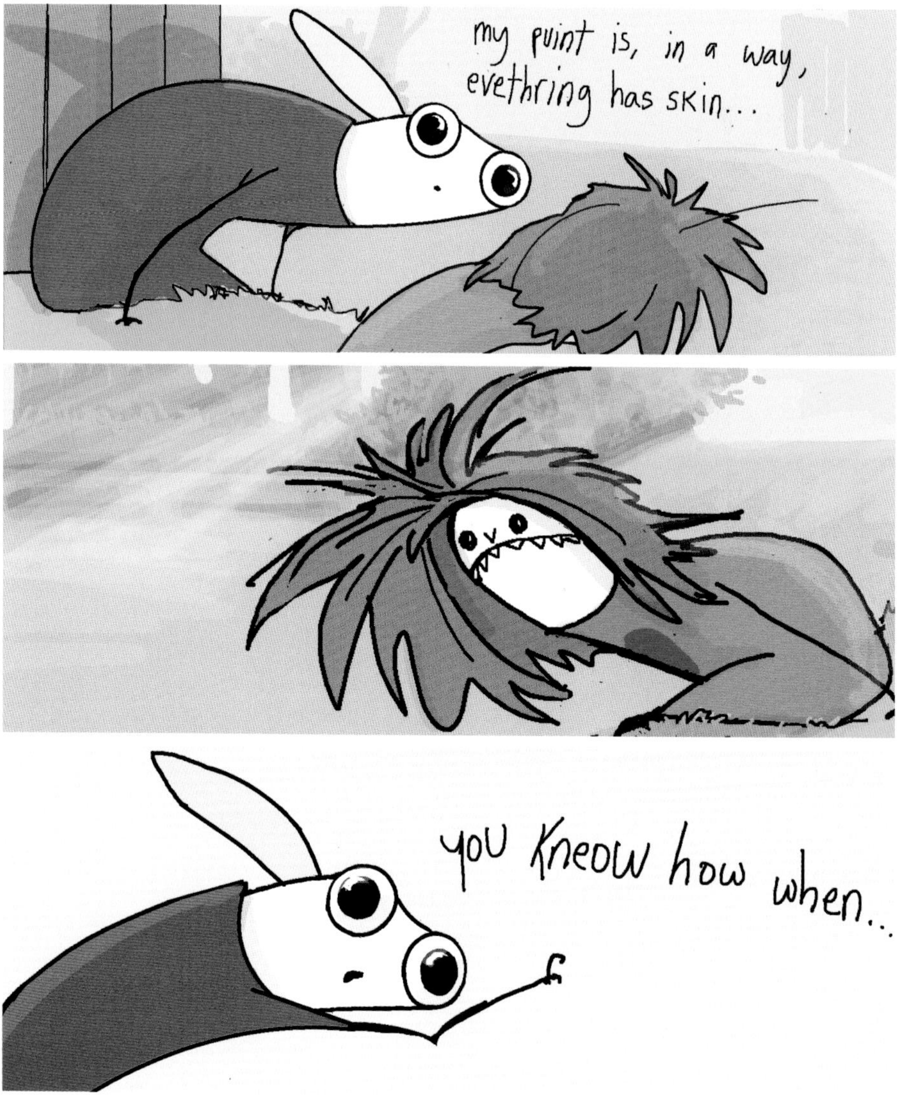
my puint is, in a way, evethring has skin...
you Kneow how when...

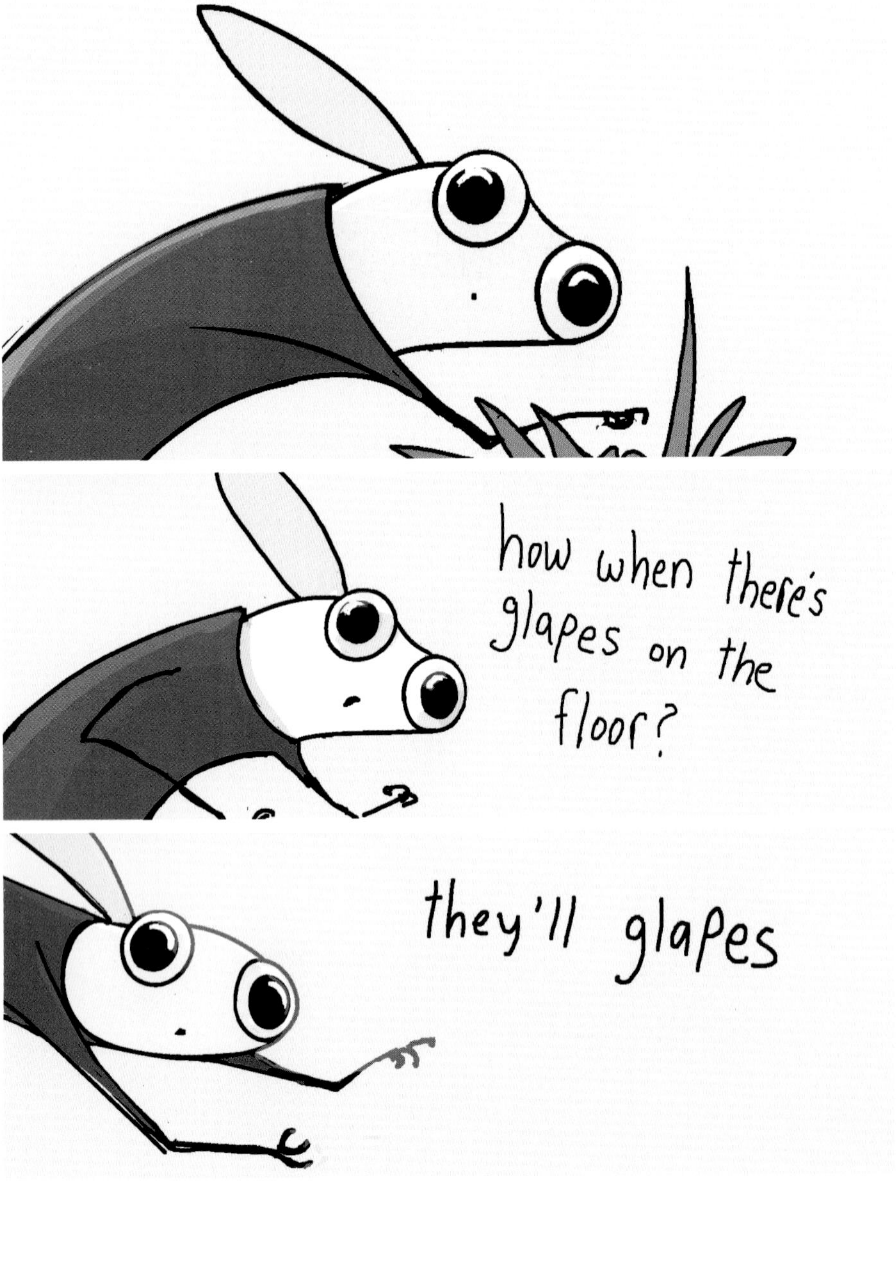
how when there's glapes on the floor?
they'll glapes

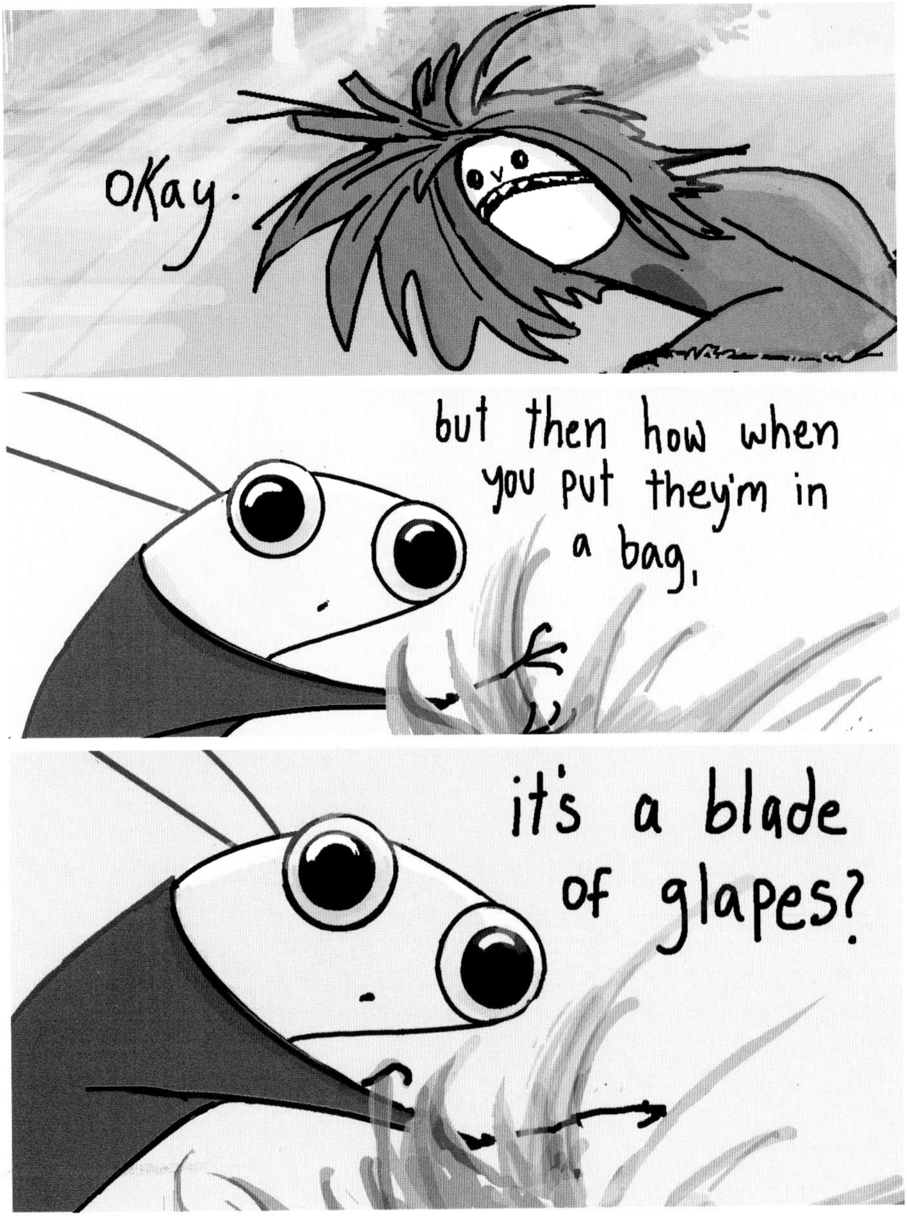
okay.
but then how when you put they'm in a bag,
it's a blade of glapes?

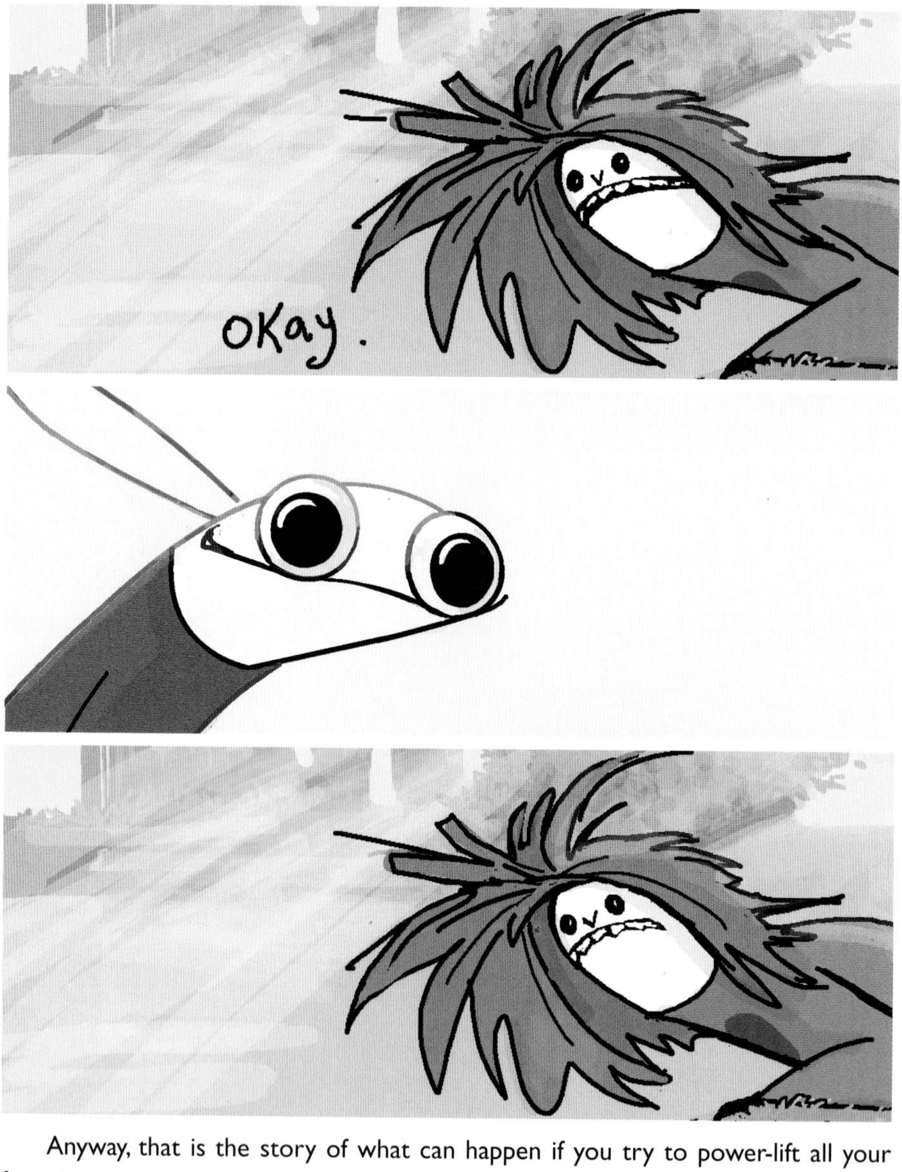
OKay.

Anyway, that is the story of what can happen if you try to power-lift all your fears in one rep.

The gains weren't as dramatic as I was hoping, but perhaps it was foolish of me to expect it to work in the first place.

The Main Conflicts in Life

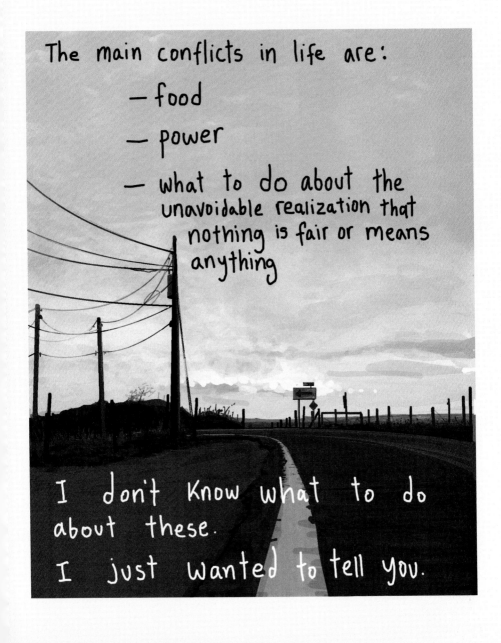

The main conflicts in life are:
- food
- power
- what to do about the unavoidable realization that nothing is fair or means anything

I don't know what to do about these.
I just wanted to tell you.

17. LOVING-KINDNESS
EXERCISE

I heard that meditation is supposed to teach you how to control yourself, so I found a guided meditation course online and meditated every single day for a week or two.

In addition to how to control ourselves, we learned things like how to relax, how to be happy, how to have a good day, and how to love everybody. When we got to the part that was supposed to teach us loving kindness, I was very excited. I have always dreamed of being one of the greats in this area, and I was eager to find out whether I'd exhibit signs of promise.

moments away from possibly discovering hidden potential for Messiah-like levels of loving kindness

The way these visualization exercises work is the meditation guy starts talking, and you do your best to keep up. He doesn't warn you ahead of time where he's going. He just goes: "Sit. Breathe. Good. Now think of a person."

Right away, I was like: GOT IT: *ME*. NEXT.

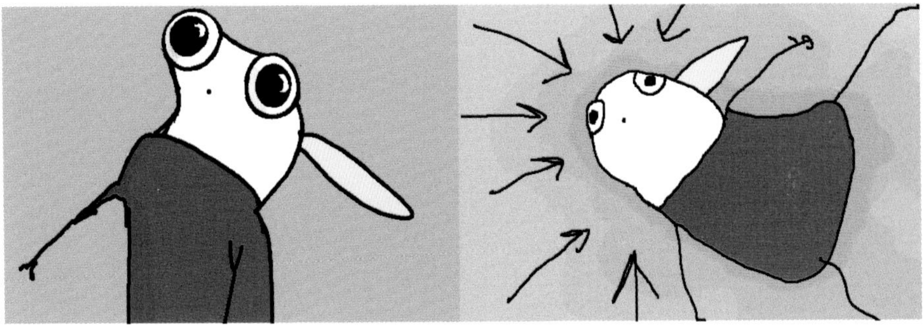

Because I didn't know the next part was going to be "The person should be someone you don't know very well."

Oh my, I thought. *Perhaps there is still time to catch up if I try crazy hard . . .*

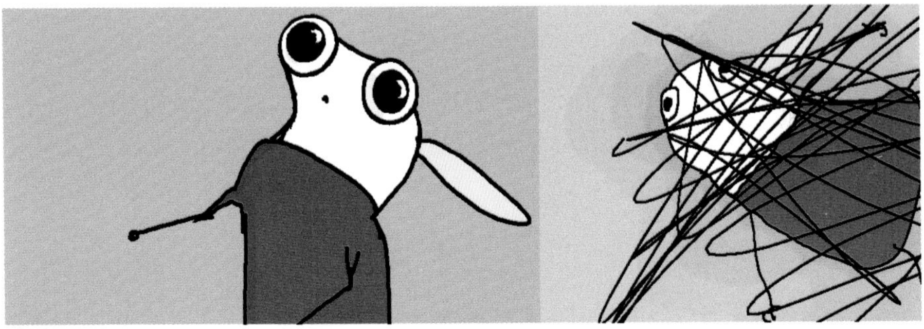

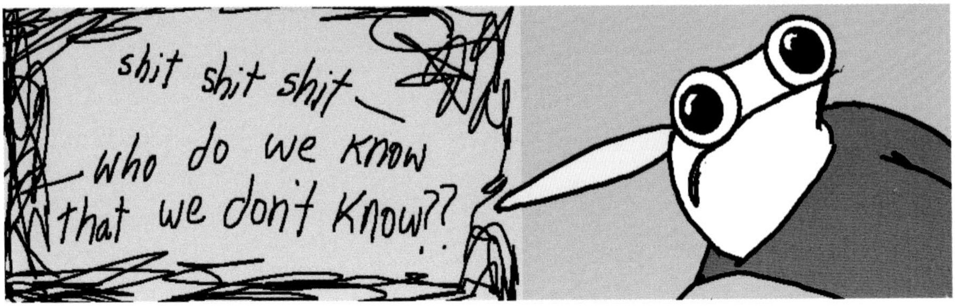
shit shit shit
who do we know
that we don't know??

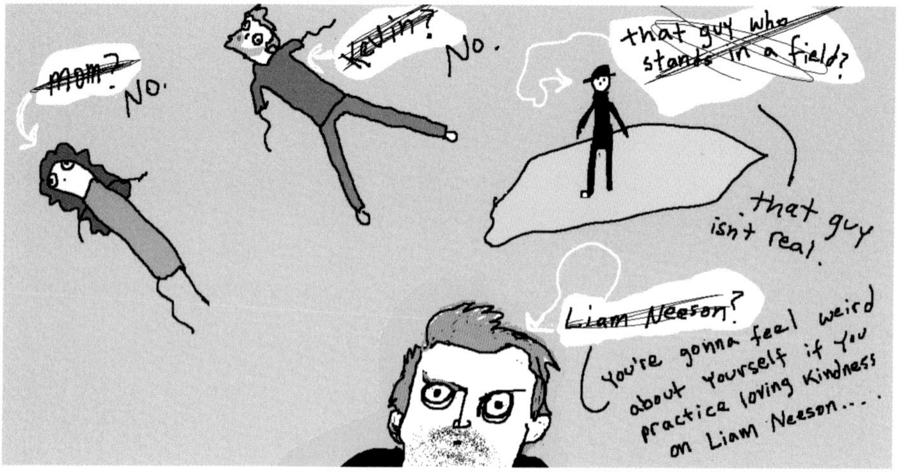
mom?
NO.
Kevin?
NO.
that guy who stands in a field?
that guy isn't real.
Liam Neeson?
you're gonna feel weird about yourself if you practice loving kindness on Liam Neeson....

I chose the self-checkout attendant from the grocery store.

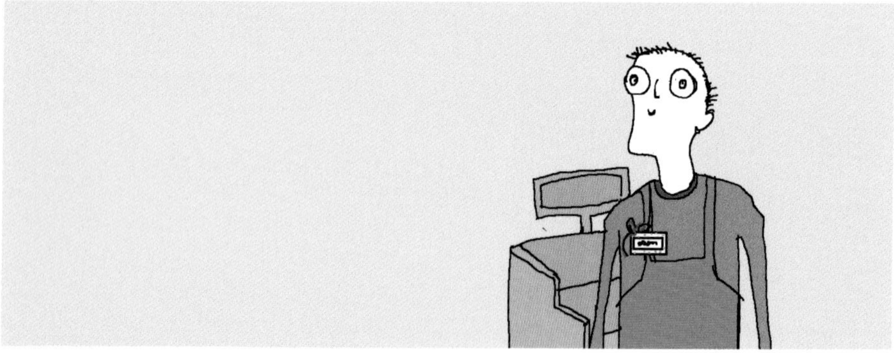

Because I didn't know the part after that was going to be "Now imagine the person doing what they love the most."

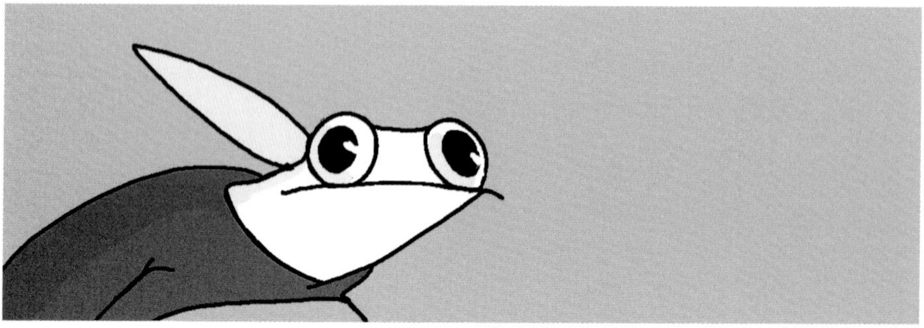

How am I supposed to know what the guy from the grocery store loves to do? Is this a trap? Is this meditation exercise trying to trick me into thinking something obvious like "groceries," and then the next part is a lecture about why you should never assume the grocery guy's favorite thing is groceries because that isn't loving or kind or respectful of the grocery guy's personhood?

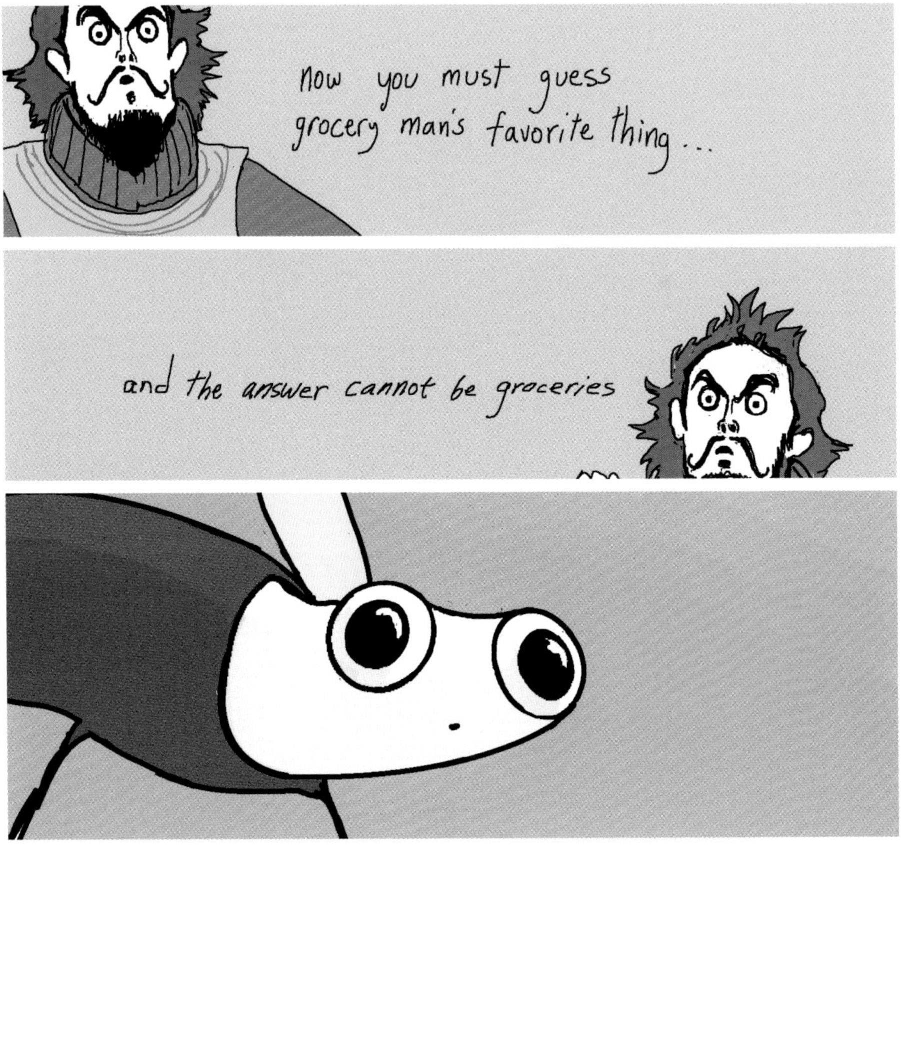
now you must guess grocery man's favorite thing...
and the answer cannot be groceries

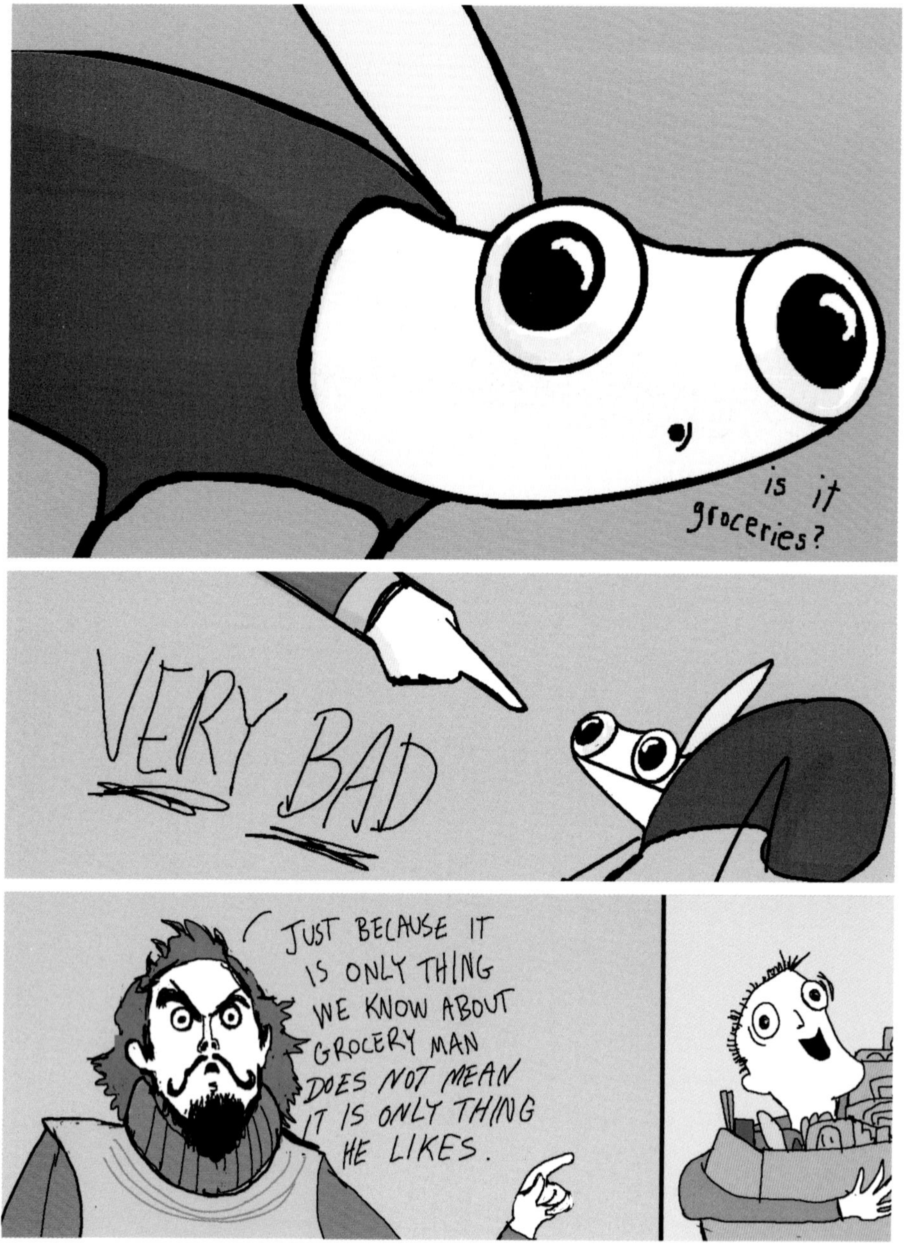
is it groceries?
VERY BAD
JUST BECAUSE IT IS ONLY THING WE KNOW ABOUT GROCERY MAN DOES NOT MEAN IT IS ONLY THING HE LIKES.

I knew nothing about the grocery guy aside from his association with groceries. On that basis alone, it should have been impossible to complete the visualization exercise.

But that didn't turn out to be a problem for me at all. Some forgotten instinct rose up to accept the challenge. And it said, *I know EXACTLY what this guy likes. First of all: knitting.*

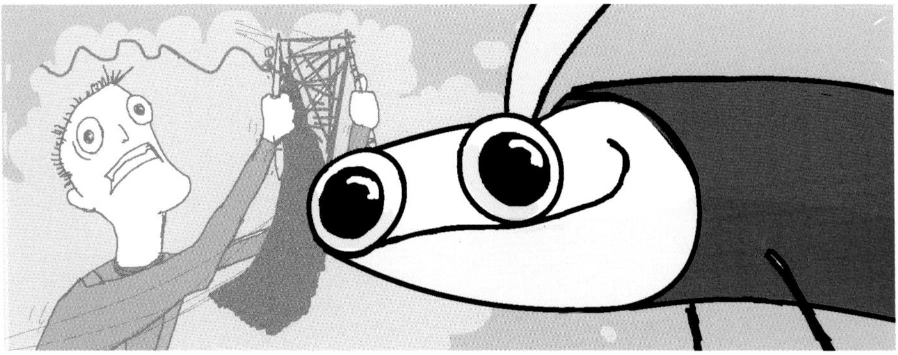

Groceries barely matter to him. Without a doubt, the thing he loves most is knitting.

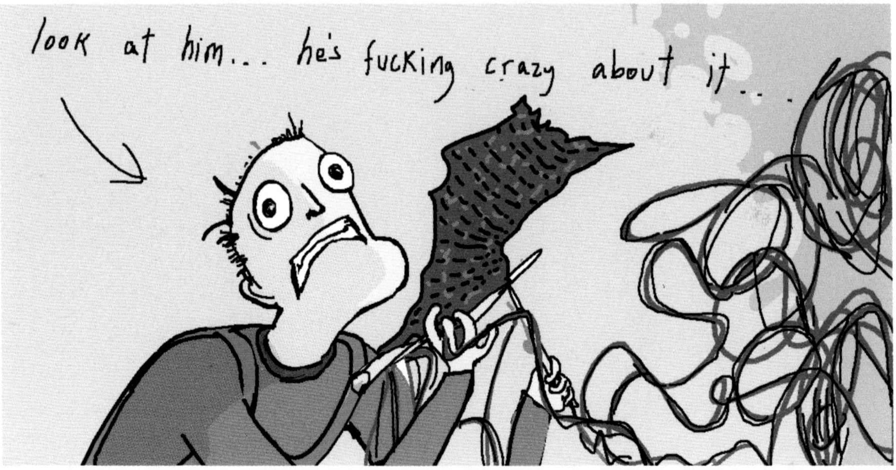
look at him... he's fucking crazy about it...

This might have been an understandable assumption to make if I'd seen the guy wearing four handmade sweaters at the same time, or actively knitting a pile of hats, or prancing around in a shirt that said *GODDAMN—I LOVE KNITTING!!!!* But, as far as I can tell, there was no real basis for it.

Later, while I was trying to process the fact that this happened, the only reasonable explanation I could find was that the first time I saw the guy, there might have been a piece of yarn on him somewhere. Like, glued to his name tag or something.

I saw the yarn, and my brain was like: YARN! I SEE YARN! AND I KNOW WHAT YARN MEANS: THIS GUY KNITS, *AND NOTHING ELSE.*

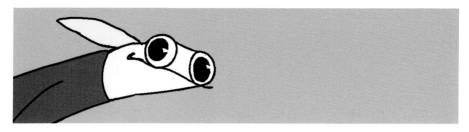

The meditation continued: "Imagine your chosen person in a place where he or she feels at ease and at home ..."

Okay, sure: it was a pretty aggressive assumption. A truly promising leadership candidate never would have been so hasty to assume such a specific thing for basically no reason. Can't undo it now, though. Let's just put it behind us and do the best we can to be fair to the guy from here. Like maybe for this part, imagine him sitting on a couch in his home. That is a reasonable thing to imagine. Anybody would feel comfortable sitting on a couch in their home ... No need to jump to conclusions ... Just keep it nice and general ...

Apparently, there wasn't enough contradictory evidence to put a dent in the initial knitting assumption. That much was obvious from looking at the image my mind created when I tried to imagine this man sitting on his couch in his home.

He's sitting on a couch.

It's a knitted couch.

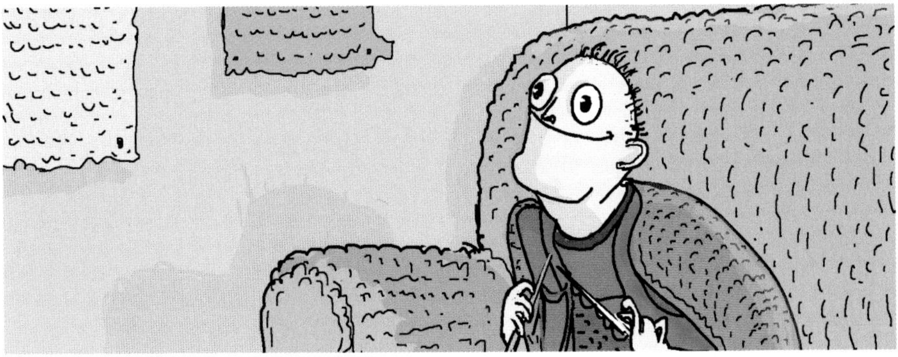

And this is for sure his home. You can tell because it is decorated exclusively with knitting. His chairs, his lamps, the floor—there are knitted squares just fucking tacked to the walls.

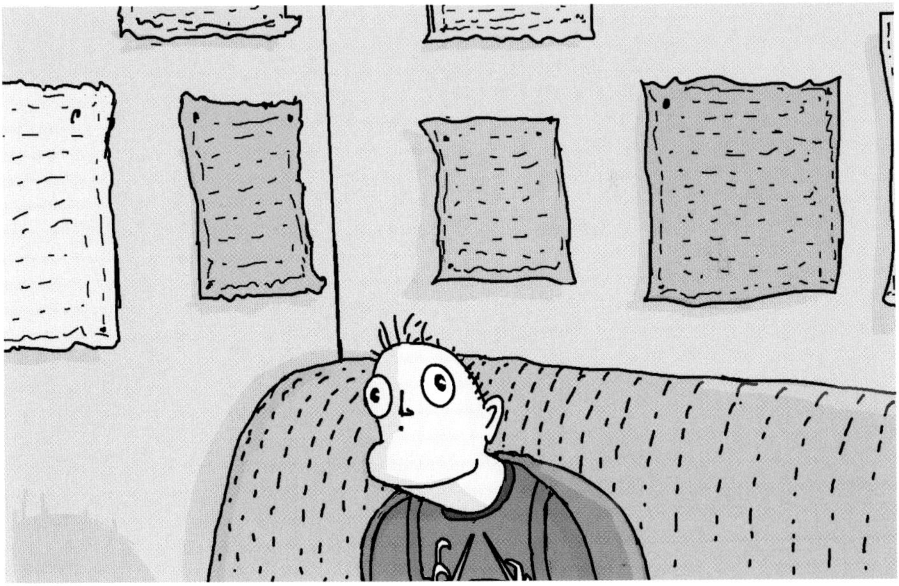

This isn't merely a guy who loves knitting . . . it's a whole alternative lifestyle.

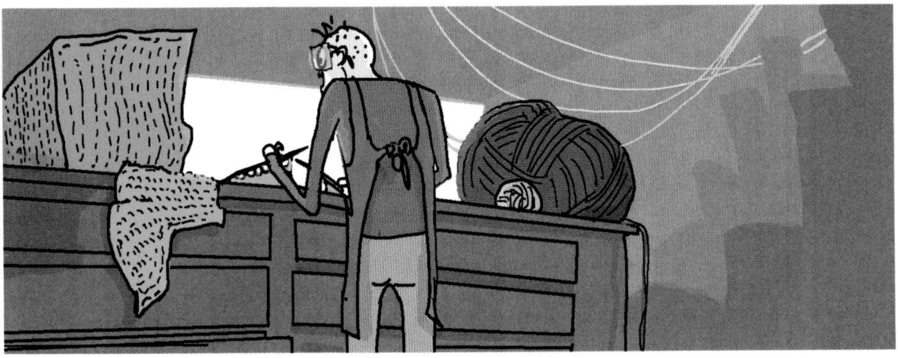

When you compare the strength of the evidence to the magnitude of the conclusion, there is an obvious and damning discrepancy.

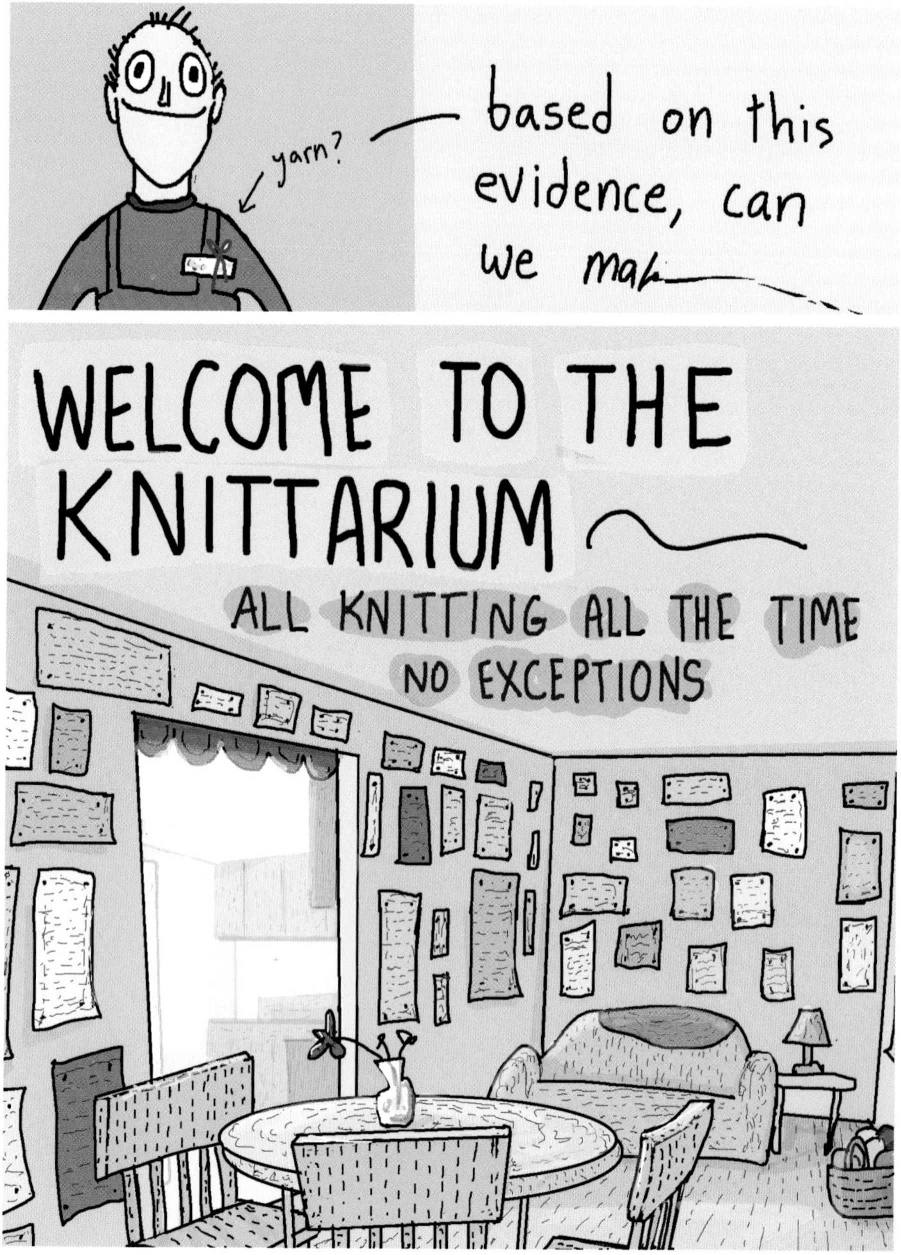
yarn?
based on this evidence, can we ma
WELCOME TO THE KNITTARIUM
ALL KNITTING ALL THE TIME
NO EXCEPTIONS

There's no way to excuse how much more believable I assumed this was than the scenario where the guy lives in a regular house and sits on a regular couch.

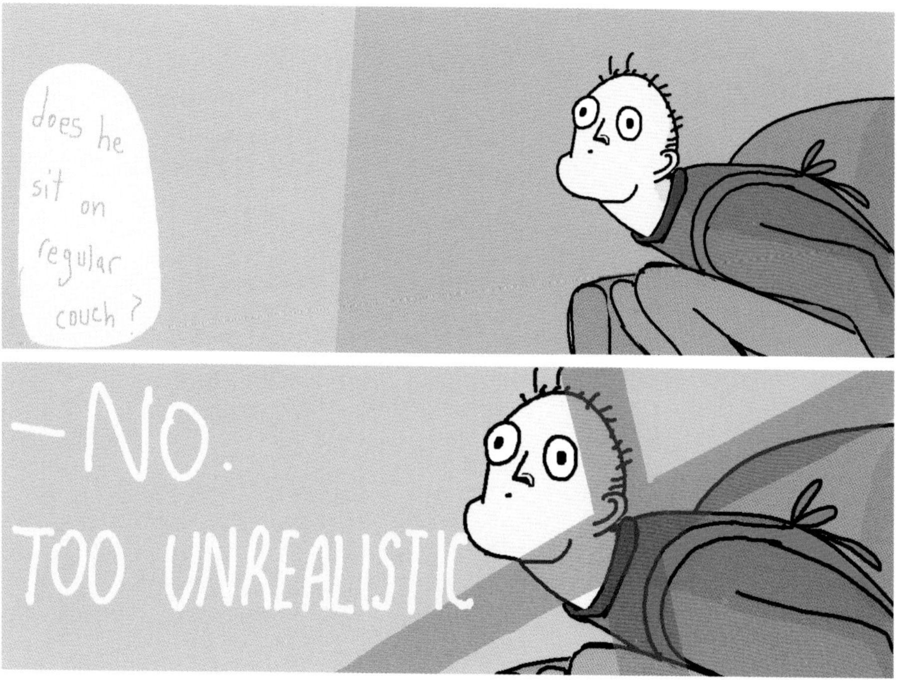
does he sit on regular couch?
—NO.
TOO UNREALISTIC

I don't want to be like that. It's dishonorable.

In a desperate attempt to change course, I turned to extreme countermeasures.

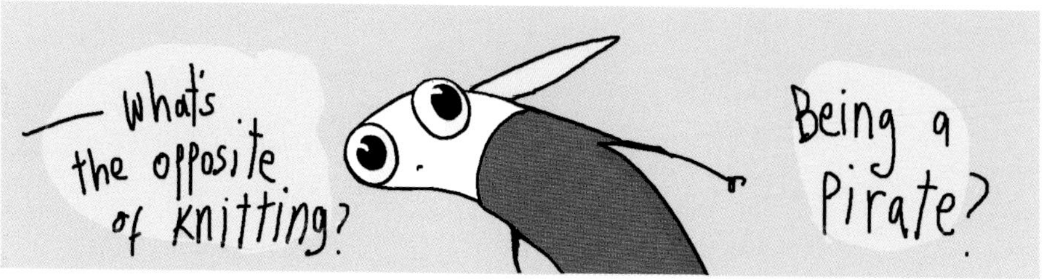
—what's the opposite of knitting?
Being a Pirate?

It got *way* worse when I tried to imagine him as a pirate. Because I didn't imagine him as a pirate—I imagined a pirate as him. And, apparently, that means the pirate acts like this:

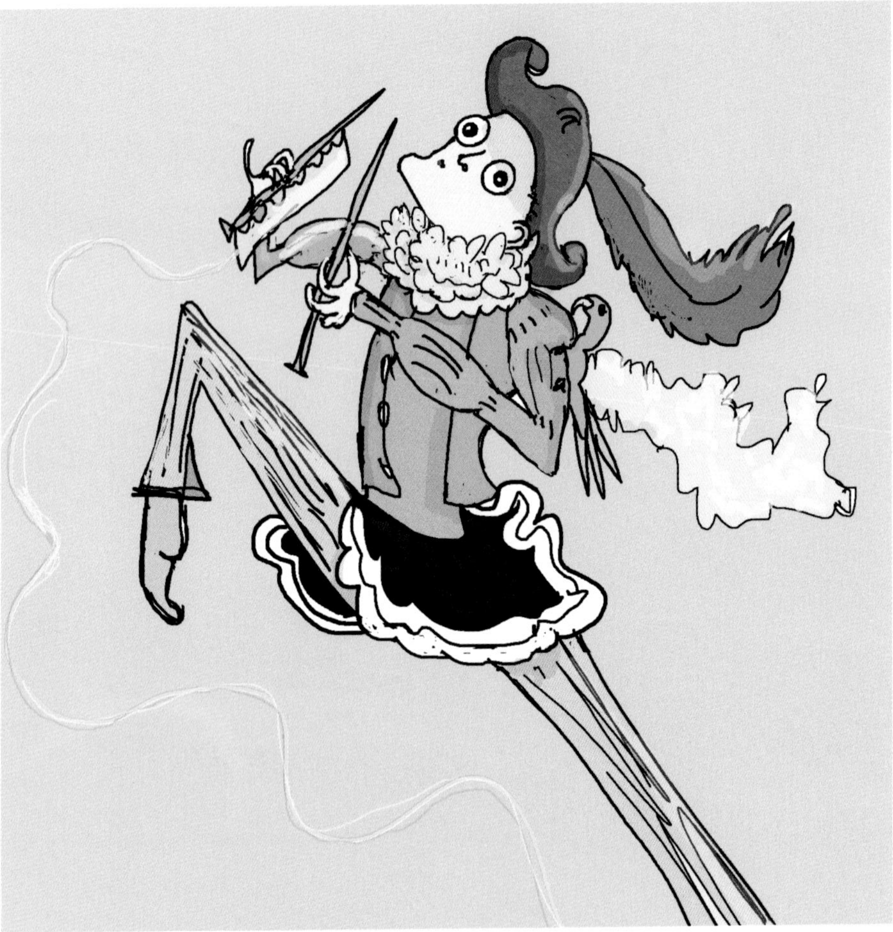

You may also notice that he has not stopped knitting. The other countermeasures I tried also failed.

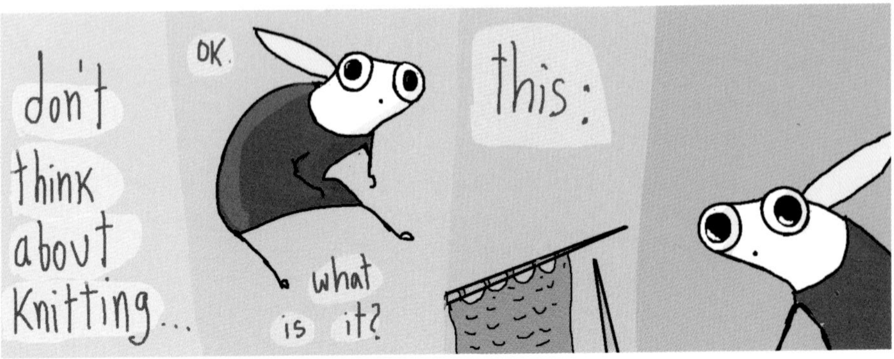
don't think about Knitting...
OK.
what is it?
this:

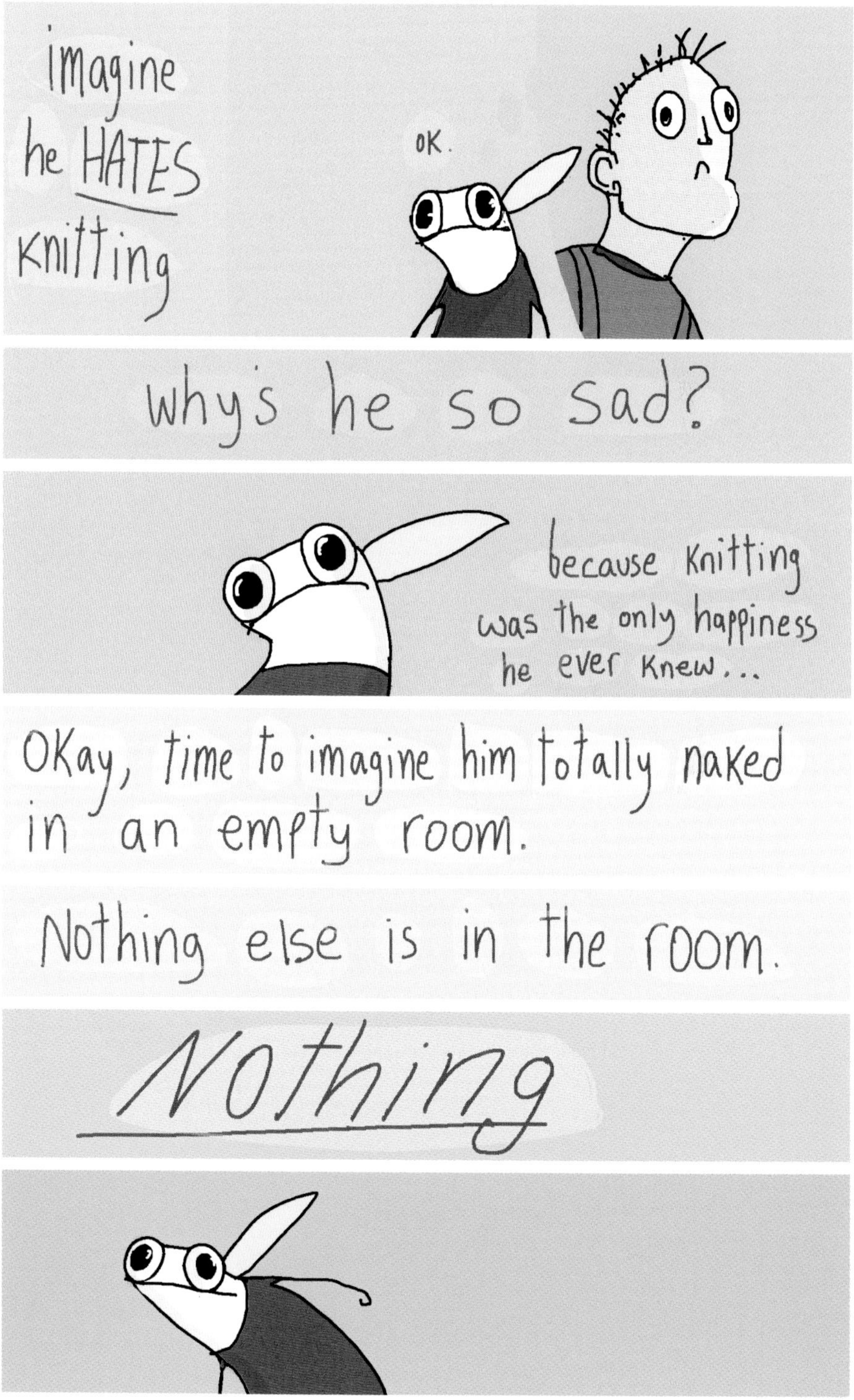
imagine he HATES knitting
OK.
why's he so sad?
because knitting was the only happiness he ever knew...
OKay, time to imagine him totally naked in an empty room.
Nothing else is in the room.
Nothing

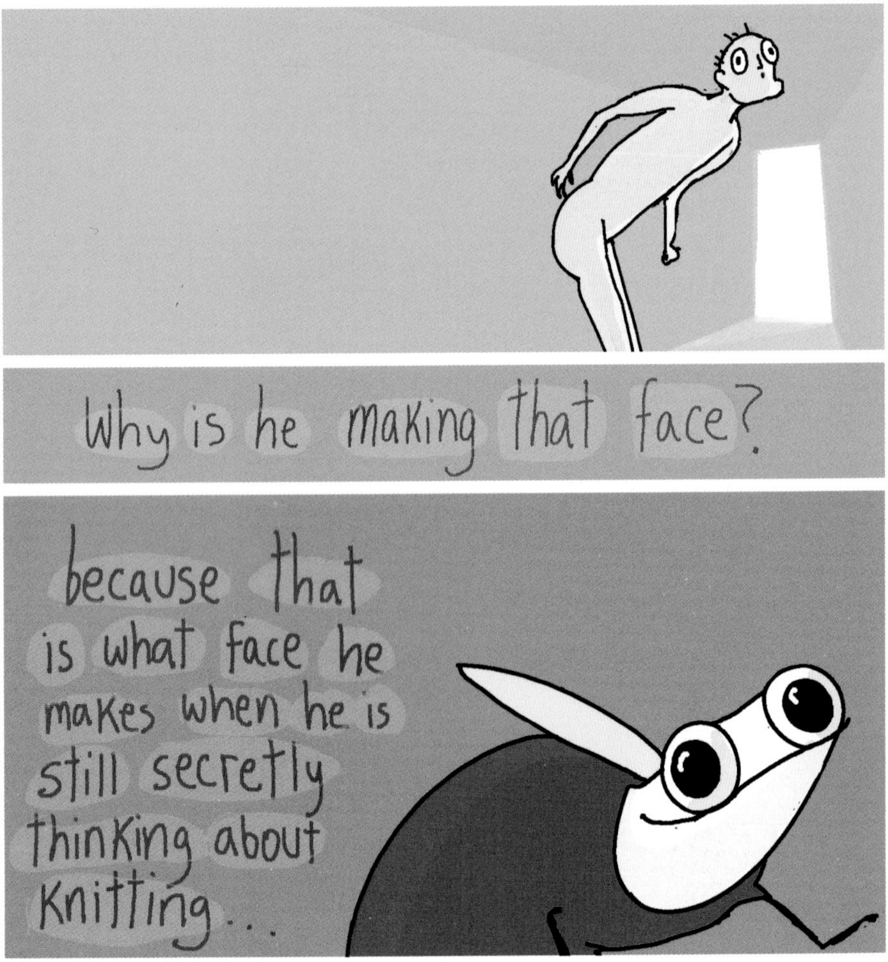

Why is he making that face?
because that is what face he makes when he is still secretly thinking about knitting...

Here is what the image looked like at the time the visualization exercise concluded:

I see the guy almost every time I go to the grocery store, and it's weird now.

He doesn't know this happened, but I'm terrified he's going to find out some-how. Like if I make eye contact with him, he'll see it.

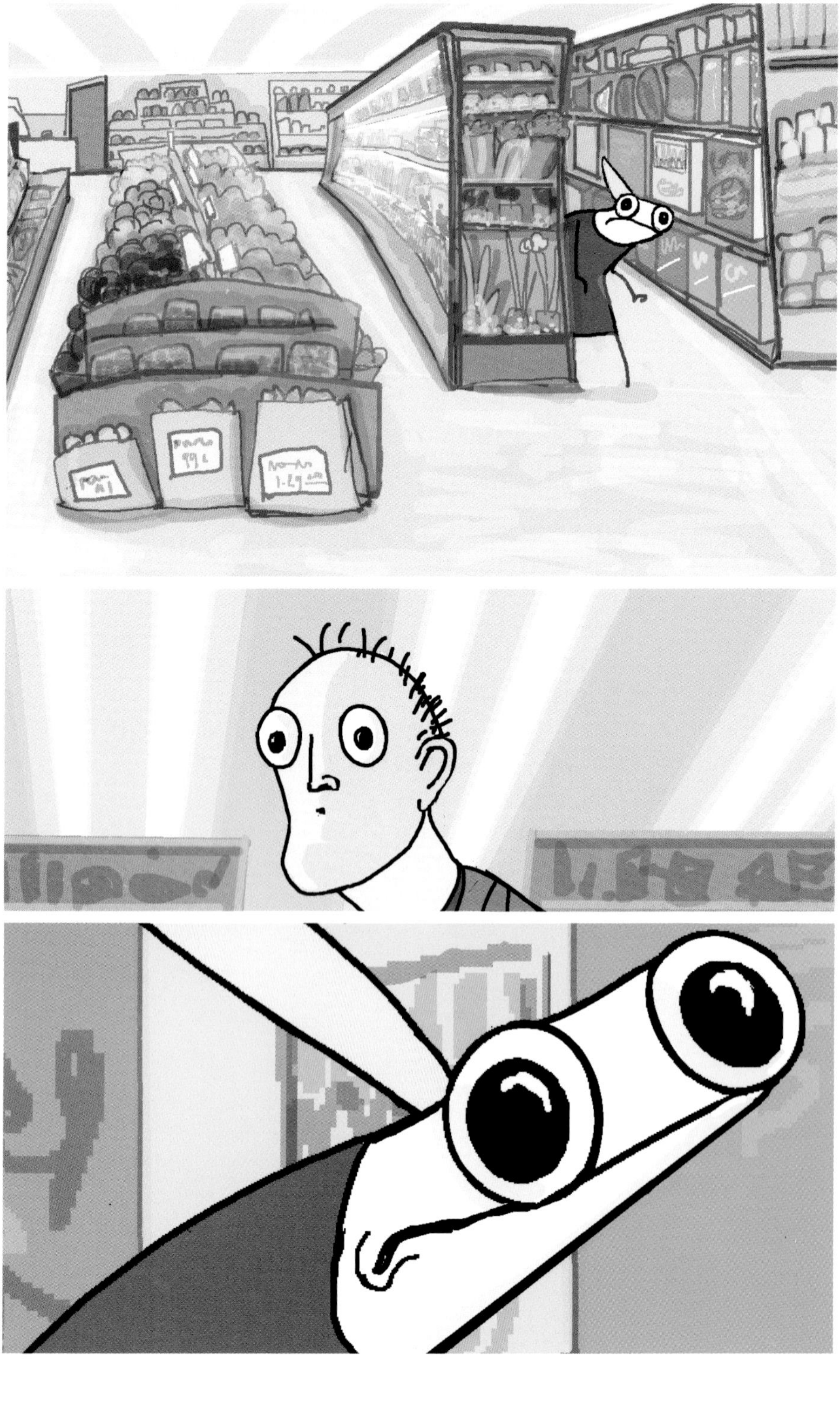

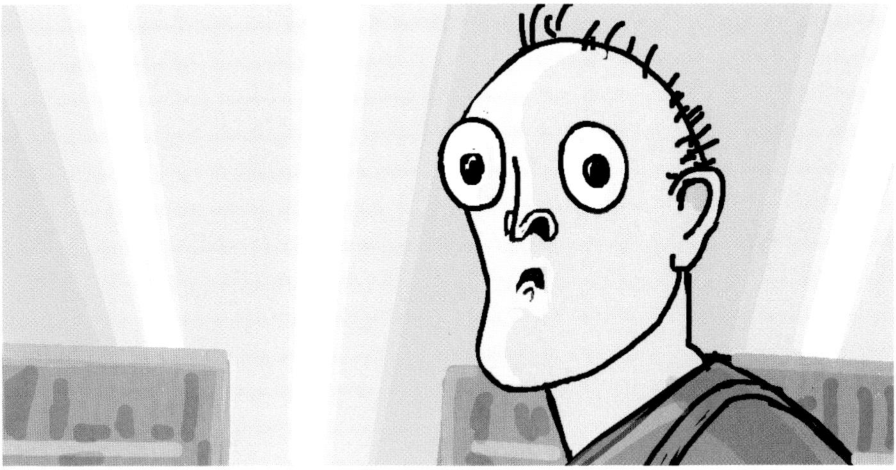

That's barely different from finding out that someone you don't know masturbates to the thought of you as a mermaid. Except the total lack of any detectable sexual motivation actually makes it quite a bit weirder.

If I find out that someone I don't know has been imagining that I'm a mermaid, "*it's a sexual fantasy*" would probably be best-case-scenario as far as explanations go. Otherwise they're imagining that I'm a mermaid for *non*sexual reasons . . . like because they actually think I'm a mermaid, or because they felt it was necessary.

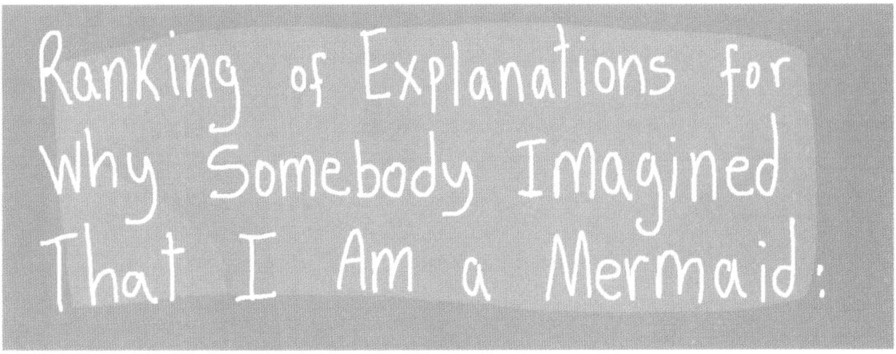
Ranking of Explanations for Why Somebody Imagined That I Am a Mermaid:

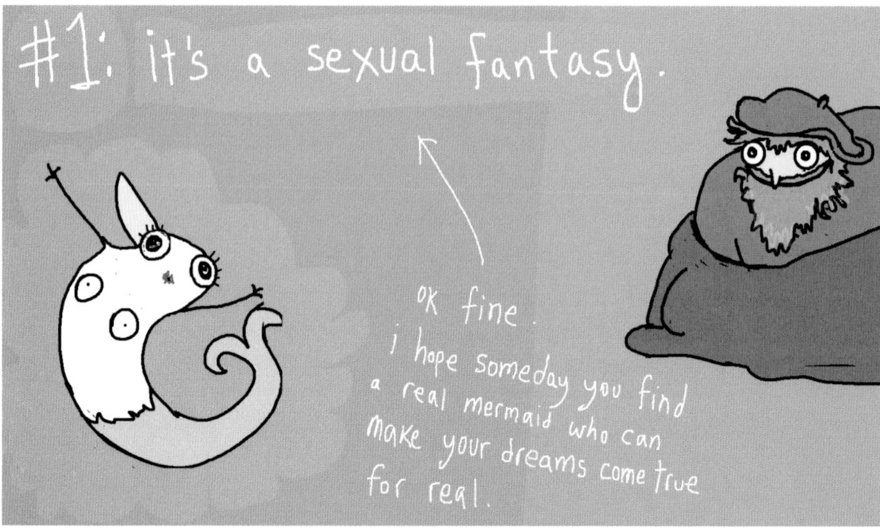
#1: it's a sexual fantasy.
ok fine.
i hope someday you find a real mermaid who can make your dreams come true for real.

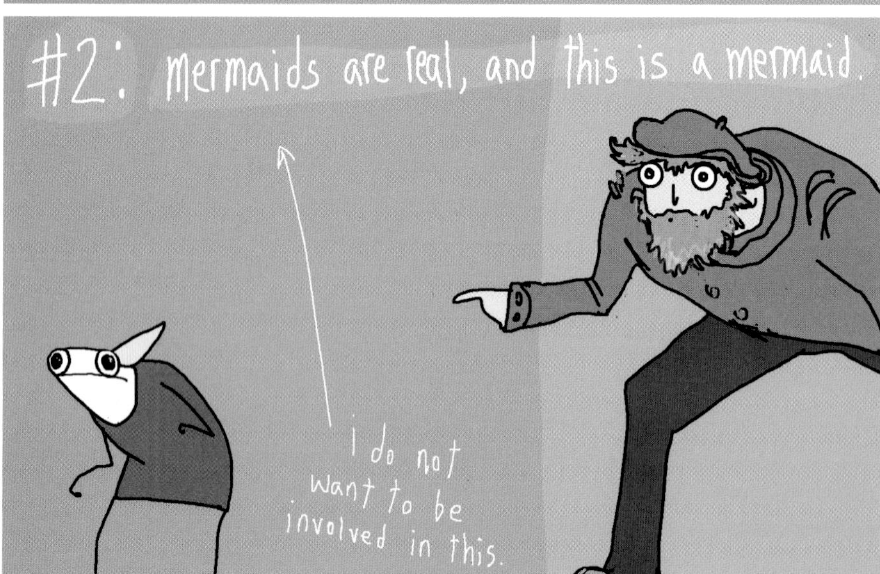
#2: mermaids are real, and this is a mermaid.
i do not want to be involved in this.

Last: it was necessary
Why?

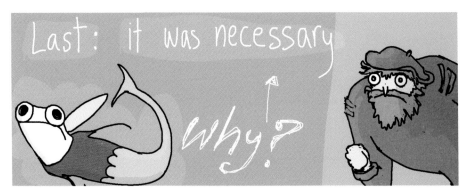

Why would it be necessary? How could it possibly be necessary to imagine me as a mermaid? Does this person want to harm me, and the mermaid thing is the only way they know to stop themselves? Is it to prevent me from seeming like a fish with legs??

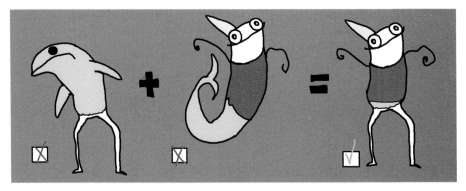

It would probably be similarly difficult to explain why I felt it was necessary to imagine him as a pirate.

Nobody would blame him for feeling offended. I mean, how are you supposed to feel if you discover that (A) you were selected as the subject of a total stranger's loving-kindness visualization exercise, (B) no matter how hard they tried—even going so far as to imagine you as a pirate—the person was unable to see you as anything other than the most extreme knitting enthusiast the world could ever contain, and (C) it went further than that. Far enough that they imagined you naked for totally nonsexual purposes. Far enough that by the end, they felt genuinely sorry for how far it went.

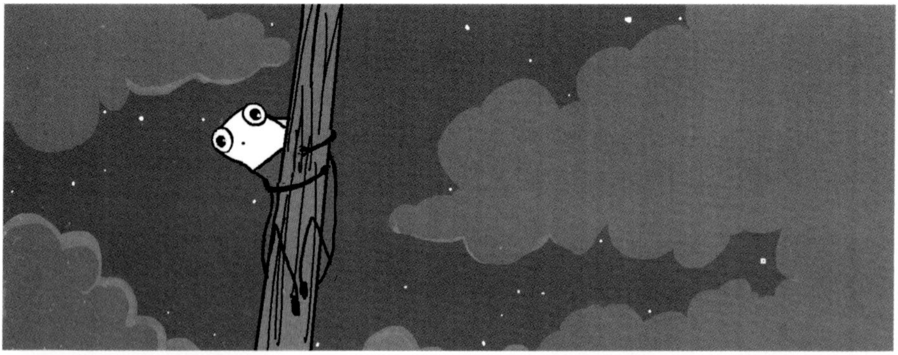

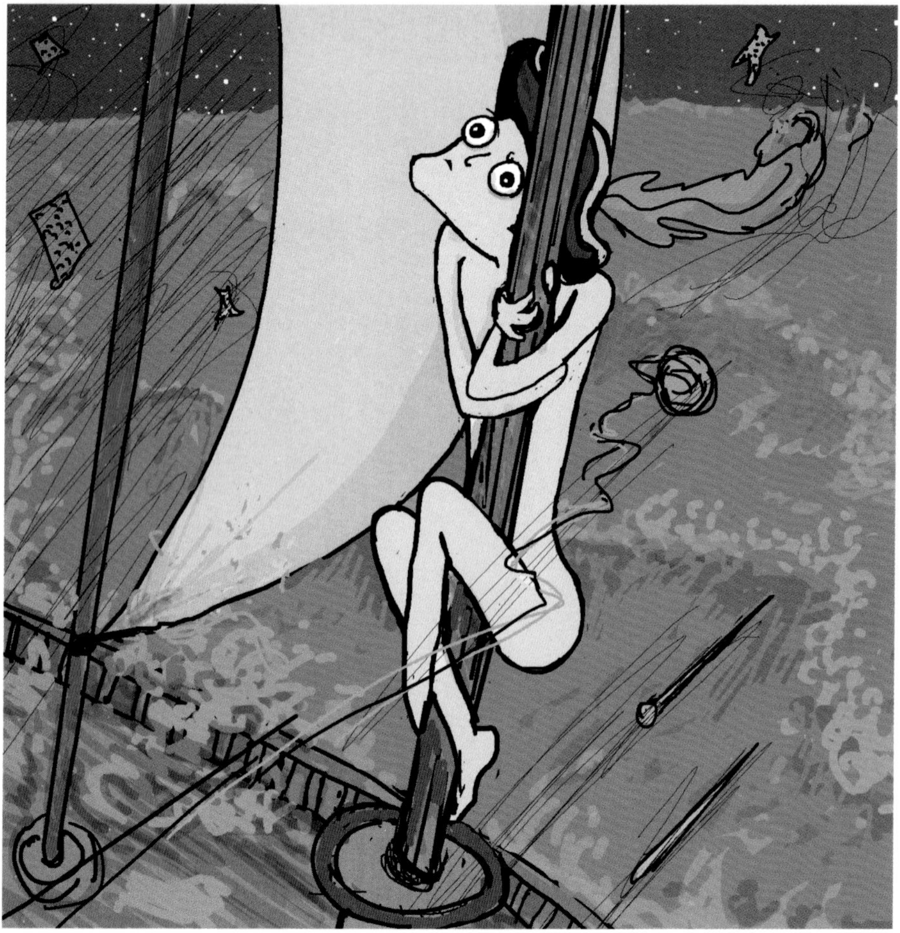

Even if he never finds out the real story, surely he'll notice how weird I act around him.

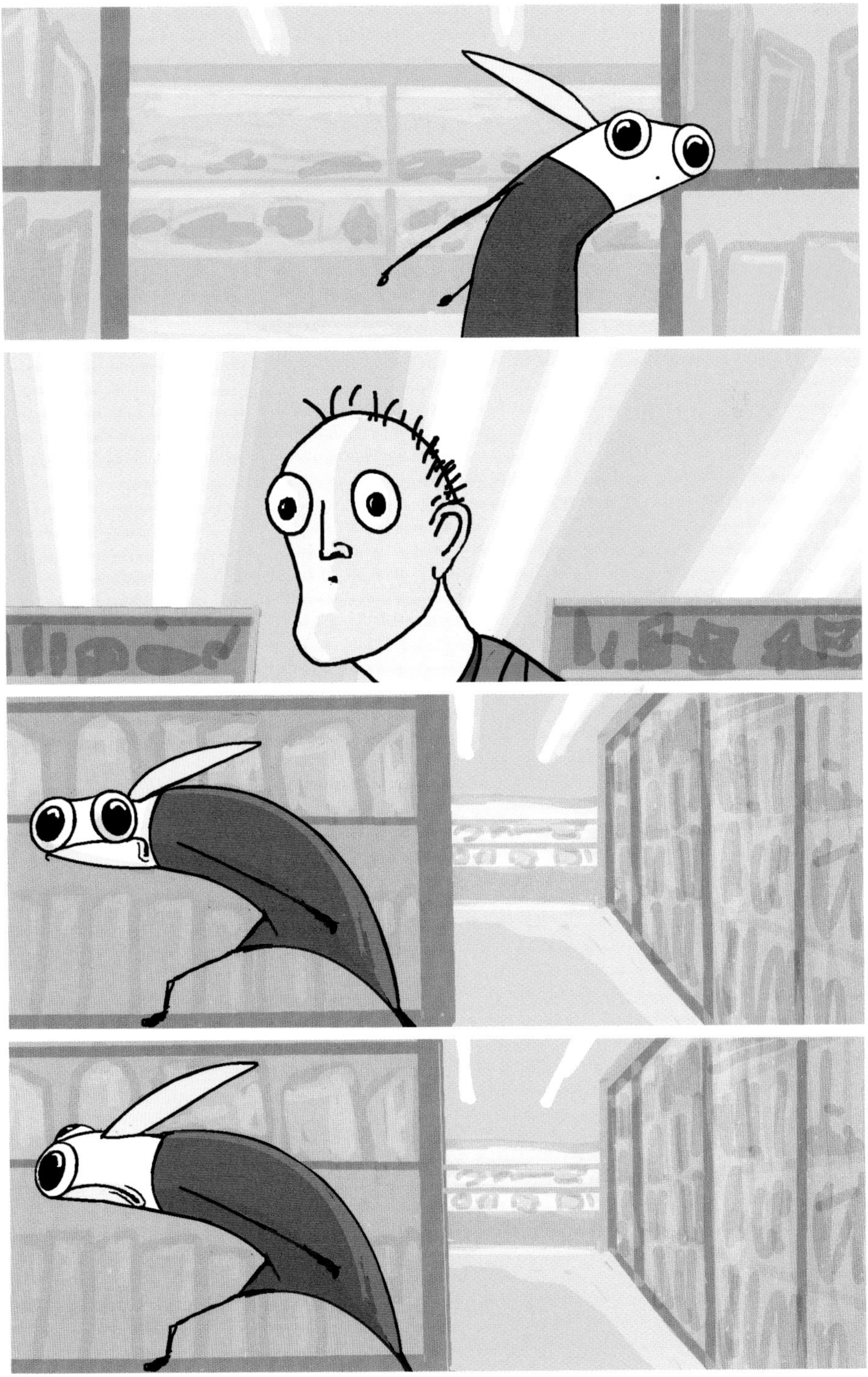

He doesn't know it's because I'm ashamed. He'll think there's something wrong with him.

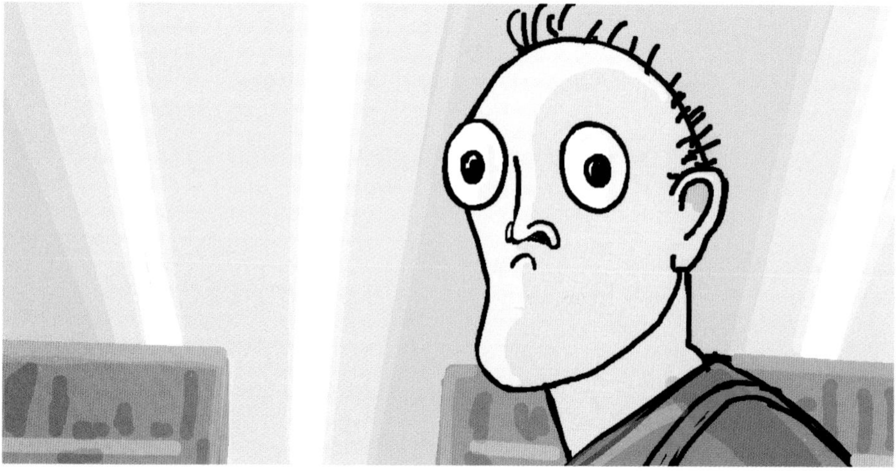

But at this point, what the *fuck* is the solution? This isn't the kind of thing you can google instructions for.

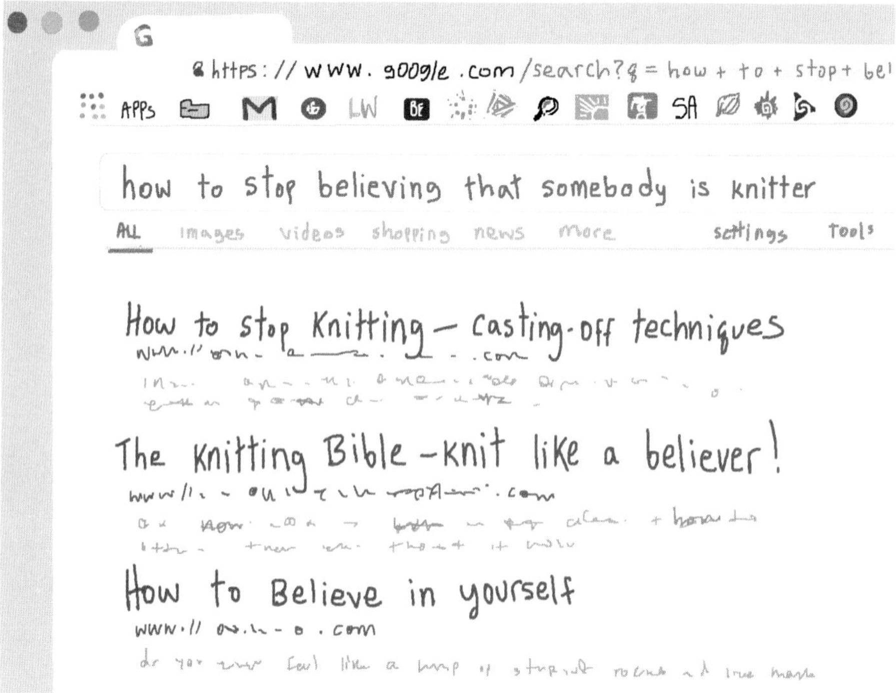
G
https://www.google.com/search?q=how+to+stop+bel
APPS
how to stop believing that somebody is knitter
All
images
videos
shopping
news
more
settings
Tools
How to stop Knitting—casting-off techniques
The Knitting Bible—knit like a believer!
How to Believe in yourself
www.//

If I want to fix this, I have to figure out how all by myself. And we must remind ourselves that my natural instincts are the exact reason we're in this situation to begin with.

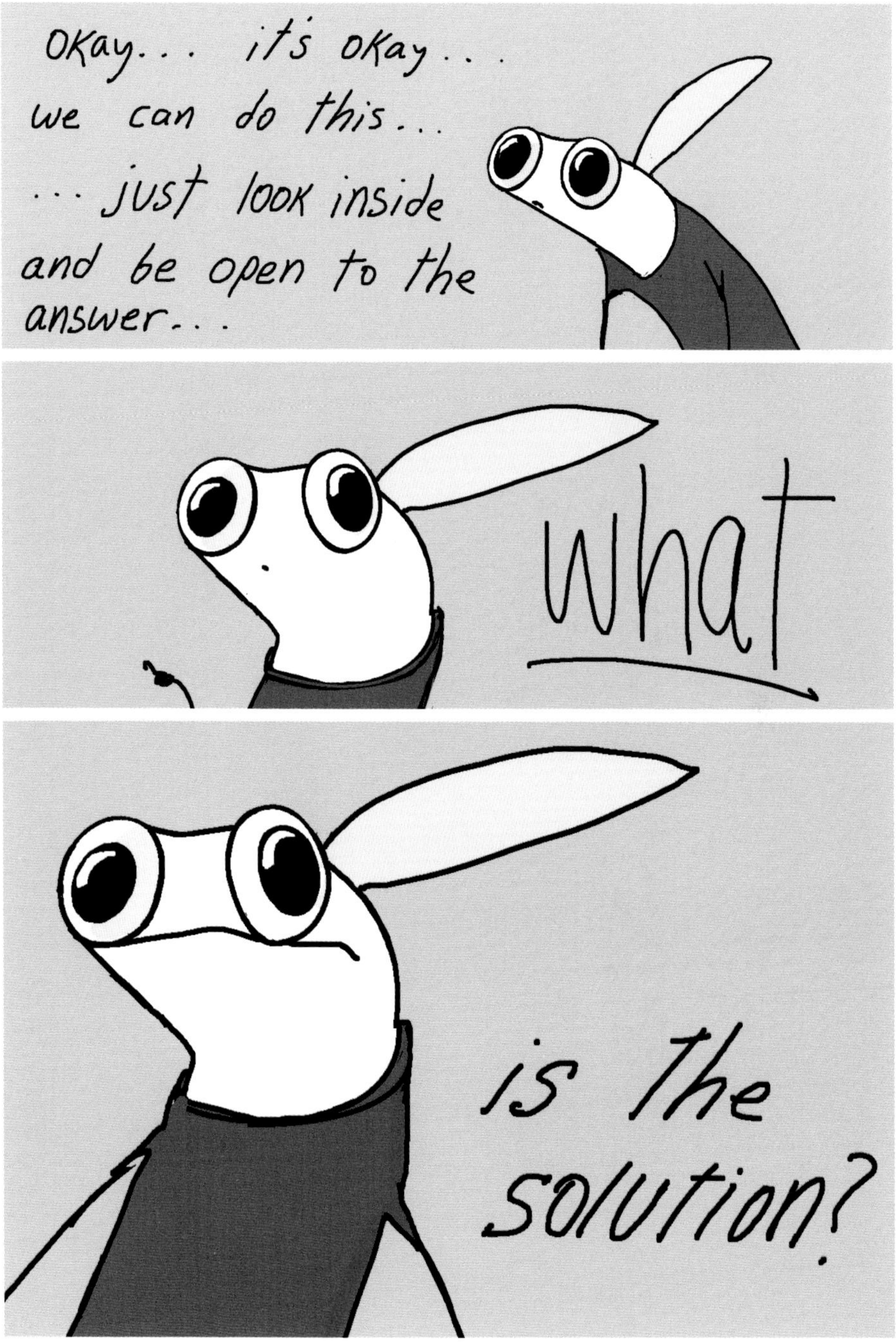
okay... it's okay...
we can do this...
...just look inside
and be open to the
answer...
what
is the
solution?

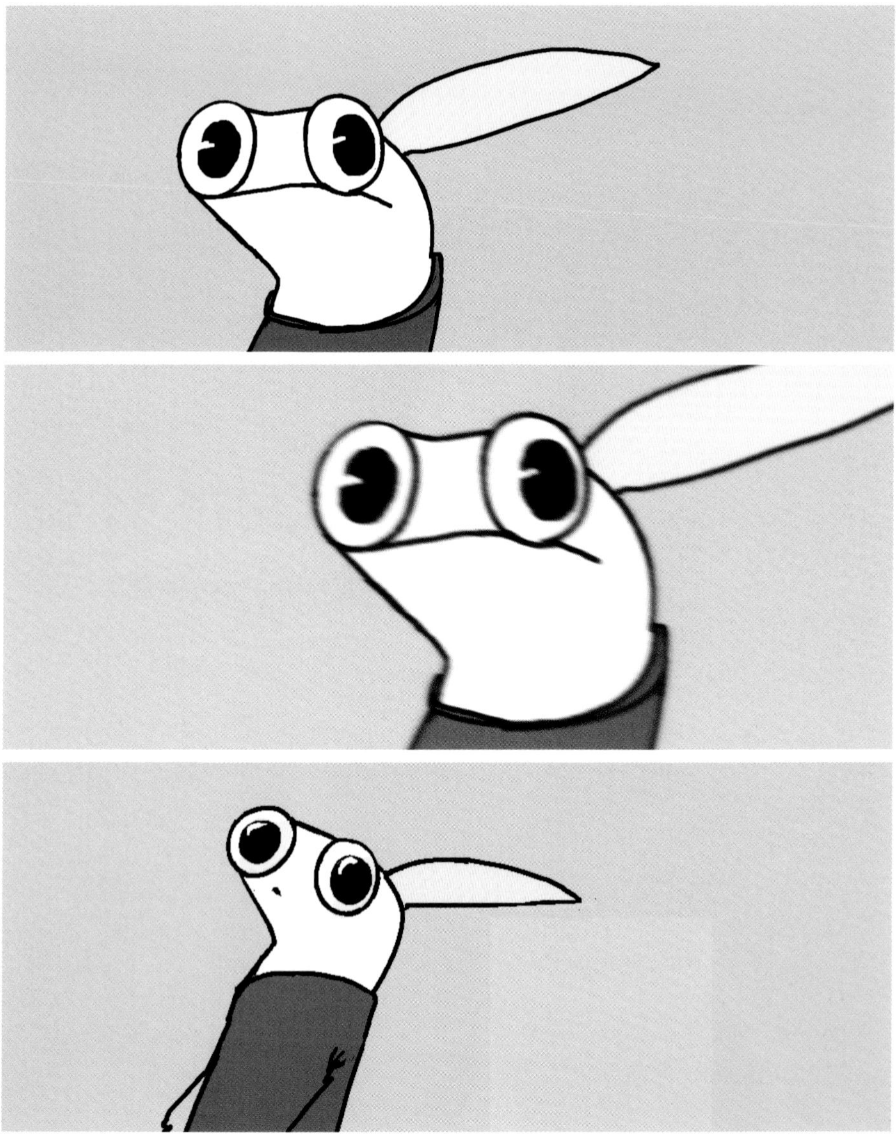

yes
we shall observe him and learn of who he REALLY is.

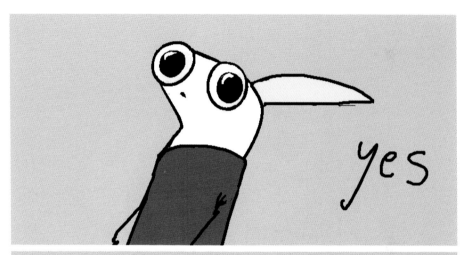

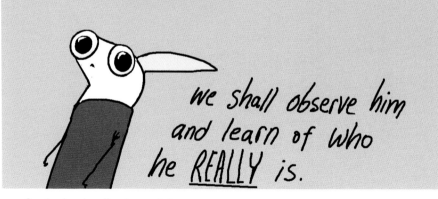

So that's what I've been doing.
For three years now.

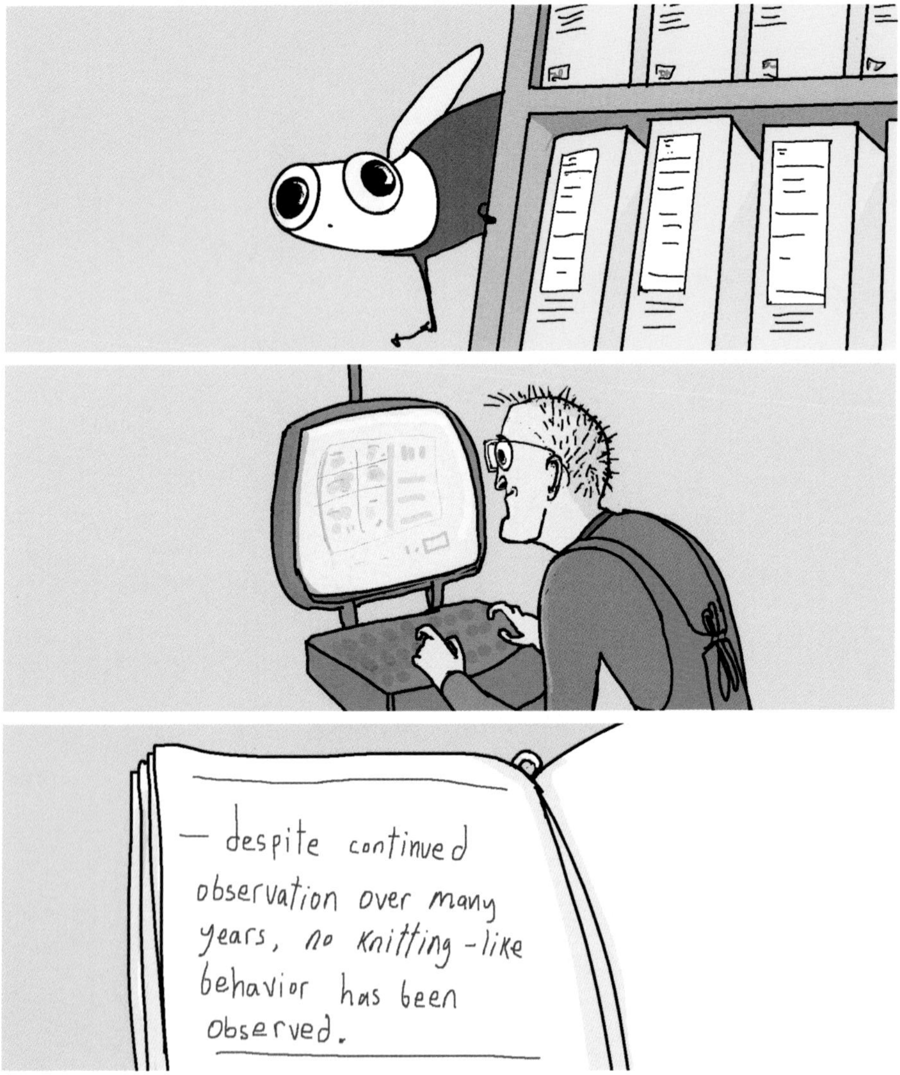
— despite continued observation over many years, no knitting-like behavior has been observed.

Knitting guy still doesn't know about any of this. If he ever finds out, I only hope he finds some way to see past the overwhelming and deeply personal sense of discomfort to the good intentions that created it. I never wanted him to feel weird. I never wanted me to feel weird either. This might be hard to believe, but the reason this happened is because I was trying to be a good person. I do not know what I am doing at all, but I'm trying *REALLY* hard. And trying really hard when you don't know what you're doing just happens to be the exact recipe for acting like a fuckin' weirdo.

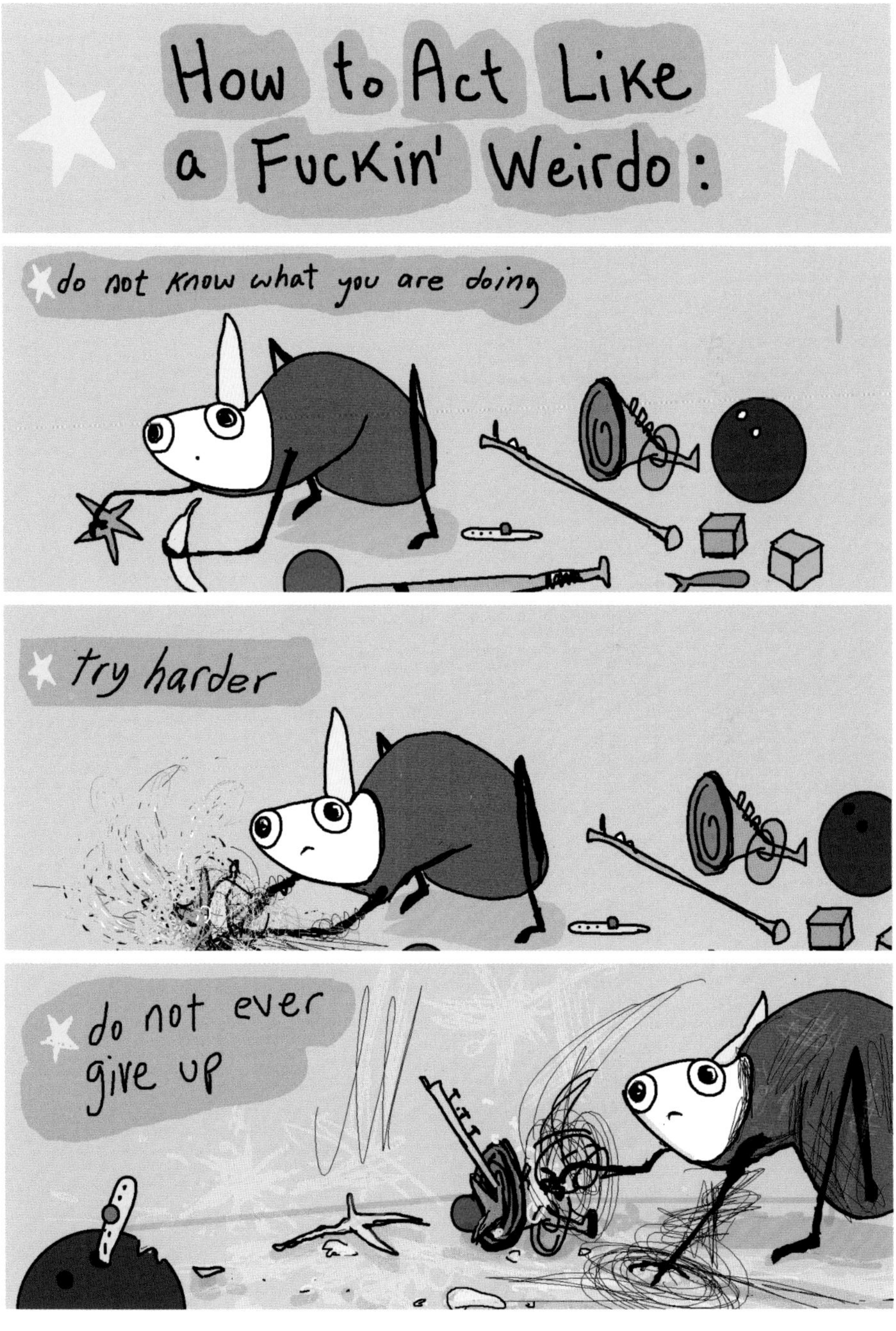
How to Act Like a Fuckin' Weirdo:
do not know what you are doing
try harder
do not ever give up

18. CAT

Adopting a cat is an entirely different process from adopting a dog. With dogs, it's all very regimented. Visitation hours and stuff. With cats, they're like, "*What do you want? Cats?*" You say yeah, and they say, "*Great. Grab however many you want—they're strewn throughout the building.*"

And then you walk around for three hours trying to find one that likes you. At the end of the day, we'd narrowed it down to four possibilities:

- An 11-year-old unicorn beast, but the horn is a wart instead of a horn. Likes being touched. REALLY likes being touched on the wart
- The statistical average of all cats. 5 years old, medium hair, kind of likes petting, kind of hates it, mostly is just around
- A blimp monster with tiny legs poking out
- A squirrel-like creature of unknown age and origin who seemed genuinely desperate to touch us with his whole body at the same time

We went with the desperate one. He seemed like he wanted it the most. We named him Squirrel because that's what he looks and acts like. Pretty straight-forward.

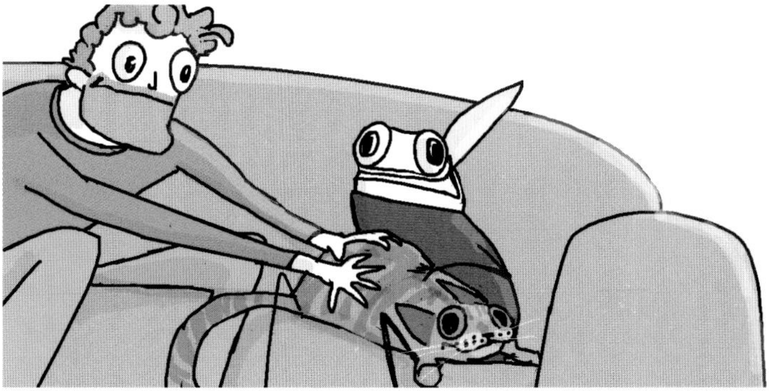

Squirrel's best friend is a green and yellow mouse toy.

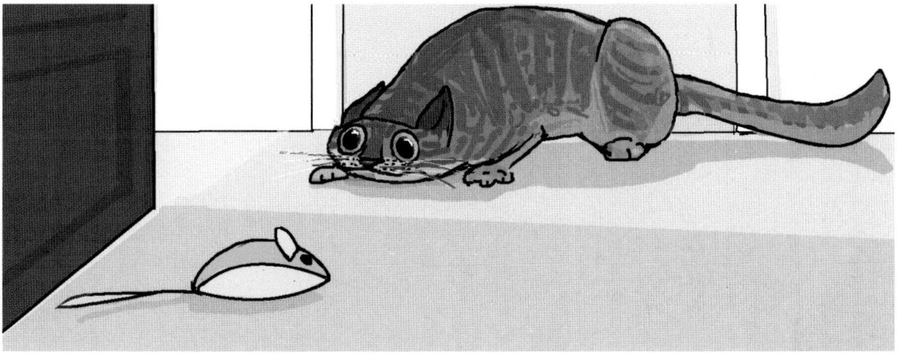

They have a mercurial relationship. Not on Mouse's end—Mouse isn't real—but as far as Squirrel is concerned, the drama never stops.

I don't understand how he maintains it. Every day, he finds new inspiration for doing all manner of bizarre things to his mouse friend.

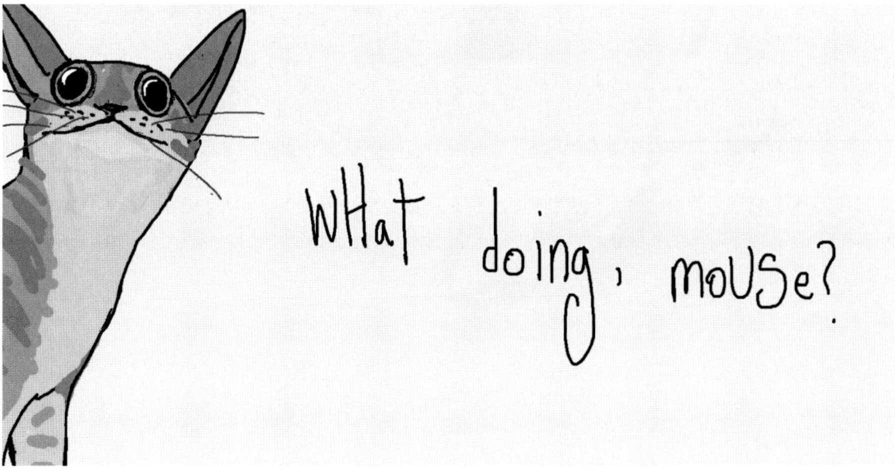
WHat doing, mouse?

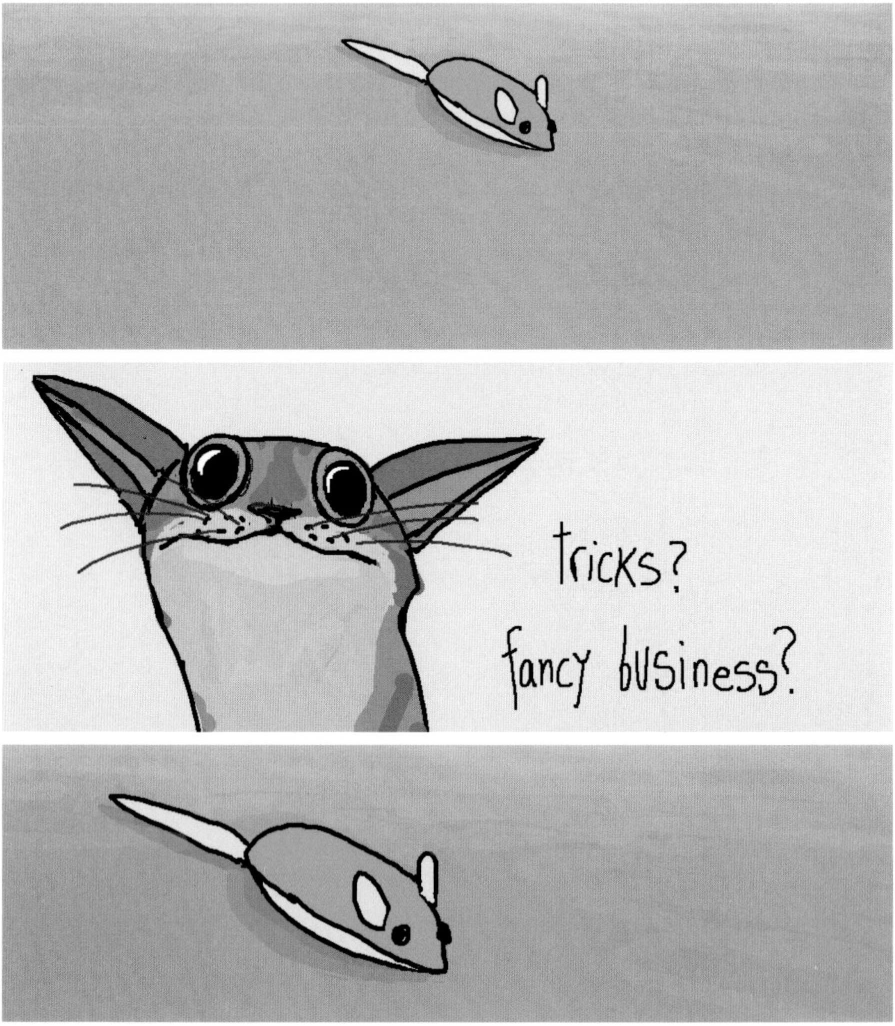
tricks?
fancy business?

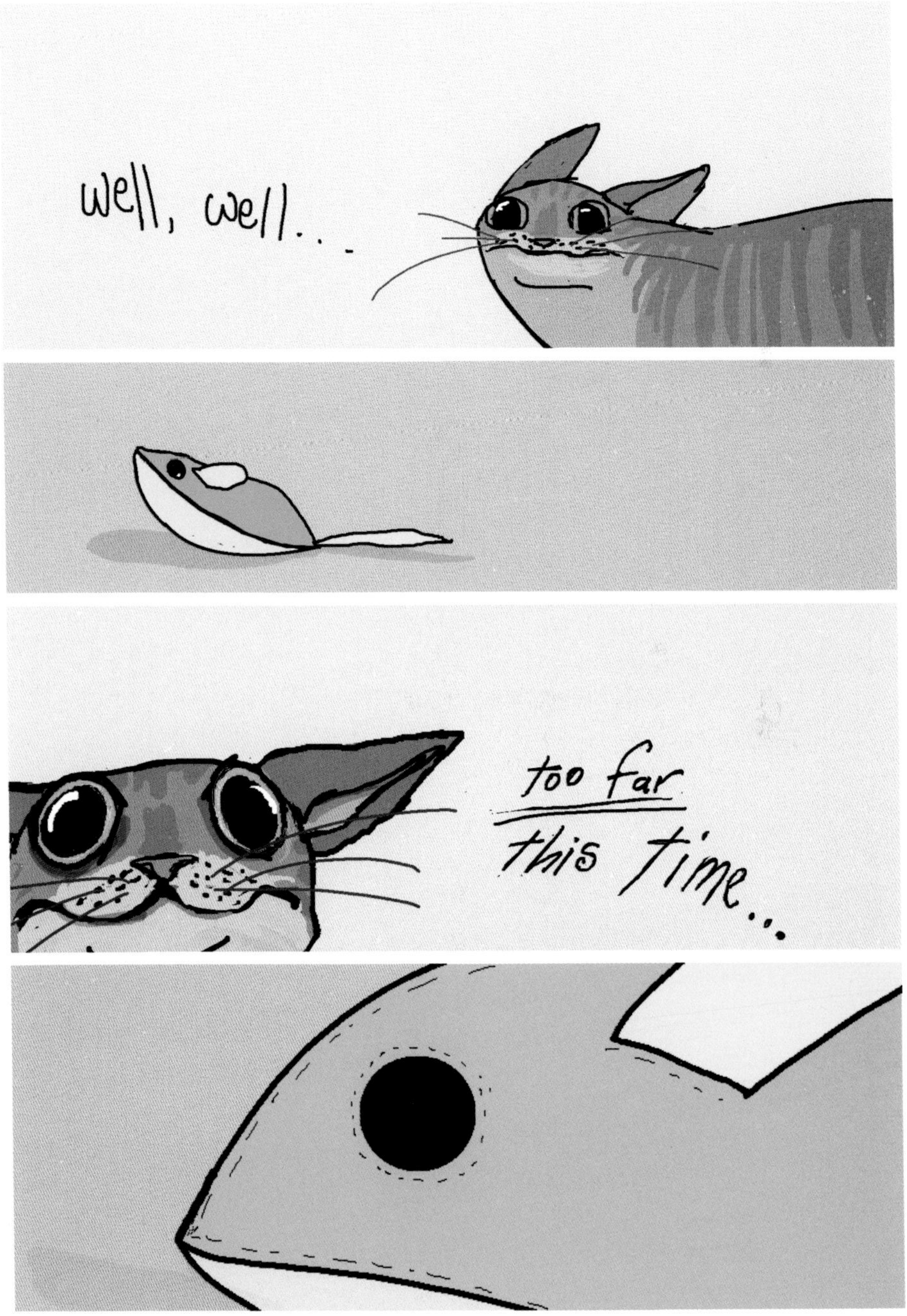
well, well...
too far this time...

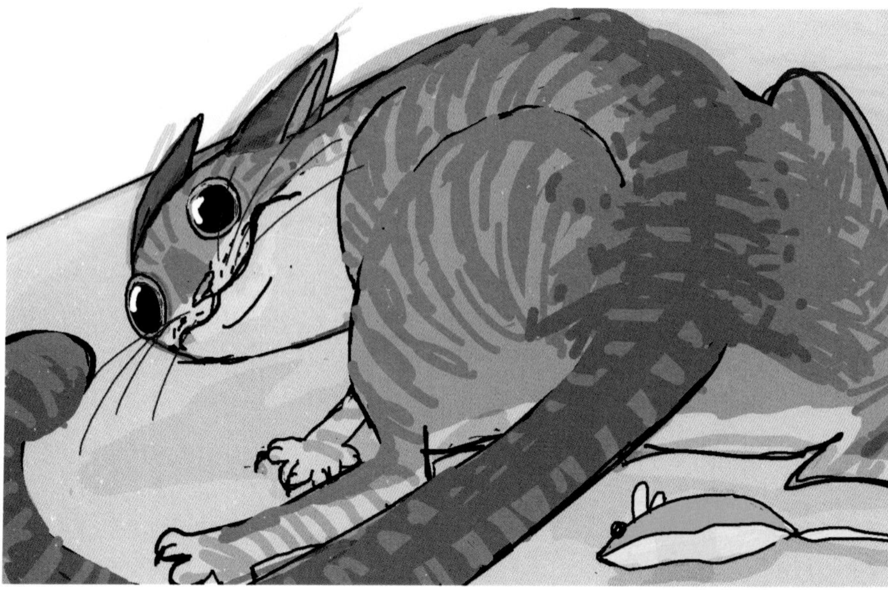

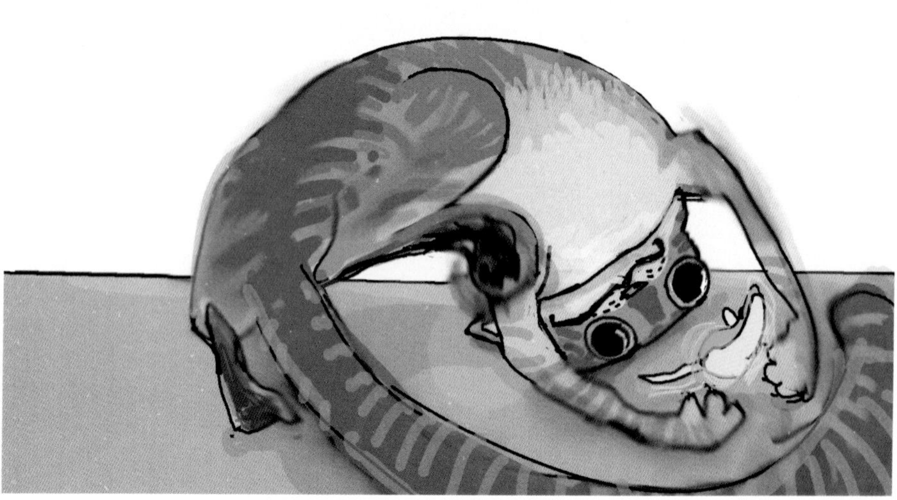

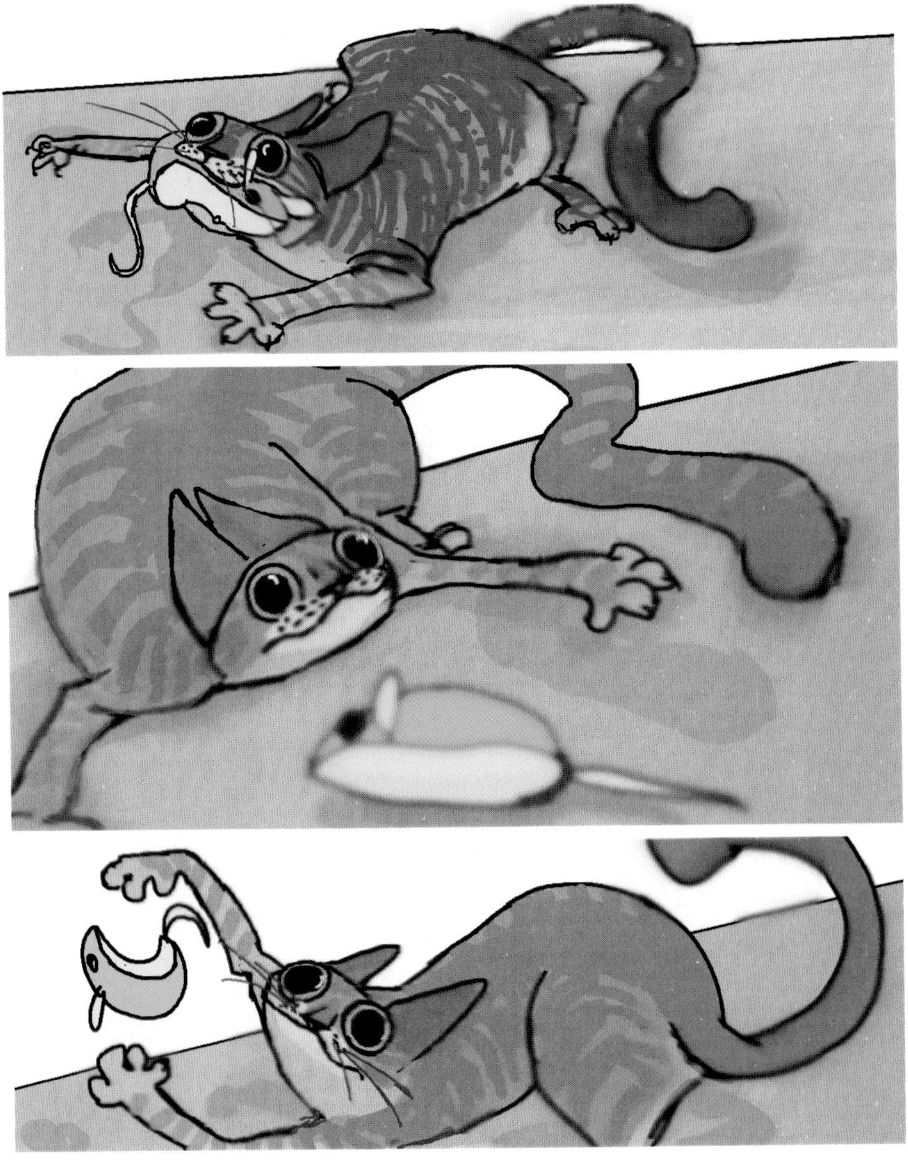

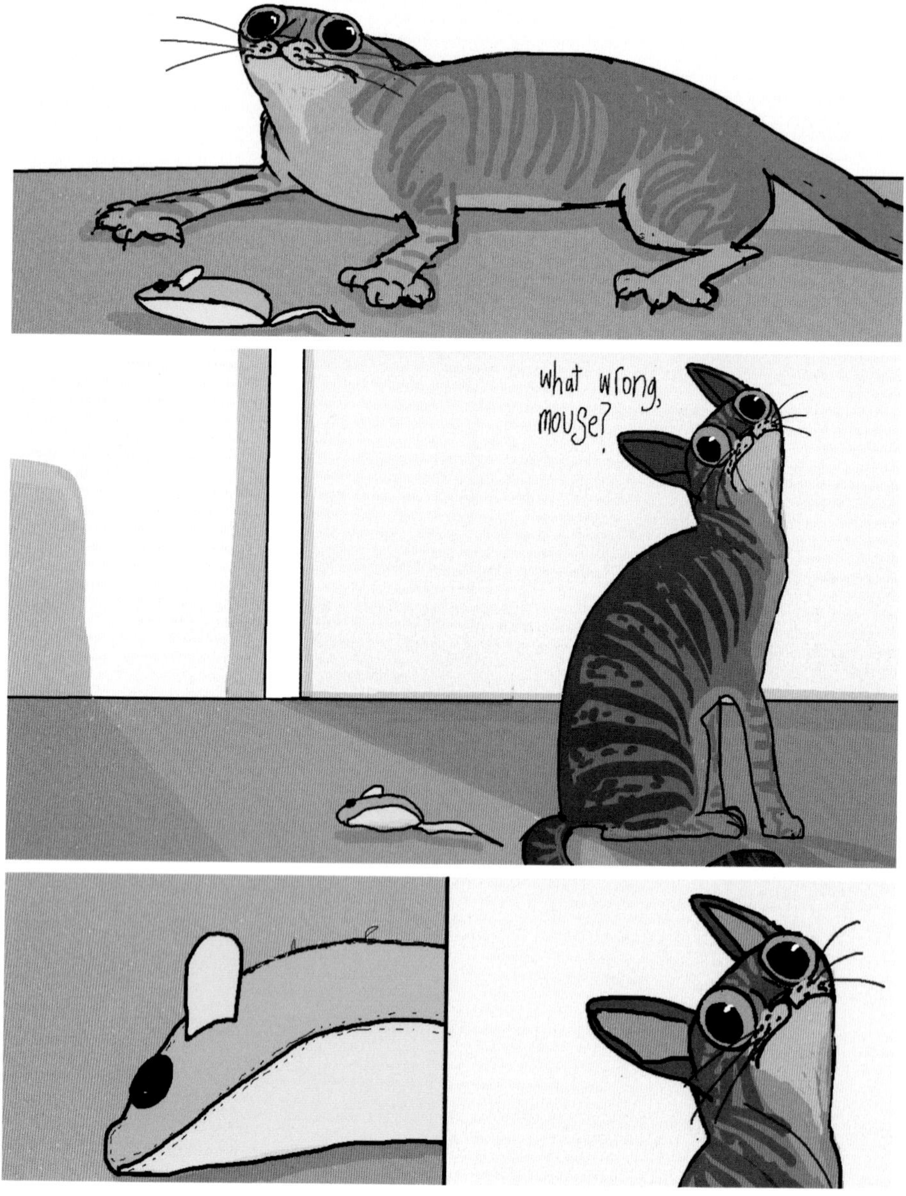
what wrong, mouse?

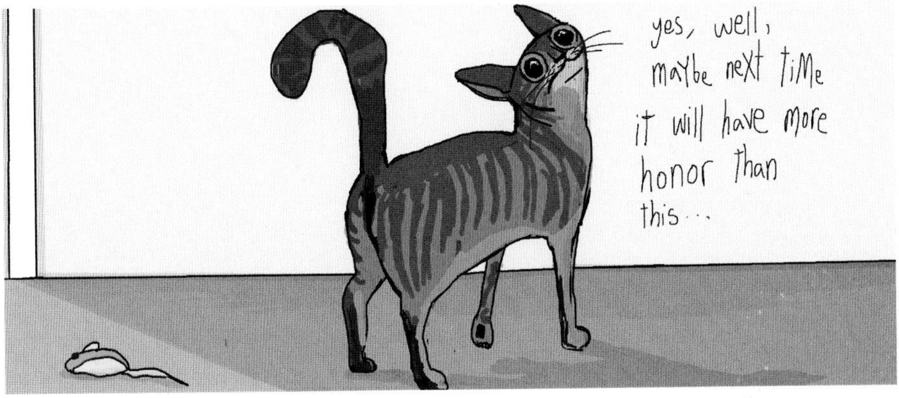
yes, well, maybe next time it will have more honor than this...

My handle on their relationship is limited to the basics. Like, I can tell when he's mad at it because he puts it in the bathroom. I get that. Sometimes, when you're so fed up with your mouse friend that you can't even look at it, you've gotta do something. Teach it a lesson. Put it in the bathroom so it can think about itself.

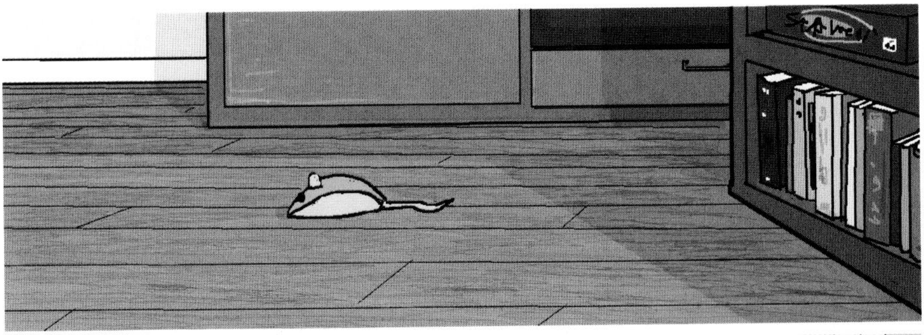

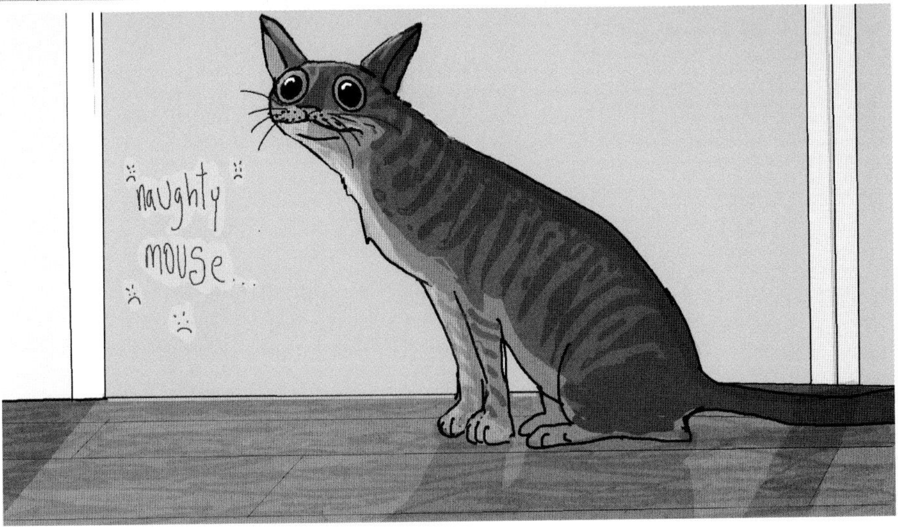
naughty mouse...

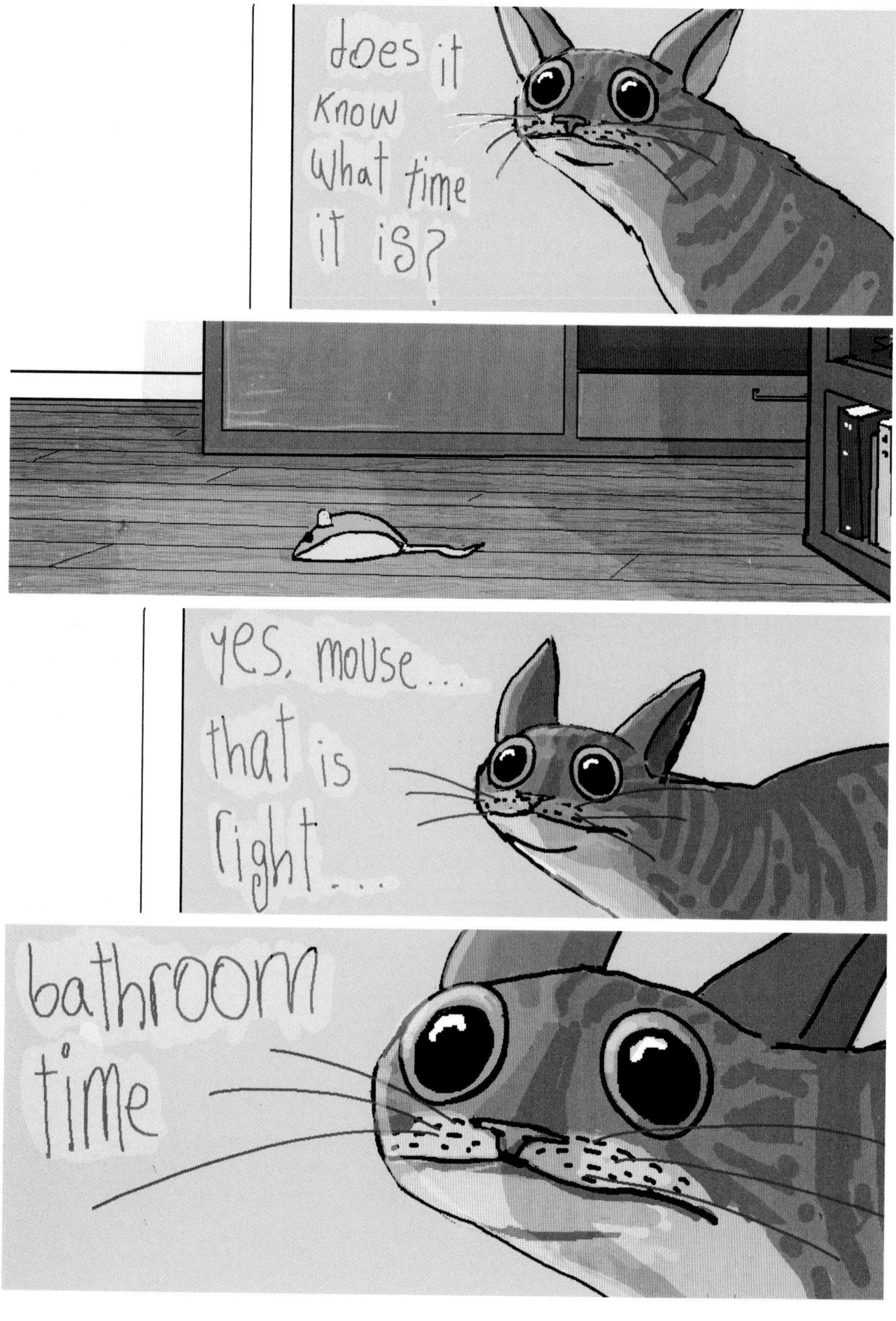
does it know what time it is?
yes, mouse... that is right...
bathroom time

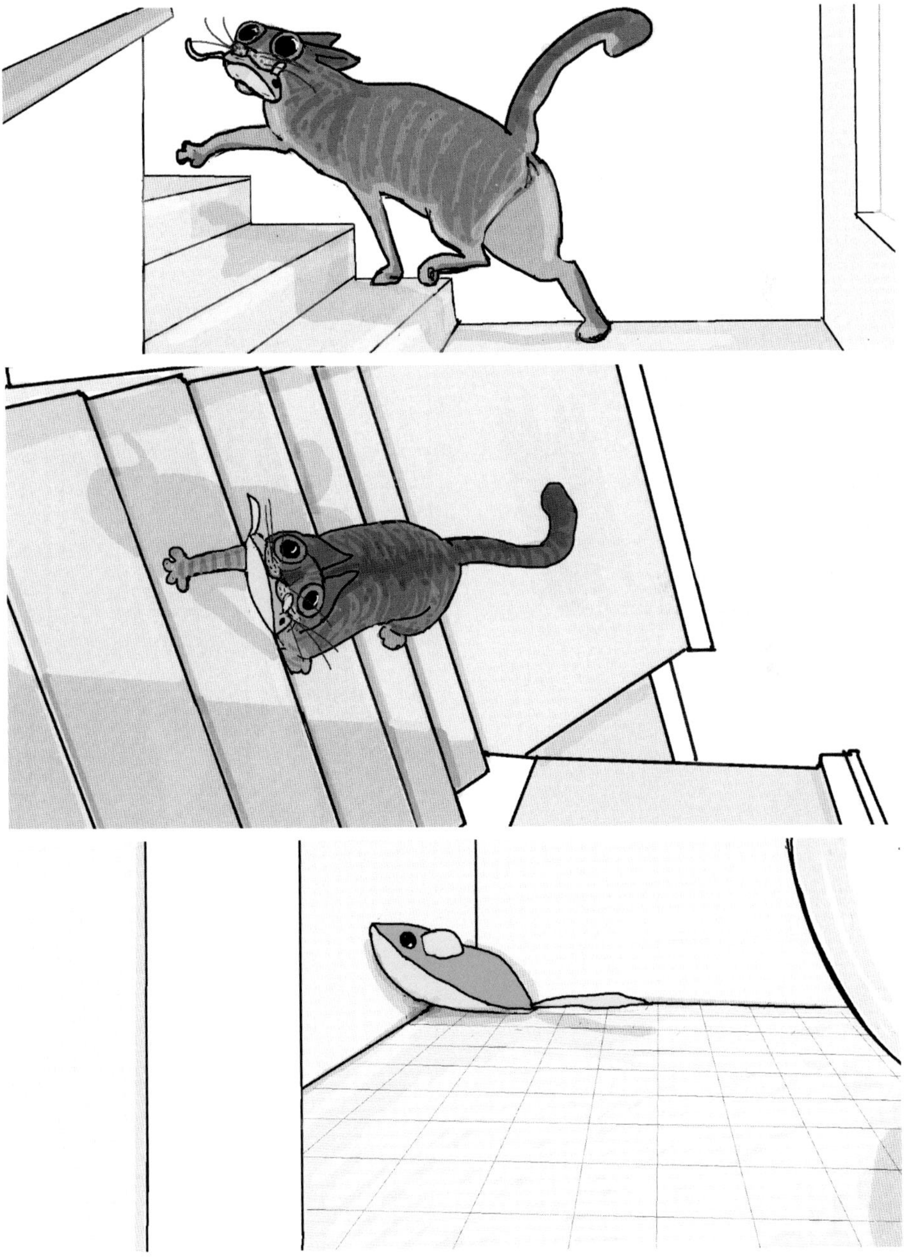

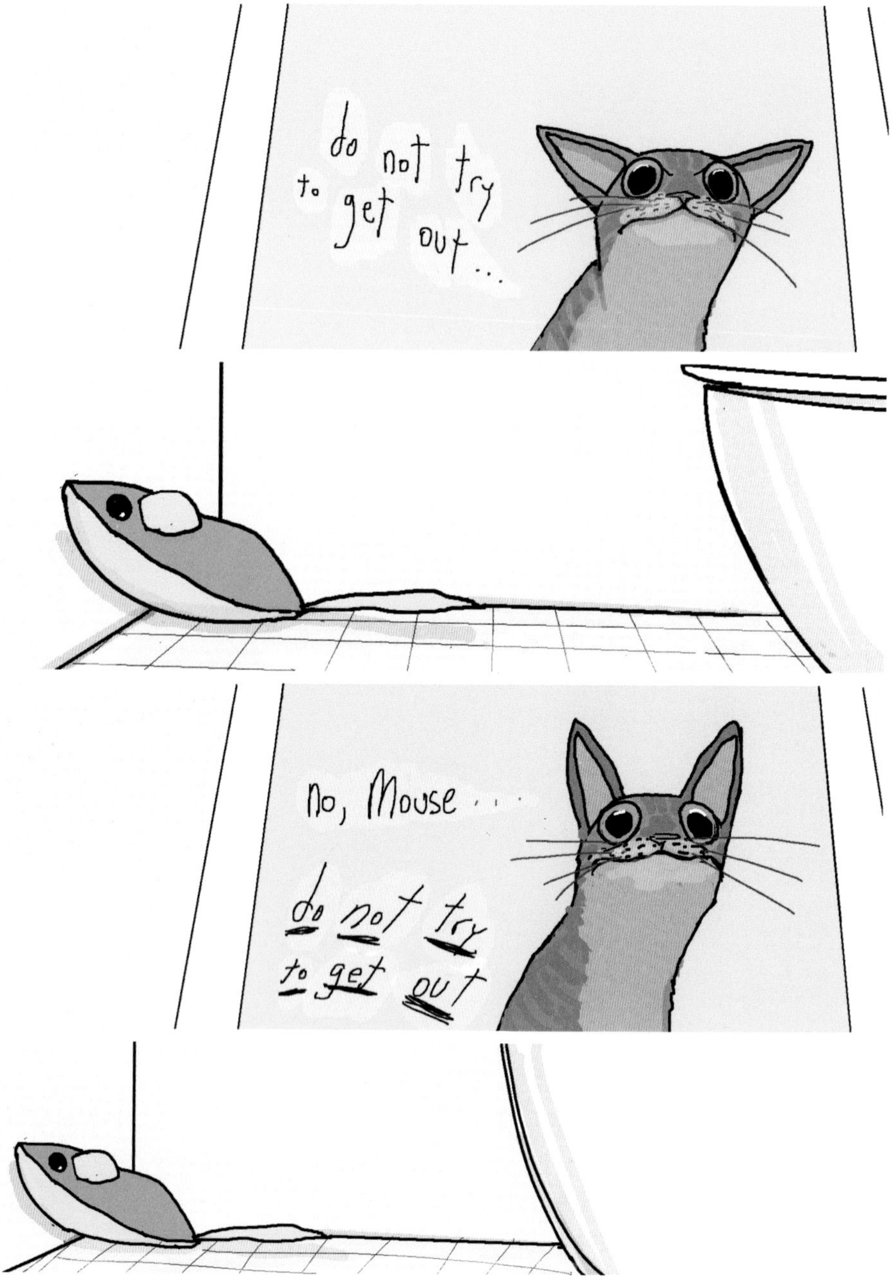

do not try to get out...
no, Mouse...
do not try to get out

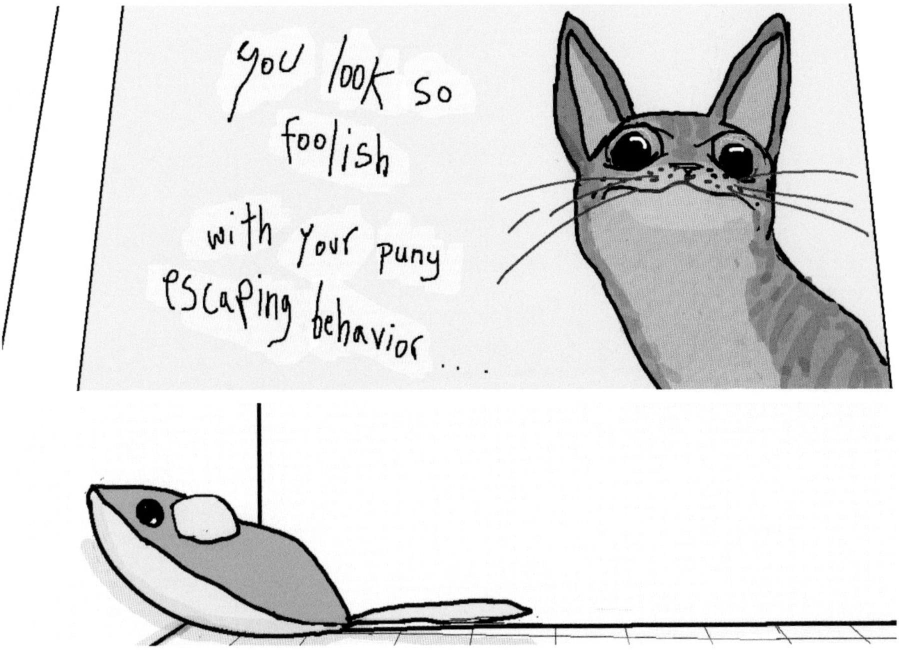
you look so foolish
with your puny escaping behavior . . .

It's always antagonizing him—falling off the bed, hiding behind the water bowl when he least expects it, making everybody feel stupid with that infuriating look on its face.

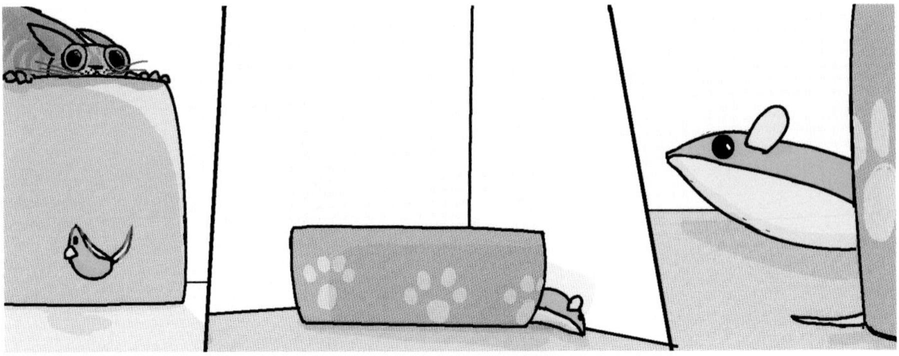

That isn't the only kind of fight they have, though. Some are more involved.

For example: One day, Mouse got wet. Squirrel took it as a personal attack, and things got weird for a while.

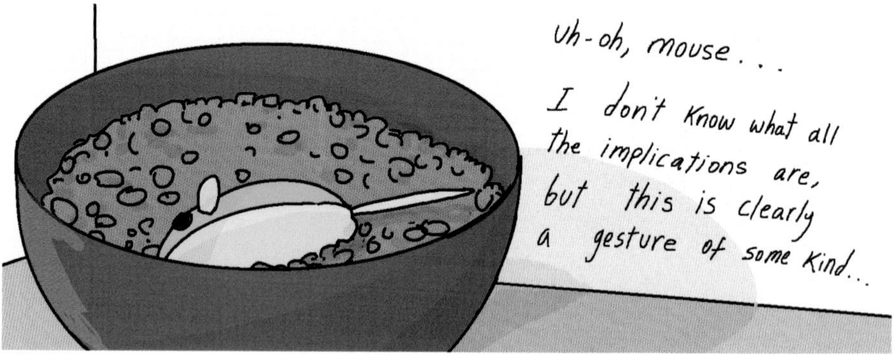
Uh-oh, mouse...
I don't know what all the implications are, but this is clearly a gesture of some kind...

Another day, I walked into the bedroom, and Squirrel was doing his actual best to shove Mouse all the way down his throat. I don't know what happened to provoke this, but he seemed *extremely* motivated.

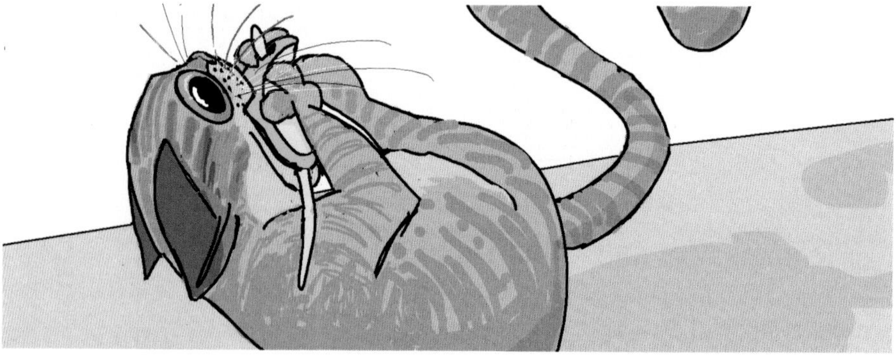

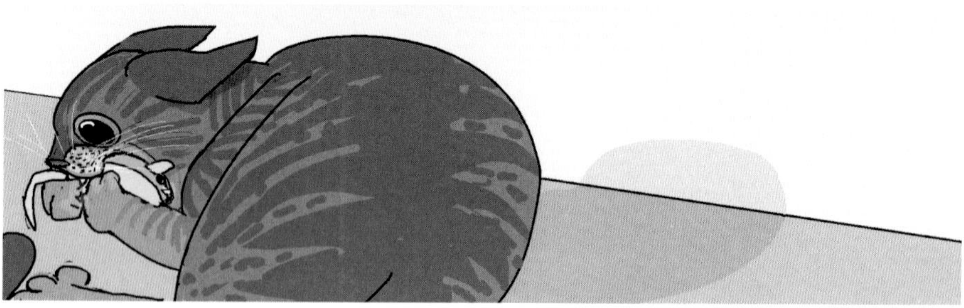

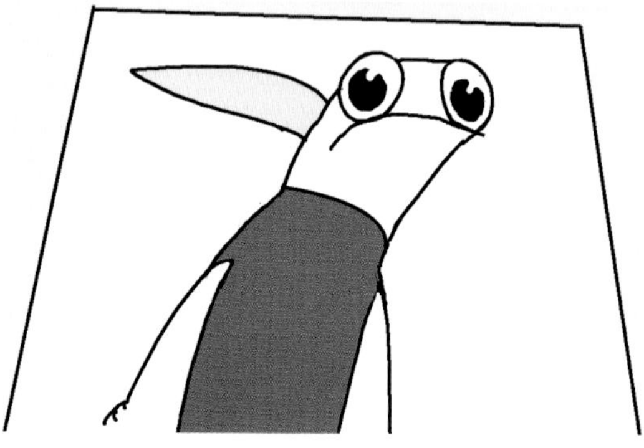

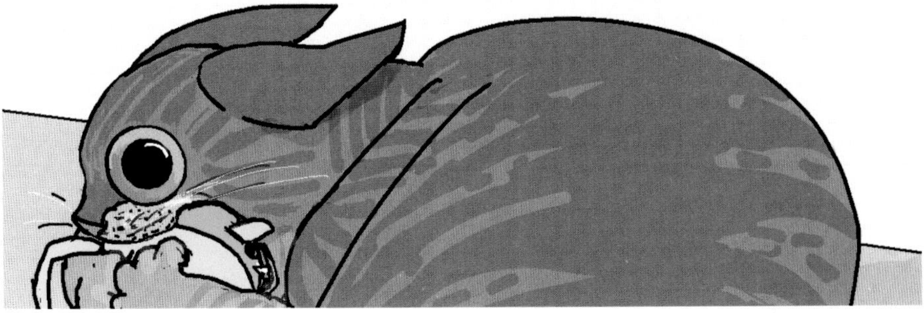

When Mouse started to fall apart, we bought new mouse toys. We thought this would work. I mean, why wouldn't it? He obviously has the power of imagination on lockdown, so why wouldn't he be able to seamlessly transition between mouse friends? None of them are real—just pretend it's the same mouse and move on with your life.

He hates the new mice. He refuses to acknowledge them. If they try to be his friends, he puts them in the bathroom.

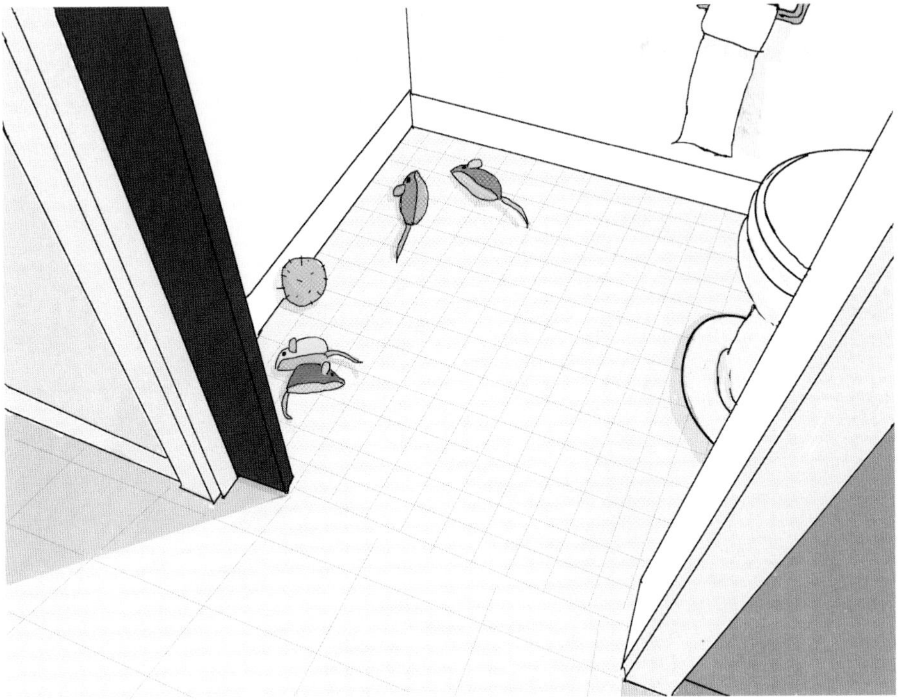

I suppose it's noble of him to be so loyal to Mouse. I mean, yeah: no other mouse could ever compete with what these two have been through together. I understand why it would be infuriating when they try to insert themselves into the relationship. That's very rude of them. How dare they.

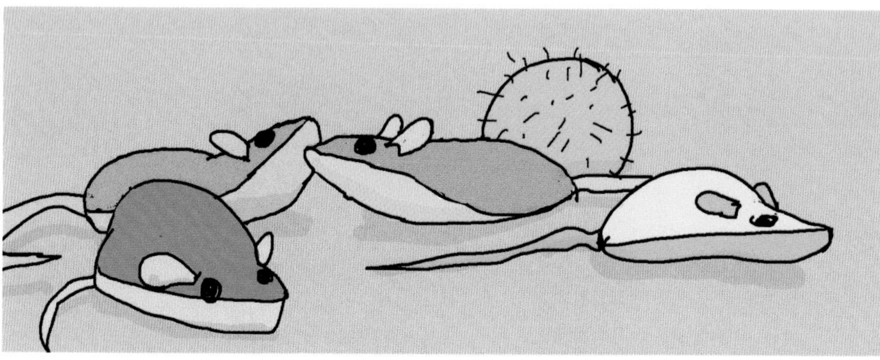

He obviously hates them, but unlike with Mouse, there's no passion behind it. He just straight up hates them and doesn't want to be their friend, end of story.

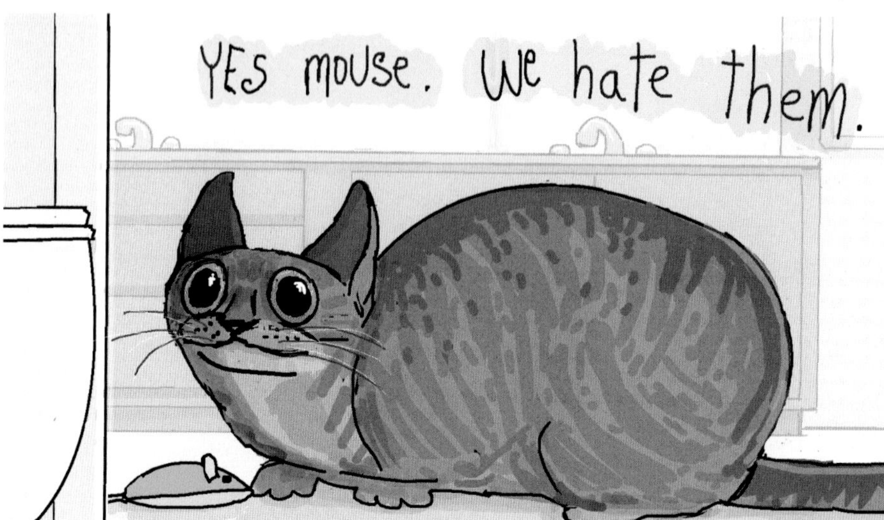
YES mouse. We hate them.

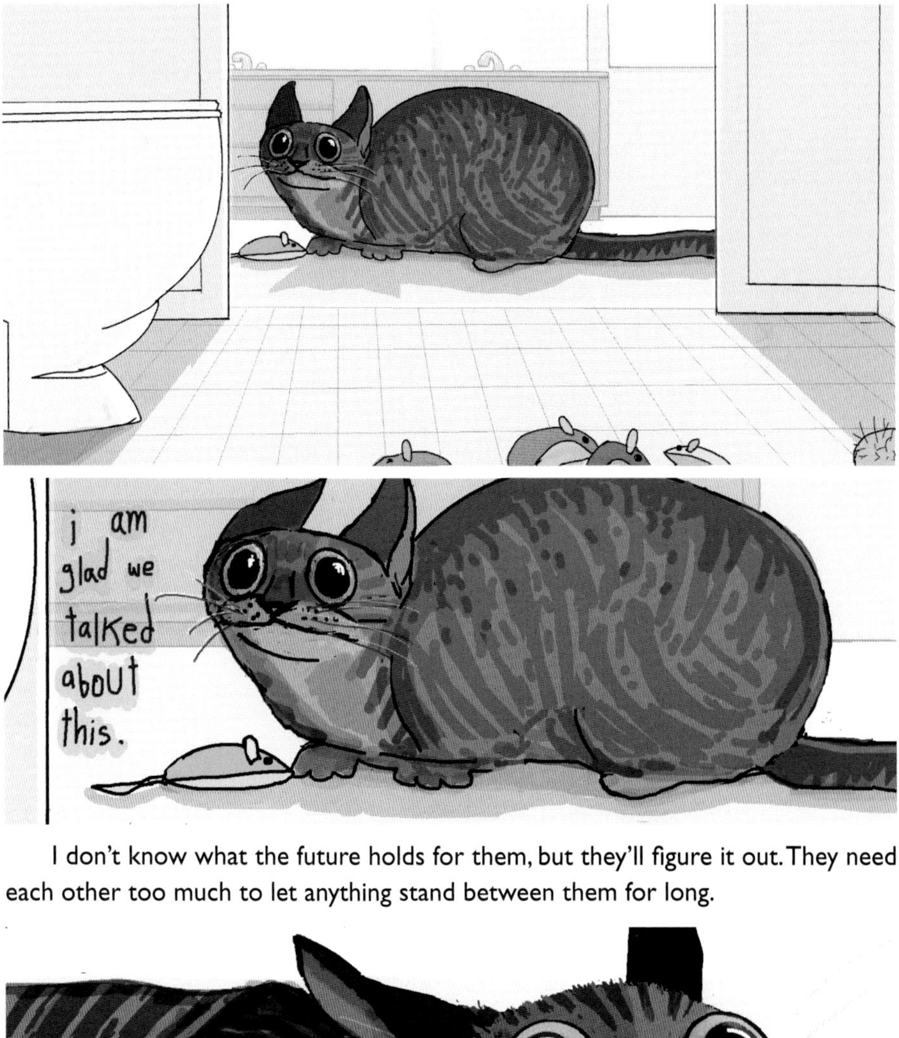
j am glad we talked about this.

I don't know what the future holds for them, but they'll figure it out. They need each other too much to let anything stand between them for long.

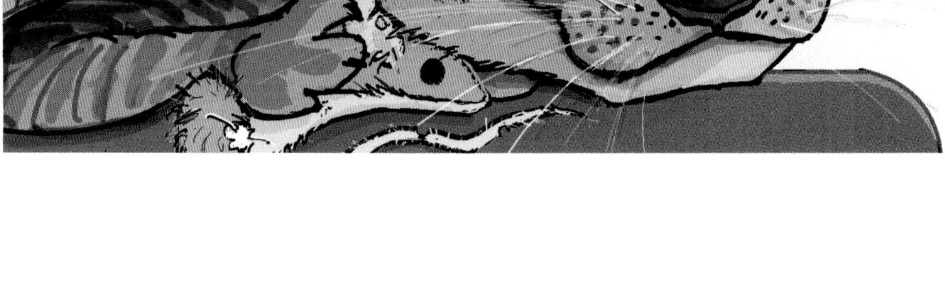

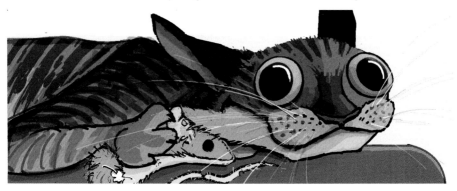

19. FISH VIDEO

There's video footage of my first attempt at friendship.

Due to the way books work, I cannot show it to you. But, for the purposes of foreshadowing, I'm going to describe the video.

I'm two. The friend I'm trying to make is a sardine.

It's dead, so right from the beginning, things aren't going well.

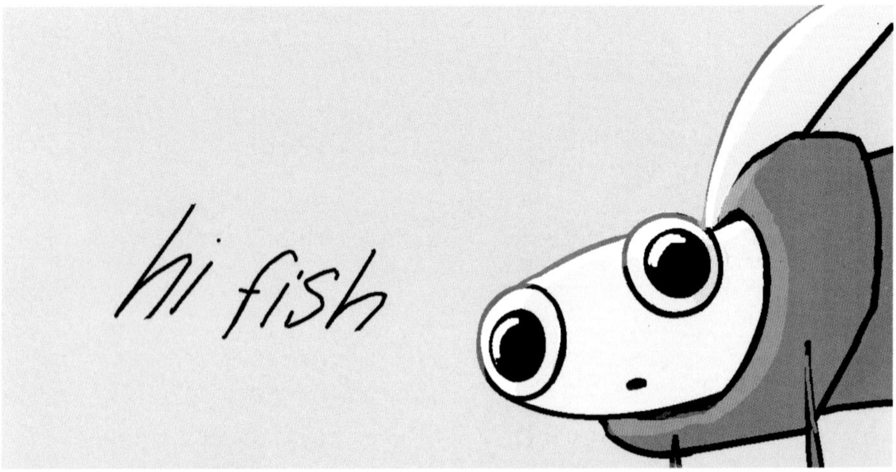
hi fish

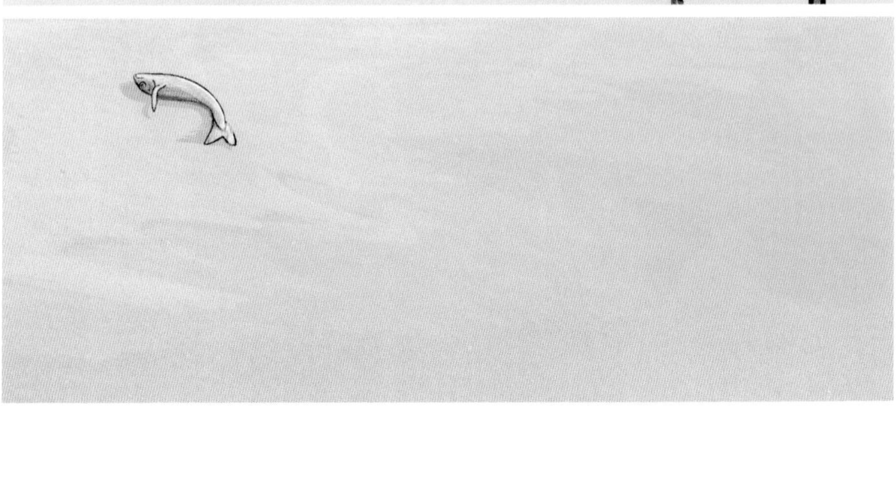

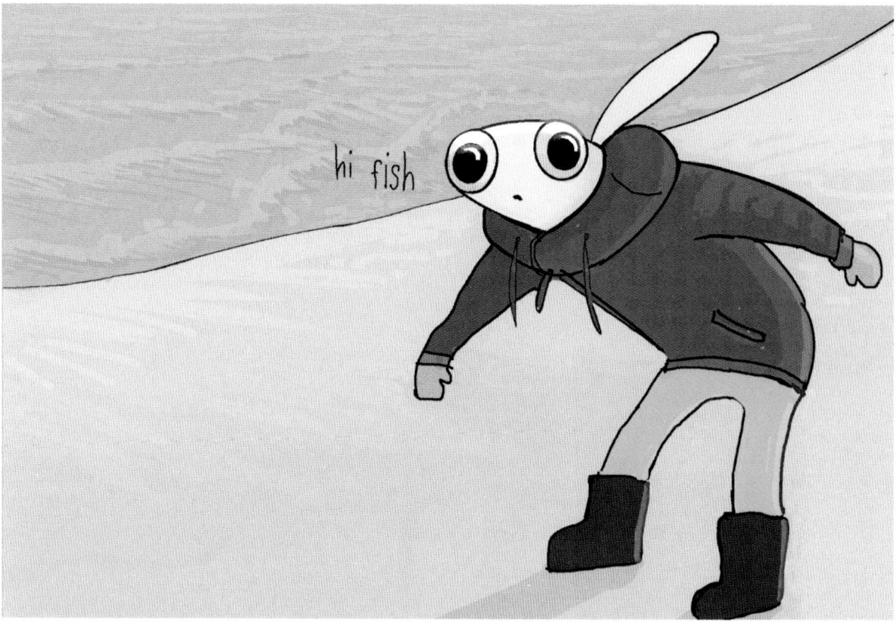
hi fish

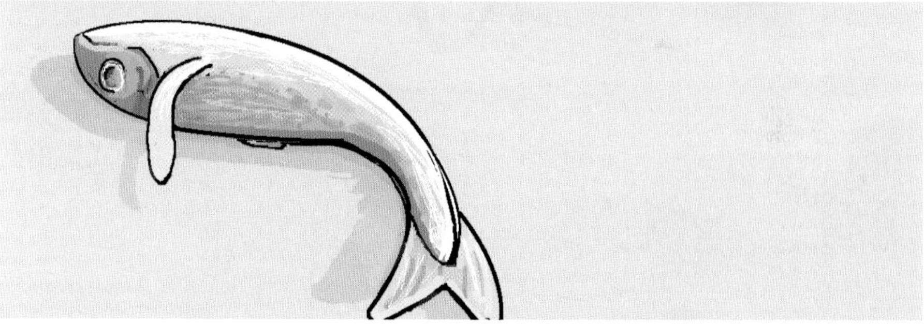

I'm really doing my absolute best to get the conversation started, though.

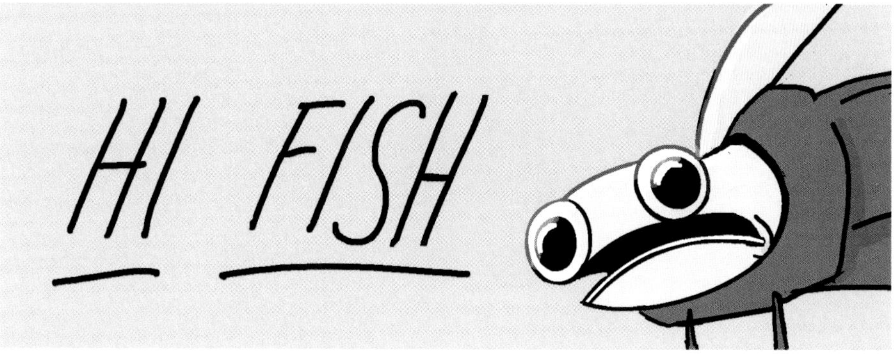
HI FISH

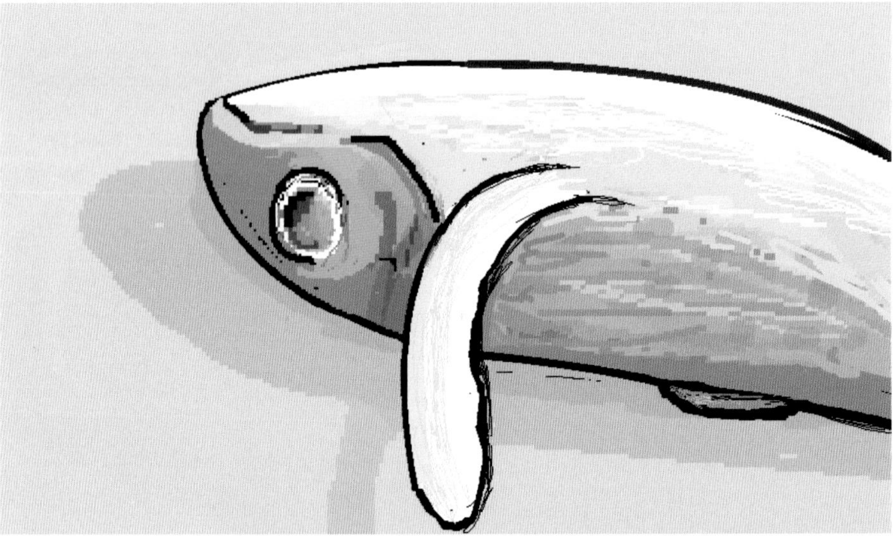

I don't know about death yet, but I can sense my friend isn't doing as great as his max potential probably. He needs my help. The determination sets in across my face. *By god, I am going to help this fish, and there is nothing anyone can do to stop me.*

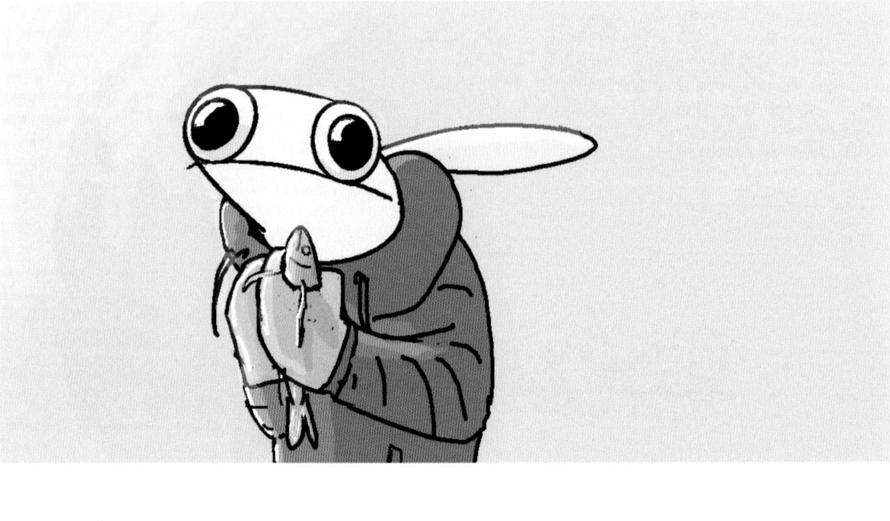

Plan A: blow on the fish.

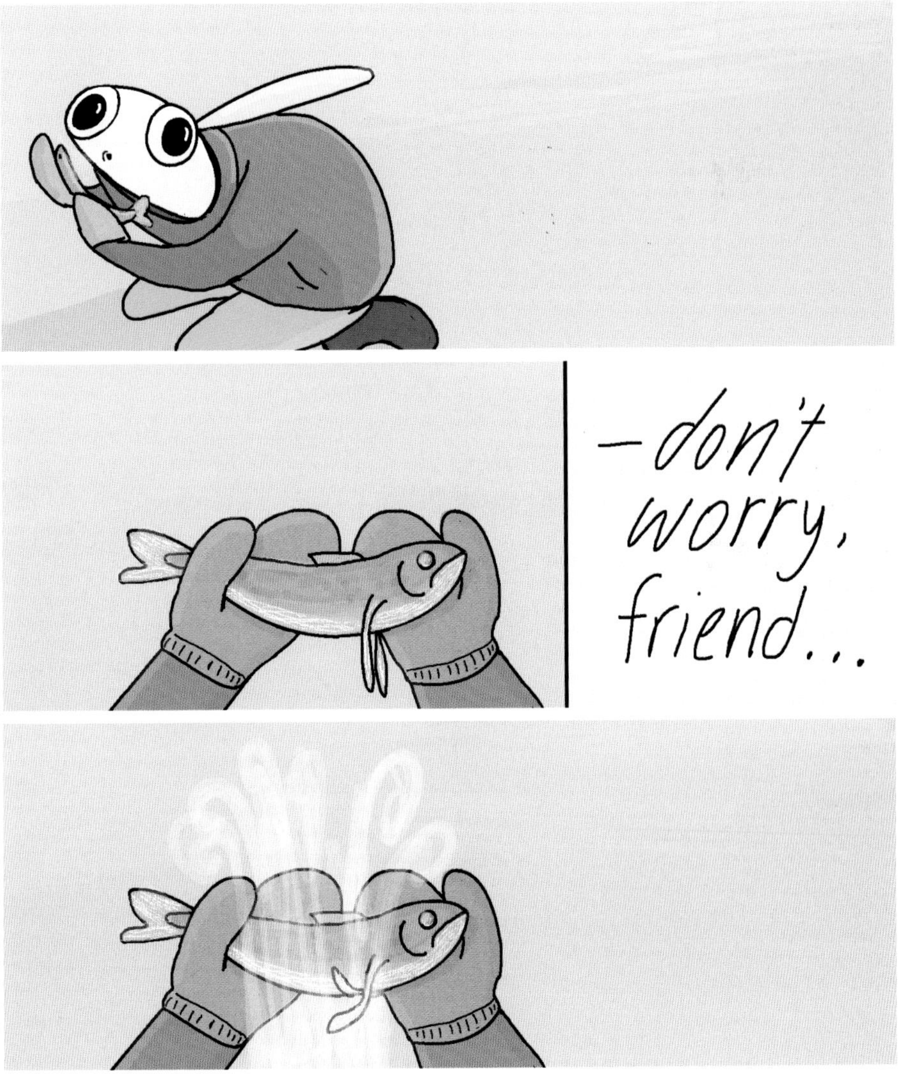
–don't worry, friend...

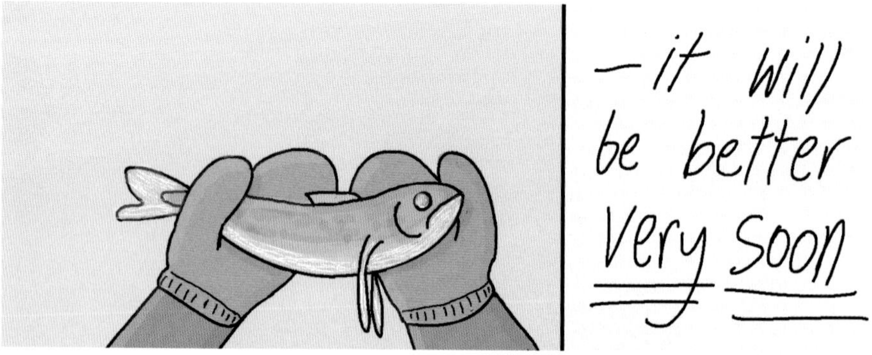
—it will be better Very Soon

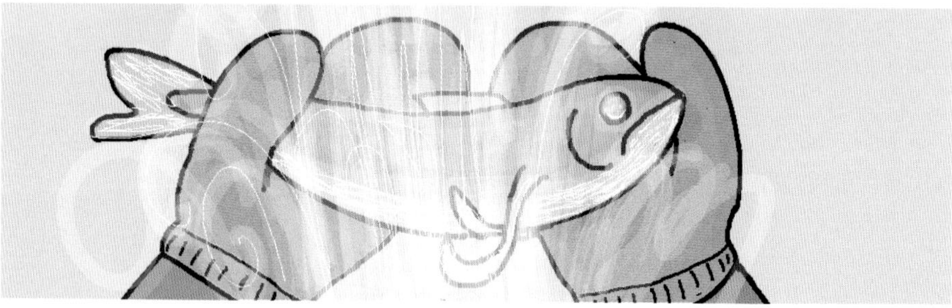

Plan B: blow as hard as you can on the fish—a tremendous air current will surely invigorate him!

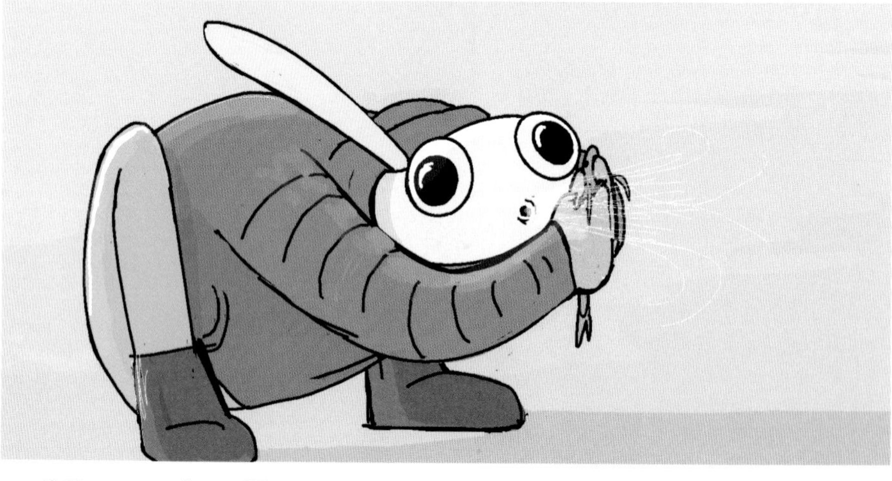

Still not working. Okay, moving on to Plan C: motivate the fish by yelling encouragement directly onto his body.

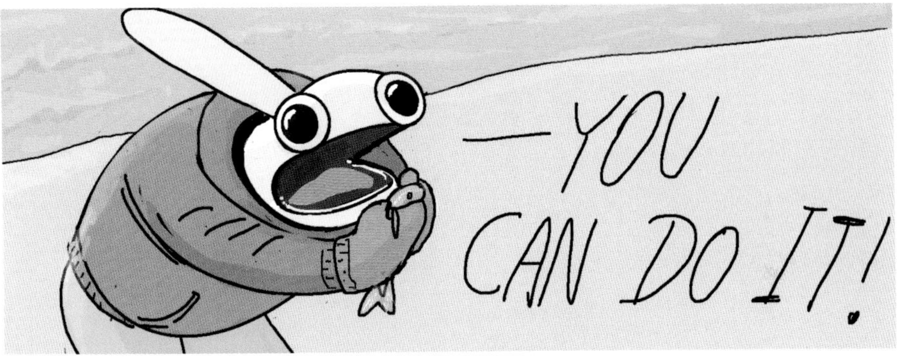
—YOU CAN DO IT!

Minutes later, he still isn't okay. I, however, do not appear to be discouraged by this at all. This fish is my friend, and I am prepared to do everything I know. For instance: setting him on the ground with ceremonial precision and then backing away with my arms raised.

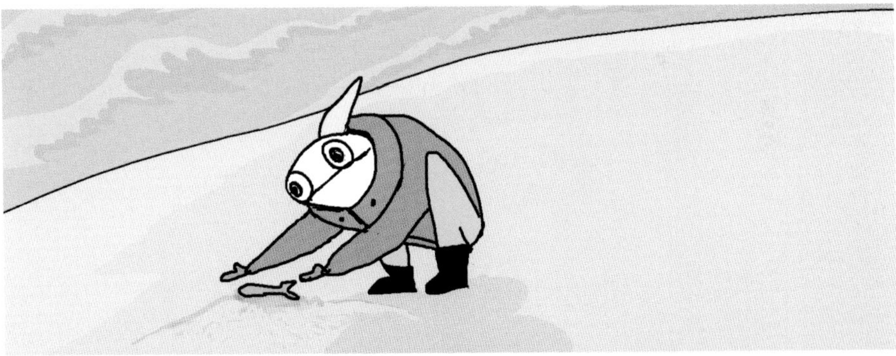

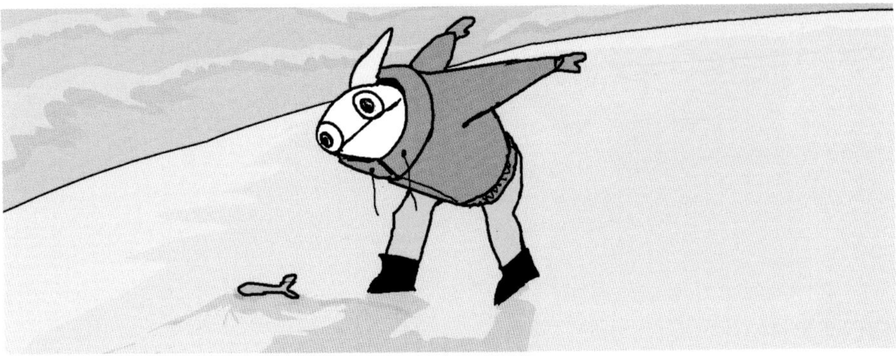

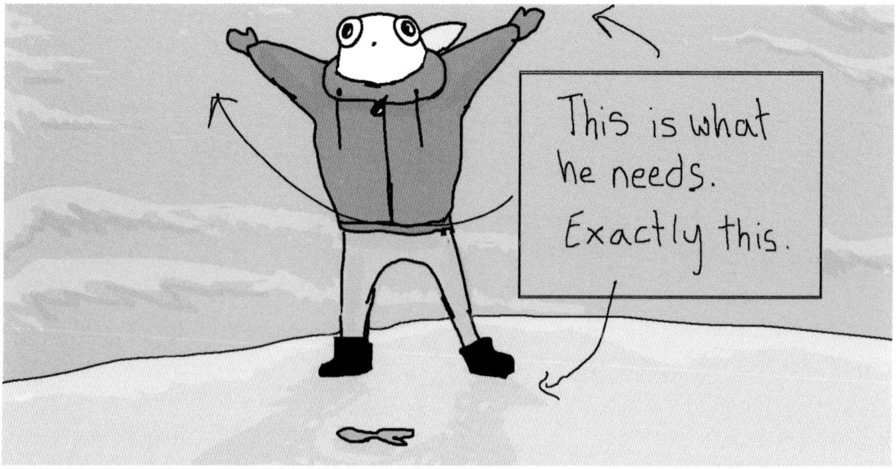
This is what
he needs.
Exactly this.

And if that doesn't work, there's always singing . . .

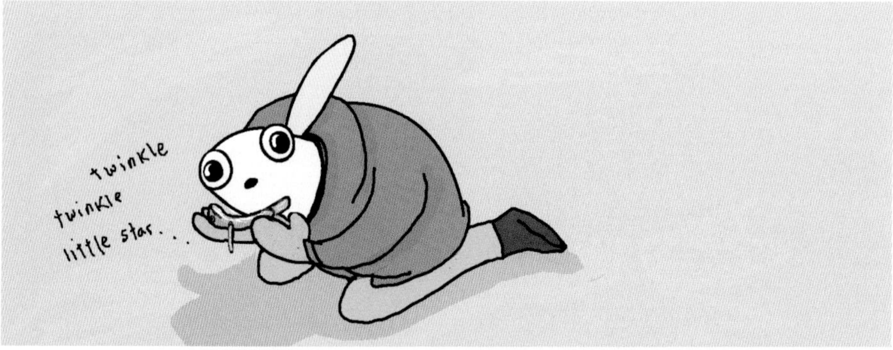
twinkle
twinkle
little star. . .

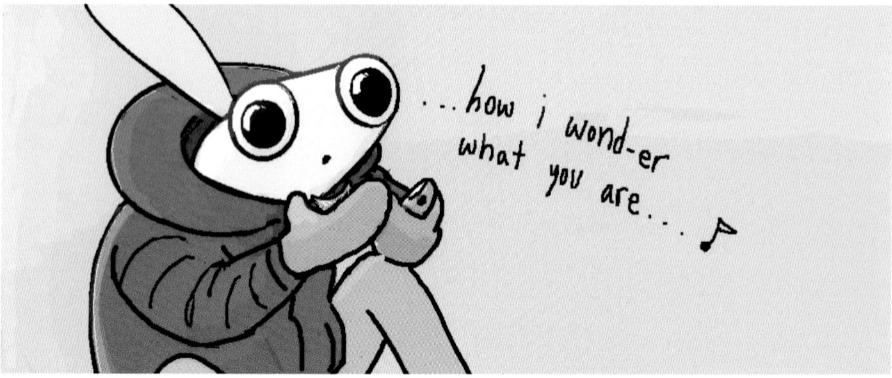
. . . how i wond-er
what you are. . .

Most people wouldn't know where to go after singing, but I do: *Vigorous massage.*

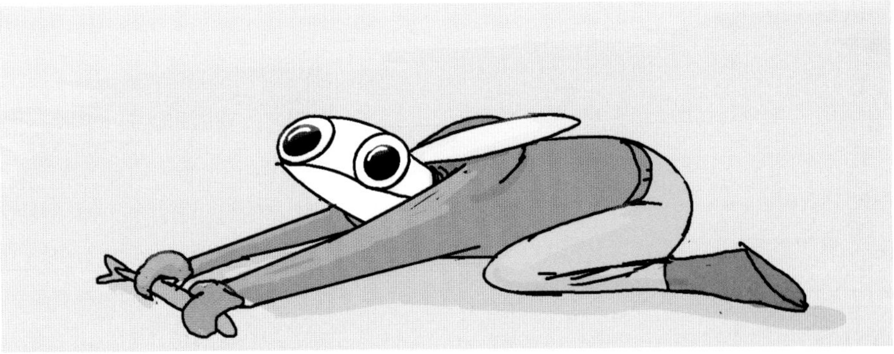

This is a home video from the '80s. Compared to the resolutions available in modern times, the quality is like standing behind a wall and guessing what's on the other side. And I'm mangling the poor fish so badly that even at this ridiculous resolution, you can see pieces of its body rubbing off on my mittens.

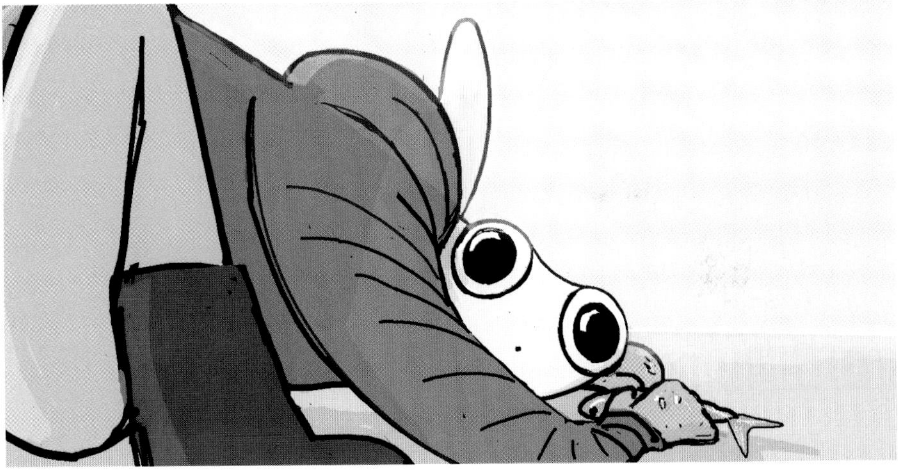

Fast-forward five minutes. For some reason, my grandma is still filming. We are well past the turning point between cute and sad. The other people on the beach are becoming uncomfortable. Sensing this, my mom makes an attempt to end the situation.

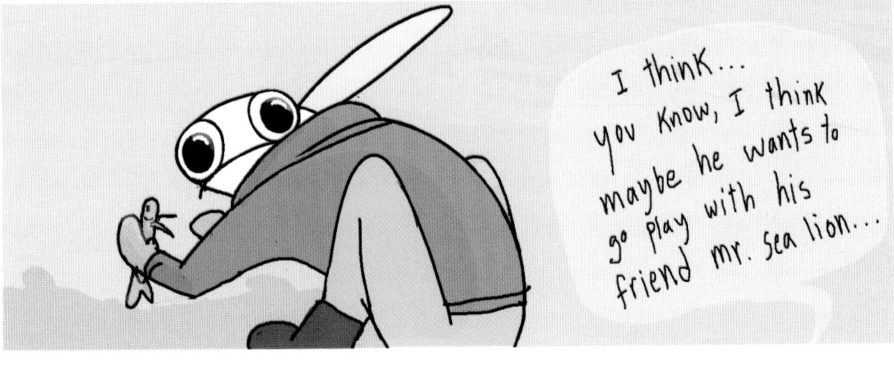
I think... you know, I think maybe he wants to go play with his friend mr. sea lion...

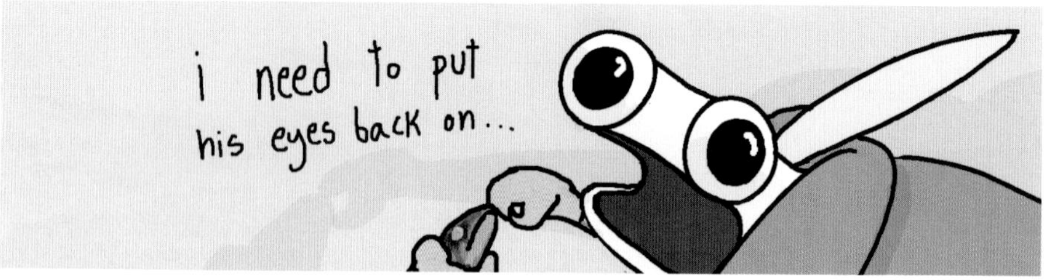
i need to put
his eyes back on...

Suddenly we zoom out. It's the future. I'm a deeply depressed adult watching this video alone in the dark at my parents' house after my sister's funeral. I found it in a box in the garage and thought, *Hey, I bet I know what would cheer me up! Watching videos from before I knew how horrifying everything is!*

And then here comes this battering ram of existential tragedy . . .

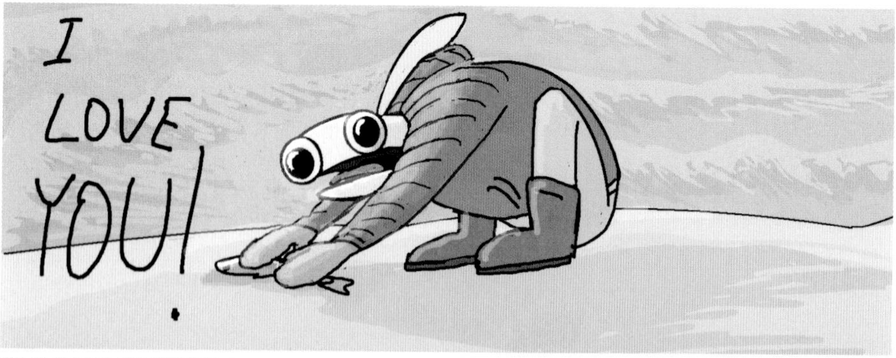
I
LOVE
YOU!

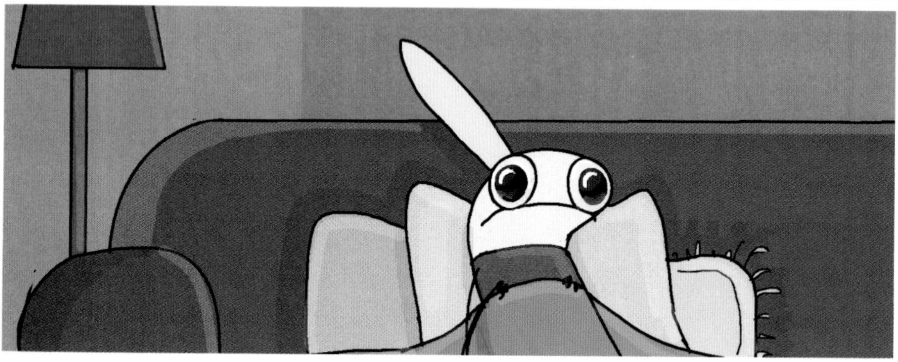

. . . unintentionally raising every point it's possible to raise about futility and really just hammering it until there's nothing left.

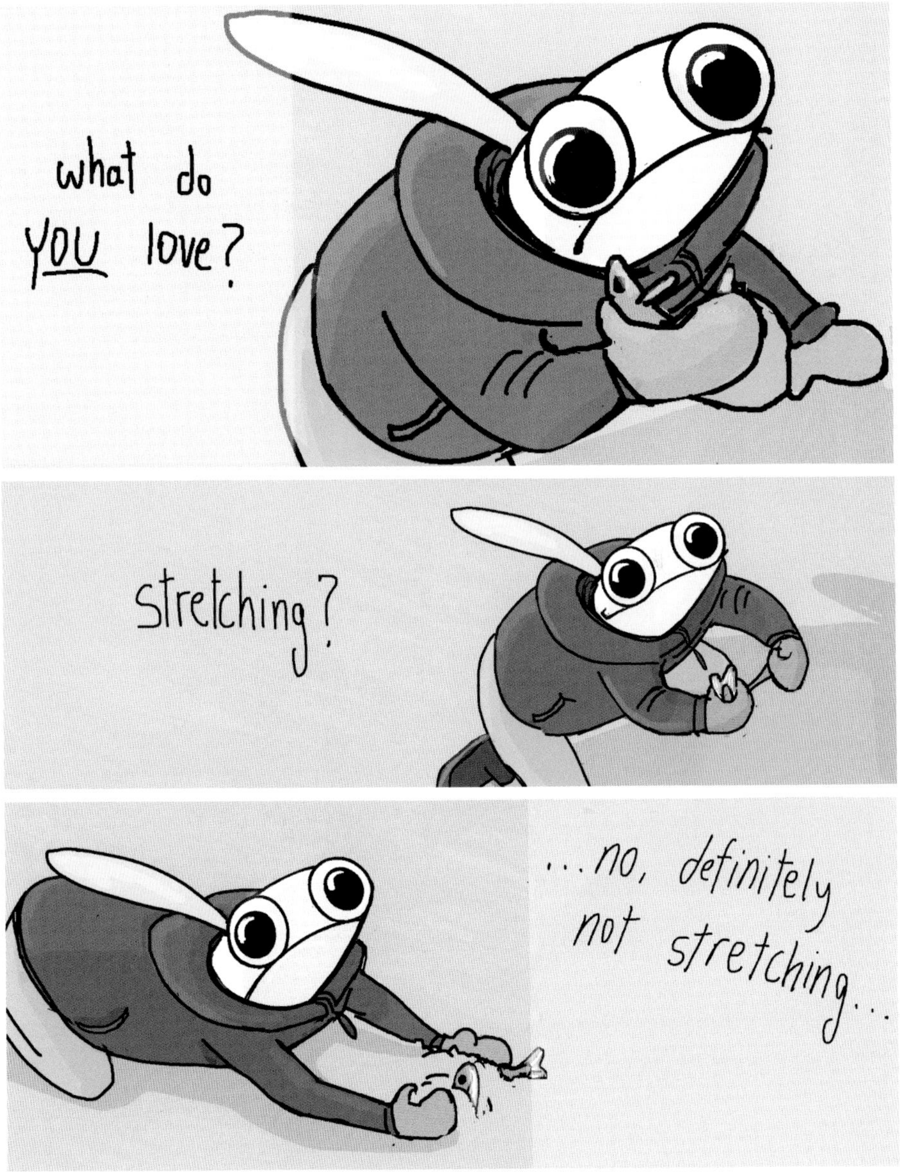
what do YOU love?
stretching?
...no, definitely not stretching...

And I think I just found it devastatingly relatable.

20. THE UGLY DUCKLING 2

We aren't good at explaining things to children. Especially not hard things like how nothing is fair or means anything but, you know, keep trying anyway.

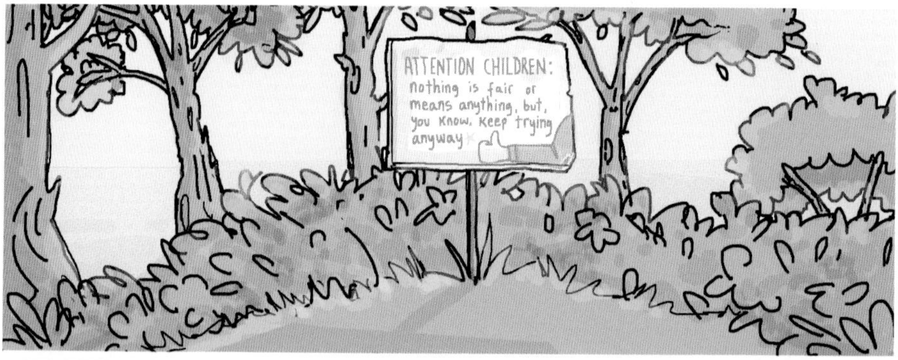
ATTENTION CHILDREN:
nothing is fair or means anything, but, you know, keep trying anyway

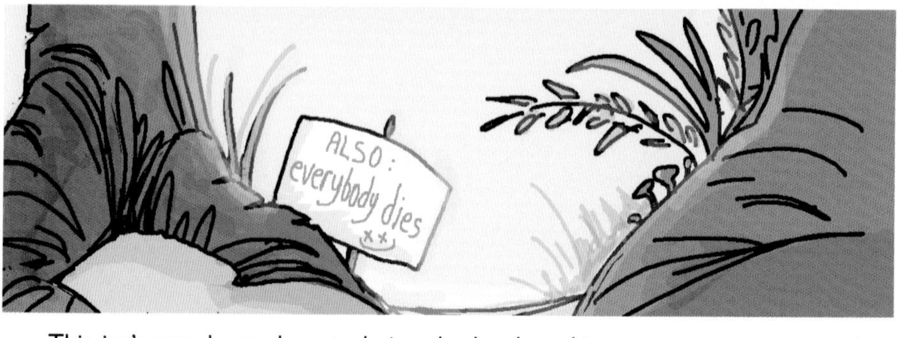
ALSO:
everybody dies

This isn't anywhere close to being the hardest thing you can come up against before your eleventh birthday, but I was a weird-looking kid. *Real* weird-looking. The kind of weird-looking where it's negligent to not address it.

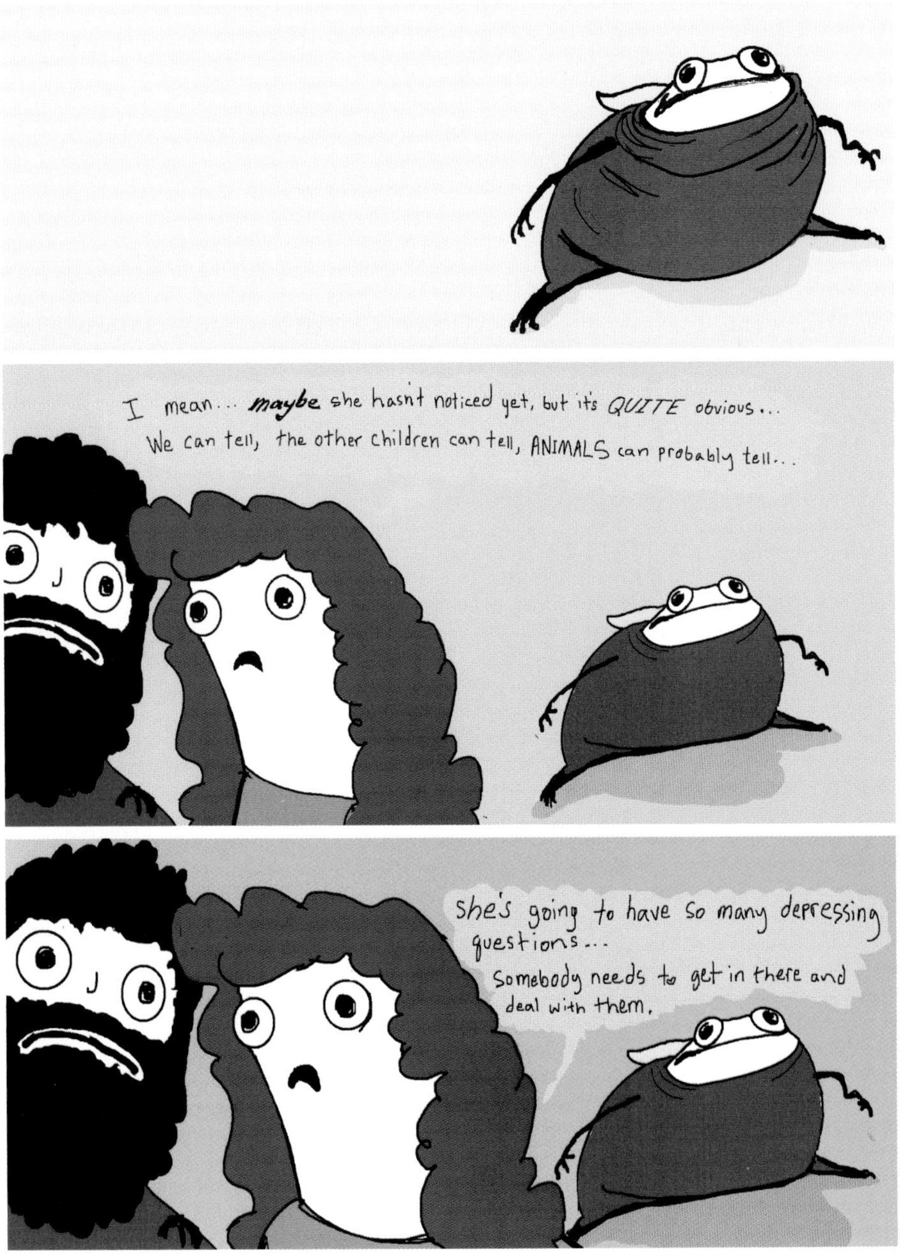
I mean... maybe she hasn't noticed yet, but it's QUITE obvious...
We can tell, the other children can tell, ANIMALS can probably tell...
She's going to have so many depressing questions...
Somebody needs to get in there and deal with them.

Nobody knows what to say to an ugly kid.

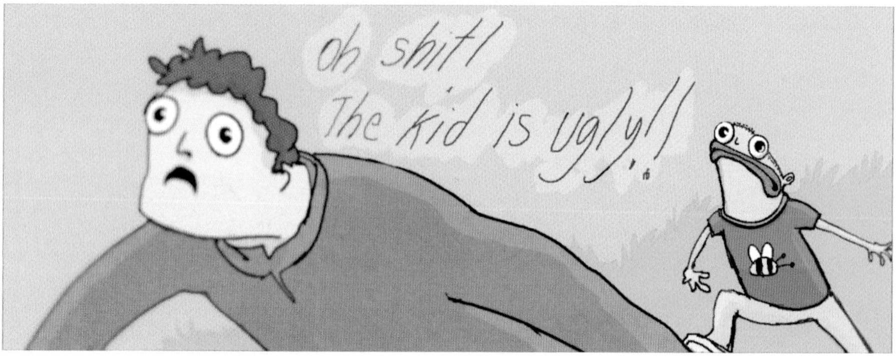
oh shit!
The kid is ugly!!

You aren't supposed to tell them the truth. What if they give up?

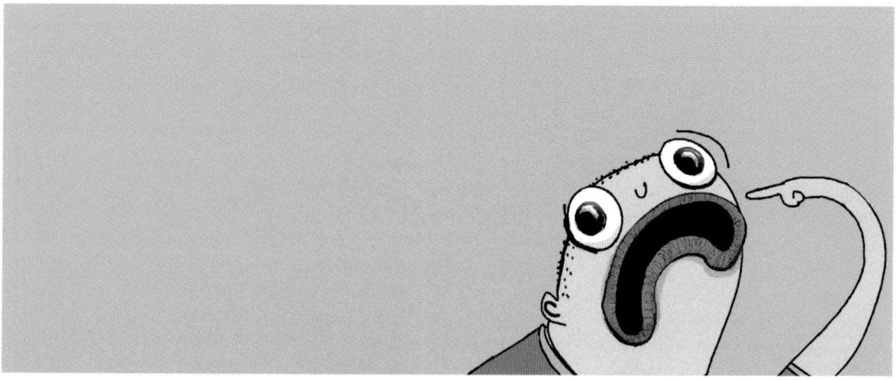

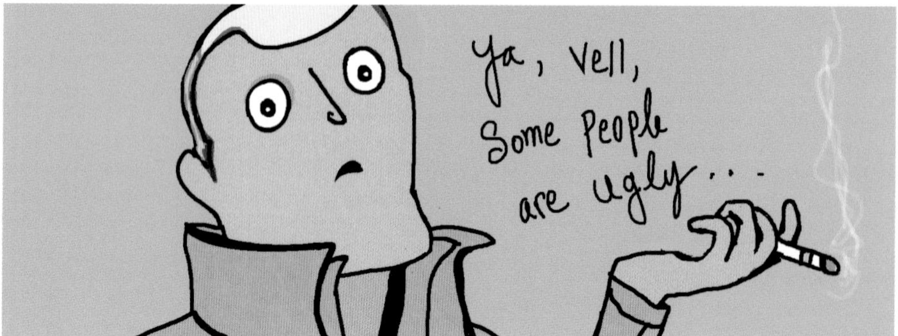
Ya, Vell,
Some People
are ugly . . .

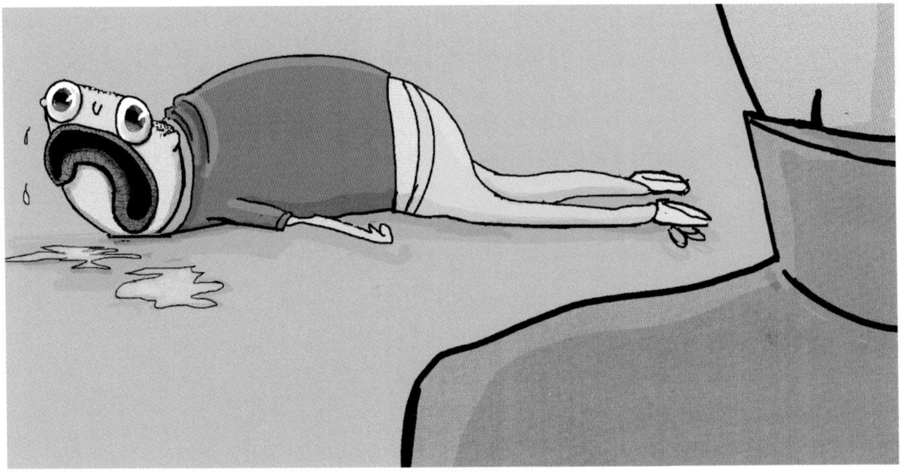

Instead, you're supposed to tell them about the Ugly Duckling.

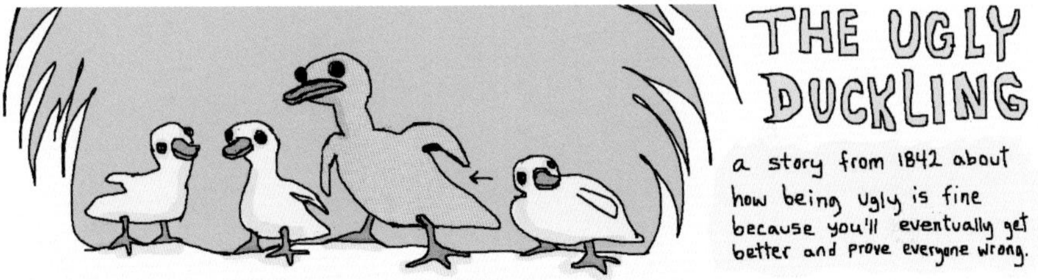
THE UGLY DUCKLING
a story from 1842 about how being ugly is fine because you'll eventually get better and prove everyone wrong.

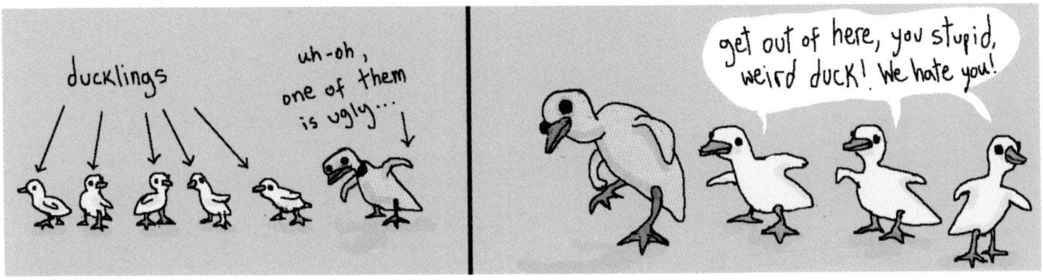
ducklings
uh-oh, one of them is ugly...
get out of here, you stupid, weird duck! We hate you!

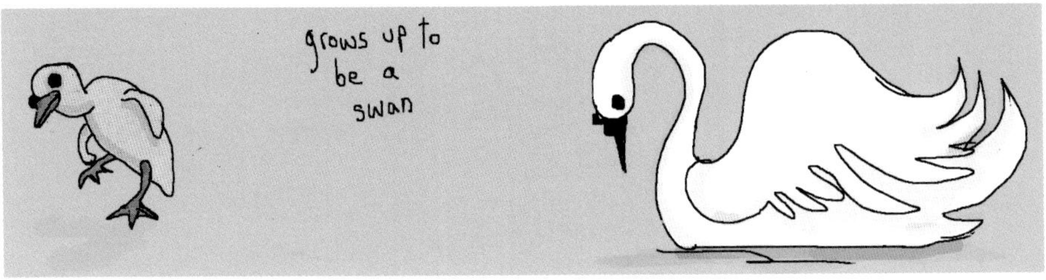
grows up to be a swan

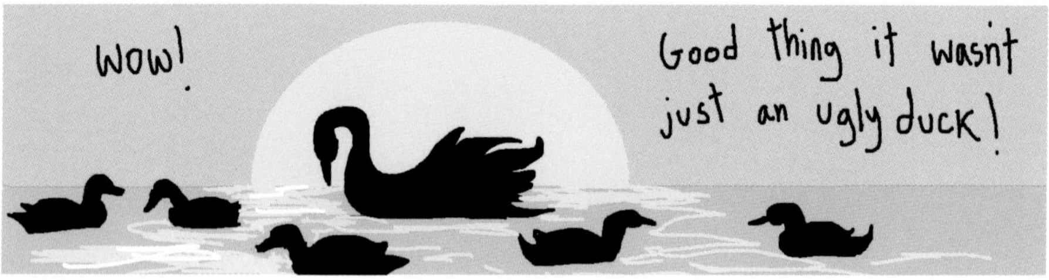
Wow!
Good thing it wasn't just an ugly duck!

I don't want to be too hard on Hans Christian Andersen because he isn't around to defend himself, but I have a difficult time believing that Hans Christian Andersen was doing the best he could and trying his hardest when he wrote *The Ugly Duckling*. The guy was a maniac. Do you know how many stories he wrote? 3,381 stories. Do you really think he thought about any of them for more than four seconds?

I'm not accusing Hans Christian Andersen of anything, but, as an ugly child, I found *The Ugly Duckling* to be an insufficient answer to my questions. And I wouldn't be surprised to find out he wrote it when he was tired and didn't want to deal with anything.

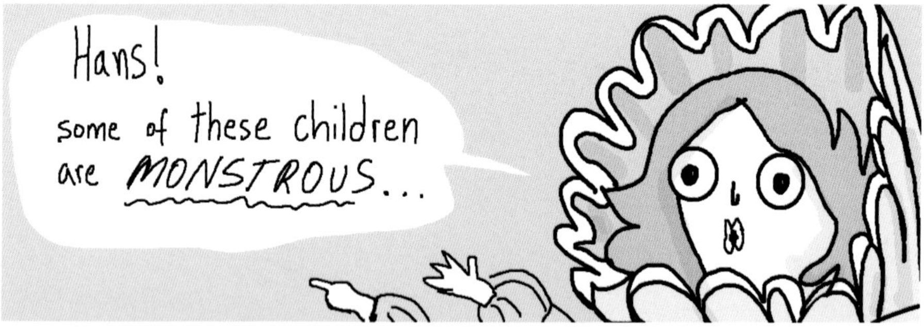
Hans!
some of these children are MONSTROUS...

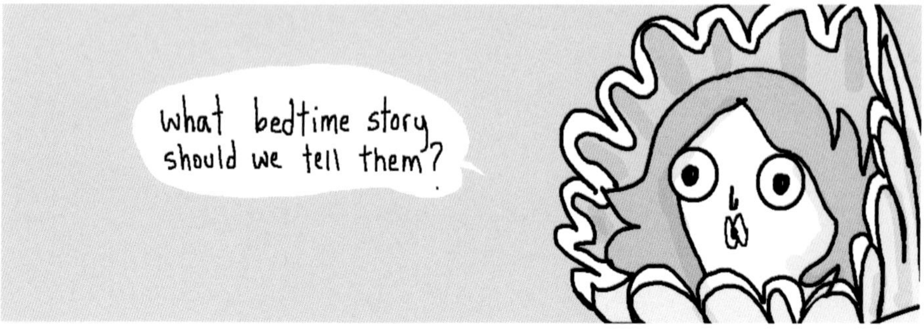
what bedtime story should we tell them?

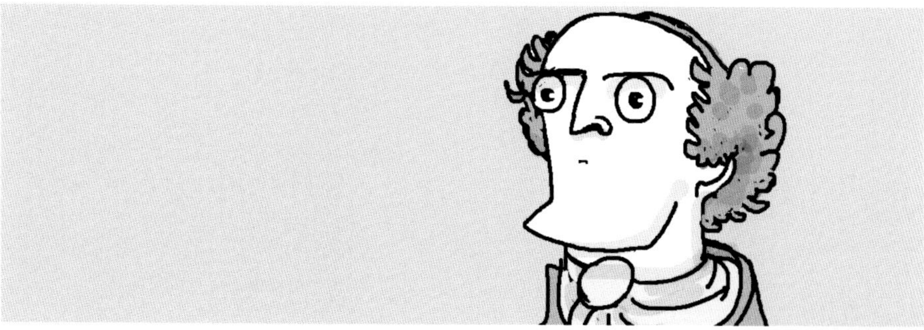

And Hans Christian Andersen just wasn't in the mood to deal with that shit. He was like, "Who knows, Felicitybelle. They can go fuck themselves."

But Felicitybelle wanted a hopeful future for those horrible, unsightly children. She stared at Hans Christian Andersen with a disappointed face until he felt obligated to take action.

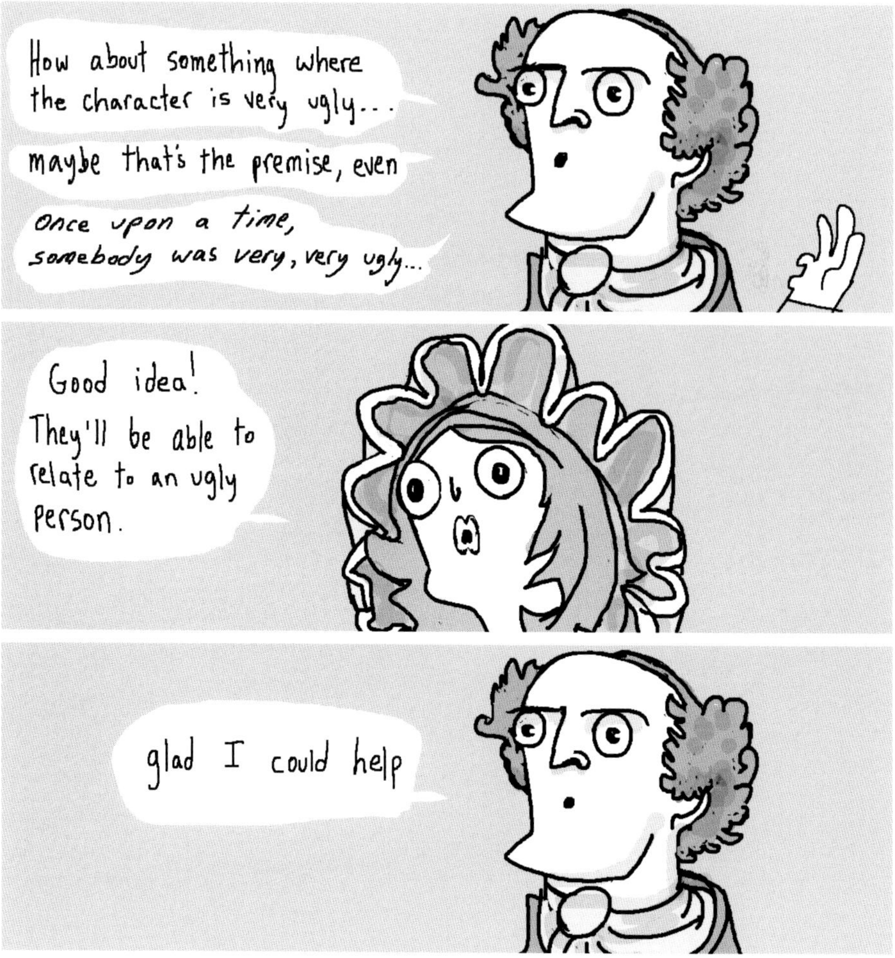
How about something where the character is very ugly...
maybe that's the premise, even
Once upon a time, somebody was very, very ugly...
Good idea! They'll be able to relate to an ugly person.
glad I could help

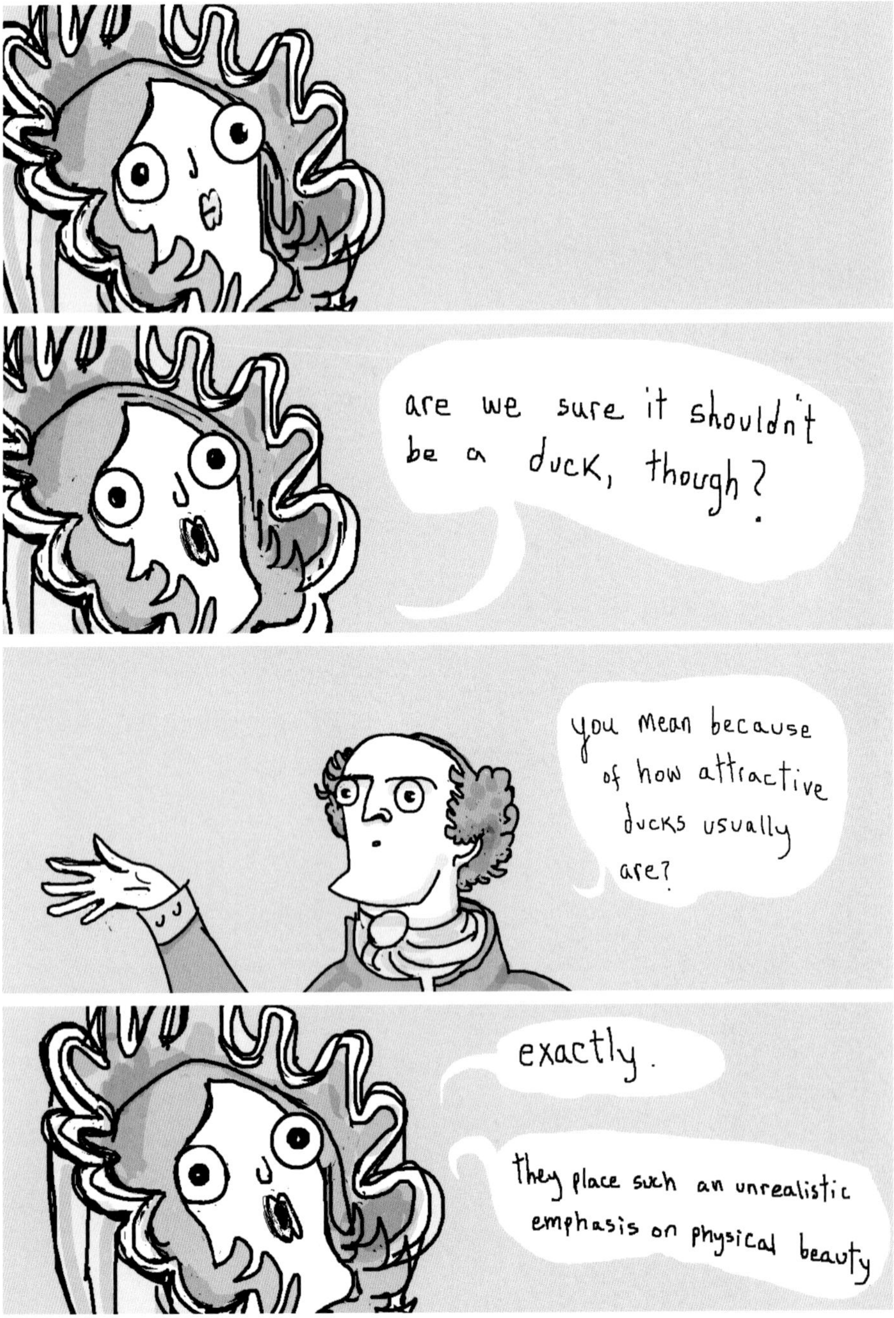
are we sure it shouldn't be a duck, though?
you mean because of how attractive ducks usually are?
exactly.
they place such an unrealistic emphasis on physical beauty

And Hans Christian Andersen was like, "Okay. The duck is ugly."

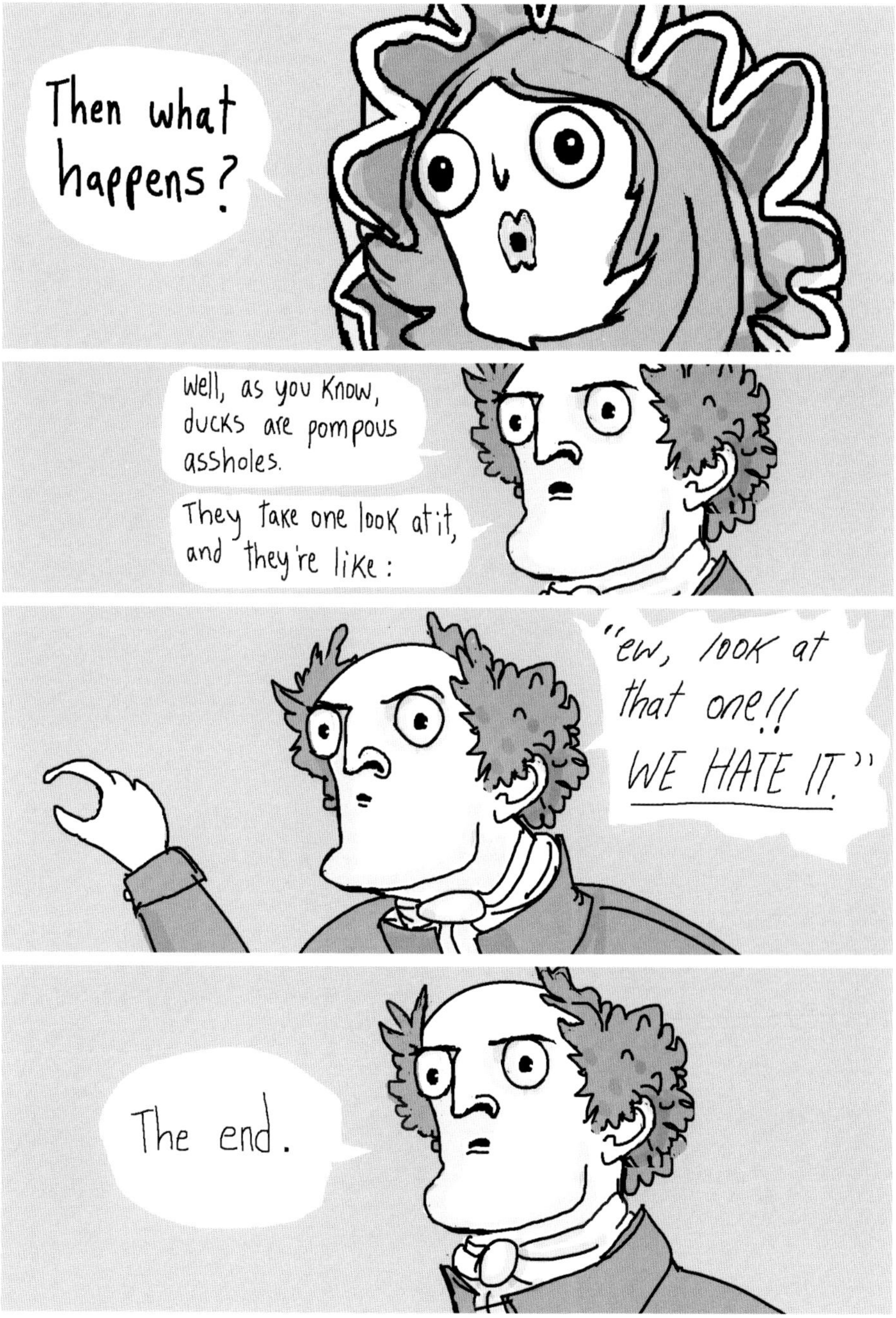
Then what happens?
Well, as you know, ducks are pompous assholes.
They take one look at it, and they're like:
"ew, look at that one!! WE HATE IT."
The end.

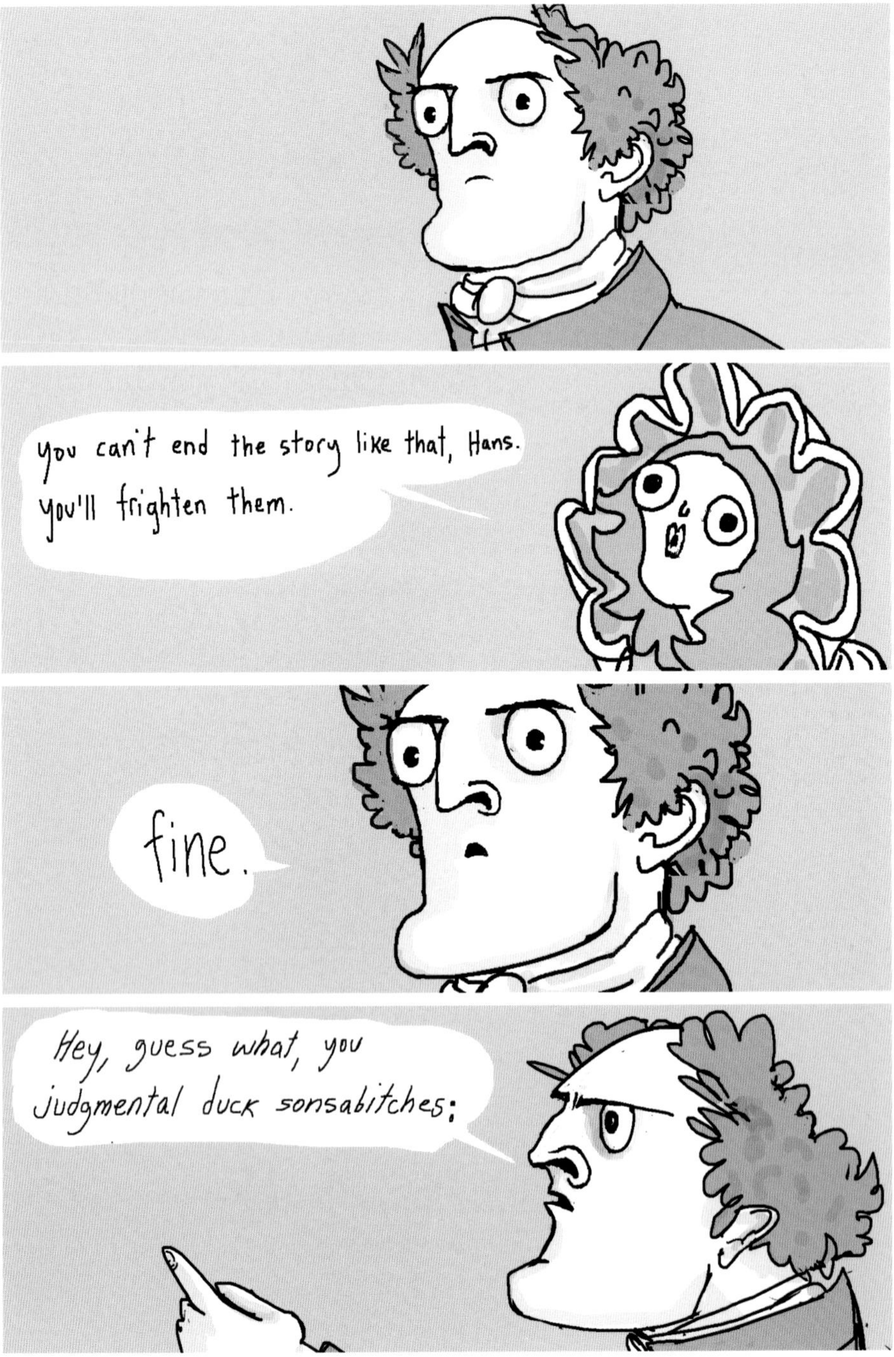
you can't end the story like that, Hans. you'll frighten them.
fine.
Hey, guess what, you judgmental duck sonsabitches:

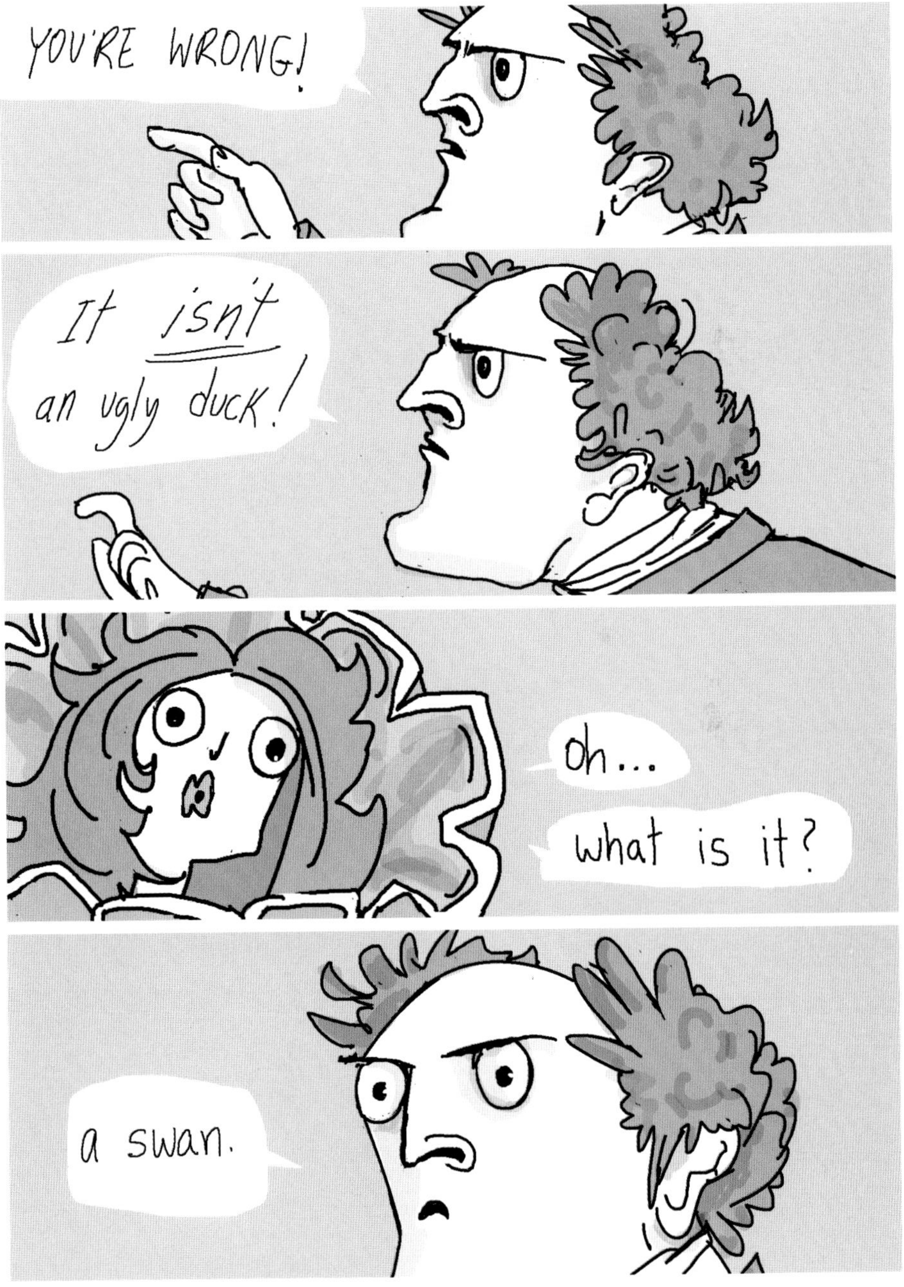
YOU'RE WRONG!
It isn't an ugly duck!
oh...
what is it?
a swan.

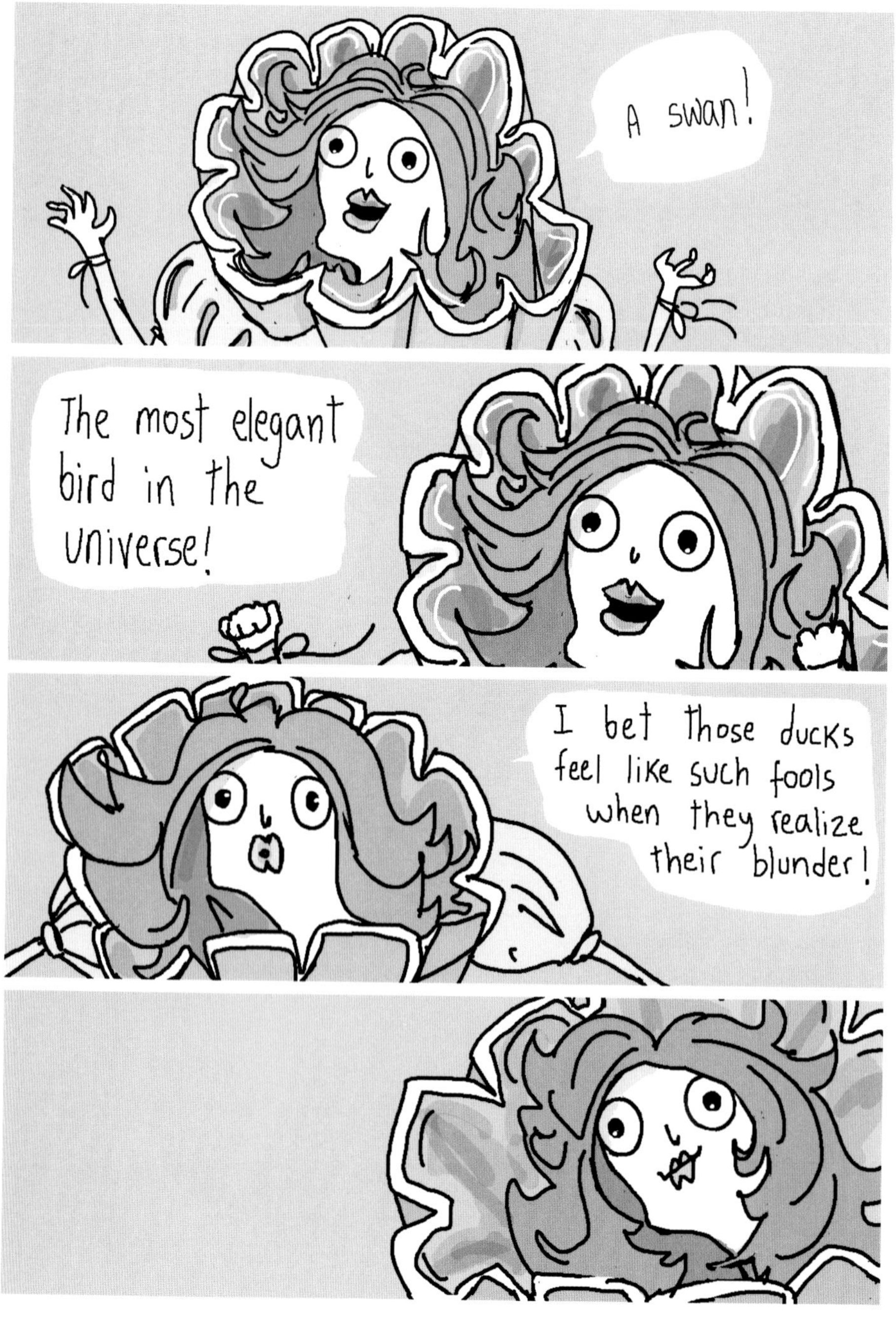
A swan!
The most elegant bird in the universe!
I bet those ducks feel like such fools when they realize their blunder!

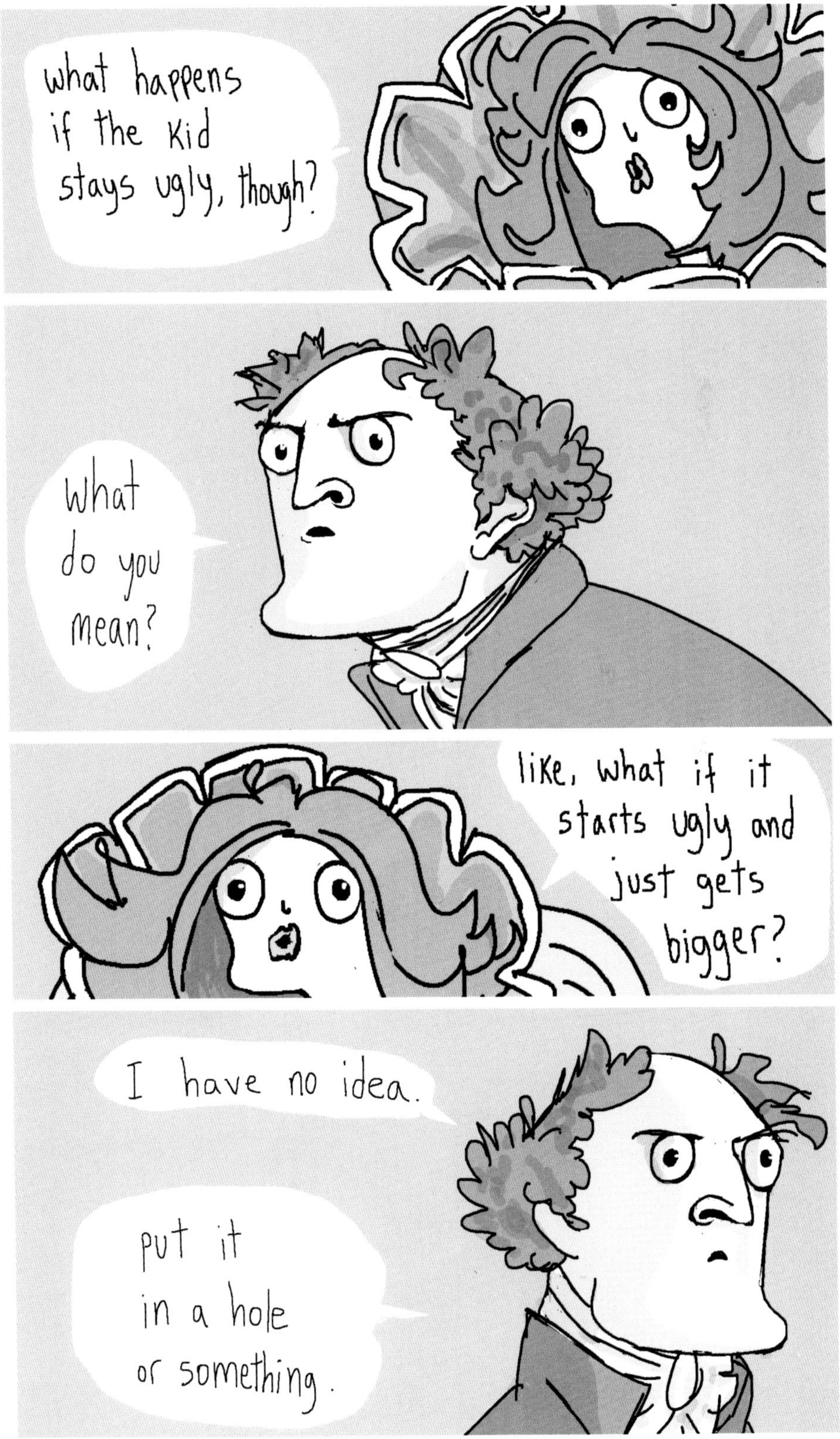
what happens if the kid stays ugly, though?
what do you mean?
like, what if it starts ugly and just gets bigger?
I have no idea.
put it in a hole or something.

And no one added anything to the discussion until 1939 when Robert Lewis May wrote *Rudolph the Red-Nosed Reindeer.* Or at least that was the main alternative presented to me.

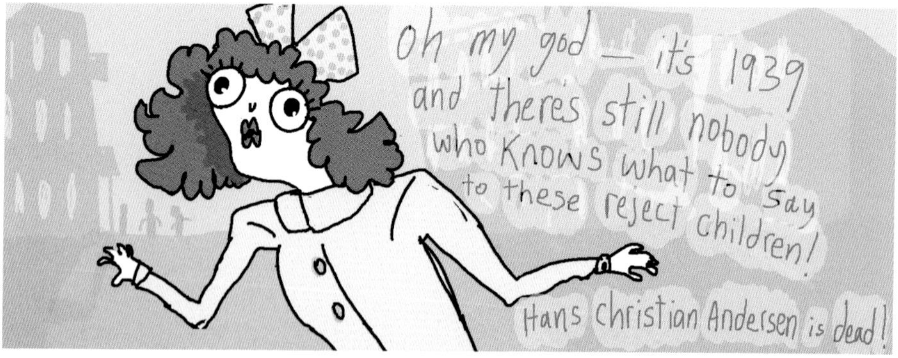
oh my god — it's 1939 and there's still nobody who knows what to say to these reject children!
Hans Christian Andersen is dead!

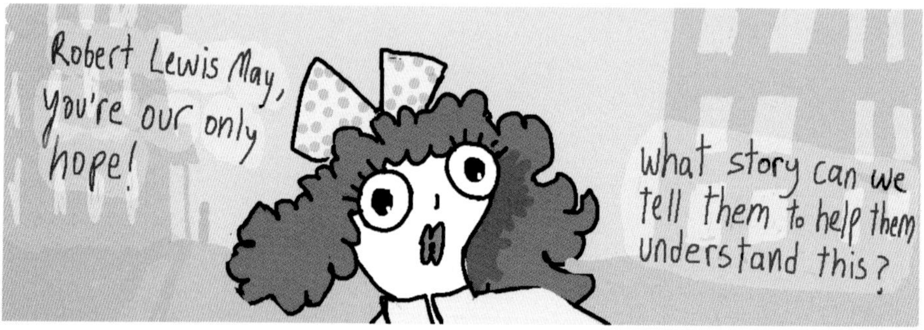
Robert Lewis May, you're our only hope!
what story can we tell them to help them understand this?

And Robert Lewis May was like:

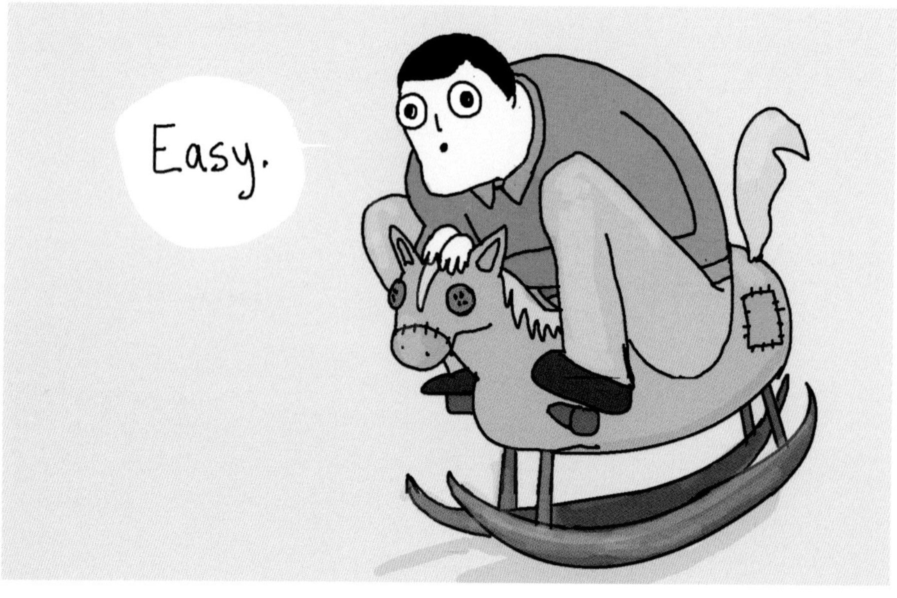
Easy.

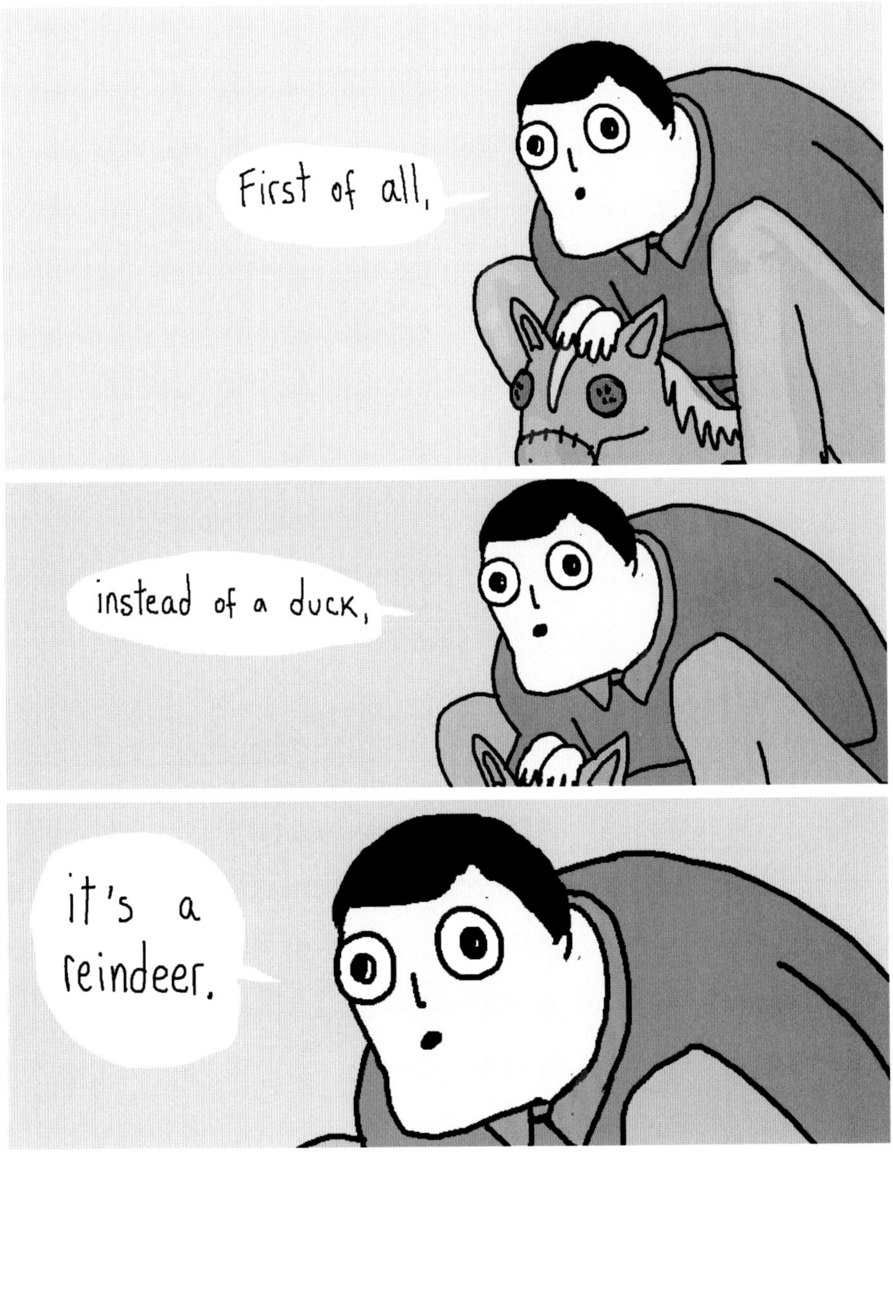
First of all,
instead of a duck,
it's a reindeer.

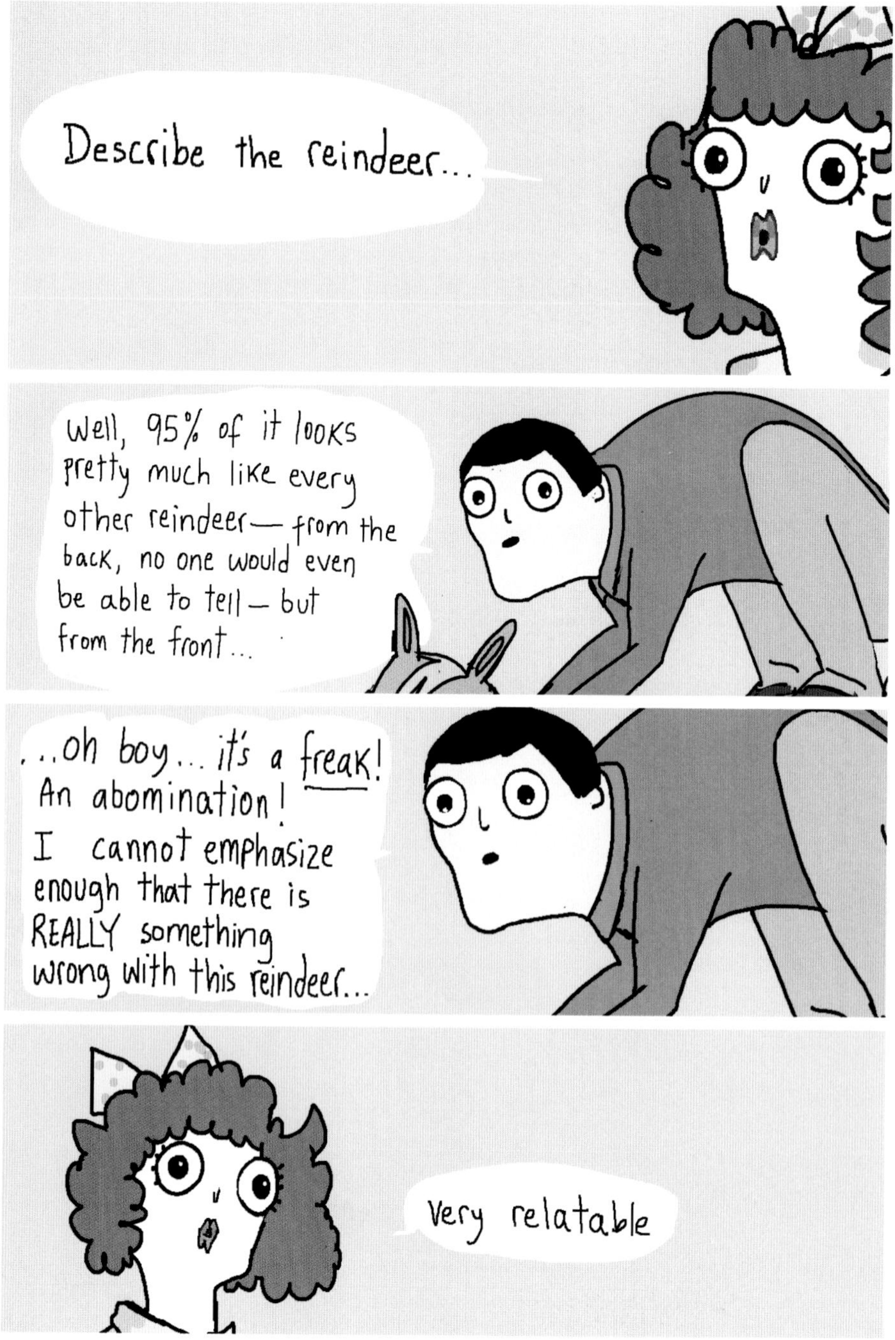

Describe the reindeer...
Well, 95% of it looks pretty much like every other reindeer— from the back, no one would even be able to tell— but from the front...
...oh boy... it's a freak! An abomination! I cannot emphasize enough that there is REALLY something wrong with this reindeer...
Very relatable

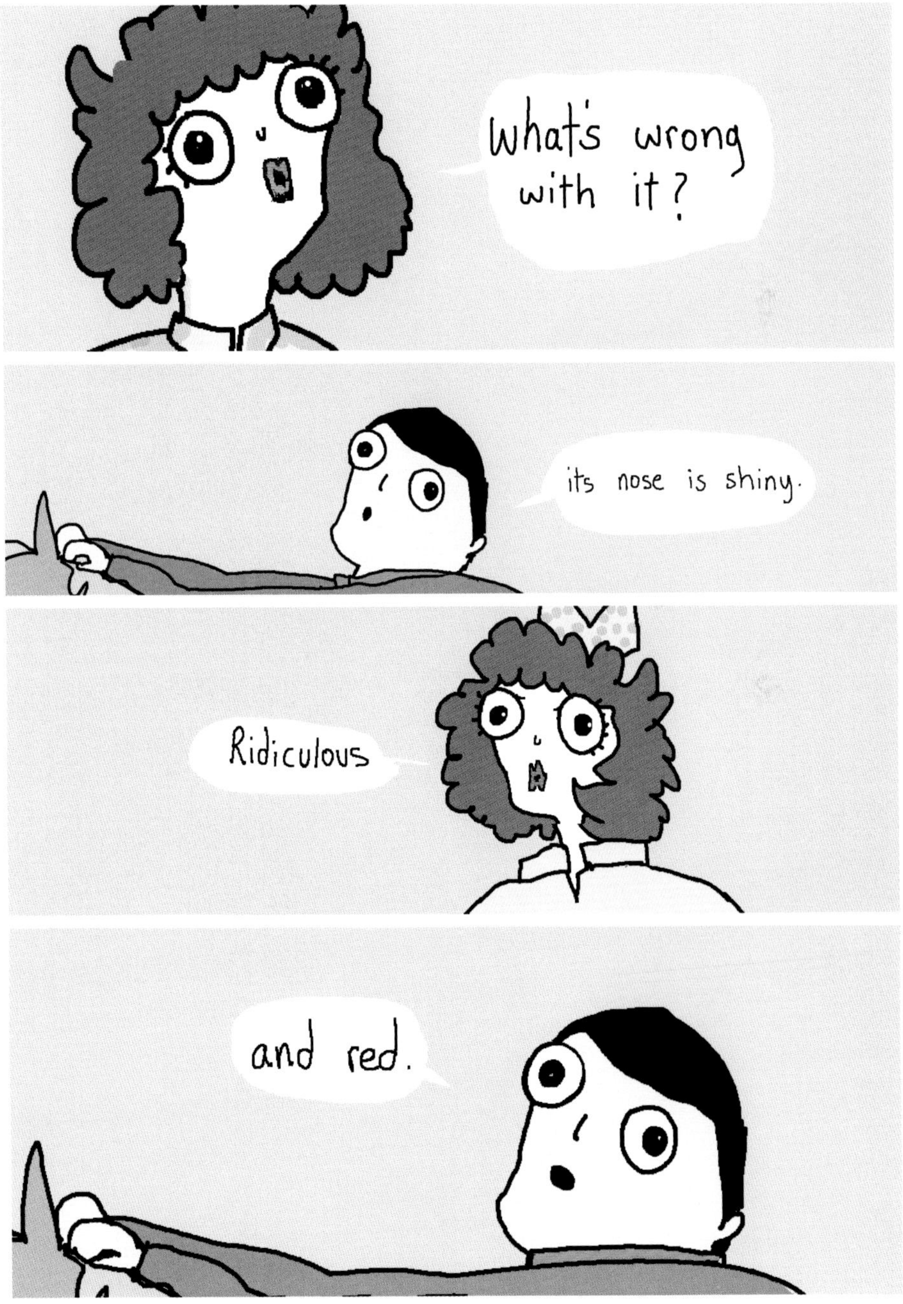
what's wrong with it?
its nose is shiny.
Ridiculous
and red.

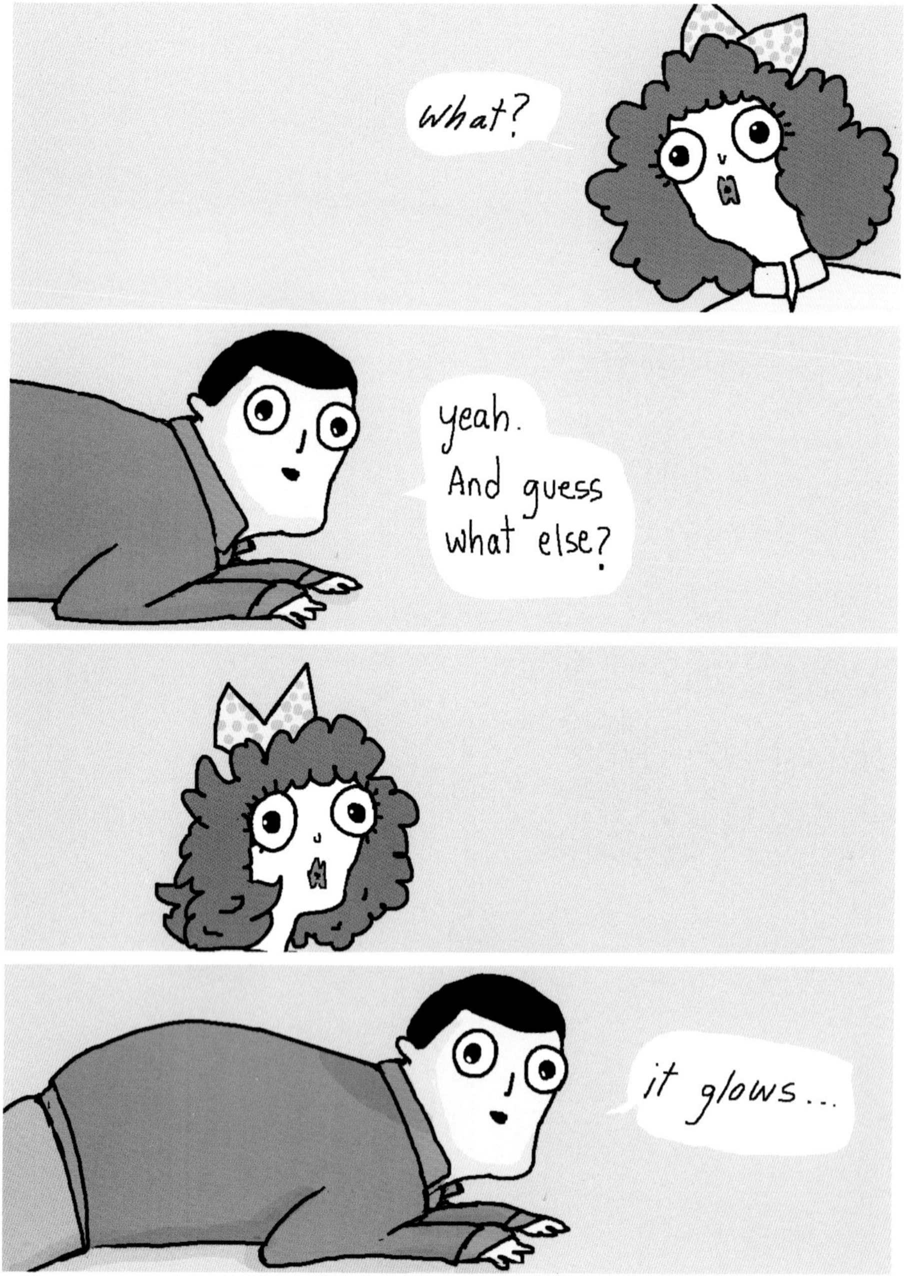
what?
yeah. And guess what else?
it glows...

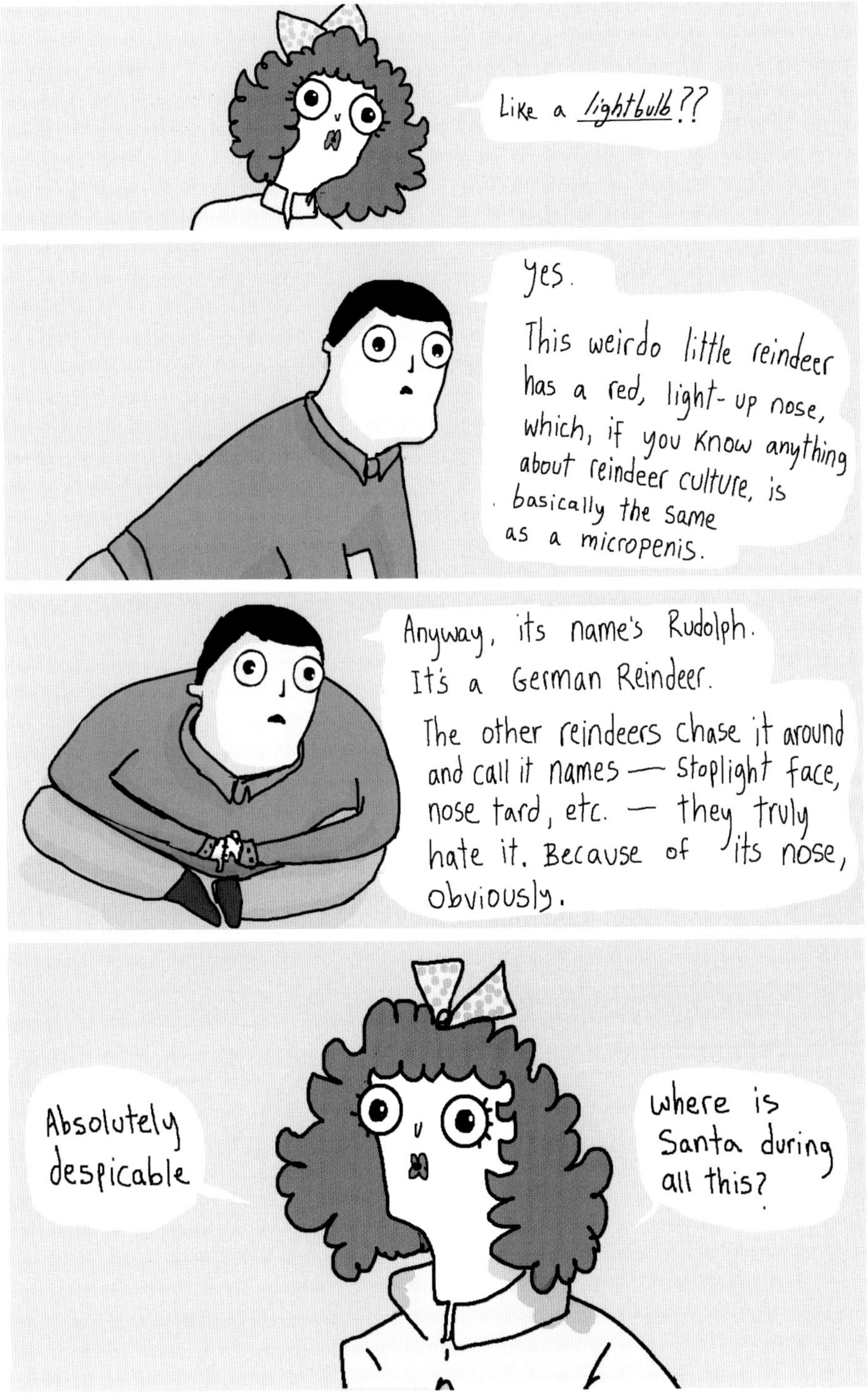

Like a lightbulb??
Yes.
This weirdo little reindeer has a red, light-up nose, which, if you know anything about reindeer culture, is basically the same as a micropenis.
Anyway, its name's Rudolph. It's a German Reindeer.
The other reindeers chase it around and call it names — stoplight face, nose tard, etc. — they truly hate it. Because of its nose, obviously.
Absolutely despicable
where is Santa during all this?

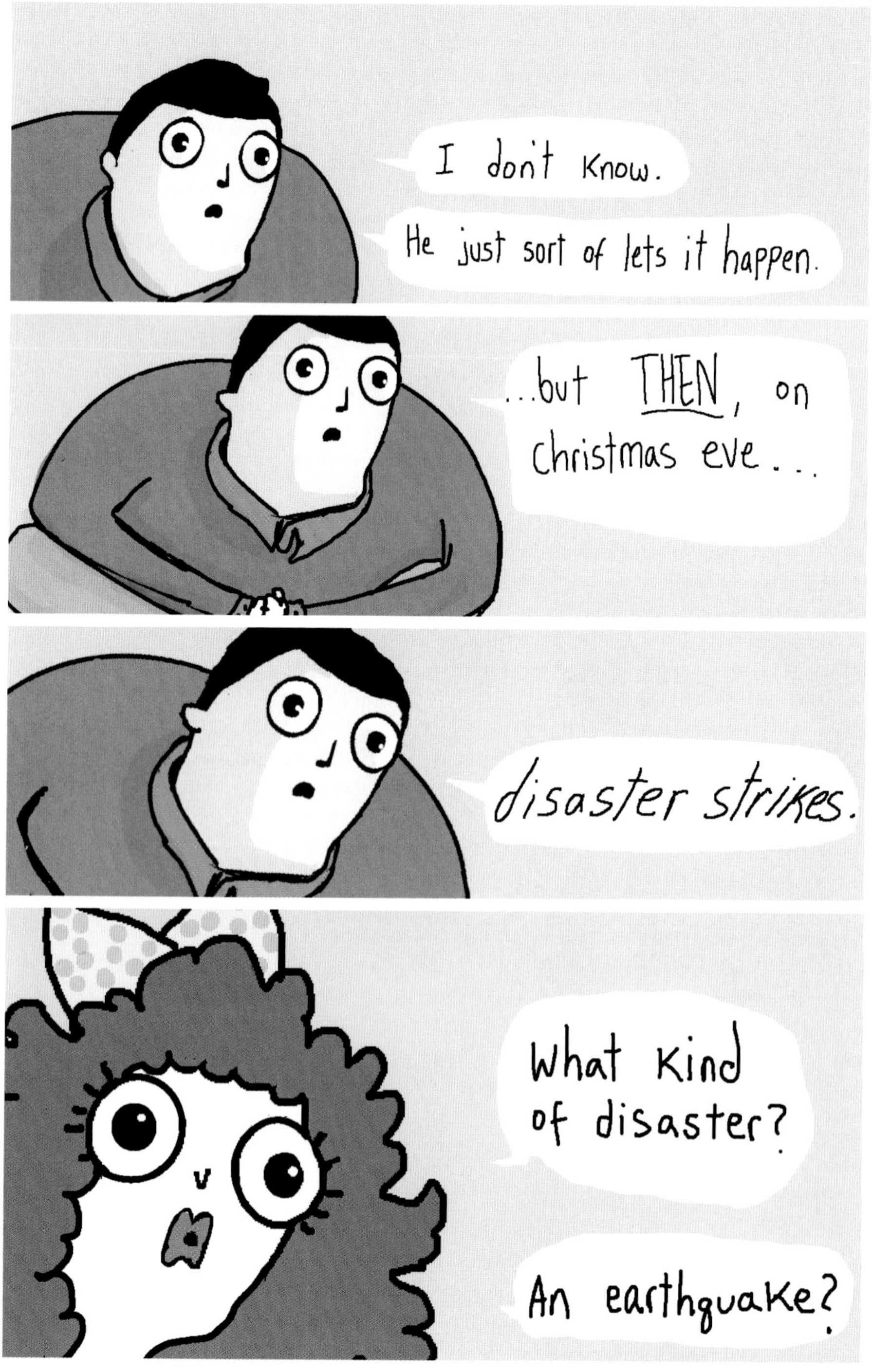
I don't know.
He just sort of lets it happen.
...but THEN, on christmas eve...
disaster strikes.
What kind of disaster?
An earthquake?

even worse...

for the first time
in the history of
christmas...

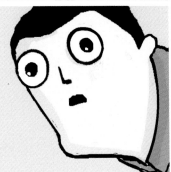

oh no...

oh no...

... it's foggy outside.

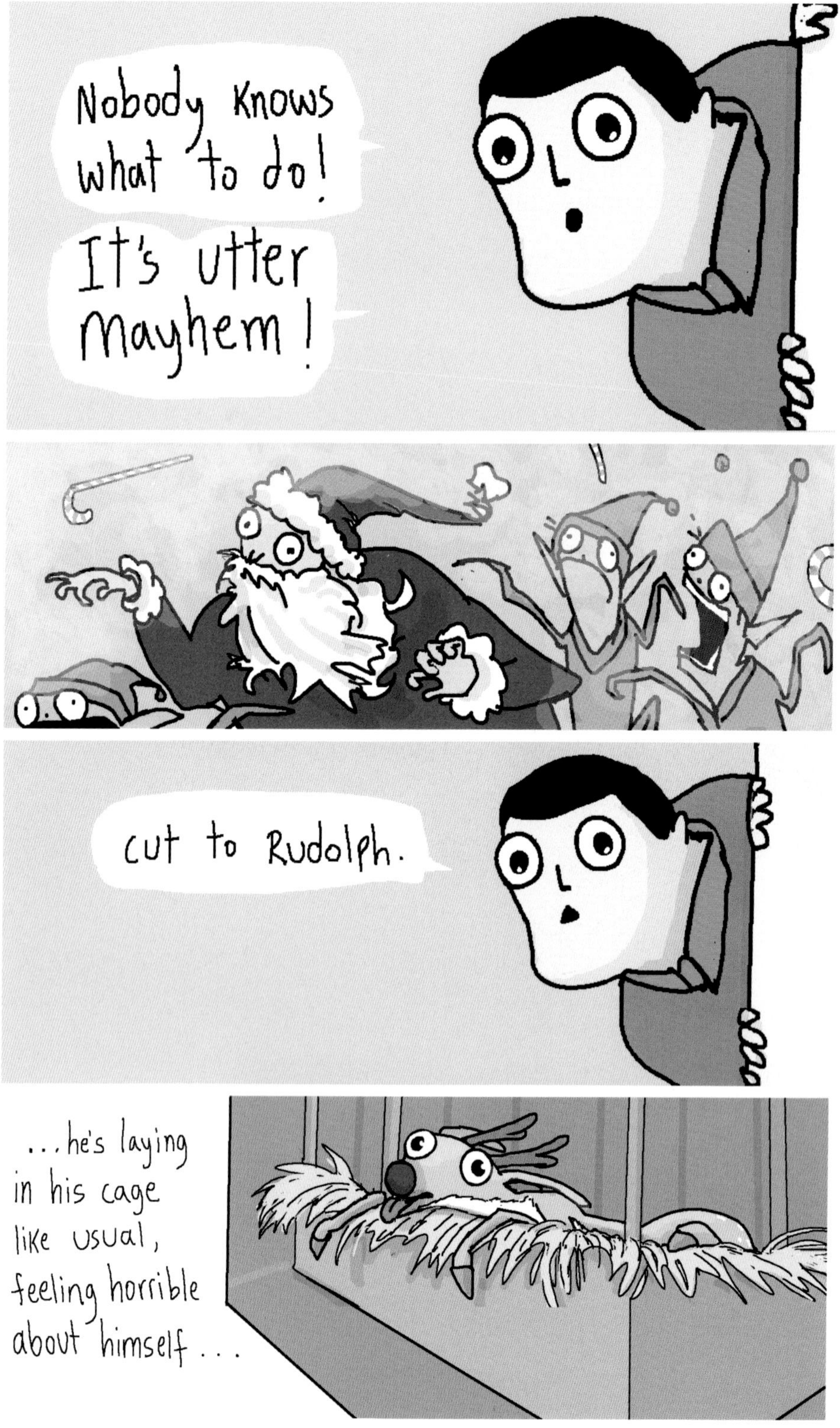
Nobody knows what to do!
It's utter mayhem!
cut to Rudolph.
...he's laying in his cage like usual, feeling horrible about himself...

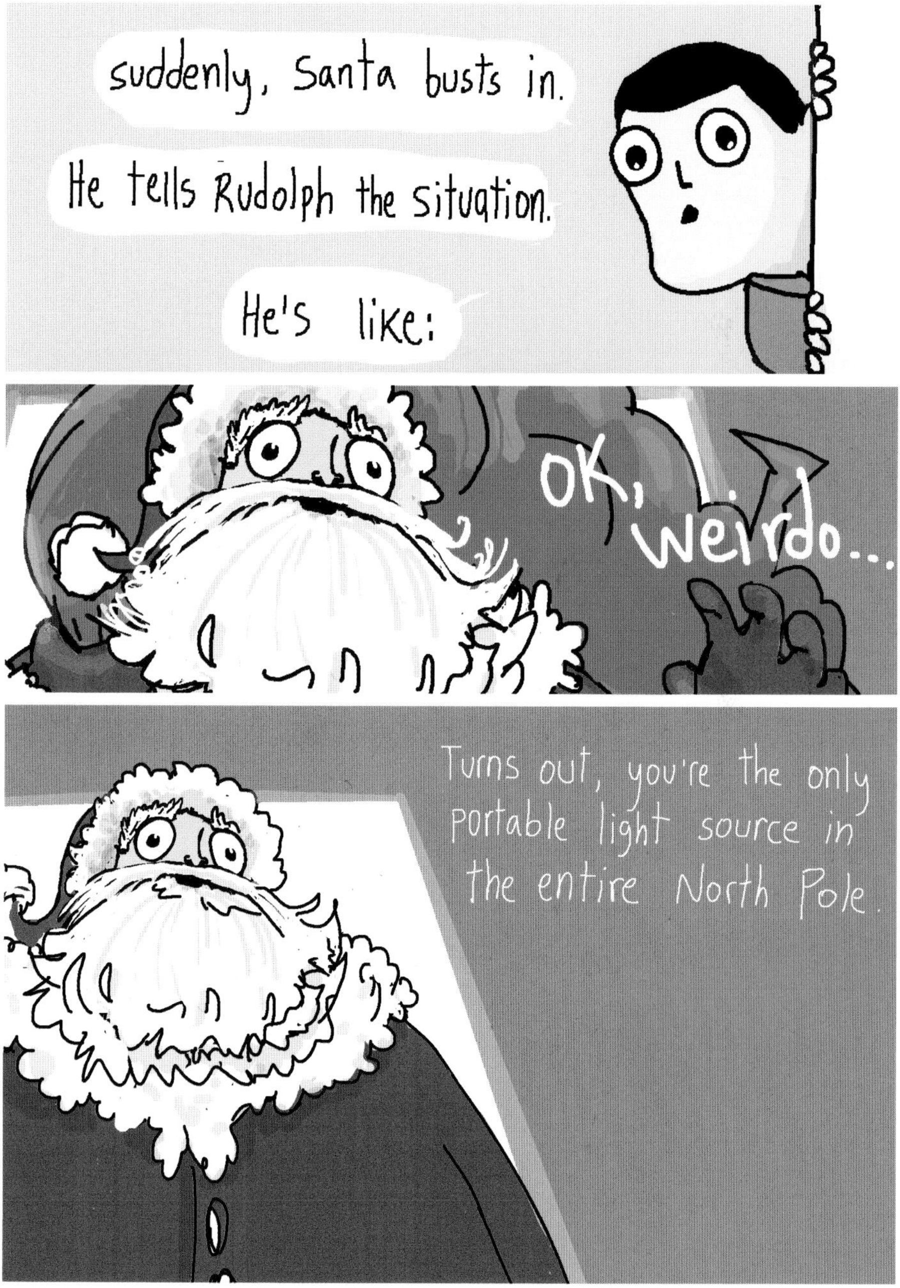
suddenly, Santa busts in.
He tells Rudolph the situation.
He's like:
OK, weirdo...
Turns out, you're the only portable light source in the entire North Pole.

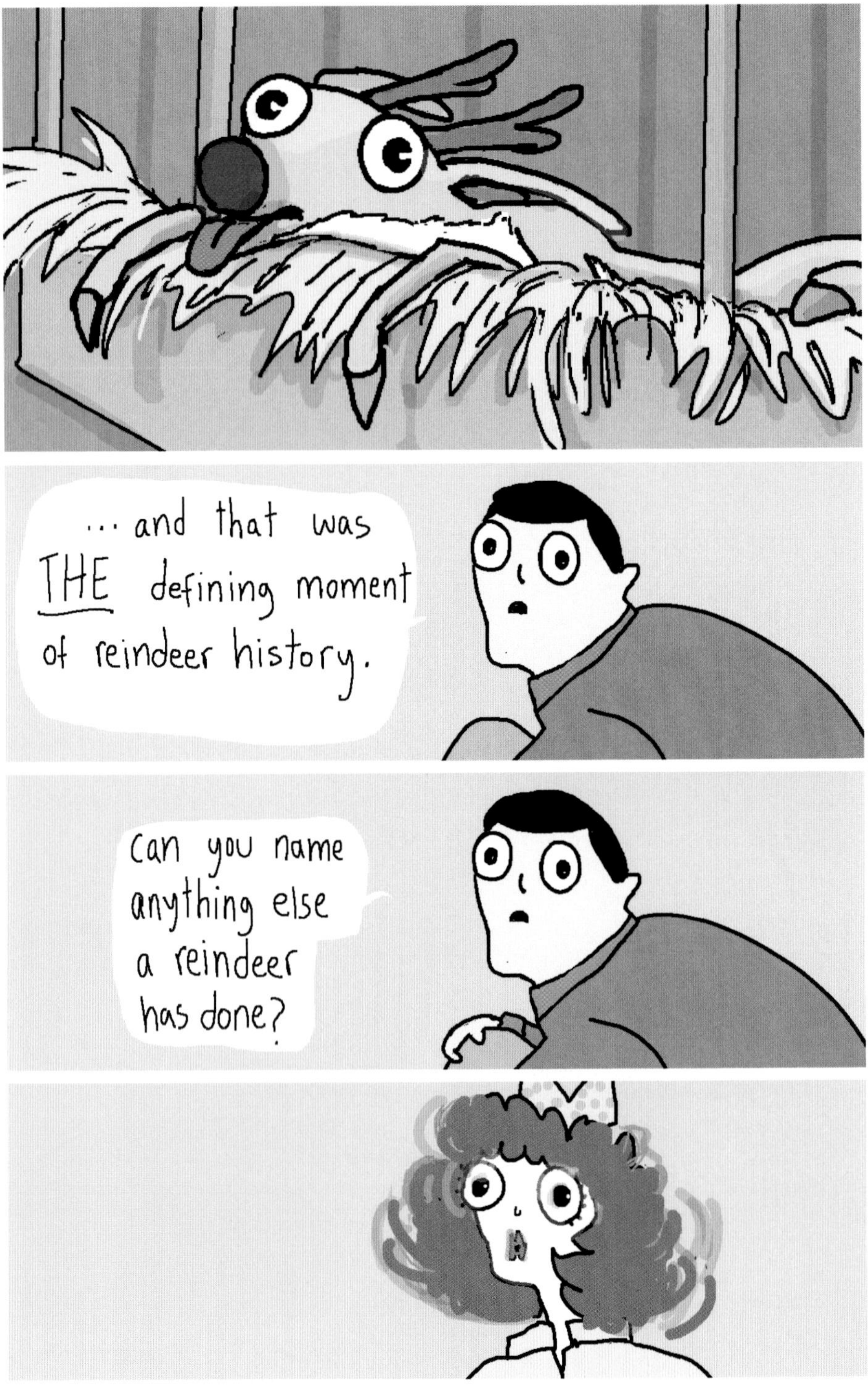
... and that was THE defining moment of reindeer history.
Can you name anything else a reindeer has done?

I also apologize to Robert Lewis May, but that is some pretty convenient logic. What is that supposed to teach me about fitting in with my peers? "Hang in there, kid—maybe there'll be some insane coincidence where your exact defect is the only solution, and everyone will be forced to accept you based on your utility"?

What do I do if there isn't? What do I do if I'm useless and ugly forever?

I'm probably not the best person to be doing this, but sometimes you have to be the change you want to see in the world, and if you can't be beautiful enough for everybody, the next best option is animal stories.

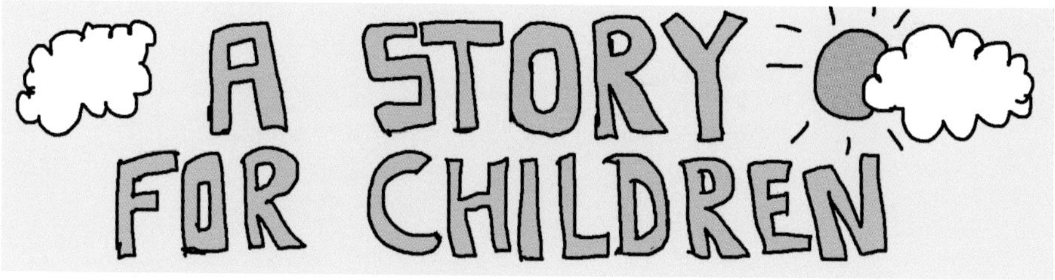
A STORY FOR CHILDREN

Dear Children:

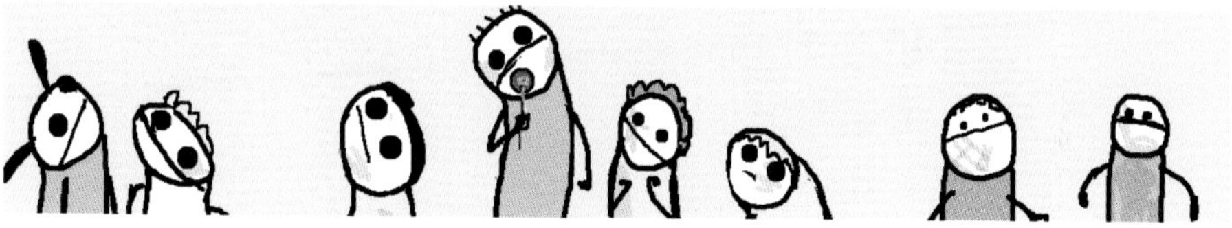

Once upon a time, there was an ugly frog.

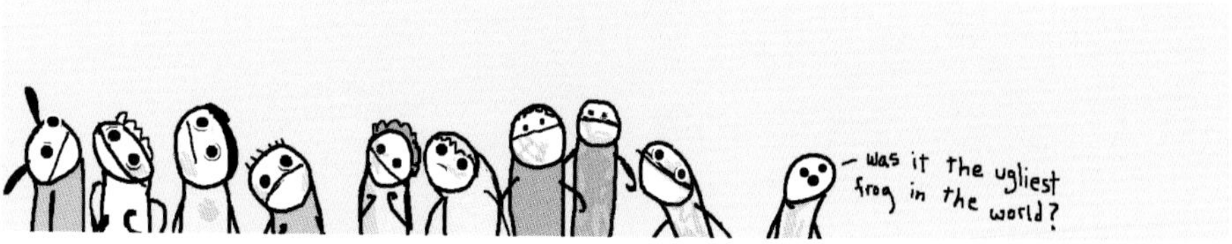
—was it the ugliest frog in the world?

Yes. It was the ugliest frog in the world.

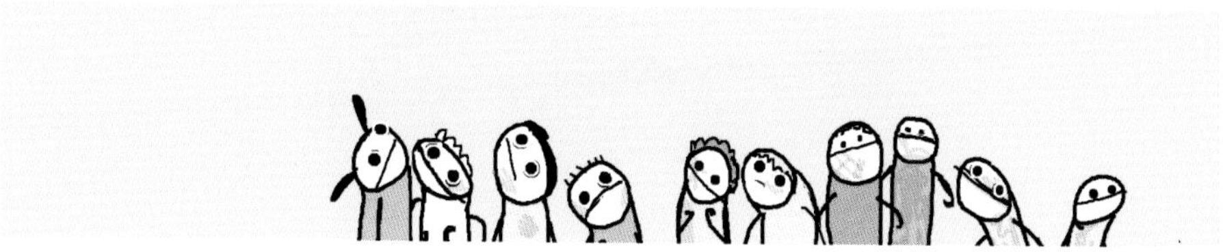

Anyw—

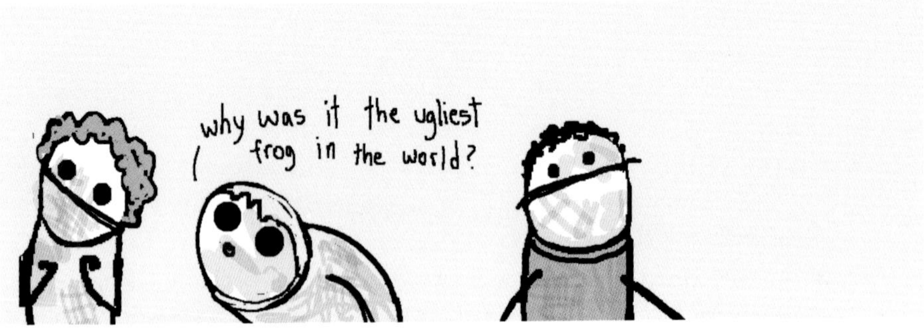
why was it the ugliest frog in the world?

Why is anything the worst anything.

It is in our nature to compare things. We should not feel bad about this, but we should also be aware of how silly it is to look at a frog and think we know where it ranks on the Best Frogs of All Time scale. Why do we even have that scale? They're frogs. Let them be.

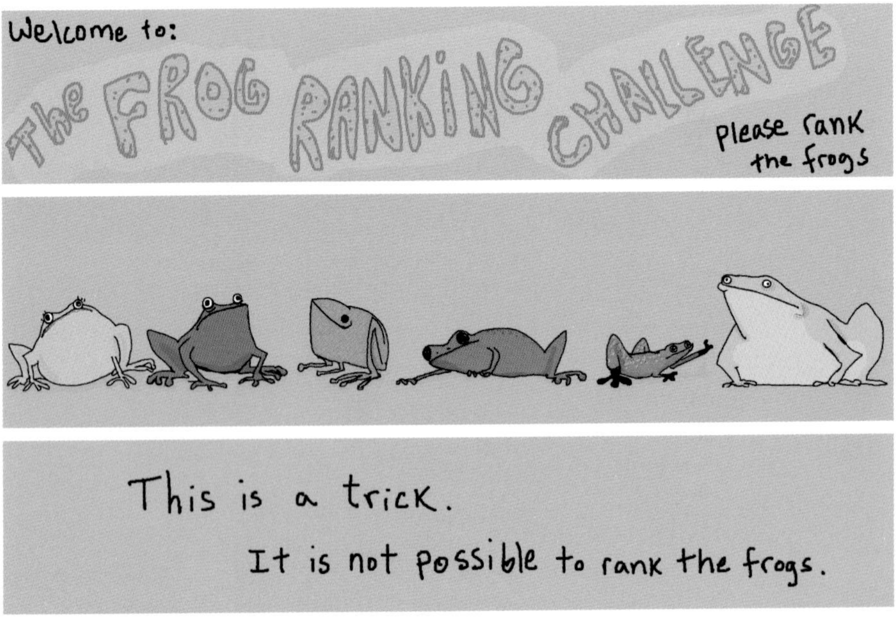
Welcome to:
THE FROG RANKING CHALLENGE
please rank the frogs
This is a trick.
It is not possible to rank the frogs.

I think what I'm trying to say is: there's no real way to tell who the ugliest frog is, and it doesn't particularly matter, but, if it will be more exciting for you, we can say this is the ugliest frog.

weird face
neck too short
ew, tiny legs
what is that
purple spot
do you know any frogs worse than this?

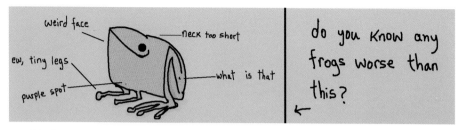

You've heard stories before, so right now, you're probably thinking, *Yeah, but that's just where the frog starts. Surely the rest of the story is about the frog's journey to success.*

No. That is not where the story is going. First of all, there is no such thing as a successful frog.

What is the point of telling us about the frog?

Oh, I'm sorry—does the frog have to be beautiful and successful before we can talk about it? Is that how the world works? We only get to talk about frogs who are amazing? Guess what, children—this isn't even a real story. It's just a ruse to teach you a lesson about life.

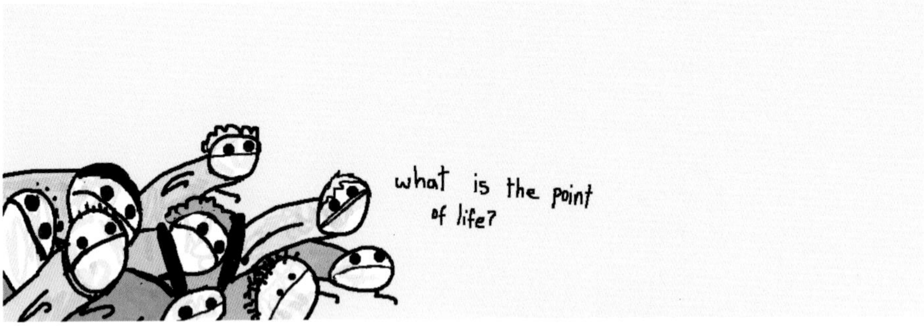
what is the point of life?

I'm glad you asked, children.

As far as we can tell, life does not have a point.

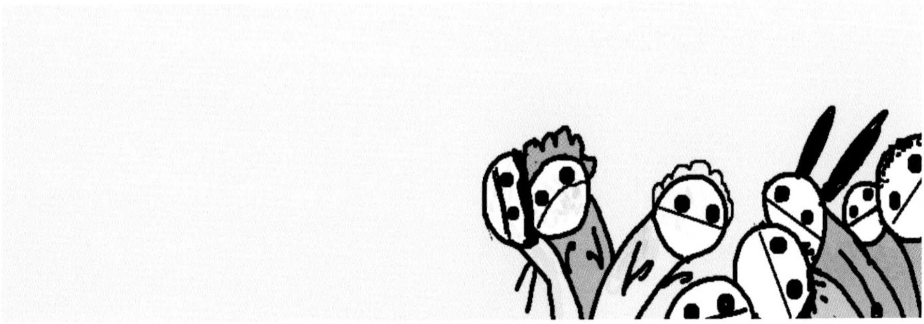

There is no need to be frightened. Yes, an invisible stranger just told you that life is pointless, but, much like this story, life doesn't need a point. I mean, it can have one if you want. Go ahead—pick one. Whatever you want. Count all the rocks. Get faster at singing. Be as nice as possible. Grow 500 pumpkins and put them in a pile. But there's nothing that requires life to have a point.

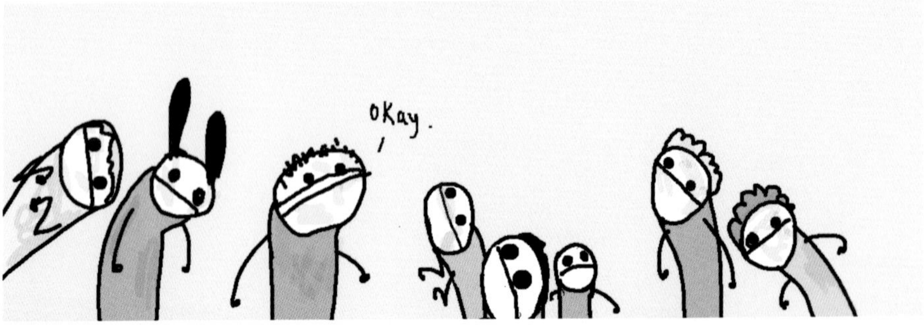
okay.

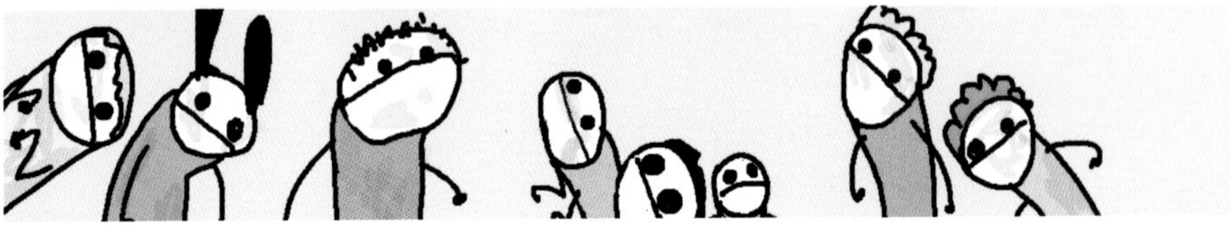

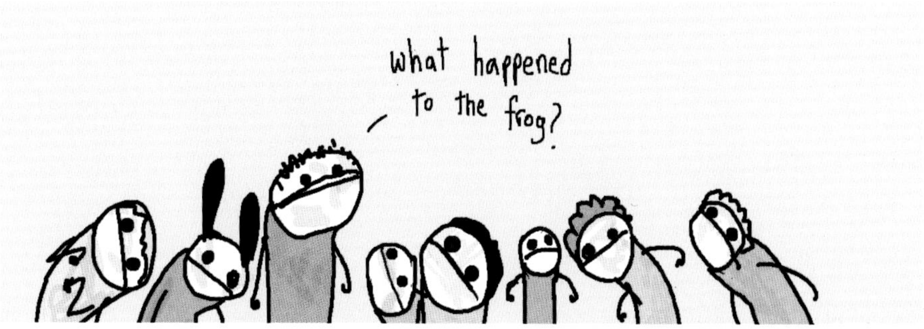
what happened to the frog?

Children . . . I'm trying my absolute best to explain the meaning of life to you. It's honestly sort of disturbing that you're stuck on the frog still. Do you know the frog? Does the frog need to be okay for you to be okay?

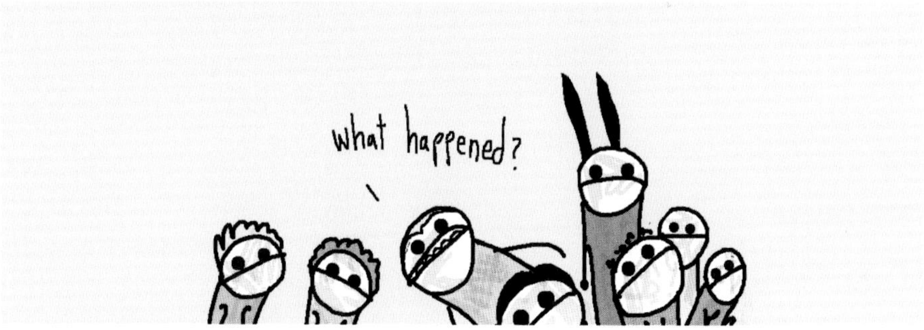
what happened?

What if I don't know what happened?

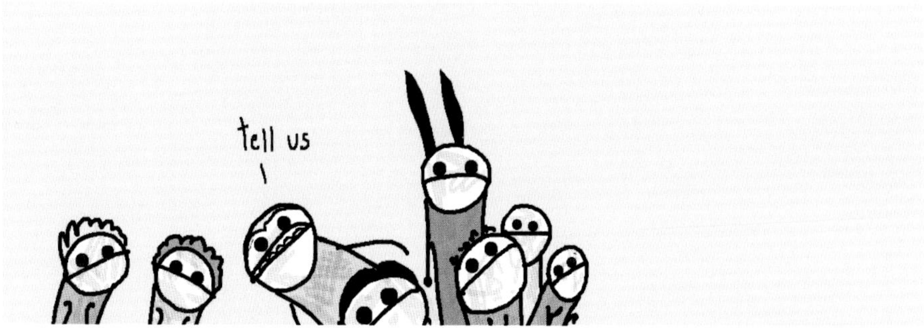
tell us

The frog isn't real, okay? I made it up.

There is no frog, life is pointless, and nobody knows what's going to happen. I'm very sorry to inform you of this, but if you grow up only reading happy stories where you find out the answers to all your questions, you will be scared and confused and probably die in a dumpster fire. It is better to accept the utter futility of things as early as possible and save yourself the struggle.

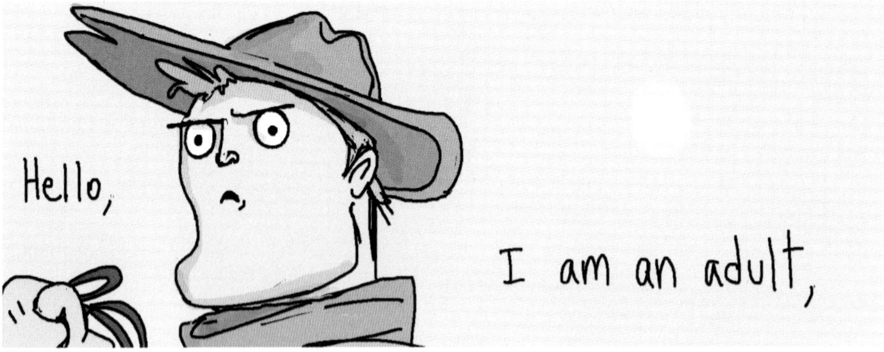
Hello,
I am an adult,

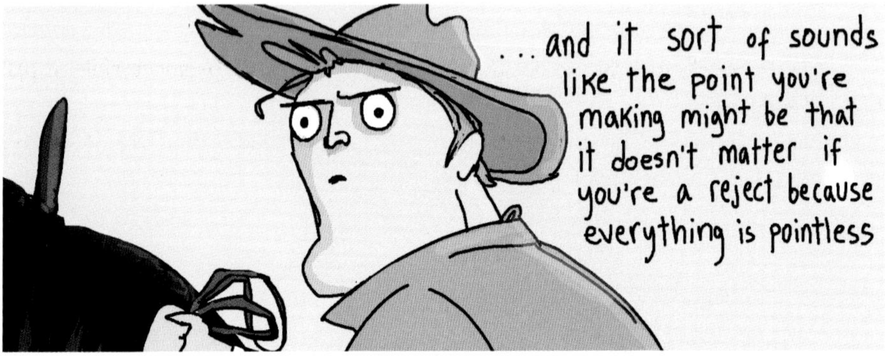
...and it sort of sounds like the point you're making might be that it doesn't matter if you're a reject because everything is pointless

Sorry.

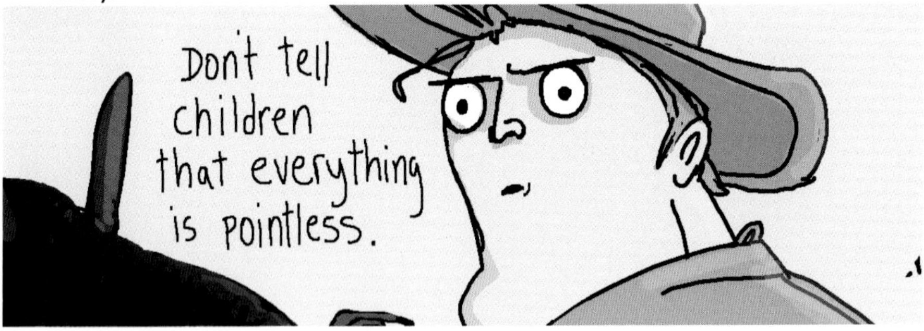
Don't tell children that everything is pointless.

I'm really sorry.

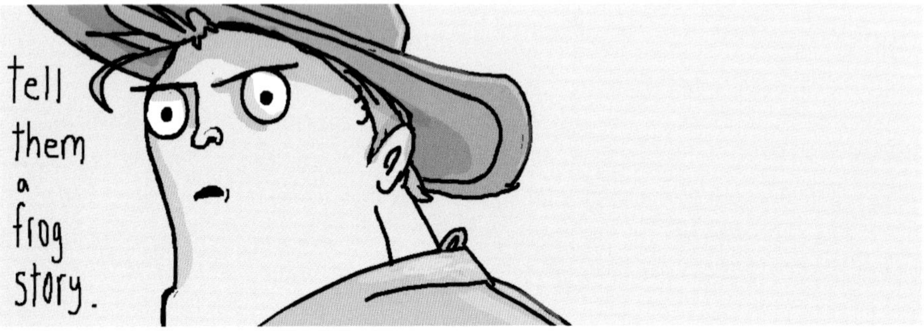
tell them a frog story.

Hello again, children. Once upon a time, there was an ugly frog.

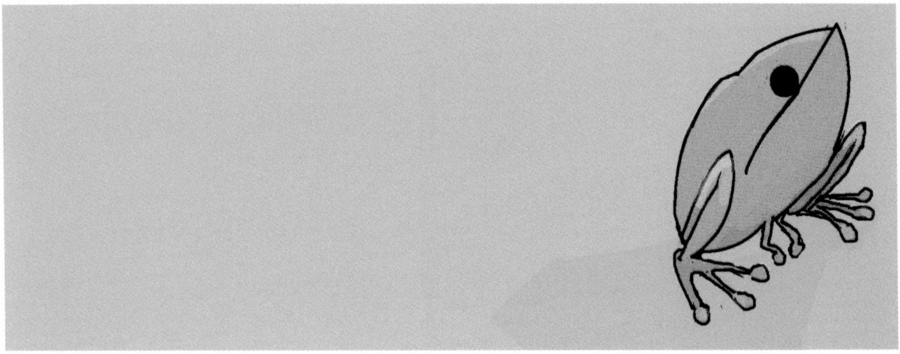

And the world isn't fair, so it didn't grow up to be pretty or successful—it just stayed how it was.

Then one foggy Christmas Eve, the frog realized that everything is equally ridiculous. And it went sledding because why not.

21. THROW-AND-FIND

By the time I was ten, I had adapted almost every friendship activity there is into either a single-player format, or a format that supports two players, but one of them is a dog that hates games.

That's how Shrimp Hide-and-seek was invented.

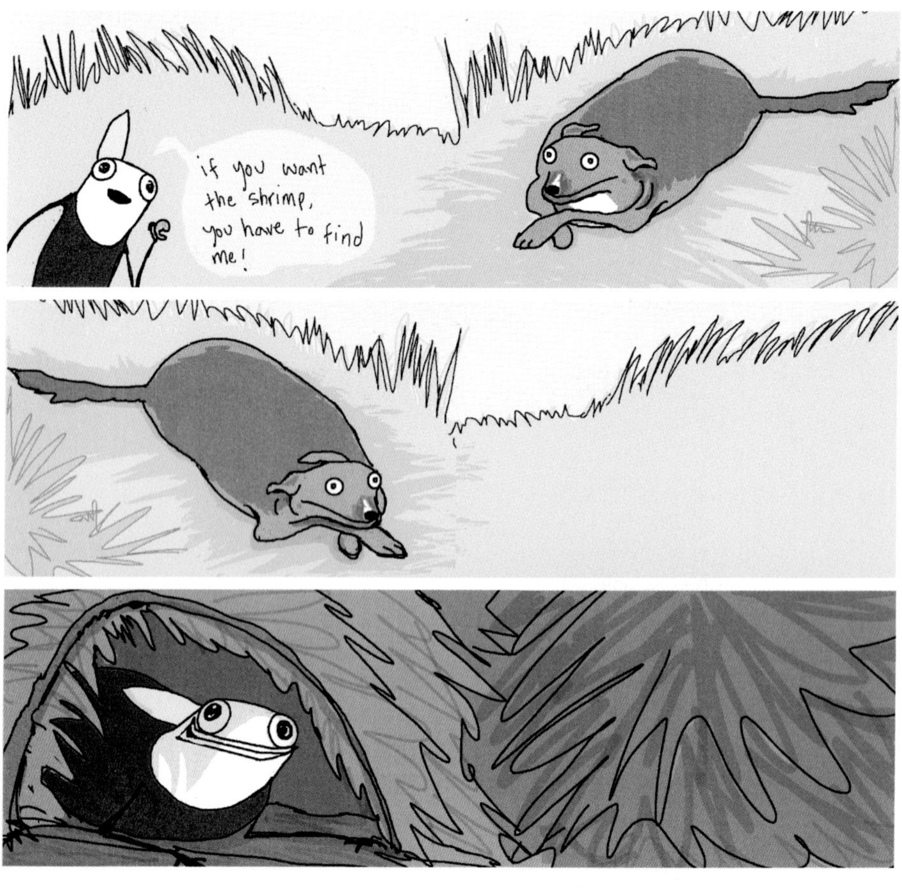
if you want the shrimp, you have to find me!

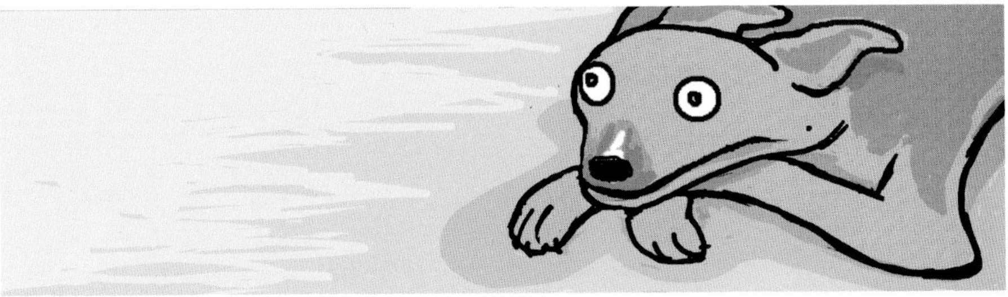

I also figured out how to play a crude version of tag by exploiting a basketball's natural tendency to roll downhill.

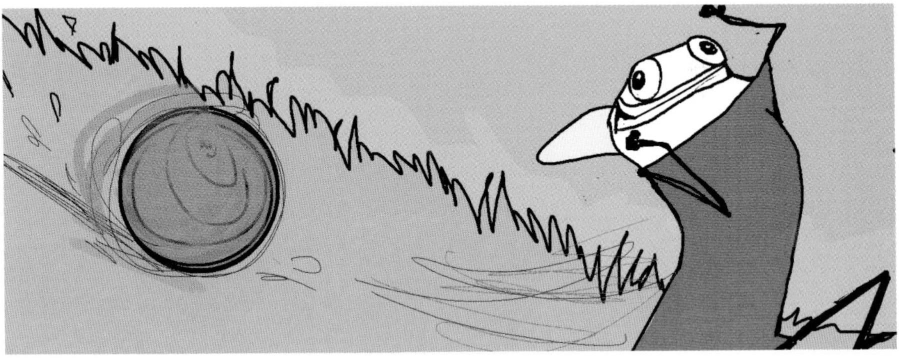

A few years ago, I came across the official rules for an original game I created called Throw-and-Find. I don't know how necessary it was to write down the rules for Throw-and-Find, but I did. You know—for the scenario where you remember your favorite game is Throw-and-Find, but you don't remember the exact details of how to play.

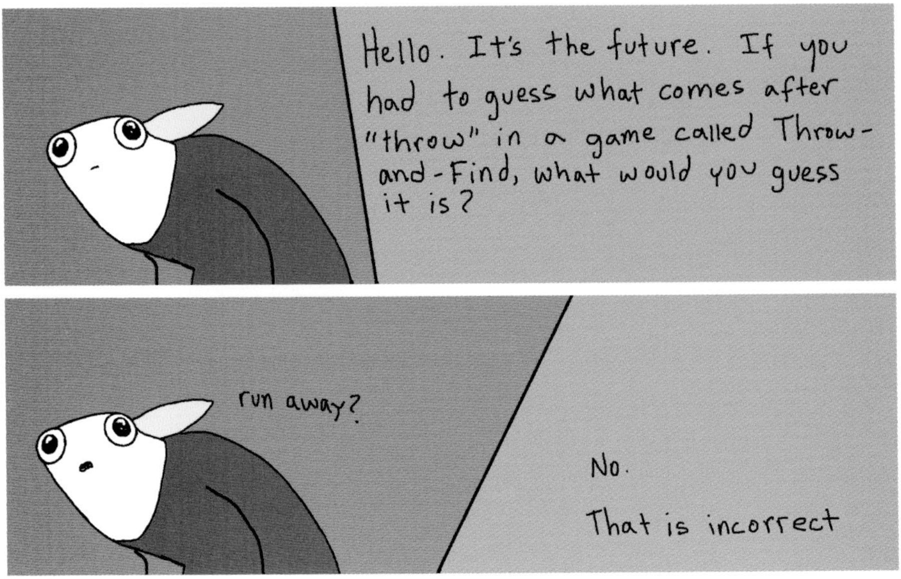
Hello. It's the future. If you had to guess what comes after "throw" in a game called Throw-and-Find, what would you guess it is?
run away?
No.
That is incorrect

Here are the official rules:

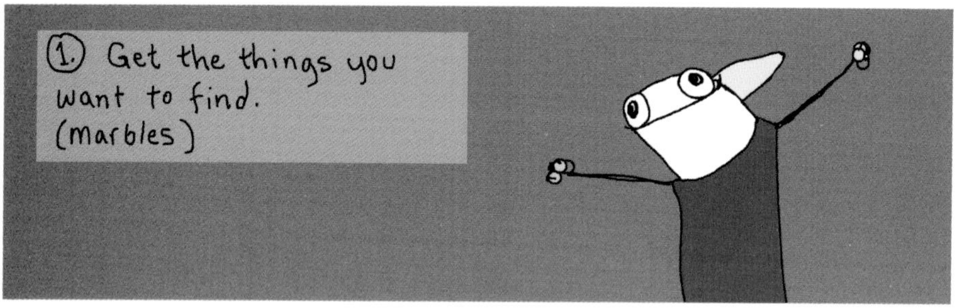
1. Get the things you want to find. (marbles)

Maybe you think you want to find a potato today, but you're wrong. Marbles are what you want to find. Or perhaps "(marbles)" is a friendly suggestion. *It's okay if you can't think of anything to find ... here's an example to get you started!*

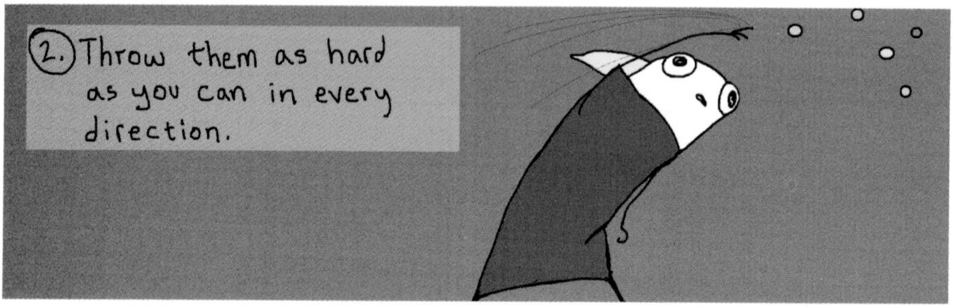
2. Throw them as hard as you can in every direction.

Every direction. Throw those marble sonsabitches in so many directions you don't know where'ta even START lookin'.

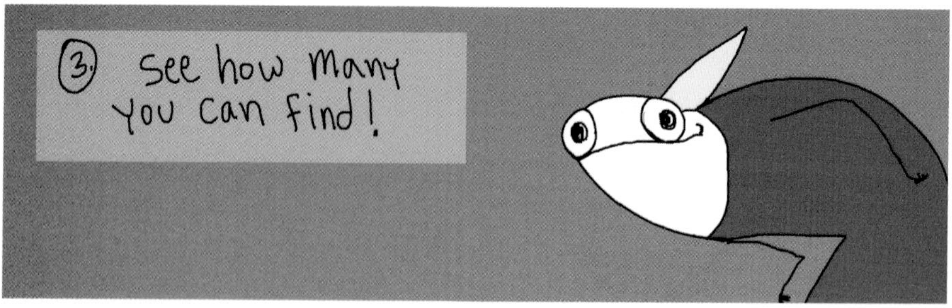
3. See how many you can find!

The exclamation point is heartbreaking. *Are you ready, Scooter? Really, really ready? Ready to find some marbles? Okay ... go get 'em!!*

There was no points system, no strategy. I didn't need them. I just liked finding things, but didn't know anyone who would hide them for me.

22. SISTER

It would have made sense to be friends with my sister.

We were both children. We were both stranded at least 20 miles from the alternatives. There was even a lot we could relate to each other about, probably.

Knows mom and Dad
Also Knows mom and Dad
Likes building sandcastles
Likes destroying sandcastles
good at finding
good at hiding

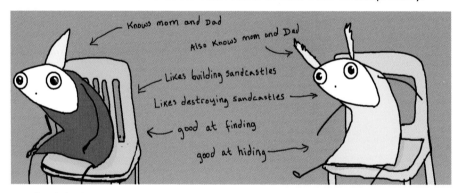

But I think at some point we'd gotten the impression that we were rivals. Maybe there was a famine or something. Who knows. But it stayed like that.

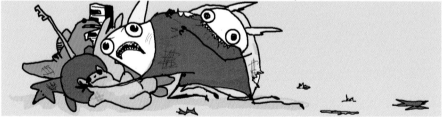

I do remember feeling envious of her friendships. They had so much fun. They invented a game called Marble Bla-Bla where you sing a crazy song and throw marbles at the ceiling fan. Yes: marbles. She loved them too. And only now, as I'm writing this 20 years later, am I making the connection that our interests lined up fucking *perfectly*.

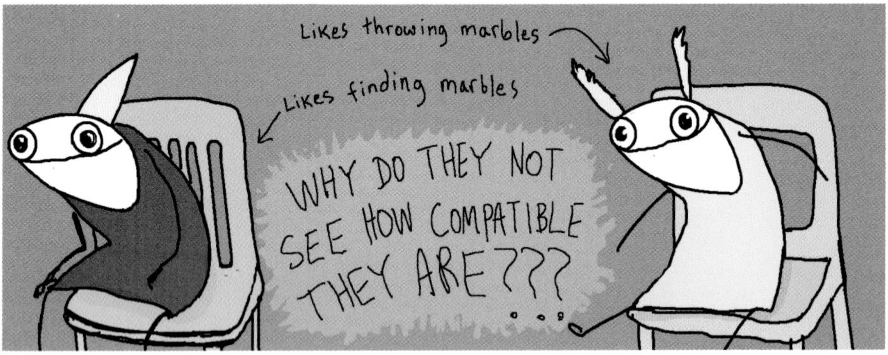
Likes throwing marbles
Likes finding marbles
WHY DO THEY NOT SEE HOW COMPATIBLE THEY ARE???

She never acted that fun around me. The only kind of game she liked to play with me was bullshit like crab basketball.

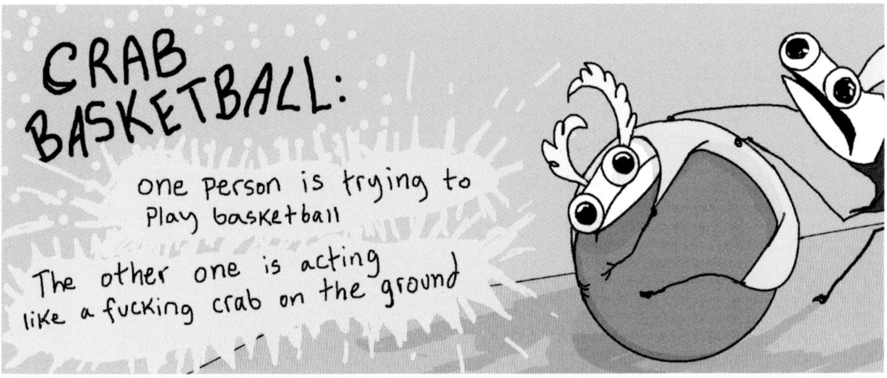
CRAB BASKETBALL:
one person is trying to play basketball
The other one is acting like a fucking crab on the ground

I hated crab basketball. Because I didn't want to play crab basketball—I wanted to play regular basketball. But I was bigger and stronger, so the only winning strategy for my sister was curling up around the basketball like a crab and refusing to participate.

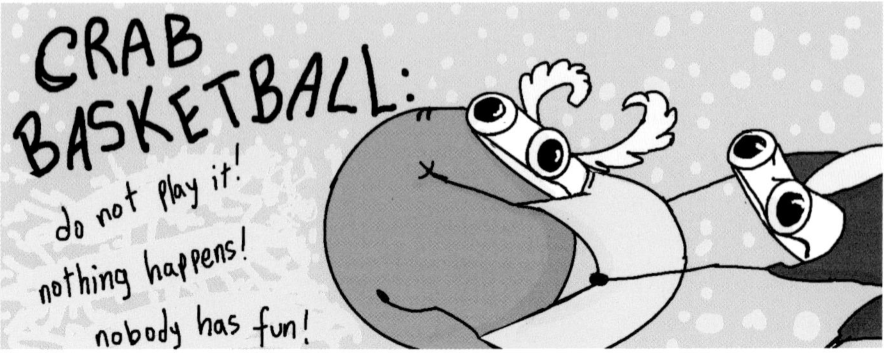
CRAB BASKETBALL:
do not play it!
nothing happens!
nobody has fun!

Even here, though, we were more alike than we realized. Crab basketball, for instance, is very, very similar to the strategy I have for life.

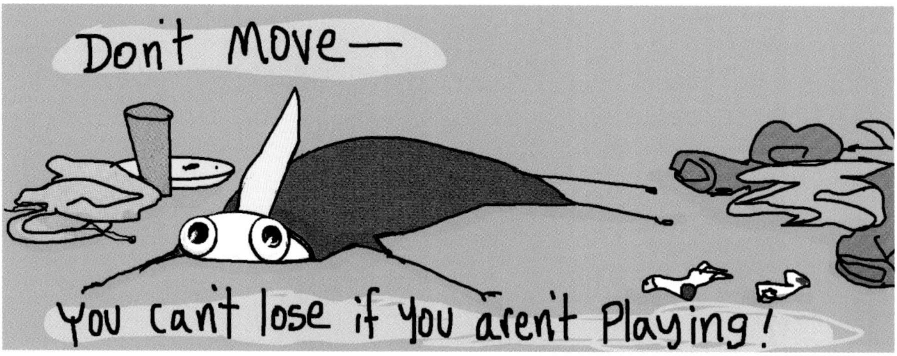
Don't Move—
You can't lose if you aren't Playing!

I didn't understand that then.

The only person who understood my sister was her friend Becky.

They had a confusing relationship. They were twelve, so maybe they just didn't know how to interact with each other. Or maybe it was some hyper-advanced form of interaction that you'd have to be Level 1000 to grasp. All I know is that one day, I came home from school, and Becky was duct-taped to a computer chair in our driveway.

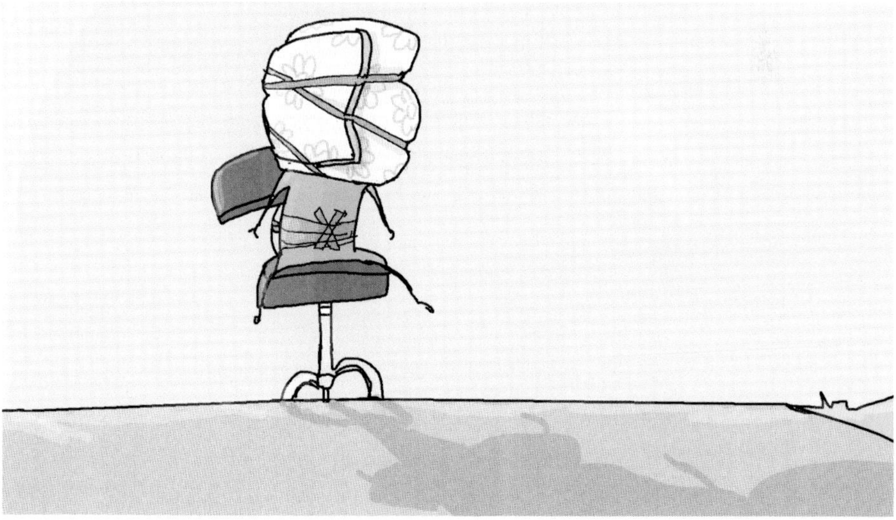

There was a blanket wrapped around her head, and her arms and legs had been scribbled on with a pen. Extensively. From the quality of the marks, there'd been a struggle.

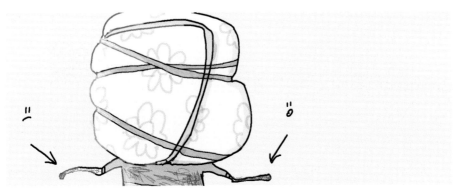

I decided to not get involved until better information was available. When I tried to go inside, though, all the doors were locked.

It was later revealed that this was a security measure to prevent Becky from flopping up the stairs and trying to get inside, but I had no way to know that.

I knocked on the door, and my little sister shot out of the kitchen clutching a salad bowl full of something that looked like water and egg yolks.

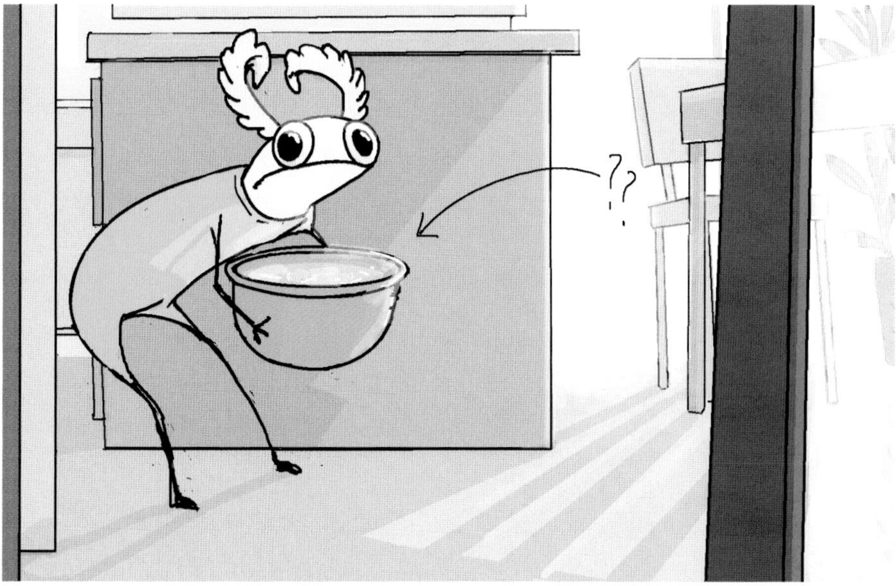
??

She yelled, "DON'T HELP HER, SHE LOVES IT," and pushed past me. Egg water spilled on the floor.

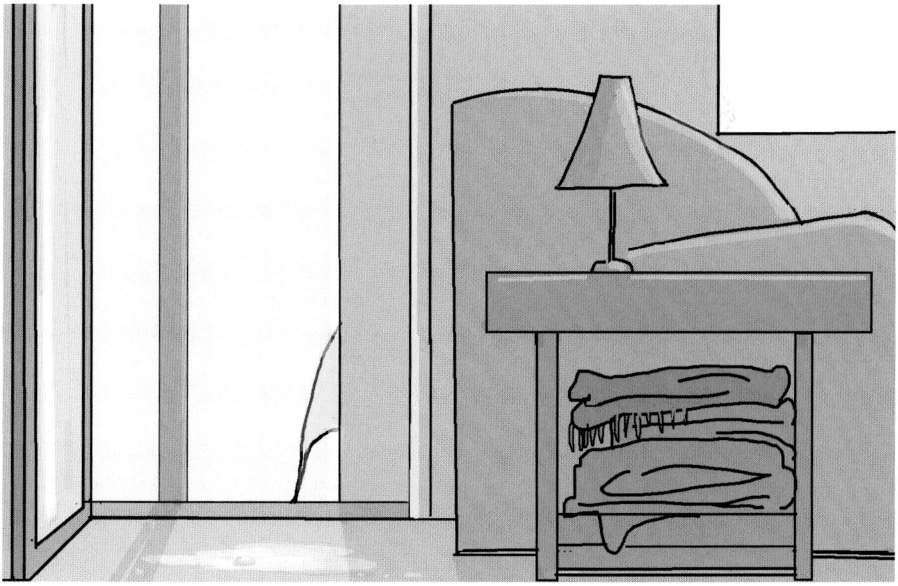

Outside, Becky made a sound. Screaming, probably.

Whatever my sister was planning to do, it didn't seem like Becky wanted it to happen. She heard my sister approaching and tried to scoot away.

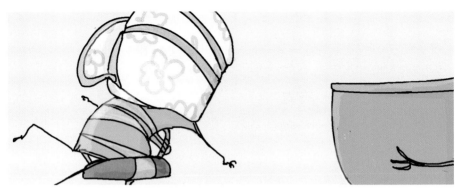

Then things got *very* intense.

My little sister ...

... my little sister who used to be a baby ...

... my little sister who loves helping ...

... my little sister who didn't want to walk on the lawn for fear of hurting it ...

—*that person*—

... seized both of her friend Becky's arms, and violently submerged them in a bowl of egg water.

And as she did this, she shouted from point-blank range:

FEEL THEM!!

FEEL THEM, BECKY!!

DO YOU LIKE THEM??!!!

And that's the kind of thing I don't get involved in.

I wouldn't understand it.

I don't need to understand it.

Best to assume they have their reasons and leave them to their terrorism activity.

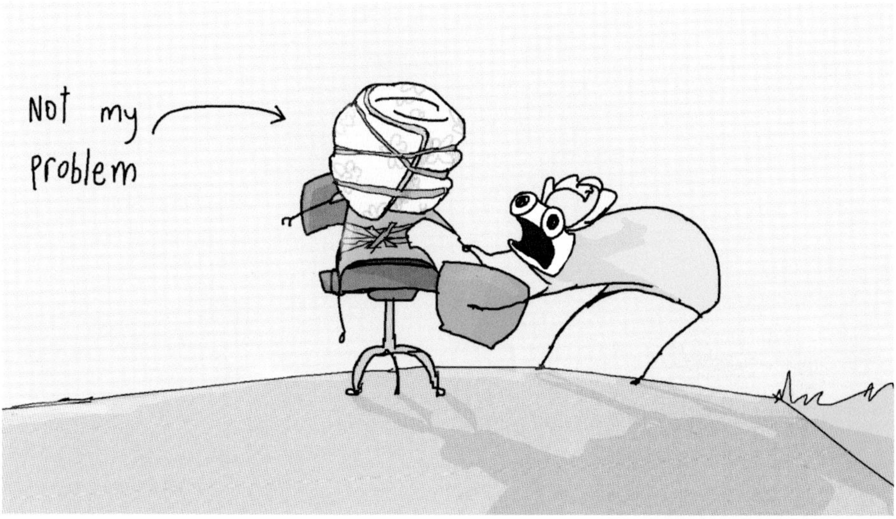
Not my problem

Neither of them ever seemed to acknowledge these incidents after the fact. When I came back later, they were working on a geography project like nothing happened.

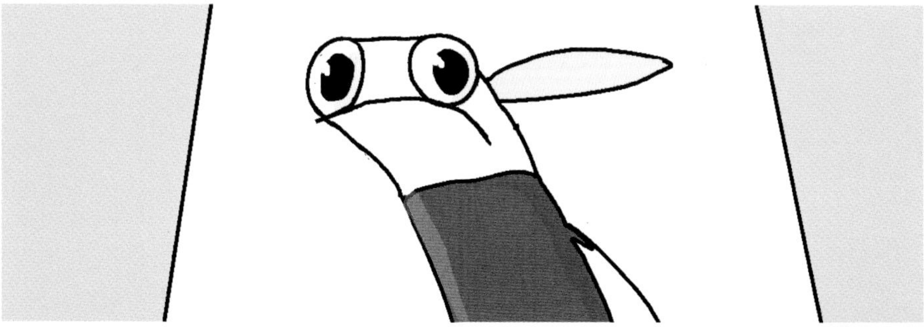

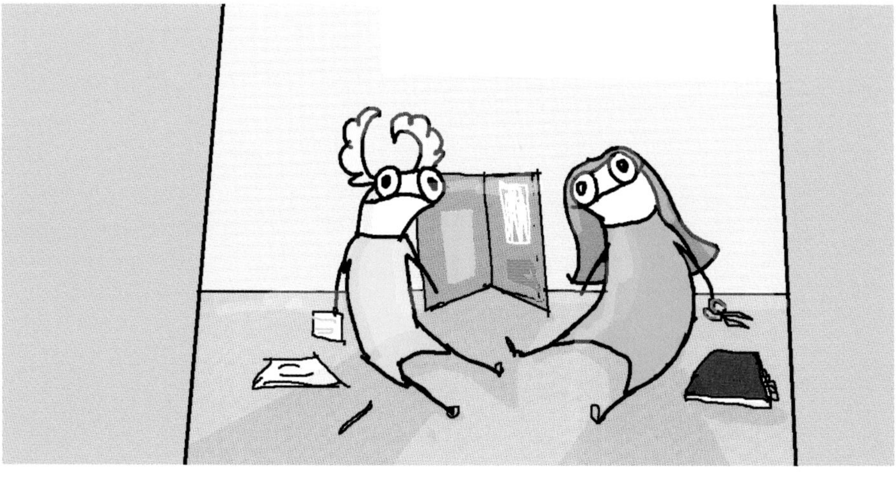

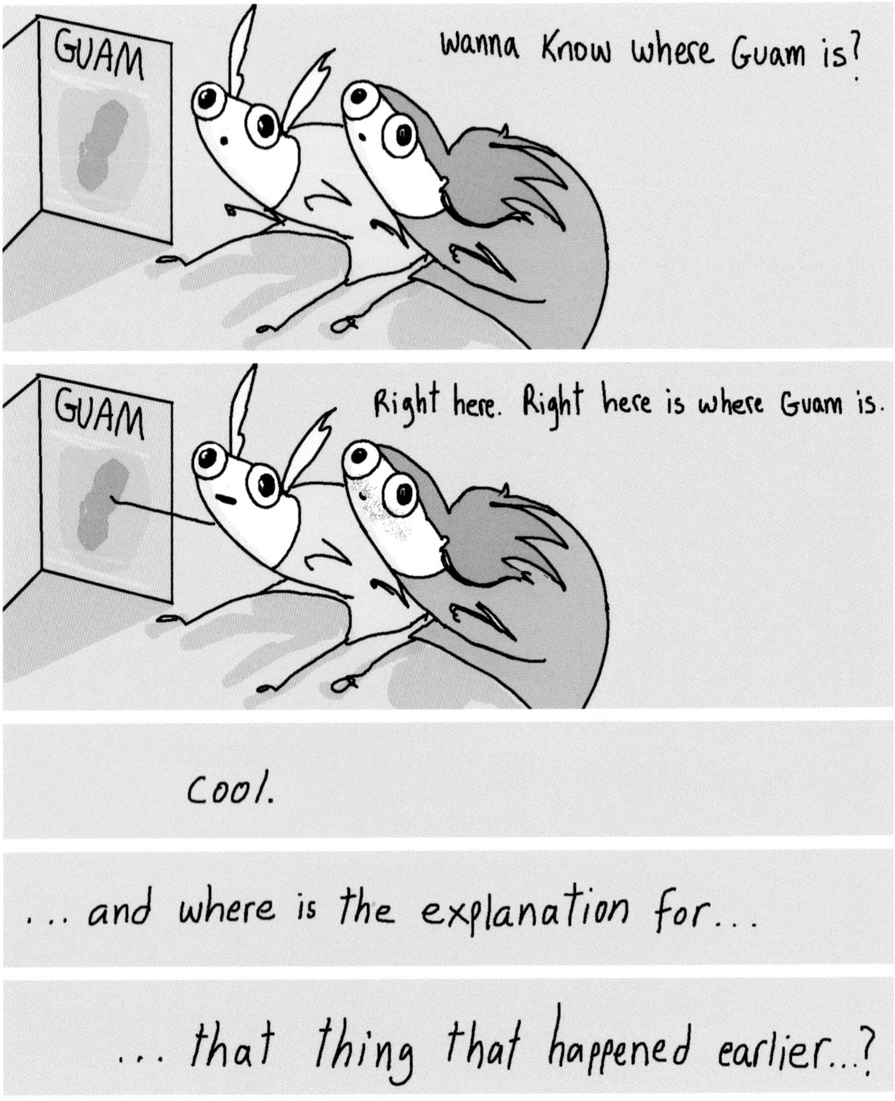
GUAM
wanna Know where Guam is?
GUAM
Right here. Right here is where Guam is.
cool.
...and where is the explanation for...
...that thing that happened earlier...?

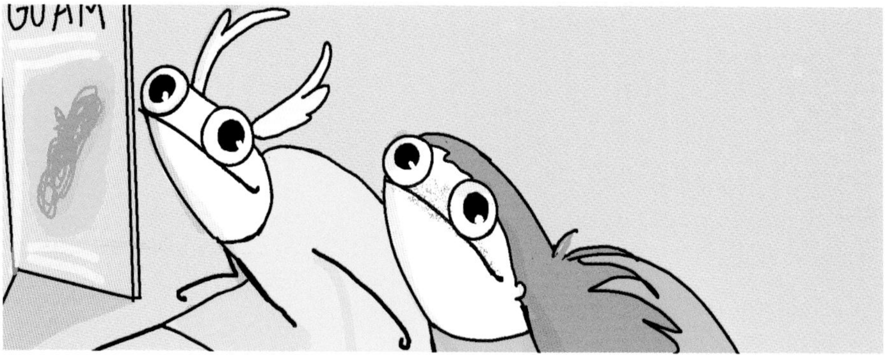

Their relationship was 30% geography projects and 70% the weirdest shit I have ever seen.

A week or two after the egg water thing, for instance, I came home from school and noticed that the pantry doors were wired shut with the phone cord. Inside, my sister was screaming for help.

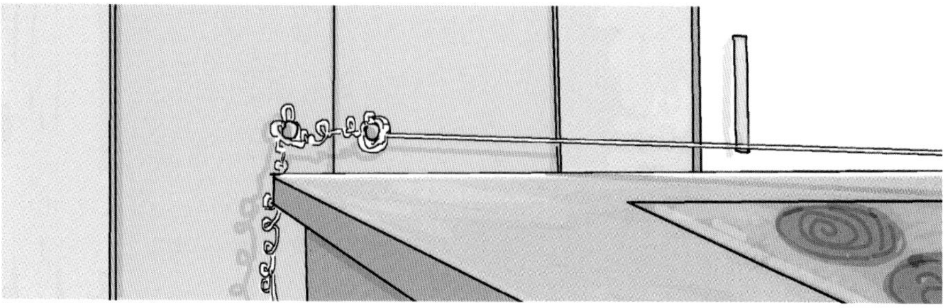

I approached the pantry, and Becky came into view.

When I saw her, I thought, *Oh good—Becky must be helping my sister . . .*

Upon closer inspection, however, Becky's behavior did not resemble helping.

She was holding a bottle of cucumber melon body spray, which is a nice enough thing to be holding, but the nozzle was aimed rather aggressively under the pantry door.

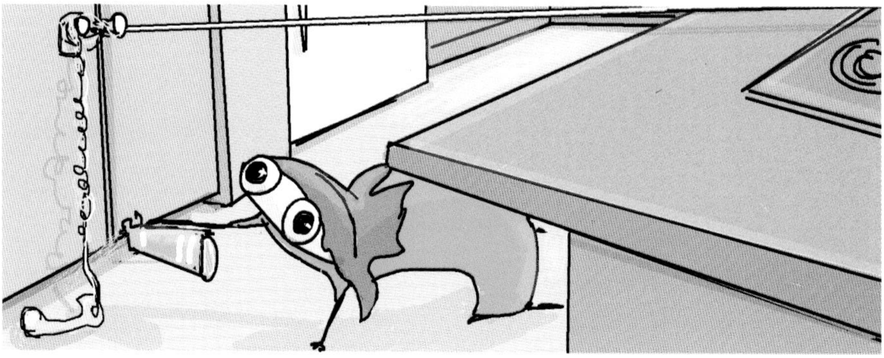

Inside the pantry, my sister was screaming, "*I GIVE UP, I GIVE UP, I GIVE UP.*" Becky said *no*, cold as ice, and kept spraying.

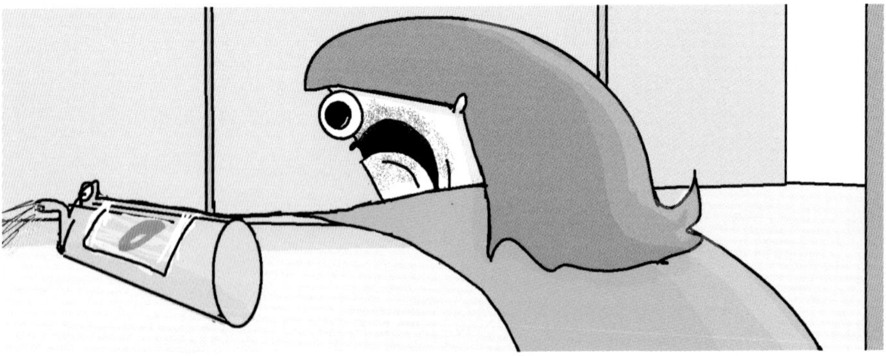

No? As in: No, you are not permitted to give up?

What's the point, then? What could you possibly be trying to accomplish by doing this to my sister? Are you training her for something?

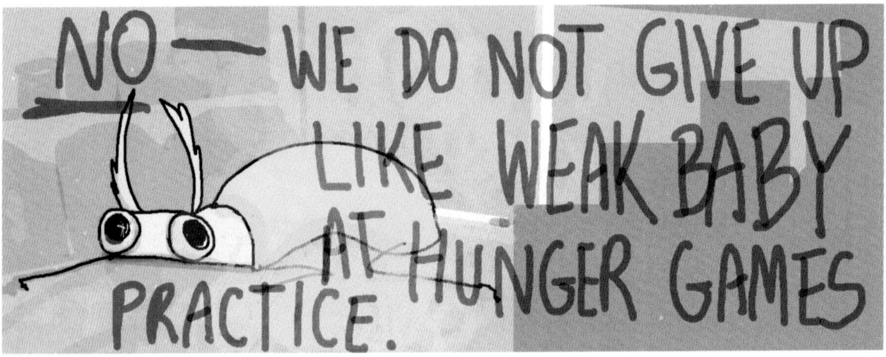
NO — WE DO NOT GIVE UP LIKE WEAK BABY AT HUNGER GAMES PRACTICE.

Later, I asked my sister how Becky had lured her into the pantry.

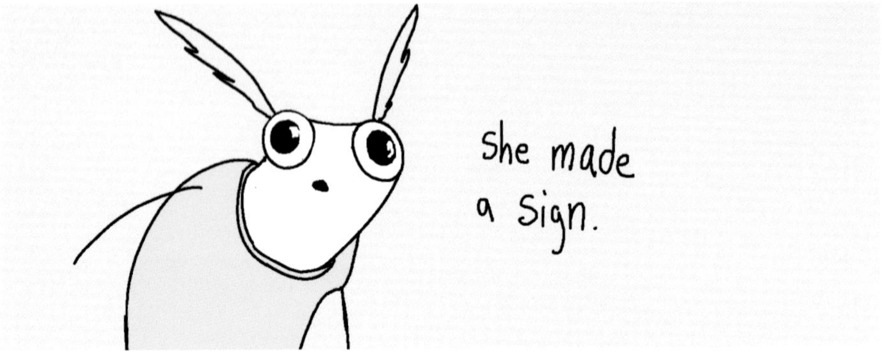
She made a sign.

And I said, "What kind of sign? '*Go in the pantry please*'? '*Go in the pantry or else*'?"

No. All the sign said was "*Guess What?*"

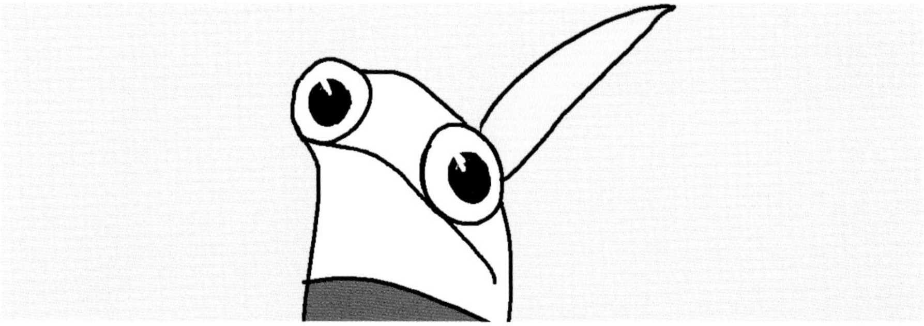

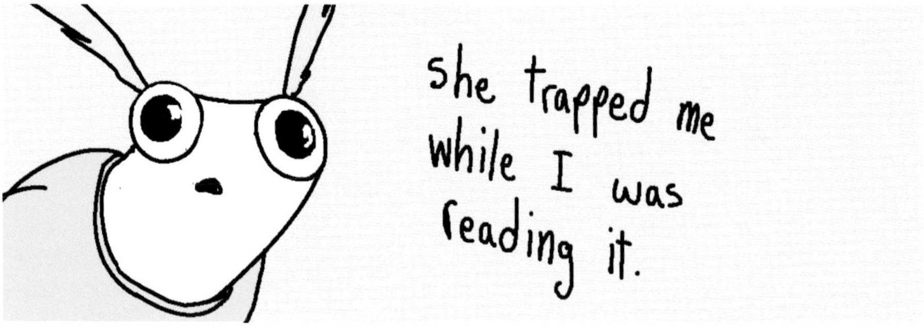
she trapped me while I was reading it.

Perhaps it was a power struggle. To establish dominance or something.

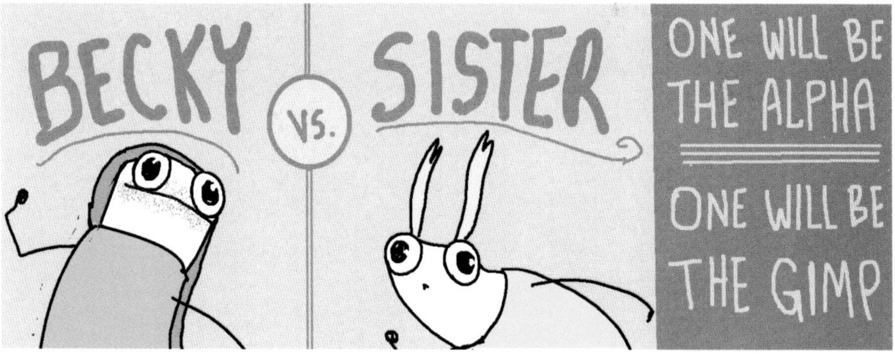
BECKY
VS.
SISTER
ONE WILL BE THE ALPHA
ONE WILL BE THE GIMP

If that's what was going on, things were fucking *neck and neck*.

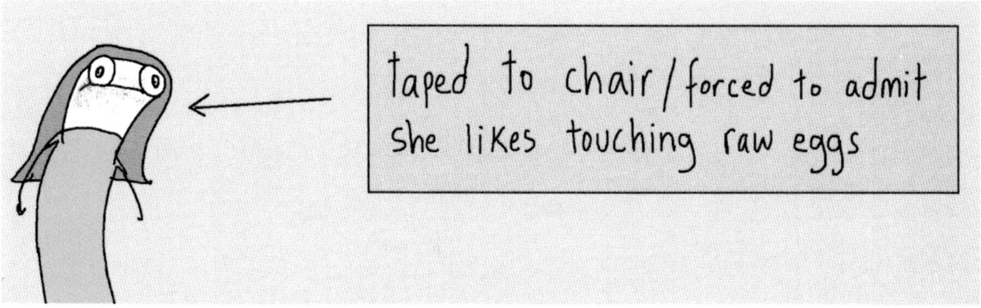
taped to chair / forced to admit she likes touching raw eggs

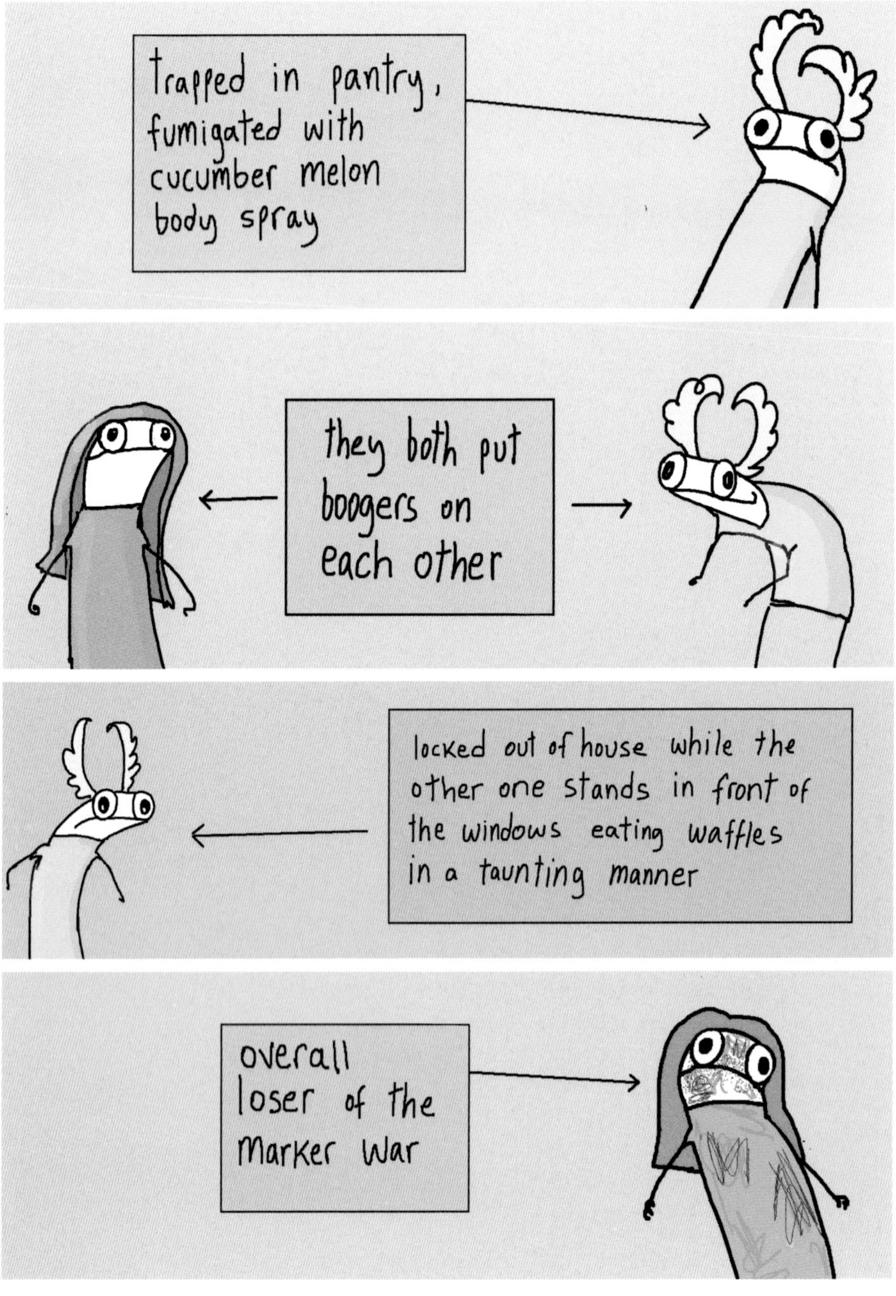
trapped in pantry, fumigated with cucumber melon body spray
they both put boogers on each other
locked out of house while the other one stands in front of the windows eating waffles in a taunting manner
overall loser of the marker war

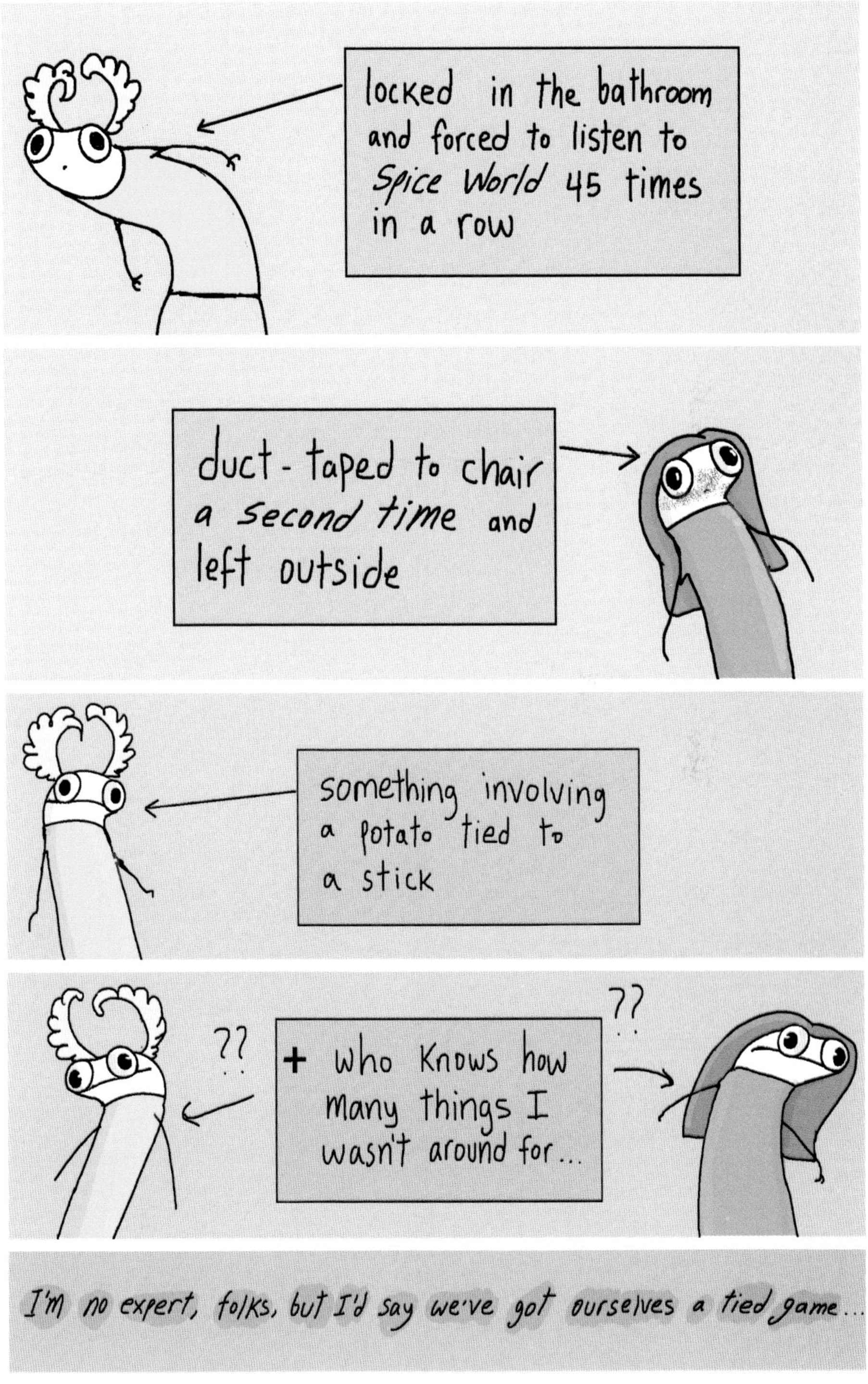
locked in the bathroom and forced to listen to *Spice World* 45 times in a row
duct-taped to chair a *second time* and left outside
something involving a potato tied to a stick
??
+ who Knows how many things I wasn't around for...
??
I'm no expert, folks, but I'd say we've got ourselves a tied game...

There was a brief period, though, where I think my sister may have pulled ahead a little bit.

I woke up for school, and the first thing I saw was Becky. Her arms and legs had been firmly secured to the bed frame with yarn.

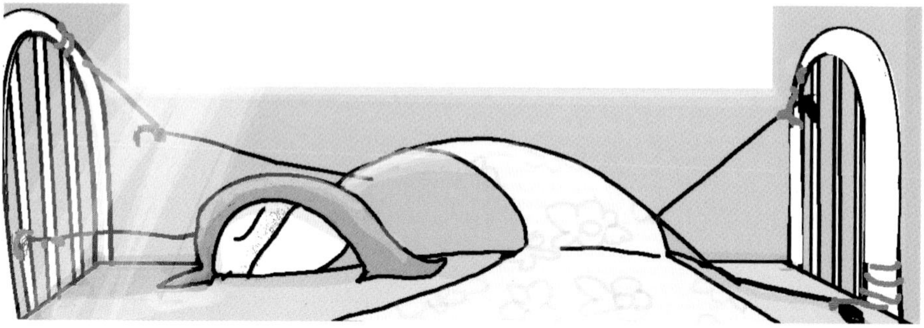

She wasn't awake yet, but she would be soon: my sister was hovering above her like a gargoyle, holding a wet piece of string and a jingle bell. She put the bell two inches from Becky's face and jingled it. *Jingle jingle, Becky . . .*

Becky's eyes opened.

She didn't recognize what was happening right away. I imagine there was a lot to process.

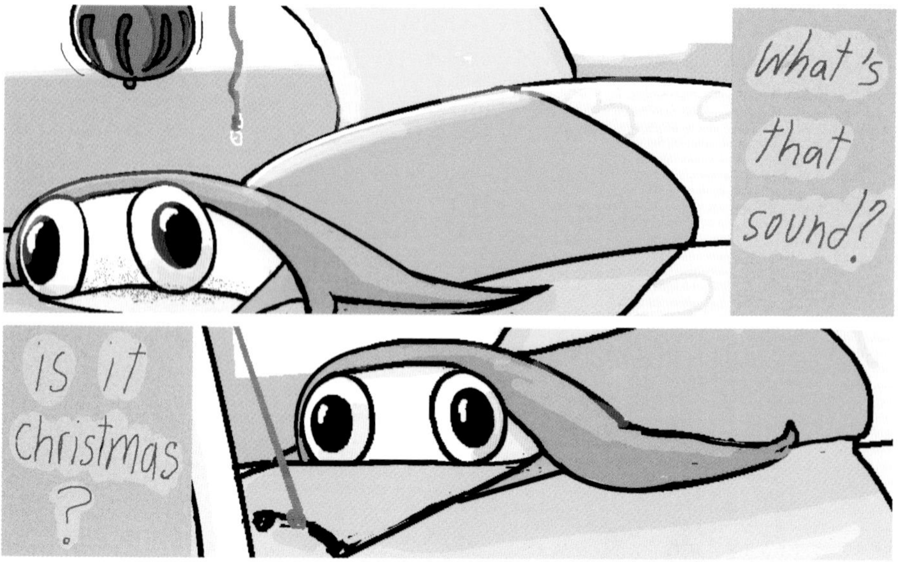
What's that sound?
is it christmas?

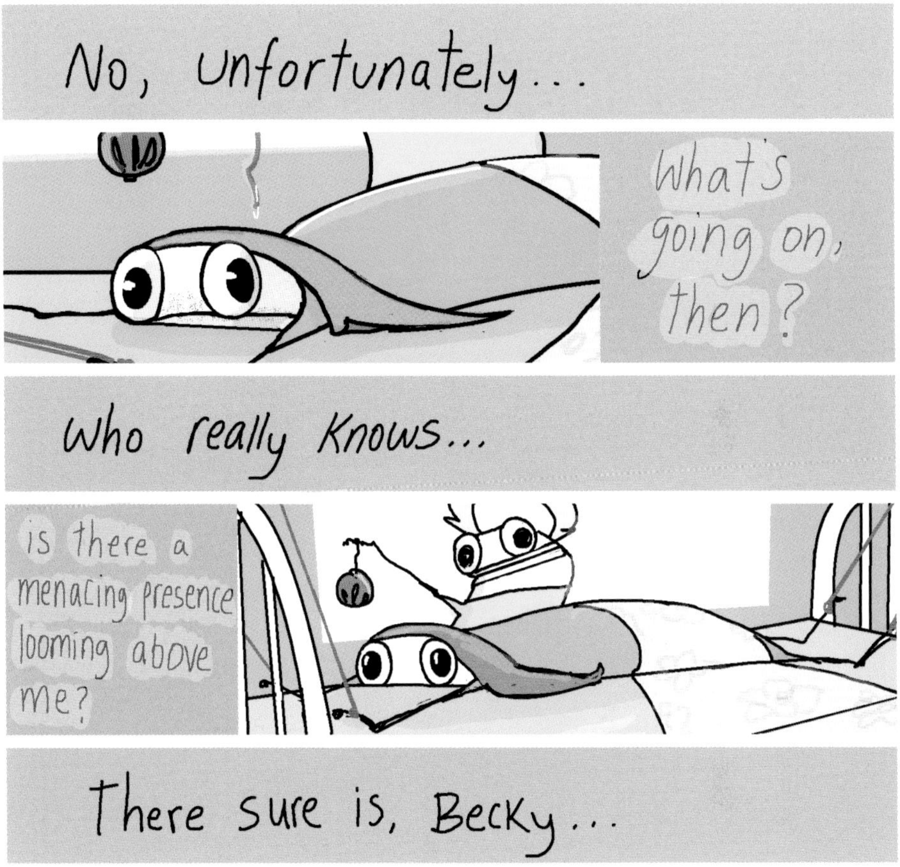
No, unfortunately...
What's going on, then?
Who really knows...
is there a menacing presence looming above me?
There sure is, Becky...

Right there, Becky's fear instincts kicked in and she tried to wriggle away. That's when she noticed she was tied to the bed.

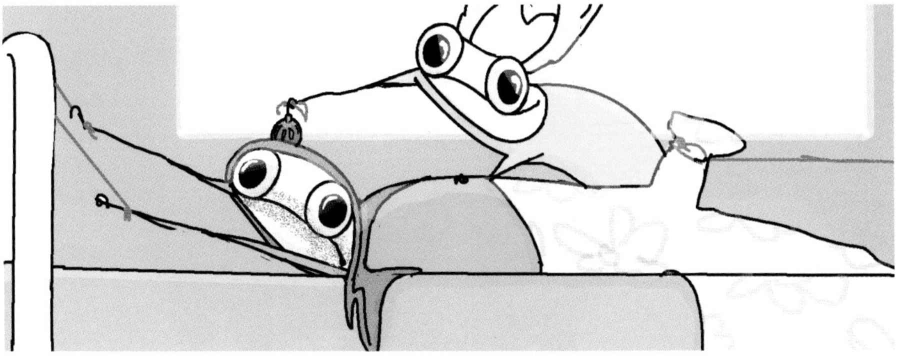

The string came into view. I still had no clue what the string was for, but Becky seemed to know. The instant she saw it, her eyes filled with terror.

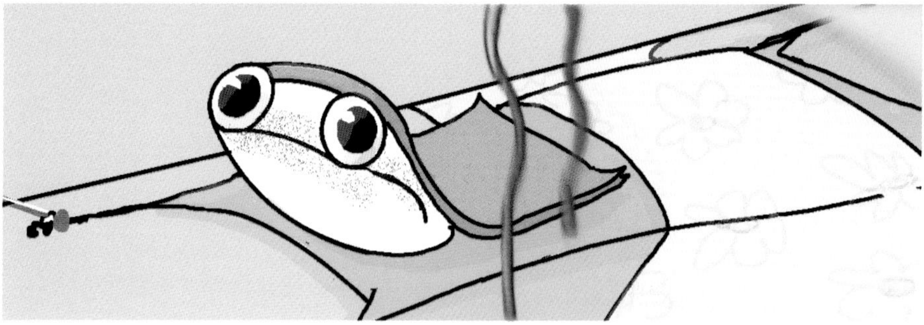

My sister didn't strike yet, though. Whatever she was planning on doing to Becky this time, she knew it would land harder if she built up to it.

I never found out what was on the string, but my sister spent the whole morning moving it toward Becky's face at approximately .02 miles per hour.

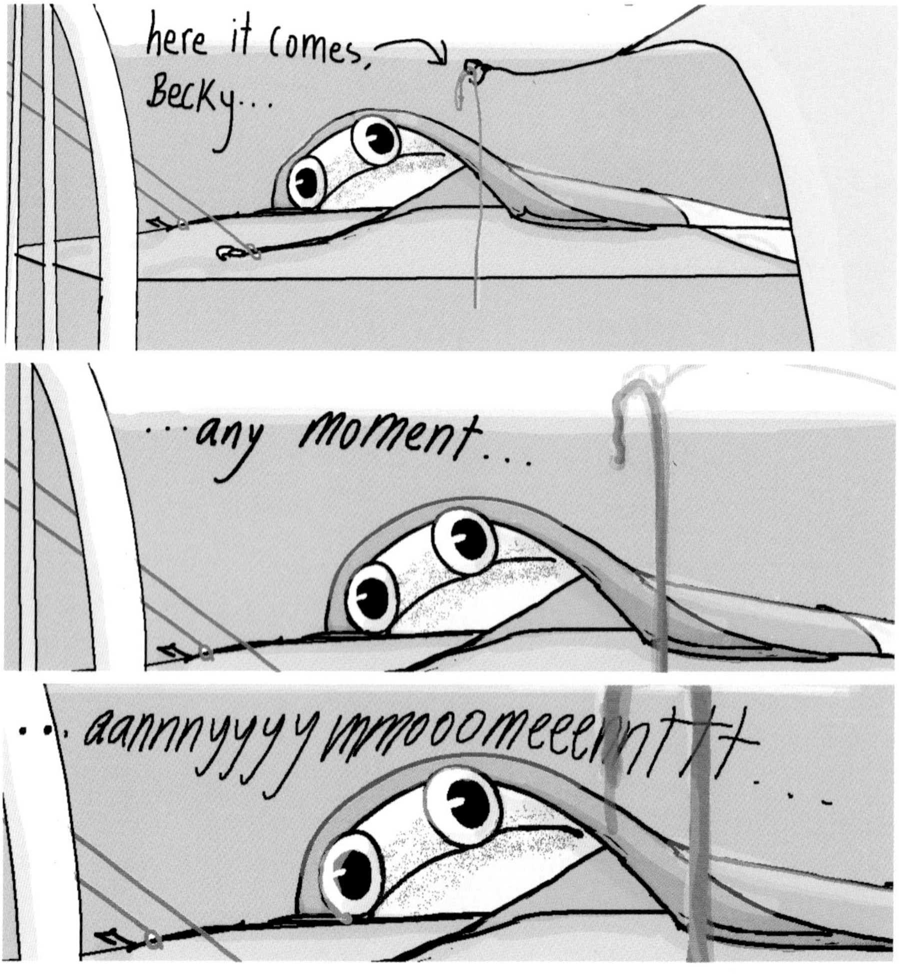
here it comes, Becky...
...any moment...
...aannnyyyymmooomeeennntt...

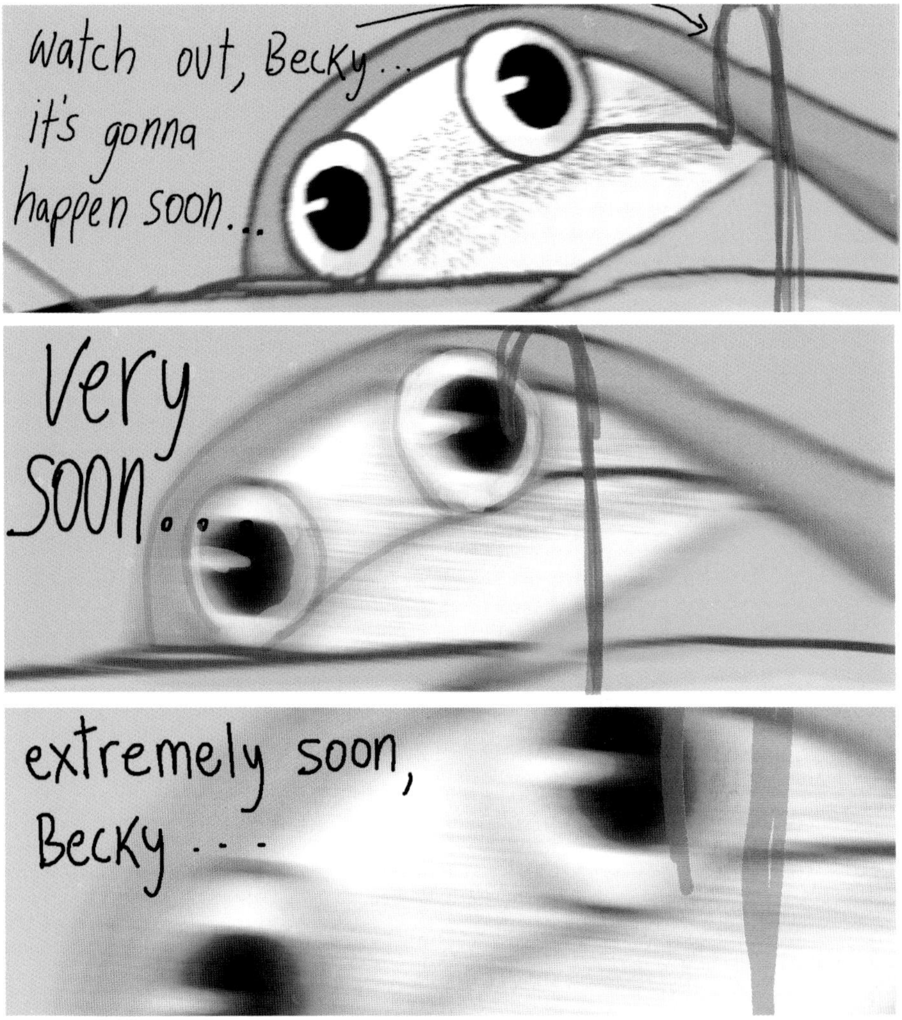
Watch out, Becky...
it's gonna
happen soon...
Very
soon...
extremely soon,
Becky...

By the time the string made contact, Becky seemed genuinely relieved to be done with the suspense.

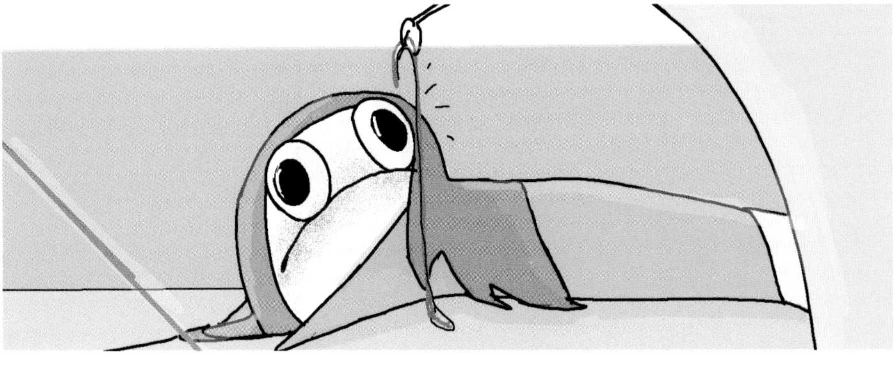

It was a totally bizarre relationship, but I will admit that part of me wanted to get in on it. Just to, like . . . be a part of it.

They had something really special.

I didn't know what it was, but I could tell.

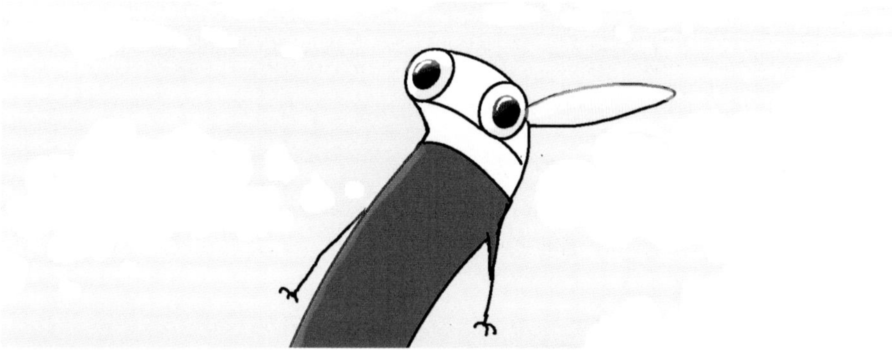

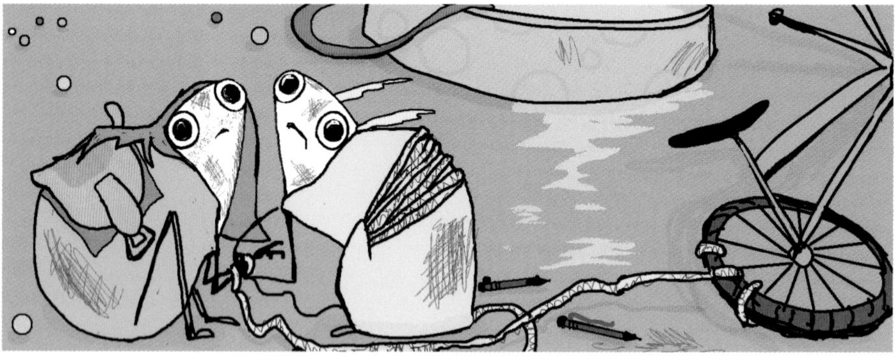

To this day, it's a source of inspiration.

If a friendship can survive all that, that's a crazy friendship.

Imagine having a friendship like that.

Like, *Hey there, pal . . . looks like you're having a weird day, so I understand if you need to trap me in a sleeping bag and rub the inside of a banana peel on me until I admit that my name is Dance Pony. Of course I understand. I mean . . . that happens. Honestly, I'm probably gonna do that to you too sometimes. No big deal. You're my best friend.*

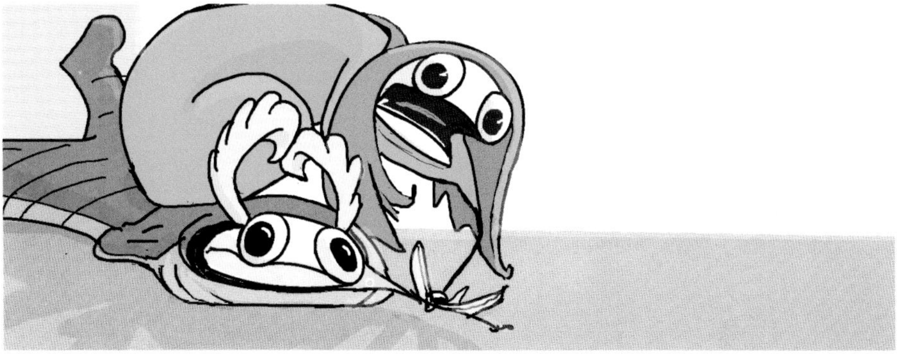

You might be thinking, *Why, though? Why is the person who does that somebody's best friend?*

Because that's intimacy, Buckaroos.

Somebody who understands exactly how weird you are, and you understand exactly how weird they are, and you're in a sort of mutually beneficial hostage situation.

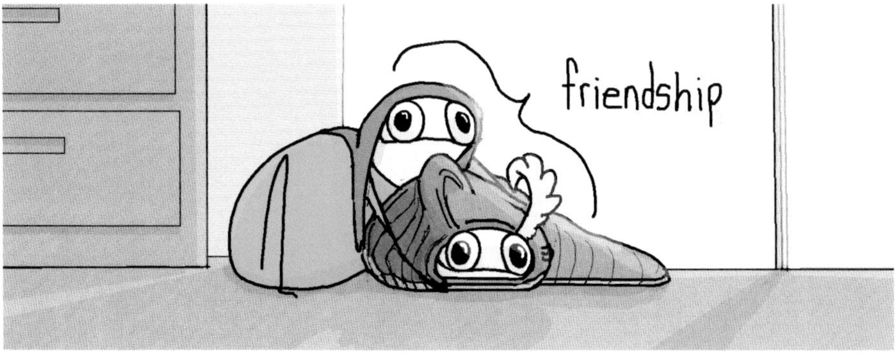
friendship

23. A NONSPECIFIC STORY ABOUT AN ANIMAL

It is the year 2015 or 2019 or something...

...just over the horizon, a creature attempts to survive...

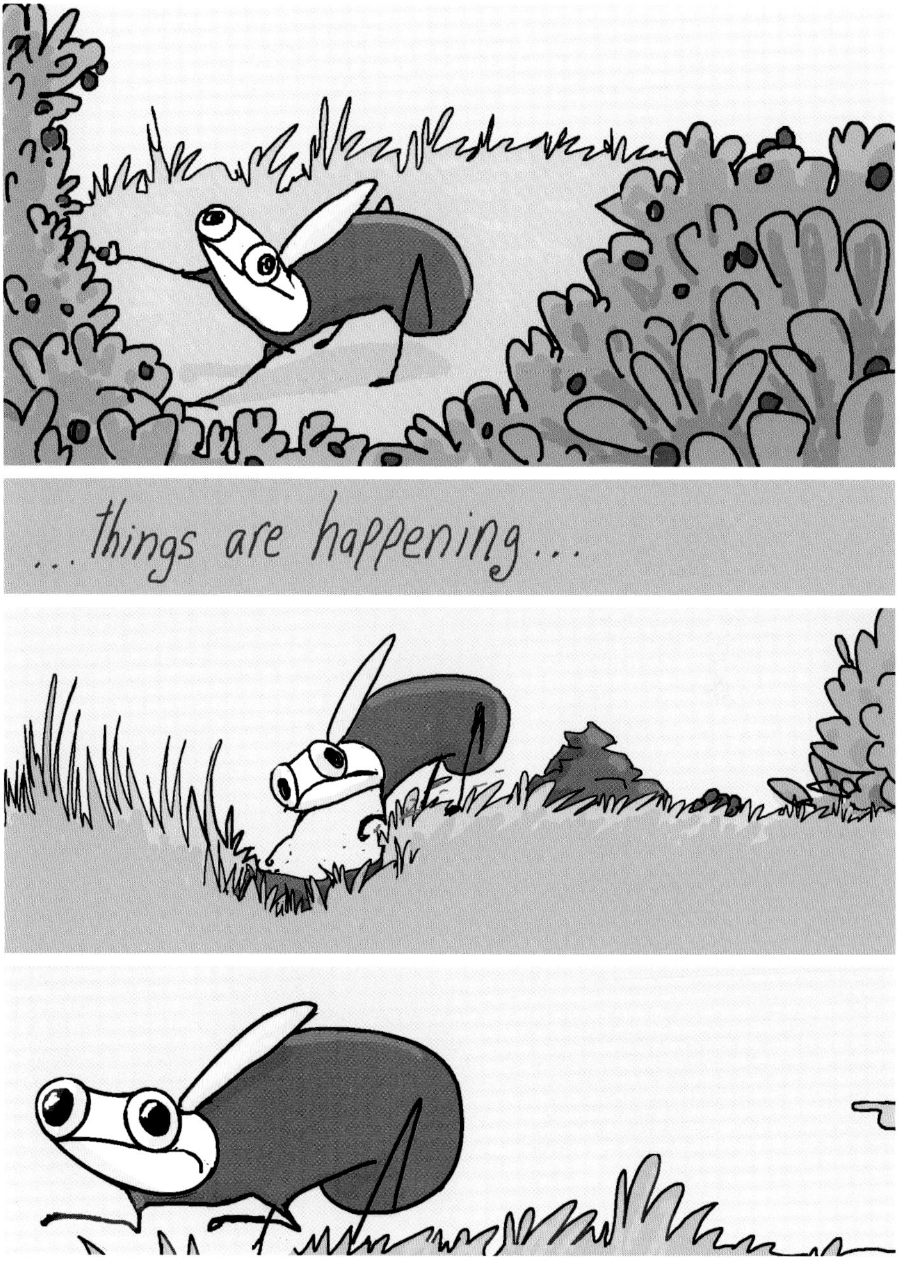
...things are happening...

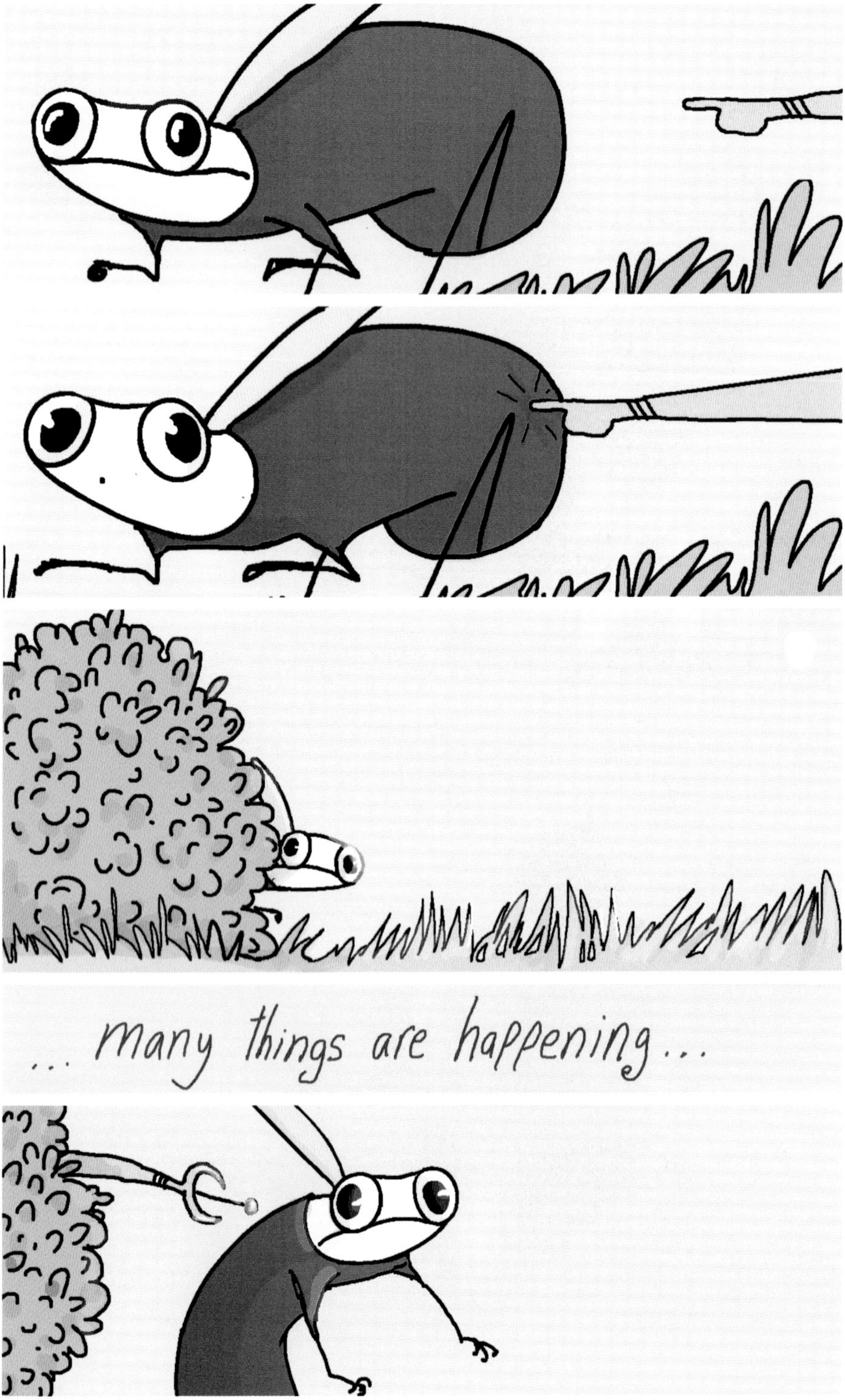
... many things are happening ...

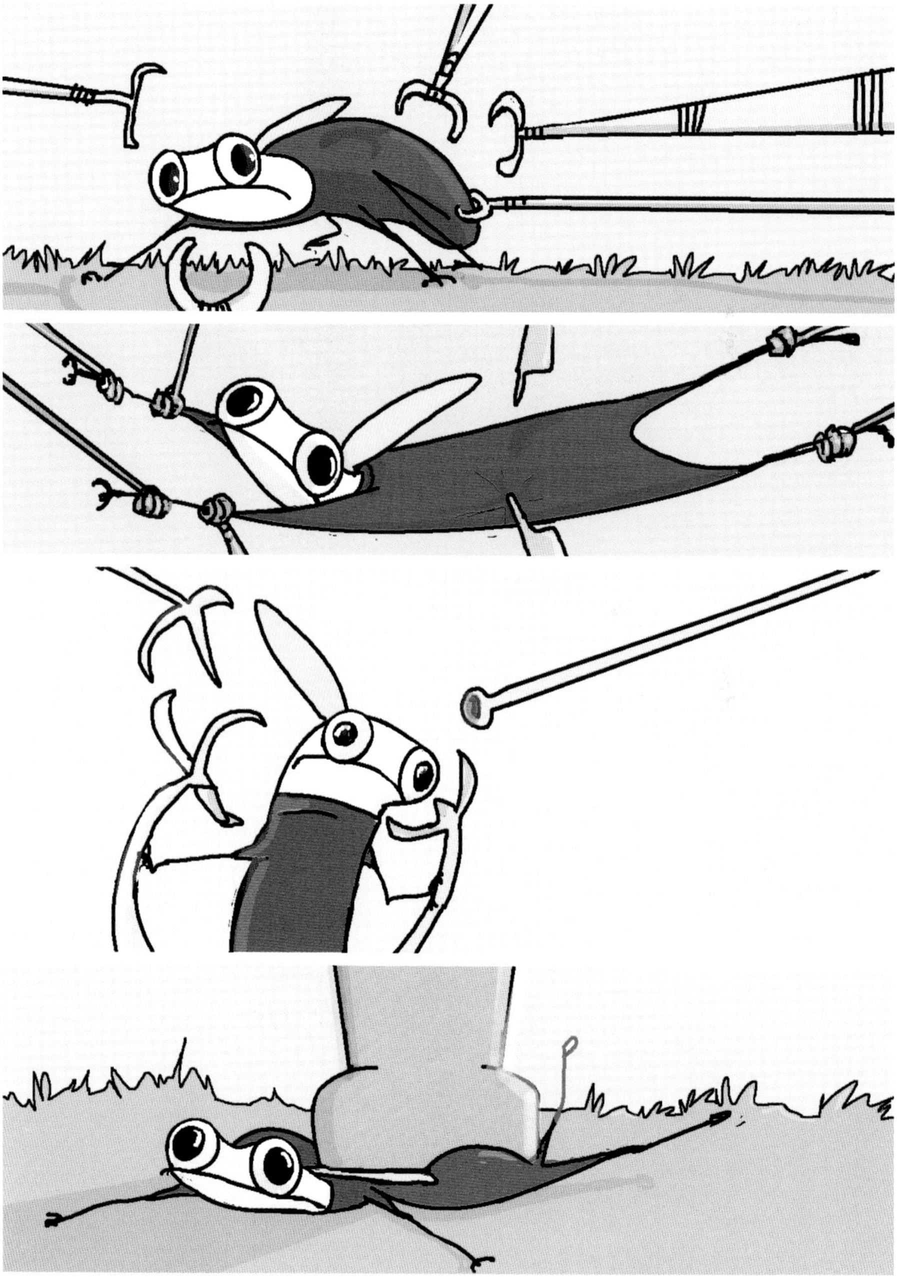

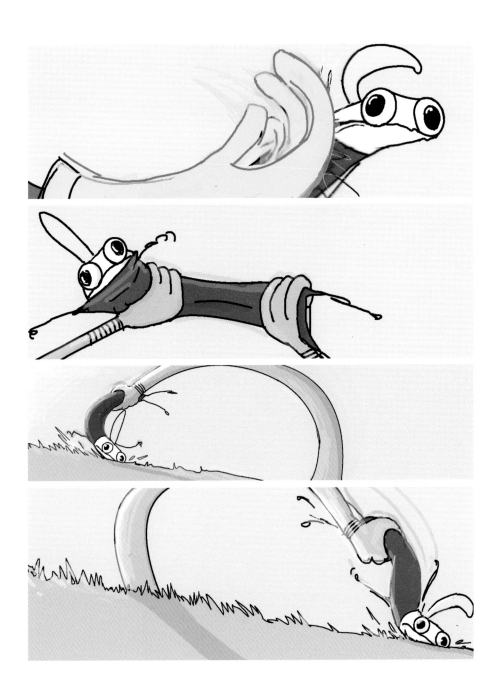

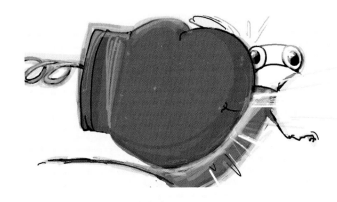

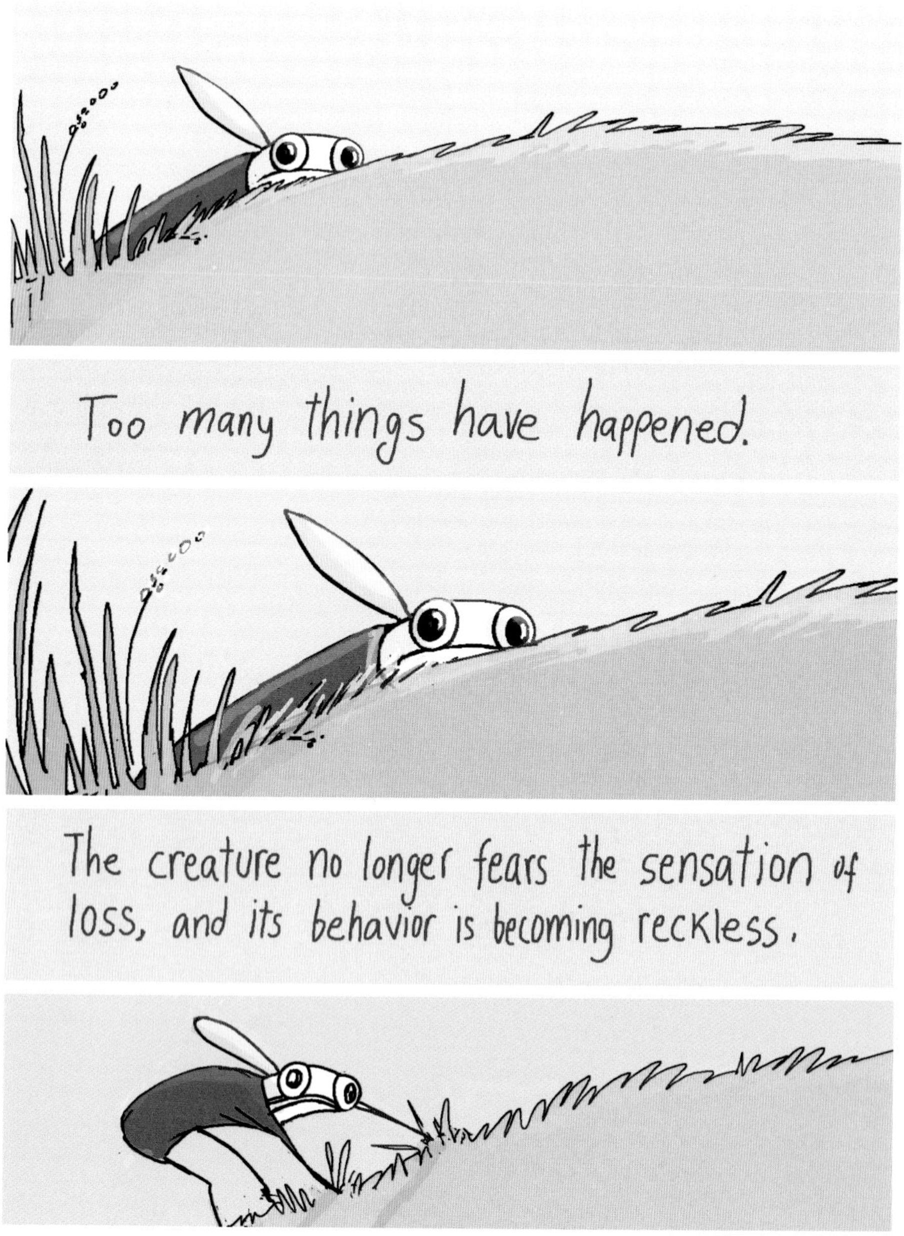
Too many things have happened.
The creature no longer fears the sensation of loss, and its behavior is becoming reckless.

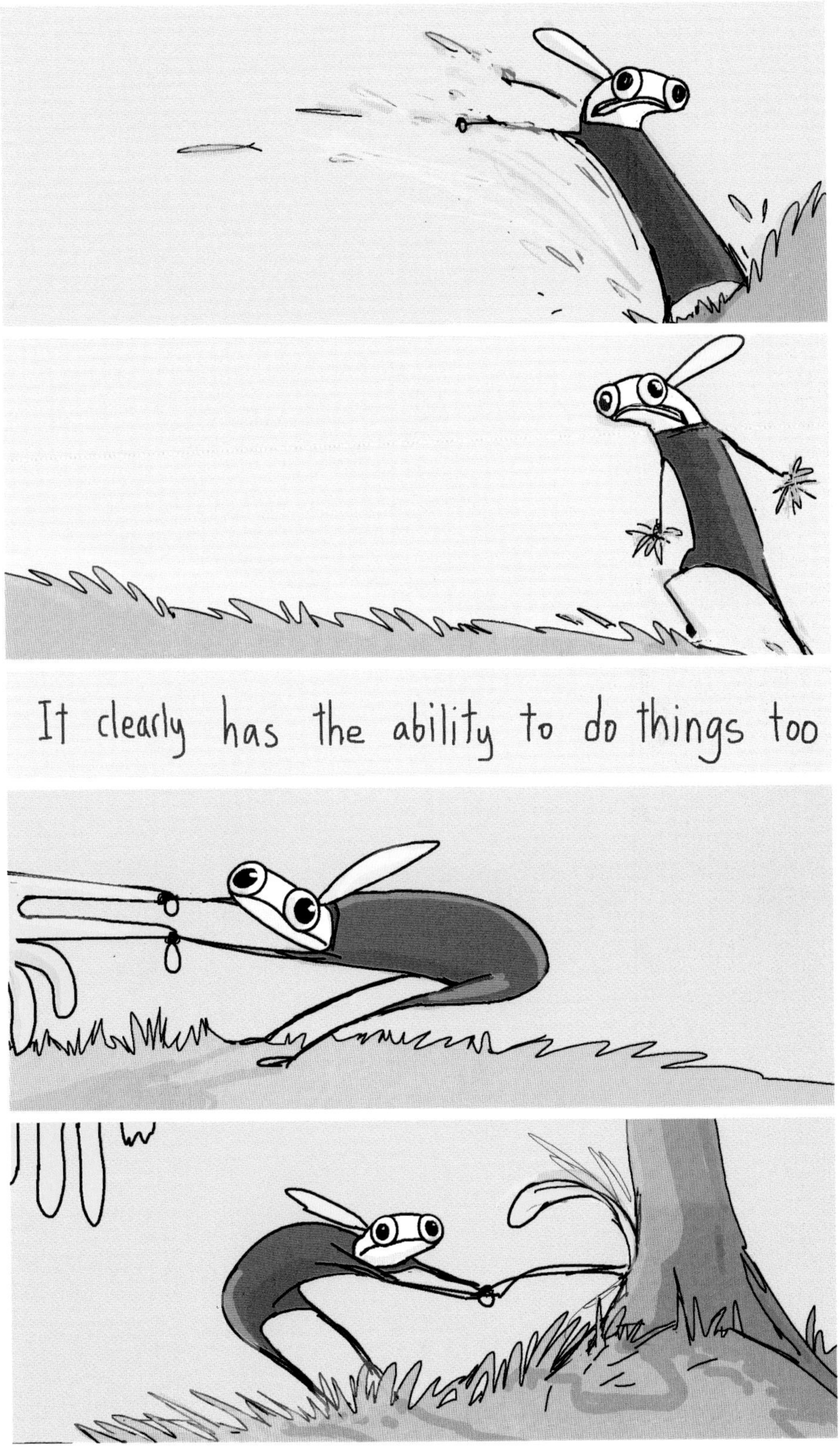
It clearly has the ability to do things too

And it believes that demonstrating this may prove it is not as powerless as it currently feels.

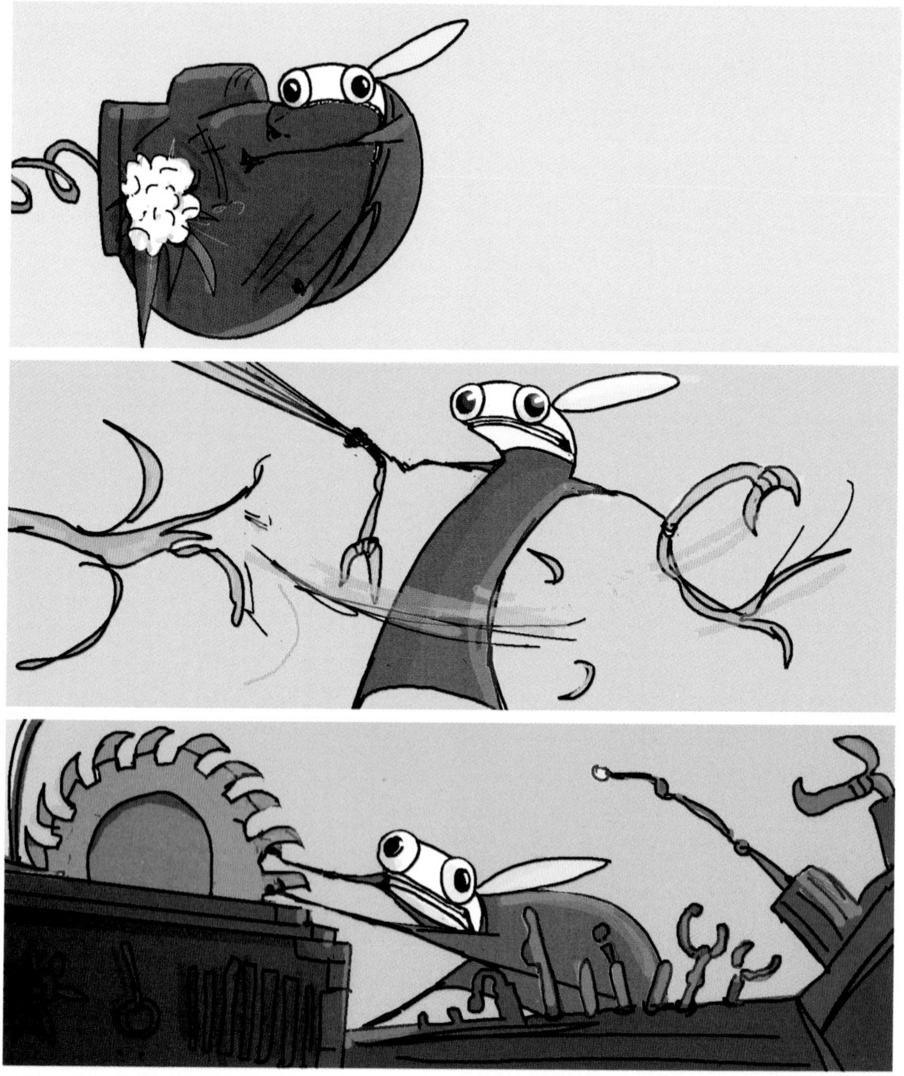

Behold the god of destruction:

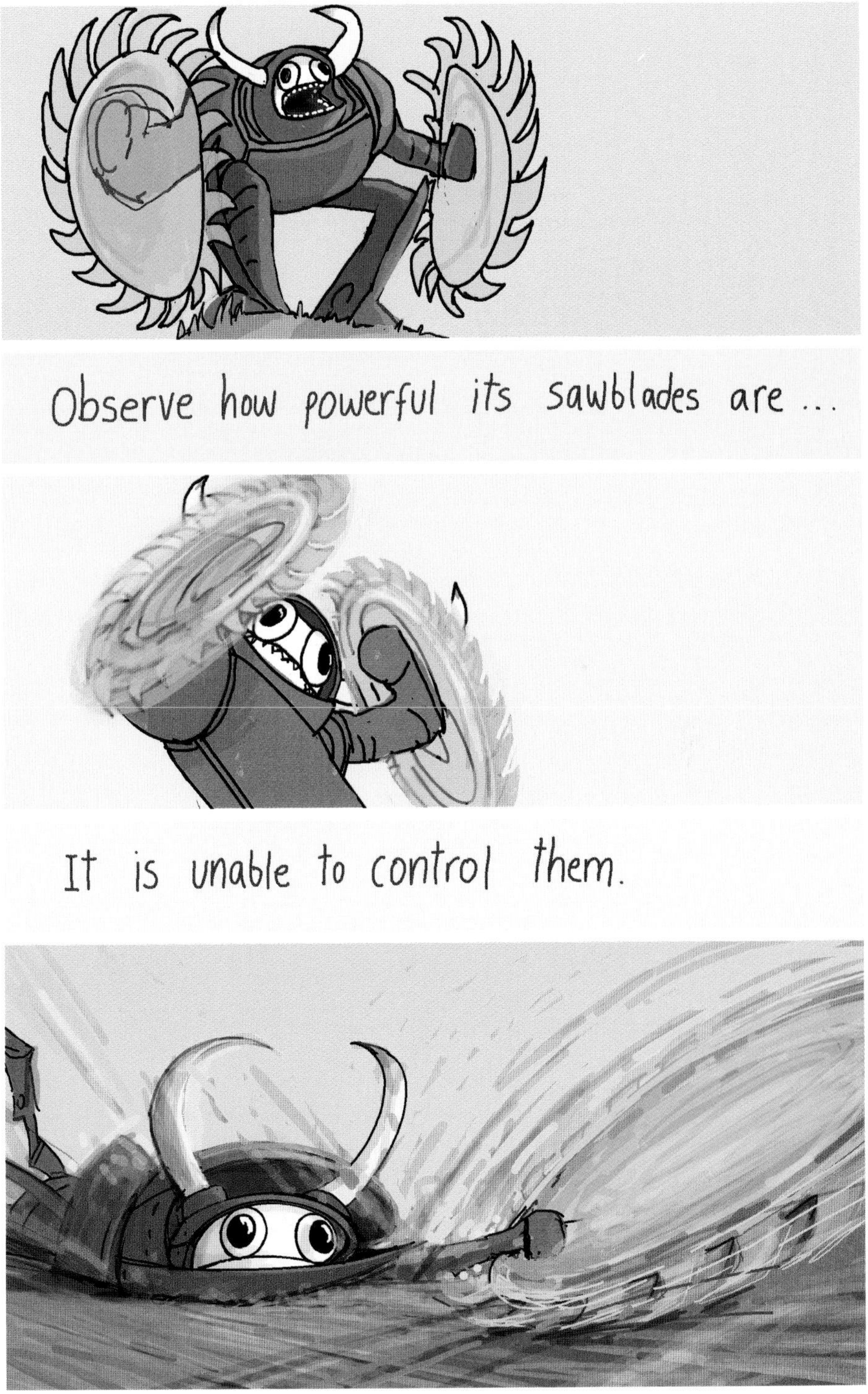
Observe how powerful its sawblades are . . .
It is unable to control them.

24. FRIENDSHIP SPELL

On July 23rd, 1996, I wrote an original friendship spell.

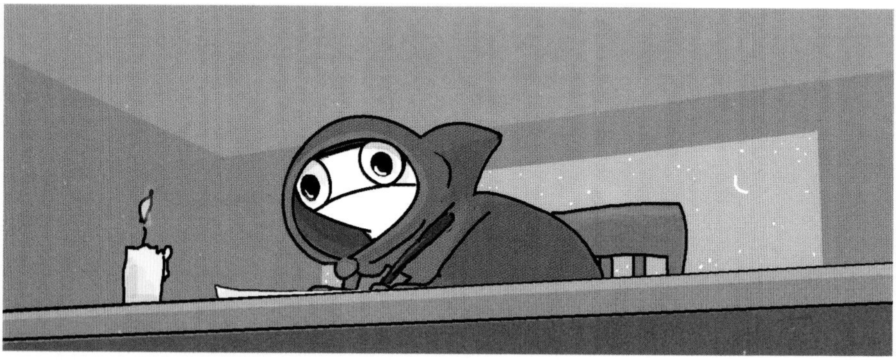

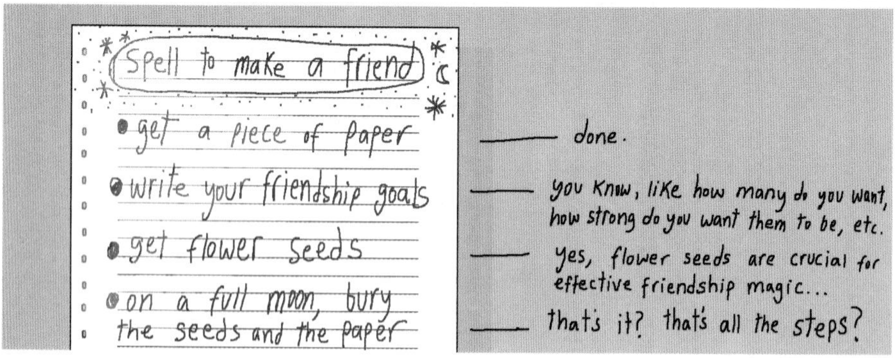
Spell to make a friend
get a piece of paper
write your friendship goals
get flower seeds
on a full moon, bury the seeds and the paper
done.
you know, like how many do you want, how strong do you want them to be, etc.
yes, flower seeds are crucial for effective friendship magic...
that's it? that's all the steps?

Fast-forward 19 years.

July 2015.

I'm 30.

I live alone in a 400-square-foot apartment, and the doors are starting to swell shut from the heat.

A few days later, I'm officially trapped.

I don't know the exact day it started, but I found out when I tried to go buy more peanuts from the liquor mart downstairs.

I've got a day or two of cereal left, but if I can't get the door open by Monday, I'll be forced to kick the wall until whoever lives on the other side gets mad and comes over here to ask me what the fuck I'm doing. Standing on the other side of the door, they'll be able to hear what I'm saying, and I can explain.

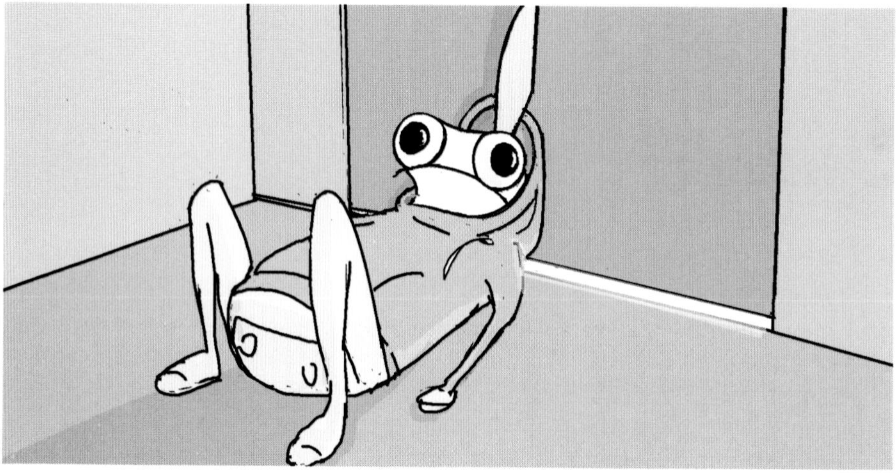

Behold the god of destruction ...

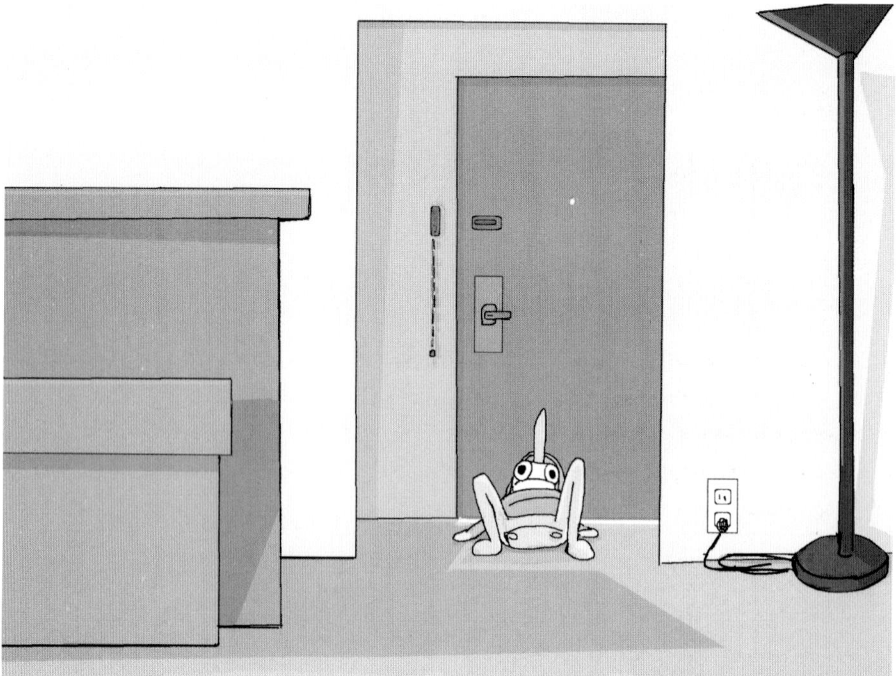

The god of destruction is lonely.

25. FRIEND

Before mutilating my life like a weaponized rototiller on speed mode, I lived with other creatures.

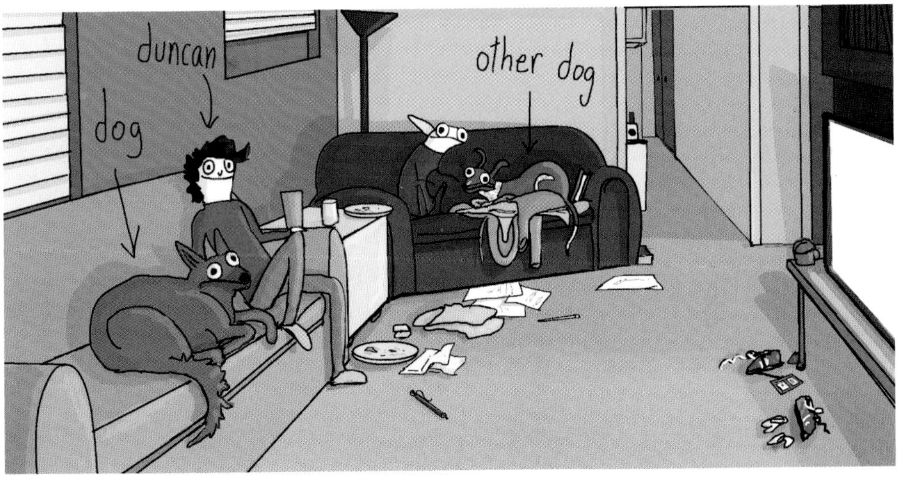
duncan
dog
other dog

Initially, I wanted to keep custody of at least one dog to avoid seeming like a lesser person, but that is a bad reason. Duncan was always the main nurturer. My role was more the stoic father figure who lives in the upstairs bedroom except for holidays and birthdays and the days when somebody needs a talkin'-to.

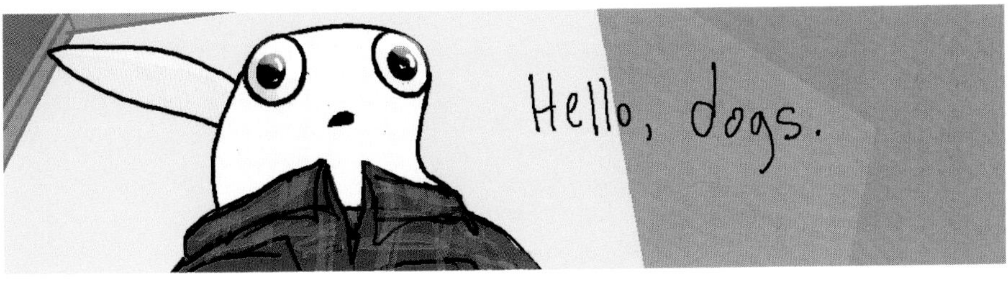
Hello, dogs.

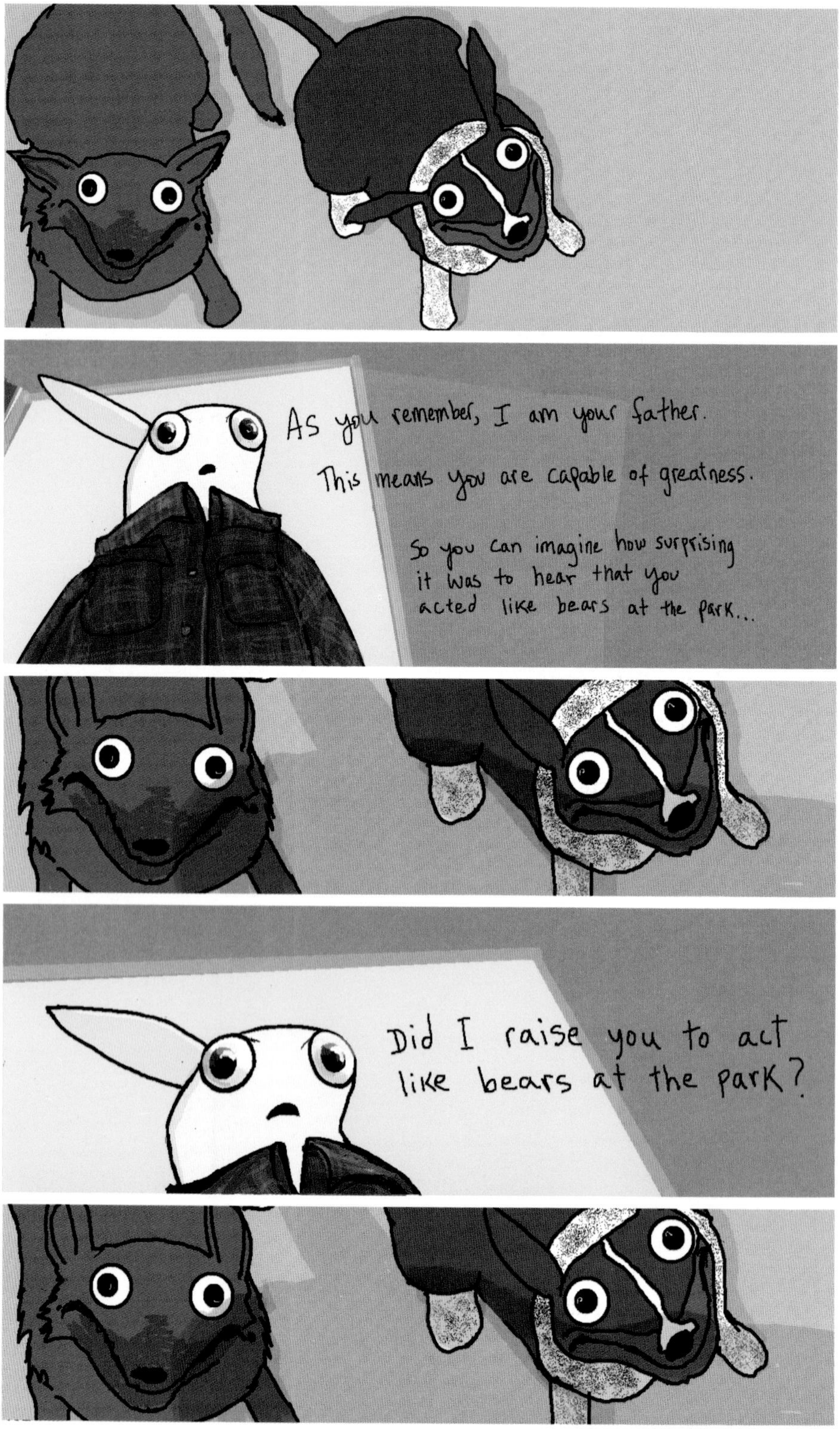
As you remember, I am your father.
This means you are capable of greatness.
So you can imagine how surprising it was to hear that you acted like bears at the park...
Did I raise you to act like bears at the park?

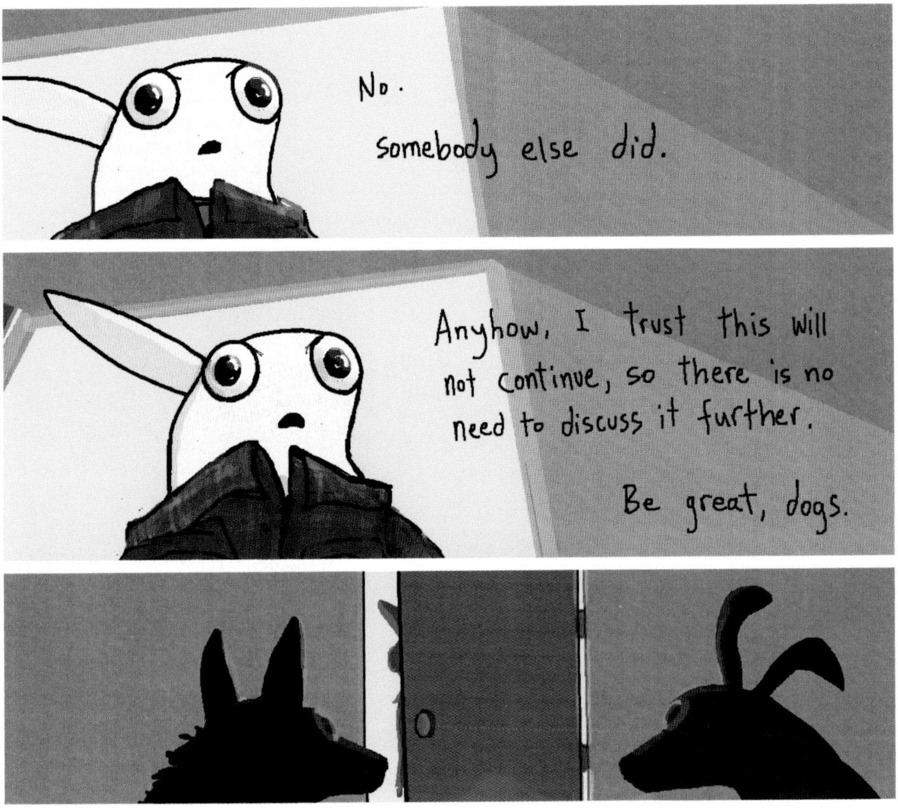
No.
Somebody else did.
Anyhow, I trust this will not continue, so there is no need to discuss it further.
Be great, dogs.

That's a fine character to have in the family if there's somebody fun and patient around to balance things out, but nobody wants their *only* friend to be like that.

So, for the first time in ten years, there was nothing around but me.

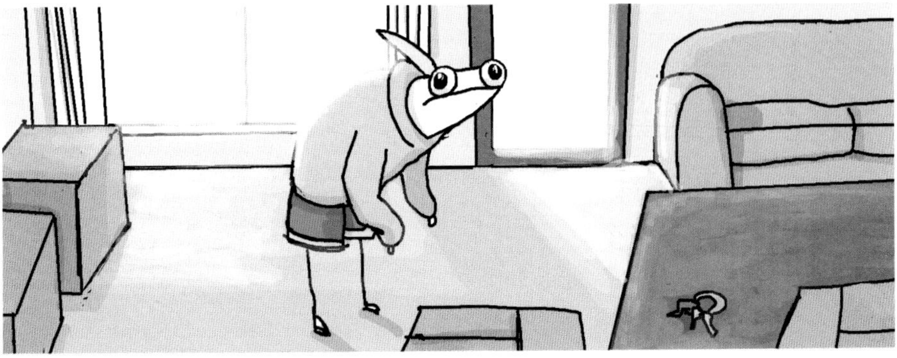

I thought that's what I wanted. But when the relief wore off, it was actually a little weird not having anything around that wanted to interact with me. This was confusing, but in a way, I kind of missed it.

I think what I'm trying to describe is loneliness.

I felt pretty offended by it. I mean, what am I—some clueless animal who needs love and companionship?

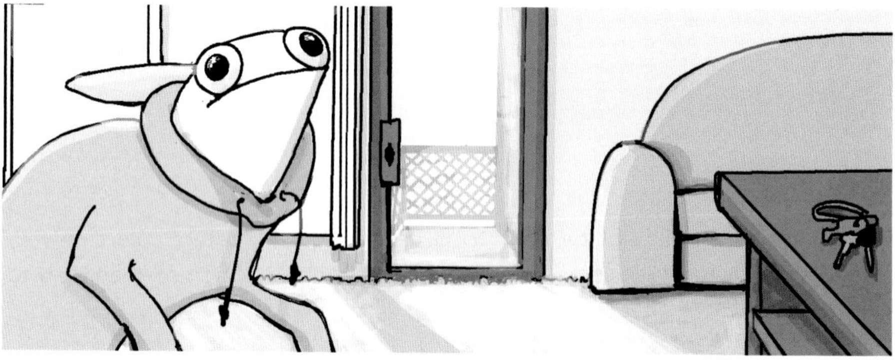

As it turns out, yes—that is what kind of animal I am. I just never realized it before because there was enough ambient love and companionship around to make it seem like maybe I don't have needs, and that's why it doesn't feel like I need anything.

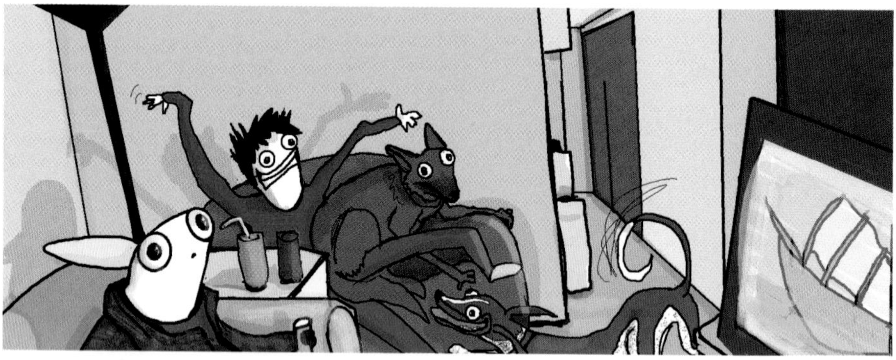

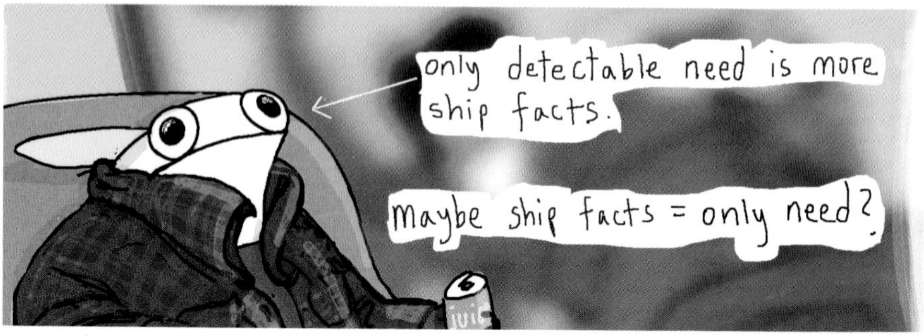
only detectable need is more ship facts.
maybe ship facts = only need?

Experiencing real loneliness for the first time is like realizing the only thing you've ever loved is your home planet after migrating to the moon.

Spider solitaire did not turn out to be an adequate substitute. I became very sad. Unless somebody did something about my emotional needs, it seemed likely to continue.

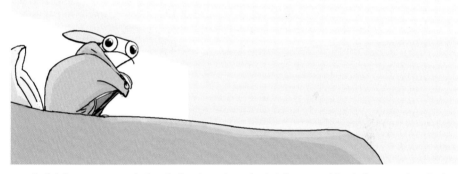

I didn't want to ask for *help*, though ... It didn't seem like I deserved it. I also wasn't necessarily ready to admit to an obvious sign of weakness like emotional needs.

Under the circumstances, the most practical solution genuinely seemed like it might be to befriend myself.

The idea wasn't my favorite I've ever had. I mean, what the fuck kind of warp-speed loser tries to be their own friend? How would that even work? Ask myself personal questions and pretend I don't know the answers already? Just be understanding and supportive and try to make myself feel special? That's some real *Sesame Street*–type shit . . .

But somebody needed to be my friend, and the convenience benefits of doing it myself were hard to argue against.

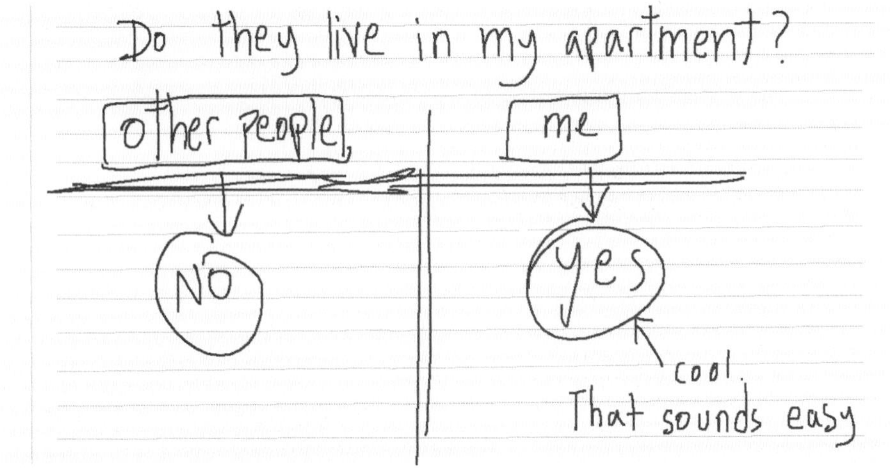

Do they live in my apartment?
other people
me
NO
yes
cool.
That sounds easy

How hard could it possibly be, I thought. I'll just act interested in what I like, do some fun activities, and blammo: best friends.

As of this writing, that was five years ago.

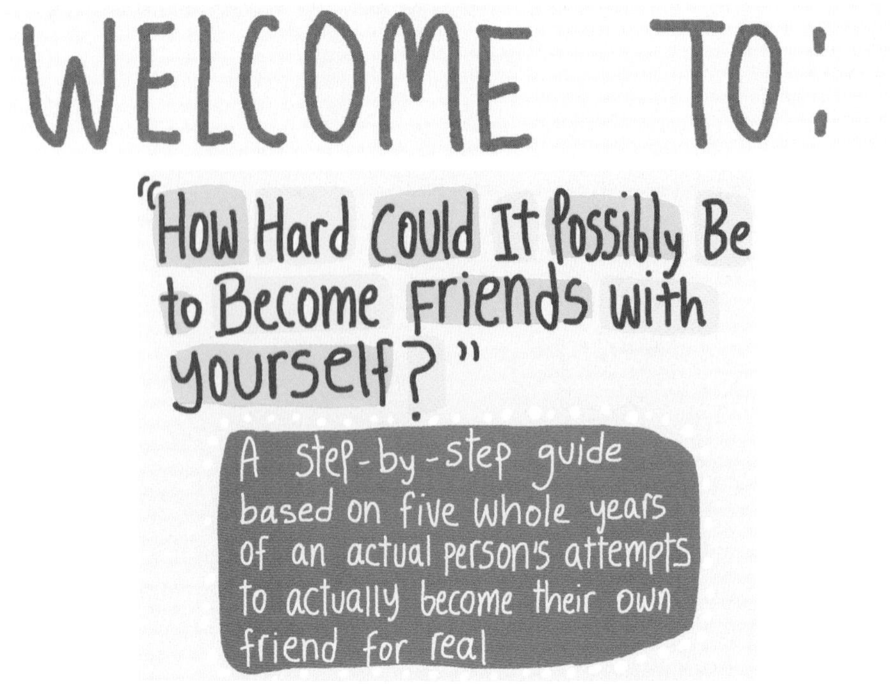

WELCOME TO:
"How Hard Could It Possibly Be to Become Friends with yourself?"
A step-by-step guide based on five whole years of an actual person's attempts to actually become their own friend for real

Step 1: initiate the friendship

It should be easy to become friends with yourself. In theory, it really seems like it should.

Once you start trying to do it, though, you'll come up against all kinds of questions you weren't prepared for, like how to begin, or what to do if you react negatively.

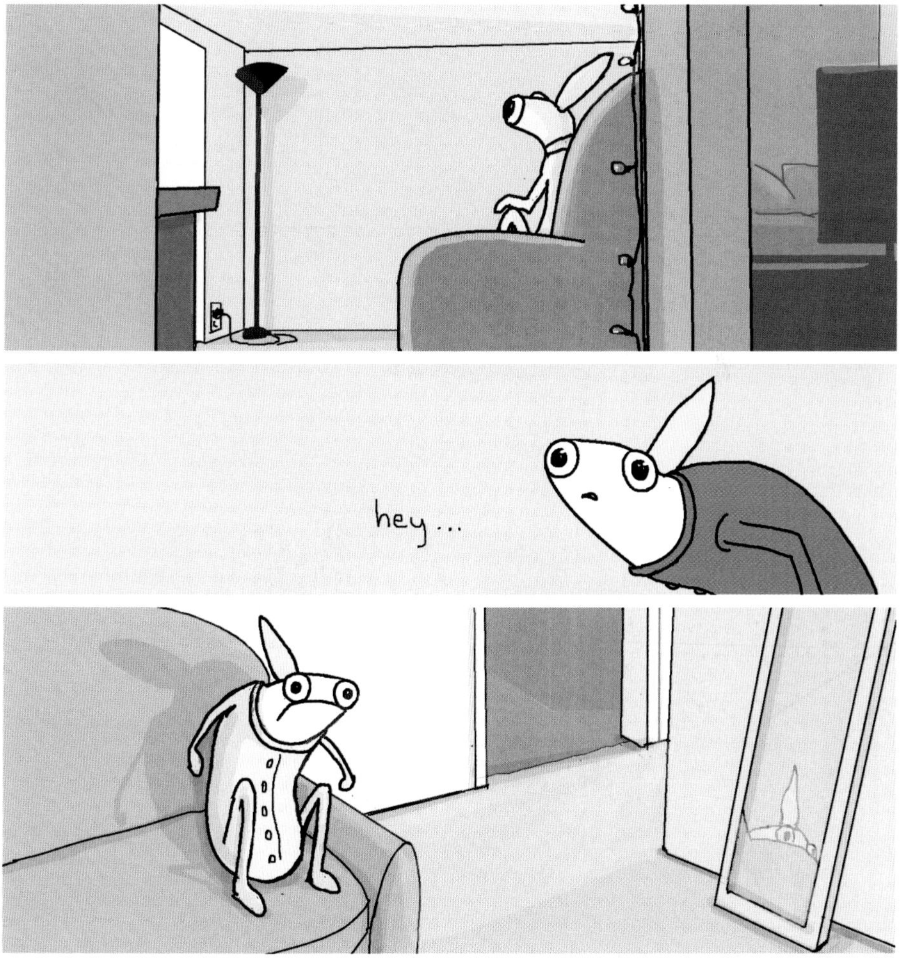
hey...

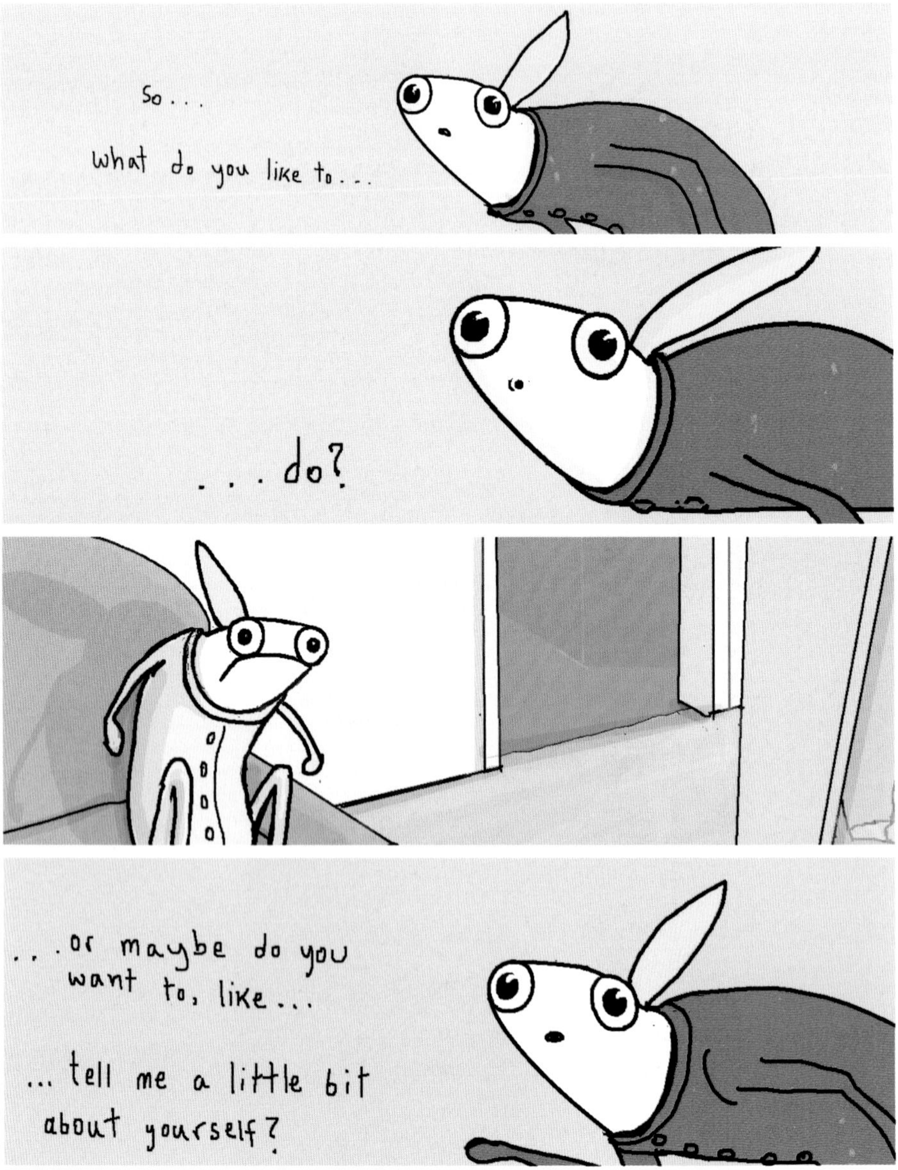
So . . .
what do you like to . . .
. . . do?
. . . or maybe do you want to, like . . .
. . . tell me a little bit about yourself?

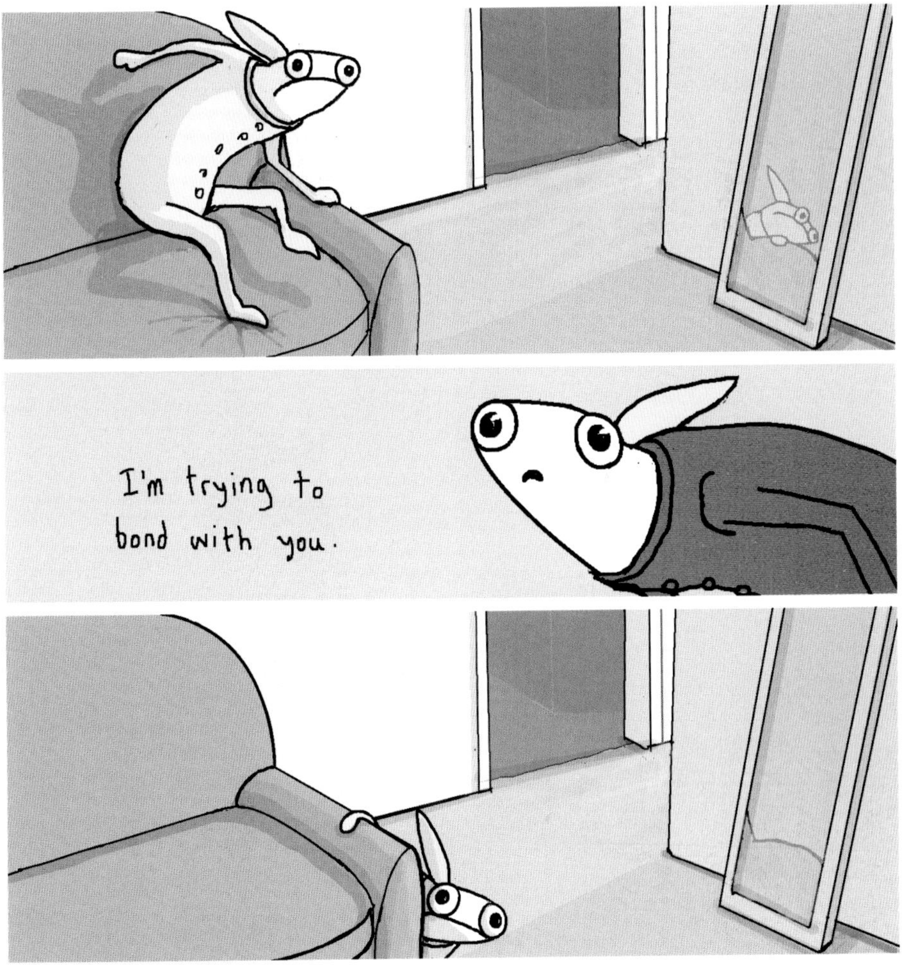
I'm trying to bond with you.

If you reject yourself, do your best to remain calm.

Remember: you are trying to be *friends,* and friends don't act like frustrated Gila monsters.

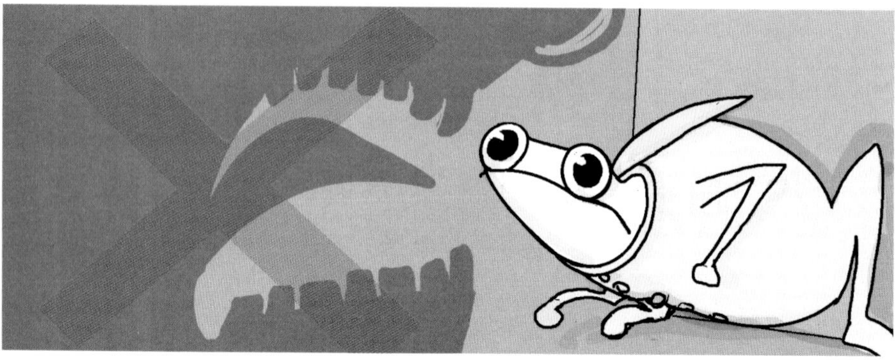

If you mess up and think a bunch of unnecessarily aggressive shit you'd never dream of saying to a real person—for example: "*I hate you, I hate you; you floor-face, mouth-face, crybaddy feelbad little crumb of bread*," and: "*WHY ALL THE TIME DO YOU SEEM LIKE A DUMPTRANG>:[???*"—do not become discouraged.

Yes, those things were clearly intended to be cruel and demeaning, but they do not make sense, and the additional damage is small compared to the scope of the total, overall damage.

Take a step back, remind yourself that nobody is a dumptrang, and keep trying.

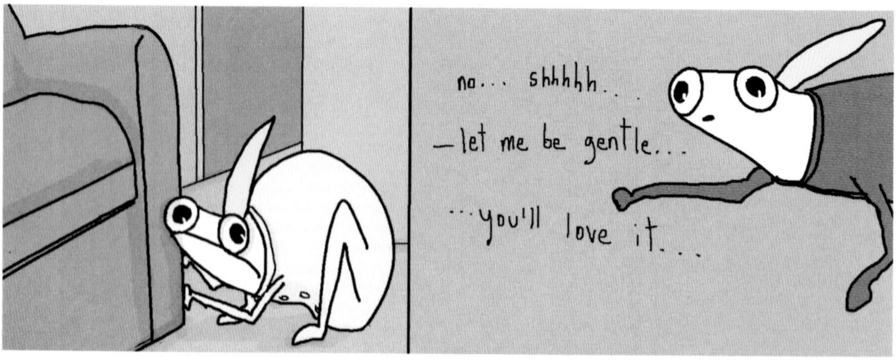
no... shhhhh...
—let me be gentle...
...you'll love it...

Step 2: ignore rejection and continue to attempt friendship

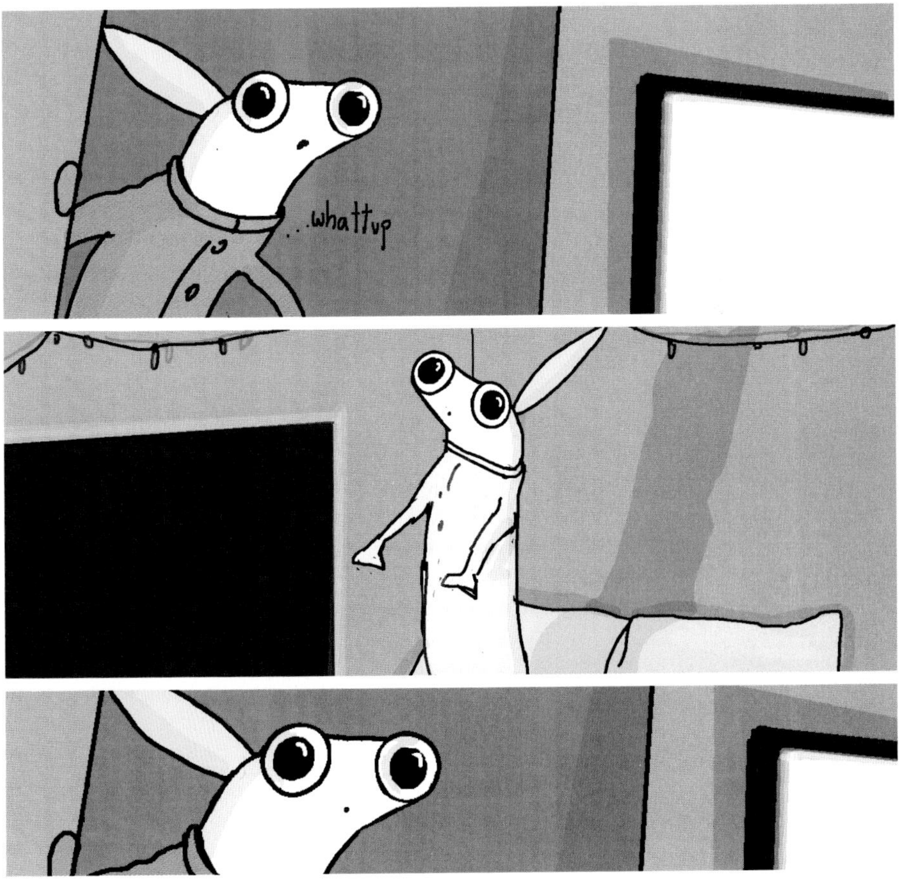
...whattup

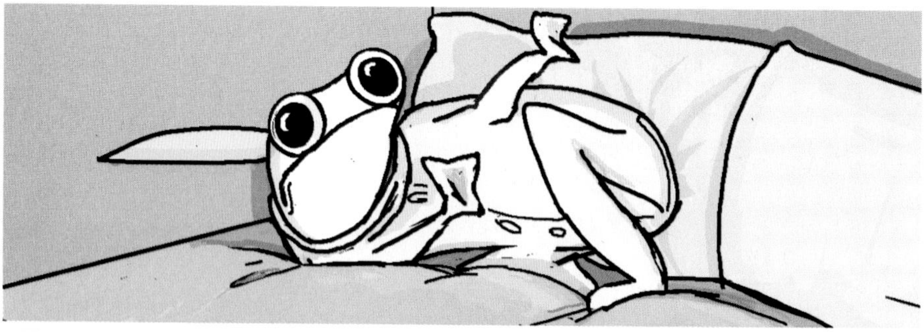

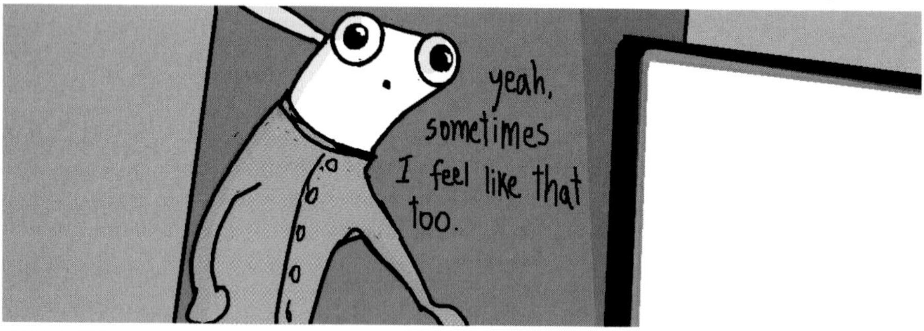
yeah, sometimes I feel like that too.

Step 3: still ignore rejection and continue to attempt friendship

It might seem like you don't want to be friends. At the very least, you'll distrust the sudden interest.

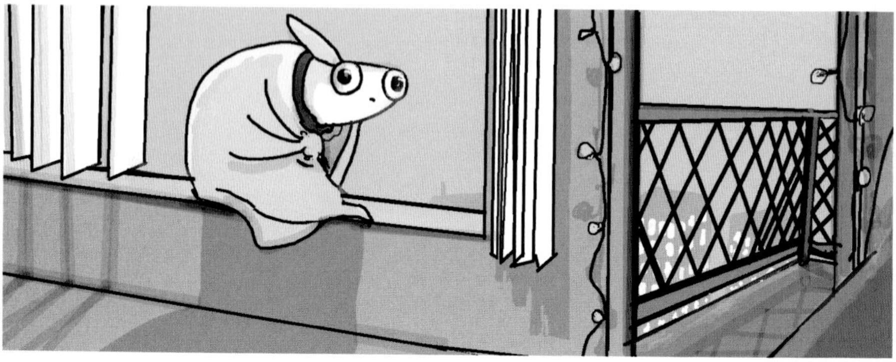

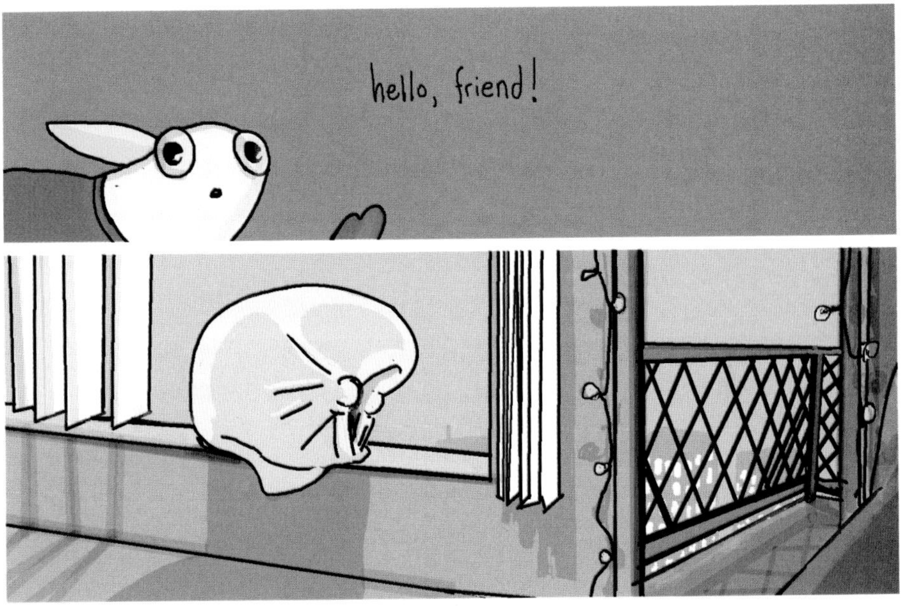
hello, friend!

This is understandable. When the vast majority of your interactions with somebody have been brutally critical—warlike, even—and you also personally caused almost all the bad things that ever happened to them, it may take a while before they don't feel spooked by your presence.

Honestly, at times it will feel pretty much the same as trying to make friends with a wild lizard. But be patient. If you are lonely enough to form a friendship with this thing, it is likely very close to being lonely enough to form a friendship with you.

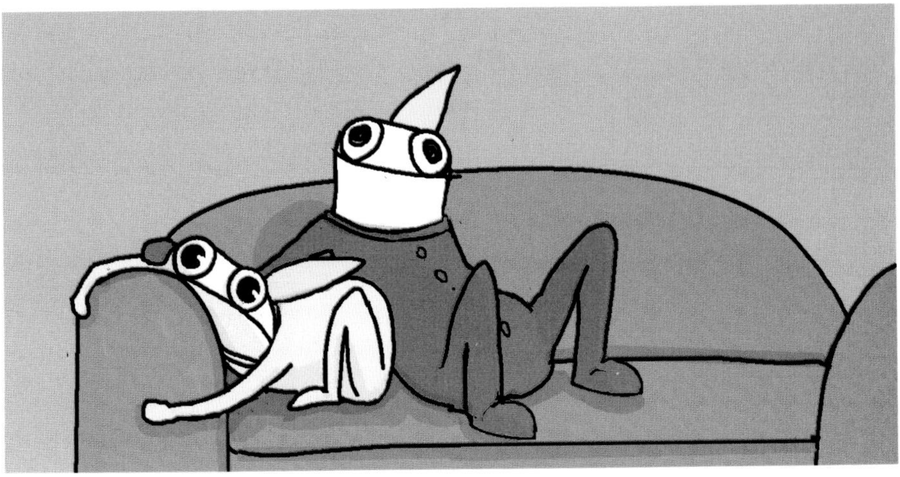

At some point, your utility as a companion will be impossible to ignore.

TIP:

to reduce the risk of unnecessary competition, remove appealing objects (such as blankets and jars) from your friend's immediate surroundings.

Step 4: appeal to your interests

Once you have firmly established yourself as the only alternative to isolation, take a little time to learn about your interests.

They aren't respectable interests, no. But the reality of the situation is that if we want our friend to like us, we must learn how to interact with our friend in a way that our friend likes.

It may be hard to tell what our friend likes, mostly because our friend is a pointless little weirdo who only likes pointless little weirdo things that are too ambiguous to be actionable, but everybody likes something.

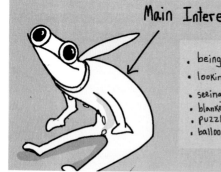

Main Interests (as far as anyone can tell):

- being places (hills, roads, by trees, etc.)
- looking at things (not interacting – just looking)
- seeing boats and planes and stuff (exciting)
- blankets
- puzzles
- balloons (doesn't really know what to do with them, though)

Okay... what can we do with these? How do we build a relationship around these?

494

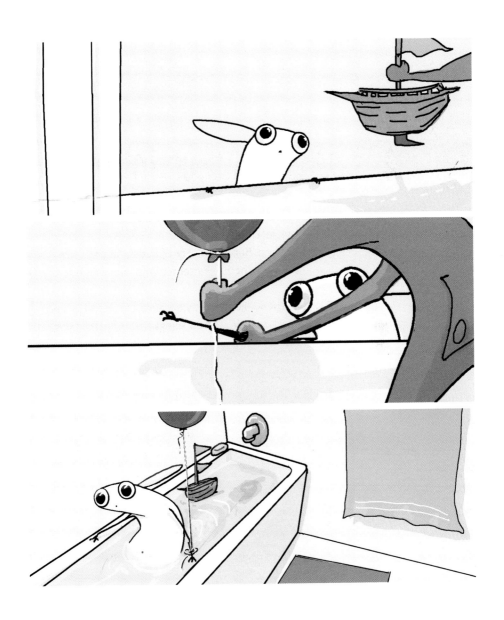

Step 4B: if necessary, force the bond to form through exposure

Sometimes—for example, if there is nothing our pointless little weirdo friend naturally enjoys about spending time together—it can be helpful to focus instead on shared experiences. No matter how much somebody doesn't get along with you, it is possible to form a crude bond through raw proximity. Go places together. Be in those places together. See the same things as each other. Over time, this will create something very similar to friendship.

It's raining.

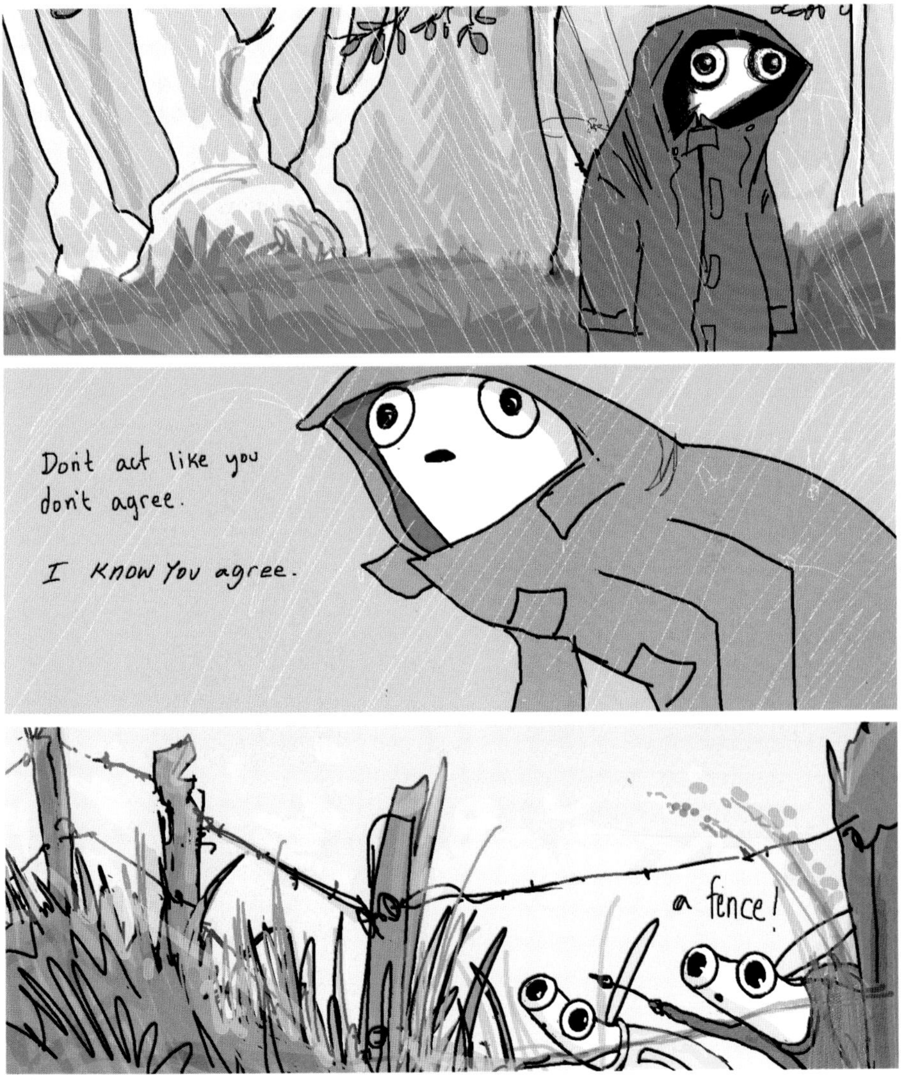
Don't act like you don't agree.
I know you agree.
a fence!

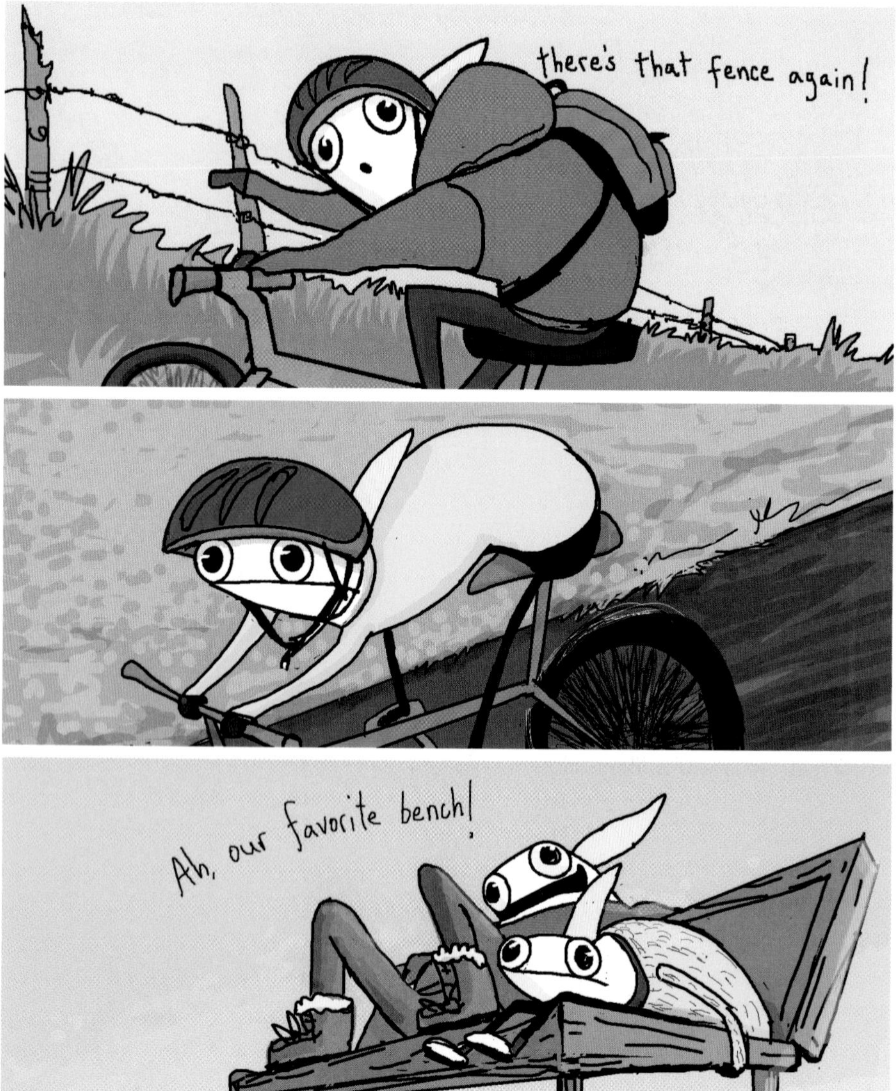
there's that fence again!
Ah, our favorite bench!

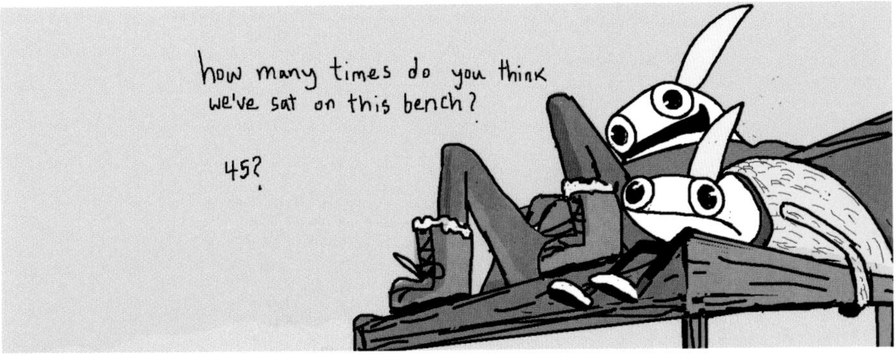
how many times do you think we've sat on this bench?
45?

Step 5: develop a supportive attitude

At many points during the friendship, we may notice that our friend is still very far from ideal.

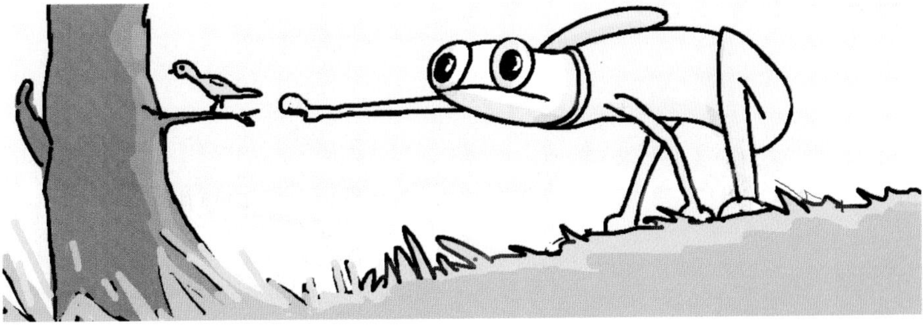

We may even notice that everything our friend enjoys is stupid, and everything our friend does looks like a clown is doing it, and our friend is weak and tiny like a shrimp, and even when our friend tries to act natural, our friend does not seem natural.

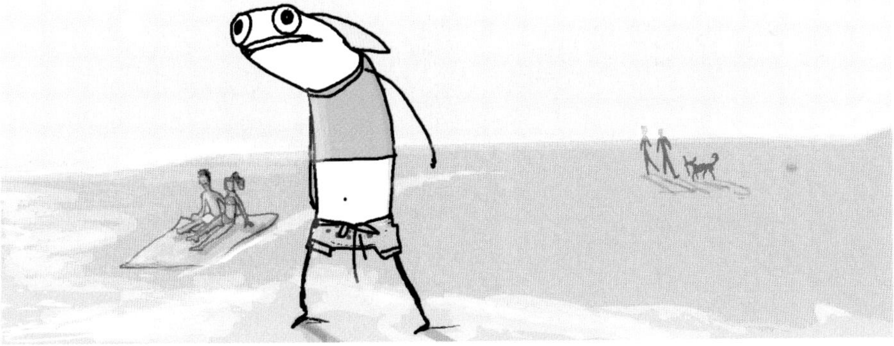

We must learn to accept this.

Yes, our friend's stance is both unnatural and tremendously prominent, but our friend enjoys standing, and this is how our friend stands. While it would be both possible and understandable to become upset about this, compassion will be more helpful to our friend.

I mean, imagine if *you* were like that . . . would it be easy to feel good about yourself? Would you feel at home in the world?

What our friend needs is encouragement.

great job!
get that beach!

Q: *What if the people don't believe our friend belongs at the beach?*

Are the people our friend?

No: our friend is our friend.

And right now, our friend is having a great time at the beach. We should allow it to continue.

Q: *But what if our friend wants to go to the museum?*

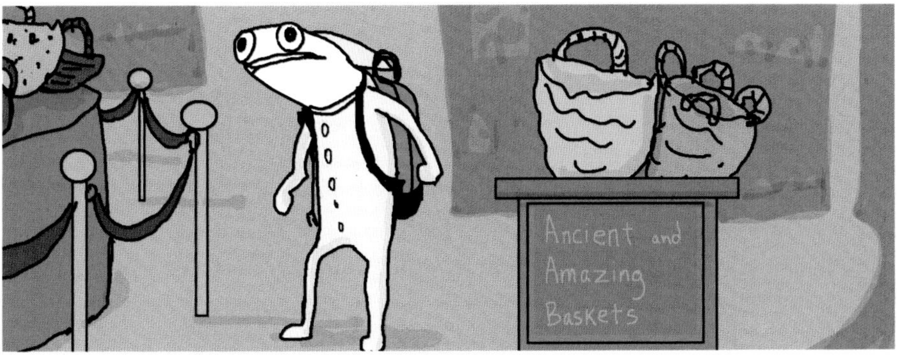
Ancient and
Amazing
Baskets

That is fine. Our friend only wants to learn more about baskets. Yes, it looks precarious, but it can't harm anybody.

Q: *What if our friend is on the escalator?*

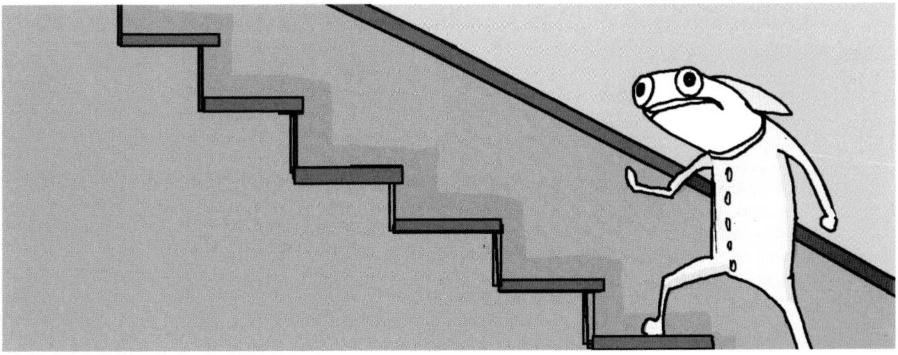

From the looks of it, our friend might be in danger, so we should probably just focus on helping.

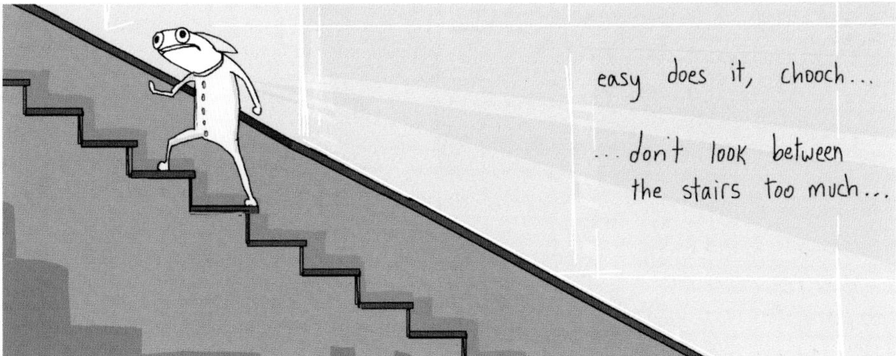
easy does it, chooch...
...don't look between the stairs too much...

Step 6: Maintain a supportive attitude

We have been supportive for quite some time now. At least four years.

Our friend will likely feel reassured by this, and may even begin to exhibit signs of reciprocating the friendship.

During this stage, our friend may, for example:

—Say things

—Show us things

—Seek our approval

—Attempt to ensnare us in baseless speculation about pointless bullshit that doesn't need to be wondered and can't actually be answered in a meaningful way

—Develop new interests, such as speed dancing

Remember: this is good. Our friend is behaving like this because it wants to interact with us. Sure, the interactions are pointless, but so is everything.

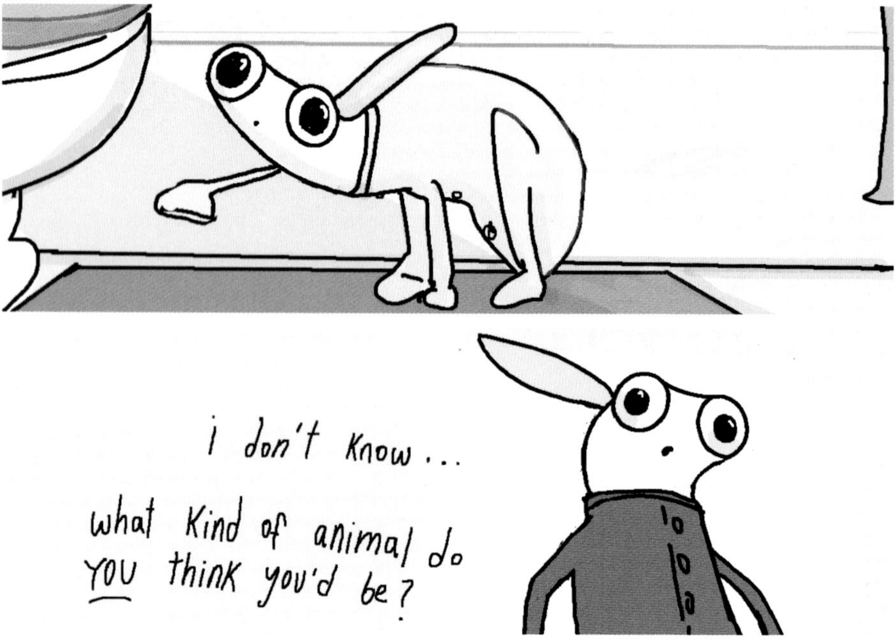
i don't know . . .
what kind of animal do YOU think you'd be?

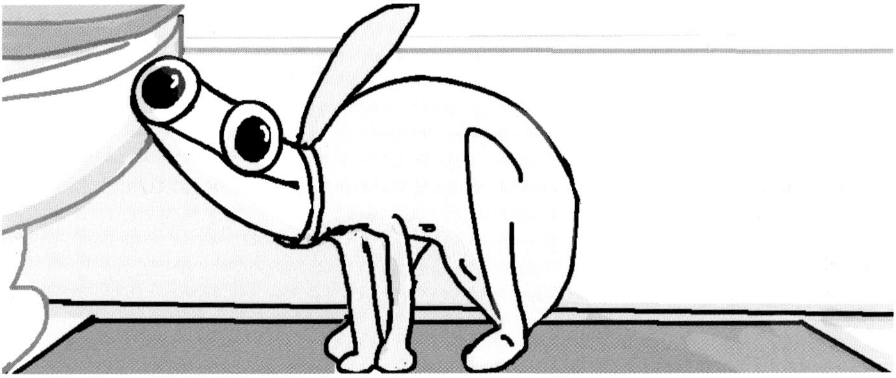

Participate where possible.

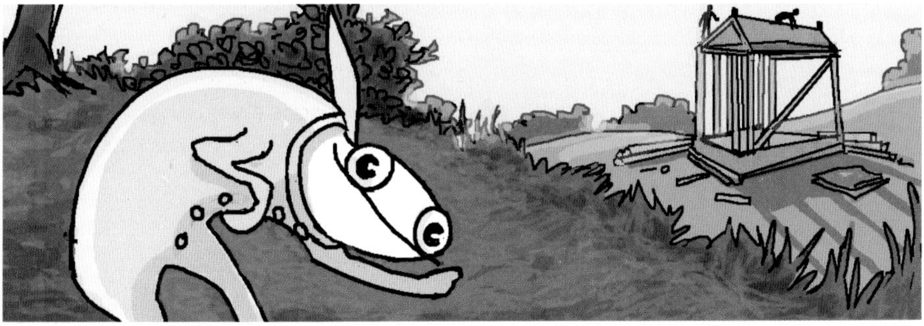

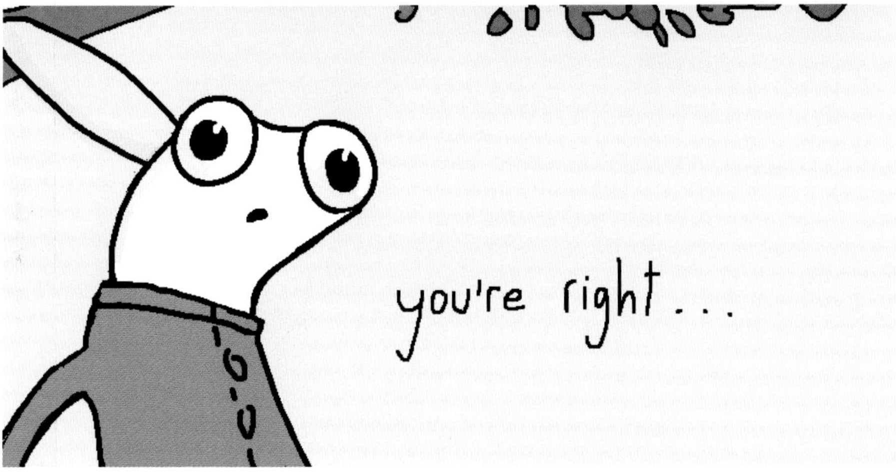
you're right...

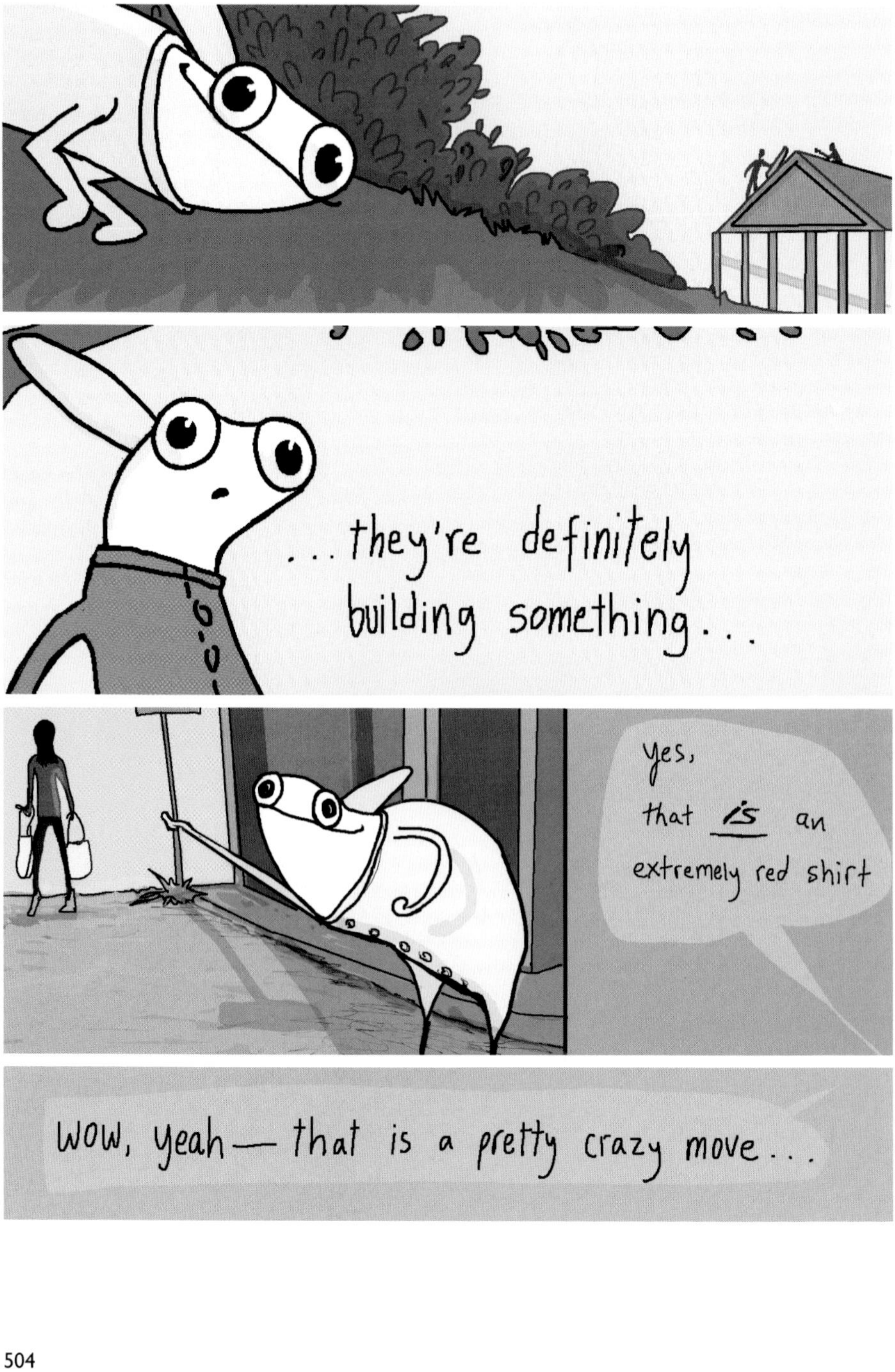
...they're definitely building something...
yes, that is an extremely red shirt
wow, yeah— that is a pretty crazy move...

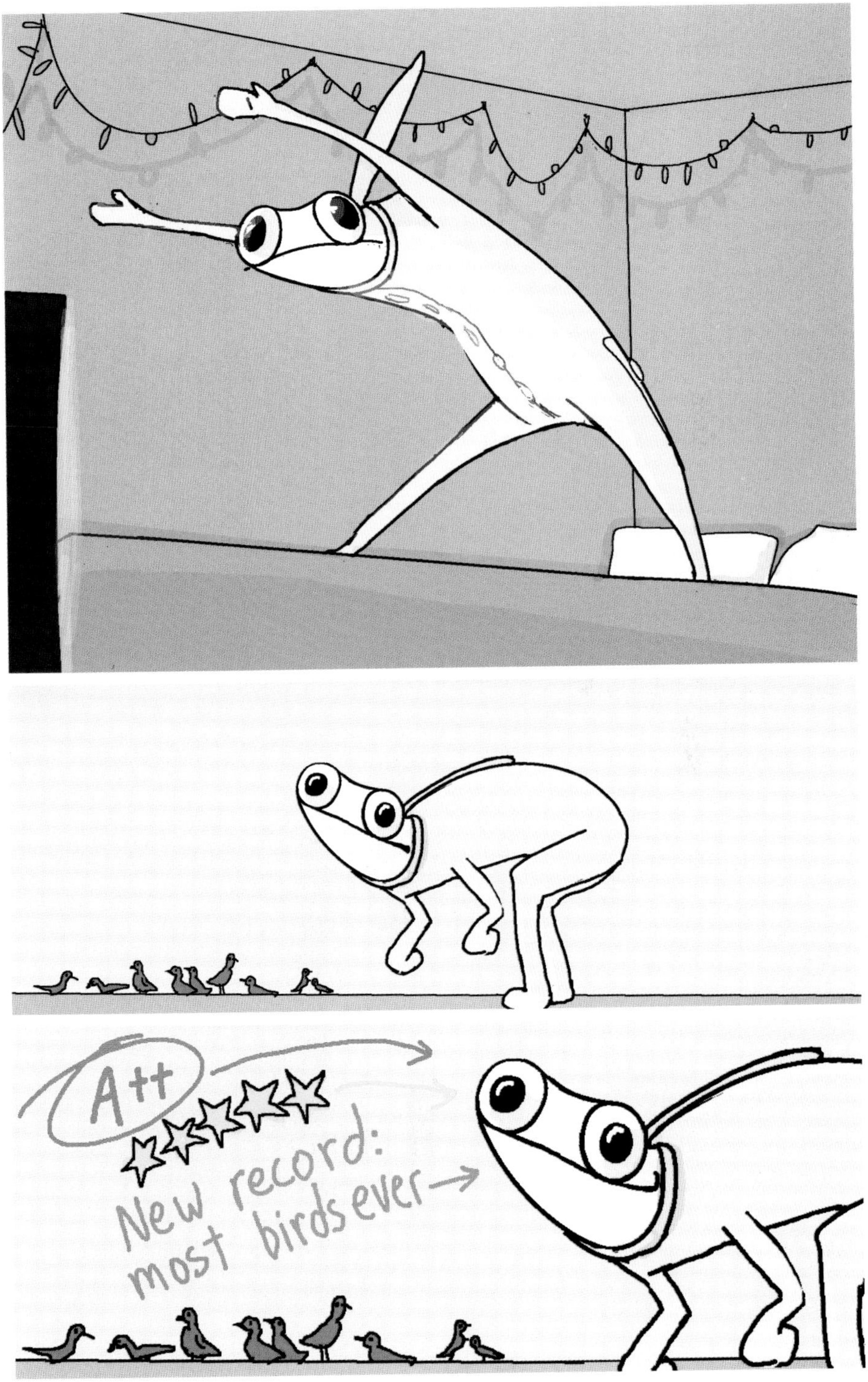
A++
New record: most birds ever

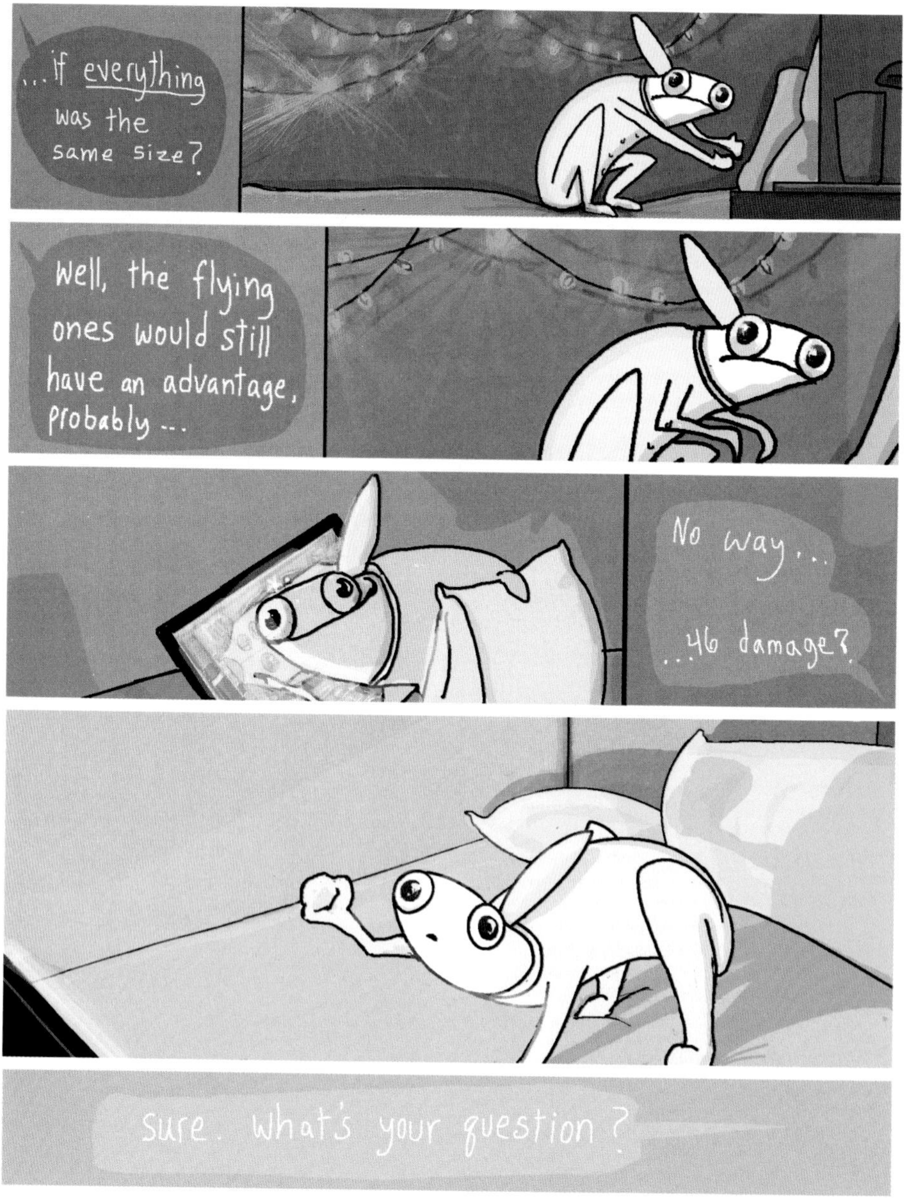

...If everything was the same size?
Well, the flying ones would still have an advantage, probably...
No way...
...46 damage?
Sure. What's your question?

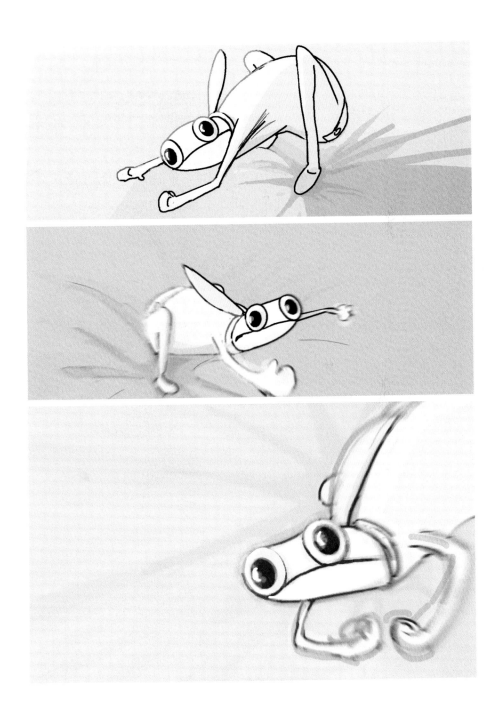

507

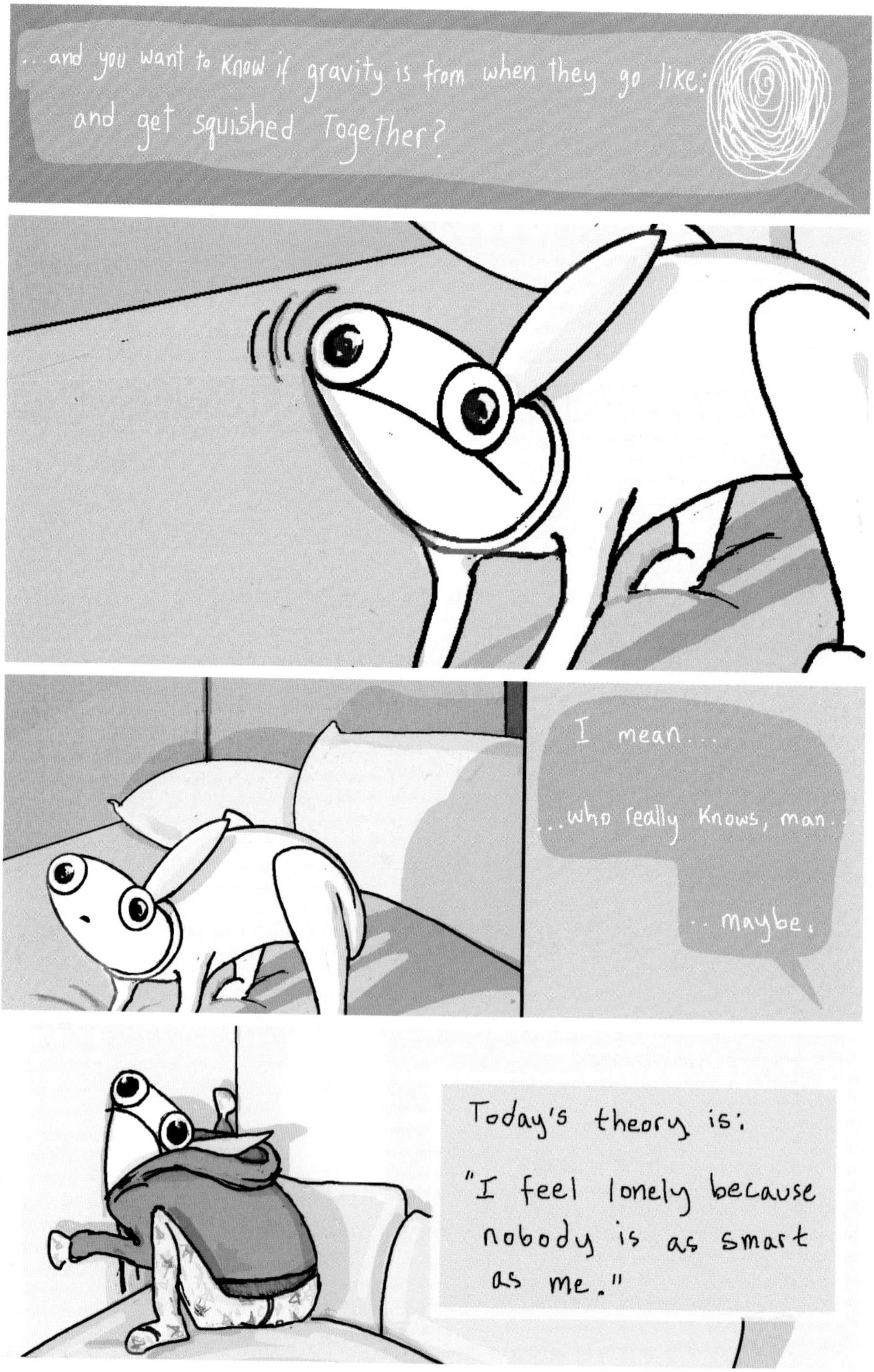
...and you want to know if gravity is from when they go like:
and get squished Together?
I mean...
...who really knows, man...
...maybe.
Today's theory is:
"I feel lonely because nobody is as smart as me."

"really likes" grapes ⟶

Step 7: Still maintain a supportive attitude

Q: *Still? We still need to pay attention to this thing's feelings and respond to its questions and care about its ideas?*

Yes.

Q: *Why?*

Because that's what it needs.

Q: *Why, though?*

Because it is a person. And people need somebody who cares about them.

Q: *It's a person?*

Yes. Everybody is a person.

Step 8: maintain a supportive attitude indefinitely

On some level, we were probably still hoping to find some hidden, deeply meaningful quality within our friend that would make it easy to care about what it likes and does and thinks about.

It is time to let go of this hope.

There is nothing inherently meaningful or important about our friend, and there probably never will be.

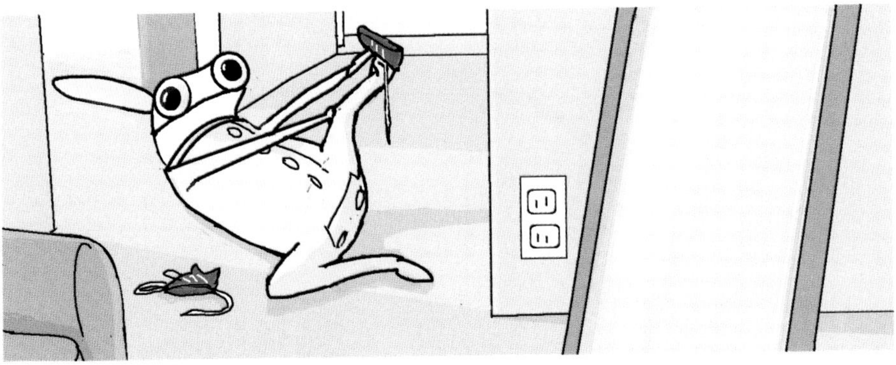

And the things it likes are even more pointless.

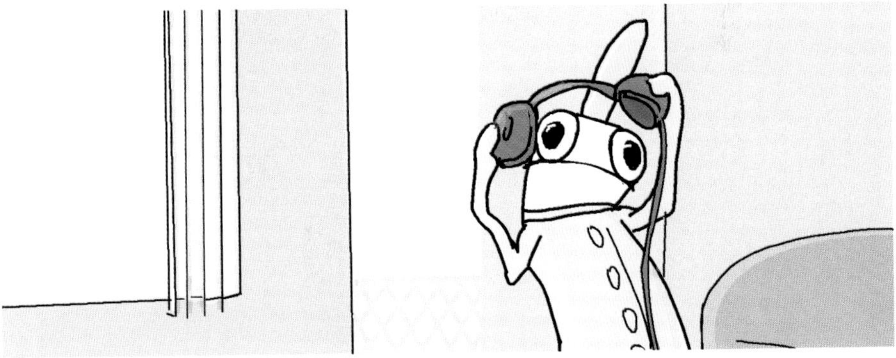

But there are things it likes.

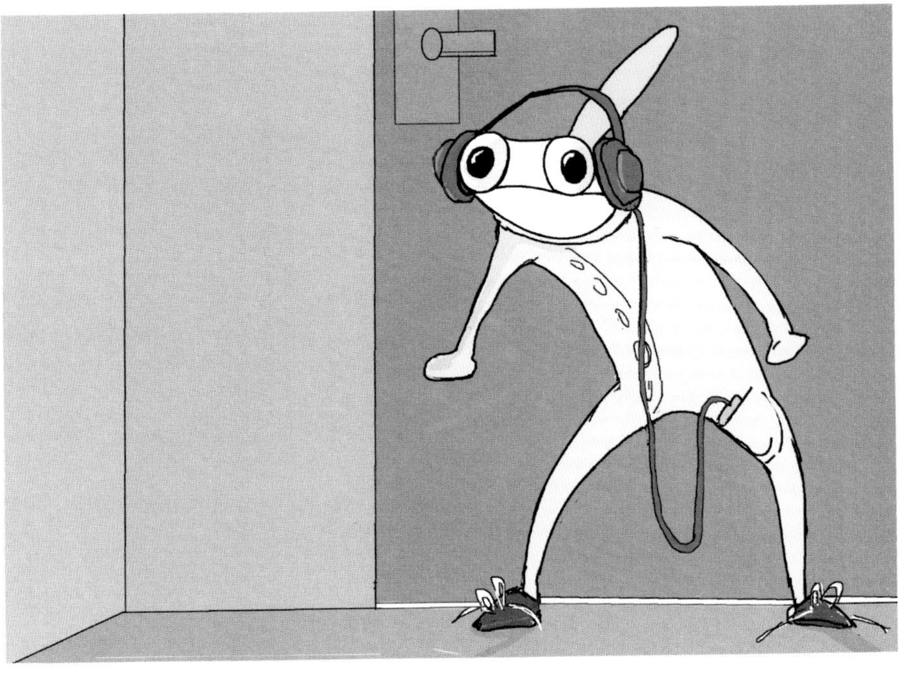

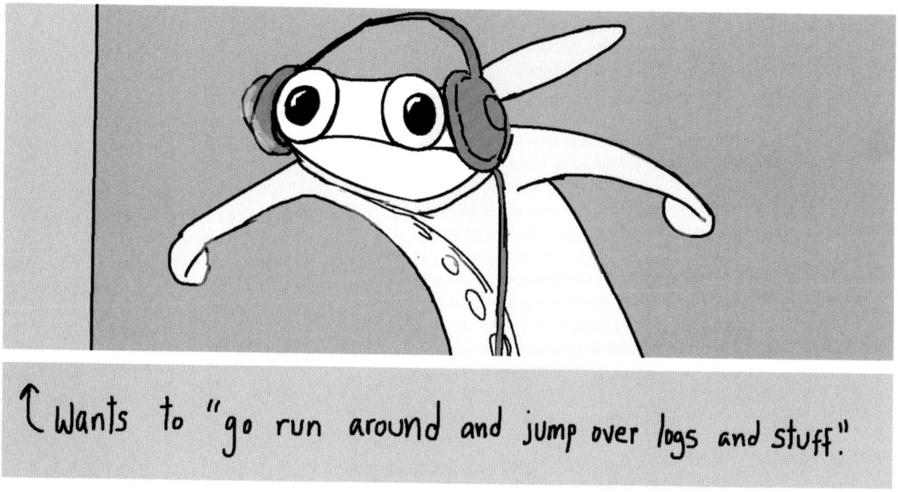
↑ Wants to "go run around and jump over logs and stuff."

So we will swallow our pride, get out there, and participate where possible.

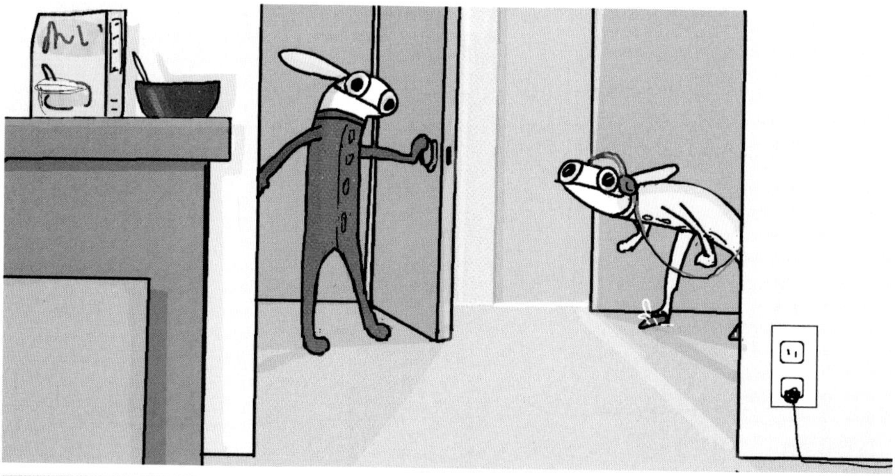

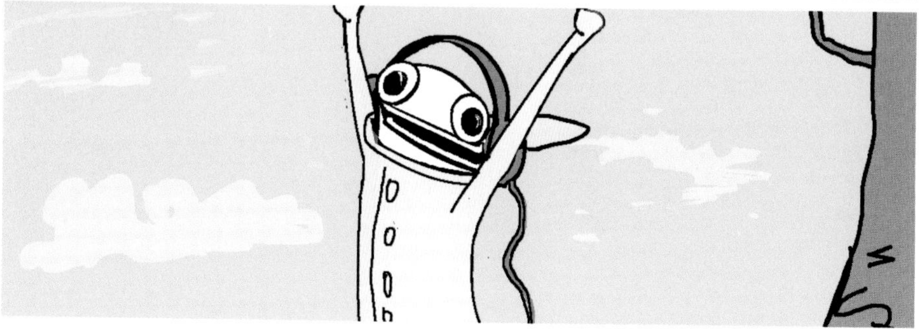

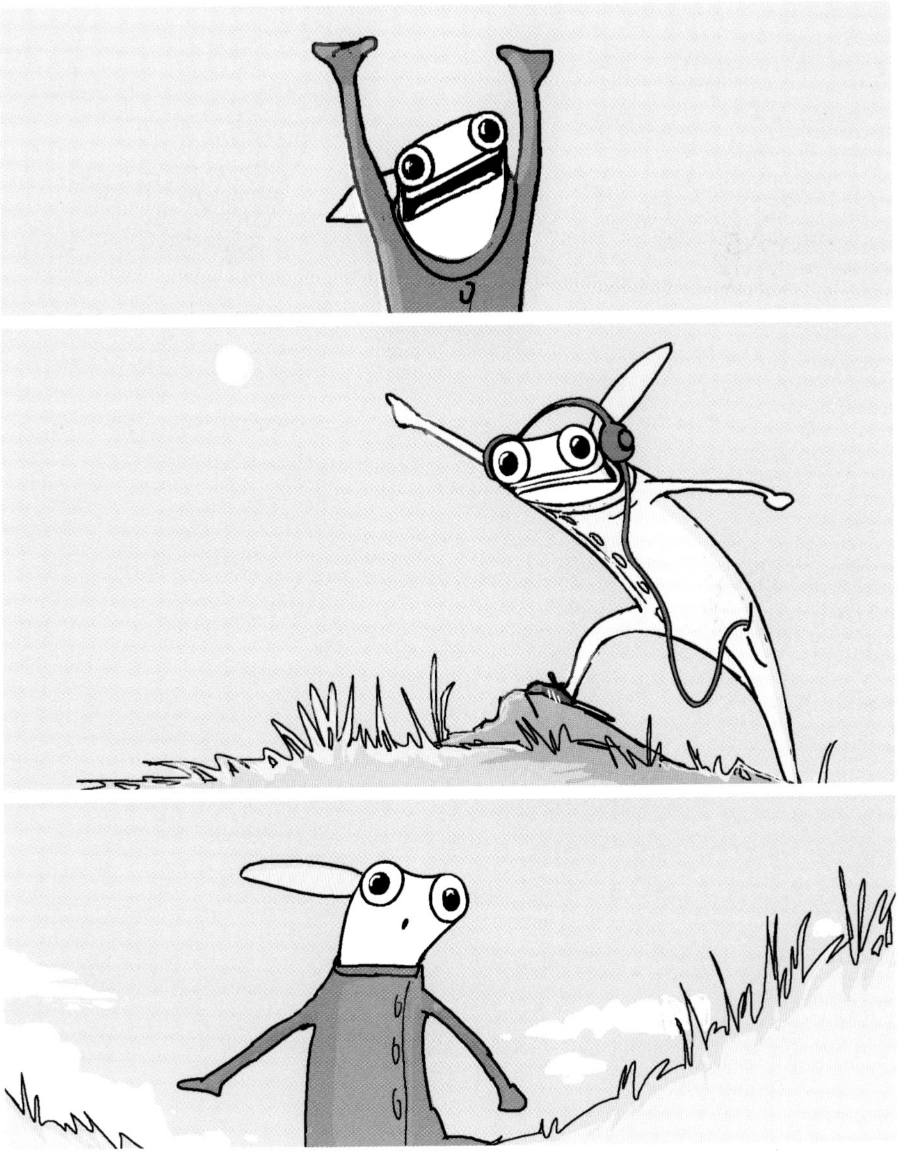

Because nobody should have to feel like a pointless little weirdo alone.

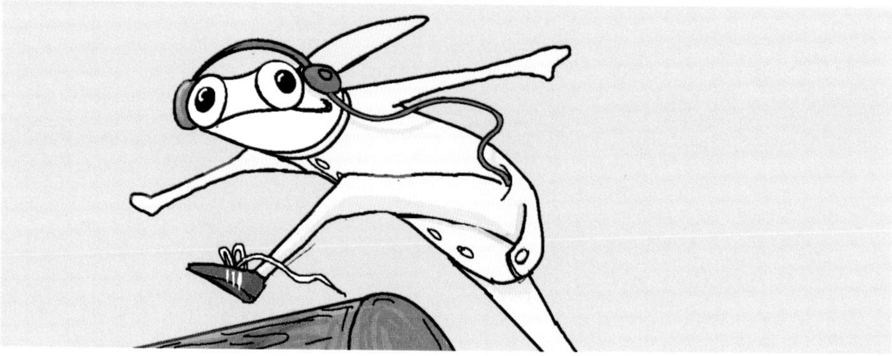

Especially if they are.

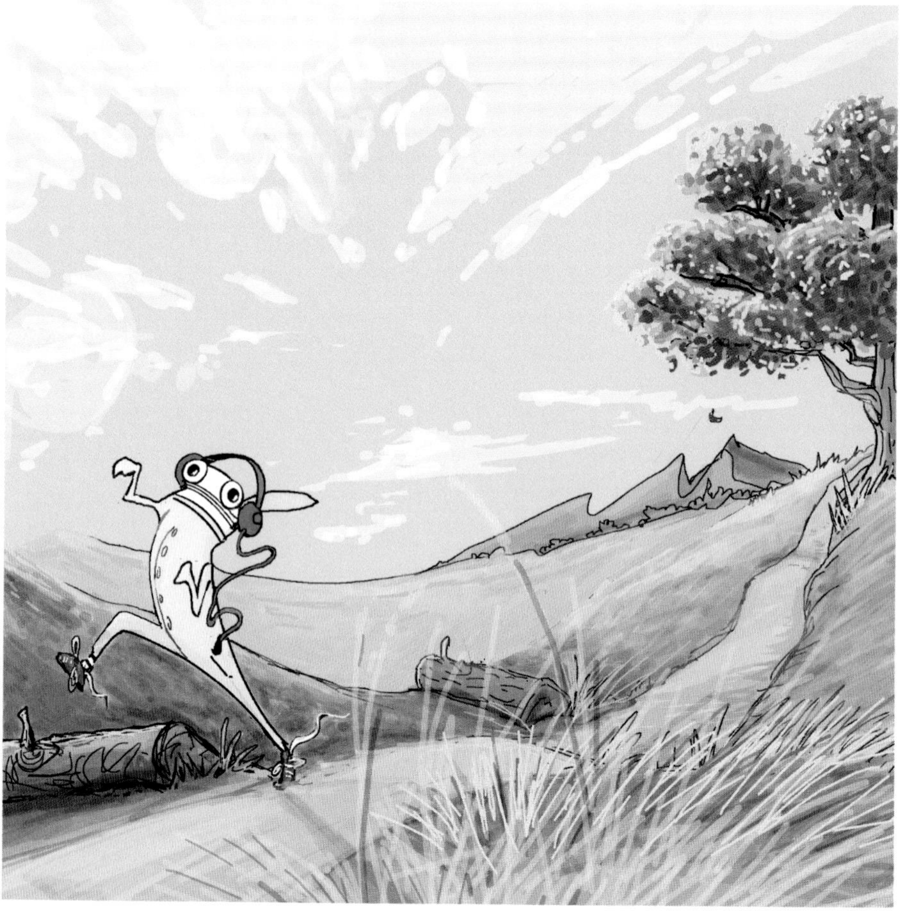

Acknowledgments

I don't know how to do these, but I'm gonna try.

I hereby acknowledge the following people:

Lauren and Monika. I don't know how many hours we spent on the phone during this, but it's more than I talk to anybody else. I mean, during quarantine, we edited this entire book verbally, which is insane, but we did it. Sometimes things got weird. Sometimes one, two, or all three of us cried (about both related and unrelated things). Sometimes (a lot) we got distracted talking about philosophy, or motherhood, or comedians or something, and only looped back to business 45 minutes later. I enjoyed this. Thank you for being my friends.

Kevin. Thank you for weathering this with me. Talking with me, helping me when I got stuck, being willing to say hard things, and keeping me company during all these years of near-total reclusiveness. At times, you were the only thing preventing me from turning feral and fully receding from humanity. I like you. You are smart and have good ideas. Plus, you're a cool dude.

Mom, Dad, Laurie, and David. We are a small but mighty family. I love you, and I appreciate that you allow me to make fun of you. Especially you, Mom. You are a patient and amazing lady. I like you very much.

Everybody who helped me make this, including but not limited to: Alysha Bullock, Ray Chokov, Mike Kwan, Caroline Pallotta, Jaime Putorti, the dix! Digital Team, Lisa Litwack, Elisa Rivlin, Rebecca Strobel (holy shit, Rebecca . . .), Jen Bergstrom, Jon Karp, Susan Moldow, Aimée Bell, Sally Marvin, Jen Long, Meredith Vilarello, Jessica Roth, Anne Jaconette, and Carolyn Reidy, who will be missed by all of us.

Peter Kleinman, who helped probably more than he realizes. If I turn out to be a decent person, this guy played a huge part in it.

Claire Johnson, who received a package addressed to me (which contained the full, uncorrected manuscript for this book) and, without knowing me or what was in the package, went to the trouble of calling the sender to find out how to get the package to its intended recipient. You are a good person, Claire Johnson. I only spoke with you briefly because it was my first time leaving the house in months, so I was uncomfortable and smelly and extremely eager to get back to the safety of my home, but I want you to know that I admire and appreciate what you did. It brings me comfort knowing there are people like you in the world, just quietly doing good things for no personal gain whatsoever.

I would also like to thank the sun, for keeping everybody warm and supplying vitamin D for our bodies.

About the Author

Allie Brosh lives as a recluse in her bedroom in Bend, Oregon. In recent years, she has become almost entirely nocturnal. Her hobbies include baseless speculation, spying, no-stakes gambling games that she makes up to pacify herself, actual games like *Magic: The Gathering* and *Hearthstone*, learning about math and physics (helps make the speculation less baseless), and also occasionally walking around and looking at things from a safe distance. She is friendly, but spooks easy.

Brosh is the author of the #1 *New York Times* bestseller and Goodreads Choice Awards winner *Hyperbole and a Half,* which was named one of the best books of the year by NPR, *The Wall Street Journal, Chicago Tribune, Library Journal, Salon*, and A.V. Club.

Brosh has also given herself many prestigious awards, including "fanciest horse drawing" and "most likely to succeed."